2007

Children's Writer's & Illustrator's Market®

P9-DER-412

Alice Pope, Editor

WRITER'S DIGEST BOOKS
CINCINNATI, OH

Editorial Director, Writer's Digest Books: Jane Friedman
Managing Editor, Writer's Digest Market Books: Alice Pope

Writer's Market Web site: www.writersmarket.com
Writer's Digest Books Web site: www.writersdigest.com

2007 Children's Writer's & Illustrator's Market. Copyright © 2006 by Writer's Digest Books.
Published by F+W Publications, 4700 East Galbraith Road, Cincinnati, Ohio 45236. Printed
and bound in the United States of America. All rights reserved. No part of this book may be
reproduced in any form or by any electronic or mechanical means including information
storage and retrieval systems without written permission from the publisher, except by reviewers who may quote brief passages to be printed in a magazine or newspaper.

Distributed in Canada by Fraser Direct
100 Armstrong Avenue
Georgetown, ON, Canada L7G 5S4
Tel: (905) 877-4411

Distributed in the U.K. and Europe by David & Charles
Brunel House, Newton Abbot, Devon, TQ12 4PU, England
Tel: (+44) 1626 323200, Fax: (+44) 1626 323319
E-mail: postmaster@davidandcharles.co.uk

Distributed in Australia by Capricorn Link
P.O. Box 704, Windsor, NSW 2756 Australia
Tel: (02) 4577-3555

ISSN: 0897-9790
ISBN-13: 978-1-58297-435-4
ISBN-10: 1-58297-435-7

Cover design by Kelly Kofron/Claudean Wheeler
Interior design by Clare Finney
Production coordinated by Robin Richie

Attention Booksellers: This is an annual directory of F+W Publications.
Return deadline for this edition is December 31, 2007.

Contents

© 2005 Nathan Hale

© 2006 Randy Cecil

MARKETS

RESOURCES

© 2006 Margie Moore

INDEXES

From the Editor

© 2001 Amy Wilson Sanger.

My son Murray hates *Goodnight Moon*. Every so often he inadvertently pulls it from his basket of board books and plops onto my lap. Two pages in, he violently flings Margaret Wise Brown's classic across the room, tumbling his stuffed animals and terrifying the cat.

There are lots of books he loves—*Good Night, Gorilla*, by Peggy Rathmann; *Eating the Alphabet*, by Lois Ehlert, Dav Pilkey's Big Dog and Little Dog books, and a certain DK title full of pictures of trucks (and covered in toddler schmutz). It's exciting to see him exhibit such passion for his books whether I'm on my 25th reading of the day or ducking a projectile board book.

A few Saturdays ago, we got an unexpected package in the mail. The big brown box was filled with board books—tons of them—courtesy of the ever-generous Kelly Milner Halls (see her article Creating Books for the Youngest Readers on page 55).

I opened the box and let the little guy have at it. He squealed with happiness; my lap was at the ready. Lift-the-flap books by Karen Katz were a hit; a cool book called *Art* (that I'm wild about) was not. *Bear and Ball*—no. *First Book of Sushi*—yes! It was fascinating to watch him react. Why do some books appeal to him and others get tossed? Why *Good Night, Gorilla* and not *Goodnight Moon*? Why did that editor at Viking send a form rejection for the same manuscript Simon & Schuster loved?

Of course, the mind of an editor doesn't work the same way as the mind of a toddler when it comes to accepting or rejecting a book. For Murray, it's simply *I love this* or *I hate this*. Editors must also consider what's appropriate for their lists and what's marketable, among other factors. Using *Children's Writer's & Illustrator's Market* can help you get inside editors' minds and, hopefully, send them manuscripts they'll love. After all, just as Murray's not going to sit still for a book that doesn't enrapture him, editors won't sign books they aren't passionate about.

And, really, it all comes down to passion. You have the passion to write and illustrate books for young readers. Editors have the passion to shine them up and get them into bookstores. Readers, no matter their age, have love-it or hate-it passion for books. Some we can't put down. Some we won't pick up. And a few we simply must throw across the room (with apologies to Ms. Brown).

Alice Pope
cwim@fwpubs.com
Watch for www.cwim.com.

Editor's note: The illustration above is from the cover of First Book of Sushi, *written and illustrated by Amy Wilson Sanger. (Murray's favorite line: . . .hot, hot, HOT!—though he's never actually tried wasabi).*

How to Use This Book

As a writer, illustrator, or photographer first picking up *Children's Writer's & Illustrator's Market*, you may not know quite how to start using the book. Your impulse may be to flip through the book and quickly make a mailing list, then submit to everyone in hopes that someone will take interest in your work. Well, there's more to it. Finding the right market takes time and research. The more you know about a company that interests you, the better chance you have of getting work accepted.

We've made your job a little easier by putting a wealth of information at your fingertips. Besides providing listings, this directory includes a number of tools to help you determine which markets are the best ones for your work. By using these tools, as well as researching on your own, you raise your odds of being published.

USING THE INDEXES

This book lists hundreds of potential buyers of freelance material. To learn which companies want the type of material you're interested in submitting, start with the indexes.

Names Index

This new index lists book and magazine editors and art directors as well as agents and art reps, indicating the companies they work for. Use this index to find company and contact information for individual publishing professionals.

Age-Level Index

Age groups are broken down into these categories in the Age-Level Index:

- **Picture books or picture-oriented material** are written and illustrated for preschoolers to 8-year-olds.
- **Young readers** are for 5- to 8-year-olds.
- **Middle readers** are for 9- to 11-year-olds.
- **Young adults** are for ages 12 and up.

Age breakdowns may vary slightly from publisher to publisher, but using them as general guidelines will help you target appropriate markets. For example, if you've written an article about trends in teen fashion, check the Magazines Age-Level Index under the Young Adult subheading. Using this list, you'll quickly find the listings for young adult magazines.

Subject Index

But let's narrow the search further. Take your list of young adult magazines, turn to the Subject Index, and find the Fashion subheading. Then highlight the names that appear on

2007 CHILDREN'S WRITER'S & ILLUSTRATOR'S MARKET KEY TO SYMBOLS

[N] market new to this edition

⬛ Canadian agency

🌐 listing outside U.S. and Canada

🍎 publisher producing educational material

⬛ electronic publisher or producer

📖 book package/producer

[A] publisher accepts agented submissions only

🏆 award-winning publisher

ms, mss manuscript(s)

SCBWI Society of Children's Book Writers and Illustrators

SASE self-addressed, stamped envelope

SAE self-addressed envelope

IRC International Reply Coupon, for use in countries other than your own

b&w black & white

(For definitions of unfamilliar words and expressions relating to writing, illustration and publishing, see the Glossary.)

Find a handy pull-out bookmark, a quick reference to the icons used in this book, right inside the front cover.

both lists (Young Adult and Fashion). Now you have a smaller list of all the magazines that would be interested in your teen fashion article. Read through those listings and decide which ones sound best for your work.

Illustrators and photographers can use the Subject Index as well. If you specialize in painting animals, for instance, consider sending samples to book and magazine publishers listed under Animals and, perhaps, Nature/Environment. Since illustrators can simply send general examples of their style to art directors to keep on file, the indexes may be more helpful to artists sending manuscripts/illustration packages who need to search for a specific subject. Always read the listings for the potential markets to see the type of work art directors prefer and what type of samples they'll keep on file, and obtain art or photo guidelines if they're available through the mail or online.

Photography Index

In this index you'll find lists of book and magazine publishers, as well as greeting card, puzzle, and game manufacturers, that buy photos from freelancers. Refer to the list and read the listings for companies' specific photography needs. Obtain photo guidelines if they're offered through the mail or online.

USING THE LISTINGS

Many listings begin with one or more symbols. Refer to the inside covers of the book for quick reference and find a handy pull-out bookmark (shown at left) right inside the front cover.

Many listings indicate whether submission guidelines are available. If a publisher you're interested in offers guidelines, get them and read them. The same is true with catalogs. Sending for and reading catalogs or browsing them online gives you a better idea of whether your work would fit in with the books a publisher produces. (You should also look at a few of the books in the catalog at a library or bookstore to get a feel for the publisher's material.)

Especially for artists & photographers

Along with information for writers, listings provide information for illustrators and photographers. Illustrators will find numerous markets that maintain files of samples for possible future assignments. If you're both a writer and an illustrator, look for markets that accept manuscript/illustration packages and read the information offered under the **Illustration** subhead within the listings.

If you're a photographer, after consulting the Photography Index, read the information under the **Photography** subhead within listings to see what format buyers prefer. For example, some want 35mm color transparencies, others want black-and-white prints. Note the type of photos a buyer wants to purchase and the procedures for submitting. It's not uncommon for a market to want a résumé and promotional literature, as well as tearsheets from previous work. Listings also note whether model releases and/or captions are required.

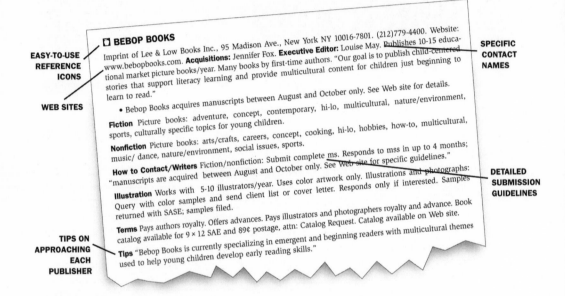

EASY-TO-USE
REFERENCE
ICONS

WEB SITES

SPECIFIC
CONTACT
NAMES

DETAILED
SUBMISSION
GUIDELINES

TIPS ON
APPROACHING
EACH
PUBLISHER

□ **BEBOP BOOKS**
Imprint of Lee & Low Books Inc., 95 Madison Ave., New York NY 10016-7801. (212)779-4400. Website: www.bebopbooks.com. **Acquisitions:** Jennifer Fox. **Executive Editor:** Louise May. Publishes 10-15 educational market picture books/year. Many books by first-time authors. "Our goal is to publish child-centered stories that support literacy learning and provide multicultural content for children just beginning to learn to read."

• Bebop Books acquires manuscripts between August and October only. See Web site for details.

Fiction Picture books: adventure, concept, contemporary, hi-lo, multicultural, nature/environment, sports, culturally specific topics for young children.

Nonfiction Picture books: arts/crafts, careers, concept, cooking, hi-lo, hobbies, how-to, multicultural, music/ dance, nature/environment, social issues, sports.

How to Contact/Writers Fiction/nonfiction: Submit complete ms. Responds to mss in up to 4 months; "manuscripts are acquired between August and October only. See Web site for specific guidelines."

Illustration Works with 5-10 illustrators/year. Uses color artwork only. Illustrations and photographs: Query with color samples and send client list or cover letter. Responds only if interested. Samples returned with SASE; samples filed.

Terms Pays authors royalty. Offers advances. Pays illustrators and photographers royalty and advance. Book catalog available for 9 × 12 SAE and 89¢ postage, attn: Catalog Request. Catalog available on Web site.

Tips "Bebop Books is currently specializing in emergent and beginning readers with multicultural themes used to help young children develop early reading skills."

Especially for young writers

If you're a parent, teacher, or student, you may be interested in Young Writer's & Illustrator's Markets. The listings in this section encourage submissions from young writers and artists. Some may require a written statement from a teacher or parent noting the work is original. Also watch for age limits.

Young people should also check Contests & Awards for contests that accept work by young writers and artists. Some of the contests listed are especially for students; others accept both student and adult work. These listings contain the phrase **open to students** in bold. Some listings in Clubs & Organizations and Conferences & Workshops may also be of interest to students. Organizations and conferences which are open to or are especially for students also include **open to students**.

Quick Tips
for Writers
& Illustrators

I f you're new to the world of children's publishing, buying *Children's Writer's & Illustrator's Market* may have been one of the first steps in your journey to publication. What follows is a list of suggestions and resources that can help make that journey a smooth and swift one:

1. Make the most of *Children's Writer's & Illustrator's Market*. Be sure to read How to Use This Book on page 2 for tips on reading the listings and using the indexes. Also be sure to take advantage of the articles and interviews in the book. The insights of the authors, illustrators, editors, and agents we've interviewed will inform and inspire you.

2. Join the Society of Children's Books Writers and Illustrators. SCBWI, more than 19,000 members strong, is an organization for both beginners and professionals interested in writing and illustrating for children. They offer members a slew of information and support through publications, a Web site, and a host of Regional Advisors overseeing chapters in almost every state in the U.S. and in a growing number of locations around the globe (including France, Canada, Japan, and Australia). SCBWI puts on a number of conferences, workshops, and events on the regional and national levels (many listed in the Conferences & Workshops section of this book). For more information, contact SCBWI, 8271 Beverly Blvd., Los Angeles CA 90048, (323)782-1010, or visit their Web site: www.scbwi.org.

3. Read newsletters. Newsletters, such as *Children's Book Insider*, *Children's Writer*, and the *SCBWI Bulletin*, offer updates and new information about publishers on a timely basis and are relatively inexpensive. Many local chapters of SCBWI offer regional newsletters as well. (See Helpful Books & Publications on page 357 for contact information on the newsletters listed above and others. For information on regional SCBWI newsletters, visit www.scbwi .org and click on "Publications.")

4. Read trade and review publications. Magazines like *Publishers Weekly* (which offers two special issues each year devoted to children's publishing and is available on newsstands), *The Horn Book*, and *Booklinks* offer news, articles, reviews of newly-published titles, and ads featuring upcoming and current releases. Referring to them will help you get a feel for what's happening in children's publishing.

5. Read guidelines. Most publishers and magazines offer writer's and artist's guidelines that provide detailed information on needs and submission requirements, and some magazines offer theme lists for upcoming issues. Many publishers and magazines state the availability of guidelines within their listings. Send a self-addressed, stamped envelope (SASE) to publishers who offer guidelines. You'll often find submission information on publishers' and magazines' Web sites.

6. Look at publishers' catalogs. Perusing publishers' catalogs can give you a feel for their line of books and help you decide where your work might fit in. If catalogs are available (often stated within listings), send for them with a SASE. Visit publishers' Web sites, which often contain their full catalogs. You can also ask librarians to look at catalogs they have on hand. You can even search Amazon.com (www.amazon.com) by publisher and year. (Click on "book search" then "publisher, date" and plug in, for example, "Lee & Low" under "publisher" and "2006" under year. You'll get a list of Lee & Low titles published in 2006, which you can peruse.)

7. Visit bookstores. It's not only informative to spend time in bookstores—it's fun, too! Frequently visit the children's section of your local bookstore (whether a chain or an independent) to see the latest from a variety of publishers and the most current issues of children's magazines. Look for books in the genre you're writing or with illustrations similar in style to yours, and spend some time studying them. It's also wise to get to know your local booksellers; they can tell you what's new in the store and provide insight into what kids and adults are buying.

8. Read, read, read! While you're at that bookstore, pick up a few things, or keep a list of the books that interest you and check them out of your library. Read and study the latest releases, the award winners, and the classics. You'll learn from other writers, get ideas, and get a feel for what's being published. Think about what works and doesn't work in a story. Pay attention to how plots are constructed and how characters are developed or the rhythm and pacing of picture book text. It's certainly enjoyable research!

9. Take advantage of Internet resources. There are innumerable sources of information available on the Internet about writing for children (and anything else you could possibly think of). It's also a great resource for getting (and staying) in touch with other writers and illustrators through listservs and e-mail, and it can serve as a vehicle for self-promotion. (Visit some authors' and illustators' sites for ideas. See Useful Online Resources on page 361 for a list of Web sites.)

10. Consider attending a conference. If time and finances allow, attending a conference is a great way to meet peers and network with professionals in the field of children's publishing. As mentioned above, SCBWI offers conferences in various locations year round. (See www.scbwi.org and click on "Events" for a full conference calendar.) General writers' conferences often offer specialized sessions just for those interested in children's writing. Many conferences offer optional manuscript and portfolio critiques as well, giving you a chance for feedback from seasoned professionals. See the Conferences & Awards section for information on SCBWI and other conferences. The section features a new Conferences & Workshops Calendar to help you plan your travel.

11. Network, network, network! Don't work in a vacuum. You can meet other writers and illustrators through a number of the things listed above—SCBWI, conferences, online. Attend local meetings for writers and illustrators whenever you can. Befriend other writers in your area (SCBWI offers members a roster broken down by state)—share guidelines, share subscriptions, be conference buddies and roommates, join a critique group or writing group, exchange information, and offer support. Get online—sign on to listservs, post on message boards, visit chatrooms. (The Institute of Children's Literature offers regularly scheduled live chats and open forums. Visit www.institutechildrenslit.com and click on Scheduled Events. Also, visit author Verla Kay's Web site, www.verlakay.com, for information on workshops. See Useful Online Resources on page 361 for more information.) Exchange addresses, phone numbers, and e-mail addresses with writers or illustrators you meet at events. And at conferences, don't be afraid to talk to people, ask strangers to join you for lunch, approach speakers and introduce yourself, or chat in elevators and hallways.

12. Perfect your craft and don't submit until your work is its best. It's often been said that a writer should try to write every day. Great manuscripts don't happen overnight;

there's time, research, and revision involved. As you visit bookstores and study what others have written and illustrated, really step back and look at your own work and ask yourself—honestly—*How does my work measure up? Is it ready for editors or art directors to see?* If it's not, keep working. Join a critique group or get a professional manuscript or portfolio critique.

13. Be patient, learn from rejection, and don't give up! Thousands of manuscripts land on editors' desks; thousands of illustration samples line art directors' file drawers. There are so many factors that come into play when evaluating submissions. Keep in mind that you might not hear back from publishers promptly. Persistence and patience are important qualities in writers and illustrators working toward publication. Keep at it—it will come. It can take a while, but when you get that first book contract or first assignment, you'll know it was worth the wait. (For proof, read First Books on page 96.)

Getting Started

Before Your First Sale

I f you're just beginning to pursue your career as a children's book writer or illustrator, it's important to learn the proper procedures, formats, and protocol for the publishing industry. This article outlines the basics you need to know before you head to the post office with your submissions.

FINDING THE BEST MARKETS FOR YOUR WORK

Researching publishers thoroughly is a basic element of submitting your work successfully. Editors and art directors hate to receive inappropriate submissions; handling them wastes a lot of their time, not to mention your time and money, and they are the main reason some publishers have chosen not to accept material over the transom. By randomly sending out material without knowing a company's needs, you're sure to meet with rejection.

If you're interested in submitting to a particular magazine, write to request a sample copy or see if it's available in your local library or bookstore. For a book publisher, obtain a book catalog and check a library or bookstore for titles produced by that publisher. Most publishers and magazines have Web sites that include catalogs or sample articles (Web sites are given within the listings). Studying such materials carefully will better acquaint you with a publisher's or magazine's writing, illustration, and photography styles and formats.

Most of the book publishers and magazines listed in this book (as well as some greeting card and paper product producers) offer some sort of writer's, artist's, or photographer's guidelines for a self-addressed, stamped envelope (SASE). Guidelines are also often found on publishers' Web sites. It's important to read and study guidelines before submitting work. You'll get a better understanding of what a particular publisher wants. You may even decide, after reading the submission guidelines, that your work isn't right for a company you considered.

SUBMITTING YOUR WORK

Throughout the listings, you'll read requests for particular elements to include when contacting markets. Here are explanations of some of these important submission components.

Queries, cover letters & proposals

A query letter is a no-more-than-one-page, well-written piece meant to arouse an editor's interest in your work. Many query letters start with leads similar to those of actual manuscripts. In the rest of the letter, briefly outline the work you're proposing and include facts, anecdotes, interviews, or other pertinent information that give the editor a feel for the manuscript's premise—entice her to want to know more. End your letter with a straightforward request to write or submit the work, and include information on its approximate length, date it could be completed, and whether accompanying photos or artwork are available.

In a query letter, think about presenting your book as a publisher's catalog would present it. Read through a good catalog and examine how the publishers give enticing summaries of their books in a spare amount of words. It's also important that query letters give editors a taste of your writing style. For good advice and samples of queries, cover letters, and other correspondence, consult *Formatting & Submitting Your Manuscript*, Second Edition, by Cynthia Laufenberg and the editors of *Writer's Market* and *How to Write Attention-Grabbing Query & Cover Letters*, by John Wood (both Writer's Digest Books). Also be sure to read 10 Tips for Writing a Great Query Letter on page 31.

For More Info

• **Query letters for nonfiction.** Queries are usually required when submitting nonfiction material to a publisher. The goal of a nonfiction query is to convince the editor your idea is perfect for her readership and that you're qualified to do the job. Note any previous writing experience and include published samples to prove your credentials, especially samples related to the subject matter you're querying about.

• **Query letters for fiction.** More and more, queries are being requested for fiction manuscripts. For a fiction query, explain the story's plot, main characters, conflict, and resolution. Just as in nonfiction queries, make the editor eager to see more.

• **Cover letters for writers.** Some editors prefer to review complete manuscripts, especially for fiction. In such cases, the cover letter (which should be no longer than one page) serves as your introduction, establishes your credentials as a writer, and gives the editor an overview of the manuscript. If the editor asked for the manuscript because of a query, note this in your cover letter.

• **Cover letters for illustrators and photographers.** For an illustrator or photographer, the cover letter serves as an introduction to the art director and establishes professional credentials when submitting samples. Explain what services you can provide as well as what type of follow-up contact you plan to make, if any. Be sure to include the URL of your online portfolio if you have one.

• **Résumés.** Often writers, illustrators, and photographers are asked to submit résumés with cover letters and samples. They can be created in a variety of formats, from a single page listing information to color brochures featuring your work. Keep your résumé brief, and focus on your achievements, including your clients and the work you've done for them, as well as your educational background and any awards you've received. Do not use the same résumé you'd use for a typical job application.

• **Book proposals.** Throughout the listings in the Book Publishers section, publishers refer to submitting a synopsis, outline, and sample chapters. Depending on an editor's preference, some or all of these components, along with a cover letter, make up a book proposal.

A *synopsis* summarizes the book, covering the basic plot (including the ending). It should be easy to read and flow well.

An *outline* covers your book chapter by chapter and provides highlights of each. If you're developing an outline for fiction, include major characters, plots and subplots, and book length.

Sample chapters give a more comprehensive idea of your writing skill. Some editors may request the first two or three chapters to determine if she's interested in seeing the whole book.

For more tips on crafting proposals see Writing the Nonfiction Book Proposal on page 39.

Manuscript formats

When submitting a complete manuscript, follow some basic guidelines. In the upper-left corner of your title page, type your legal name (not pseudonym), address, and phone number. In the upper-right corner, type the approximate word count. All material in the upper corners should be single-spaced. Then type the title (centered) almost halfway down that page, the word ''by'' two spaces under that, and your name or pseudonym two spaces under ''by.''

The first page should also include the title (centered) one-third of the way down. Two spaces under that type ''by'' and your name or pseudonym. To begin the body of your manuscript, drop down two double spaces and indent five spaces for each new paragraph. There should be one-inch margins around all sides of a full typewritten page. (Manuscripts with wide margins are more readable and easier to edit.)

Set your computer on double-space for the manuscript body. From page two to the end of the manuscript, include your last name followed by a comma and the title (or key words of the title) in the upper-left corner. The page number should go in the top right corner. Drop down two double spaces to begin the body of each page. If you're submitting a novel, type each chapter title one-third of the way down the page. For more information on manuscript formats, read *Formatting & Submitting Your Manuscript*, by Cynthia Laufenberg and the editors of *Writer's Market* (Writer's Digest Books). SCBWI members and nonmembers can refer to their publication *From Keyboard to Printed Page: Facts You Need to Know*. Visit their Web site www.scbwi.org and click on ''Publications.''

For More Info

Picture book formats

The majority of editors prefer to see complete manuscripts for picture books. When typing the text of a picture book, don't indicate page breaks and don't type each page of text on a new sheet of paper. And unless you are an illustrator, don't worry about supplying art. Editors will find their own illustrators for picture books. Most of the time, a writer and an illustrator who work on the same book never meet or interact. The editor acts as a go-between and works with the writer and illustrator throughout the publishing process. *How to Write and Sell Children's Picture Books*, by Jean E. Karl (Writer's Digest Books), offers advice on preparing text and marketing your work.

If you're an illustrator who has written your own book, consider creating a dummy or storyboard containing both art and text, and then submit it along with your complete manuscript and sample pieces of final art (color photocopies or computer printouts—never originals). Publishers interested in picture books specify in their listings what should be submitted. For tips on creating a dummy, refer to *How to Write and Illustrate Children's Books and Get Them Published*, edited by Treld Pelkey Bicknell and Felicity Trotman (North Light Books), or Frieda Gates' book, *How to Write, Illustrate, and Design Children's Books* (Lloyd-Simone Publishing Company).

For More Info

Writers may also want to learn the art of dummy making to help them through their writing process with things like pacing, rhythm, and length. For a great explanation and helpful hints, see *You Can Write Children's Books*, by Tracey E. Dils (Writer's Digest Books).

Mailing submissions

Your main concern when packaging material is to be sure it arrives undamaged. If your manuscript is less than six pages, simply fold it in thirds and send it in a #10 (business-size) envelope. For a SASE, either fold another #10 envelope in thirds or insert a #9 (reply) envelope which fits in a #10 neatly without folding.

Another option is folding your manuscript in half in a 6×9 envelope, with a #9 or #10 SASE enclosed. For larger manuscripts, use a 9×12 envelope both for mailing the submission and as a SASE (which can be folded in half). Book manuscripts require sturdy packaging for mailing. Include a self-addressed mailing label and return postage.

If asked to send artwork and photographs, remember they require a bit more care in packaging to guarantee they arrive in good condition. Sandwich illustrations and photos between heavy cardboard that is slightly larger than the work. The cardboard can be secured by rubber bands or with tape. If you tape the cardboard together, check that the artwork doesn't stick to the tape. Be sure your name and address appear on the back of each piece of art or each photo in case the material becomes separated. For the packaging, use either a manila envelope, a foam-padded envelope, brown paper, or a mailer lined with plastic air bubbles. Bind nonjoined edges with reinforced mailing tape and affix a typed mailing label or clearly write your address.

Mailing material first class ensures quick delivery. Also, first-class mail is forwarded for one year if the addressee has moved, and it can be returned if undeliverable. If you're concerned about your original material safely reaching its destination, consider other mailing options, such as UPS or certified mail. If material needs to reach your editor or art director quickly, use overnight delivery services.

Remember, companies outside your own country can't use your country's postage when returning a manuscript to you. When mailing a submission to another country, include a self-addressed envelope and International Reply Coupons, or IRCs. (You'll see this term in many listings in the Canadian & International Book Publishers section.) Your postmaster can tell you, based on a package's weight, the correct number of IRCs to include to ensure its return.

If it's not necessary for an editor to return your work (such as with photocopies), don't include return postage. You may want to track the status of your submission by enclosing a postage-paid reply postcard with options for the editor to check, such as "Yes, I am interested," "I'll keep the material on file," or "No, the material is not appropriate for my needs at this time."

Some writers elect to include a deadline date. If you don't hear from the editor by the specified date, your manuscript is automatically withdrawn from consideration. Because many publishing houses and companies are overstocked with material, a minimum deadline should be at least three months.

Unless requested, it's never a good idea to use a company's fax number or e-mail address to send manuscript submissions. This can disrupt a company's internal business. Some publishers, however, may be open to e-mail submissions. Study the Book Publishers listings for specifics and visit publishers' Web sites for more information.

Keeping submission records

It's important to keep track of the material you submit. When recording each submission, include the date it was sent, the business and contact name, and any enclosures (such as samples of writing, artwork, or photography). You can create a record-keeping system of your own or look for record-keeping software in your area computer store.

Keep copies of articles or manuscripts you send together with related correspondence to make follow-up easier. When you sell rights to a manuscript, artwork, or photos, you can "close" your file on a particular submission by noting the date the material was accepted, what rights were purchased, the publication date, and payment.

Often writers, illustrators, and photographers fail to follow up on overdue responses. If you don't hear from a publisher within their stated response time, wait another month or so and follow up with a note asking about the status of your submission. Include the title or description, date sent, and a SASE for response. Ask the contact person when she anticipates making a decision. You may refresh the memory of a buyer who temporarily forgot about your submission. At the very least, you'll receive a definite "no" and free yourself to send the material to another publisher.

Simultaneous submissions

If you opt for simultaneous (also called "multiple") submissions—sending the same material to several publishers at the same time—be sure to inform each editor to whom you submit that your work is being considered elsewhere. Many editors are reluctant to receive simultaneous submissions but understand that for hopeful writers and illustrators, waiting several months for a response can be frustrating. In some cases, an editor may actually be more inclined to read your manuscript sooner if she knows it's being considered by another publisher. The Society of Children's Book Writers and Illustrators cautions writers against simultaneous submissions. They recommend simultaneously submitting to publishers who state in their submission guidelines that they accept multiple submissions. In such cases, always specify in your cover letter that you've submitted to more than one editor.

It's especially important to keep track of simultaneous submissions, so if you get an offer on a manuscript sent to more than one publisher, you can instruct other publishers to withdraw your work from consideration.

AGENTS & ART REPS

Most children's writers, illustrators, and photographers, especially those just beginning, are confused about whether to enlist the services of an agent or representative. The decision is strictly one that each writer, illustrator, or photographer must make for herself. Some are confident with their own negotiation skills and believe acquiring an agent or rep is not in their best interest. Others feel uncomfortable in the business arena or are not willing to sacrifice valuable creative time for marketing.

About half of children's publishers accept unagented work, so it's possible to break into children's publishing without an agent. Some agents avoid working with children's books because traditionally low advances and trickling royalty payments over long periods of time make children's books less lucrative. Writers targeting magazine markets don't need the services of an agent. In fact, it's practically impossible to find an agent interested in marketing articles and short stories—there simply isn't enough financial incentive.

One benefit of having an agent, though, is it may speed up the process of getting your work reviewed, especially by publishers who don't accept unagented submissions. If an agent has a good reputation and submits your manuscript to an editor, that manuscript will likely bypass the first-read stage (which is generally done by editorial assistants and junior editors) and end up on the editor's desk sooner.

When agreeing to have a reputable agent represent you, remember that she should be familiar with the needs of the current market and evaluate your manuscript/artwork/photos accordingly. She should also determine the quality of your piece and whether it is saleable. When your manuscript sells, your agent should negotiate a favorable contract and clear up any questions you have about payments.

Keep in mind that however reputable the agent or rep is, she has limitations. Representation does not guarantee sale of your work. It just means an agent or rep sees potential in your writing, art, or photos. Though an agent or rep may offer criticism or advice on how to improve your work, she cannot make you a better writer, artist, or photographer.

Literary agents typically charge a 15 percent commission from the sale of writing; art and photo representatives usually charge a 25 to 30 percent commission. Such fees are taken from advances and royalty earnings. If your agent sells foreign rights to your work, she will deduct a higher percentage because she will most likely be dealing with an overseas agent with whom she must split the fee.

Be advised that not every agent is open to representing a writer, artist, or photographer who lacks an established track record. Just as when approaching a publisher, the manuscript, artwork, or photos and query or cover letter you submit to a potential agent must be attractive and professional looking. Your first impression must be as an organized, articulate person.

For listings of agents and reps, turn to the Agents & Art Reps section. For additional listings of art reps, consult *Artist's & Graphic Designer's Market*; for photo reps, see *Photographer's Market*; for more information and additional listings of agents see *Guide to Literary Agents* (all Writer's Digest Books).

Running Your Business

The Basics for Writers & Illustrators

A career in children's publishing involves more than just writing skills or artistic talent. Successful authors and illustrators must be able to hold their own in negotiations, keep records, understand contract language, grasp copyright law, pay taxes, and take care of a number of other business concerns. Although agents and reps, accountants and lawyers, and writers' organizations offer help in sorting out such business issues, it's wise to have a basic understanding of them going in. This article offers just that—basic information. For a more in-depth look at the subjects covered here, check your library or bookstore for books and magazines to help you. We also tell you how to get information on issues like taxes and copyright from the federal government.

CONTRACTS & NEGOTIATION

Before you see your work in print or begin working with an editor or art director on a project, there is negotiation. And whether negotiating a book contract, a magazine article assignment, or an illustration or photo assignment, there are a few things to keep in mind. First, if you find any clauses vague or confusing in a contract, get legal advice. The time and money invested in counseling up front could protect you from problems later. If you have an agent or rep, she will review any contract.

Sources for Contract Help

Writers organizations offer a wealth of information to members, including contract advice:

Society of Children's Book Writers and Illustrators members can find information in the SCBWI publication Answers to Some Questions About Contracts. Contact SCBWI at 8271 Beverly Blvd., Los Angeles CA 90048, (323)782-1010, or visit their Web site: www.scbwi.org.

The Authors Guild also offers contract tips. Visit their Web site, www.authorsguild .org. (Members of the guild can receive a 75-point contract review from the guild's legal staff.) See the Web site for membership information and application form, or contact The Authors Guild at 31 E. 28th St., 10th Floor, New York NY 10016, (212)563-5904. Fax: (212)564-5363. E-mail: staff@authorsguild.org. Web site: www .authorsguild.org.

A contract is an agreement between two or more parties that specifies the fees to be paid, services rendered, deadlines, rights purchased, and for artists and photographers, whether original work is returned. Most companies have standard contracts for writers, illustrators, and photographers. The specifics (such as royalty rates, advances, delivery dates, etc.) are typed in after negotiations.

Though it's okay to conduct negotiations over the phone, get a written contract once both parties have agreed on terms. Never depend on oral stipulations; written contracts protect both parties from misunderstandings. Watch for clauses that may not be in your best interest, such as "work-for-hire." When you do work-for-hire, you give up all rights to your creations.

When negotiating a book deal, find out whether your contract contains an option clause. This clause requires the author to give the publisher a first look at her next work before offering it to other publishers. Though it's editorial etiquette to give the publisher the first chance at publishing your next work, be wary of statements in the contract that could trap you. Don't allow the publisher to consider the next project for more than 30 days and be specific about what type of work should actually be considered "next work." (For example, if the book under contract is a young adult novel, specify that the publisher will receive an exclusive look at only your next young adult novel.)

For More Info

(For more information about SCBWI, The Authors Guild, and other organizations, turn to the Clubs & Organizations section and read the listings for the organizations that interest you.)

Book publishers' payment methods

Book publishers pay authors and artists in royalties, a percentage of either the wholesale or retail price of each book sold. From large publishing houses, the author usually receives an advance issued against future royalties before the book is published. Half of the advance amount is issued upon signing the book contract; the other half is issued when the book is finished. For illustrations, one-third of the advance should be collected upon signing the contract; one-third upon delivery of sketches; and one-third upon delivery of finished art.

After your book has sold enough copies to earn back your advance, you'll start to get royalty checks. Some publishers hold a reserve against returns, which means a percentage of royalties is held back in case books are returned from bookstores. If you have a reserve clause in your contract, find out the exact percentage of total sales that will be withheld and the time period the publisher will hold this money. You should be reimbursed this amount after a reasonable time period, such as a year. Royalty percentages vary with each publisher, but there are standard ranges.

Book publishers' rates

According to figures from the Society of Children's Book Writers and Illustrators, first-time picture book authors can expect advances of $2,000-3,000; first-time picture book illustrators' advances range from $5,000-7,000; text and illustration packages for first-timers can score $6,000-8,000. Rates go up for subsequent books: $3,500-5,000 for picture book text; $7,000-10,000 for picture book illustration; $8,000-10,000 for text and illustration. Experienced authors can expect higher advances. Royalties for picture books are generally about five percent (split between the author and illustrator) but can go as high as 10 percent. Those who both write and illustrate a book, of course, receive the full royalty.

Advances for hardcover novels and nonfiction can fetch authors advances of $4,000-6,000 and 10 percent royalties; paperbacks bring in slightly lower advances of $3,000-5,000 and royalties of 6-8 percent.

As you might expect, advance and royalty figures vary from house to house and are affected by the time of year, the state of the economy, and other factors. Some smaller houses may not even pay royalties, just flat fees. Educational houses may not offer advances or offer smaller amounts. Religious publishers tend to offer smaller advances than trade publishers. First-time writers and illustrators generally start on the low end of the scale, while established and high-profile writers are paid more. For more information SCBWI members can request or download SCBWI publication "Answer to Some Questions About Contracts." (Visit www.scbwi.org.)

Pay rates for magazines

For writers, fee structures for magazines are based on a per-word rate or range for a specific article length. Artists and photographers have a few more variables to contend with before contracting their services.

Payment for illustrations and photos can be set by such factors as whether the piece(s) will be black and white or four-color, how many are to be purchased, where the work appears (cover or inside), circulation, and the artist's or photographer's prior experience.

Remaindering

When a book goes out of print, a publisher will sell any existing copies to a wholesaler who, in turn, sells the copies to stores at a discount. When the books are "remaindered" to a wholesaler, they are usually sold at a price just above the cost of printing. When negotiating a contract with a publisher, you may want to discuss the possibility of purchasing the remaindered copies before they are sold to a wholesaler, then you can market the copies you purchased and still make a profit.

KNOW YOUR RIGHTS

A copyright is a form of protection provided to creators of original works, published or unpublished. In general, copyright protection ensures the writer, illustrator, or photographer the power to decide how her work is used and allows her to receive payment for each use.

Essentially, copyright also encourages the creation of new works by guaranteeing the creator power to sell rights to the work in the marketplace. The copyright holder can print, reprint, or copy her work; sell or distribute copies of her work; or prepare derivative works such as plays, collages, or recordings. The Copyright Law is designed to protect work (created on or after January 1, 1978) for her lifetime plus 70 years.

If you collaborate with someone else on a written or artistic project, the copyright will last for the lifetime of the last survivor plus 70 years. The creators' heirs may hold a copyright for an additional 70 years. After that, the work becomes public domain. Works created anonymously or under a pseudonym are protected for 120 years, or 95 years after publication. Under work-for-hire agreements, you relinquish your copyright to your "employer."

Copyright notice & registration

Some feel a copyright notice should be included on all work, registered or not. Others feel it is not necessary and a copyright notice will only confuse publishers about whether the material is registered (acquiring rights to previously registered material is a more complicated process).

Although it's not necessary to include a copyright notice on unregistered work, if you don't feel your work is safe without the notice, it is your right to include one. Including a copyright notice—© (year of work, your name)—should help safeguard against plagiarism.

Registration is a legal formality intended to make copyright public record, and it can help you win more money in a court case. By registering work within three months of publication or before an infringement occurs, you are eligible to collect statutory damages and attorney's fees. If you register later than three months after publication, you will qualify only for actual damages and profits.

Ideas and concepts are not copyrightable, only expressions of those ideas and concepts. A

Getting Started

character type or basic plot outline, for example, is not subject to a copyright infringement lawsuit. Also, titles, names, short phrases or slogans, and lists of contents are not subject to copyright protection, though titles and names may be protected through the Trademark Office.

You can register a group of articles, illustrations, or photos if it meets these criteria:

- the group is assembled in order, such as in a notebook
- the works bear a single title, such as "Works by (your name)"
- it is the work of one writer, artist, or photographer
- the material is the subject of a single claim to copyright

It's a publisher's responsibility to register your book for copyright. If you've previously registered the same material, you must inform your editor and supply the previous copyright information, otherwise, the publisher can't register the book in its published form.

For more information about the proper way to register works and to order the correct forms, contact the U.S. Copyright Office, (202)707-3000. The forms available are TX for writing (books, articles, etc.); VA for pictures (photographs, illustrations); and PA for plays and music. For information about how to use the copyright forms, request a copy of Circular I on Copyright Basics. All of the forms and circulars are free. Send the completed registration form along with the stated fee and a copy of the work to the Copyright Office.

For More Info

For specific answers to questions about copyright (but not legal advice), call the Copyright Public Information Office at (202)707-3000 weekdays between 8:30 a.m. and 5 p.m. EST. Forms can also be downloaded from the Library of Congress Web site: www.copyright.gov. The site also includes a list of frequently asked questions, tips on filling out forms, general copyright information, and links to other sites related to copyright issues. For members of SCBWI, information about copyrights and the law is available in their publication: Copyright Facts for Writers.

The rights publishers buy

The copyright law specifies that a writer, illustrator, or photographer generally sells one-time rights to her work unless she and the buyer agree otherwise in writing. Many publications will want more exclusive rights to your work than just one-time usage; some will even require you to sell all rights. Be sure you are monetarily compensated for the additional rights you relinquish. If you must give up all rights to a work, carefully consider the price you're being offered to determine whether you'll be compensated for the loss of other potential sales.

Writers who only give up limited rights to their work can then sell reprint rights to other publications, foreign rights to international publications, or even movie rights, should the opportunity arise. Artists and photographers can sell their work to other markets such as paper product companies who may use an image on a calendar, greeting card, or mug. Illustrators and photographers may even sell original work after it has been published. And there are a number of galleries throughout the U.S. that display and sell the original work of children's illustrators.

Rights acquired through the sale of a book manuscript are explained in each publisher's contract. Take time to read relevant clauses to be sure you understand what rights each contract is specifying before signing. Be sure your contract contains a clause allowing all rights to revert back to you in the event the publisher goes out of business. (You may even want to have the contract reviewed by an agent or an attorney specializing in publishing law.)

The following are the rights you'll most often sell to publishers, periodicals, and producers in the marketplace:

First rights. The buyer purchases the rights to use the work for the first time in any medium. All other rights remain with the creator. When material is excerpted from a soon-to-be-published book for use in a newspaper or periodical, first serial rights are also purchased.

One-time rights. The buyer has no guarantee that she is the first to use a piece. One-time permission to run written work, illustrations, or photos is acquired, then the rights revert back to the creator.

First North American serial rights. This is similar to first rights, except that companies who distribute both in the U.S. and Canada will stipulate these rights to ensure that another North American company won't come out with simultaneous usage of the same work.

Second serial (reprint) rights. In this case, newspapers and magazines are granted the right to reproduce a work that has already appeared in another publication. These rights are also purchased by a newspaper or magazine editor who wants to publish part of a book after the book has been published. The proceeds from reprint rights for a book are often split evenly between the author and his publishing company.

Simultaneous rights. More than one publication buys one-time rights to the same work at the same time. Use of such rights occurs among magazines with circulations that don't overlap, such as many religious publications.

All rights. Just as it sounds, the writer, illustrator, or photographer relinquishes all rights to a piece—she no longer has any say in who acquires rights to use it. All rights are purchased by publishers who pay premium usage fees, have an exclusive format, or have other book or magazine interests from which the purchased work can generate more mileage. If a company insists on acquiring all rights to your work, see if you can negotiate for the rights to revert back to you after a reasonable period of time. If they agree to such a proposal, get it in writing.

Note: Writers, illustrators, and photographers should be wary of "work-for-hire" arrangements. If you sign an agreement stipulating that your work will be done as work-for-hire, you will not control the copyrights of the completed work—the company that hired you will be the copyright owner.

Foreign serial rights. Be sure before you market to foreign publications that you have sold only North American—not worldwide—serial rights to previous markets. If so, you are free to market to publications that may be interested in material that's appeared in a North American-based periodical.

Syndication rights. This is a division of serial rights. For example, if a syndicate prints portions of a book in installments in its newspapers, it would be syndicating second serial rights. The syndicate would receive a commission and leave the remainder to be split between the author and publisher.

Subsidiary rights. These include serial rights, dramatic rights, book club rights, or translation rights. The contract should specify what percentage of profits from sales of these rights go to the author and publisher.

Dramatic, television, and motion picture rights. During a specified time, the interested party tries to sell a story to a producer or director. Many times options are renewed because the selling process can be lengthy.

Display rights or electronic publishing rights. They're also known as "Data, Storage, and Retrieval." Usually listed under subsidiary rights, the marketing of electronic rights in this era of rapidly expanding capabilities and markets for electronic material can be tricky. Display rights can cover text or images to be used in a CD-ROM or online, or they may cover use of material in formats not even fully developed yet. If a display rights clause is listed in your contract, try to negotiate its elimination. Otherwise, be sure to pin down which electronic rights are being purchased. Demand the clause be restricted to things designed to be read only. By doing this, you maintain your rights to use your work for things such as games and interactive software.

STRICTLY BUSINESS

An essential part of being a freelance writer, illustrator, or photographer is running your freelance business. It's imperative to maintain accurate business records to determine if you're making a profit as a freelancer. Keeping correct, organized records will also make your life easier as you approach tax time.

When setting up your system, begin by keeping a bank account and ledger for your business finances apart from your personal finances. Also, if writing, illustration, or photography is secondary to another freelance career, keep separate business records for each.

You will likely accumulate some business expenses before showing any profit when you start out as a freelancer. To substantiate your income and expenses to the IRS, keep all invoices, cash receipts, sales slips, bank statements, canceled checks, and receipts related to travel expenses and entertaining clients. For entertainment expenditures, record the date, place, and purpose of the business meeting, as well as gas mileage. Keep records for all purchases, big and small. Don't take the small purchases for granted; they can add up to a substantial amount. File all receipts in chronological order. Maintaining a separate file for each month simplifies retrieving records at the end of the year.

Record keeping

When setting up a single-entry bookkeeping system, record income and expenses separately. Use some of the subheads that appear on Schedule C (the form used for recording income from a business) of the 1040 tax form so you can easily transfer information onto the tax form when filing your return. In your ledger include a description of each transaction—the date, source of income (or debts from business purchases), description of what was purchased or sold, the amount of the transaction, and whether payment was by cash, check, or credit card.

Don't wait until January 1 to start keeping records. The moment you first make a business-related purchase or sell an article, book manuscript, illustration, or photo, begin tracking your profits and losses. If you keep records from January 1 to December 31, you're using a calendar-year accounting period. Any other accounting period is called a fiscal year.

There are two types of accounting methods you can choose from—the cash method and the accrual method. The cash method is used more often: You record income when it is received and expenses when they're disbursed.

Using the accrual method, you report income at the time you earn it rather than when it's actually received. Similarly, expenses are recorded at the time they're incurred rather than when you actually pay them. If you choose this method, keep separate records for ''accounts receivable'' and ''accounts payable.''

Satisfying the IRS

To successfully—and legally—work as a freelancer, you must know what income you should report and what deductions you can claim. But before you can do that, you must prove to the IRS you're in business to make a profit, that your writing, illustration, or photography is not merely a hobby.

The Tax Reform Act of 1986 says you should show a profit for three years out of a five-year period to attain professional status. The IRS considers these factors as proof of your professionalism:

- accurate financial records
- a business bank account separate from your personal account
- proven time devoted to your profession
- whether it's your main or secondary source of income
- your history of profits and losses
- the amount of training you have invested in your field
- your expertise

If your business is unincorporated, you'll fill out tax information on Schedule C of Form

1040. If you're unsure of what deductions you can take, request the IRS publication containing this information. Under the Tax Reform Act, only 30 percent of business meals, entertainment and related tips, and parking charges are deductible. Other deductible expenses allowed on Schedule C include: car expenses for business-related trips; professional courses and seminars; depreciation of office equipment, such as a computer; dues and publication subscriptions; and miscellaneous expenses, such as postage used for business needs.

If you're working out of a home office, a portion of your mortgage interest (or rent), related utilities, property taxes, repair costs, and depreciation may be deducted as business expenses—under special circumstances. To learn more about the possibility of home office deductions, consult IRS Publication 587, Business Use of Your Home

The method of paying taxes on income not subject to withholding is called "estimated tax" for individuals. If you expect to owe more than $500 at year's end and if the total amount of income tax that will be withheld during the year will be less than 90 percent of the tax shown on the current year's return, you'll generally make estimated tax payments. Estimated tax payments are made in four equal installments due on April 15, June 15, September 15, and January 15 (assuming you're a calendar-year taxpayer). For more information, request Publication 533, Self-Employment Tax.

The Internal Revenue Service's Web site (www.irs.gov) offers tips and instant access to IRS forms and publications.

For More Info

Social Security tax

Depending on your net income as a freelancer, you may be liable for a Social Security tax. This is a tax designed for those who don't have Social Security withheld from their paychecks. You're liable if your net income is $400 or more per year. Net income is the difference between your income and allowable business deductions. Request Schedule SE, Computation of Social Security Self-Employment Tax, if you qualify.

If completing your income tax return proves to be too complex, consider hiring an accountant (the fee is a deductible business expense) or contact the IRS for assistance. (Look in the White Pages under U.S. Government—Internal Revenue Service or check their Web site, www.irs.gov.) In addition to offering numerous publications to instruct you in various facets of preparing a tax return, the IRS also has walk-in centers in some cities.

Insurance

As a self-employed professional, be aware of what health and business insurance coverage is available to you. Unless you're a Canadian who is covered by national health insurance or a full-time freelancer covered by your spouse's policy, health insurance will no doubt be one of your biggest expenses. Under the terms of a 1985 government act (COBRA), if you leave a job with health benefits, you're entitled to continue that coverage for up to 18 months—you pay 100 percent of the premium and sometimes a small administration fee. Eventually, you must search for your own health plan. You may also choose to purchase disability and life insurance. Disability insurance is offered through many private insurance companies and state governments. This insurance pays a monthly fee that covers living and business expenses during periods of long-term recuperation from a health problem. The amount of money paid is based on the recipient's annual earnings.

Before contacting any insurance representative, talk to other writers, illustrators, or photographers to learn which insurance companies they recommend. If you belong to a writers' or artists' organization, ask the organization if it offers insurance coverage for professionals. (SCBWI has a plan available to members in certain states. Look through the Clubs & Organizations section for other groups that may offer coverage.) Group coverage may be more affordable and provide more comprehensive coverage than an individual policy.

A Writing Teacher's Do's & Don't

by Esther Hershenhorn

The scene is oh, so familiar, repeating itself with each new adult Writing for Children class I teach.

A writing student arrives the first day of class, manuscript in hand like a gift-bearing Magi.

"Hurrah!" I exclaim. I pat my student on his back. "You kept your body in the chair. You kept your fingers on the keyboard. You kept your eye on the prize to tell your tale from start to finish."

But honesty prevails if I'm to do my job right.

A heart-felt sigh soon punctuates my words.

"Now," I say, "Let's do it again. Now," I say, "let's tell your story to your reader."

The Truth is: a story's *first* draft is vital. It's in this all-important first draft that you tell *yourself* the story.

It's in the second draft, however, that you tell it to your *reader*, making choices as you go to tell a good story well.

The following list of Do's and Don't, gleaned from years of teaching and reviewing manuscripts, can help you make the necessary choices.

Good choices insure a page-turning reader, the story sounding in his heart the way it first *thrumped* in yours.

#1: Do know your characters from their insides-out

A story is about a character *who*_____. Complete the blank with a dream/wish/fear or problem.

> A mouse with big ears who longs to know love.
> Four motherless sisters who want to help a very interesting boy.
> A stuffed toy bear who needs to find his lost button.

Immerse yourself in the lives of your characters. Imagine your way into their heads, hearts and guts. Widen your camera lens to view each and every character, to see what came before

ESTHER HERSHENHORN is a Chicago-based children's book author and Writing Coach. She teaches adult Writing for Children classes at the University of Chicago's Writer's Studio, the Newberry Library, and Ragdale, an artist residency program in Lake Forest, Illinois. Visit www.estherhershenhorn.com to learn more about her books, teaching, and coaching.

as well as what came after. Doing so leads to fully-realized (and thus believable) characters who pull a reader in. Doing so also leads to character-driven plotlines.

You, the storyteller, must know *what* your characters want. That *what* determines a character's physical plotline. You must also know the *why* behind that *what*. The *why* determines a character's emotional plotline.

Notice above the use of *characters* plural. To get your story right, it's important to invest equally in all of your characters—your main character's friends as well as his enemies. Their actions and reactions impact those of your main character. You, the storyteller, must know their *what's* and *why's*, too.

Check out Marian Dane Bauer's book *What's Your Story?* from your local library. Chapters Three and Four offer writers of all ages creative exercises to help grow well-rounded characters.

#2: Do create a flawless story logic

John Gardner writes in *The Art of Fiction*, "Fiction does its work by creating a dream in the reader's mind."

For a reader to experience a story, that fictional dream must remain continuous. The reader cannot be distracted. He can never leave the story. He must never be given reason to pause to ask, "Hey! How can *that* be?"

Chinks in a story's logic always distract.

Make sure each character's actions and *re*actions are not only true to his nature, to his quest, to his motivation—but accurately reflect the character you've presented.

Make sure there are no loose story threads, no characters introduced but soon left withering on the vine. Finally, make sure you foreshadow your story's inevitable yet surprising

Articles & Interviews

MORE DO'S FROM WRITING TEACHERS...

Paula Morrow

"Do read," advises Paula Morrow, a veteran faculty member of the Institute of Children's Literature and long-time Cricket Group editor.

Morrow believes nearly all mistakes, whether in plot, voice, characterization, technique, manuscript submission or lesson completions, can be traced to the basic failing of not reading.

"I always know when my students write an assignment without reading the manual: most if not all the mistakes in their manuscripts are things that were clearly explained in the lesson. At Cricket Group, it's obvious which manuscripts in the slush pile were submitted by someone who had not bothered to read the guidelines or had never looked at a copy of the magazine to which the manuscript was addressed. Book submissions, too, betray an author who has not looked carefully at our catalog and actually read at least one book we've published."

Morrow suggests writers read children's books and magazines, guidelines publishers' catalogues. "Read to see what works—and what doesn't. Read for pleasure. Read for knowledge. Read for inspiration. Read to laugh and to cry."

She concludes, "Just read."

The Institute of Children's Literature offers students one-on-one personalized instruction in the traditional home-study method. Lessons are exchanged through the mail or via the Internet. Visit www.writingforchildren.com.

satisfactory resolution. Lay the groundwork for your story's ending. And, let that ending arise from all your character learned.

To keep both you and your reader on track, fully-invested in your fictive dream, read Christopher Vogler's *The Writer's Journey*. Vogler's insights can help you draft a road map of your characters and their actions, one you can consult should you ever lose your way.

#3: Do choose an appropriate format in which to tell your story

When children comprise your readership, you have a wealth of formats in which to tell your story.

A story may be ripe for illustrations, yet not able to go the distance of a 32-page picture book. A slice-of-life moment might be best served by a magazine story or a series of connected ''moments'' in an early chapter book. Some true-to-life tales deserve true-to-life tellings.

Think about your reader's chronological age.

Think about your reader's cognitive skills.

Think about your reader's emotional age, too.

Then, think about your story—its subject matter and likely child interest—and the language necessary to tell such a story.

Familiarize yourself with the available formats published today in the trade, educational, magazine, religious and Web site markets. Barbara Seuling's *How to Write a Children's Book and Get It Published* and Harold Underdown's *The Complete Idiot's Guide to Publishing Children's Books* include not only explanations of available formats but representative works for you to study.

#4: Do consider your viewpoint opportunities

Choose carefully when selecting your story's narrator. The choice affects your story's tone, your story's style, and certainly, your story's ''voice.''

First person? Third person? Limited third person? Each has its perks; each has its pitfalls.

The first person narrator offers intimacy, yet cannot offer the reader a sweeping landscape; the omniscient third person narrator offers a fuller cast of characters, yet often fails to give the young reader that one single character in whom he can invest; the third person limited viewpoint offers some degree of intimacy, yet cannot bring the immediacy of a first person telling.

Experiment with each viewpoint before making your choice. Try telling your story through the eyes of your main character's best friend or much-admired older sibling, or better yet, his archenemy or life-long competitor. Ask yourself: which viewpoint allows the reader to best hear your character, to best experience his actions and re-actions, to best get inside his state of mind. Choose the viewpoint that allows the reader to see instantly who claims your story. Young readers need to know: whose story is it?

Whichever viewpoint you choose, honor it, so the reader knows *always* with whom he's traveling.

#5: Do begin your story at the right moment

Most editors agree: begin at that one moment when everything changes for your story's character, when his world becomes different, when he now must categorize his life as Before and After.

Your opening pages or first chapter need to hook the reader. They are not the place to offer up back history. Weave the important facts the reader needs to know into the opening dialogue, briefly, subtly.

Make sure you're not writing text to warm yourself up, to ready your spirit to go on to tell the tale.

Test yourself: choose a favorite book, past and/or present; read the plot's summary in a book review or on the flap copy; then return to the opening pages to note the story's start. Determine its importance to the character and the story.

#6: Do move your story forward in rendered scenes

Once you know what your story is about and what happens, render scenes to move your story forward.

Think of a scene as a small story unto itself, on stage. There's a beginning, a middle and an end. There's a setting. There are characters speaking to reveal their true selves, to inform the reader, to advance the plot.

Select a favorite book that utilizes a format comparable to yours. Bracket the scenes. Color-code the characters and their lines of dialogue within each scene. Note the balance between narrative and dialogue. Characters who speak help you show your reader the story.

William Sloane writes in *The Craft of Writing*, "A scene is a unit of events . . . containing nothing except characters in action. In theatre, it's what goes on between people, and it begins when the curtain rises and it ends when the curtain falls. No characters not germane to the purpose of the scene should be allowed on stage. No information for its own quaint sake should be included as window dressing."

#7: Do create a palpable story tension

You want your reader needing to turn the pages. You want him worrying. You want him to care. You want him thinking, "Oh?" then "Oh, my!" then *"Oh, dear!"* then, "OH, NO!" Then, finally, *"Oh, yes."*

Leave your reader with a compelling question at the end of Chapter One or your picture book's opening scenes or your article's first paragraph: "Will he or won't he?" or "Can he?" or *"Now* what?"

MORE DO'S FROM WRITING TEACHERS...

Anastasia Suen

Prolific author Anastasia Suen teaches online intensive writing workshops, focusing on varied and various formats, genres and sides of the writing business. She offers an emphatic *ibid* to Paula Morrow's comment. "Do read, read, read!"

Suen believes the writing process actually has three steps: first you read, then you think and then . . . you write. What she finds with many writers is that they skip the first step. They don't read.

She asks all of her workshop students to read, read, read while they are writing with her.

"When you immerse yourself in books," Suen tells her students, "writer's block disappears and your writing deepens. When you eat, drink and sleep *story*, your writing grows. You see the worst and the best, and you discover what you like. Reading helps you find your voice."

Suen commands, "Give me five!" She asks her students to read five books a day. For books with chapters, she recommends a book a day, or five books a week. "Read in your genre *every* day," she advises, "and watch your writing grow!"

Visit www.anastasiasuen.com to learn more about Anastasia Suen and her online workshops. Writer's Digest Books published her picture book writing text *Picture Writing*.

Turn-of-the-century novelists who tied the Heroine to the railroad tracks knew what they were doing. Usually, the Union Pacific Zephyr was due to barrel through moments later and the likely rescuing Sheriff was tied up to a chair.

Escalate the danger as you build your scenes. Raise the ante. Raise what's at stake. Implement a now-or-never deadline. Insert a ticking bomb or a ticking clock. Giving the reader a clear grasp of the story's reasonable chronology—one day, one week, one month, one season—can also tighten your story's tension.

Make sure conflict is always present. The reader needs to see the forces opposing your story's character.

#8: Do ground your reader in a time and a place

A story's *when* and *where* are important, too. Young readers especially need to be grounded. They need a firm footing before they take off with your characters.

The concrete and hopefully sensory details of your story's time and place not only give your characters a world in which to live and breathe; they do the same for your reader.

Connie Epstein writes in *The Art of Writing for Children* that "background gives the reader something to look at. It establishes an atmosphere and helps to make a story emotionally strong."

Time and setting can also serve your story, in ways not possible when you first told yourself your story. Now, let your word choice—your phrasing, your language structure, your character and place names—intentionally reflect the world in which your characters live.

Epstein also reminds writers, "Setting affects the action of the plot and the personality of the characters. In every piece of fiction, setting is one of the three major elements, along with characterization and plot, that the writer must weave together to create the narrative."

#9: Do pay attention to language

Telling your good story well often demands a third retelling, a more careful examination of the words, the sentences, the paragraphs, the chapters, and how they work together to serve the greater whole. Maybe rhyme isn't in keeping with the kind of story you're telling, with the characters you're presenting. Maybe less florid writing would showcase the simplicity of your story and its plotline.

Removing clumsy writing, however, is always advisable.

Gardner speaks at length on this subject in *The Art of Fiction*, stating that clumsy writing removes the reader from the fictional dream as well as undercuts the writer's authority.

"Where lumps and infelicities occur in fiction, the sensitive reader shrinks away a little, as we do when an interesting conversationalist picks his nose."

Gardner's obvious forms of clumsiness are worth noting: (1) inappropriate or excessive use of the passive voice; (2) inappropriate use of introductory phrases containing infinite verbs; (3) shifts in diction level or the regular use of distracting diction; (4) lack of sentence variety; (5) lack of sentence focus; (6) faulty rhythm; (7) accidental rhyme; (8) needless explanation; (9) careless shifts in psychic distance; and (10) mannered writing.

Once you've finished your second draft, tuck it away in a drawer for a while, so you can re-read a few weeks later with thoroughly refreshed eyes. Consider recording your text, then playing it back, looking and listening for the story's flow and sentence rhythm. It also helps to listen to an "innocent reader" read aloud your story.

#10: Don't preach

Let the theme of your good story do all the talking. Give your reader concrete telling details in a character-driven plot and let *him* draw the Universal Truths.

It also helps to have the story's characters *speak* of what they've learned while out and about on their various plotlines. It's always a Red Flag when an adult character enters and *tells* the reader of some greater moral lesson.

If you came to your story wanting to teach, rethink your choice to do so in a story. As Seuling informs her readers, the theme of Frank Baum's *The Wonderful Wizard of Oz* is "Be it ever so humble, there's no place like home." The plot, on the other hand, focuses on how Dorothy needs to get herself out of trouble and home again after a tornado drops her in the fantastical world of Oz.

To this Writing Teacher's way of thinking, making your manuscript reader-ready is an opportunity—indeed, a second chance, to tell your good story well to a waiting world of children.

MORE DO'S FROM WRITING TEACHERS...

Barbara Seuling

Do plot!" counsels author Barbara Seuling.

Seuling directs The Manuscript Workshop in Vermont, a summer writing workshop to which she brings techniques of successful writing through informal but structured guidance.

She believes that children want stories that are well plotted, that have clear beginnings, middles and ends, with the necessary interesting characters, tension, conflict and satisfying ending. "That's what makes a story stick, stay with the reader long after the book is closed, and long into one's memory," she says.

According to Seuling, "Plot problems become evident when the writer loses sight of what she set out to say, or accomplish, and goes off on a track that takes her someplace else that doesn't connect smoothly to her original plan."

Seuling admits to knowing this problem well. "As a beginning writer, I had written a novel that got good feedback from editors, but couldn't pass muster because there was no clear plot! When I found the 25-words-or-less exercise in Phyllis Reynolds Naylor's book *The Craft of Writing*, it all came clear and I've been using it myself—and with my students—ever since."

Barbara Seuling's book *How to Write a Children's Book and Get It Published* (Wiley) is now in its third edition. Visit www.barbaraseuling.com to learn more about her Vermont workshop.

Successful Rewriting

Viewing the Big Picture

by Sue Bradford Edwards

Once upon a time, I *thought* I knew how to rewrite. After all, I'd rewritten numerous manuscripts for various editors and had over 100 sales to my credit.

Then came my young adult novel. Chapter by chapter, I read my critique groups' comments and altered the hard copy. Around Chapter 6, I bogged down. I looked at page after page of detailed comments and just couldn't get going.

What was I doing wrong? To find out, I talked to seven multipublished authors. I learned that the rewrite process starts the moment you receive an editor's letter.

Am I on Candid Camera?

How do you react to comments on your work? Author Kathryn Lay's reaction is fairly typical if somewhat understated. "First I read it quickly, panic awhile, then put it away for a day or two and reread. I panic a little less the second time," she says.

On a good day, most authors sit in shocked dismay after reading a lengthy rewrite request. On a bad day, we gripe about our editor and fire off heated e-mails to our writer friends. At the very least, most of us get annoyed when a critique buddy or editor doesn't adore our work as is. Face it, a really good rewrite is a lot of work.

Even before talking to these writers, I did one thing right. I limited my "tantrum time." "Take three days to get over being mad. You're allowed only three days and then get busy and get to work," says Darcy Pattison.

This is vital because some writers never get beyond this knee-jerk reaction. Instead they put editors who ask for extensive rewrites on a "no submission" list made up of those who just don't "get" their work. These writers lose out because they never look calmly at the editor's comments. "An editorial letter," says Pattison, "you're not going to get better direction than that."

What direction is that?

When they've had a chance to mellow, the pros set aside a block of time to reread their editor's letter. They make sure the editor's comments are systematically grouped so that evaluating the manuscript is easier. "I mark up their letter. I make notes. Some editors are very organized in their notes and some are very scattered," says Pattison. "I make sure I have the similar things together."

SUE BRADFORD EDWARDS writes and rewrites from her Missouri home. She specializes in nonfiction, especially history and archaeology. Her work can regularly be found in a variety of testing publications, *Children's Writer* newsletter and the St. Louis *Post-Dispatch*. Visit her Web site www.suebradfordedwards.8m.com.

Next the pros read their manuscript in one sitting. "I make sure I have a long stretch of time when I'm not going to be interrupted, and I do a read-through of my manuscript from scratch," says Amanda Jenkins. "I don't make long notes, but just mark places where I'm bored, or can't follow the story, or where something trips me up. The editorial letter is in the back of my mind the whole time, so I'm especially looking for things that corroborate what the editor found lacking."

This read-through helps the author wrap her mind around the manuscript as a single piece of work in relationship to the letter. "Generally if I have a chance to focus first on what the editor is telling me, then reread my manuscript straight through," says Dori Butler, "I see exactly what the editor is saying and I can go from there."

I had always read short manuscripts through before beginning my rewrite, but skipped this with my novel. By rereading both the comments on my work and the novel itself, I would have better defined my direction and been prepared to look deep.

Don't be shallow

Failed revisions often dance across the surface of the work—polishing sentences, moving punctuation and dealing only with the most basic comments from the editor. A professional rewrite goes beyond the cosmetic surface of rhythmic words and well-grouped paragraphs. It alters the deeper structure, quickening plot, strengthening theme and bulking up character.

To do this, look deeper than the editor's comments. "I don't always look at what specific changes the editor asks for, so much as what she wants changed. In other words, I look closely at what the editor says is *not* working," says Jenkins. This may mean addressing characterization issues vs. individual actions that don't ring true. "Sometimes editors may suggest a change that won't fix what's really wrong, and if you go blindly plugging in their suggestions, you'll get mixed up and lose your feel for the characters and story," says Jenkins. "I feel that it's more productive to see what's wrong, decide whether the editor's suggestion will work, and if not, to figure out a fix that comes naturally from the characters."

Pattison's approach is similar. "I try to understand not *what* they're saying to me but *why* they're saying it," she says. "When my editor at Harcourt wrote back and told me a couple of things, I summarized it and said 'the voice is wrong and the tone is wrong.' What mattered to me was the summary. Not the specifics. If you do just what they say, it will be rejected."

Superficial rewrites fail when suggestions don't mesh with the original manuscript. "When I was working on *River Dragon*, I had the dragon appear three times and his voice sounded like the clink of copper coins because that's what I'd found in my research," says Pattison. Her editor wanted a progression in the metals and suggested copper, silver, and gold which wasn't a good fit. "I put in a progression to baser metals, copper to brass to the clang of a hammer on an anvil which worked well because the main character was a blacksmith," says Pattison. "Don't look at the details, look at the heart of what they want you to change." By going beyond her editor's suggestions, Pattison found a fix that grew from within for a better fit.

Knowing the general issues the editor wants addressed also keeps the goal in sight. "*Saving the Griffin* came back from my editor with writing on every single page of the manuscript," says Kristin Nitz. "Usually, I'll check all the comments in one quick sitting. But this time, I went through the manuscript page by page for an hour and a half until I became too depressed to continue." Fortunately, Nitz's editor had called her and let her know that the comments, written throughout the manuscript, were made to help her address three major concerns: the relationships between the characters, the need to work in the Italian characters more smoothly, and making the fantasy element work throughout the story as a whole. This enabled Nitz to put the comments in perspective and keep her eyes on the big picture.

Because I failed to reread my novel and focus on it as a whole, I was overwhelmed by the many suggestions from my critiquers. I needed Nitz's lesson to look for the big picture. This would have made it easier for me to decide which of the suggested changes to make.

Even for the pros this isn't always an easy decision.

We fear change

No matter how good a suggestion is, sometimes writers will resist making the change. Butler did this to protect a good friend—her POV character. "I have a book coming out Spring 2006 called *Tank Talbott's Guide to Girls*. At the very end, Tank gets a final report card. I didn't want to fail him in any subject because he was really trying and well . . . because I *like* the kid!" says Butler. "But pieces of his writing are shown throughout the book. He's *not* a very good speller. My editor insisted he needed to fail spelling, even at the end. The more I thought about it, the more I realized she was right. Tank didn't deserve a passing grade. No real teacher would've passed him. So it wasn't right for me to pass him, either."

Sometimes they resist because of the scope of the changes involved. "In my middle-grade novel *Crown Me!*, I originally ended it with my character preparing to run for student council president the next semester. My editor said this was an important part of the novel," says Lay. What her editor suggested meant making the subplot, the campaign for office, the central

More Lessons from the Pros

Rewriting isn't a static process, done the same way manuscript after manuscript. Perhaps the greatest variation is in how a beginner and a pro use the term. "I now recognize there are several different kinds of revision. When I first started writing, I only knew the 'polishing' kind, where you're really only working with words and sentences," says Dori Butler. "Now I might be revising the shape of the story as a whole, I might be tightening subplots, looking at character arc, rising conflicts, raising stakes, theme, setting . . ."

No two rewrite requests are exactly alike. "Every story is different and every story has to be attacked in a slightly different way," says Kristin Nitz. "Even editors have different ways of editing the same writer." For *Defending Irene*, Nitz's Peachtree editor sent her a two-page letter suggesting changes, but *Saving the Griffin* came back with comments on every single page.

As writers hone their craft, they identify their strengths and their weaknesses. "I have more confidence in my process. I write short and I have to go back in and layer things in. Rarely do I have to do much cutting," says Darcy Pattison. "People need to know what types of drafts they turn out. You don't always know that early in your career."

They also learn when to stand firm. "On the one hand, I'm more open to suggestions, and on the other hand, I'm firmer about sticking by my guns. I've learned how to pick my battles, in other words. Editorial suggestions no longer hurt my feelings the way they did at the beginning," says Tracy Barrett, "but when I feel strongly about something, I don't change it. I tell the editor why I've left the text the way it was, but I don't change it."

Lastly, they learn that rewrites don't always necessitate a full-scale makeover of a project. "The changes tend to be less intensive and more insightful the more experienced you get," says Kelly Milner Halls. "They tend to *better* a project if you've been at this a while, rather than mandating a full-fledged makeover."

plot. "When I'd finished it all, I felt it was much stronger and satisfying," says Lay. "Kids who have e-mailed me about the book or reviewed it have almost always mentioned that they liked the way it ended. Thanks to my editor, I feel the storyline, and characters, became much more rounded with this addition."

Other times the editor's direction is clear but unacceptable, leading to a compromise. "In *Dinosaur Mummies,* my editor wanted to soften the pure science of the fossil record—imply it wasn't fact but theory. I understand her concerns, in a pro-Bush environment. But I have worked hard to be credible with paleontologists," says Kelly Milner Halls whose editor suggested replacing "scientists believe" with "some scientists believe." "I compromised by saying, 'Most scientists believe,' which is in fact true," says Hall. "*Most* consider the fossil record fact. A few do not. I could live with *most* because it was accurate. She could live with *most* because it left a tiny bit of wiggle room for those who don't."

Mission impossible

But even a pro sometimes refuses to make a change, perhaps because she and editor have different visions for the finished piece or a different world view. This happened with the first publisher that accepted Tracy Barrett's *The Trail of Tears: An American Tragedy.* "They said that I had been too hard on Andrew Jackson, the president who had ordered the brutal and illegal Indian Removal Act. They said that he was a man of his times," says Barrett. "I answered that he was *not* a man of his times, that many people had been against the Act, and that the debate over it in Congress was the longest debate on record. I cited editorials, letters, etc. from contemporaries who were horrified by it."

Barrett stuck to her version, which meant pulling the project from that publisher. "They said that if I didn't soften it they wouldn't publish it," she says. "I said, 'Genocide is genocide' and sent them back their advance." In Barrett's case, all's well that ends well as a hi-lo version was later accepted by Perfection Learning Corporation.

Pros also fight for the integrity of fictional stories that serve a targeted readership. "*Alexandra Hopewell, Labor Coach* is about a girl who wants to be there when her baby brother or sister is born," says Butler. "It never received a form rejection, but it did receive many requests for rewrite." Largely these requests said one of two things. The first version was that Butler tackled "childbirth from an interesting angle" but Alexandra needed further development. The second version, which Butler received most often, stated Alexandra was "an interesting character," but the childbirth scene was too graphic.

The reason Butler refused to tone down the scene is the story behind the story. "I was present for a friend's home birth. My 'job' was to take care of my friend's 4-year-old daughter, be with her in the room if she wanted to be there to see the baby be born or take her out if things got too intense," says Butler. "One year later, my then 4-year-old got the idea in his head that *he* wanted to come to the hospital with us to see his baby brother be born. Both of these kids had very positive experiences attending the births of their siblings. But I think part of why they were positive is because both kids were *very* prepared for what they were about to see. I always knew I would use that in a story someday."

Because the realism of this scene was so important to her, Butler chose instead to strengthen her main character. "I took a closer look at what the other editors were telling me, and I did a pretty major character revision."

Although the book was accepted and published by Albert Whitman with the scene intact, Butler's win came at a price. "I've noticed that book isn't in anywhere near as many schools as my other books are. I'm disappointed about that, but I understand," she says. "It's *not* a book for every child, just like being there to see a baby be born isn't right for every child. But it's the *right* book for a child who *is* contemplating being there with Mom and Dad when a baby brother/sister is born."

Articles & Interviews

Sometimes even a pro will let themselves be talked into a change that's a bad fit. Pattison did this in her upcoming picture book *19 Girls and Me*. "I had the teacher call the class in for lunch," says Pattison. "They ate *soup de jour*." Her editor objected that this term was too hard for first graders. Pattison reluctantly agreed to the change although *chicken soup* didn't have the same playful feel and perfect fit that had brought her to chose *soup de jour*. When the final proofs came, Pattison still disliked the new phrase and the original text was restored. "Just because they said no at one stage doesn't mean they'll say no again at another stage if you have a good reason for it," she says. "The editors are more than willing to look at your point of view. They want the best manuscript possible. We're both on the same team."

Proceed like a pro

Even when sweeping changes are for the better, it's unnerving to make major alterations. Like the pros, I put up a safety net by saving the original file. "I always keep old files because if I write something out of existence in the new file, I want to be able to recapture it," says Nitz, "because some of the old words work well."

This enables them to verify how a change functions. "Save the file as you originally wrote it, then create a new file and make the edits requested," says Halls. "Sleep on it a day or two, then read *both* pieces. Odds are good you'll agree the edited piece really is better for the revisions."

Pros know that the goal in learning to rewrite in not necessarily a sale but a better manuscript. "Rewrite in service of the story," says Jenkins, "*not* in service of one particular editor. That way you'll end up with a stronger manuscript, no matter what happens with that editor." For a variety of reasons, an improved manuscript may not sell, but it can lead to something even better long term. "Rewrites don't always lead to contracts, but they may lead to relationships," says Nitz, "which is a good thing and can lead to future books."

Remember, many writers never get beyond shocked indignation. Some of us get mired in the details. But if we can learn from the pros, we too can impress editors with our professional approach and join the ranks of multipublished professionals.

Check It Out

See for yourself what a rewrite can produce—read these books by the authors we interviewed.

- **By Kelly Milner Halls:** *Dinosaur Mummies, Wild Dogs, Albino Animals, I Bought a Baby Chicken.*
- **By Amanda Jenkins:** *Breaking Boxes, Damage, Out of Order.*
- **By Darcy Pattison:** *The River Dragon, The Journey of Oliver K. Woodman, The Wayfinder, Searching for Oliver K. Woodman.*
- **By Kristin Nitz:** *Defending Irene, Fundamental Softball, Play-by-Play Track, Play-by-Play Field Events.*
- **By Dori Butler** *Sliding Into Home*; *Do You Know the Monkey Man*; *Alexandra Hopewell, Labor Coach*; *Trading Places with Tank Talbott*; *Whodunit? How the Police Solve Crimes.*
- **By Kathryn Lay:** *Crown Me!, The Organized Writer is a Selling Writer*, "The Healing Truth" in Bruce Coville's *A Glory of Unicorns.*
- **By Tracy Barrett:** *Cold in Summer, On Etruscan Time, The Ancient Greek World, Growing Up in Colonial America, Ann of Byzantium, Trail of Tears, The Ancient Chinese World.*

10 Tips for Writing a Great Query Letter

by Lauren Barnholdt

Imagine you're an editor or agent. Your work day is filled with phone calls, meetings, and appointments. Weekends and evenings are the only time you have to read prospective manuscripts, so you're forced to lug your slush pile home from the office, which is time consuming (and heavy). You're anxious to find the "next big thing" but you just don't have the time to go through all the manuscripts that are arriving at your office. Enter the query letter, savior of editors and agents, and the bane of a writer's existence.

A query letter is a short (usually one page) letter to an agent or editor, describing yourself and your project and inviting her to read your manuscript. "I get anywhere from 50 to 100 query letters a week," says Nadia Cornier of Firebrand Literary. "It would be impossible to have that many manuscripts arriving at my office. I'd never be able to get anything else done!"

Queries have always been required for nonfiction pieces, and now, with the growing number of people writing picture books and novels for children and teens, a query letter is an essential part of the publication process for full-length fiction. (Usually for short stories, you send the whole story.) Great writing, an original idea, and well-developed characters mean nothing if you don't have a good query letter, because without an enticing query, no one will see your work.

Writing a successful query letter is fairly easy, yet not many writers seem to be able to accomplish it. They don't know what a good query letter is composed of, or they're intimidated by the fact that this one page will determine whether or not their work will be considered. "I used to have query letter phobia," admits Amanda Marrone, author of *Uninvited* (Aladdin Books, 2008.) "I didn't think I could pitch my book well and the thought of summarizing my stories was daunting. I wanted to be able to send to someone who I had already been introduced to or had given me a critique so I could just say 'Here's the manuscript you requested,' or 'You said you liked edgy books and thought you might be interested in my YA.'"

Once you get a handle on it, writing a query letter can be easy and fun. But how *do* you write a good query letter? And how can you possibly be expected to get the brilliance

LAUREN BARNHOLDT is the author of *Reality Chick* (Simon Pulse). Her articles and short stories have appeared in *Elements* magazine, *Girls' Life*, and on www.mensclick.com. She resides in Central Connecticut, and when she's not writing, she spends most of her time reading and watching lots and lots of reality TV. She teaches How to Write the YA Chick Lit Novel as an e-course and is very active on YA writing-related web groups. Visit her Web site, www.laurenbarnholdt.com.

Articles & Interviews

of your work across in one page? Here are 10 tips on writing a query letter that will hook an agent or editor, followed by examples of query letters that resulted in publication—and some that didn't.

1. Address your query to a specific person, and greet them by "Mr." or "Ms."

If you send your query letter to a specific person at a publishing house or literary agency, you'll have a much better chance of getting read. Addressing to a specific person gets your letter in the right hands faster, and shows you've done your research. You don't want to give an editor the impression you're sending your book out to everyone you can find, and some editors and agents will dismiss you right off the bat if you don't address your query to a specific person. So show you've done your research. Be careful, though—the publishing agency is always changing, with editors and agents transitioning to different houses and jobs. Make sure your information is accurate and up-to-date.

2. Know your project.

The first paragraph of your query letter should be a brief explanation of why you are querying that agent or editor. For example, "I am currently seeking representation for my middle grade novel, *Title*. I am querying you because I read in the current issue of *Children's Writer's & Illustrator's Market* that you are looking for humorous stories with a contemporary voice, and I think my manuscript meets those criteria."

There are differences in word count between children's books, middle grade books, and young adult projects. Knowing the differences in word count categories, as well as genres such as fantasy, contemporary, and paranormal demonstrates knowledge of the market, and shows the agent or editor you have what they're looking for. You'll have a higher success rate if you send a batch of custom-tailored letters to those who are actively seeking what you write, rather than sending a query to agents and editors at random, hoping one will stick. "I queried my current agent because I knew she was looking for upper YA novels," says Marrone. "Because I described my project as such, she immediately wanted to read it."

3. Keep it brief.

Editors and agents get a ton of mail every day. If you can't keep your query to a page or so, you risk losing their interest. *But how am I supposed to show how good my book is in just one page?* authors often wail. The purpose of a query letter isn't to describe your project in minute detail—it's to entice the agent or editor to want to read it. Briefly explain what you're thinking for your article, or what your book is about. Think of back cover copy of a novel when you're writing your project summary—short, succinct, and enticing.

4. Always include a self-addressed stamped envelope.

A #10, self-addressed stamped envelope (fold it into thirds), should always be included with your query letter. Whether or not the agent or editor wants to see your manuscript, they'll reply using this envelope. Agents and editors don't have the time or money to spend addressing envelopes and buying postage for every random person who sends them a query. If you don't include a SASE, you risk not getting a response, making your query letter obsolete.

5. Know what to mention.

The last paragraph of your query letter should list your writing credits and qualifications. You can say things like, "My short story, 'A Great Story' has appeared in *This & That* magazine." You can also mention any writing organizations you're in, or any classes you may have taken. But you don't have to limit your qualifications to writing. If you're writing a historical YA, and you have particular knowledge about that topic (i.e., you have a Ph.D in history), mention it. If you're writing a book set at a summer camp, and you used to work at one, mention that as well.

If you have no previous publishing credits, don't say things like, "Although I haven't been published, all the kids in my daughter's first grade class loved my picture book." The last thing you want to do is make note of the fact you're unpublished, and editors and agents really won't care if your daughter's first grade class loved your book.

6. Keep your letter professional.

Send it on plain white paper in a plain white, #10 envelope. Don't send photos. Don't decorate your envelope with stickers or glitter. Don't send gifts or pictures of your children. "I always get asked by people if they should do something to stand out, because otherwise, how will they get noticed?" says Cornier. "The answer is no. You're trying to sell your writing, not yourself, your kids, or your creativity." If your query is good, your materials will get requested. Let your writing speak for itself.

7. Avoid sweeping comparisons.

If you've written an edgy YA, along the lines of Gossip Girl, definitely mention it in your query. "My book will appeal to readers of the Gossip Girl series, as it's an edgy YA for the 14-plus crowd" is fine, and shows you know where your book fits into the marketplace. Saying something like, "This manuscript is going to be the next Harry Potter/Junie B. Jones/Goosebumps" is not. "I get queries every day that claim to be the next big thing," Cornier says. "You don't need to make these claims to get an agent or editor interested in your work. Write a great query letter, and let the writing stand for itself."

8. Include your contact info.

If you get someone interested in your work, the last thing you want is for that person to be unable to contact you! Always include your name, address, phone number, and e-mail.

9. Follow instructions.

Read each publisher's or agency's submission guidelines, and submit accordingly. If they only take e-mail queries, don't send one through the regular mail and vice versa. Sometimes for picture books, they'll ask to see the whole manuscript in addition to the query letter. For longer works, they may ask for just a query letter, or a query letter and a chapter or two. "This is really the easiest thing to do," says Cornier. "And yet you'd be surprised at the number of authors who don't follow directions." Many agencies and publishers have their submission guidelines right on their Web sites, and offer information on what and how to submit in *Children's Writer's & Illustrator's Market*. So make a good first impression, and show the editor or agent you can follow directions.

10. Just do it!

Sending out query letters can be intimidating, but in the end, it's an essential part of the process. "Sending out a query letter is necessary," says Marrone. "If I hadn't done it, I never would have sold my book. It's hard not to be intimidated, but if you want to get published, it's just something that has to be done." So just do it—getting your stuff out there may be the hardest part of the process for some people, but remember—no guts, no glory.

Articles & Interviews

Good Fiction Query

Megan Atwood
Submissions Editor
Acquisitions Department/Children's Division
Llewellyn Worldwide
P.O. Box 64383
St. Paul, MN 55164-0383

Addressed to a specific editor.

Dear Ms. Atwood:

Shows she's done her research, and that this editor is looking for the kind of book she's writing.

I was pleased to read in *Children's Book Insider* of your interest in acquiring Young Adult and Middle Grade manuscripts. I believe my humorous Young Adult novel, *Stuck Down*, may be an appropriate fit for Llewellyn.

Short summary of the book, shows that it is indeed YA, and gives a good idea of what the book is about, so the editor can decide if it's something she might be interested in.

Stuck Down is about Kevin Martin, a deceased, 18-year-old boy who spans the gap between Nirvanaville and Earth by delivering letters to loved ones. On Earth, he lands in jail for allegedly stealing his motorcycle and another's identity. After all, Kevin Martin is dead. To complicate matters, he suffers loss of flying powers so there's no escape—not from Earth or from Morty, a quirky, bully spirit. On the day of trial, Kevin is stunned to learn that his dad, a prosecuting attorney, is trying the case against him. Now he's face-to-face with a gap of a more personal nature—his unresolved relationship with his dad, and perhaps the key to getting unstuck.

She knows their submission requirements, and has included a SASE for their response.

Enclosed for your consideration are the first three chapters and a synopsis of *Stuck Down*, which in its entirety consists of approximately 37,000 words. Also enclosed is a self-addressed, stamped envelope for your response. I'd be happy to send you the full manuscript if you are interested.

Short paragraph listing her credentials without sounding like she's bragging—her credits are applicable and impressive.

In the past two years, I've had published twelve short stories/articles in Focus on the Family's *Brio Magazine*, *On the Line, Guide, My Friend, Wee Ones*, and *First-Time Authors Anthology* (Inst. of Children's Lit.) as well as two essays in *Big Ones* and *Valley-Kids Parent News*. Additionally, I am a member of the Society of Children's Book Writers and Illustrators.

Thanks editor for her time—always a nice touch.

Thank you for your time and consideration.

Sincerely,

Eileen Rosenbloom
Enclosures
Contact Info

(*Stuck Down* was released by Llewellyn Publishing in June 2005.)

Articles & Interviews

Good Nonfiction Query

January 28, 2002
Pelican Publishing Co. Inc.
1000 Burmaster St.
Gretna LA 10053-2246

Dear Ms. Kooij:

First paragraph tells exactly what kind of book it is, and what the book is about.

Enclosed is a manuscript for a 1100-word biography picture book, *Trailblazer: The Life of Daniel Boone*. "High on a knoll in the Pennsylvania backwoods in 1734, a small cabin was home to the Quaker family. It pleasured Squire and Sarah Boone that their sixth child was a boy. They named him Daniel." This manuscript covers Daniel's life from birth to old age, but concentrates on his life as a trailblazer.

Shows she's done her research and knows there's a market for her project.

The story of Daniel Boone has been told in numerous children's books, but usually in a more advanced academic level. Today, famous Americans are being studied in the primary grades as students are introduced to biographies. As a librarian in a primary school, I have noticed the trend.

Impressive and relevant credentials.

I taught Kentucky history, in which Daniel Boone's pioneering plays a prominent role, for seven years and have a master's degree in elementary education and a second master's degree in library and information science. In 1999, Charlesbridge published my picture book, *Once Upon a Dime*. In Feburary, 2002, I will receive a grant for writing picture books from the Kentucky Foundation of Women. I have had several articles published in the following magazines: *Book Links*, *Good Apple*, *Back Home in Kentucky*, *M Magazine*, *Kudzu*, and most recently, in the January and February issues of *Children's Book Insider*.

If this manuscript meets your editorial needs, please contact me at:

Includes contact information.

Nancy Kelly Allen
Address
Phone Number
E-mail

Sincerely,

Nancy Kelly Allen

(*Daniel Boone: Trailblazer* was released by Pelican Publishing in October 2005.)

Good Agent Query

Articles & Interviews

Stephen Fraser
Jennifer Dechiara Literary Agency
254 Park Avenue South
New York, NY 10010

Dear Mr. Fraser:

Floe Ryan is a cryogenically preserved Venice Beach teen who is thawed ten years from now, and suddenly has to adjust to being the ward of her younger (now older) sister, while crushing on the boy from the vat next door, and, oh, adjusting to a whole new world. (Ashton Kutcher as Vice President, anyone?)

I Was a Teenage Popsicle is a 60,000 word young adult novel, possibly the first in a series I'm calling "The Frozen Zombies of Venice Beach." I am a former romance editor, and a twice published romance author. My latest romantic comedy, *Wanted: An Interesting Life* (Harlequin Flipside, 2004), was cited by *Romantic Times Magazine* as one of the five best Flipsides of 2004.

Writing young adult novels has long been a dream of mine, and as I live with two pre-teens, the time is definitely right—they're constant inspirations! I would love it if you could help me navigate the young adult publishing world, which is new to me. I've heard wonderful things about your agency.

Aside from *I Was a Teenage Popsicle* and its sequel, I am also working on a young adult novel called *Retest*, about a teen who finds herself reliving a test day over and over again. I am also working on a "mom lit" novel, about a woman who finds a way to travel back in time and make different life choices.

You can reach me anytime at [*telephone number*], or by e-mailing me at [*e-mail address*]. I do hope my book premises intrigue you! I look forward to hearing from you.

Yours very sincerely,

Bev Katz Rosenbaum
Address
Phone and e-mail info

Short, enticing summary that gives us an idea of what the book is about.

Shows she knows the word counts for YA books, and that the book works as a stand alone or in a series.

Good credentials.

Shows that she's plugged into the YA demographic, but doesn't use it to sell her writing—she knows the writing should stand alone, but wants the agent to know she has an idea of what will appeal to YA readers.

Shows she has other projects and is interested in working on her craft.

(*I Was a Teenage Popsicle* is an October 2006 release from Berkley Publishing.)

Bad Agent Query

Who? Always address to a specific person.

Doesn't tell us anything regarding what the book is about.

Her daughter's opinion doesn't mean anything, and she's projecting that editors and agents will feel the same way—very unprofessional.

This is way too long for most middle grade books, which shows she doesn't know her market.

A middle grade series wouldn't follow characters through high school, and 10 books is a bit of a stretch unless it really catches on.

Never send agents or editors to a Web site to read your work—follow their submission guidelines. If they want to see the book, they'll request it.

Dear Agent,

I am looking for someone to sell my middle grade fiction book, *Rose Sullivan, Queen of the Seventh Grade*. It is about Rose Sullivan, queen of the seventh grade and all the escapades she gets into with her friends.

I have a daughter who is in seventh grade, and all her friends have read it and loved it. Her friend Jennifer said, "I love this book! It's hilarious!" I am sure editors and other readers will feel the same way.

The manuscript runs about 115,000 words, which is about the size of some of the Harry Potter novels. I plan for the book to be the first of a 10-book series, which will follow Rose and her friends all the way through high school.

If you would like to read the manuscript, you can find it online at my Web site, www.rosesullivanqueen.com. If you like the first chapters that you read there, I would be glad to send you the rest of the manuscript—I know you will just love it!

Sincerely,

Jane Bad Writer

Bad Fiction Query

Always use Mr. or Ms. —

Dear Michelle,

Recently, I read that you are interested in acquiring books that have a male protagonist. Well, look no further! My YA novel, *Billy Shark Knows It All*, has a boy protagonist!

The summary is long and confusing and not well-written. It should be cut down and organized.

Billy and his father, Walter, are mobsters. Billy got into the mob because of his dad, even though he's only 13. But don't worry, because the book isn't violent. At least not graphically so. It is more about Billy and the relationship he has with his dad, as they go on mob missions.

Billy and his father have to travel the world as hitmen, and go on missions in Brazil, Argentina, Africa, and Japan. Finally, they are caught by the men who have a hit out on Billy's father's life, and have to get out of the trap with a blowtorch. Along the way, they meet many new friends and contacts, including a girl named Tracy, whose dad is also a hitman and her and Billy start up a romance. He has to leave her, however, when Billy and Mr. Shark have to return home and pretend to be a normal family.

Never give an editor or agent a deadline for when you want to sell your book—selling a book is hard, and no one wants to take on an author who is impatient and bothersome.

But then, once they get home, Billy finds out Tracy will be moving next door to him, and he perks up. After going through a lot of hardships, like their families not wanting them to be together, Billy and Tracy finally get together. The book ends with the two fathers getting out of the mob and Billy and Tracy dating.

I would be happy to send you this book. I have to let you know that I'm looking for a fast response, as I'd like to sell it before the summer, since my kids will be out of school then, and I won't have much time.

Not enough info in this query letter. How long is the book? What are his qualifications?

Thanks for reading.

Too informal. —

Take care,

Bobby Slushpile

Writing the Nonfiction Book Proposal

by Connie Goldsmith

Writing a nonfiction book before selling it to a publisher is like putting a note in a bottle and tossing it overboard while adrift at sea in a bobbling dinghy. What are the chances that someone will actually find your note and come to rescue you? When I tried to sell my first nonfiction book, 16 editors sailed by before the 17th threw me a life preserver and shouted, "Welcome aboard!"

Now I know better. I didn't write a single word of my next six books until I'd found a publisher, signed a contract, and received an advance. You too, can sell your book *before* you write it by first submitting a book proposal to that ever-so-carefully selected editor. Not only does a formal proposal let you tailor your manuscript to the publisher, it also helps to organize your work. Once you get that coveted contract, you'll be ready to write.

"A book proposal is a job interview. It is well written with good grammar and no typos, showing that the author is a professional who takes the job seriously," says Joelle Riley, Senior Science Editor with Lerner Books. "A good proposal puts the proposed book and its author in the best possible light. It is well thought out and makes a strong case for why the publisher should publish the book." Riley requires a formal proposal from writers who don't have a strong track record with Lerner.

According to Hannah Rodgers, formerly an Associate Editor with Houghton Mifflin, "Formal proposals are always a good idea when it comes to nonfiction writing. Proposals give writers the chance to pique an editor's interest by saying, 'You may think you know this story, but here's something new.' A good proposal will act as a teaser for the book, the way a preview can capture your interest at the movie theater."

ELEMENTS OF A PROPOSAL

A book proposal "includes a concise, to-the-point cover letter; a short overview of the topic; a detailed, annotated outline of the material to be covered; a writing sample tailored to the intended audience; and a brief summary of the author's background and qualifications," says Riley. Let's take a close look at those elements and others that are often included in proposals.

CONNIE GOLDSMITH is a registered nurse who writes books and magazine articles for adults and children. She has four juvenile books coming out in 2007 from Lerner Books and Millbrook Press, all on health-related topics. She also writes a monthly children's book review column for a regional parenting magazine in Sacramento, California where she lives.

The overview

Introduce the editor to your book. Drum up some excitement. What would you tell her if you had five minutes of face time? At a minimum, she wants to know:

- What is the book about? Develop a clear and concise statement describing your book. Think 25-word sales pitch, a hook to snag the editor's attention.
- Why should it be written? To keep the editor's attention, offer a compelling reason why your book should be published.
- What will the book look like in terms of structure, sidebars, art, end material?

Advice from the Pros

Lerner editor Joelle Riley says my proposal for *Superbugs Strike Back*, a book about the increase in antibiotic-resistant infections threatening our health, immediately caught her attention. "The topic was timely and I knew it would fill a hole in our list. The proposal was well-written, so I could expect the full manuscript to arrive in good shape. The author demonstrated that she'd taken the time to familiarize herself with our list and that she'd researched the potential competition."

Are you ready to write a book proposal? Here a few more hints to boost your confidence and get your creativity flowing.

From the editors

"Write about what fascinates you," recommends Hannah Rodger, "and make it clear in your proposal why it fascinates you. If you can spark an editor's interest in the subject and teach him or her something new right away, your proposal will have added depth and impact. Even if your topic is well-known, a thorough proposal demonstrates your own knowledge as well as your research abilities, and can highlight any special affinity you might have for the topic."

Riley says, "Familiarize yourself with the book publishing industry so you can target your proposal to the market for which it is best suited. Don't send a proposal unless you can make a strong argument for your book's sales potential. Instead of trying to follow trends, be on the lookout for fresh topics and approaches."

From the authors

Janet Fox has this advice for nonfiction children's writers: "Target your idea to the right publisher. Check their Web site and catalog. Do the market research and assess the competition so you can make a course correction before you write. Don't write the whole book before you submit it. The publisher will buy the idea and your ability to deliver, not your first golden words."

Pamela Turner urges writers, "Think about story. The best nonfiction always tells a story. What's the narrative thread? How can you set up each chapter so the reader wants to turn the page to find out what happens next?"

Cindy Blobaum says, "A well-written proposal helps the author create a realistic vision of the project, which helps immensely once it's accepted. Although you should invest a considerable amount of time in creating a top-notch proposal, don't write your entire book until you have a contract in hand. Each publisher has different styles and different requirements, and it's much easier to change a sample chapter than it is to rewrite an entire book."

- Why are you the best person for the job? Focus on a few key points here—personal expertise, writing experience, professional credentials, or passion for the topic? You'll detail your full qualifications in the author background section.
- How do you plan to write it? Will you interview experts, call upon your own experience, research historical archives, read extensively, surf the Web, or visit exotic locations, like Pamela Turner did when she wrote *Gorilla Doctors* (Houghton Mifflin, 2005)?

Turner, who traveled to Rwanda to research *Gorilla Doctors* says, "I think the overview is the most important part of the proposal. It needs to be short, snappy, and compelling. If you can't sell a book idea to an editor in a paragraph, how will the publisher be able to sell it to libraries and booksellers? In my overview, I stated the subject, the angle, and how the book would complement school curricula."

Cindy Blobaum (*Insectigations*, Chicago Review Press, 2005) wrote her overview as a vision statement. "It probably took the most time. I included my hook, references to how *Insectigations* would compare to CRP's recent publications, and a bulleted summary of highlights. Every word had to have impact!"

Sizing up the competition

Show the acquiring editor you've done your homework. No matter what your idea is, someone has probably thought of it before. The competition section is where you tell the editor about books that are similar to yours. The editor probably knows about those books. What she wants to know is what you'll bring that's new and exciting. "Gorillas are not a new topic, but Pam went out of her way to distinguish her approach so I could tell immediately how [*Gorilla Doctors*] would stand out in the marketplace," says Rodgers.

When Turner prepared her proposal, she discovered nearly a dozen children's books in print about gorillas. Only one was about mountain gorillas, and she didn't find any books about the health care of wild gorillas. She capitalized on her unique angle. "Gorillas are a subject. Scientists helping to protect gorillas from human diseases is an angle." Turner's proposal also promised original photographs, while the book most like hers was illustrated with paintings and sketches

When compiling a list of books similar to yours, include the book's name, author, publisher, date of publication, and target audience. Say a few words about each book. Point out how it differs from the one you're proposing. Be objective while avoiding negative or derogatory comments about the competing books.

Marketing & promoting

Your editor works together with the publisher's sales department to determine if your proposed book will sell or not. This is the place to clearly define your target market, to give the editor the ammunition she needs when she presents your proposal at the crucial acquisitions meeting. Say your proposed topic is luminescent sea creatures. Your target market could be children over 10 years old who are interested in sea life. The book could be a cross-over title, perhaps fitting into the trade market as well as the school and library market. Special niche markets might include gift shops at aquariums, large zoos with marine exhibits, and big stores that sell fish and supplies.

How will you help promote your book? Few publishers send authors on national book tours anymore, but any of us can help promote our book when it comes out. Can you approach regional booksellers to arrange book signings? Will you do library visits or school presentations? Do you have contacts with organizations for biology and science teachers who would be interested in a new book about luminescent sea creatures? Can you link it to appropriate Web sites? Talk to your published friends to see what they've done to promote

Articles & Interviews

Elements of a Book Proposal

- Cover letter (1 page)
- Overview (1-2 pages)
- Competition (1 page)
- Marketing/promoting (1 page)
- Author Background (1 page)
- Outline (4-6 pages)
- Additional material can include complete list of publishing credits, professional résumé, and samples of published material

their work. Read a book on the subject. You might be surprised at how many ways you can find to promote your book.

Author background

The editor wants to know about you. What experience do you have that relates to the proposed book? Do you have another career or some unusual accomplishments? This is where you share your writing experience as well as applicable information about your professional and personal life. Find a balance between modesty and overconfidence. If you plan to include a complete list of publishing credits with your proposal, detail only the highlights of your writing experience here. Picture this section as the bio on the inside back flap of your book. Turner says, "Writing the author section was easy for me—it's just a chatty version of a résumé."

If you're short on writing experience, strengthen your credentials by writing a magazine article on your topic. Perhaps *Odyssey* would be interested in a piece about your glowing sea critters. Join The Society of Children's Book Writers and Illustrators, or an organization applicable to your topic. For example, if your proposal is about health or science, try the American Medical Writers Association or the National Association of Science Writers. Think about your day job. Do you belong to professional groups such as those for teachers and librarians that would spiff up your credentials? Chances are, once you start brainstorming, you'll realize you've got the qualifications to write the proposed book. Your job is to convince the editor.

Outline

Completing a well-done outline gives you a head start when it's time to begin writing the book. The outline may be written in several ways. Janet Fox (*Get Organized Without Losing It*, Free Spirit Publishing, 2006), says, "I wrote one paragraph to describe each chapter. This section was the easiest for me because I was having so much fun."

My own proposals are similar, except I add topical sidebars to the chapter outline. For example in my proposal for *Superbugs Strike Back* (Lerner, 2007), I added a sidebar titled, "A 16th Century German Pharmacy" describing some of the wacky things used to treat human illness. Another sidebar titled, "Ashley's Science Project" told how a 16-year-old won an international science prize by finding antibiotics in drinking water at her high school.

Blobaum "wrote a detailed, three-page table of contents which served as the outline, and I also included an 11-page sample chapter." Turner chose a somewhat different approach.

Articles & Interviews

"I chose a narrative outline with one or two snappy paragraphs per chapter. I decided that was the best way to show there was a narrative thread that ran throughout the book. I might not do that if I was proposing a book on something that already had an obvious story thread, such as a historical event. However, science books usually lack a clear story structure."

GET GOING

No matter how exciting the topic or well-written the proposal, if the publishers have a similar book in the works, they won't be interested in yours. Consider querying before sending your proposal to an editor. A proposal query letter should contain all the usual elements of any query letter: who you are and what you are proposing, why you are the best person to write it, and publication credits, if any. It should close with a clear request: May I send you my complete proposal?

This worked for Blobaum when she started her proposal for *Insectigations*. First, she learned everything she could about Chicago Review Press. She studied its Web site, its writer's guidelines, and attended a presentation by a CRP editor at an SCBWI event. "Then, I sent a query with a sample activity to gauge their interest." she says. "When they responded that they would like to see more, I created the outline, some marketing ideas, a market survey, a table of contents, a fully referenced sample section, my résumé, and a list of publishing credits."

The proposal format is not set in stone. While most proposals include similar information, they may be structured differently. Because Turner's book was heavily dependent on experts, she included a section called, "About the Subjects," in which she detailed the academic and professional credentials of the three scientists she traveled with as she wrote her book. Rodger says, "Pam Turner's proposal for *Gorilla Doctors* had all the elements I look for," says Rodgers. "It was thorough, professional and informative—plus she had experience in the field and ready access to research, which I knew would ensure the book's integrity."

A month should be enough time to write a good proposal. In the August, 2005 issue of *Writer's Digest* magazine, Kevin Alexander says he first read a book about proposals before setting out to write his own. Once he started, it took a month of concentrated effort to complete his proposal. Fox had a similar experience. "From the time I had the idea until I put the proposal in the mail was about one month. I worked quickly because I was so excited about the idea, and wanted to capture that initial enthusiasm in my proposal."

Don't wait for an editor to pluck your note-in-a-bottle from the stormy publishing sea. Write a proposal then find an editor before starting your nonfiction book. It could be just what you need to score both a contract and an advance check!

Recommended Reading

- *Write the Perfect Book Proposal*, by Jeff Herman and Deborah Levine Herman (John Wiley & Sons).
- *How to Write a Book Proposal*, by Michael Larsen (Writer's Digest Books).
- *Nonfiction Book Proposals Anybody Can Write: how to get a contract and advance before writing your book*, by Elizabeth Lyon (Perigree Books).
- *An Author's Guide to Children's Book Promotion*, by Susan Salzman Raab (Two Lives Publishing).

The Newest Children's Book Imprints

by Alicia Potter

Since 2004, the children's book world has welcomed a raft of new imprints—those small, specialized, oh-so-selective lines within a publishing house. Several are the result of an exploding young adult market; others, high-profile rewards for proven editorial stars. While their arrival is undoubtedly good news, it also begs some questions. What makes a Ginee Seo book, well, so Ginee Seo? And how can you tell if your YA novel is a Graphia or an Amulet? To find out, we asked the heads of six recently christened imprints about their visions, their likes and dislikes, and how aspiring authors can squeeze onto these often incredibly targeted lists.

Ginee Seo is the editorial director of Ginee Seo Books at Atheneum Books for Young Readers, where she publishes four to seven titles each season. In addition to the National Book Award finalist *Inexcusable*, by Chris Lynch, recent works include *Ask Me No Questions*, by Marina Budhos; *What Athletes Are Made Of*, by Hanoch Piven; and *Totally Joe*, by James Howe.

What distinguishes a Ginee Seo book?

I like to think that I'm doing things that are a little edgy or different or quirky or show some sort of uniqueness. Anytime you have an imprint with your name on it I think it reflects who you are as a person. Each book is something I've felt passionately about and I think contributes to children in some way. If a manuscript is review-driven and literary and offers something different, then it's for me.

Any room for first-time authors?

Yes. I'll have quite a few first novels. I'm always interested in people who have a fresh perspective and something new to offer.

What do you wish wasn't in your slush pile?

Really marketing-driven picture books that don't have soul or heart. I'm also getting some very religious picture books that seem much more about the market. Anything that presents a marketing plan first, rather than an idea and characters, is a turn-off for me. I'm not interested in trends. Write about what your passion is, about what you're interested in. Don't be afraid to take risks.

ALICIA POTTER is a Boston-based freelance journalist who writes about children's books for *FamilyFun*.

Is there any predictability to the mix of genres on your list?

My love has always been novels. My first list was all novels and, in the future, there are going to be a lot of novels on the list. I'd say probably half to three-quarters of the list will be novels. But I really love picture books. It's a pleasure to edit them and it's not something that initially I had a great deal of experience with. It's been wonderful fun to learn and work on more picture books.

What is your vision for the imprint?

To make books that last and that make people think. I would like to publish books that inspire, provoke, entertain—and make readers for life.

Senior editor Eden Edwards oversees Graphia, Houghton Mifflin's paperback imprint for young adults. The line unveils four to six new titles each season; among the latest are *Whatcha Mean, What's a 'Zine?*, by Mark Todd and Esther Watson; *All Q, No A: More Tales of a 10th-Grade Social Climber*, by Lauren Mechling and Laura Moser; and *The Candy Darlings*, by Christine Walde.

What distinguishes a Graphia book?

We're very welcoming of books for older teenagers and have a wide variety of nonfiction, poetry, and fiction. Some of our

Eden Edwards

books are original paperbacks and some are reprints from our hardcover lists. We really focus on quality writing with a protagonist who, generally, is 14 or older.

Any room for first-time authors?

Most of our original paperbacks are first-time authors. It's a nice opportunity for a first-time author to break out and have a book that might be a little more experimental or older. Most of our original books are by first-time authors, too, and a lot of these authors are still very young. One book that's just beautiful is *A Certain Slant of Light*, by Laura Whitcomb, and then we have a series—the first book was *The Rise and Fall of a 10th-Grade Social Climber*— by two young authors who write as a team.

What's your advice to writers looking to publish with Graphia?

I'd say read a lot of great books for teenagers and then read what's being published now. Talk to teenagers and learn what they want to read. We are still looking for great books of interest to teenage boys and also nonfiction for teenagers.

What do you wish wasn't in your slush pile?

Sometimes I'd love to see more inventiveness. A lot of people try to write the same stories as what's doing well; you see a lot of imitation. But I've always welcomed something just really fresh and different. That's what grabs my eye.

What is your vision for the imprint?

Well-written, great books that speak to today's teenagers and respect their intelligence and the sophistication of their lives.

Articles & Interviews

Anne Schwartz collaborates with Lee Wade to co-direct Random House's Schwartz & Wade imprint. Together, they oversee a list of 20 children's books, including *Moxie Maxwell Does Not Like* Stuart Little, by Peggy Gifford; *Sky Boys: How They Built the Empire State Building*, written by Deborah Hopkinson, illustrated by James Ransome; and *Toys Go Out*, by Emily Jenkins.

Anne Schwartz

What distinguishes a Schwartz & Wade book?

The list is extremely small and selective. It's mostly picture books with some innovative nonfiction and middle grade and very little YA. It's basically our taste, what strikes a chord in us. My tastes tend to be a little offbeat, a little quirky, and Lee's taste is more mainstream. We expect all our books to be something out of the ordinary.

Any room for first-time authors?

We have so many new writers on our list! For Spring '07, there are three writers completely new to children's books out of seven titles. I love working with new people, and I actually think that it's a myth that their books don't do as well. Books that really break on the scene and are huge successes are often by brand new people. Tad Hills had never written and illustrated a trade book, and his *Duck and Goose* is our first list's lead book!

What's your advice to writers looking to publish with Schwartz & Wade?

I don't want people to send me their 12 favorite manuscripts. I want one manuscript that they love, that they are passionate about. So much of the work that goes into a picture book manuscript comes before you sit down at a desk. So much is just the basic idea and trying to figure out a new way to express it. What I care about is a spark of originality, even just a tiny piece of something new. That's the hardest thing to do but it's the most important.

What do you wish wasn't in your slush pile?

The usual. Rhyming text with some sort of Seussian thing going on. Sweet day-in-the-life stories. Mood pieces.

What's your vision for the imprint?

To stay small, to stay innovative, to focus on every part of making a wonderful book from the beginning to the end. To make sure that everything is as perfect as can be.

Eloise Flood is the publisher of Razorbill, an imprint of Penguin Putnam Books for Young Readers. She turns out 35 books a year, with recent titles including *Magic Lessons*, by Justine Larbalestier; *Teach Me*, by R.A. Nelson; and *Thicker Than Water*, by Carla Jablonski.

What distinguishes a Razorbill book?

We do not publish books for the youngest readers. We do not publish picture books. We do not publish early chapter books. Our age range is 9 and up, but our focus is really 12 and up. We do hardcover fiction and paperback original fiction. We have some nonfiction titles that tend to be in the health, wellness, or self-help arena. One of the first books we published is the novel *So Yesterday*, by Scott Westerfield, and a lot of people hold that up as the quintessential Razorbill book. It's very modern and hip. We believe it speaks directly to teens. Our books are the kind that teenagers pick up on their own instead of their parents buying them.

Any room for first-time authors?
Absolutely. I would say the majority of our authors are new. We are definitely looking to develop new talent.

How do you decide what's hardcover and what's paperback original?
It's a bit of a blurry line. Some of the books we published in hardcover are probably less literary and more commercial than other children's book publishers', and some of our paperback originals are beautifully written. If we're going to do a series, we almost always do that in paperback. One of the reasons we publish paperback originals is because we really want them to be accessible to teenagers. Teenagers may not want to shell out $17 for a book, but they may be much more willing to shell out $8 or $9. We published a book called *Catch*, by Will Leitch; it's his first novel and it's a really beautiful story. We could have easily published this in hardcover, but we published it in paperback because we wanted to be sure that kids would be able to buy it.

What do you wish wasn't in your slush pile?
I'm not particularly fond of problem novels. We get a lot of them because a lot of what is written for teens are novels where the teenager's issue is the main point of the story. We try to do things like that but to put it into a context of a larger story—for example, *The Bermudez Triangle*, by Maureen Johnson. Some people might see it as a problem novel, but for us, that book is a friendship story. It's about girls who have been life-long best friends and two of them fall in love with each other, but we don't look at it as a book about teenage lesbians. We tend not to go for things that focus overly on the issue to the detriment of the rest of the story.

What is your vision for the imprint?
We want to keep it small. I like that we have an identity—more so than a lot of other imprints because of where our focus is. We're going to keep publishing books that teenagers are really going to want to pick up on their own.

Carolyn Yoder heads up Calkins Creek, a new historical fiction and nonfiction imprint from Boyds Mill Press. At this point, Yoder does not publish a set number of books each season, but among the imprint's first offerings are *Two in the Wilderness*, by Sandra Weber; *Blue*, by Joyce Moyer Hostetter, and *By the Sword*, by Selene Castrovilla.

Carolyn Yoder

What distinguishes a Calkins Creek title?
Calkins Creek is totally devoted to U.S. history. We publish nonfiction and historical fiction mostly for ages 8 and up. Our mission is to publish books that achieve a balance of solid research and strong writing and put history front and center. I tend not to look for the encyclopedic or a straightforward biography. I want to open up the world of the past to young readers.

Any room for first-time authors?
Absolutely. A person's credentials are helpful, but they aren't the only thing I look for. I'll go through the cover letter first and see what drew the author to the subject, why they're

Articles & Interviews

the best person to write it. Then I'll go to the bibliography; that will really tell me if I am going to read something new and different and accurate. And then I'll read the manuscript.

What's your advice to writers looking to publish with Calkins Creek?

Authors need to value the importance of research as a writing tool. Tiny details really lend themselves to the storytelling and voice. If writers take a deep breath and read the research, they're going to find those gems. In most of our manuscripts, the research is stressed in the finished product, and the back matter is a big part of it. For example, in one picture book, there's an afterword, a timeline, a fairly extensive bibliography, and a research note from the author and even the designers.

What do you wish wasn't in your slush pile?

I was seeing a lot of Revolutionary War subjects and Quaker history. I don't get a lot of nonfiction manuscripts, and I would like to see more. I was getting historical fiction manuscripts lacking historical and cultural context. There was no setting or atmosphere; it was as if characters were in a vacuum. I also get manuscripts that don't have a bibliography. A lot of times those manuscripts will go back, or I will e-mail the author and ask for the bibliography.

What is your vision for the imprint?

To build a rich, diverse look at American history. Hopefully, with all different kinds of books—picture books, chapter books and novels—we'll offer kids an exciting approach to the study of their country.

Senior editor Susan Van Metre runs the show at Amulet Books, the imprint for older readers from Harry N. Abrams Books for Young Readers. She publishes eight books a year. Recent titles include Lauren Myracle's best-selling young-adult novel *ttyl,* its sequel *ttfn,* and *The Hour of the Cobra,* by Maiya Williams.

Susan van Metre

What distinguishes an Amulet book?

We differ from some of the other new imprints in that we're really just the older half of the Abrams children's list. Because Abrams is primarily known as an illustrated book publisher, we decided we should have a separate imprint for our novels. So we don't have as narrow parameters as some of the other imprints that are succeeding at edgy YA. We're young adult and middle grade fiction. I particularly like fantasy and historical fiction and genre fiction. The contemporary stuff tends to be humorous or has an interesting element to it like Lauren Myracle's instant-messaging novels.

Any room for first-time authors?

Definitely. We're always eager to find new talent.

What's your advice to writers looking to publish with Amulet?

Unfortunately, because of sheer volume, it is difficult for me to cope with unsolicited manuscripts. The best advice would be to try to see me at a conference or come to us through an agent. We are looking to diversify our list and we have a lot of fantasy right now, so we would be interested in getting more contemporary fiction, especially for boys. I like my contemporary stories to be more humorous than problem-oriented.

What do you wish wasn't in your slush pile?

I feel like everything I receive is a proposed series. It's not that we're not interested in publishing series, but I would love to see somebody who is genuinely focused on producing a great single novel. What often happens is that people are saving their strength for the second or third book, or the strength is stretched over three books. I'd like authors to be focused on one great book and then we'll see what happens.

What is your vision for the imprint?

That we'll continue to be a small "boutique" house that publishes beautiful books. Our interest is being very child-friendly. We're happy to get the great reviews, but we want to publish titles that are of high interest to children.

U.S. vs. U.K. Children's Fiction

by Sara Grant

What do Jacqueline Wilson, Enid Blyton, and J.K. Rowling have in common? You must have lived under a rock for the last 10 years not to recognize Rowling and her magical world of wizardry. If you are an American living in the U.S., I'd wager that the other names aren't familiar.

If you grew up in the U.K., these names have the same reference point—award-winning, bestselling children's book authors. Jacqueline Wilson, the current U.K. children's laureate, has written more than 80 books, which have sold more than 20 million copies in the U.K. During her lifetime Enid Blyton wrote more than 600 books. The U.K.-based magazine *Books for Keeps* ranks her as one of the all-time bestselling children's book authors along with Dr. Seuss, Beatrix Potter and Lewis Carroll.

"In America when the discussion is about children's books you don't realize until you get out of America that you've only been talking about American children's books," says Lissa Paul, professor at Brock University in St. Catharines, Ontario, Canada.

More than an ocean separates the worlds of U.S. and U.K. children's books. Sure we speak the same language, but cultural, philosophical and practical differences diminish the number of children's books that cross the Atlantic. And some worry that U.S. children's book publishing is slowly closing its borders.

Market size

Many practical differences distinguish the two markets. The U.S. and U.K. are influenced by different forces. The U.S. children's book market is significantly larger than the U.K. market. Some estimate that U.S. publishers sell more than three times as many children's books and enjoy profits four times those of U.K. publishers. Surprisingly, although U.S. publishers sell more total children's books, U.K. publishers publish more individual titles.

Book rights

U.K. children's book publishing is more globally focused. Because of the U.K.'s market size, a children's book's chances for publication may depend on the ability of the publisher to secure co-editions or sell rights to other countries. "We look at picture books as a global

SARA GRANT is a published author, freelance writer and public relations consultant. Her publication credits include stories in *Spider* and *Pockets* children's magazines. She's also written on assignment for *U*S* Kids* and *Indianapolis Monthly* magazines and past editions of *Children's Writer's & Illustrator's Market*. She lives, works and studies in London, England. In 2006, she earned an MA in creative and life writing at Goldsmiths College, University of London.

operation,'' says Natascha Biebow, senior commissioning editor at Random House Children's Books U.K. "But in the U.S., global rights are icing on the cake.''

British publishers endeavor to retain all publication rights for a book, yet more and more often in the U.S. agents hold the rights. U.S. agents may only offer U.K. publishers commonwealth rights for their authors' work. Adding to this confusion, hardback and paperback rights may belong to different U.S. publishers.

These market forces have changed the relationships between U.S. and U.K. publishers. Often British publishers sell rights to American publishers on a book-by-book basis. An increasing number of British publishers have created American subsidiaries or forged partnerships to secure U.S. distribution. For example, Candlewick Press in Cambridge, Mass., has first right of refusal on all books from London-based Walker Books and vice versa.

Market influences

There are powerful forces in the U.S. children's book market that are diminished or even nonexistent in the U.K. "The library market in the U.S. still seems to be healthy and strong,'' says Rachel Wade, senior editor for London-based Hodder Children's Books. "U.S. publishers can sell hardbacks, which is something we could do 10 years ago in Britain. Now Hodder publishes very few hardbacks. The U.S. still publishes nearly everything in hardback first.''

Mara Bergman, an American senior commissioning editor at Walker Books, concurs: "In the U.S., the support from libraries is huge, which provides another buoyancy for American book publishing. [In the U.K.] the library market is, sadly, dying, due to lack of funding for books.'' U.S. libraries spend about 10 times as much on children's materials as do their U.K. counterparts.

Conservative pressure

U.S. publishers may be more sensitive to topics such as evolution, nudity and offensive language because of a strong library market and an influential religious community. Laura Atkins, a doctoral student who lectures in children's literature at Roehampton University in London and the University of Newcastle, has worked in children's book publishing in both countries and says that there is more censorship in the U.S. than in the U.K. From 1990 to 2004, the American Library Association's Office for Intellectual Freedom recorded more than 8,300 formal written complaints filed with a library or school requesting that certain material be removed because of content or appropriateness. No similar list or means to record complaints exists in the U.K.

"The perception is that American parents are more likely to complain,'' says Biebow. "For example, they worry about a child being pictured unsupervised in a bath tub. British parents aren't so fussed about that kind of thing.''

Cultural differences

Beyond a story's setting, what makes a book American or British? The countries' health care and educational systems are different. Few American kids make copious cups of tea. But beyond the obvious, what more abstract cultural ethics distinguish U.S. from U.K. children's fiction?

"[This Britishness] encompasses a whole sensibility: family life, school life, the way you relate to friends,'' says Bergman. "Some things that come from the States are too sentimental with some books for young children deemed too sickeningly sweet.''

Julia Eccleshare, children's book editor for *The Guardian*, one of the U.K.'s premier national newspapers, agrees: "Look at [the U.K.'s] classic children's fiction. These children's novels are all about orphans and about people who are being badly treated. It's a key part of the English tradition of childhood, over coming adversity . . . In general, Americans have a more sentimental view of childhood even now. There's still a protection of children in children's fiction in America that we don't have.''

British and American books even look different. Wade says you *can* judge a book by its cover: ''You can usually tell at a glance, which children's books are American and which are British. British books hardly ever depict the main character on the cover, while it seems that U.S. covers generally highlight the main character.''

Endings may provide the most distinguishable difference between many British and American children's stories. ''Americans prefer the happy ending. Brits allow the ending to be more sad or dark,'' says Sara O'Connor, who has edited children's books for U.S. and U.K. publishers. ''Brits are just happy to let things be. Americans like to change for the better.''

According to Margaret Meek's *Children's Literature and National Identity*, ''No study of English children's books can ignore the issue of *class*. It is the most pervasive aspect of social life in England, historically and contemporarily. It includes a subtle network of social, linguistic and literary codes that entwine children's books and the development of their readers as literates.'' Classic inequality exists in both countries, of course, but, as Bergman notes, ''The U.K. class system is more obvious . . . Here it's almost a built-in system. First- and second-class stamps, first- and second-class rail travel. You don't get that in the States . . . Maybe it's so imbedded here that people don't see it anymore.''

Another obvious but tricky difference is sense of humor. Still humor seems to translate well. Louise Rennison's U.K.-set Georgia Nicolson series has sold well in the U.S. Similarly, American author Meg Cabot's Princess Diaries series appears on U.K. bestseller lists. ''Americans have a lighter touch on young adult fiction,'' says Eccleshare. ''[U.K. teen fiction] became very issues-based early on.''

Although the trend is hard to quantify, many experts believe that the U.S. market publishes more multicultural books than the U.K. ''The size of the American market allows them to publish more niche books targeted to ethnic minorities,'' says Kelly Cauldwell, senior editor at Random House Children's Books U.K. Atkins adds that these U.S. multicultural books are created by a more diverse group of authors and illustrators than in the U.K.

''Although the quantity [of multicultural books published in the U.K.] is lower, my impression is that you get more books published here that don't focus on the issue of race or racism,'' says Atkins, whose doctoral dissertation will focus on U.K. multicultural children's literature. ''Proportionally, in the United States it seems more of the books are issues books with race being the issue.''

Picture book challenges

Picture books have additional hurdles when trying to appeal to multiple markets. ''Picture books in the U.S. are more touchy-feely,'' says Biebow. ''Americans publish books with a more preachy tone. U.K. parents don't like an overt message.'' British and American artwork styles also differ. The illustrations in picture books destined for both markets must have a universal appeal—no big red buses or American flags. Illustrators must also carefully construct groups of children because the racial composition is unique to each culture.

''Any individuality was bred out of picture books a long time ago because of the co-edition market,'' says Eccleshare. ''We've known for a long time that pictures books must have a universal quality to work in other territories—which they have to do to survive.''

Editing foreign authors

When a book makes the journey across the Atlantic, publishers generally try to maintain the book's integrity. They may change the title, redesign the cover, or alter slang or unfamiliar words to make the meanings clear in the context of the story. Both Linda Summers, associate publisher for rights at Random House Children's Books U.K., and Atkins agree that American

Articles & Interviews

publishers edit more heavily than their British counterparts. Atkins attributed this, in part, to a "tradition in the U.S. of publishers being trained in editing."

Success stories

So what makes a book successful in both countries? David Fickling, publisher of David Fickling Books, the first children's book publisher to publish simultaneously in the U.S. and U.K., provides a simple answer: "Good stories travel. Bad stories don't. Huge allowances will be made for good stories."

You don't have to be a wizard to guess the genre that most easily moves between countries. "Fantasies can transcend cultural differences," says Cauldwell. These imaginary places are equally strange and fascinating to both cultures. England has a heritage of fantasy works that cross boundaries of space and time: *The Wind in the Willows*, *Peter Pan*, Winnie the Pooh, The Chronicles of Narnia, *Alice in Wonderland*, The Lord of the Rings, Philip Pullman's His Dark Materials trilogy, and, of course, J.K. Rowling's Harry Potter series. U.S. fantasy writers also succeed in the U.K. market. Christopher Paolini's *Eragon* and *Eldest* have topped children's book bestseller lists in both countries.

Teen fiction also crosses borders. Brit Mark Haddon has gained critical acclaim from both countries for *The Curious Incident of the Dog in the Night-Time*. U.K. author Melvin Burgess stirred controversy in the U.S. and U.K. with *Smack* (titled *Junk* in the U.K.) and *Doing It*. American Jennifer Donnely won the British Library Association's Carnegie Medal for *A Northern Light* (titled *A Gathering Light* in the U.K.) "U.S. teen fiction travels because U.K. kids of that age have seen so much of American entertainment," says Bergman.

Lost in translation

But don't let Hollywood fool you. Many topics don't hold the same attraction for British and American children and may make a book less marketable globally.

- American football, basketball or baseball. These sports aren't well-known to British children. In the U.K. soccer (which Brits call "football") and cricket are top sports.
- Social issues. "Social realism is quite a new genre [but it closes] borders and markets," says Eccleshare. Immigration, for example, is a big issue for a small island. Immigrants and the immigration experience create a different feeling when the destination country is known as a melting pot.
- Unique cultural references. For example, Brits don't know the acronym WWJD, so Jack Ganto's book *What Would Joey Do?* doesn't have the same connotation in the U.K.
- Historical settings unique to the U.S., including stories set during the Great Depression or the U.S. Civil War.

Covering these topics doesn't mean a book won't succeed in other markets, but it might make it more challenging. Still Fickling believes it's a mistake to consider markets first. "I don't publish stories to make money," he says. "But I know if you publish good stories you will make money. I think it's a mistake to think of the market before the [product]."

Talent scouts

Keeping up on the trends and talent in one country is tough enough. Now editors and publishers rely on literary scouts to find promising talent in other countries. Literary scouts have existed for more than 20 years in the U.S., but they've been focused on the adult market. Harry Potter changed that. New York-based Lina Sion of Franklin and Siegal Associates was the first literary scout to focus solely on children's fiction. She researches new children's books and alerts foreign publishers, such as Hodder Children's Books, to up-and-coming

American authors. Similar scouts work in Europe to inform American publishers of hot properties overseas.

Shrinking borders

Even though U.S. publishers are on the lookout for the next J.K. Rowling, some industry experts believe that U.S. children's book publishing is becoming more ethnocentric. "I think there's less cross-over," says Eccleshare. "As long as we worry about children reading, we work harder and harder to make a book relevant. That means the focus gets narrower. Because we think relevant means *like* and that's not what relevant really means. We think if you can say to a child that [a story] is set in a school that's just like your school . . . or this is a divorce just like your divorce, [this similarity] will engage them in reading. Instead of saying that this is a concern that we can explore in an interesting way, and you can extrapolate what is relevant to you. We don't do that."

Not only are gatekeepers in the way, market forces also have hindered the exportation of British fiction to the States. "The market is tougher," says Biebow. "American publishers aren't buying as much as they used to. They have a huge market, so they don't need to be more global."

And fewer picture books travel west. "The picture book market is flat," says Summers. "When it's a difficult market, you look to publish your own authors. No longer is *good* good enough."

Regardless of cultural differences and market pressures, exceptional writing resonates with readers around the world. "There are features in all lives, wherever and whenever they are lived, that are recognizable to all of us," said British author David Almond when accepting the Boston Globe-Horn Book award for *Fire-Eaters*. "One of the functions of stories is to bring together two more opposites: the local and the universal."

Articles & Interviews

Creating Books for the Youngest Readers

by Kelly Milner Halls

There is one audience so special, so unique only the most skillful writers can capture its heart—on extra thick pages. They are baby readers; tiny toddlers who can't speak, much less make out letters or words. But they are learning faster in those early days of life than they will ever learn again. Board book authors and editors know how important their mission is.

According to Beginning with Books (www.beginningwithbooks.org), a Pittsburgh-based early literacy program, babies have heard more than 30 million different words by the time they reach their third birthdays. Those who absorb some through reading lock into learning with far greater ease than those who don't experience toddler books.

What makes a board book a classic? A cuddly keeper? A gem? And is writing for babies as easy as some people would like to think? We turned to a panel of experts to find out.

Jabari Asim is no stranger to the world of children's books. As a long-time editor for the *Washington Post's BookWorld,* Asim has heralded some of the finest titles ever written to a cross-country readership in the hundreds of thousands, if not millions. But he has also written two charming board books for Little Brown—*Whose Toes are Those?* and *Whose Knees are These?* (both June 2006 releases).

Margaret Ferguson and **Frances Foster** edit/publish Frances Foster Books, an imprint at Farrar, Straus & Giroux's Books for Young Readers. They have published such winning young adult titles as *Keesha's House*, by Helen Frost, and *Buddah Boy*, by Kathe Koja. And when they see a board book winner, they add it to their distinctive list.

Emily Jenkins can attest to the wisdom of Margaret Ferguson and Frances Foster. They published Bea and Ha Ha, her four book series for toddlers in 2006—*Num, num, num!*; *Hug, hug, hug!*; *Plonk, plonk, plonk!*; and *Up, up, up!*

Karen Katz is one of Little Simon's board book anchors, responsible for such magical, lift-the-flap board books as *Where is Baby's Belly Button?*, *Toes, Ears & Nose!*, *Grandpa and Me* and *Counting Kisses*, to name only a few of her expansive and award-winning list.

Summer Dawn Laurie edits distinctive titles for young readers at Berkeley's Tricycle Press. She may be best known for the controversial and important picture book *King and King*, but her distinctive board book series are just as noteworthy. From John Schindel's *Busy*

KELLY MILNER HALLS is a full-time freelance children's writer with nearly 2,000 articles and more than 15 books published. Her latest book is *Tales of the Cryptids* (Darby Creek Publishing, Fall 2006), a look at mysterious animals that may or may not exist. She lives in Spokane with two daughters and too many animals and fights censorship in her spare time.

Articles & Interviews

Monkeys, Busy Kitties, Busy Penguins and *Busy Doggies* to Amy Wilson Sanger's delicious food board books—*First Book of Sushi*; *A Little Bit of Soul Food*; *Let's Nosh*; and *Mangia, Mangia!*—Laurie offers fresh options every time.

What are the most common misconceptions about baby board books?

Jabari Asim

Jabari Asim: I'm not sure if I can call these "common" misconceptions, but I know some people may believe that not much thought goes into their creation as into other books, that they're sort of throwaways. But they require some deep thinking because you have very little space and time to communicate an idea.

Emily Jenkins: I think the biggest misconception is that quality doesn't matter. People assume a junky, badly written thing is fine for a baby, because the baby doesn't know the difference and is only going to suck on it anyway. My thinking is that beautiful, emotional, or comical pictures and text with pleasing rhythms and genuine feelings are going to engage children more strongly than junk. Even the very youngest children. Why on earth would you read your child something you think is no good? But people do it all the time.

Karen Katz: A common misconception about baby board books is that babies grow out of them or get to old for them. I think babies love looking at their board books well beyond the age you would think. I have had teachers tell me that they use my board books to teach reading in the lower grades and to teach English as a second language. My daughter loved pointing and flipping the flaps on her board books well past her baby days.

Another misconception about board books is that they are really easy to do. Sometimes they are simple but to come up with something that is a little different and will stand out is a challenge. There are a lot of board books out there and very few stay in print, but a truly special one will last.

Summer Dawn Laurie: That any book can be taken, shrunk down, printed on board stock and there you have it . . . a board book! We've seen loads of best selling picture books

© 2006 LeUyen Pham.

Whose Toes Are Those? and *Whose Knees Are These?* are the first board books by long-time editor and father of five Jabari Asim. He says many people believe not much thought goes into the creation of board books, "but they require some deep thinking because you have very little space and time to communicate an idea."

converted into board book format. So many of these books are too long, the language is too sophisticated, subject matter too complex. Picture books and board books are intended for wholly different audiences. The flip side to that, of course, is seeing publishers take picture books from years past and bringing them out in board book format to better effect. Before there was a real market in board books, everything would be brought to market as a picture book. Now, some of those books are being released in a more appropriate fashion. Tricycle, for example, is publishing a book called *P. Bear's New Year's Party*—black-and-white illustrations, counting book, perfect board book candidate, but we originally published it in hardcover with a jacket before board books really had a place in stores. Now it should see a second life in a more comfortable skin.

What elements are crucial to a special baby board book?

Asim: The language should be clean, simple and engaging. Even if it manages to embody all those qualities, it is still dependent on the illustrations. Without top-quality artwork, preliterate children will not be attracted to them.

Ferguson and Foster: [That they meet] our standards for aesthetically appealing, age-appropriate picture books for the very young. Pearson's books offer a completely fresh way of reading and interpreting familiar nursery classics, making these rhymes truly accessible to children today. They are old friends in new dress. Emily Jenkins and Tomek Bogacki introduce Bea and HaHa, new characters in everyday situations, best friends who don't always get along but always work things out. These are books that invite parents and caretakers to read with their babies—and no baby is too young to engage in conversation sparked by a book.

Frances Foster

Jenkins: I think repetition and rhythm are especially important in this kind of book. *Max's First Word*, by Rosemary Wells, is a great example. Max keeps saying ''bang'' over and over, while his big sister Ruby tries to teach him other words. Very young children love that repetition, and they master it. They can predict it and laugh at it.

Katz: A book should be fun! Books that have bright colors, bold illustrations and are interactive capture a baby's attention. That is why lift-the-flap books and books that include an activity are so popular. Babies love to be engaged. They also love to look at other babies.

There are many reasons why a board book can be special from its vibrant artwork, to a gentle lulling refrain, to pages of interactive pulling, flipping and fluffing. One thing that is important is it has to have an element of surprise. There needs to be, as we call it in publishing, a ''payoff'' at the end. Something that will make that baby smile.

Laurie: Artwork. With 10 spreads and only 50-100 words, what can really set a board book apart is illustration style. For the audience, it is especially difficult to create images that are at once simple and interesting, comprehensible yet engaging.

What elements are most likely to sink a board book submission?

Laurie: Length, inappropriate subject matter.

Why did you elect to devote some part of your career to this unique kind of book and readership?

Asim: I'm a father of five. I have four boys and one girl. My oldest is 22 and my youngest is four. I'm working on writing something that will appeal to each of them. My youngest can pick out a few words here and there but mostly he is being read to. The board books were written with him in mind.

Ferguson and Foster: We can hardly be said to have devoted even a small part of our careers to publishing board books. We have, however, over the years followed a few favorite authors who have presented us with hard-to-resist proposals for board books. These include picture book authors like Leo Lionni and Satachi Kitamura, and most recently Tracy Campbell Pearson, Emily Jenkins, and Tomek Bogacki.

Jenkins: I had a baby. I read a million board books. I was intrigued by telling a story with meaningful conflicts and characters in such a small space. That is, I was interested in the formal challenge. I also wanted to amuse babies, since I suddenly knew so many and saw how much they could be amused by good books intended for them.

Emily Jenkins

Katz: As an author and illustrator, I find doing board books so much fun. I started out doing books for older kids. One day, I went up to Simon & Schuster to show my work to Lee Wade, the creative director. She said to me, ''Why don't you try a book for really, really young kids?'' It immediately excited me. My work is very bold and colorful and so it becomes a perfect format for me to work with. That was my first board book, *Where is Baby's Bellybutton?*

Laurie: Honestly, just an aesthetic love for the format and the challenge of the constraints of the format. I've found it to be a great way to introduce the world to fledgling illustrators.

What board books have been overdone?

Ferguson and Foster: The only thing that dampens our enthusiasm for these books is the large chain bookstores' preference for board books featuring licensed characters or already well-established ones. Unless they show more interest in supporting newcomers, it's unlikely that we'll be able to continue publishing them.

Laurie: As with almost every genre, licensed character books.

Where do you see holes in the genre? What's on your wish list?

Asim: I'm always eager to see comical stuff that makes kids laugh out loud.

Jenkins: There are artists I'd love to see do some board book originals, as Helen Oxenbury

Links

- For more about Jabari Asim:
  www.postwritersgroup.com/Asim.htm

- For more about Margaret Ferguson and Frances Foster:
  www.fsgkidsbooks.com/

- For more about Emily Jenkins:
  www.emilyjenkins.com/kids.html

- For more about Karen Katz:
  www.karenkatz.com/

- For more about Summer Dawn Laurie:
  www.tenspeedpress.com/catalog/tricycle/index.php3

and Rosemary Wells have done. Mary Murphy and Chris Rashka, too. But there are many more whose work is well-suited to very young readers, and I'd love to see them making board book originals. Margaret Chodos-Irvine, for example. Or Eric Rohmann. Or Simms Taback. However, the royalty structure and the challenges in marketing board books make this development somewhat unlikely. On the other hand, some great artists (David Shannon, Mo Willems, Ian Falconer) have done board books recently as tie-ins to popular characters they originated in hardcover. Some people might feel cynical about this development, but I'm glad to see their work available for littler kids.

Katz: I have a lot on my wish list and in fact some of it I am doing right now. Board books with foil and fluffy yarns and lots of tactile elements. I have a bunch of books coming out this next year and I did get to use those materials. I would also like to do a series of board books that feature ethnic kids on the covers. Adorable chunky African-American babies, and smiling laughing Hispanic babies and giggly cooing Asian babies, but ethnic babies are generally not featured on the covers. Also I would like to have a character (that is in the works too) to be loved by kids. Then I could do tons of books about that character's adventure.

Karen Katz

Are there any board books you wanted to do but couldn't get through editorial committee?

Asim: I've been lucky so far. I'm working on a couple more for Little Brown. Beyond that I want to develop them as series in which I can use the same identifiable characters.

© Karen Katz. Reprinted with permission.

Mini-readers get three books by Karen Katz in Baby's Box of Fun, released in 2004 by Little Simon. The collection includes *Where Is Baby's Mommy?*, *Where Is Baby's Belly Button?*, and *Toes, Ears, & Nose*, delightful lift-the-flap board books written and illustrated by Katz.

Articles & Interviews

Articles & Interviews

Katz: I've written a few board books that we haven't decided yet if they are picture books or board books. The amount of text in a book some times defines what format it will be published in. I use so little text in most of my books they can sometimes go either way. This is a good point to keep in mind if you are writing board books. . . . the text should be short and simple.

Laurie: Happens all the time. One of the most difficult issues with board books is the price point. What is such a plus for the end consumer, can be a huge hurdle for the publisher. Our initial investment to create a board book is only slightly lower than what we lay down for a $15.95 picture book, so we must be discerning and only publish those board books we believe we can make up in volume what they lack in retail [price].

Where do you see the future of the genre headed?

Asim: I think we'll continue to see new and different approaches from illustrators, as well as features that will make them interactive—tabs, wheels, bells, and other tactile items for children to manipulate, as well as accompanying software that will enable parents and their children to use them in conjunction with computers.

Summer Dawn Laurie

Jenkins: Alas, somewhat downhill, as the chain stores are not particularly supportive of board books that don't feature already established characters. I guess I'd say the future of the genre is probably in abridged reprints of hardcover hits, but I am not an editor.

Katz: I don't know where the future of board books is going but I do know that babies will always want to ''read,'' touch, sleep and play with their board books.

Amy Wilson Sanger's *First Book of Sushi* is one of a series of World Snacks Books from Tricycle Press featuring rollicking rhyme about ethnic cuisine and tasty, textural mixed-media illustrations. The bestselling book is a favorite of Tricycle editor Summer Dawn Laurie.

© 2001 Amy Wilson Sanger.

Laurie: Certainly it will continue on a positive track, perhaps diversifying into two tracks . . . very hip, kitchy books using the format, but primarily intended for an adult audience to gift. And then an expansion of books even more targeted for the very young on a developmental level. I can see black-and-white, wordless books specifically with the pre-reader in mind, a more up-market Baby Einstein.

Why are board books important?

Asim: They are so perfect for children who can't read yet. Because they're so plush and colorful and cuddly, board books introduce the very necessary notion that books are worthwhile and rewarding companions, not just in childhood but throughout one's life.

Jenkins: They don't break or tear in the hands of young readers. They are much more affordable than hardcovers and cheaper even than paperbacks. They are portable. They are small enough for a baby to hold. In other words, they can get people reading and owning books very young, and very cheaply—and they last.

Katz: Board books are babies' first experience with language in the written form. It is the beginning of identifying a word with a picture and that is the beginning of reading. But more importantly board books provide a tool for sharing, cuddling and having interaction with parents, caregivers and everyone in the family. Board books stimulate babies to see, and hear, and touch and begin to get to know this big world that is opening up to them. What is more amazing than the first time your little baby shrieks ''toes!'' and points to his own!

Laurie: The physical format of a board book enables even the youngest of children to interact with a book. From a publishing community standpoint, I think the expansion of the board book genre is wonderfully productive in that it opens a whole new world for a lot of authors and illustrators. Board books open up a world to prereaders to ''read.'' The format gives us as publishers the opportunity to publish appropriately for young children. The more sophisticated the consumer becomes with this genre, the more appropriately publishers can make their creations.

Best Books for Babies

These board books were named ''Best Books for Babies'' in 2005 by Beginning with Books Center for Early Literacy. Visit www.beginningwithbooks.org for more about the organization.

- *Buenos Dias Baby!*, by Libby Ellis (Chronicle Books).
- *Tomie's Baa Baa Black Sheep and Other Rhymes*, by Tomie DePaola (Putnam).
- *Little Bo Peep*, by Tracey Pearson (Farrar Strauss Giroux).
- *Truck Duck*, by Michael Rex (Putnam).
- *Baby Danced the Polka*, by Karen Beaumont, illustrated by Jennifer Plecas (Dial).
- *Te Amo, Bebe, Little One*, by Lisa Wheeler, illustrated by Maribel Suarez (Little, Brown,).
- *Duckie's Rainbow*, by Frances Barry (Candlewick Press).
- *Me Baby You Baby*, by Ashley Wolff (Dutton).
- *Snug in Mama's Arms*, by Angela Shelf Medearis, illustrated by John Sandford (McGraw Hill Children's Publishing).
- *Wynken, Blynken, and Nod*, by Eugene Field and illustrated by David McPhail (Cartwheel Books).

Do you believe board books lay the foundation for a love of books later in life? And if so, does the physical part (teething on the books, snuggling in a big person's lap, being able to touch the fat pages) help make that happen?

Jenkins: Anyone with a baby knows that they rip paper. If you want to read to a baby regularly, a board book is best. I do not know if it creates a love of books later in life, but it is a very good way to amuse a small person; a way to snuggle and have quiet time; a way to build vocabulary; and a good way to create family rituals early in life, like reading before bed, that can last throughout childhood.

Katz: I absolutely believe that the teething, cuddling, chewing, touching and snuggling in a big person's lap is all part of learning to love books, whether it is for the words or they just simply love the pictures.

Laurie: Yes, yes, yes. I think interaction of any kind of book, even seeing a parent immersed in reading, can lay a solid foundation, and simple respect for the written word, down the road. And I like to believe that for very young children, being able to physically manipulate a page and take some control of the book helps them internalize that connection. But I'd prefer to leave that to the scientific community. I do know that a board book is much easier to fit in a diaper bag than a full size picture book, and therefore has a better chance of being brought along through out the day.

The New Rules of Teen Lit

(Hint: There Are No Rules)

by Megan McCafferty

'm an imposter. I shouldn't be included in this book because I'm neither a children's book writer nor an illustrator. Technically, I'm not even a Young Adult writer. My books (the novels *Sloppy Firsts*, *Second Helpings* and *Charmed Thirds* and a short story collection I edited, *Sixteen: Stories About That Sweet and Bitter Birthday*) are published by Crown, a subsidiary of Random House that doesn't put out children's books. Though my core audience consists of teenagers, my books are most often shelved in the regular fiction section of bookstores.

I always viewed my books as crossovers between the teen and adult markets. I began the first novel in 1999, and there were numerous examples of the teen-adult pop culture overlap. TV shows like *Dawson's Creek*, movies like *American Pie* and music by the likes of Britney, Backstreet Boys and *NSYNC weren't exclusively for teenagers. I argued to my agent that my books could capitalize on a similar multigenerational appeal. It seemed like a no brainer to me. One book, two markets, many copies sold. I could retire to the Caribbean before I was 30.

Or not.

Most publishers saw it differently. In fact, when my novel was being pitched for publication, the response was nearly unanimous: Editors loved the book, but had no idea what to do with it. Was it YA? Adult? Who was the audience? Where would it be shelved in bookstores? How would it be marketed? I explained how *Sloppy Firsts* was a comic coming-of-age novel that could be enjoyed by older teens and adults. Therefore, it had a better chance of reaching both if it were shelved in Fiction versus YA, as teen readers tend to read "up" to adult fiction, but not vice-versa. And—hey!—maybe it could even be shelved in both!

I was told by more than one editor that I was dead wrong. Whether it's YA, Sci-Fi, Chick Lit or Mystery, I was told that my book, like all books, must fit into an easily-categorized niche. Otherwise it would get lost on the shelves. And *Sloppy Firsts*, with its contemporary voice and ageless appeal, simply didn't fit into a single category. If I tried to put a book about teens in the adult section of the bookstore, I was warned that I would confuse and lose everyone. Editors advised me to either make it more "literary" so it would be more appropriate for adults, or to "dumb it down" for teens.

MEGAN McCAFFERTY is the author of *Sloppy Firsts, Second Helpings* and *Charmed Thirds*. She also edited a short story collection, *Sixteen: Stories About That Sweet (and Bitter) Birthday*. She lives in Princeton, New Jersey with her husband and young son, and is currently working on the fourth Jessica Darling novel. For more info, visit www.meg anmccafferty.com.

Articles & Interviews

Charmed Thirds is the latest installment in Megan McCafferty's mega-popular series about Jessica Darling, a series published by Crown as adult— not YA—titles. Says *Publishers Weekly*: "The snappy writing, au courant wordplay and easy-to-relate-to plot turns will keep eager teens—and teens-at-heart— turning the pages."

Reprinted with permission.

Fortunately, Kristin Kiser at Crown loved my book enough to go against this conventional wisdom and publish my book as it was—and as an adult title. Any author who is lucky enough to find an editor or agent who is passionate about your book should work with that person regardless of what else she publishes. As I learned, these zealous insiders are often in the best position to champion your books, and just might make the difference between a bestseller and the remainders bin. In my own case, it's now six years, two sequels, 10 foreign translations and nearly 500,000 copies later. I can definitely say that I was glad to have disregarded the rule dictating that I shouldn't work with an untraditional publisher.

Of course, I am not advising you to shut out others' criticism in favor of your own grand vision all the time. I appreciate input from my editors and my agent and know that their hard work has always improved my books. But as authors, we're often told what we can and can't do with our writing. And quite often, that advice is misguided. Herewith follows other rules for teen lit that were meant to be broken.

Rule #1: Don't write about sex and drugs.

I was ecstatic when a very famous editor offered me a generous six-figure deal for my first novel. Then she dropped the bomb: "The title has got to go. *Sloppy Firsts* is depraved." Warning sirens went off: WHOOP! WHOOP! WHOOP! The title was a joke, albeit one that plays off a crude bit of sexual slang. If this editor didn't get the joke, that *Sloppy Firsts* referred to all the first-time mistakes one makes as a teenager, how could I be sure that she would approve of other edgier aspects of the novel? What would stop her from cutting out other "depraved" things, like when Jessica discusses her confusion about orgasms? Would she also want to edit out when the very underage Jessica gets drunk at a beach party? In the end, I turned down this editor's offer and took less money from my editor at Crown, who told me she loved the title and everything else.

I don't take sex or drug use lightly. As the daughter of two high school teachers, I took great pains in depicting this particular slice of suburban life as it really is, and not, alas, as many people wish it would be. When I was writing *Sloppy Firsts* I remember thinking: *Okay, I can either tone this down so it won't offend anyone or write the book I want to write.* Ultimately I figured that if this stuff is being talked about in the hallways of my former high school, I would be doing a disservice by not writing about it, and in the real language that teens actually use. (More on that later.)

Since my books have been published, I've been told that if anything I've toned-down teens' frankness about sexual activity and drug use. Thousands of readers—teenagers, librarians, teachers, and yes, even some parents!—have told me via e-mail and in-person that they appreciate Jessica's candor about controversial subjects and can identify with her hormonally-charged confusion. Jessica makes mistakes and learns from them. That's what my fans love about her. It's what I love about her, too.

That doesn't mean everyone has to love it. And so, I understand when more conservative parents keep my books out of their daughters' hands because they don't like my use of four-letter words. (Though I can't help but wonder what would happen if they tried discussing the content of the books instead of censoring them . . .)

Rule-Breaking Lesson

There seems to be societal pressure to be safe and wholesome, and commercial pressure to be sexy and edgy. While being shocking for the sake of being shocking is never a good idea, teens do appreciate candid characters and honest portrayals of controversial subjects.

Rule #2: Don't be too sophisticated—teens won't get it.

So much of the material about teenagers—especially girls—is insipid, insulting or inaccurate (or all three). All too often, writers resort to horrifying plot twists in order to give their teenage narrators a story "worth telling." I have a deep respect for the ordinary trials and tribulations of teenagerdom and I've always been disappointed when a promising story gets ruined by over-the-top, soap-opera developments. That's why I kept the plot of my first novel simple: *You're sixteen years old. Your best friend moves 1,000 miles away. You hate all your other friends and your parents don't understand you. What happens next?*

I was confident that if I wrote honestly, *Sloppy Firsts* would relate to anyone who survived high school, a time when the tiniest event takes on the hugest significance, and a best friend moving away is nothing short of catastrophic. Maybe Jessica's troubles aren't earth-shaking in the grand scheme of things, but they are to *her*, which is why so many teens can relate. By treating these intense issues with the intelligence and respect they deserve my work transcends the fluff.

And yet, some critics suggested that Jessica was *too* intelligent, too insightful. Others were afraid that teen readers would be turned off by her impressive vocabulary. All fears proved to be unfounded. By refusing to dumb down or overdramatize her plight, Jessica Darling is both universally identifiable, yet unique. Since no one in her world provides the model for the type of person she wants to become, she has to experience the pain and pleasure of creating herself through trial-and-error. Who can't relate to that? And in terms of her SAT-ready vocabulary, I've had countless fans tell me over the years that they appreciate Jessica's wordplay, and that mine is the first novel that ever inspired them to consult a dictionary because they didn't want to miss a joke!

Just because she's a sophomore in high school doesn't mean her wit is sophomoric. Jessica's biting observations are funny on two levels. First, because they are *so true*, with an in-your-face comedic value that can be enjoyed by readers of all ages. Her insights are also funny because they often reflect her youthful ignorance, which only more mature readers will fully appreciate.

I'm happy to say that my books aren't alone. The quality of writing for teens has improved immensely in the six years since I pitched *Sloppy Firsts*. The best YA books have become much more sophisticated and give young readers a lot more credit. Authors such as Ann Brashares, Rachel Cohn, David Levithan, and Carolyn Mackler have really elevated the genre to the point that the YA label doesn't do their books justice. They appeal to teen readers who are turned-off by babyish YA, *and* charm older readers who (like me) are suckers for anything in the teen angst genre. In fact, their novels are better written and more entertaining than many so-called "adult" books.

Rule-Breaking Lesson

Don't underestimate the teen reader's capacity for understanding and appreciating complex storytelling. But don't make it like homework for them either. The books they love best are those that enlighten *and* entertain.

Rule #3: Don't use slang or reference pop culture. You'll date your book.
Rule #4: Don't forget slang or references to pop culture. Your book will seem dated without them.

Obviously, these rules contradict themselves, as many rules do. This is something many writers for teens struggle with—and not without good reason. When I worked at a teen magazine I observed a focus group of high school students talking about their favorite (and least favorite) books. I'll never forget the way one 16-year-old voiced the most serious complaint about young adult novels. "I hate it when like, *old farts* try too hard to sound cool." At the time, I was 23. I already qualified as an "old fart." Now, at 33, I'm a relic. How do I avoid embarrassing myself?

I write my books in "real time," so whatever happens in the world immediately affects the tone and content of novel. But I don't worry about my books getting outdated because I go out of my way to set them during very specific periods. That way, all pop culture details contribute to a time capsule effect: *This is how it was then.* My inspiration is J.D. Salinger's *The Catcher in the Rye*, a book written in the mid-1940s that still resonates today. Do I know all the actors, movies, songs that Holden refers to in the book? No. Does anyone say "crumby" anymore? Nope. Do these throwbacks distract from my enjoyment of the story? Not one bit.

To mimic the particular patois of a millennial New Jersey teen, I became a chronic eavesdropper. (Note: This was hardly an invasion of privacy because they're usually shouting out their personal, private business as if they *want* strangers to get involved.) It helped that my mom was, until very recently, a high school teacher at my alma mater. I could learn more about how suburban teens act by sitting in on one of her classes than I could by poring over every teen magazine on the newsstand. I'm lucky enough to live within one mile of a major university, so virtually any trip outside of my door doubled as research for *Charmed Thirds,* the novel about Jessica's college years.

On the surface, many things have changed since I graduated high school. Music, TV, movies, fashion, and technology are nothing like they were in the late '80s and early '90s. I mean, back then I was wearing spandex and shoulder pads, listening to M.C. Hammer and typing up papers on a word processor that weighed more than I did. But what I agonized over in my journals back then—unrequited crushes, catty girl fights, brain-numbing boredom, too many zits and too little boobage—are the same subjects many teen bloggers obsess about today. I tap into my feelings from when I was young, combine that with my eavesdropped observations from now and—hopefully—come up with a realistic depiction of teen life in the '00s.

I'm familiar enough with teen culture to write about it without feeling like an "old fart" who's faking it. But if you feel like a fraud when you incorporate slang into your work, find another way to tell your story. Set your book in the era in which you the author came of age, like Stephen Chbosky's *Perks of Being a Wallflower.* Or create an alternate universe in which you invent the slang and trends, as in M.T. Anderson's *Feed.* Cater to your strengths as a writer, and don't force yourself to conform to the foreign language of teendom.

Rule-Breaking Lesson

There is nothing more cringeworthy to a teen than a writer who *gets it wrong.* But take heart: The 3 A's of adolescence—awkwardness, alienation and angst—are evergreen. Focus on the emotions, and not buzzwords of the era, and you'll write a book that teens will enjoy for generations.

Rule #5: Don't write a *blank* novel. It won't sell.

Why write another teen angst novel? I was asked. Wasn't the market saturated with novels about moody teenage girls and the boys who love them? At the time, I was told that I'd be better off if I wrote: (a) an "issue" book about some traumatizing event like rape or drug addiction and how the protagonist "came of age" as a result of it; (b) an "otherwordly" book, where a character is blessed (or cursed) with some superhuman ability; or (c) a gossipy, supertrendy book that is forgotten as soon as its finished.

None of these ideas interested me in the slightest.

I've accepted that there are a finite number of themes in this literary universe. There have been a bizillion romantic coming-of-age novels, but that didn't stop me from adding one more to the stacks. I believed I could handle a familiar theme in a refreshing way. I cared so much about Jessica, and all the characters in her world, and was genuinely excited to find out what would happen to them as I typed away at my laptop. Writing a novel isn't easy, and you need to be enthusiastic about your idea or you'll never make it through the rough spots. If you don't care about your work, you're just a hack. How often have you read a novel and gotten the impression that the author was as bored as you are? I know that I had tried to write one of those other books, my heart wouldn't have been in it. And it would have *suuuuuucked.*

Rule-Breaking Lesson

A good if well-tread idea, beautifully and creatively handled, transcends all publishing trends. It's better to pursue an idea you're passionate about than a marketable idea that doesn't interest you at all.

Rule #6: Don't write for teens. Period.

Before I was a novelist, I was an editor at the most popular women's magazine on the planet. Many assumed I'd write a novel that would cash in on the lucrative chick lit market. Or that I'd write a "literary" novel for adults that would give me a certain kind of credibility that magazines couldn't provide. Why waste my time writing for teens?

I couldn't stop thinking about how I, like many teens before me, was blown away by *The Catcher in the Rye* when I read it in seventh grade, and how it still amazed me each time I revisited it. I devoured novels written from a first-person female point-of-view, hoping that I'd finally find Holden Caulfield's female counterpart: a teenage protagonist that is highly-observant, hilarious and wise-beyond her years, yet still has a lot to learn about life. Though I found a few well-written and entertaining books, none came close to reflecting my high school reality.

Fortunately, I wasn't alone in my longing. Hundreds of thousands of readers have also found a fictional friend in Jessica Darling, and they care about her almost as much as I do. Which brings me to the greatest perk of writing for teens: When teens love a character, they *reeeeeeeeeeeeeeeeeallly* love that character with an unbridled enthusiasm that simply cannot be matched in adulthood. The best compliment I can get is when a teen says, "I *hate* to read. But I loved your book!" Every time I make one nonreader into a fan, that's more than enough to silence the critics—real or imagined—inside my head.

Rule-Breaking Lesson

Regardless of what type of book you write, there will always be naysayers. Writing takes courage because you put something out there that's very personal, and people will judge not only the work, but you as an individual—even if they don't know you. That's scary. But I've accepted that no writer can control the audience's reaction. There will always be people who don't like your writing because it's impossible to please everyone, so you shouldn't bother trying. Instead, write the story that *you* would have read when you were a teen—or now! There's sure to be many others out there who have been searching for the same book.

Mainstreaming the Graphic Novel

by Patricia Newman

Faster than a speeding bullet. Able to leap tall buildings in a single bound. And now appearing on your library and bookstore shelves. No, it's not Superman. It's a super-comic, popularly called the graphic novel. Today's graphic novels are a far cry from the stories featuring buxom women with impossibly tiny waists being snatched from the clutches of doom by buff superheroes. Instead they are closer to the wit and wisdom of truly great comic strips.

Comic strips are as American as Old Glory: Peanuts, Doonesbury, Bloom County, Pogo, and Calvin and Hobbes. The creators of these strips are humorists, philosophers and chroniclers of American history. But in the last 15 years or so, the phrase graphic novel has crept into the lexicon. Superhero stories are certainly one genre covered by graphic novels, but other genres are appearing in the catalogs of mainstream publishing houses. The time has come for a new look at the art of what many cartoonists in the field refer to as sequential storytelling.

LEARNING THE LANGUAGE

The first thing you should know is that not everyone likes the term graphic novel. Cartoonist Grady Klein says the word "graphic" reminds him of pornography. While some graphic novels tend toward the more lurid, truly literary works like Joann Sfar's *The Rabbi's Cat* are currently being published. Klein also says that many graphic novels are not novels at all. A novel is a genre and graphic novels tend to jump across genres. Klein's *The Lost Colony* is historical fiction; *Maus*, by Art Spiegelman, is nonfiction; *Persepolis*, by Marjan Satrapi, is a memoir. "Graphic novels slip outside conventional boxes, blurring age categories, genres, and markets," says Mark Siegel, Editorial Director of First Second, the new graphic novel imprint of Roaring Brook Press.

Back in the 1940s and 1950s, censorship crashed down on American comics causing creators to split into two camps: those who produced commercial comic books like *Archie* and *Richie Rich*, material that kids tended to outgrow quickly; and those who produced subversive, underground material that didn't hit the mass market. Morphing comics into

PATRICIA NEWMAN is the author of *Jingle the Brass* (Farrar, Straus & Giroux), a Junior Library Guild Selection recommended by *Publishers Weekly*, *Kirkus Reviews*, *The Horn Book*, *Booklist*, and *School Library Journal*. She has also written for *National Geographic Explorer*, *Spider*, *Highlights*, *Appleseeds*, *Boys' Quest* and *Storyworks*, and local publications serving her Sacramento, California home. Her profiles about other children's authors have appeared in several regional parenting magazines and can also be found on her Web site at www.patriciamnewman.com.

© 2006 Jennifer L. Holm and Matthew Holm.

Articles & Interviews

Sister and brother graphic novel team Jennifer L. Holm and Matthew Holm created the character Babymouse, star of several recent and upcoming graphic novels for 4- to 8-year-old readers including *Babymouse: Queen of the World, Babymouse: Our Hero*, and *Babymouse: Beach Babe*.

comix or *commix* (a co-mixing of words and pictures), today's artists and writers want to differentiate themselves from what Scott McCloud in *Understanding Comics* calls "the usually crude, poorly drawn, semiliterate, cheap disposable kiddie fare" that spawned the contempt of parents and teachers.

In contrast, it's not unusual to see adults and children in Japan cradling a *manga* (the Japanese version of graphic novels) under their arms. More graphic novels are sold in Japan than in the rest of the world combined. Europe has also had a long love affair with comics or graphic novels. "I was pickled in them," says Siegel who grew up in France where he and his fellow Europeans discovered novels and great writers through comics. "In France, people who love to read comics love to read, period."

THE POWER OF COMICS

Whatever associations you bring to the term comics, American librarians now recognize the popularity of Japanese *manga* and American comics among school children. Rich Thomas, a Senior Editor at Hyperion, says, "Comics empower reluctant readers to open up a book instead of their game consoles." Random House editor, Shana Corey, says, "Most of the major review journals—including those geared to librarians—cover graphic novels now. And many teachers use them in their classrooms. In fact, some school systems have begun incorporating comics into curriculums."

According to Mike Chin in *Writing and Illustrating Graphic Novels*, the form is the new voice for the 21st century. "Taking the far-reaching emotional world of conventional novels, the familiar visual techniques of comics, and tossing in a few ideas from the movies, graphic novels have created their own space and become something unique."

McCloud's definition of graphic novels includes *all* genres, *all* art materials, and *all* schools of art. Similarly, cartoonist James Sturm defines graphic novel as a medium encompassing all genres: "Graphic novels are not just illustrated text. The images tell the story and function as a picture language." Sturm adds, "The images are read instead of viewed. Each panel needs to articulate something very specific while being integrated with the visual grammar and rhythms of the page." This is the art of sequential storytelling.

GRAPHIC NOVEL TOOL KIT

To understand the nuances of graphic novels, Siegel recommends Scott McCloud's *Understanding Comics*. "It is conceptually unrivaled and [McCloud] gives you a tool kit for creating your own comics."

The first tool in your kit is a familiarity with several types of graphic novel art (see Resources & Reading sidebar on page 74). In many of the books, you will see a characteristic tendency toward cartoon images. McCloud says, "When we abstract an image through cartooning, we're not so much eliminating details as we are focusing on specific details. By stripping down an image to its essential meaning, an artist can amplify that meaning in a way that realistic art can't." Sturm, Klein, Siegel, and brother-sister team Jennifer Holm and

Articles & Interviews

Matt Holm prefer a less cluttered style of art. According to Sturm, art that is too detailed is not readily absorbed by the reader and bogs down the story. In McCloud's words, ''The cartoon . . . is an empty shell that we inhabit which enables us to travel in another realm. We don't just observe the cartoon, we become it.'' All of this is not to say that realism doesn't have a place in graphic novels. For example, Hergé, creator of the Tintin comics, contrasts abstract characters against realistic backgrounds.

Closure—the reader's ability to observe the parts (the individual panels) but perceive the whole (the flow of the story)—is another essential element in your tool kit. Think of it this way—unlike movies, comic panels fracture time and space, offering staccato bits of an entire sequence of action. For example, in the *Satchel Paige* sequence below, we *see* the baseball player swing the bat. We *assume* he hits the ball because we *see* the crowd looking skyward

© James Sturm. Reprinted with permission.

These four panels from James Sturm's *The Return of Satchel Paige*, illustrated by Rich Tomossa (Hyperion), showing a baseball player hitting a homerun, illustrate the way comics capture small bits of action in a sequence but still give readers the whole story.

Articles & Interviews

in the second panel. In panel three, we *see* the treetops, and *assume* the hit soars out of the park. Panel four confirms our suspicion with the boys searching the woods for the home run.

Closure allows you to read the story as one continuous, unified whole. McCloud says, ''The reader's deliberate and voluntary closure is comics' primary means of simulating time and motion.'' Pretty powerful stuff for a bunch of cartoons.

The magic of closure lies between the panels. Although this blank space requires nothing from you is at precisely this point that all of your senses are engaged.

Setting the mood and engaging your reader's senses are another set of tools for the graphic novelist. Larger panels suggest longer time periods. Borderless panels and art that ''bleeds'' off the edge of the page suggest timelessness. Dotted speech balloons infer whispering, while a few simple lines simulate the crack of a bat against a ball and the arc in which the bat travels.

TRADITIONAL BOOKS VS. GRAPHIC NOVELS

The characteristic that most distinguishes comic art from illustrations is the immediacy of the drawings. When you read comics, the words and images on the page generate a flow. Remember flip-books—individual images drawn on different pages in varying degrees of motion, so when the pages are fanned the images are ''animated?'' Sequential storytelling creates that kind of movement in your mind as the story unfolds.

Creating graphic novels for children requires the same attention to story and characters as with picture books, chapter books, and novels. A compelling story line with well-developed characters is of primary importance. With the exception of novels, all of the above forms also require the writer to leave some room for the artist. In both picture books and graphic

© 2006 Grady Klein. Reprinted with permission.

The Lost Colony, Book 1: The Snodgrass Conspiracy is the first in a series of historical fiction graphic novels by Grady Klein set in 19th-century America on a mysterious unknown island full of colorful characters. These pages offer a glimpse into Klein's process from early sketch (left) to final art (right) as he works out both his illustrations and dialogue.

Sample Script

Here is an early script for *The Lost Colony, Book 1: The Snodgrass Conspiracy*, by Grady Klein (First Second Books).

Stoop—(puts down the mug without drinking it)
Pepe—(glares hard at Birdy, says quietly) "I know that Miss Birdy."
Stoop—"no thanks."
Stoop—(hands Pepe a poster) "Here! Put this . . . up . . . in your . . . store."
Pepe—(sneaks around and pushes the mug back in front of Stoop)
Stoop—(looks down) "Say . . ."
Stoop—(points at the mug) "What's this about anyway?"
Stoop—(waves his hand) "That's not beer."
Pepe—(smiles congenially) "But it's very good!"
Birdy—(elbows him) "Say Mister"
Birdy—"It's a magic drink!"
Pepe—"Shush!"
Pepe—(laughs nervously) "Hahahahahahah, please excuse the funny girl"
Birdy—(yells as Pepe carries her away) "It's a crazy drink! It'll make you strange!"
Stoop—(eyes the mug a little differently)

novels, the words and pictures have to work together creating something bigger than the sum of its parts.

But the similarities end there. "Illustrating and cartooning have about as much in common as creative writing and sign painting," Sturm says. Where the illustrator of a picture book seeks to capture one specific moment in a scene on a page spread, the graphic artist captures multiple actions. According to Klein, writing and drawing graphic novels is more akin to graphic design. "Every picture has to be specific in what it is trying to communicate."

With traditional books, the writer and artist often work independently of each other—never meeting, never speaking. As the publishing industry takes on graphic novels, it's finding that the old way doesn't work. "With graphic novels, we have to reconsider how writers and artists work," says Jennifer Holm. "We can't just say here's a manuscript like we do with a picture book. It has to be a collaboration."

Graphic novel manuscripts look different than picture book or traditional novel manuscripts. Generally, the manuscript looks like a play script or a screenplay. (See Sample Script sidebar above.) At Hyperion, editor Rich Thomas says some of his authors create scripts as detailed as screenplays with specifics on close-ups, angles, and stage directions. Others create a general overview of the plot and hand it over to the artist who interprets the action. The author then fills in the dialogue after the artist has sketched out the story.

Klein, who is both author and artist, writes his manuscripts out like a three-act play. Because graphic novels are longer than short stories or picture books, the three-act format helps him with the pacing of his story. He suggests that you think about your writing in terms of page spreads, flowing from the top left to the bottom right. Each page will be like a comic strip in its own right. "It is the [author's/artist's] responsibility to invite the reader to turn the page to find out what happens next." Random House editor, Shana Corey, adds, "I think for a very young audience, graphic novels need to be clear. These are kids who are

Articles & Interviews

still mastering reading, so you don't want to trip them up over which panel or thought bubble to read next.''

Jennifer Holm, who had no previous instruction in cartooning or submitting graphic novels, uses an approach that worked for her when she made commercials in her advertising days. She and Matt Holm create a storyboard. Together they nail down the text before Matt completes the rough pencil sketches. According to Jennifer, ''The storyboard is a paper form of animation.''

No matter how you choose to format your manuscript, editors Siegel and Thomas agree that some finished pages are essential. A short proposal that outlines the concept but doesn't overwhelm the editors is perfect. In addition, the ''treatment'' should consist of between five and 20 pages of finished art to show editors how the dialogue and action work together in several scenes to fulfill the stated aims of your proposal. The finished pages are critical because, according to Sturm, the content of a graphic novel has a shape that is determined by the way in which the images are drawn and arranged.

THE NEXT STEP

If you're thinking about tweaking that picture book manuscript that won't sell into a graphic novel, STOP! Picture books, chapter books, and novels all have special challenges that have to be mastered before producing a manuscript worthy of publication. So too, does the graphic novel form. If you're an author, challenge yourself to think of your story as a movie and your characters moving from one scene to the next. Graphic novels will allow you to collaborate

Resources & Reading

Want to learn more? Visit the Center for Cartoon Studies at www.cartoonstudies .org. Read *Understanding Comics* by Scott McCloud and *Graphic Storytelling and Visual Narrative* by Will Eisner. Read books published by Fantagraphics, Drawn and Quarterly, Marvel Comics, DC Comics, First Second Books

Check out these graphic novels!
- Babymouse (series), by Jennifer Holm and Matt Holm
- *The Complete Peanuts*, by Charles Schultz
- *A Contract with God*, by Will Eisner
- *The Golem's Mighty Swing*, by James Sturm
- Johnny Mutton (series), by James Proimos
- *Krazy and Ignatz*, by George Herriman
- *The Lost Colony*, by Grady Klein
- *Marvel 1602*, by Neil Gaiman
- *Maus*, by Art Spiegelman
- *Palestine*, by Joe Sacco
- *Persepolis*, by Marjan Satrapi
- *The Rabbi's Cat*, by Joann Sfar
- The Sandman (series), by Neil Gaiman (*Dream Country* includes a full-length script at the end)
- *To Dance: A Ballerina's Graphic Novel*, by Mark Siegel and Siena Cherson-Siegel
- *X-Men: The Dark Phoenix Saga*, by Chris Claremont, et. al

Gallery of Characters

James Sturm is the creator of *The Golem's Mighty Swing*, named the Best Comic 2001 by *Time Magazine*. He's the founder of The National Association of Comics Art Educators and his work has appeared in *The Chronicle of Higher Education, The Onion, The New York Times*, and on the cover of *The New Yorker*. Currently, he's the director of the Center for Cartoon Studies in White River Junction, Vermont.

© James Sturm

© Matthew Holm

Jennifer Holm is a Newbery Honor medallist for *Our Only May Amelia*. She's a comics reader from way back, and her father was a huge Prince Valiant and Flash Gordon fan. The Babymouse books are her first foray into the world of graphic novels and a collaboration with her brother **Matthew Holm**.

Grady Klein is an award-winning illustrator, animator, and designer. His new graphic novel, *The Lost Colony*, digs into a few thorny issues in America's past. Editor Mark Siegel describes it as "an important book in the American literary landscape." He began creating editorial cartoons in high school and majored in Philosophy at the University of Chicago.

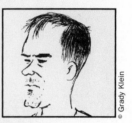

© Grady Klein

© Mark Siegel

Mark Siegel is Editorial Director for First Second Books, www.firstsecondbooks.com. He is a cartoonist whose newest work, *To Dance: A Ballerina's Graphic Novel*, is available from Simon & Schuster. He recommends reading graphic novels from America, Europe and Asia. Favorite reads include: *Tintin* (Hergé), *Persepolis* (Marjan Satrapi), *The Rabbi's Cat* (Joann Sfar).

Rich Thomas used to work for DC Comics before moving to Disney's Hyperion. His pet projects include adapting the Haunted Mansion attraction into a "cool, hip, and edgy" graphic novel with the help of SLG Publications. Hyperion has also contracted with James Sturm's Center for Cartoon Studies to produce graphic novel biographies.

© Rich Thomas

© Matthew Holm

Shana Corey's first experience with publishing graphic novels occurred when Jennifer Holm pitched the Babymouse series. Holm and Corey worked together on Holm's middle-grade novels. Corey is now an avid *shojo* reader—Japanese *manga* starring girls!

Articles & Interviews

with the artist, but you must be able to communicate your vision to the artist and allow the artist to contribute to your vision. If you're an illustrator, challenge yourself to master the art of cartooning in combination with the art of graphic design. No small task!

The good news for budding graphic novelists is that you can now make a living at it. "The model for [graphic novel] publishing is evolving into a regular advance and royalty system," says Siegel. The market is wide open and ready to receive new material from authors, artists, playwrights, and screenwriters.

Klein says, "There's a whole slew of people out there who we artists and authors need to court because there's a lot in the [graphic novel] form, in its history, in its traditions that is so very challenging on so many levels." In the current market, graphic novels have exploded in influence and quality. Klein's challenge to you is to find ways to present your ideas to captivate and appeal to these people.

Blogging for Authors & Illustrators

by Roz Fulcher

nitially I created a blog so I would have a venue to share my process and network with other illustrators. Soon, I discovered that it was also a fantastic way to promote myself, and learn more about children's publishing and a way for editors to get to know me better.

You're probably thinking that "blogging" is the last thing in the world you have time for. But, before you dismiss it completely, I want to share with you what a vital tool you can add to your author and illustrator arsenal simply by creating a blog.

WHAT'S A BLOG?

"Blog" is a short term for the words "Web log" and means a journal/newsletter that is available on the Web.

When you update your blog it is referred to as "blogging" and someone who keeps a blog is a "blogger."

Your entries are saved in chronological order and can be updated as often or as seldom as you like. Visitors can then visit your blog, post comments, link to or just read on a weekly/hourly basis.

The content and purpose of blogs are very individual and vary greatly which is what makes them so interesting and entertaining!

NETWORKING

I am amazed at the invaluable information that is being provided on blogs regarding the children's publishing industry. It is so important for us to stay current on what is going on and many of our peers make it easier by generously providing timely, invaluable information through their blogs. And as we become more educated authors and illustrators, we create more professional submissions.

For example, check out Cynthia Leitich Smith's blog, "Cynsations" (http://cynthialeitich smith.blogspot.com/). It's a treasure trove of insightful information about children's writing and publishing. Smith's blog includes author/illustrator interviews, reading recommendations, event announcements, analysis of trends, and numerous links to other sites of interest.

ROZ FULCHER spent several years learning the craft of children's books, then "cut out" a niche for herself when she began illustrating with felt. She has completed illustration assignments for McMillan/McGraw Hill and Perfection Learning and *Ladybug*, *Click*, *Hopscotch*, *Boys' Quest* and *New Moon* magazines. You can find her blogging about her illustration work at www.rozzieland.blogs.com.

On her blog "Cachibachis" (http://cachibachis.blogspot.com/), Amy Moreno has used her passion for the children's book market to provide a blog full of interesting "odds and ends" that will appeal to both authors and illustrators alike.

MARKETING

You've heard it before—having a Web site is a key element to marketing. And even more important than having a Web site is getting visitors *to* your site. If you want to increase traffic to your existing site, creating a blog can help.

Before I began blogging, visits to my online portfolio were random at best. As soon as I added a link to my Web site on my blog page, I started getting visitors daily.

Blogging is a very interactive medium that thrives on URL links. For example, visitors to my blog "link" or refer to my site on their own blogs. In turn, every time I comment on someone else's blog (be sure to leave your URL address), that's a link back to mine. This helps your online presence in two ways: (1) All of these links bring traffic to your blog which increases the likelihood of more bloggers linking to it. (2) Search engines give high priority to sites that others link to, so your blog is more likely to show up on the first page of search engines.

The bottom line: by keeping a blog you are gaining more exposure and bringing more traffic to your existing Web site, attracting visitors who may not have known it even existed.

Because images and information are normally updated infrequently on an author's or illustrator's Web site, having your blog linked to your site keeps it interesting and alive. People will be more prone to visit regularly if they know they'll find fresh updates and content.

WEB SITE ALTERNATIVE

Maybe you don't have a Web site yet and feel a bit intimidated by the time and investment involved in creating one. A blog is an inexpensive and informal way of introducing your work to the public and you can still receive a lot of the benefits that you would with a traditional Web site.

Author, Chris Barton (www.chrisbarton.info/blog/blog.html) shares how he has made his blog work for him: "I was about to finish the final manuscript for my first book, *The Day-Glo Brothers*, (Charlesbridge Publishing) but the publication date was still a couple of years away. I wanted to use the time in between to establish a community of writers who might be interested in the first-time-author's view of the publication process and who would share in my enthusiasm for the book. In other words, I started the blog as a marketing vehicle," says Barton. "I received part of my advance upon finalizing the manuscript, and I had been planning to put that money toward paying someone to develop a full-fledged Web site for me. But with my book still 20 months in the future, that seemed premature. For the time being, I figured, 'Bartography' was the perfect amount of exposure, and for an unbeatable price—nothing. I use my real name on my blog, so 'Chris Barton' is very visible through the major search engines. Plus, a lot of what I've written on the blog can be used in the 'About Me,' 'About My Book,' etc. sections of my Web site, so I won't have to create all of that content for the Web site all at once."

OPPORTUNITY KNOCKS

There is tangible proof that exposure through a blog can result in some exciting and unexpected opportunities.

Illustrator Jenny B. Harris (www.allsorts.blogs.com) received several assignments from American Greetings after an art director came across her artwork while surfing the Internet. Although Jenny has a well-established portfolio Web site, it was actually a personal piece of artwork she posted on her blog that caught the art directors' attention and landed her the assignment.

Don Tate (www.devasrantsandraves.blogger) is a successful illustrator who started a blog that has lead to some interesting and unexpected results: "I started my blog as a way of developing my writing skills. Up until then, I wasn't comfortable with words—writing them, and definitely not sharing them with an editor or critique group." says Tate. "I thought that by starting a blog, I could first promote my freelance illustration business by letting the publishing world know more about me, the artist behind the children's books. Second, I could get used to putting my words out for public scrutiny. Third, I started a blog as a way of networking with others in the business. As a result of daily blogging, I am much more comfortable writing children's manuscripts, and I now have several in the works. As I became more comfortable with writing, it began to take on many new directions. One of my blog posts was picked up and republished in my hometown newspaper. Another poem has been requested for republication in a children's collection of poems tentatively to be published by Simon & Schuster."

SENSE OF COMMUNITY

Blogging can definitely serve you well as a marketing tool. But I truly believe the sense of community that blogging provides is just as important for a freelance author/illustrator.

There is no doubt that the children's publishing field is competitive and can be hard on the ego—we all need encouragement along the way. I've found that my blogging community helps me feel connected and continually inspired. Freelancing can be an isolating experience and knowing that there are others out there who are as passionate about the business as I am keeps me going.

Fellow authors and illustrators can become each other's greatest fans. This is not to be neglected. When we are experiencing a lulls in our careers we can identify with each other and show support. When we have something to celebrate who better to share this news with than others in the same field who fully comprehend our achievement?

BLOG SPACE

Most of the blogging services I have researched are very easy to use and provide ample space for uploading files and images. Visit other writers' and illustrators' blogs to help you decide on the best service for yourself. I chose Typepad because I enjoyed the look of other blogs using this platform. Plus, I had many friends using it and I knew I could rely on them for help if I needed it.

Here are links to some popular blog services to get you started:

- **Blogger:** www.blogger.com/start. Free and easy to use.
- **Typepad:** www.typepad.com/. Minimal monthly fee dependent upon the amount of space you need. It has a great archiving system and has easy access to uploading image files.
- **Live journal:** www.sixapart.com/livejournal. This is a favorite among authors due to the interactive feature and ease of leaving comments back and forth.
- **Moveable type:** www.sixapart.com/movabletype. This is an affordable system to incorporate blog programming to your existing Web site.
- **Xanga:** http://www.xanga.com. This is another Web log community offering both free and premium blog space.

STARTING A BLOG

Getting started is probably the most difficult part of blogging. You want to create an identity but you're not sure how to define that identity. That's a common feeling—you must just jump in and get started. Again, visit other blogs to get a sense of what others are doing and then start writing about what interests you.

My own blog has been growing and evolving along with me. When I first started, I thought I would use it as a way to show my experimentation with different media. Instead it became more of a place where I share sketches, assignments and a little bit of what goes on behind the scenes, hopefully inspiring other illustrators who are pursuing children's book illustration.

If you're worried that your blog won't be interesting, think again. So often we take what we have to offer for granted. We all have individual takes on the industry and can provide information that others will enjoy and find helpful.

Since we are primarily talking about the *children's* publishing industry, it's best to keep your posts as child-friendly as possible, especially if you're planning to link it to your existing Web site. Also avoid bashing editors, agents and publishing houses in this public forum. No need to burn valuable bridges.

Many authors and illustrators are concerned that blogging will such away valuable work time. Remember, though, that you have control over how much time to invest. You should write regularly enough to build your readership, but only commit as much time as you need to. Weekly and monthly updates can be just as affective as daily posts.

Here are some brainstorming ideas to get your blog rolling:

- Whether you are a beginner or professional, connecting with others in the field is a fun way not to feel so isolated and alone. You can write about your own experiences or share links that inspire you.
- If you want to use a blog for purely professional purposes then create one that will keep librarians, teachers and students in the loop of your upcoming events, news and visiting schedule. Little tidbits here and there about what you're working on are always entertaining to your fan base.
- Writing begets writing. Authors, use your blog posts as a daily warm up exercise!
- Illustrators, participate in blog forums that offer weekly illustration prompts to help inspire new ideas (www.illustrationfriday.com).

POSTING COMMENTS

Comments can play an important role when it comes to linking and increasing search engine stats. On a more personal level, they are also a great way to connect with our peers. I admit

Blog Hubs

- **Illustration Friday:** www.illustrationfriday.com. Not a blog but a great place to start if you want to connect with other illustrators.

- **Anastasia Suen's Blog central:** www.asuen.com/blog.central.html. A smorgasbord full of author, illustrator, editor, agent and children's literature blogs!

- **Children's Illustrator Blog Ring:** www.ringsurf.com/netring?ring=RozArt;action=list. This is a group of blogs written by children's book illustrators.

- **Bloglines:** www.bloglines.com. A free online service for searching, subscribing, creating and sharing news feeds. This is a great service once you find several blogs that you enjoy reading. It will notify you when someone has added a new post to their blog. What a great time saver!

that I have a love hate relationship with comments—I hate that I love them so much! I love posting and receiving feedback. Comments can be encouraging, insightful and a way for me to receive support from fellow authors and illustrators, but I have to be careful not to become too reliant on them. Sometimes, we can get too caught up with the popularity aspect of comments if we start comparing blogs and the feedback they receive. This is not a popularity contest—it's simply another way to connect with our audience. If comments become overwhelming or don't interest you, you can simply disable the comment option on your blog and still benefit from the blogging experience.

If you do want your blog to be interactive and would like to receive comments, reap what you sow. Make time to visit other blogs and comment when you can. Fellow bloggers appreciate the time you take to comment and will often reciprocate. This is a fun way to build relationships and bond with like minds.

I love the blogging community and all that it has to offer. Not only has it helped me bring more traffic and exposure to my online portfolio, but equally important, it has brought me in touch with fellow authors and illustrators who love this industry as much as I do. I encourage you to enter the blogosphere. It's bound to enrich your freelancing experience as much as it has my own.

Articles & Interviews

Conquering Home Office Clutter

by Hope Vestergaard

Have you ever uttered any of the following statements about your work space? A cluttered office is the hallmark of a creative mind. Where is that %$#&! receipt?! Calgon, take me away!

So many people think of getting organized as a chore, a punishment, or some kind of a straightjacket. I think it's an adventure. I find stuff I need and things I'd forgotten I had. I create an attractive space that makes "butt-in-chair" time so much more pleasant. By setting up systems to manage receipts, manuscripts, and paperwork, I save myself time and money. And last, but certainly not least, I find that periodically taking time to unclutter my workspace helps me unclutter my mind—manuscripts that stopped making sense start falling into place on an unconscious level as I sort, shelve, and toss.

As you roll up your sleeves to tackle your own office demons, a systematic approach will keep you on track:

- Identify your personal pitfalls.
- Prioritize your needs.
- Break big jobs into manageable tasks.
- Set a reasonable timeline and stick to it.

That's just four simple steps to the office of your dreams. *Shall we?*

WHAT TO KEEP AND HOW TO KEEP IT

The piles that used to accumulate in my office fell into a few basic categories: stuff I needed to keep, stuff I needed to do, and stuff I didn't know what to do with. Unfortunately, with that "filing system," putting my hands on an important piece of paper took about as long as finding a bestseller in a slushpile. To make the most of your time and storage space, try to be a little more specific. For writers and illustrators, the following categories will cover most of the "stuff" in your home office.

- Business papers
- Office supplies
- Promotional materials

HOPE VESTERGAARD works from a relatively uncluttered office in Ann Arbor, Michigan. She's the author of eight books for children including *Hillside Lullaby* and *What Do You Do When a Monster Says Boo?* (both by Dutton, 2006) and *Weaving the Literacy Web: Creating Curriculum Based on Books Children Love* (Redleaf Press, 2005). For other teacher resources and more articles on the writing life, visit her Web site: www.hopevestergaard.com.

- School and conference materials
- Tools
- Work by-products

Business papers

Business papers include tax documentation, contracts, and royalty statements. These can all be filed in hanging file folders.

For **taxes**, you'll need files for recent returns, checking accounts, credit cards, receipts and mileage logs, and blank forms for monthly or quarterly returns. A mileage log is easy: a small spiral-bound notebook in your car can easily last a year. If you forget to write down a trip, use MapQuest.com or http://maps.yahoo.com to chart the route for events you have driven to. Write the name of the event on the MapQuest print-out and tally up your mileage at the end of the year.

Expense receipts are easy to tame. Use a large envelope for each month. Every time you come home from a trip, put your receipts in the envelope. Total the expenses by category on the outside of the envelope itself. Keep a catch-all clear plastic envelope in your purse or car and deposit all stray receipts there. When the envelope is full, sort the receipts and put them away. If you use a separate credit card for all business expenses, tax documentation is even easier. Many card companies will send quarterly or annual expense management reports. Programs such as Quickbooks, Microsoft Money, TurboTax, and others also make money management quick and easy.

Contracts should be kept in one place, all together. You'll only need to look at them a couple times a year, so one a legal-sized accordion envelope should suffice. If you have so many contracts that you need more than one envelope, write on the envelope which books'

Photo: Hope Vestergaard.

Hope Vestergaard advises writers with messy offices (you know who you are) to think of getting organized as an adventure. Adhering to the belief that a cluttered desk makes for a cluttered mind, Vestergaard has created a neat and inviting workspace complete with big, bright windows with flowing curtains. Her office supplies are in reach, her desktop is clear of papers and knickknacks, and she has easy access to the files and reference material she needs.

Articles & Interviews

Tricks of the Trade

Before you start sifting through the detritus in, on, and around your desk, keep in mind these general tips:

- **What's in a name?** Everything, if you're trying to alphabetize. Be consistent in the way you name your file folders. For example, if you use key words from book titles, do the same for all of your books.

- **Color coding can be fun!** Besides the pretty rainbow effect, using different color file folders for different kinds of information can help you find things fast. Once you group colored files together, alphabetize within each category. (An extra file tab will designate the heading on the first folder in a new section.)

- **Maintain your cool.** Whether it's developing the habit to save computer files to the appropriate folder, cleaning off your desk daily, or making an appointment to pay bills and file papers weekly, the key to an organized workspace is maintenance.

contracts are inside or use a cardboard file box. File them alphabetically or by date in an out-of-the-way spot.

Royalty statements fit nicely in hanging file folders. Put them in order by date and clip together the statements for each book for quick reference.

Office supplies

In addition to the basic writing utensils, tape, scissors, etc., writers' and illustrators' office supplies include art supplies and special papers, inkjet and laser printer cartridges, copy paper, and CDs or DVDs for digital back-ups. Basically, if there's any supply you need to do your work that you *can't* get at a 24-hour store, you should have a stash on hand. If you don't have much room, clear, flat under-bed plastic storage containers are a great way to store many of these essential items. These containers can also be stacked securely in a closet, basement, or garage. If you have room for cabinets and drawers in your workspace, smaller storage boxes, drawer dividers, and portable accordion files can keep papers, pencils, and such sorted and easily accessible. Several artists I spoke to mentioned map-sized drawers as an ideal way to store art papers and completed illustrations without crumpling or wrinkling.

If you choose remote storage such as the basement or an out-of-way drawer for any basic supplies, keep a running list of what you have and keep the list on your desk or in your purse so you don't keep buying the same things. If your storage area is humid or extremely dry, it may affect your materials so keep that in mind as you select containers and locations.

Many artists use cups, cans, or kitchenware crocks to store pencils, paintbrushes, and vertical tools on a countertop or desk. Some use plastic toolboxes. If your office is a multi-function room, storing supplies in plastic drawer stacks makes it easy to tuck them away and wheel them out when you need them or pull a single drawer out of the stack to take it to your workspace.

One final type of office supply that's nice to keep on hand: packing materials and postage for the packages you typically send.

Promotional materials

Promotional materials include review copies, newspaper articles, work clips, flyers, postcards, and contact lists. These fit nicely in hanging file folders. Be sure to make photocopies or scans of newspaper articles and tearsheets that you use a lot so you don't give away your originals. If you do a lot of school visit mailings, pre-pack some envelopes with your standard mailing pieces (flyer, postcard, etc.) so all you have to add is a personalized letter and mailing label. I keep 25-30 of each promo postcard in my office, but store the big boxes of postcards in my basement (with the book name written on the side of the box because those boxes all look alike). I don't keep a lot of pre-printed flyers on hand because the information on them changes frequently. I either print as many as I need from my computer, or have a copy shop do a large printing for a special mailing. Either way, keep 10-20 single sheets or tri-folds in a hanging file folder so you always have some ready to go. I keep reviews, articles, personal notes and photos for my books in individual folders by book. The promotional section of my file drawer also includes a folder for **contacts**. When I attend a conference, I highlight names of people I met and make notes on the attendee roster, then file it in my contacts folder. People who are really gung-ho about promotion, can type those names and addresses directly into a mailing list database.

Author Hope Vestergaard writes picture books for very young readers like *Hillside Lullaby* in her well-organized office in her farmhouse outside of Ann Arbor. "*Hillside Lullaby* is a cozy bedtime book," she says. "A little girl unwinds as she listens to the sounds of various (adorably illustrated!) critters outside her window." Visit www.hopevestergaard.com/lullaby.php to hear her book set to music.

Articles & Interviews

"What Do You Do When a Monster Says Boo?" is a playful peek into a day in the life of a harried big brother and his attempts to get along with his monstrous little sister," and it's inspired by real life, says author Hope Vestergaard—a mother of two boys and second oldest of 12 siblings. "It's a book about chaos—and calming it. As is my article," she notes.

© 2006 Maggie Smith.

School & conference materials

Materials for school visit and conferences include contracts, correspondence, maps, handouts, props, and flyers. I make a new file folder for each visit. This holds the contract, correspondence, driving directions, my schedule at the school and a list of things I need to bring. After each visit, I add my contact person's name to my mailing list and put the check stub in my taxes file. I keep preprinted copies of my handouts in files. This way it's easy to make copies for a specific visit or pull various worksheets together for a new workshop. My workshop files are labeled by age group: elementary, mid-grade, YA, or adult, and within each file I have separate folders for each worksheet. I use note cards for some of my talks, and I store these in a separate hanging file called "speeches." Keep index cards together with clip rings, rubber bands, or in little plastic cases for big stacks.

One important aspect of conferences and school visits is the **visual aids**. Overheads fit well in hanging file folders or portable accordion files. If you mount them on cardboard frames (available at most office supply stores), they won't crumple or curl. I number my frames in pencil so I can easily re-sort them for new presentations. I also write a caption for each picture in bold marker on the frame. This helps me keep my train of thought as I speak and shows me quickly which way to put the overhead on the projector. As more schools and venues acquire digital projectors, I'm converting most of my presentations to digital PowerPoint files, which will eventually save me a lot of storage space. Some school visit materials don't fit well in a drawer. I have a collection of stuffed animals, oversized writers' tools, editorial artifacts and other props that I use when I speak. I store these in large clear plastic storage containers or cardboard file boxes.

Tools

Most children's book authors and illustrators have a collection of **favorite books** in their work-space. I have a designated shelf for the books and other printed material that I use as writing tools. These reference materials include books on craft, style, and markets; non-fiction books;

Organizing Your Computer

If you would be lost without your computer, you should treat yours with the TLC and respect it deserves. The default save location for Microsoft Word is usually the "My Documents" folder. If you don't modify this, it's equivalent to stuffing each new manuscript into a drawer full of manuscripts. When you create and save documents or images, organize them as specifically as you would organize your paper files. Create separate folders for different projects, and within each project, use a system that designates the version of each that you're saving. Using a simple, consistent system such as TITLE.date or TITLE.version will make tracking changes and finding the right files much easier.

The beauty of computers is that we can save so much space and paper by saving most things digitally. The downside of working digitally rears its ugly head when computers crash, which is why writers and illustrators must back up their files religiously. Put it on your calendar—once a week, at least, more often if you're working toward a deadline. Always operate as though your computer could go kaput tomorrow morning. Utility programs, external hard drives, jump (or thumb) drives, and online storage sites make backing up so easy that there's really no excuse not to.

If the unthinkable happens—something on your computer crashes and you can't get to important files, don't panic. Most places that service computers offer data retrieval for starting at around $75, which, if it works, is a small price to pay for days and weeks of lost work. But don't count on that! Some information is irretrievable, so use data retrieval as a last-ditch fix, not back-up plan.

The last digital danger is a biggie: computer viruses and worms. If your Internet provider doesn't offer strong antivirus protection, purchase your own and keep it updated. Windows security updates are another important tool against hackers. If you're likely to forget to do either kind of updating, set your system to automatically download and install updates.

E-mail correspondence is another computer quagmire. First, print a copy of anything you absolutely must save. Second, file e-mail just as you file paperwork and computer files: create separate inboxes for school visits, editors, critique groups, etc. Create a system for reading and responding to mail so that you don't forget important messages. For example, try not to read mail unless you have time to respond; if your server allows you to, save messages requiring a response as unread so they'll pop up every time you open your mailbox. Periodically purge or print old messages so you don't go over your allotted space and to keep things manageable. Use a spam-blocker to reduce junk mail and tweak the settings so important messages don't get waylaid.

Articles & Interviews

newsletters and magazines. Stow magazines and newsletters in stand-up magazine files. If a periodical only has one or two articles you want to re-read, pull the article out and file it. Illustrators often have photo books, photos, and small models or shapes that need a place to perch while they're being used; a shelf or basket on a shelf can keep these within reach.

Work by-products

The last kind of office clutter is the actual work you do—before, during, and after completion. Work products include idea files, manuscripts, sketches, finished art, and research. Many writers and illustrators keep **idea files** of varying designs. I like index card boxes, which hold scraps of paper and folded up clippings as well as index cards with notes. Some people use a notebook, others use a hanging file folder, still others, a shoebox. Whatever format you choose, I do recommend you pick one place to stow your ideas so you can easily find them when you need a kick start!

For **works-in-progress**, most writers save every draft. I do this digitally and only print when I do a major overhaul. Keep paper copies of unfinished work in a file folder, each draft numbered or dated. Once a manuscript sells and has been accepted in final form, cull through paper drafts and only keep the ones that show big changes. File revision notes, and any sketches, etc. in each book's file.

Many writers and illustrators use a large bulletin board, magnetic board, or tack strip to organize their picture book spreads or chapters during the course of a book. If you're really short on space, Post-it® notes on the inside of kitchen cabinet doors can do the job. Illustrators who don't work digitally can use large cardstock ''portfolios'' or envelopes to store their drafts; a shelf mounted to the underside of a large worktable or desk is one way to keep these flat if you don't have a lot of room for map-sized drawers or vertical storage. For work that is mounted on heavy cardstock or mats, poster-sized moving boxes can keep art together in a dry, pest-free environment. For digital archivists, instead of keeping your CDs and DVDs in jewel cases, save space by putting them in sleeves within binders, properly organized and labeled, of course.

Storing **research materials** can be a big challenge. For nonfiction work, I use index cards to take notes. For each project, I keep a master card with all of my sources. On the top of each note card, I put the title and number of the card (1/10 for a particular book, for example.) In addition to note cards, I make photocopies of any source that would be hard to find again. Beyond the notes, I don't save hard copies for sources that are stored elsewhere digitally or which are widely available. I save all research materials in a tie-close accordion folder, which goes into remote storage after the book has been published.

WORKSPACE: THE FINAL FRONTIER

Now that you have de-cluttered the rest of your office, it's time to explore the final frontier: the prime piece of real estate known as Your Desk. In order to have room to actually work on it, remove everything that's not essential. My own desk has an in-box (with two sections, one for ''to-do'' and one for ''to-file''), a small basket with supplies (pens, pencils, and scissors, stapler, and correction tape), a task light, and my computer. Instead of arranging picture frames or personal knickknacks on your desk, make a special spot for them elsewhere in the room— somewhere you can see and touch them, but in a place that they won't get lost amid the clutter.

Phew! That's it! The first time you see the surface of your desktop, it might look a little naked, but you'll get used to it once you experience the many benefits of decluttering. After you've done all this hard work, don't forget to maintain. Taking 20 minutes every week to keep up your system can save you hours of frustration. Instead of spending time chasing down articles or receipts, you will create more time and space—physical and mental—to let your creative brain do the stuff it's best suited for: create.

William Joyce

Picture Books from the Shelves
to the Big Screen

Photo: Philip Gould.

by Ramona Wood

I t's a safe bet that his houseful of eccentric relatives sowed the seeds of William Joyce's zany imagination. An uncle would casually drop by after a trip to Mars. His grandfather had a glass eye he swore could see when it wasn't in place, and a missing thumb to boot. The family relished opera singing at the dinner table—on the days they ate at the table. Bongo players, artists and actors proliferated among his relatives. Often one or more of them will slip into one of Joyce's creations.

It's no wonder Joyce is a top creator in children's media today. His characters from George Shrinks and Rolie Polie Olie are seen in Joyce's picture books as well as in highly acclaimed children's TV programs. For the 1995 movie *Toy Story*, Joyce designed the look of characters Woody, Buzz Lightyear and comrades. Since then he continues to expand his own books into large productions with the major animation studios.

But Joyce is not an uptown media tycoon living near one of the large animation studios. In fact, he hasn't strayed far from his childhood home near Shreveport, Louisiana. The library he visited as a child was an actual log cabin way back in the woods, and the children's librarian passed on her appreciation for books to the young Joyce. He loved books by Maurice Sendak, Bill Peet and Beatrix Potter, among others. The family TV set caught his attention as well— offering a steady stream of incredible shrinking men, courageous dogs, and people from other planets.

Joyce began "drawing stories" in grade school, starting with one about a kid who was really bad at math. Although his preference of stories over homework assignments got him in trouble, it set the groundwork for his career.

After high school, Joyce went to art school where his style didn't fit the curriculum. He left to study filmmaking, and today animation fuels his storytelling.

Joyce never lost that *what-if* and *why-not* curiosity from his childhood. He builds an idea for a Rolie Polie Olie story with questions like: *What if the planet's made of ice cream?* Characters can go sledding on the mounds of ice cream. They can just reach down and eat a handful of it. *Why not?*

A large part of Joyce's success stems from his art. His award-winning illustrations have a retro feel to them—even in futuristic settings. His techniques are unconventional as well. In

RAMONA WOOD is a writer and illustrator who is drawn to stories about extraordinary people. Her first book, *The Goat Woman of Smackover* (Abc Press, 2001), won an award from the National Museum of Women in the Arts. Her latest book *Now Caitlin Can: A donated organ helps a child get well* (Abc Press, 2004) is a picture book about an actual child organ recipient. She has also written and illustrated for *Pocket's* and various curricular publications.

Articles & Interviews

Bentley and Egg, Joyce used acrylic paints in a watercolor style. *Dinosaur Bob* was created with oil paints on watercolor paper (coated with Gesso). In the original book, *George Shrinks*, Joyce used watercolors—without much water—but dabbled on the computer for the animated version.

Joyce's innovative attitude was a sure-fire catalyst to his writing and illustration success. Add an unorthodox upbringing, a driving passion and the know-how to put it all together and you've got a recipe for success in the field of children's books.

Tell me about your start writing and illustrating children's books.

I guess there were two venues that were my spark. I wanted to tell stories, but I always liked to draw, so as a little kid I would sit and draw stories.

Writing or illustrating—which comes more naturally?

Since they've always gone hand in hand for me I hardly make a differentiation, especially with pictures books. When it's a longer thing—like a screenplay—the writing is really hard.

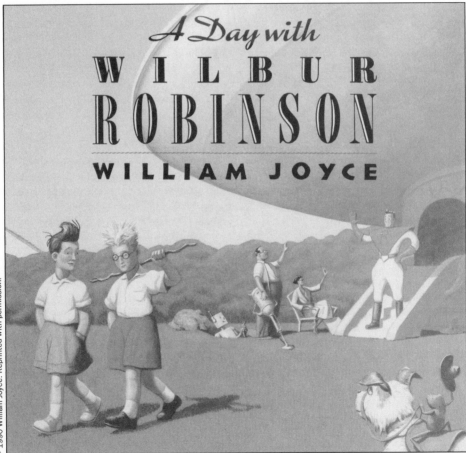

© 1990 William Joyce. Reprinted with permission.

An exaggerated version of William Joyce's childhood, as raised by a "congenial horde of Southern screwballs," when *A Day with Wilbur Robinson* came out in 1990, it made the year-end best lists of *Publishers Weekly, Newsweek,* the *L.A. Times,* and the American Library Association among other accolades. An animated Disney movie version is planned for a 2006 release.

Do you use an outline in your writing?

Yeah, but not always. I outline on longer things like screenplays where there's too much to juggle without one. On picture books I mainly need to know what the ending is. The hardest part is, I'll get an idea like, "I really want to write a book about a dinosaur." And then I'm like . . . *so what*. I've got to figure out the ending first. From there I'll know at least some of what I need to do to get there.

What are the challenges in writing screenplays for your TV shows?

For the *Rolie Polie Olie* series, each segment is seven minutes long and there are three segments in a show. Writing each seven-minute segment felt like writing a picture book because each needed a beginning, a middle, and an end and I really had to get to the point in a hurry. It's just as much work to come up with a seven-minute segment as for a 30-minute show like *George Shrinks* because there's not enough room to goof around. But the best of children's books feel like there's not one ounce of wasted fat in them. Like the picture book *Harold and the Purple Crayon* just seems perfect [in its simplicity.] Crockett Johnson reportedly worked long and hard and agonized over them. It wasn't easy at all.

How did the *Rolie Polie Olie* television series come about?

The people from the animation studio came to me and said, "We want to do an animated TV show with you." At first I said, "I'm not interested. And I hate TV cartoons." Then they said I'd have complete control and oversee production if a company wanted to do it.

Then I'm like, "Well, okay."

I had worked on *Toy Story* so I knew something about it and was really excited about what computer animation could do. The computer has problems with some things like hair, fabric and skin—which are time-consuming and expensive to do, but it's good at basic shapes and hard surfaces.

I had started a picture book about robots a few years before and had gotten tired of drawing all the circles by hand. But that is actually perfect for computers, so I designed the program. They said, "This is the most insane thing we've ever seen." They tested it before an audience and came back with the highest numbers on one of these things. They said to go ahead with it. It's a rare thing when they say, "We feel good about this guy, give him a few million dollars" . . . and hope for the best.

As an illustrator, have you worked quite a bit at drawing figures accurately and keeping your characters consistent?

I still struggle with all that stuff. I'm drawing a dinosaur right now and it ain't easy. I mean, I love it, but it ain't easy.

Drawing for animation: Is computer or hand-drawn art more prevalent?

When we started on the movie *Robots* in 2001, most of the animation guys drew with pencil on paper. By the time we finished the movie, [three years later] there were only two of us [out of about 50 artists] who still drew on a piece of paper. Everyone was painting on computer.

How do you feel about using the computer for your art?

You just think of the computer as just another set of paints. The computer is faster and it's easier to fix a mistake on one, but the thing is, when you're done, there's nothing there. Although you can make a printout on archival paper, you can print a limited number and it will look for all the world like it was painted. But to me it's still not a genuinely tactile thing. And I miss that.

Articles & Interviews

Articles & Interviews

© 2002 William Joyce. Reprinted with permission.

Part of William Joyce's Rolie Polie Olie series, *Big Time Olie* takes the lead character on big and small adventures courtesy of a shrink-and-grow-a-lator. "The brightly colored characters, fashioned out of round balls, metal springs, and simple shapes, and the slightly futuristic, but somehow old-fashioned cartoon quality of the illustrations meet for a wonderfully playful effect," says *School Library Journal*. "The spare, rhythmic text perfectly captures the conflicting desires of preschoolers to grow up and venture out, yet to be safe and close to home and family."

Tell me about the animators you work with.

I work with the animators from studios like Nelvana. I don't usually do the hiring but I've been lucky to work with people I connect with and really get along with—collaborating. I really didn't think I'd ever be an adept people person. But you've got to be, to get a project done.

What kind of skills and training does an animator need?

It would behoove an aspiring animator to go to art school or learn filmmaking and screenwriting. But it's not essential. Some of the best people come from unlikely places. If you can tell a story, if you can draw, then you can sit down at the computer and do this stuff. Animators are a particular breed of people. They're technical virtuosos, but they also have skill as actors to be able to move a character around.

With so many projects going on, how do you stay sane?

That's why there are doors on offices! [*laughs*] You have to learn to be the master of your day and get people to understand. There are parts of a job—writing especially—when I have

Articles & Interviews

to go off where I can't hear anybody else. But at other times I actually enjoy being around people. When I'm painting it's much easier in a roomful of people. I don't know—I guess the energy makes me focus.

It's a strange thing. When I'm illustrating for a book I will agonize and try to get everything just right. But when I sketch something for a movie I know it's not the final product so I can just sit down and get it done. I don't fret about it at all and it'll be as good as anything I've done for a book because I'm less precious about it. I wish I had that mindset all the time.

Do you ever have creative block?

I wish I did. I'd love to sit and not think about this stuff. It never stops . . . But I'd probably get cranky if it did.

What do you do when you're in the middle of a book and it's not working?

That happens a lot. You break through or you don't. I have all sorts of half-baked projects lying around. You get all excited about it and halfway through you think, this isn't going anywhere. You think, "this isn't as cool as you thought it was." If the fire's really in my belly I'll figure it out. But if it dissipates after a period of time . . . it's time to move on.

© 1985 William Joyce. Reprinted with permission.

In what *Publishers Weekly* called "a fast and funny" debut, after 20-plus years, William Joyce's *George Shrinks* has not only become a classic in the world of picture books, it's also a PSB Kids series. "George is three inches tall. He lives with a normal-sized family. But no one ever makes reference to his size difference," Joyce told CNN.com. "George is so ingenious and clever and optimistic [as] he faces his monumental struggle to have a regular everyday American childhood that he never complains, and manages with casual aplomb to reign victorious."

William Joyce Timeline

Books

The following are picture books unless otherwise noted.

1985   *George Shrinks*, first edition (later became a PBS animated children's television series)

1988   *Dinosaur Bob and His Adventures with the Family Lazardo*

1990   *A Day with Wilbur Robinson* (movie version, 2006)

1992   *Bentley and Egg* (ALA Notable Book Award)

1993   *Santa Calls* (ALA Book of the Month)

1996   *The Leaf Men and the Brave Good Bugs*

1997   *Buddy* (movie version co-written and produced by Joyce)
        The World of William Joyce Scrapbook

1999   *Dinosaur Bob*; *Life with Bob*; Baseball Bob board books; *Rolie Polie Olie* (picture book and Emmy award-winning Disney channel animated preschool show); *Sleepy Time Olie*; *Big Time Olie*; *George Shrinks*, second edition; *How Many Howdy's*

2000   Rolie Polie Olie board books

Movies

1995   *Toy Story* (designed and created inspirational character paintings)

1998   *A Bug's Life* (created conceptual character paintings)

2005   *Robots* (executive producer)

Illustration facts

- Created periodic *New Yorker* cover illustrations from 1994 through 2000.

- First published work: *Tammy and the Gigantic Fish*, 1983.

- Illustrated the following between 1984 and 1990: *My First Book of Nursery Tales*, *Mother Goose*, *Waiting for Spring Stories*, *Shoes*, *Humphrey's Bear*, *Nicholas Cricket*, and *Some of the Adventures of Rhode Island Red*.

What needs do you see in the field of children's book publishing?

Publishers need to support the titles they have instead of pushing for more. It's like fashion, what's in this season is out next season. They're wearing out their talent by saying ''You need another book on the list, you need another book on the list.'' Why don't they support the one I did last year that got a lot of awards and a lot of press? For a while I got one Rolie Polie book out a year, but then I'm like I'm not going to worry about having a book on every list. That'll drive you crazy. The problem is when you crank 'em out sometimes they're not good enough and never feel right. When people are pressured to get something out, it doesn't get to be everything it could've been.

What is television production like?

In TV you know there's another show next week so if this one isn't perfect, you'll try to get it the next week. But you know that going in, you know you cannot get them all perfect, but if you've got a good team of people, you do the best you can with the schedule you have. By the way, the schedule actually works to your benefit.

Articles & Interviews

To me it's good to have a deadline. It makes you think on your feet and go with your instincts. You don't second-guess yourself too much. You have just so much money to spend on each episode—it's a challenge that's sort of fun.

Tell me about your involvement in making movies.

I've always liked movies—it's my second love, so getting to make this stuff come alive and dance around is really cool and rewarding.

But what bugs me about the movies is that they throw so much money at it, but the schedule is the most important thing. When they've decided this movie's coming out then it's almost impossible to change that date. They don't want to change it. And when that date changes—it's *catastrophic*. It's in the paper. There's a certain part of them that wants to make as good a movie as they can, but if it's too tough and they're not going to make a schedule, then well . . . it will be what it will be.

You seem to handle the stress amazingly well.

You're not there in the middle of it. [*laughs*] Sometimes you have to go with what Alfred Hitchcock used to tell his actors: "It's *only* a movie." Everyone works so hard on those movies and they work so long. You want it to be as great as it can be, but sometimes there's just not time. You just have to cope, do it anyway, hope for the best and sometimes it magically falls together.

You've received more than 50 awards for your books, television shows and movies. Which do you take the most pride in?

I really liked getting a couple ALA (American Library Association) awards. I liked winning my gold medals at the Society of Illustrators, but the books mean more to me. Maybe it's because the book awards came first. And I never had a book come out that I didn't feel was exactly the way I wanted it to be. When I get that book out I feel like I've done everything I could, within reason and it's what I wanted it to be.

First Books

New Novelists

by Alice Pope

As I was gearing up to work on this piece, I posted to a well-populated children's writing listserv asking for first-time authors and illustrators to interview—and got upwards of 70 e-mails in 24 hours. I heard from picture book writers and illustrators, mid-grade and YA novelists, nonfiction writers, poets, even an editor and a publicist or two. I read enthusiastic book descriptions. I visited Web sites. I read reviews and excerpts. And I printed out a huge stack of e-mails. It was fun!

Trouble was, I had to choose only four.

I decided to come up with a theme to help narrow down my list. I tossed around a few ideas (books with colors in their titles, books with Jewish main characters, books written in verse), but I kept coming back to a few of the debut novels. The four that interested me most did have some similarities. They all had titles that drew me in, whether cute, provocative, or mysterious. They all had appealing covers. They were all told in first person points of view, narrated by girls. They were all contemporary novels. They all had storylines that piqued my interest or hit home with me. Each of the main characters was a creative type (dancer, writer, poet, artist). And, ultimately, I wanted to spend time with these characters. I wanted Kayla, Sarah, Felicia, and Catherine to tell me their stories. And I'm positive the editors who signed these books felt the same way.

So what's my theme? *New Novelists* worked for my subhead. (*New Novelists Who Wrote in First Person POV with Tween or Teen Girl Main Characters and Good Titles and Cover Art* was a tad wordy.) After some thought, my theme became clear: *Novels I Had to Read*. I would have picked up each and every one of these titles if I'd been browsing in a bookstore. Now let's hear about how these four first books got from the writers' imaginations to the store shelves.

Cynthia Lord
Rules (Scholastic Press)
www.cynthialord.com

Wake up each day by 4 a.m. to write could be first on Cynthia Lord's list of Rules for Her Writing Life. Lord began her wee-hours writing habit about five years ago when she came across her college writing texts. "I had stopped writing when my children were small, and seeing those books suddenly filled me with loss," she says.

"I knew there would never be an easy time to fit writing into my life, so I decided I either had to walk away from those

Rubber duck photo © Gary Doak/Photonica. Goldfish detail © G.K. & Vikki Hart/Photonica.
Jacket design by Kristina Albertson.

Articles & Interviews

As the idea for her story brewed in Cynthia Lord's mind, she wrote a line: "At our house, we have a rule," From there, she says, the first draft of *Rules* took shape. In Lord's book, Catherine, who has an autistic younger brother, longs for a "normal" household. She writes rules to help her brother navigate the world. As the story unfolds, Catherine gains insights about herself and her brother, and learns lessons about friendship, all with a little help from a boy who can't speak and the wisdom of *Frog & Toad*.

books and not look back with regret or I had to find a way to include writing in my already full day." Waking up early was a good decision for Lord. Her first book, the mid-grade novel *Rules*, was released by Scholastic in 2006.

Rules' main character is Catherine, a 12-year-old with an autistic younger brother, David. Catherine longs for a normal family life, one that does not revolve around David's disability. In an attempt to get closer to that normalcy, she keeps a running list of rules for her brother to help him navigate the world. (*No toys in the fish tank. Not everything worth keeping has to be useful. Late doesn't mean not coming.*) Along the way, readers see how these rules apply to Catherine's life too, as they are seamlessly woven into the text.

Lord's character David is loosely based on her own son who is autistic. "The family in *Rules* is not my own family," says Lord, "though I did borrow some of my son's younger behaviors and used a few rules we've had at our house." But the heart of Lord's book is not Catherine's home life and her relationship with David—it's Catherine's relationship with Jason, a boy she befriends as she accompanies her brother on his weekly trips to occupational therapy.

Jason is in a wheelchair and cannot speak—he has conversations using a "communication book," a binder he flips through pointing to the appropriate word cards. Catherine, a budding

Articles & Interviews

artist, adds words to Jason's book each week, words inspired by the challenges of her own life with an autistic younger brother, parents who don't always pay enough attention to her, a best friend away for the summer, and a new girl next door she's hoping to befriend.

"When Catherine says about David, 'Our quarrels fray instead of knot,' that's the whole challenge with David as an opposing character," says Lord. "He couldn't purposefully and steadily escalate tension for me due to his autism. For Catherine to grow, Jason was truly the person she needed most."

For Lord's manuscript to grow from first draft to publishable, she had the insights and support of a critique group and retreat-mates. "Some of my writing friends bought me cake and flowers when I sold *Rules*. Some told me with kind firmness when I wasn't telling the whole truth of the story yet," she says. "And when I wanted to quit, they all listened with genuine empathy and then told me to get back to work."

Lord met agent Tracey Adams, who would eventually take her on as a client, at a New England SCBWI conference, "where she gave me a lot of encouragement and a wonderful critique on the first 10 pages of *Rules*." When she felt ready to seek publication, Lord sent queries and sample copies to four publishers and got three requests for the entire manuscript, and one form rejection. "It took about eight months from sending my full manuscript to receiving an offer from Scholastic."

When it looked like an offer was looming, Lord asked Adams if she'd consider representing her and she sent off her manuscript. "I came home one afternoon to find the message on my answering machine that every new writer dreams of hearing: 'Everyone here loves your book.' "

More good news came via telephone when Lord got her acceptance call from Scholastic. "At one point during that phone call, I wondered how life around me could simply be continuing in its usual way—the kitchen clock ticking, cars going by on the road outside—when between my hand on the phone receiver and my ear, a dream was coming true."

Through the revision process Lord learned a lot about herself as a writer and about the writer-editor exchange. "The most wonderful surprise was seeing what an insightful and talented editor brings to a book," she says. "Leslie Budnick, my editor as Scholastic, guided *Rules* in a way that pushed me past where I'd ever been as a writer. She moved my own concept of 'my best' to a new level, and she did it in a way that always asked everything of me, but never overwhelmed me."

Lord also learned a new rule: *When your work is done, let the book go. It's no longer yours.* "A book going out into the world is not about the author; it's about the reader's connection to the story," she explains. "When people write to me about *Rules*, it's most often about their own relationships with my characters or the emotions the story brought forth from that individual reader. It's an amazing, amazing moment as a writer to watch characters step beyond me."

Maryrose Wood
Sex Kittens and Horn Dawgs Fall in Love (Delacorte Press)
www.maryrosewood.com

With years of experience writing for theatre, Maryrose Wood had not envisioned herself as a YA novelist. But, she says, "I had been including teen characters in play after play—I even wrote a whole musical called *The Tutor* about a 16-year-old goth girl who falls in love with her SAT tutor." It was a writer friend, YA and picture book author E. Lockhart, who encouraged Wood to write a book if she wanted to make a living writing about teens.

Maryrose Wood's first novel, *Sex Kittens and Horn Dawgs Fall in Love*, is set in the Manhattan Free Children's School (aka the Pound), where the students "pass the time by digging deeply into our passions,"—which include violin, sitar, karate and genius rabbits. Fourteen-year-old poet Felicia sets out to win the heart of her unrequited crush Matthew by working with him on a science fair project: The Search for X (the thing that makes the one you love, love you back.)

Jacket illustration © 2006 Linda Ketelhut.

"It was a 'eureka' moment for me as a writer," says Wood. "I honestly had never noticed how many stories about young people I'd written, but there it was: the 10-minute musical drama about a school shooting; the futuristic play about two girls who rebel against the strict population control measures of their society by trying to get pregnant; the comedy about the teen who decides to lose her virginity while her mother is in the hospital having plastic surgery. I'd been writing YA plots for years; I just needed a little sideways nudge into a much more receptive marketplace for them."

So on her friend's advice, Wood called Lockhart's agent, Elizabeth Kaplan, and pitched the idea for what would eventually become her first book *Sex Kittens and Horn Dawgs Fall in Love*. "Elizabeth listened to me babble a fairly garbled description of *Kittens* over the phone—at the time I had not written one word of it." Kaplan asked for a written treatment of the book, and in a couple of weeks Wood sent one off. Kaplan "asked good questions, and I revised it based on her notes," says Wood.

Articles & Interviews

Kaplan sent the revised treatment to editor Marissa Walsh at Delacorte, Wood revised some more, and Delacorte made an offer shortly thereafter. "I think the whole process, from gleam in my eye to two-book contract, took about two months. I later found out that this is ridiculously fast."

The idea for *Sex Kittens* was sparked by Wood's own experiences re-entering the dating world after being married for many years. "They say dating makes you feel like a teenager all over again, and it's certainly true. It was all so hilarious and heart-breaking," she says. "Why were some first dates death-by-tedium, and others love-at-first-sight? Why would I be drooling for someone and he'd say, 'Well, obviously there's no chemistry, but let's definitely be friends?' "

So Wood's leap from her own curiosity about how love really works to her 14-year-old character, Felicia, asking the same question "was quite organic." In *Sex Kittens*, Felicia hatches a plan to get closer to Matthew, the boy she has a crush on, by working with him on a science fair project, The Search for X, "X" being that elusive ingredient that actually makes the one you love, love you back. Felicia hopes she'll win Matthew's heart and maybe win the science fair, too.

Wood said she didn't have much trouble capturing her character's teen voice. "Felicia's voice is probably the closest thing to my own inner mental monologue I've ever written. All that hyper-articulate riffing and noticing odd little details and compulsively turning ideas into poems, not to mention the propensity for crazy unrequited crushes—no, it wasn't tough to capture at all!"

What was a little more challenging to the first-time novelist was adjusting to a new way of working as she wrote *Sex Kittens*. "My background had been working in theatre, where everybody is in one room jumping up and down saying, 'I have an idea!' and acting things out and talking in funny accents, so I found it a bit sad and lonely to send my poor, vulnerable first draft off to this strange corporate silence, waiting weeks with no word at all and then getting formal written notes," she says. " I was revved up to brainstorm and improvise and instead I was left alone with a piece of paper, trying to transform my response to it into the same sense of back-and-forth collaborative energy that I was used to."

After a few phone conversations, Wood and her editor came to understand each other's process. "I learned that I have the freedom to take those notes and dig into them and find my own creative solutions to the issues they raised, even if it meant jumping around the room talking in funny accents all by myself," she says. "Believe it when the how-to books tell you that you have to write, revise, accept criticism, revise again, and keep writing! There's no shortcut."

In edition to input from her agent and her editor, Wood also recruited a group of early readers, two of them in the age range of her audience. "From the younger-teen girls, I got solid reassurance that the level of the writing (which, like the book's narrator, is rather precocious) and the story (which is comic and romantic, but 'squeaky clean,' as one reviewer said) were truly enjoyable for their age group."

And for Wood, the story is paramount. "If you can sharpen one skill, make it your storytelling," she says. "All the lovely language in the world will not save you if you can't tell a story."

Dorian Cirrone
Dancing in Red Shoes Will Kill You
(HarperCollins)
www.doriancirrone.com

The idea for Dorian Cirrone's debut novel came from a situation she remembered from her years studying and teaching dance. "One of my colleagues at the studio was a beautiful ballerina who was told early on that she would never be a professional ballet dancer because her breasts were too large," says Cirrone. "She went to Las Vegas and became a

Articles & Interviews

Kayla, a budding bal-
lerina, has been danc-
ing since she learned
to walk, and is set on
a career in the ballet.
There is one thing
(um, make that two
things) standing in
her way—her breasts
are too large by ballet
standards, and she's
passed over for a solo
part in her high
school's production
of *Cinderalla*. Dorian
Cirrone's debut *Danc-
ing in Red Shoes Will
Kill You* grapples with
gender issues and the
feminine ideal (with a
healthy dose of boob
jokes) as Kayla grap-
ples with the decision
of whether or not to
have the breast re-
duction surgery her
dance instructor
recommends.

Jacket art © 2005 Kate Turning. Jacket design by Sasha Illingworth.

showgirl for a while, but her true love was ballet. She eventually had [breast reduction] surgery and got a position in a company, though she was already somewhat old for a ballerina by then. I always thought it was an interesting story, but I wanted my readers to ponder the issue of breast reduction surgery a little more."

So Cirrone created the character of Kayla, a talented high-school-age dancer who's passed over for the lead in her school's production of *Cinderella* (and relegated to the role of an ugly step-sister) because of her non-ballerina proportions. Her dance teacher suggests Kayla consider a breast reduction, polarizing her classmates into two camps, Whack the Rack vs. Save the Hooters.

Cirrone rounded out the plot for *Dancing in Red Shoes Will Kill You* with a mystery surrounding pairs of red pointe shoes which begin appearing throughout the school and a censorship subplot featuring Kayla's feminist sister Paterson who's not allowed to use her painting of a male nude as her senior art project.

Paterson's story, like Kayla's, was inspired by real life incident Cirrone had read about. "In that incident a girl was prevented from displaying her sculpture, which depicted a man

Articles & Interviews

with overly large genitalia, even though female nudes were allowed in the school exhibit. She protested, but the school refused to display the sculpture," says Cirrone.

A member of a critique group for more than a decade, Cirrone had a lot of encouragement as she forged ahead with her manuscript. "I had been in a writing group run by my mentor, young adult author Joyce Sweeney, since the mid-'90s," she says. "During that time I wrote two novels, dozens of picture book manuscripts, and hundreds of poems and short stories for children and adults, but had only published a few poems and essays for adults in journals and anthologies."

Cirrone took a brief hiatus from the group to work on a dissertation, but she eventually abandoned that work in favor of writing fiction. "When I returned, author Alex Flinn was in the group and was just about to publish her novel *Breathing Underwater*. I was working on *Dancing In Red Shoes Will Kill You* by then and Alex asked me if I wanted to join an online group of writers."

Through a tip from her online group, Cirrone learned that Steven Chudney, who would become Cirrone's agent, was looking for new clients. "I sent him a picture book, a chapter book, and five chapters of the novel. He sent me an e-mail the next day telling me how much he loved the novel. His enthusiasm made me work much faster and I wrote the next 10 chapters in a few months," she says. "About six weeks after he sent the novel to HarperCollins, Steven called me to talk about another project. In between the conversation, he said, 'Oh, by the way, we got an offer.' It was a funny and wonderful surprise and the best non sequitur I'd ever heard."

Once her contract was signed, Cirrone found the editorial process pleasing. "My editor Tara Weikum knew exactly what parts of the manuscript to cut and what parts to strengthen. Her comments were very clear and I was able to accomplish our mutual goals for the manuscript easily," she says. "The only surprise was that her notes were so easy to follow and made so much sense to me. I was coming from an academic background where there's a lot of jargon and I was afraid I wouldn't understand what she was talking about."

In addition to her writing groups, her agent, and her editor, Cirrone got a little help with her novel from a doctor. "I have a great friend who is a plastic surgeon and he allowed me to come to his office and pretend I was the character in my book," says Cirrone. "I filled out papers, sat in the waiting room, and consulted with him. It was just like a regular appointment—but without the physical exam. I asked him questions about breast reduction surgery as if I were a 16-year-old dancer. I have to say he never once broke character even though it had to be a stretch to pretend that I was a teenager with a perfect ballet body except for huge breasts."

In the end of *Dancing in Red Shoes*, Kayla opts (at least for the moment) not to have surgery. "I always wanted to leave the ending open because I felt it would be an opportunity for the reader to decide," says Cirrone. "I think some readers felt I was saying she should never have the surgery because of what Paterson and Gray [her boyfriend] told her. But the real reason for leaving it open was so Kayla would realize it had to be her decision, not her choreographer's, her teacher's, her friends' or her relatives' decision."

With her first book under her belt (or tutu), Cirrone awaits the publication of her next books, two mid-grades featuring Lindy Blues, "a spunky, self-confident, fourth-grade investigative reporter who solves mysteries in her neighborhood, while her little brother follows her with a camcorder," say Cirrone. "She does a weekly newscast on LBN (the Lindy Blues Network)." *Lindy Blues: The Missing Silver Dollar* is a spring 2006 release, with *Lindy Blues: The Big Scoop* following in fall 2006. "I also have another young adult novel called *Prom Kings and Drama Queens* coming out in 2008."

Getting her first book published, says Cirrone, offered her validation that "I did know what I was doing after all these years." She advises aspiring writers to read and study books like those they want to write—lots of them. "Join a writing community, either in person or online. Try to find a mentor. Don't expect to sell the first things you write—that's your practice work. Write constantly," she says. "Don't give up."

Susan Amessé
Kissing Brendan Callahan (Roaring Brook)

"October 16, 2003 at 3:11 p.m. At that moment, I found out that the glass slipper really did fit." That's the precise time Susan Amessé learned her first book, *Kissing Brendan Callahan* would be published by Roaring Brook Press with editor Deborah Brodie.

Amessé had hoped to someday work with Brodie since taking a class with the editor at the New School in Manhattan. "Deborah covered all the elements of writing a novel. She inspired me to persevere and to dig much deeper," says Amessé. "I spent years struggling with my characters and the plot, but I always returned to my notes from Deborah's class."

As Amessé worked through her manuscript for *Kissing Brendan Callahan*, she got to know her characters that same way she'd become acquainted with new friends. "The more you get to know them, the more well-rounded and interesting they become," she says. "I was surprised by some of the things I found out about my characters. Whenever I got stuck, I would quietly wait until my characters revealed things to me."

Sarah, the main character in Amessé's debut novel, "popped up during a writing exercise. I saw a young girl who was in love with the idea of writing and becoming famous," says Amessé. In the book, Sarah longs to be a "best-selling author of high-quality romances" just like her favorite writer Antonia DeMarco. But Sarah's mother quashes the budding writer's plans by not letting her enter a writing contest judged by Antonia. "I was engrossed in the struggle between this dreamer and her overly realistic mother. I'm a dreamer. I was rooting for Sarah, but I didn't know what was going to happen to her, so I had to continue writing to find out."

Amessé admits that there is a lot of herself in her main character. "A dear friend on mine, whom I have known since first grade, read the book and was thrilled to be meeting me for the second time. I was a dramatic child. I even had visions of being a movie star." Amessé even spent some time working in theatre, and drew upon those days as she created diva romance author Antonia DeMarco, who is a big mess beneath her dramatic, confident façade. "I encountered a lot of highly insecure people who came across as happy, confident, independent and successful," says Amessé. "But if you caught them off-guard, they would suddenly slip into sadness, insecurity, needfulness or depression. These people and their illusions fascinated me."

Fortunately, Amessé's crowd these days is full of friends and fellow writers who support her career and helped her as she worked on her book. "It's important to share your manuscript with people you trust," she says. "How else can you learn to communicate? And writing is all about communicating. Learning to accept critique can be tricky. For me, it took a lot of practice to listen without defending every word. Someone pointed out to me that when you send your manuscript to an editor or an agent, you won't be able to pop out of the manuscript and explain anything."

In addition to learning to accept constructive criticism, as she revised *Kissing Brendan Callahan* Amessé also learned that she loves to rewrite. "I cut my original draft from nearly 300 pages to about 150, and it retained its essence. I didn't feel like I was losing an arm," she says. "I have a tendency to be redundant. But now the sweetest surprise occurs each time a reader compliments me on writing a tight, fast-paced book!"

And for Amessé, the best part of getting her first book published "was that people were

Articles & Interviews

Articles & Interviews

actually going to read it. The scariest part was that people were going to read it. You can get overwhelmed trying to guess what people are thinking of your writing. Will they hate it? Will they see me differently?'' say says. ''But it's great fun to get unsolicited comments from readers about their impressions and which character they liked best.''

With *Kissing Brendan Callahan* under her belt, Amessé is working on a new novel. ''I'm having fun discovering who my characters are,'' she says. She advises other writers of mid-grade novels to read as many as they can to see different styles and techniques employed by authors. Writers groups are also helpful, she says, because you not only get a critique, but a deadline. ''Most importantly, don't give up on a character you really love, even if you are having problems with him or her. Do something to see them from a different angle. You might even try standing on your head.''

Susan Amessé's debut, *Kissing Brendan Callahan*, features budding novelist Sarah, who aspires to be ''a best-selling author of high-quality romances,'' just like her favorite writer Antionia De-Marco. All she has to do to get noticed is win a writing contest judged by her idol—one that her mother won't let her enter. When her scheming to get noticed by Antionia causes unexpected consequences, Sarah learns that things—and people—aren't always as they seem.

Jacket photo: Geoff Graham, © 2005 Echos-nonstock.com. Jacket design by BTDNYC.

Book Publishers

There's no magic formula for getting published. It's a matter of getting the right manuscript on the right editor's desk at the right time. Before you submit it's important to learn publishers' needs, see what kind of books they're producing and decide which publishers your work is best suited for. *Children's Writer's & Illustrator's Market* is but one tool in this process. (Those just starting out, turn to Quick Tips for Writers & Illustrators on page 5.)

To help you narrow down the list of possible publishers for your work, we've included several indexes at the back of this book. The **Subject Index** lists book and magazine publishers according to their fiction and nonfiction needs or interests. The **Age-Level Index** indicates which age groups publishers cater to. The **Photography Index** indicates which markets buy photography for children's publications. The **Poetry Index** lists publishers accepting poetry.

If you write contemporary fiction for young adults, for example, and you're trying to place a book manuscript, go first to the Subject Index. Locate the fiction categories under Book Publishers and copy the list under Contemporary. Then go to the Age-Level Index and highlight the publishers on the Contemporary list that are included under the Young Adults heading. Read the listings for the highlighted publishers to see if your work matches their needs.

Remember, *Children's Writer's & Illustrator's Market* should not be your only source for researching publishers. Here are a few other sources of information:

- The Society of Children's Book Writers and Illustrators (SCBWI) offers members an annual market survey of children's book publishers for the cost of postage or free online at www.scbwi.org. (SCBWI membership information can also be found at www.scbwi.org.)
- The Children's Book Council Web site (www.cbcbooks.org) gives information on member publishers.
- If a publisher interests you, send a SASE for submission guidelines (or check publishers' Web sites for guidelines) *before* submitting. To quickly find guidelines online, visit The Colossal Directory of Children's Publishers at www.signaleader.com/childrens-writers/.
- Check publishers' Web sites. Many include their complete catalogs that you can browse. Web addresses are included in many publishers' listings.
- Spend time at your local bookstore to see who's publishing what. While you're there, browse through *Publishers Weekly* and *The Horn Book*.

SUBSIDY & SELF-PUBLISHING

Some determined writers who receive rejections from royalty publishers may look to subsidy and co-op publishers as an option for getting their work into print. These publishers ask writers to pay all or part of the costs of producing a book. We strongly advise writers and illustrators to work only with publishers who pay them. For this reason, we've adopted a policy not to include any subsidy or co-op publishers in *Children's Writer's & Illustrator's Market* (or any other Writer's Digest Books market books).

If you're interested in publishing your book just to share it with friends and relatives, self-publishing is a viable option, but it involves time, energy, and money. You oversee all book production details. Check with a local printer for advice and information on cost or check online for print-on-demand publishing options (which are often more affordable).

Whatever path you choose, keep in mind that the market is flooded with submissions, so it's important for you to hone your craft and submit the best work possible. Competition from thousands of other writers and illustrators makes it more important than ever to research publishers before submitting—read their guidelines, look at their catalogs, check out a few of their titles and visit their Web sites.

ADVICE FROM INSIDERS

For insight and advice on getting published from a variety of perspectives, be sure to read the Insider Reports in this section. Subjects include authors and illustrators **Elizabeth Bluemle** (page 116), **Christopher Paolini** (page 130), **Tanya Lee Stone** (page 144), and **Audrey Couloumbis** (page 158), and illustrator and author **Nathan Hale** (page 180).

Information on book publishers listed in the previous edition but not included in this edition of *Children's Writer's & Illustrator's Market* may be found in the General Index.

ABINGDON PRESS

The United Methodist Publishing House, 201 Eighth Ave. S., Nashville TN 37203. (615)749-6384. Fax: (615)749-6512. E-mail: jstjohn@umpublishing.org. Web site: www.abingdonpress.com/ Estab. 1789. **Acquisitions:** Judy Newman-St. John, children's book editor. "Abingdon Press, America's oldest theological publisher, provides an ecumenical publishing program dedicated to serving the Christian community."
Nonfiction All levels: religion.
How to Contact/Writers Query or submit outline/synopsis and 1 sample chapter. Prefers submissions by e-mail. Responds to queries in 3 months; mss in 6 months.
Illustration Uses color artwork only. Reviews ms/illustration packages from artists. Query with photocopies only. Samples returned with SASE; samples not filed.
Photography Buys stock images. Wants scenic, landscape, still life and multiracial photos. Model/property release required. Uses color prints. Submit stock photo list.
Terms Pays authors royalty of 5-10% based on retail price. Work purchased outright from authors ($100-1,000).

☝ HARRY N. ABRAMS BOOKS FOR YOUNG READERS

115 W. 18th St., New York NY 10011. (212)519-1200. **Director, Children's Books:** Howard W. Reeves.
• Abrams Books for Young Readers no longer accepts unsolicited works of fiction. Nonfiction manuscripts may be sent via mail. Abrams title *Maritcha: A Nineteenth-Century American Girl*, by Tonya Bolden, won a 2006 Coretta Scott King Author Honor Award.
Nonfiction Picture books, young readers, middle readers, young adult.
How to Contact/Writers Nonfiction: Submit complete ms or proposal with SASE. Responds in 6 months only with SASE. Will consider multiple submissions.
Illustration Illustrations only: Do not submit original material; copies only. Contact: Tad Beckerman.

☐ ABSEY & CO.

23011 Northcrest Dr., Spring TX 77389. (281)257-2340. Fax: (281)251-4676. E-mail: abseyandco@aol.com. Web site: www.absey.com. New York address: 45 W. 21st Street, Suite 5, New York NY 10010. (212)277-8028. (Send mss to Spring TX address only.) **Publisher:** Edward Wilson. "We are looking primarily for education books, especially those with teaching strategies based upon research." Publishes hardcover, trade paperback and mass market paperback originals. Publishes 5-10 titles/year. 50% of books from first-time authors; 50% from unagented writers.
Fiction "Since we are a small, new press, we are looking for good manuscripts with a firm intended audience."

Recently published *Saving the Scrolls*, by Mary Kerry; and *Regular Lu*, by Robin Nelson (winner of Mom's Choice Award).

How to Contact/Writers Fiction: Query with SASE. Nonfiction: Query with outline and 1-2 sample chapters. Does not consider simultaneous submissions. Responds to queries in 3 months.

Illustration Reviews ms/illustration packages. Send photocopies, transparencies, etc.

Photography Reviews ms/photo packages. Send photocopies, transparencies, etc.

Terms Pays 8-15% royalty on wholesale price. Publishes book 1 year after acceptance of ms. Manuscript guidelines for #10 SASE.

Tips "Absey publishes a few titles every year. We like the author and the illustrator working together to create something magical. Authors and illustrators have input into every phase of production."

ADVOCACY PRESS

P.O. Box 236, Santa Barbara CA 93102. (805)962-2728. Fax: (805)963-3580. E-mail: advocacypress@girlsincsb.org. Web site: www.advocacypress.com. **Publisher:** Joan Bowman. Publishes 1-2 children's books/year. Specializes in life skills development books for youth, and children's titles with a gender equity focus.

- Advocacy Press title *My Way Sally* won the Benjamin Franklin Award for Best Children's Picture Book from the Publishing Marketing Associaion.

Fiction Picture books, young readers, middle readers: adventure, animal, concepts in self-esteem, contemporary, fantasy, folktales, gender equity, multicultural, nature/environment, poetry. "Illustrated children's stories incorporate self-esteem, gender equity, self-awareness concepts." Published *Father Gander Nursery Rhymes*, by Doug Larche, illustrated by Carolyn Blattel; *Minou*, by Mindy Bingham, illustrated by Itoko Maeno; *My Way Sally*, by Penelope Paine, illustrated by Itoko Maeno; *Shadow in the Ready Time*, by Patty Sheehan, illustrated by Itoko Maeno. "Most publications are 32-48 page picture stories for readers 4-11 years. Most feature adventures of animals in interesting/educational locales."

Nonfiction Middle readers, young adults: careers, multicultural, self-help, social issues, textbooks.

How to Contact/Writers "Because of the required focus of our publications, most have been written in-house. We are not currently publishing new titles, but would like samples to keep on file."

Illustration "Require intimate integration of art with story. Therefore, almost always use local illustrators." Average about 30 illustrations per story. Reviews ms/illustration packages from artists. Submit ms with dummy. Contact: Ruth Vitale. Responds in 2 months. Samples returned with SASE.

Terms Authors paid by royalty or outright purchase. Pays illustrators by project or royalty. Book catalog and ms guidelines for SASE.

Tips "We are not presently looking for new titles."

ALADDIN PAPERBACKS/SIMON PULSE PAPERBACK BOOKS

1230 Avenue of the Americas, 4th Floor, New York NY 10020. (212)698-2707. Fax: (212)698-7337. Web site: www.simonsays.com. Vice President/Associate Publisher, Aladdin: Ellen Krieger; Vice President/Editorial Director, Simon Pulse: Bethany Buck; Julia Richardson, Editorial Director (Aladdin); Jennifer Klonsky, Executive Editor (Aladdin); Michelle Nagler, Senior Editor (Pulse). **Manuscript Acquisitions:** Attn: Submissions Editor. **Art Acquisitions:** Karin Paprocki, Aladdin; Russel Gordon, Simon Pulse. Paperback imprints of Simon & Schuster Children's Publishing Division. Publishes 250 titles/year.

- Aladdin publishes reprints of successful hardcovers from other Simon & Schuster imprints as well as original beginning readers, chapter books, and middle grade single title and series fiction. They accept query letters with proposals for originals. Simon Pulse publishes original teen series and single title fiction, as well as reprints of successful hardcovers from other Simon & Schuster imprints. They accept query letters for originals.

Fiction Recently published Robin Hill School beginning reader series (Julia Richardson, editor); Blast to the Past chapter book series (Jennifer Klonsky, editor); Nancy Drew and the Clue Crew chapter book series (Molly McGuire, editor); Ziggy and the Black Dinosaurs middle grade series (Ellen Krieger, editor); Pendragon middle grade series (Julia Richardson, editor); SpyGear Adventures middle grade series (Jennifer Klonsky, editor); Edgar & Ellen middle grade series (Ellen Krieger, editor).

ALASKA NORTHWEST BOOKS

Imprint of Graphic Arts Center Publishing Co., P.O. Box 10306, Portland OR 97296-0306. (503)226-2402. Fax: (503)223-1410. E-mail: editorial@gacpc.com. Web site: www.gacpc.com. **Executive Editor:** Tim Frew. Imprints: Alaska Northwest Books. Publishes 3 picture books/year; 1 young reader/year. 20% of books by first-time authors. "We publish books that teach and entertain as well as inform the reader about Alaska or the western U.S. We're interested in wildlife, adventure, unusual sports, inspirational nature stories, traditions, but we also like plain old silly stories that make kids giggle. We are particular about protecting Native American story-telling traditions, and ask that writers ensure that it's clear whether they are writing from within the culture or about the culture. We encourage Native American writers to share their stories.''

Fiction Picture books, young readers: adventure, animal, contemporary, fantasy, history, humor, multicultural, nature/environment, poetry. Middle readers, young adult/teens: adventure, animal, anthology, contemporary, history, humor, multicultural, nature/environment, suspense/mystery. Average word length: picture books—500-1,000; young readers—500-1,500; middle readers—1,500-2,000; young adults—35,000. Recently published *Seldovia Sam and the Wildfire Rescue*, by Susan Woodward Springer, illustrated by Amy Meissner (ages 6-10, early chapter book); *Ten Rowdy Ravens*, by Susan Ewing, illustrated by Evon Zerbetz (age 5 and up, humor); *Berry Magic*, by Teri Sloat and Betty Huffmon, illustrated by Teri Sloat (age 6 and up, legend).

Nonfiction Picture books: animal. Young readers: animal, multicultural, sports. Middle readers, young adults/teens: animal, history, multicultural, nature/environment, sports, Alaska- or Western-themed adventure. Average word length: picture books—500-1,000; young readers—500-1,500; middle readers—1,500-2,000; young adults—35,000. Recently published *Big-Enough Anna: The Little Sled Dog Who Braved the Arctic*, by Pam Flowers and Ann Dixon, illustrated by Bill Farnsworth (5 and up); *Recess at 20 Below*, by Cindy Lou Aillaud (ages 6-10).

How to Contact/Writers Fiction: Submit complete ms for picture books or submit outline/synopsis and 2 sample chapters for YA novels. Nonfiction: Submit complete ms for picture books or submit 2 sample chapters for YA nonfiction chapter books. Responds to queries/mss in 3-5 months. Publishes book 2 years after acceptance. Will consider simultaneous submissions.

Illustration Works with 4-5 illustrators/year. Uses color artwork only. Reviews ms/illustration packages from artists. Submit ms with dummy or scans of final art on CD. Contact: Tricia Brown. Illustrations only: Query with résumé, scans on CD. Responds only if interested. Samples not returned; samples filed.

Photography Buys stock and assigns work. ''We rarely illustrate with photos—only if the book is more educational in content.'' Photo captions required. Uses color and 35mm or 4×5 transparencies. Submit cover letter, résumé, slides, portfolio on CD, color promo piece.

Terms Pays authors royalty of 5-7% based on net revenues. Offers advances (average amount: $2,000). Pays illustrators royalty of 5-7% based on net revenues. Pays photographers royalty of 5-7% based on net revenues. Sends galleys to authors; dummies to illustrators. Originals returned to artist at job's completion. Book catalog available for 9×12 SASE and $3.85 postage; ms, art, and photo guidelines available for SASE. All imprints included in a single catalog. Catalog available on Web site.

Tips ''As a regional publisher, we seek books about Alaska and the West. We rarely publish YA novels, but are more interested in the preschool to early reader segment. A proposal that shows that the author has researched the market, in addition to submitting a unique story, will get our attention.''

ALL ABOUT KIDS PUBLISHING

117 Bernal Rd. #70, PMB 405, San Jose CA 95119. (408)846-1833. Fax: (408)846-1835. E-mail: lguevara@aakp.com. Web site: www.aakp.com. **Acquisitions:** Linda Guevara. Publishes 5-10 picture books/year; 3-4 chapter books/year. 80% of books by first-time authors.

Fiction Picture books, young readers: adventure, animal, concept, fantasy, folktales, history, humor, multicultural, nature/environment, poetry, religion, suspense/mystery. Average word length: picture books—450 words. Recently published *A, My Name is Andrew*, by Mary McManus-Burke (picture book).

Nonfiction Picture books, young readers: activity books, animal, biography, concept, history, multicultural, nature/environment, religion. Average word length: picture books—450 words. Recently published *Shadowbox Hunt: A Search & Find Odyssey*, by Laura L. Seeley (picture book).

How to Contact/Writers Fiction: Submit complete ms. Nonfiction: Submit complete ms for picture books; outline synopsis and completer ms for young readers. Responds to mss in 3 months. Publishes a book 2-3 years after acceptance. Manuscript returned with SASE only.

Illustration Works with 5-10 illustrators/year. Reviews ms/illustration packages from artists. Submit ms with dummy or ms with 2-3 pieces of final art. Contact: Linda Guevara, editor. Illustrations only: Arrange personal portfolio review or send résumé, portfolio and client list. Responds in 3 months. Samples returned with SASE; samples filed.

Photography Works on assignment only. Contact: Linda Guevara, editor. Model/property releases required. Uses 35mm transparencies. Submit portfolio, résumé, client list.

Terms Pays author royalty. Offers advances (average amount: $1,000). Pays illustrators by the project (range: $3,000 minimum) or royalty of 3-5% based on retail price. Pays photographers by the project (range: $500 minimum) or royalty of 5% based on wholesale price. Sends galleys to authors; dummies to illustrators. All imprints included in a single catalog. Writer's, artist's and photographer's guidelines available for SASE.

Tips ''Write from the heart and for the love of children. Submit only one manuscript per envelope. We do not accept queries of submissions via e-mail.''

AMERICAN GIRL PUBLICATIONS

8400 Fairway Place, Middleton WI 53562-2554. (608)836-4848. Fax: (608)836-1999. Web site: www.americangirl.c om. **Manuscript Acquisitions:** Submissions Editor. Jodi Evert, editorial director fiction; Michelle Watkins, editorial director, American Girl Library. Imprints: The American Girls Collection, American Girl Library, History Mysteries, AG Fiction, Girls of Many Lands. Publishes 30 middle readers/year. 10% of books by first-time authors. Publishes fiction and nonfiction for girls 8-12. "Pleasant Company's mission is to educate and entertain girls with high-quality products and experiences that build self-esteem and reinforce positive social and moral values."

- American Girl Publications does not accept ideas or manuscripts for The American Girls Collection, but does accept manuscripts for stand-alone historical fiction, and is seeking manuscripts for AG Fiction, its contemporary middle-grade fiction imprint for girls 10 and up. Request writers' guidelines for more information. Also publishes *American Girl* magazine. See the listing for *American Girl* in the Magazines section.

Nonfiction Middle readers: activity books, arts/crafts, cooking, history, hobbies, how-to, self help, sports. Recently published *A Smart Girl's Guide to Friendship Troubles*, by Patti Kelley Crisswell, (ages 8 and up; self-help); *Paper Punch Art*, by Laura Torres (ages 8 and up; craft); *Quiz Book 2*, by Sarah Jane Brian, illustrated by Debbie Tilley (ages 8 and up; activity).

How to Contact/Writers Nonfiction: Submit well-focused concepts for activity, craft or advice books. "Proposals should include a detailed descripton of your concept, sample chapters or spreads and lists of previous publications. Complete manuscripts also accepted." Responds in 3 months. Will consider simultaneous submissions.

Illustration Works with 10 illustrators/year. Reviews ms/illustration packages from artists. Illustrations only: Query with samples. Contact: Art Director. Responds only if interested. Samples not returned.

Photography Buys stock and assigns work. Submit cover letter, published samples, promo piece.

Terms Pays authors royalty or work purchased outright. Pays illustrators by the project. Pays photographers by the project. Sends galleys to authors; dummies to illustrators. Originals returned to artist at job's completion. Book catalog available for 8½×11 SAE and 4 first-class stamps. All imprints included in a single catalog.

Tips "We want nonfiction specifically targeted to girls. If the approach would appeal to boys as well as girls, it is not right for American Girl Library."

☐ AMIRAH PUBLISHING

P.O. Box 541146, Flushing NY 11354. E-mail: amirahpbco@aol.com. Web site: www.ifna.net. **Acquisitions:** Yahiya Emerick, president. Publishes 2 young readers/year; 5 middle readers/year; 3 young adult titles/year. 25% of books by first-time authors. "Our goal is to produce quality books for children and young adults with a spiritually uplifting application."

- Amirah accepts submissions only through e-mail.

Fiction Picture books, young readers, middle readers, young adults: adventure, animal, history, multicultural, religion, Islamic. Average word length: picture books—200; young readers—1,000; middle readers—5,000; young adults—5,000. Recently published *Ahmad Deen and the Curse of the Aztec Warrior*, by Yahiya Emerick (ages 8-11); *Burhaan Khan*, by Qasim Najar (ages 6-8); *The Memory of Hands*, by Reshma Baig (ages 15 to adult).

Nonfiction Picture books, young readers, middle readers, young adults: history, religion, Islamic. Average word length: picture books—200; young readers—1,000; middle readers—5,000; young adults—5,000. Recently published *Color and Learn Salah*, by Yahiya Emerick (ages 5-7, religious); *Learning About Islam*, by Yahiya Emerick (ages 9-11, religious); *What Islam Is All About*, by Yahiya Emerick (ages 14 and up, religious).

How to Contact/Writers Fiction/nonfiction: Query via e-mail only. Responds to queries in 2 weeks; mss in 3 months. Publishes a book 6-12 months after acceptance. Will consider electronic submissions via disk or modem.

Illustration Works with 2-4 illustrators/year. Reviews ms/illustration packages from artists. Query. Contact: Qasim Najar, vice president. Illustrations only: Query with samples. Contact: Yahiya Emerick, president. Responds in 1 month. Samples returned with SASE.

Photography Works on assignment only. Contact: Yahiya Emerick, president. Uses images of the Middle East, children, nature. Model/property releases required. Uses 4×6, matte, color prints. Submit cover letter.

Terms Work purchased outright from authors for $1,000-3,000. Pays illustrators by the project (range: $20-40). Pays photographers by the project (range: $20-40). Sends galleys to authors; dummies to illustrators. Originals returned to artist at job's completion. Book catalog available for SASE and 2 first-class stamps. All imprints included in a single catalog. Catalog available on Web site.

Tips "We specialize in materials relating to the Middle East and Muslim-oriented culture such as stories, learning materials and such. These are the only types of items we currently are publishing."

AMULET BOOKS

Abrams Books for Young Readers, 115 W. 18th St., New York NY 10001. (212)229-8000. Web site: www.hnaboo ks.com. Estab. 2004. Specializes in trade books, fiction. **Manuscript Acquisitions:** Susan Van Metre, executive editor. **Art Acquisitions:** Becky Terhune, art director. Produces 6 middle readers/year, 6 young adult titles/year. 10% of books by first-time authors.

Fiction Middle readers: adventure, contemporary, fantasy, history, science fiction, sports. Young adults/teens: adventure, contemporary, fantasy, history, science fiction, sports, suspense. Recently published *The Sisters Grimm: The Fairy-Tale Detectives*, by Michael Buckley (mid-grade series); *ttyl*, by Lauren Miracle (YA novel); *The Hour of the Cobra*, by Maiya Williams (middle grade novel).

How to Contact/Writers Fiction: Query. Responds to queries in 2-3 months. Publishes book 18-24 months after acceptance. Considers simultaneous submissions.

Illustration Works with 10-12 illustrators/year. Uses both color and b&w. Query with samples. Contact: Becky Terhune, art director. Samples filed.

Photography Buys stock images and assigns work.

Terms Offers advance against royalties. Illustrators paid by the project . Author sees galleys for review. Illustrators see dummies for review. Originals returned to artist at job's completion. Catalog available for 9×12 SASE and 4 first-class stamps.

ATHENEUM BOOKS FOR YOUNG READERS

1230 Avenue of the Americas, New York NY 10020. (212)698-2715. Web site: www.simonsayskids.com. Book publisher. Vice President, Associate Publisher: Emma D. Dryden. Estab. 1960. **Manuscript Acquisitions:** Send queries with SASE to Kristy Raffensberger or Jordan Brown, editorial assistants. "All editors consider all types of projects." **Art Acquisitions:** Ann Bobco, executive art director. Imprint of Simon & Schuster Children's Publishing Division. Publishes 20-30 picture books/year; 20-25 middle readers/year; 15-25 young adult titles/year. 10% of books by first-time authors; 60% from agented writers. "Atheneum publishes original hardcover trade books for children from preschool age through young adult. Our list includes picture books, chapter books, mysteries, biography, science fiction, fantasy, graphic novels, middle grade and young adult fiction and nonfiction. The style and subject matter of the books we publish is almost unlimited. We do not, however, publish textbooks, coloring or activity books, greeting cards, magazines or pamphlets or religious publications. The lists of Charles Scribner's Sons Books for Young Readers have been folded into the Atheneum program."

- Atheneum does not accept unsolicited manuscripts. Send query letter only. Atheneum title *Hot Air: The (Mostly) True Story of the First Hot-air Balloon Ride*, written and illustrated by Marjorie Priceman (an Anne Schwartz book), won a 2006 Caldecott Honor Award.

How to Contact/Writers Send query letters for picture books; send synopsis and first 3 chapters or first 30 pages for novels. Responds to queries in 1 month; requested mss in 3-4 months. Publishes a book 24-36 months after acceptance. Will consider simultaneous queries from previously unpublished authors and those submitted to other publishers, "though we request that the author let us know it is a simultaneous query." Please do not call to query or follow up.

Illustration Works with 40-50 illustrators/year. Send art samples résumé, tearsheets to Ann Bobco, Design Dept. 4th Floor, 1230 Avenue of the Americas, New York NY 10020. Samples filed. Responds to art samples only if interested.

Terms Pays authors in royalties of 8-10% based on retail price. Pays illustrators royalty of 5-6% or by the project. Pays photographers by the project. Sends galleys and proofs to authors; proofs to illustrators. Original artwork returned at job's completion. Manuscript guidelines for #10 SAE and 1 first-class stamp.

Tips "Atheneum has a 40+ year tradition of publishing distinguished books for children. Study our titles."

AVISSON PRESS, INC.

3007 Taliaferro Rd., Greensboro NC 27408. (336)288-6989. Fax: (336)288-6989. **Manuscript Acquisitions:** Martin Hester, publisher. Publishes 5-7 young adult titles/year. 70% of books by first-time authors.

Nonfiction Young adults: biography. Average word length: young adults—25,000. Recently published *I Can Do Anything: The Sammy Davis, Jr. Story*, by William Schoell (ages 12-18, young adult biography); *The Girl He Left Behind: The Life and Times of Libbie Custer*, by Suzanne Middendorf Arruda (ages 12-18, young adult biography); *Randolph Caldecott: An Illustrated Life*, by Claudette Hagel.

How to Contact/Writers Accepts material from residents of U.S. only. Nonfiction: Submit outline/synopsis and 2 sample chapters. Responds to queries/mss in 3 weeks. Publishes a book 9-12 months after acceptance. Will consider simultaneous submissions.

Terms Pays author royalty of 8-10% based on wholesale price. Offers advances (average amount: $400). Sends galleys to authors. Book catalog available for #10 SAE and 1 first-class stamp; ms guidelines available for SASE.

Tips "We publish *only* YA biographies. All artwork is done in-house. We need a few experienced writers for house-generated titles."

AVON BOOKS/BOOKS FOR YOUNG READERS

1350 Avenue of the Americas, New York NY 10019. (212)261-6500. Fax: (212)261-6668. Web site: www.harperchildrens.com.

- Avon is not accepting unagented submissions. See listing for HarperCollins Children's Books.

BALLYHOO BOOKWORKS INC.

P.O. Box 534, Shoreham NY 11792. E-mail: ballyhoo@optonline.net. **Acquisitions:** Liam Gerrity, editorial director. Publishes 2 picture books/year; 1 young reader/year. 30% of books by first-time authors. "We are a small press, but highly selective and want texts that flow from the tongue with clarity and are infused with the author's passion for the piece."

> • Ballyhoo is not accepting new manuscripts until Spring 2007 due to a full schedule and an overwhelming increase in unsolicited submissions.

Fiction Young readers: animal, nature/environment. Average word length: picture books—up to 500; young readers—up to 1,000. Recently published *The Alley Cat* and *The Barnyard Cat*, by Brian J. Heinz, illustrated by June H. Blair (ages 5-9, picture books).

Nonfiction Picture books: arts/crafts, how-to. Young readers, middle readers: activity books, arts/crafts, hobbies, how-to. Average word length: picture books—up to 500; young readers—up to 1,000; middle readers—up to 10,000. Recently published *Metal Detecting for Treasure*, by Dorothy B. Francis (ages 10 and up, how-to).

How to Contact/Writers Accepts material from residents of U.S. only. Fiction/nonfiction: Query or submit outline/synopsis or outline/synopsis and 2 sample chapters. Responds to queries in 1 month; mss in 2 months. Publishes book 12-18 months after acceptance. Will consider simultaneous submissions.

Illustration Accepts material from residents of U.S. only. Works with 2-3 illustrators/year. Reviews ms/illustration packages from artists. Query or send ms with dummy. Contact: Editorial Director. Illustrations only: Send résumé, promo sheet and tearsheets. "We file all samples for future reference."

Terms Pays authors royalty of 5% based on retail price. Offers advances (average amount: $1,000-2,500). Pays illustrators 5% based on retail price. Sends galleys to authors. Originals returned to artist at job's completion. Manuscript guidelines available for SASE.

Tips "We don't see any value in trends, only in good writing."

⏏ BANCROFT PRESS

P.O. Box 65360, Baltimore MD 21209. (410)358-0658. Fax: (410)637-7377. E-mail: bruceb@bancroftpress.com. Web site: www.bancroftpress.com. **Manuscript Acquisitions:** Bruce Bortz, publisher. **Art Acquisitions:** Bruce Bortz, publisher. Publishes 1 middle reader/year; 2-4 young adult titles/year.

Fiction Middle readers, young adults: adventure, animal, contemporary, fantasy, humor, multicultural, problem novels, religion, science fiction, special needs, sports, suspense/mystery. Average word length: middle readers—40,000; young adults—50,000. Recently published *Finding the Forger: A Bianca Balducci Mystery*, by Libby Sternberg (ages 10 and up); *The Reappearance of Sam Webber*, by Jonathon Scott Fuqua (ages 10 and up); *Jake: The Second Novel in the Gunpowder Trilogy*, by Arch Montgomery (ages 13 and up); *Like We Care*, by Tom Matthews (ages 15 and up).

Nonfiction Middle readers, young adults: animal, biography, concept, health, history, multicultural, music/dance, nature/environment, reference, religion, science, self help, social issues, special needs, sports, textbooks.

How to Contact/Writers Fiction/nonfiction: Submit complete ms or submit outline/synopsis and 3 sample chapters. Responds to queries/mss in at least 6 months. Publishes book 18 months after acceptance. Will consider e-mail submissions, simultaneous submissions or previously published work.

Terms Pays authors royalty of 8% based on retail price. Offers advances (average amount: $1,000-3,000). Sends galleys to authors. Catalog and ms guidelines available on Web site.

Tips "We advise writers to visit our Web site and to be familiar with our previous work. Patience is the number one attribute contributors must have. It takes us a very long time to get through submitted material, because we are such a small company. Also, we only publish 4-6 books per year, so it may take a long time for your optioned book to be published. We like to be able to market our books to be used in schools and in libraries. We prefer fiction that bucks trends and moves in a new direction. We are especially interested in mysteries and humor (especially humorous mysteries)."

Ⓐ BANTAM BOOKS FOR YOUNG READERS

Imprint of Random House Children's Book, Division of Random House, Inc., 1745 Broadway, New York NY 10019. (212)782-9000. Web site: www.randomhouse.com/kids. Book publisher.

> • See listings for Random House/Golden Books for Young Readers Group, Delacorte and Doubleday Books for Young Readers, Alfred A. Knopf and Crown Books for Young Readers, and Wendy Lamb Books.

How to Contact/Writers Not seeking manuscripts at this time.

Illustration Contact: Isabel Warren-Lynch, executive director, art & design. Responds only if interested. Samples returned with SASE; samples filed.

Terms Pays illustrators and photographers by the project or royalties. Original artwork returned at job's completion.

BAREFOOT BOOKS

2067 Massachusetts Ave., 5th Floor, Cambridge MA 02140. Web site: www.barefootbooks.com. **Manuscript/ Art Acquisitions:** U.S. editor. Publishes 35 picture books/year; 10 anthologies/year. 35% of books by first-

Book Publishers

Book Publishers

time authors. "The Barefoot child represents the person who is in harmony with the natural world and moves freely across boundaries of many kinds. Barefoot Books explores this image with a range of high-quality picture books for children of all ages. We work with artists, writers and storytellers from many cultures, focusing on themes that encourage independence of spirit, promote understanding and acceptance of different traditions, and foster a life-long love of learning."

Fiction Picture books, young readers: animal, anthology, concept, fantasy, folktales, multicultural, nature/environment, poetry, spirituality. Middle readers, young adults: anthology, folktales. Average word length: picture books—500-1,000; young readers—2,000-3,000; anthologies—10,000-20,000. Recently published *We All Went on Safari*, by Laurie Krebs, illustrated by Julia Cairns (ages 3-7, picture book); *Thesaurus Rex*, by Laya Steinberg, illustrated by Debbie Harter (ages 2-6, concept book); *Goddesses: A World of Myth and Magic*, by Burleigh Muten, illustrated by Rebecca Guay (ages 7 to adult, anthology).

How to Contact/Writers Fiction: Submit complete ms for picture books; outline/synopsis and 1 sample story for collections. Responds in 4 months if SASE is included. Will consider simultaneous submissions and previously published work.

Illustration Works with 20 illustrators/year. Uses color artwork only. Reviews ms/illustration packages from artists. Send query and art samples or dummy for picture books. Illustrations only: Query with samples or send promo sheet and tearsheets. Responds only if interested. Samples returned with SASE.

Terms Pays authors royalty of 5% based on retail price. Offers advances. Sends galleys to authors. Originals returned to artist at job's completion. Book catalog available for 9 × 12 SAE and 5 first-class stamps; ms guidelines available for SASE. Catalog available on Web site.

Tips "We are looking for books that inspire and are filled with a sense of magic and wonder. We also look for strong stories from all different cultures, reflecting the ways of the individual culture while also touching deeper human truths that suggest we are all one. We welcome playful submissions for the very youngest children and also anthologies of stories for older readers, all focused around a universal theme. We encourage writers and artists to visit our Web site and read some of our books to get a sense of our editorial philosophy and what we publish before they submit to us. Always, we encourage them to stay true to their inner voice and artistic vision that reaches out for timeless stories, beyond the momentary trends that may exist in the market today."

BARRONS EDUCATIONAL SERIES

250 Wireless Blvd., Hauppauge NY 11788. Fax: (631)434-3723. E-mail: waynebarr@barronseduc.com. Web site: www.barronseduc.com. **Manuscript Acquisitions:** Wayne R. Barr, acquisitions manager. **Art Acquisitions:** Bill Kuchler. Publishes 20 picture books/year; 20 young readers/year; 20 middle readers/year; 10 young adult titles/year. 25% of books by first-time authors; 25% of books from agented writers.

Fiction Picture books: animal, concept, multicultural, nature/environment. Young readers: adventure, multicultural, nature/environment, fantasy, suspense/mystery. Middle readers: adventure, fantasy, multicultural, nature/environment, problem novels, suspense/mystery. Young adults: problem novels. Recently published *Everyday Witch*, by Sandra Forrester; *Word Wizardry*, by Margaret and William Kenda.

Nonfiction Picture books: concept, reference. Young readers: how-to, reference, self help, social issues. Middle readers: hi-lo, how-to, reference, self help, social issues. Young adults: biography, how-to, reference, self help, social issues, sports.

How to Contact/Writers Fiction: Query via e-mail. Nonfiction: Submit outline/synopsis and sample chapters. "Submissions must be accompanied by SASE for response." Responds to queries in 2 months; mss in 4 months. Publishes a book 1 year after acceptance. Will consider simultaneous submissions.

Illustration Works with 20 illustrators/year. Reviews ms/illustration packages from artists. Query first; 3 chapters of ms with 1 piece of final art, remainder roughs. Illustrations only: Submit tearsheets or slides plus résumé. Responds in 2 months.

Terms Pays authors royalty of 10-14% based on net price or buys ms outright for $2,000 minimum. Pays illustrators by the project based on retail price. Sends galleys to authors; dummies to illustrators. Book catalog, ms/artist's guidelines for 9 × 12 SAE.

Tips Writers: "We publish preschool storybooks, concept books and middle grade and YA chapter books. No romance novels." Illustrators: "We are happy to receive a sample illustration to keep on file for future consideration. Periodic notes reminding us of your work are acceptable." Children's book themes "are becoming much more contemporary and relevant to a child's day-to-day activities, fewer talking animals. We have a great interest in children's fiction (ages 7-11 and ages 12-16) with New Age topics."

BEBOP BOOKS

Imprint of Lee & Low Books Inc., 95 Madison Ave., New York NY 10016-7801. (212)779-4400. Web site: www.bebopbooks.com. **Acquisitions:** Jennifer Fox. **Editor-in-Chief:** Louise May. Publishes 10-15 educational market picture books/year. Many books by first-time authors. "Our goal is to publish child-centered stories that support literacy learning and provide multicultural content for children just beginning to learn to read. We make a special effort to work with writers and illustrators of diverse backgrounds. Current needs are posted on Web site."

• Bebop Books acquires manuscripts between August and October only. See Web site for details.

Fiction Picture books: adventure, concept, contemporary, multicultural, nature/environment, sports, culturally specific topics for young children.

Nonfiction Picture books: arts/crafts, careers, concept, cooking, hobbies, how-to, multicultural, music/dance, nature/environment, social issues, sports.

How to Contact/Writers Fiction/nonfiction: Submit complete ms. Responds to mss in up to 4 months. See Web site for specific guidelines; submit between August and October only. We will not respond to manuscripts received when our call for manuscripts is not open."

Illustration Works with 5-10 illustrators/year. Uses color artwork only. Illustrations and photographs: Query with color samples and send client list or cover letter. Responds only if interested. Samples returned with SASE; samples filed. "We are especially interested in submissions from artists of color, and we encourage artists new to the field of children's books to send us samples of their work."

Terms Pays authors royalty. Offers advances. Pays illustrators and photographers royalty and advance. Book catalog available for 9×12 SAE and 89¢ postage, attn: Catalog Request. Catalog available on Web site.

Tips "Bebop Books is currently specializing in beginning readers with multicultural themes. Often called 'little books,' they are used to help young children develop early reading skills and strategies. Each book is a small paperback, with full color illustrations and a story specifically written and illustrated to support beginning readers."

BENCHMARK BOOKS

Imprint of Marshall Cavendish, 99 White Plains Rd., Tarrytown NY 10591. (914)332-8888. Fax: (914)332-1888. E-mail: mbisson@marshallcavendish.com. Web site: www.marshallcavendish.com. **Manuscript Acquisitions:** Michelle Bisson. Publishes about 100 young reader, middle reader and young adult books/year. "We look for interesting treatments of primarily nonfiction subjects related to elementary, middle school and high school curriculum."

Nonfiction Most nonfiction topics should be curriculum related. Average word length: 4,000-20,000. All books published as part of a series. Recently published First Americans (series), Family Trees (series), Bookworms (series).

How to Contact/Writers Nonfiction: Submit outline/synopsis and 1 or more sample chapters. Responds to queries/mss in 3 months. Publishes a book 2 years after acceptance. Will consider simultaneous submissions.

Photography Buys stock and assigns work.

Terms Buys work outright. Sends galleys to authors. Book catalog available online. All imprints included in a single catalog.

THE BENEFACTORY

24 Pine Circle, Pembroke MA 02359. (781)294-4715. Web site: www.readplay.com. **Manuscript/Art Acquisitions:** Cindy Germain, director, creative services. Publishes 6-12 picture books/year with the Humane Society of the United States; 6-12 picture books/year. 50% of books by first-time authors. The Benefactory publishes "classic" true stories about real animals, through licenses with many nonprofits. Each title is accompanied by a read-along audiocassette and a plush animal. A percentage of revenues benefits the licensor. Target ages: 4-10.

Nonfiction Picture books: nature/environment; young readers: animal, nature/environment. Average word length: 700-1,500. Recently published *Chessie, the Travelin' Man*, written by Randy Houk, illustrated by Paula Bartlett (ages 5-10, picture book); *Condor Magic*, written by Lyn Littlefield Hoopes, illustrated by Peter C. Stone (ages 5-10, picture book); *Caesar: On Deaf Ears*, written by Loren Spiotta-DiMare, illustrated by Kara Lee (ages 5-10, picture book).

How to Contact/Writers Query only—does not accept unsolicited mss. Responds to queries in 6 weeks. Publishes a book 1 year after acceptance. Will consider simultaneous submissions. Send SASE for writer's guidelines.

Illustration Works with 6-8 illustrators/year. Uses color artwork only. Reviews ms/illustration packages from artists. Query or send ms with dummy. Illustrations only: Send résumé, promo sheet and tearsheets to be kept on file. Responds in 6 months. Samples returned with SASE; samples filed. Send SASE for artist guidelines.

Terms Pays authors royalty of 3-5% based on wholesale price. Offers advances (average amount: $5,000). Pays illustrators royalty of 3-5% based on wholesale price. Sends galleys to authors; dummies to illustrators. Originals returned to artist at job's completion. Book catalog available for 8½×11 SASE; ms and art guidelines available for SASE.

Book Publishers

◘ BESS PRESS

3565 Harding Ave., Honolulu HI 96816. (808)734-7159. Fax: (808)732-3627. E-mail: editor@besspress.com. Web site: www.besspress.com. **Acquisitions Editor:** Reve Shapard. Publishes 3 picture books/year; 3 young readers/year. 5% of books by first-time authors. Publishes trade and educational books about Hawaii and Micronesia only. "The perspective should be that of a resident, not a visitor."

Fiction Picture books: Hawaii. Average word length: picture books—600. Recently published *How Six Little Ipu Got Their Names*, by Debi Brimmer and Julie Coleson (ages 5-10, picture books with CD); *Whose Slippers Are Those?*, by Marilyn Kahalewai (ages 2-5, picture book); *The Story of Hula*, by Carla Golembe (ages 5-8, picture book); *Waltah Melon: Local Kine Hero*, by Carmen Geshell and Jeff Pagat (ages 5-8, picture book).

Nonfiction Picture books, young readers: Hawaii. Recently published *Dangerous Sea Creatures of Hawaii A to Z Coloring Book*, by Terry Pierce and Kristen Kofsky (ages 6-10, coloring book).

How to Contact/Writers Fiction/nonfiction: Submit complete ms. Responds to queries in 2-3 weeks; mss in 4-6 weeks. Publishes book 1 year after acceptance. Will consider e-mail submissions, simultaneous submissions, and previously published work.

Illustration Works with 2-3 illustrators/year. Reviews ms/illustration packages from artists. "We prefer to use illustrators and photographers living in the region. We do not encourage samples from freelancers outside the region." Query. Contact: Reve Shapard, editor. Illustrations only: Query. Responds only if interested. Samples returned with SASE; samples filed.

Photography Works on assignment only. Uses Hawaii-Pacific photos only. Model/property releases required. Uses color and various size prints and transparencies. Submit cover letter.

Terms Pays authors royalty of 4-10% based on wholesale price or work purchased outright from authors. Pays illustrators by the project or royalty of 4-6% based on wholesale price. Pays photographers by the project. Sends galleys to authors; dummies to illustrators. Originals returned to artist at job's completion. Book catalog available for SASE; ms guidelines available for SAE. All imprints included in a single catalog. Catalog available on Web site.

Tips "As a regional publisher, we are looking for material specific to the region (Hawaii and Micronesia), preferably from writers and illustrators living within (or very familiar with) the region."

BETHANY HOUSE PUBLISHERS

11400 Hampshire Ave. S., Minneapolis MN 55438-2852. (952)829-2500. Fax: (952)829-2768. Web site: www.bethanyhouse.com. **Manuscript Acquisitions:** Youth Department. **Art Acquisitions:** Paul Higdon. Publishes 10 middle-grade readers/year; 8 young adult titles/year. "Bethany House Publishers is an evangelical Christian publisher seeking to publish imaginative, excellent books that reflect an evangelical worldview without being preachy."

Fiction Children's and young adult fiction list is full.

Nonfiction Young readers, middle readers, young adults: religion/devotional, self-help, social issues. Recently published *God Called a Girl*, by Shannon Kubiak (young teen); *Total Devotion: A Growing-Up Guide*, by Sandra Byrd (middle readers).

How to Contact/Writers Considers unsolicited 1-page queries sent by fax only. "Bethany House no longer accepts unsolicited manuscripts or book proposals." Responds in 4 months. Publishes a book 12-18 months after acceptance.

Illustration Works with 5 illustrators/year.

Terms Pays authors royalty based on net sales. Pays illustrators by the project. Pays photographers by the project. Sends galleys to authors. Book catalog available for 11 × 14 SAE and 5 first-class stamps. Write "Catalog Request" on outside of envelope.

Tips "Research the market, know what is already out there. Study our catalog before submitting material. We look for an evangelical message woven delicately into a strong plot and topics that seek to broaden the reader's experience and perspective."

BEYOND WORDS PUBLISHING, INC.

20827 N.W. Cornell Rd., Hillsboro OR 97124-1808. (503)531-8700. Fax: (503)531-8773. E-mail: info@beyondword.com. Web site: www.beyondword.com.

- Beyond Words is not accepting any new children's material at this time.

◘ BICK PUBLISHING HOUSE

307 Neck Rd., Madison CT 06443. (203)245-0073. Fax: (203)245-5990. E-mail: bickpubhse@aol.com. Web site: www.bickpubhouse.com. **Aquisitions Editor:** Dale Carlson. "We publish psychological, philosophical, scientific information on health and recovery, wildlife rehabilation, living with disabilities, teen psychology and science for adults and young adults."

Nonfiction Young adults: nature/environment, religion, science, self help, social issues, special needs. Average word length: young adults—60,000. Recently published *In and Out of Your Mind* (teen science); *Who Said What?* (philosophy quotes for teens), *What are You Doing with Your Life?*, by J. Krishnamurti (philosophy for teens), *The Teen Brain Book*, by Dale Carlson.

How to Contact/Writers Fiction: Submit outline/synopsis and 3 sample chapters. Nonfiction: Submit outline/synopsis or outline/synopsis and 3 sample chapters. Responds to queries/mss in 2 weeks. Publishes book 1 year after acceptance. Will consider simultaneous submissions and previously published work.

Illustration Works with 1 illustrator/year. Uses b&w artwork only. Reviews ms/illustration packages from artists. Submit sketches of teens or science drawings. Contact: Dale Carlson, president. Illustrations only: Query with photocopies, résumé, SASE. Responds in 2 weeks. Samples returned with SASE.

Terms Pays authors royalty of 5-10%. Pays illustrators by the project (range: up to $1,000). Sends galleys to authors; dummies to illustrators. Book catalog available for SASE with 1 first-class stamp; writer's guidelines available for SAE. Catalog available on Web site.

Tips ''Read our books!''

☐ BIRDSONG BOOKS

1322 Bayview Rd., Middletown DE 19709. (302)378-7274. E-mail: BirdsongBooks@Delaware.net. Web site: www.BirdsongBooks.com. **Manuscript & Art Acquisitions:** Nancy Carol Willis, president. Publishes 1 picture book/year. ''Birdsong Books seeks to spark the delight of discovering our wild neighbors and natural habitats. We believe knowledge and understanding of nature fosters caring and a desire to protect the Earth and all living things. Our emphasis is on North American Animals and Habitats rather than people.''

Nonfiction Picture books, young readers: activity books, animal, nature/environment. Average word length: picture books—800-1,000. Recently published *Red Knot: A Shorebird's Incredible Journey*, by Nancy Carol Willis (age 6-9, nonfiction picture book); *Raccoon Moon*, by Nancy Carol Willis (ages 5-8, natural science picture book); *The Robins In Your Backyard*, by Nancy Carol Willis (ages 4-7, nonfiction picture book).

How to Contact/Writers Nonfiction: Submit complete manuscript package with SASE. Responds to mss in 3 months. Publishes book 2-3 years after acceptance. Will consider simultaneous submissions (if stated).

Illustration Accepts material from residents of U.S. Works with 1 illustrator/year. Reviews ms/illustration packages from artists. Send ms with dummy (plus samples/tearsheets for style). Illustrations only: Query with brochure, résumé, samples, SASE, or tearsheets. Responds only if interested. Samples returned with SASE.

Photography Uses North American animals and habitats (currently shorebirds and horseshoe crabs). Submit cover letter, résumé, promo piece, stock photo list.

Tips ''We are a small independent press actively seeking manuscripts that fit our narrowly defined niche. We are only interested in nonfiction, natural science picture books or educational activity books about North American animals and habitats. Our books include back matter suitable for early elementary classrooms. Mailed submissions with SASE only. No e-mail submissions or phone calls, please. Cover letters should sell author/illustrator and book idea.''

Ⓝ BLOOMING TREE PRESS

P.O. Box 140934, Austin TX 78714. Estab. 2000. (512)921-8846. Fax: (512)873-7710. E-mail: email@bloomingtreepress.com. Web site: www.bloomingtreepress.com. **Publisher:** Miriam Hees; Madeline Smoot, senior editor, children's division; Judy Gregerson, editor, children's division; Meghan Dietsche, associate editor, children's division; Bradford Hees, senior editor, graphic novels/comics. **Art Acquisitions:** Miriam Hees. ''Blooming Tree Press is dedicated to producing high quality book for the young and the young at heart. It is our hope that you will find your dreams between that pages of our books.''

Fiction Picture books: adventure, animal, contemporary, fantasy, folktales, history, humor, multicultural, religion, science fiction, special needs, sports. Young readers: adventure, animal, contemporary, fantasy, folktales, history, humor, multicultural, religion, science fiction, special needs, sports, suspense. Middle readers: adventure, animal, anthology, contemporary, fantasy, folktales, history, humor, multicultural, poetry, religion, science fiction, suspense. Young adults/teens: adventure, animal, anthology, contemporary, fantasy, folktales, history, humor, religion, science fiction, suspense. Average word length: picture books—500-1,000; young readers—800-9,000; middle readers—25,000-40,000; young adult/teens: 40,000-70,000. Recently published *Callie and the Stepmother*, by Susan A. Meyers, illustrated by Rose Gauss (beginning reader about stepfamilies); *Lyranel's Song*, by Leslie Carmichael, illustrated by Elsbet Vance (upper mid-grade fantasy trilogy); *Little Bunny Kung Fu*, by Regan Johnson (picture book about respect for others).

Nonfiction Picture Books: biography, cooking, geography, history, self help, social issues, special needs, sports. Young Readers: animal, biography, careers, cooking, geography, history, music/dance, religion, science, self help, social issues, special needs, sports. Middle Readers: biography, cooking, geography, history, how-to, music/dance, religion, science, self help, social issues, sports. Young Adults/Teens: biography, careers, cooking, geography, history, hobbies, music/dance, religion, science, self help, social issues, sports.

How to Contact/Writers Fiction: Query. Nonfiction: submit outline/synopsis and 3 sample chapters. Responds

Elizabeth Bluemle

Read, read, read; write, write, write

Elizabeth Bluemle and Josie Leavitt, co-owners of the Flying Pig Bookstore in Charlotte, Vermont, hadn't planned on opening a children's bookstore when the two relo-
cated. "We had moved to Vermont from New York City, intending to write and teach
school," says Bluemle. "I had recently been a teacher and school librarian, and Josie was
a high school English teacher and a professional standup comic."

Their plans got sidetracked, however, when the old post office-turned-cafe in town was
suddenly for lease. "There's not much in our tiny downtown, and we wanted the building to
be a community gathering place. The only idea that made sense for us, given our interests
and backgrounds, was to open a bookstore that emphasized children's books." And they were
off—going from idea to opening day in just 10 weeks, with a starting inventory of 6,500 books.
"I still think it was impossible," says Bluemle, "like the quest in *The Phantom Tollbooth*: 'So
many things are possible just as long as you don't know they're impossible.' "

Today the Flying Pig stocks more than 40,000 books—one of which is *My Father the
Dog* (Candlewick), Bluemle's first picture book. Here, wearing her writer's hat, she talks
about earning an MFA in children's writing from Vermont College, her first publishing experience, and her upcoming projects. And, speaking as a bookseller, she offers advice to both
aspiring and published writers.

**Did co-owning a bookstore give you a leg-up when it came to getting your first
picture book published?**
In terms of knowing the marketplace and the strengths of various children's book publishers, my bookstore life absolutely helped. I knew I wanted to go to Candlewick first with
my manuscript because I love their books and thought mine would be a good fit. Working
at a bookstore also helped my manuscript reach an editor. Candlewick doesn't accept
unsolicited manuscripts, but they know my bookstore and indicated that they would certainly look at something if I sent it. Once in the door, however, the book had to stand on
its own little legs.

**Tell me a little about your experience completing the Vermont College MFA
in children's writing program. What prompted you to enter the program?**
I had just finished directing a community theatre production, and felt an enormous creative
letdown. We wouldn't be doing another play until the following year, and my craving for an
artistic outlet was so strong I knew I needed to make it a priority in my life. Writing was
my main passion, and I'd always given it a backseat to my other work. So I talked with my
partner about allowing my writing life to take over some of the time I'd been spending at

our bookstore, and she was—to my everlasting gratitude—completely supportive. I sent my application in to Vermont College. Once I was accepted, I never looked back. I loved the program, the incredible generous, demanding faculty, the focus on craft over commercialism, and the deadlines that forced me to write. I made friends there who will be my writing family forever. It's been so much fun to see them all blossom and to order their books for my bookstore.

Did anything in particular spark your idea for *My Father the Dog*? Do your own dogs have dad-like qualities?

I love this question about my dogs having dad-like qualities! Usually, people ask the reverse. Let's see, my cocker spaniels do frown at me occasionally when they disapprove (if I forget a treat I've promised them, for example), and they are cozy, like my dad. I tell my father he is of course too dignified to be dog-like, but actually, he does share many of the traits in *My Father the Dog*, beginning with the morning scratch.

The idea for the book was one of those late-at-night, bolt-upright-in-bed kind of things. I was in a dream or half-sleep, and I sort of heard the little girl's voice saying, "My father pretends to be human, but I know he is really a dog. Consider the evidence..." I scrawled those first lines and a few more ideas, then went to sleep. I actually forgot about it until some months later, when the idea walloped me over the head again and I started tinkering with it again.

How did *My Father the Dog* end up with Candlewick? Did you submit it on your own, or do you have an agent?

My submission story is unorthodox. When I was preparing to go to BookExpo in 2002 (in my bookseller guise), I stuck the manuscript in my suitcase in case I got the courage to

My Father the Dog

Elizabeth Bluemle
illustrated by Randy Cecil

Jacket illustration © 2006 Randy Cecil. Reprinted with permission.

"My father pretends to be human, but I know he is really a dog. Consider the evidence . . . ," begins Elizabeth Bluemle's debut picture book, *My Father the Dog* (Candlewick). The author, who is also co-owner of the Flying Pig Bookstore in Charlotte, Vermont, says the idea for her first book—and that first line—came to her in "one of those late-at-night, bolt-upright-in-bed" moments.

show it to Candlewick. The Saturday of the show, I had lunch with an author friend, who read the manuscript and encouraged me to submit it. So, in effect, I walked over to a Candlewick sales rep who knew I was in the Vermont College program and gave it to her. She passed the book on to the picture book committee, which is where my editor took it on. That is not the normal route for a manuscript to take, obviously.

About agents: I submitted *My Father the Dog* without an agent, but had a good literary lawyer (one who specializes in children's book contracts) look over the terms. That first time through, I didn't know that if an editor calls and offers you an advance and royalties, and you say, "Yes, sounds good, let me take a look at the contract," you've pretty much given a verbal agreement to the offered advance and royalties. (In my previous work life, numbers weren't essentially fixed until *after* you'd actually seen the contract.) I think that's an important custom peculiar to publishing for first-time authors to know. Fortunately, Candlewick is a fair house and didn't try to take advantage of my ignorance. I approached my agent when the contract for my second book looked imminent, and she's negotiated everything since then.

You host events with both well-known authors and newer or debut authors. What kind of crowds do you generally draw for signings? Would you recommend newer authors do bookstore appearances?

I think we are very lucky. Although we can never predict crowds—we've had as few as three people show up to an event, and as many as 250 (we go offsite for those)—authors seem to have a really good time at the store. However, I've heard horror stories about bad signings, where the bookstore personnel didn't even know the authors were coming, or hadn't ordered their books. Those signings would be pretty dispiriting. The authors I've talked to online are divided: some have reported that a sparsely-attended reading led to a school connection that has ended up paying off in wonderful ways, but others say they don't do bookstore appearances except locally, because they feel it's a waste of time. I'll be interested to see how I feel about signings after I do some. At the worst, though, it's a chance to get a bookstore behind you and your books.

As a first-time author, what was the editorial process like for you? Were there any surprises?

The editorial process is fascinating, and there are lots of surprises along the way. Even though I knew the field pretty well—I'd worked in what seemed like every other book-related realm: editor, production manager, librarian, teacher, bookseller—I still had (and have) so much to learn as an author. The first time through is a huge learning curve, because the author is still figuring out how to navigate requested changes: should I fight for this line, or am I being precious about it? Should I give input on the art when invited to, and if so, how do I do it without stepping on the artist's creative process? After all, it's his or her book, too. What efforts should I be making to promote my book? Am I lazy if I don't beat down doors? Will I annoy the PR department at the publisher if I do *too* much? Ack. Fortunately, editors are used to working with writers, and they help you work your way through all the questions. Frequent gut-checks to monitor your instincts don't hurt, either.

The illustrations in your book are wonderful, right down to the endpapers. How did you feel when you first saw them?

One of Candlewick's most wonderful qualities is its attention to the visual and physical qualities of a book. They take care to involve the author in those aspects, unlike many publishing houses. Randy Cecil was a perfect match for *My Father the Dog*, and I laughed out loud at his sketches. I loved seeing his process through three rounds of sketches, and when I got the final art, it took my breath away. When I saw the finished hardcover, and the richness of the colors and textures in their full glory, I cried.

I've been hearing that the picture book market is flat these days. Do you see that at your bookstore? Should that discourage budding picture book authors?

I've heard this, too, but picture books still sell solidly at our store, perhaps in part because our town keeps producing babies. It also helps that we're located next door to a preschool, and we're about a mile away from the local elementary school. So we haven't noticed a slump, except perhaps in midlist hardcover picture books. It's a shame, because many quiet treasures get lost. My philosophy is that this phase too shall pass. The pendulum will always swing back; it just takes time. When we opened the bookstore, everyone was bemoaning the death of YA. Now look at it.

Tell me about your upcoming projects *Dogs on the Bed* and *How Do You Wokka-Wokka*?

Well, if picture books are flat, I'm in trouble. But I do have great fondness for these projects.

After one particularly hazardous night when my two small spaniels managed to hog at least half the bed, I wrote a little story/song of love and annoyance. The result was a rhyming picture book about family dogs creating chaos when bedtime rolls around. *Dogs on the Bed* is slated for Fall 2007, and will be illustrated by the marvelous Anne Wilsdorf.

How Do You Wokka-Wokka? is what I call a crazy toddler jazz dance thingie. It's another rhyming picture book, about a little boy who leads his neighbors to a giant block party. I couldn't get the rhythm of this one out of my head until I'd finished the darn thing. It won't be out until at least 2008, and the artist hasn't yet been assigned.

What advice would you offer—bookseller to aspiring authors? Why is it important that writers visit bookstores regularly?

Read, read, read, read, read. Go to the library and take out stacks and stacks of books. Books that inspire you, books that make you remember why you love to write in the first place. Even books that aren't good teach you about writing. What bookstores offer that libraries may not is up-to-date information on who's publishing what *right now*. Over time, you develop a strong sense of the various publishers' lists, and save yourself time and effort by pinpointing the right kind of house for your book.

My other piece of advice, of course, is obvious: write, write, write, write, write. Writing's like any other art—one of my writer friends said that no one expects to sit down at the piano for the first time and play a Liszt concerto. Frequent practice gets the rust off and leads to wonderful things, including practical improvement and surprising artistic discoveries. That's my favorite thing about writing—the surprises.

I'd like to encourage authors not to be shy when they go to bookstores. Introduce yourselves; let us get to know you. Booksellers do a lot of handselling. (In our store, for example, I'd say we directly recommend at least 75% of what we sell. That adds up.) Booksellers can't help but feel more invested in you and your books when they get to know and like you. Then they have an extra reason to want your good book to succeed. Don't be fakey about it, of course. This appreciation works both ways; if you support their efforts as booksellers by shopping with them, and sending friends to their stores, you're helping keep alive strong community bookstores whose employees go the extra mile for authors. Those relationships may bear unexpected and long-lasting fruit. Plus, it's always delightful for a bookseller to meet people who share a genuine passion for books.

—Alice Pope

to queries in 1-3 months; mss in 3-4 months. Publishes ms 18-36 months after acceptance. Will consider simultaneous submissions.

Illustration Works with 6-20 illustrators/year. Reviews ms/illustration packages. Send manuscript with dummy and sample art. Contact: Miriam Hees, publisher. Illustration only: Query with samples to Miriam Hees, publisher. Samples not returned; sample filed.

Terms Pays authors royalty of 10% depending on the project. Pays illustrators by the project. Authors see galleys for review; illustrators see dummies. Send e-mail with mailing address for catalog. Writer's guidelines on Web site.

Tips "Send a crisp and clean one-page query letter stating your project, why it is right for the market, and a little about yourself. Write what you know, not what's 'in.' Remember, every great writer/illustrator started somewhere. Keep submitting . . . don't ever give up."

BLOOMSBURY CHILDREN'S BOOKS

Imprint of Bloomsbury PLC, 175 Fifth Avenue, Suite 315, New York NY 10010. (646)307-5858. Fax: (212)982-2837. E-mail: bloomsburykids@bloomsburyusa.co. Web site: www.bloomsbury.com/usa. Specializes in fiction, picture books. Publishes 20 picture books/year; 5 young readers/year; 10 middle readers/year; 15 young adult titles/year. 25% of books by first-time authors.

• Bloomsbury title *Princess Academy*, by Shannon Hale, won a 2006 Newbery Honor Award.

Fiction Picture books: adventure, animal, contemporary, fantasy, folktales, history, humor, multicultural, poetry, suspense/mystery. Young readers: adventure, animal, anthology, concept, contemporary, fantasy, folktales, history, humor, multicultural, suspense/mystery. Middle readers: adventure, animal, contemporary, fantasy, folktales, history, humor, multicultural, poetry, problem novels. Young adults: adventure, animal, anthology, contemporary, fantasy, folktales, history, humor, multicultural, problem novels, science fiction, sports, suspense/mystery. Recently published *Where is Coco Going?*, by Sloone Tanen (picture books); *Once Upon a Curse*, by E.D. Baker (middle reader); *Enna Burning*, by Shannon Hale (young adult fantasy).

How to Contact/Writers Submit synopsis and first 3 chapters with SASE. Responds to queries/mss in 6 months.

Illustration Works with 15 illustrators/year. Reviews ms/illustration packages from artists. Query or submit ms with dummy. Illustrations only: Query with samples. Responds only if interested. Samples returned with SASE; samples filed.

Photography Buys stock and assigns work. Uses color or b&w prints. Submit SASE.

Terms Pays authors royalty or work purchased outright for jackets. Offers advances. Pays illustrators by the project or royalty. Pays photographers by the project or per photo. Sends galleys to authors; dummies to illustrators. Originals returned to artist at job's completion. Writer's and art guidelines available for SASE. Catalog available on Web site.

Tips "Spend a lot of time in the bookstore and library to keep up on trends in market. Always send appropriate SASE to ensure response. Never send originals."

BLUE SKY PRESS

557 Broadway, New York NY 10012-3999. (212)343-6100. Fax: (212)343-4713. Web site: www.scholastic.com. **Acquisitions:** Bonnie Verburg. Publishes 15-20 titles/year. 1% of books by first-time authors. Publishes hardcover children's fiction and nonfiction including high-quality novels and picture books by new and established authors.

• Blue Sky is currently not accepting unsolicited submissions due to a large backlog of books.

Fiction Picture books: adventure, animal, concept, contemporary, fantasy, folktales, history, humor, multicultural, nature/environment, poetry. Young readers: adventure, contemporary, fantasy, folktales, history, humor, multicultural, nature/environment, poetry. Young adults: adventure, anthology, contemporary, fantasy, history, humor, multicultural, poetry. Multicultural needs include "strong fictional or themes featuring nonwhite characters and cultures." Does not want to see mainstream religious, bibliotherapeutic, adult. Average length: picture books—varies; young adults—150 pages. Recently published *To Every Thing There Is a Season*, illustrated by Leo and Diane Dillon (all ages, picture book); *Bluish*, by Virginia Hamilton; *No, David!*, by David Shannon; *The Adventures of Captain Underpants*, by Dav Pilkey; *How Do Dinosaurs Say Good Night?*, by Jane Yolen, illustrated by Mark Teague.

How to Contact/Writers "Due to large numbers of submissions, we are discouraging unsolicited submissions—send query with SASE only if you feel certain we publish the type of book you have written." Fiction: Query (novels, picture books). Responds to queries in 6 months. Publishes a book 1-3 years after acceptance; depending on chosen illustrator's schedule. Will not consider simultaneous submissions. No electronic submissions or faxes.

Illustration Works with 10 illustrators/year. Reviews illustration packages "only if illustrator is the author." Submit ms with dummy. Illustrations only: Query with samples, tearsheets. Responds only if interested. Samples only returned with SASE. Original artwork returned at job's completion.

Terms Pays 10% royalty based on wholesale price split between author and illustrators. Advance varies.
Tips "Read currently published children's books. Revise—never send a first draft. Find your own voice, style, and subject. With material from new people we look for a theme or style strong enough to overcome the fact that the author/illustrator is unknown in the market."

⊠ BOYDS MILLS PRESS

815 Church St., Honesdale PA 18431. (877)512-8366 or (570)253-1164. Fax: (570)253-0179. Web site: www.boydsmillspress.com. Estab. 1990. **Manuscript Acquisitions:** J. DeLuca. Manuscript Coordinator. **Art Acquisitions:** Tim Gillner. Imprints: Calkins Creek Books, Front Street Books, Wordsong. 5% of books from agented writers. "We publish a wide range of quality children's books of literary merit, from preschool to young adult."
- Prose fiction for middle-grade through young adult should be submitted to Boyds Mills imprint Front Street Books. See Front Street listing for address and contact information. Boyds Mills title *A Splendid Friend, Indeed*, by Suzanne Bloom, won a 2006 Theodor Seuss Geisel Honor Award.

Fiction All levels: adventure, contemporary, history, humor, multicultural, poetry. Picture books: animal. Multicultural themes include any story showing a child as an integral part of a culture and which provides children with insight into a culture they otherwise might be unfamiliar with. "Please query us on the appropriateness of suggested topics for middle grade and young adult. For all other submissions send entire manuscript."
Nonfiction All levels: nature/environment, science. Picture books, young readers, middle readers: animal, multicultural. Does not want to see reference/curricular text.
How to Contact/Writers Fiction/nonfiction: Submit complete ms or submit through agent. Query on middle reader, young adult and nonfiction. Responds to queries/mss in 3 months.
Illustration Works with 25 illustrators/year. Reviews ms/illustration packages from artists. Submit complete ms with 1 or 2 pieces of art. Illustrations only: Query with samples; send résumé and slides. Responds only if interested. Samples returned with SASE. Samples filed. Originals returned at job's completion.
Photography Assigns work.
Terms Authors paid royalty or work purchased outright. Offers advances. Illustrators paid by the project or royalties; varies. Photographers paid by the project, per photo, or royalties; varies. Manuscripts/artist's guidelines available for #10 SASE.
Tips "Picture books with fresh approaches, not worn themes, are our strongest need at this time. Check to see what's already on the market before submitting your story."

⊡ BRIGHT RING PUBLISHING, INC.

P.O. Box 31338, Bellingham WA 98228. (360)676-8645. Fax: (360)733-0722. E-mail: maryann@brightring.com. Web site: www.brightring.com. **Editor:** MaryAnn Kohl.
- Bright Ring is no longer accepting manuscript submissions.

⊡ BROADMAN & HOLMAN PUBLISHERS

LifeWay Christian Resources, 127 Ninth Ave. N., Nashville TN 37234-0115. Fax: (615)251-3752. Web site: www.broadmanholman.com. **Contact:** Attn: Children's Area. Publishes 4-6 titles/year for ages 0-10. "All books have Christian values/themes."
Nonfiction Picture books: religion. Recently published *Word & Song Bible*, by Stephen Elkins, illustrated by Tim O'Conner; *LullaBible Series for Little Ones*, by Stephen Elkins, illustrated by Ellie Colton; *A Parable About the King*, by Beth Moore, illustrated by Beverly Wamen; *When the Creepy Things Come Out*, by Melody Carlson, illustrated by Susan Reagan.
How to Contact/Writers **Only interested in agented material. Not accepting unsolicited material.** Responds to queries/mss in 6-9 months. Publishes a book 18 months after acceptance.
Illustration Works with 3-4 illustrators/year. Samples returned with SASE; samples filed.
Terms Pays authors royalty of 10-18% based on wholesale price. Offers variable advance. Original artwork returned at job's completion. Book catalog available for 9×12 SAE and 2 first-class stamps. Manuscript guidelines available for SASE.
Tips "We're looking for picture books with good family values; Bible story retellings; modern-day stories for children based on Bible themes and principles. Write us to ask for guidelines before submitting."

CALKINS CREEK BOOKS

Boyds Mills Press, 815 Church St., Honesdale PA 18431. (570)253-1164. Fax: (570)253-0179. E-mail: contact@boydsmillspress.com. Web site: www.boydsmillspress.com. Estab. 2004. **Manuscripts Acquisitions:** J. Deluca. **Art Acquisitions:** Tim Gillner, art director. "We aim to publish books that are a well-written blend of creative writing and extensive research which emphasize important events, people, and places in U.S. history."
Fiction All levels: history. Recently published *Young Patriots*, by Marcella Fisher Anderson and Elizabeth Weiss

Vollstadt (ages 10 and up, historical fiction); *Hour of Freedom*, by Milton Meltzer (ages 12 and up, American history in poetry).

Nonfiction All levels: history. Recently published *The President Is Shot*, by Harold Holzer (ages 8 and up, American history); *George Washington, the Writer*, edited by Carolyn P. Yoder (ages 8 and up, American history); *Dog of Discovery*, by Laurence Pringle (ages 8 and up, American history).

How to Contact/Writers Accepts international submissions. Fiction: Submit outline/synopsis and 3 sample chapters. Nonfiction: Submit outline/synopsis and 3 sample chapters. Considers simultaneous submissions. Responds in 3 months.

Illustration Accepts material from international illustrators. Works with 25 (for all Boyds Mills Press imprints) illustrators/year. Uses both color and b&w. Reviews ms/illustration packages. For ms/illustration packages: Submit ms with 2 pieces of final art. Submit ms/illustration packages to Tim Gillner, art director. Reviews work for future assignments. If interested in illustrating future titles, query with samples. Submit samples to Tim Gillner, art director.

Photography Buys stock images and assigns work. Submit photos to: Tim Gillner, art director. Uses color or b&w 8×10 prints. For first contact, send promo piece (color or b&w).

Terms Authors paid royalty. Offers advance against royalties. Author sees galleys for review. Illustrators see dummies for review. Catalog available for 9×12 SASE with 6 first-class stamps. Offers writer's, artist's guidelines for SASE.

Tips "Read through our recently-published titles and review our catalog. When selecting titles to publish, our emphasis will be on important events, people, and places in U.S. history. Writers are encouraged to submit a detailed bibliography, including secondary and primary sources, and expert reviews with their submissions."

CANDLEWICK PRESS

2067 Massachusetts Ave., Cambridge MA 02140. (617)661-3330. Fax: (617)661-0565. E-mail: bigbear@candlewick.com. Web site: www.candlewick.com. **Manuscript Acquisitions:** Karen Lotz, publisher; Liz Bicknell, editorial director and associate publisher; Joan Powers, editorial director; Mary Lee Donovan, executive editor; Kara LaReau, senior editor; Sarah Ketchersid, editor; Deborah Wayshak, senior editor. **Art Acquisitions:** Anne Moore. Publishes 160 picture books/year; 15 middle readers/year; 15 young adult titles/year. 5% of books by first-time authors. "Our books are truly for children, and we strive for the very highest standards in the writing, illustrating, designing and production of all of our books. And we are not averse to risk."

- Candlewick Press is not accepting queries and unsolicited mss at this time. Candlewick title *Michael Rosen's Sad Book*, by Michael Rosen, illustrated by Quentin Blake, won a 2005 Boston Globe-Horn Book Award for nonfiction.

Fiction Picture books: animal, concept, contemporary, fantasy, history, humor, multicultural, nature/environment, poetry. Middle readers, young adults: contemporary, fantasy, history, humor, multicultural, poetry, science fiction, sports, suspense/mystery. Recently published *The Earth, My Butt, and Other Big Round Things*, by Carolyn Mackler (young adult fiction); *Seeing the Blue Between*, edited by Paul B. Janeczko (young adult poetry collection); *Dragonology*, by Ernest Drake; *Encyclopedia Prehistorica: Dinosaurs*, by Robert Sabuda and Matthew Reinhart.

Nonfiction Picture books: concept, biography, geography, nature/environment. Young readers: biography, geography, nature/environment. Recently published *Top Secret: A Handbook of Codes, Ciphers, and Secret Writing*, by Paul B. Janeczko, illustrated by Jenna LaReau.

Illustration Works with approx. 40 illustrators/year. "We prefer to see a range of styles from artists along with samples showing strong characters (human or animals) in various settings with various emotions." Receives unsolicited illustration packages/dummies from artists. Color or b&w copies only, please; no originals. Illustrations only: Submit color samples to Art Resource Coordinator. Samples returned with SASE; samples filed.

Terms Pays authors royalty of 2½-10% based on retail price. Offers advances. Pays illustrators 2½-10% royalty based on retail price. Sends galleys to authors; dummies to illustrators. Pays photographers 2½-10% royalty. Original artwork returned at job's completion.

CAROLRHODA BOOKS, INC.

Lerner Publishing Group, 241 First Ave. N., Minneapolis MN 55401. Web site: www.lernerbooks.com. **Contact:** Zelda Wagner, submissions editor. Estab. 1969. Accepts submissions only in November. Publishes hardcover originals. Averages 8-10 picture books each year for ages 3-8, 6 fiction titles for ages 7-18, and 2-3 nonfiction titles for various ages.

- Carolrhoda only accepts submissions during the month of November. Also see listing for Lerner Publishing Group and Kar-Ben Publishing. Carolrhoda title *Secrets of a Civil War Submarine: Solving the Mysteries of the H.L. Hunley*, by Sally M. Walker, won the 2006 Sibert Medal.

Fiction For picture books, seeks unique stories with strong child appeal and visual potential. For longer fiction, seeks fresh voices and perspectives; open to both literary novels and high-quality genre novels (mystery, science fiction, fantasy, etc.). Recently published *The Perfect Shot*, by Elaine Marie Alphin YA novel); *Noel*, by Tony Johnston with illustrations by Cheng-Khee Chee (ages 9-12); *Happy Birthday, Mallory*, by Laurie Friedman, illustrated by Tamara Schmitz (ages 9-12); *Think Big*!, by Nancy Carlson (ages 4-8).

Nonfiction Seeks original research paired with outstanding writing on unusual, high-appeal topics that have strong visual potential. Not looking for textbooks, workbooks, songbooks, puzzles, plays, or religious material.

How to Contact/Writers No queries, please. Submit complete ms by mail in November. Responds in 8-12 months. Accepts simultaneous submissions.

Terms Pays royalty on wholesale price or makes outright purchase. Negotiates payments of advance against royalty. Average advance: varied. Book catalog 9×12 SAE with $4.05 postage. Ms guidelines online.

CARTWHEEL BOOKS, for the Very Young

Imprint of Scholastic Inc., 557 Broadway, New York NY 10012. (212)343-4804. Web site: www.scholastic.com. Estab. 1991. Book publisher. Vice President/Editorial Director: Ken Geist. **Manuscript Acquisitions:** Grace Maccarone, executive editor; J. Elizabeth Mills, editor. **Art Acquisitions:** Stephen Hughs, art director; Keirsten Geise, associate art director. Publishes 15-20 picture books/year; 20-25 easy readers/year; 40-45 novelty/concept/board books/year. "With each Cartwheel list, we strive for a pleasing balance among board books and novelty books, hardcover picture books and gift books, nonfiction, paperback storybooks and easy readers. Cartwheel seeks to acquire novelties that are books first; play objects second. Even without its gimmick, a Cartwheel book should stand alone as a valid piece of children's literature. We want all our books to be inviting and appealing, and to have inherent educational and social value. We believe that small children who develop personal relationships with books and grow up with a love of reading, become book consumers, and ultimately better human beings."

- Cartwheel title *Hi! Fly Guy*, by Tedd Arnold, won a 2006 Theodor Seuss Geisel Honor Award.

Fiction Picture books, young readers: humor, suspense/mystery. Average word length: picture books—100-500; easy readers—100-500.

Nonfiction Picture books, young readers: animal, history, nature/environment, science, sports. "Most of our nonfiction is either written on assignment or is within a series. We do not want to see any arts/crafts or cooking." Average word length: picture books—100-1,500; young readers—100-2,000.

How to Contact/Writers Cartwheel Books is no longer accepting unsolicited mss. All unsolicited materials will be returned unread. Fiction/nonfiction: For previously published or agented authors, submit complete ms. Responds to mss in 6 months. Publishes a book within 2 years after acceptance. SASE required with all submissions.

Illustration Works with 100 illustrators/year. Reviews ms/illustration packages from artists. Send ms with dummy. Illustrations only: Query with samples; arrange personal portfolio review; send promo sheet, tearsheets to be kept on file. Contact: Art Director. Responds in 2 months. Samples returned with SASE; samples filed. Please do not send original artwork.

Photography Buys stock and assigns work. Uses photos of kids, families, vehicles, toys, animals. Submit published samples, color promo piece.

Terms Pays advance against royalty or flat fee. Sends galley to authors; dummy to illustrators. Originals returned to artist at job's completion.

Tips "Know what types of books we do. Check out bookstores or catalogs to see where your work would fit best."

MARSHALL CAVENDISH CHILDREN'S BOOKS

Imprint of Marshall Cavendish, 99 White Plains Rd., Tarrytown NY 10591-9001. (914)332-8888. **Editorial Director:** Margery Cuyler. **Art Acquisitions:** Anahid Hamparian, art director. Publishes 20-25 books/year.

Fiction Publishes fiction for all ages/picture books.

How to Contact/Writers Query nonfiction. Submit 3 chapters or more for fiction. No picture book submissions. Enclose SASE.

Illustration Contact: Art Director.

Terms Pays authors/illustrators advance and royalties.

CHARLESBRIDGE

85 Main St., Watertown MA 02472. (617)926-0329. Fax: (617)926-5720. E-mail: tradeeditorial@charlesbridge.com. Web site: www.charlesbridge.com. Estab. 1980. Book publisher. **Contact:** Trade Editorial Department, submissions editor or School Editorial Department. Publishes 60% nonfiction, 40% fiction picture books and early chapter books. Publishes nature, science, multicultural, social studies and fiction picture books. Charlesbridge also has an educational division.

Fiction Picture books and chapter books: "Strong, realistic stories with enduring themes." Considers the following categories: adventure, concept, contemporary, health, history, humor, multicultural, nature/environment, special needs, sports, suspense/mystery. Recently published *Cowboy Slim*, by Julie Danneberg; *Maxwell's Mountain*, by Shari Becker.

Nonfiction Picture books: animal, biography, careers, concept, geography, health, history, multicultural, music/dance, nature/environment, religion, science, social issues, special needs, hobbies, sports. Average word length: picture books—1,000. Recently published *A Mother's Journey*, by Sandra Markle; *Mama's Wild Child/Papa's Wild Child*, by Dianna Hutts Aston.

How to Contact/Writers Send ms and SASE. Accepts exclusive submissions only. Responds to mss in 3 months. Full mss only; no queries.

Illustration Works with 5-10 illustrators/year. Uses color artwork only. Illustrations only: Query with samples; provide résumé, tearsheets to be kept on file. "Send no original artwork, please." Responds only if interested. Samples returned with SASE; samples filed. Originals returned at job's completion.

Terms Pays authors and illustrators in royalties or work purchased outright. Manuscript/art guidelines available for SASE. Exclusive submissions only.

Tips "We want books that have humor and are factually correct. See our Web site for more tips."

CHELSEA HOUSE PUBLISHERS

Facts on File, 132 West 31st Street, 17th Floor, New York, New York 10001. (800)322-8755. Fax: (917)339-0326. E-mail: authors@chelseahouse.com. Web site: www.chelseahouse.com. Specializes in nonfiction, educational material. **Manuscript Acquisitions:** Laurie Likoff, editor-in-chief. **Art Acquisitions:** Rachel Berlin, production director. Imprints: Chelsea Clubhouse; Chelsea House. Produces 150 middle readers/year, 150 young adult books/year. 10% of books by first-time authors

CHICAGO REVIEW PRESS

814 N. Franklin St., Chicago IL 60610. (312)337-0747. Fax: (312)337-5110. E-mail: csherry@chicagoreviewpress.com. Web site: www.chicagoreviewpress.com. **Manuscript Acquisitions:** Cynthia Sherry, associate publisher. **Art Acquisitions:** Gerilee Hundt, art director. Publishes 3-4 middle readers/year; 4 young adult titles/year. 33% of books by first-time authors; 30% of books from agented authors. "Chicago Review Press publishes high-quality, nonfiction, educational activity books that extend the learning process through hands-on projects and accurate and interesting text. We look for activity books that are as much fun as they are constructive and informative."

Nonfiction Picture books, young readers, middle readers and young adults: activity books, arts/crafts, multicultural, history, nature/environment, science. "We're interested in hands-on, educational books; anything else probably will be rejected." Average length: young readers and young adults—144-160 pages. Recently published *Exploring the Solar System*, by Mary Kay Carson (ages 9 and up); *Africa for Kids*, by Harvey Croze (ages 9 and up); *Our Supreme Court*, by Richard Panchyk (ages 10 and up).

How to Contact/Writers Enclose cover letter and no more than table of contents and 1-2 sample chapters; prefers not to receive e-mail queries. Send for guidelines. Responds to queries/mss in 2 months. Publishes a book 1-2 years after acceptance. Will consider simultaneous submissions and previously published work.

Illustration Works with 6 illustrators/year. Uses primarily b&w artwork. Reviews ms/illustration packages from artists. Submit 1-2 chapters of ms with corresponding pieces of final art. Illustrations only: Query with samples, résumé. Responds only if interested. Samples returned with SASE.

Photography Buys photos from freelancers ("but not often"). Buys stock and assigns work. Wants "instructive photos. We consult our files when we know what we're looking for on a book-by-book basis." Uses b&w prints.

Terms Pays authors royalty of $7\frac{1}{2}$-$12\frac{1}{2}$% based on retail price. Offers advances of $3,000-6,000. Pays illustrators by the project (range varies considerably). Pays photographers by the project (range varies considerably). Original artwork "usually" returned at job's completion. Book catalog/ms guidelines available for $3.

Tips "We're looking for original activity books for small children and the adults caring for them—new themes and enticing projects to occupy kids' imaginations and promote their sense of personal creativity. We like activity books that are as much fun as they are constructive. Please write for guidelines so you'll know what we're looking for."

CHILDREN'S BOOK PRESS

2211 Mission St., San Francisco CA 94110. (415)821-3080. Fax: (415)821-3081. E-mail: submissions@childrensbookpress.org. Web site: www.childrensbookpress.org. **Acquisitions:** Dana Goldberg. "Children's Book Press is a nonprofit publisher of multicultural and bilingual children's literature. We publish contemporary stories reflecting the traditions and culture of minorities and new immigrants in the United States. Our goal is to help broaden the base of children's literature in this country to include stories from the African-American, Asian-American, Latino/Chicano and Native American communities. Stories should encourage critical thinking about social and/or personal issues. These ideas must be an integral part of the story."

Fiction Picture books: contemporary, history, multicultural, poetry. Average word length: picture books—750-1,500.

Nonfiction Picture books, young readers: multicultural.

How to Contact/Writers Submit complete ms to Submissions Editor. Responds to mss in roughly 4 months. "Please do not inquire about your manuscript. We can only return/respond to manuscripts with a SASE." Publishes a book 1-2 years after acceptance. Will consider simultaneous submissions.

Illustration Works with 4-5 illustrators/year. Uses color artwork only. Reviews ms/illustration packages from artists. Send ms with 3 or 4 color photocopies. Illustrations only: color copies only, no original artwork. Responds in 8-10 weeks. Samples returned with SASE.

Terms Original artwork returned at job's completion. Book catalog available; ms guidelines available via Web site or with SASE.

Tips "Vocabulary level should be approximately third grade (eight years old) or below. Keep in mind, however, that many of the young people who read our books may be nine, ten, or eleven years old or older. Their life experiences are often more advanced than their reading level, so try to write a story that will appeal to a fairly wide age range. We are especially interested in humorous stories and original stories about contemporary life from the multicultural communities mentioned above by writers *from* those communities."

CHRISTIAN ED. PUBLISHERS

P.O. Box 26639, San Diego CA 92196. (858)578-4700. E-mail: jackelson@cehouse.com. Web site: www.ChristianEdWarehouse.com. Book publisher. **Acquisitions:** Janet Ackelson, assistant editor; Carol Rogers, managing editor; Clint Kruger, design coordinator. Publishes 80 Bible curriculum titles/year. "We publish curriculum for children and youth, including program and student books and take-home papers—all handled by our assigned freelance writers only."

Fiction Young readers: contemporary. Middle readers: adventure, contemporary, suspense/mystery. "We publish fiction for Bible club take-home papers. All fiction is on assignment only."

Nonfiction Publishes Bible curriculum and take-home papers for all ages. Recently published *All-Stars for Jesus*, by Treena Herrington and Letitia Zook, illustrated by Aline Heiser (Bible club curriculum for grades 4-6); *Honeybees Classroom Activity Sheets*, by Janet Miller and Wanda Pelfrey, illustrated by Brenda Warren and Terry Walderhaug (Bible club curriculum for ages 2-3).

How to Contact/Writers Fiction/nonfiction: Query. Responds to queries in 5 weeks. Publishes a book 1 year after acceptance. Send SASE for guidelines or contact Christian Ed. at cgast@cehouse.com.

Illustration Works with 6-7 illustrators/year. Query by e-mail. Contact: Clint Kruger, design coordinator (ckruger @cehouse.com). Responds in 1 month. Samples returned with SASE.

Terms Work purchased outright from authors for 3¢/word. Pays illustrators by the project (range: $300-400/book). Book catalog available for 9×12 SAE and 4 first-class stamps; ms and art guidelines available for SASE or via e-mail.

Tips "Read our guidelines carefully before sending us a manuscript or illustrations. All writing and illustrating is done on assignment only and must be age-appropriate (preschool-6th grade)."

CHRONICLE BOOKS

85 Second St., 6th Floor, San Francisco CA 94105. (415)537-4400. Fax: (415)537-4415. Web site: www.chroniclekids.com. Book publisher. **Acquisitions:** Victoria Rock, associate publisher, children's books. Publishes 50-60 (both fiction and nonfiction) books/year; 5-10% middle readers/year; young adult nonfiction titles/year. 10-25% of books by first-time authors; 20-40% of books from agented writers.

Fiction Picture books, young readers, middle readers: "We are open to a very wide range of topics." Young adults: "We are interested in young adult projects, and do not have specific limitations on subject matter." Recently published *Papa Do You Love Me?*, by Barbara Joosse, illustrated by Barbara Lavallee (ages 0-6, picture books); *I Love the Rain*, by Margaret Park Bridges, illustrated by Christine Davenier (ages 6 and up, picture book).

Nonfiction Picture books, young readers, middle readers, young adults: "We are open to a very wide range of topics." Recently published *Middle School: How to Deal*, by Sara Borden, Sarah Miller, Alex Strikeleather, Maria Valladares, and Miriam Yelton; *Postmark Paris*, by Leslie Jonath.

How to Contact/Writers Fiction/nonfiction: Submit complete ms (picture books); submit outline/synopsis and 3 sample chapters (for older readers). Responds to queries in 1 month; mss in 3-4 months. Publishes a book 1-3 years after acceptance. Will consider simultaneous submissions, as long as they are marked "multiple submissions." Will not consider submissions by fax, e-mail or disk. Must include SASE or projects will not be returned.

Illustration Works with 40-50 illustrators/year. Wants "unusual art, graphically strong, something that will stand out on the shelves. Either bright and modern or very traditional. Fine art, not mass market." Reviews ms/illustration packages from artists. "Indicate if project *must* be considered jointly, or if editor may consider text and art separately." Illustrations only: Submit samples of artist's work (not necessarily from book, but in the envisioned style). Slides, tearsheets and color photocopies OK. (No original art.) Dummies helpful. Résumé helpful. Samples suited to our needs are filed for future reference. Samples not suited to our needs are returned if SASE is enclosed; otherwise samples will be recycled. Queries and project proposals responded to in same time frame as author query/proposals.''

Photography Purchases photos from freelancers. Works on assignment only. Wants nature/natural history photos.

Terms Generally pays authors in royalties based on retail price, ''though we do occasionally work on a flat fee basis.'' Advance varies. Illustrators paid royalty based on retail price or flat fee. Sends proofs to authors and illustrators. Book catalog for 9×12 SAE and 8 first-class stamps; ms guidelines for #10 SASE.

Tips ''Chronicle Books publishes an eclectic mixture of traditional and innovative children's books. We are interested in taking on projects that have a unique bent to them—be it subject matter, writing style, or illustrative technique. As a small list, we are looking for books that will lend us a distinctive flavor. Primarily we are interested in fiction and nonfiction picture books for children ages infant-8 years, and nonfiction books for children ages 8-12 years. We are also interested in developing a middle grade/YA fiction program, and are looking for literary fiction that deals with relevant issues. Our sales reps are witnessing a resistance to alphabet books. And the market has become increasingly competitive. The '80s boom in children's publishing has passed, and the market is demanding high-quality books that work on many different levels.''

☑ CLARION BOOKS

215 Park Ave. S., New York NY 10003. (212)420-5800. Web site: www.clarionbooks.com. **Manuscript Acquisitions:** Dinah Stevenson, associate publisher; Virginia Buckley, contributing editor; Jennifer Greene, senior editor. **Art Acquisitions:** Joann Hill, art director.
- Clarion title *Good Brother, Bad Brother: The Story of Edwin Booth and John Wilkes Booth*, by James Cross Giblin, won a 2005 Boston Globe-Horn Book Honor Award for nonfiction. Their title *Children of the Great Depression*, by Russell Freedman, won the Golden Kite Award for nonfiction for 2005.

How to Contact/Writers Fiction and picture books: Send complete mss. Nonfiction: Send query with up to 3 sample chapters. Must include SASE. Will accept simultaneous submissions if informed. ''Please no e-mail queires or submissions.''

Illustration Send samples (no originals).

Terms Pays illustrators royalty; flat fee for jacket illustration. Pays royalties and advance to writers; both vary. Guidelines available on Web site.

CLEAR LIGHT PUBLISHERS

823 Don Diego, Santa Fe NM 87505. (505)989-9590. Fax: (505)989-9519. Web site: www.clearlightbooks.com. **Acquisitions:** Harmon Houghton, publisher. Publishes 4 middle readers/year; 4 young adult titles/year.

Nonfiction Middle readers and young adults: multicultural, American Indian and Hispanic only.

How to Contact/Writers Fiction/nonfiction: Submit complete ms with SASE. ''No e-mail submissions. Authors supply art. Manuscripts not considered without art or artist's renderings.'' Will consider simultaneous submissions. Responds in 3 months. Only send *copies*.

Illustration Reviews ms/illustration packages from artists. ''No originals please.'' Submit ms with dummy and SASE.

Terms Pays authors royalty of 10% based on wholesale price. Offers advances (average amount: up to 50% of expected net sales within the first year). Sends galleys to authors.

Tips ''We're looking for authentic American Indian art and folklore.''

CONCORDIA PUBLISHING HOUSE

3558 S. Jefferson Ave., St. Louis MO 63118. (314)268-1187. Fax: (314)268-1329. Web site: www.cph.org. **Contact:** Peggy Kuethe. ''Concordia Publishing House produces quality resources which communicate and nurture the Christian faith and ministry of people of all ages, lay and professional. These resources include curriculum, worship aids, books, and religious supplies. We publish approximately 30 quality children's books each year. We boldly provide Gospel resources that are Christ-centered, Bible-based and faithful to our Lutheran heritage.''

Nonfiction Picture books, young readers, middle readers, young adults: activity books, arts/crafts, concept, contemporary, religion. Picture books: poetry. ''All books must contain explicit Christian content.'' Recently published *The Shepherd's Christmas Story*, by Dandi Daley Mackall (picture book for ages 6-10); *Mommy Promises*, by Julie Stiegemeyer (ages over 5-9, picture book).

How to Contact/Writers Submit complete ms (picture books); submit outline/synopsis and sample chapters for longer mss. May also query. Responds to queries in 1 month; mss in 3 months. Publishes a book 2 years after acceptance. Will consider simultaneous submissions. ''No phone queries.''

Illustration Works with 20 illustrators/year. Illustrations only: Query with samples. Contact: Ed Luhmann, art director. Responds only if interested. Samples returned with SASE; samples filed.

Terms Pays authors royalties based on retail price or work purchased outright ($750-2,000). Sends galleys to author. Manuscript guidelines for 1 first-class stamp and a #10 envelope. Pays illustrators by the project.

Tips "Do not send finished artwork with the manuscript. If sketches will help in the presentation of the manuscript, they may be sent. If stories are taken from the Bible, they should follow the Biblical account closely. Liberties should not be taken in fantasizing Biblical stories."

N A JOANNA COTLER BOOKS

HarperCollins Children's Books. 1350 Avenue of the Americas, New York NY 10019. Web site: www.harperchild rens.com. **Senior Vice President and Publisher:** Joanna Cotler. Assistant Editor: Alyson Day. Publishes literary and commercial fiction and nonfiction. Publishes 6 picture books/year; 5 middle readers/year; 2 young adult titles/year. 15% of books by first-time authors.

Fiction Recently published *Wasteland*, by Francesca Lia Block; *Replay*, by Sharon Creech; *More Perfect than the Moon*, by Patricia MacLachlan.

How to Contact/Writers Only interested in agented material.

Illustration Will review ms/illustration packages. Reviews work of illustrators for possible future assignments. Contact: Alison Day, assistant editor. Sample are not kept on file.

Terms Illustrators see dummies for review. Originals returned to artist at job's completion.

N C COTTONWOOD PRESS, INC.

109-B Cameron Drive, Fort Collins CO 80525. Estab. 1986. (907)204-0715. Fax: (907)204-0761. E-mail: cottonwo od@cottonwoodpress.com. Web site: www.cottonwoodpress.com. Specializes in educational material. **President:** Cheryl Thurston. Cottonwood Press strives "to publish material that are effective in the classroom and help kids learn without putting them to sleep, specializing in materials for grades 5-12." Publishes 4 middle reader and young adult book/year. 60% of books by first-time authors.

Nonfiction Middle readers: textbooks. Young Adults/Teens: textbooks. Recently published: *Un-Journaling: daily writing exercises that are NOT personal, NOT introspective, NOT boring*; *Singuini: noodling around with silly songs*; *Phunny Stuph: Proofreading exercised with a sense of humor.*

How to Contact/Writers Nonfiction: Submit complete manuscript. Responds to queries in 2 weeks; mss in 2 months. Publishes a book 6 months-1 year after acceptance. Will consider simultaneous submissions if notified.

Terms Pay royalty of 10-15% based on net sales.

Tips "It is essential that writers familiarize themselves with our Web site to see what we do. The most successful of our authors have used our books in the classroom and know how different they are from ordinary textbooks."

CREATIVE EDUCATION

Imprint of The Creative Company, 123 South Broad St., Mankato MN 56001. (800)445-6209. Fax: (507)388-1364. **Manuscript Acquisitions:** Aaron Frisch. Publishes 5 picture books/year; 20 young readers/year; 30 middle readers/year; 20 young adult titles/year. 5% of books by first-time authors.

Fiction Picture books, young readers, middle readers, young adult/teens: adventure, animal, anthology, contemporary, folktales, history, nature/environment, poetry, sports. Average word length: 1,500. Recently published *The Adventures of Pinocchio*, by Carlo Collodi, illustrated by Roberto Innocanti (ages 10-adult); *A Was an Apple Pie*, illustrated by Etienne Delessert (ages 5-adult); *Galileo's Universe*, by J. Patrick Lewis, illustrated by Tom Curry (ages 12-adult).

Nonfiction Picture books, young readers, middle readers, young adults: animal, arts/crafts, biography, careers, geography, health, history, hobbies, multicultural, music/dance, nature/environment, religion, science, social issues, special needs, sports. Average word length: young readers—500; middle readers—3,000; young adults-6,500. Recently published *My First Look At Science*, by Melissa Gish (age 7, young reader); *The Wild World of Animals*, by Mary Hoff (age 11, middle reader); *Martin Luther King, Jr.*, by Jennifer Fandel (age 14, young adult/teen).

How to Contact/Writers Fiction: Submit complete ms. Nonfiction: Submit outline/synopsis and 2 sample chapters. Responds to queries in 6 weeks; mss in 3 months. Publishes book 2 years after acceptance. Do not accept illustration packages.

Photography Buys stock. Contact: Nicole Becker, photo editor. Model/property releases not required; captions required. Uses b&w prints. Submit cover letter, promo piece. Ms. and photographer guidelines available for SAE.

Tips "We are primarily a nonfiction publisher and are very selective about fiction picture books, publishing five or fewer annually. Nonfiction submissions should be in series (of 4, 6, or 8), rather than single."

CRICKET BOOKS

Carus Publishing Company, P.O. Box 300, Peru IL 61354. (815)224-5803, ext. 656. E-mail: cricketbooks@carusp ub.com. Web site: www.cricketbooks.net. **Art Acquisitions:** Ron McCutchan.

• Cricket books has a moratorium on unsolicited manuscripts. Submissions from agents and authors already working with Cricket Books or magazines are still welcome. Watch Web site for updates.

How to Contact Not accepting unsolicited mss. See Web site for details and updates on submissions policy.

Illustration Works with 4 illustrators/year. Use color and b&w. Illustration only: Submit samples, tearsheets. Contact: Ron McCutchan, 315 Fifth St., Peru IL 61354. Responds only if interested. Samples returned with SASE; sample filed.

Tips "You may consider submitting your manuscript to one of our magazines, as we sometimes serialize longer selections and always welcome age-appropriate stories, poems, and nonfiction articles."

DARBY CREEK PUBLISHING

7858 Industrial Pkwy., Plain City OH 43064. (614)873-7955. Fax: (614)873-7135. E-mail: info@darbycreekpublishing .com. **Manuscript/Art Acquisitions:** Tanya Dean, editorial director. Publishes 10-15 children's books/year.

Fiction Middle readers, young adult. Recently published *The Warriors*, by Joseph Bruchac (ages 10 and up); *Dog Days*, by David Lubar (ages 10 and up); *Four Things My Geeky-Jock-of-a-Best-Friend Must Do in Europe*, by Jane Harrington.

Nonfiction Middle readers: biography, history, science, sports. Recently published *Albinio Animals*, by Kelly Milner Halls, illustrated by Rick Spears; *Miracle: The True Story of the Wreck of the Sea Venture*, by Gail Karwoski.

How to Contact/Writers Accepts international material only with U.S. postage on SASE for return; no IRCs. Fiction/nonfiction: Submit publishing history and/or résumé and complete ms for short works or outline/synopsis and 2-3 sample chapters for longer works, such as novels. Responds in 6 weeks. Does not consider previously published work.

Illustration Illustrations only: Send photocopies and résumé with publishing history. "Indicate which samples we may keep on file and include SASE and appropriate packing materials for any samples you wish to have returned."

Terms Offers advance-against-royalty contracts.

Tips "We like to see nonfiction with a unique slant that is kid friendly, well-researched and endorsed by experts. We're interested in fiction or nonfiction with sports themes for future lists. No series, please."

⬚ MAY DAVENPORT, PUBLISHERS

26313 Purissima Rd., Los Altos Hills CA 94022-4539. (650)947-1275. Fax: (650)947-1373. E-mail: mdbooks@eart hlink.net. Web site: www.maydavenportpublishers.com. **Acquisitions:** May Davenport, editor/publisher. Publishes 1-2 picture books/year; 2-3 young adult titles/year. 99% of books by first-time authors. Seeks books with literary merit. "We like to think that we are selecting talented writers who have something humorous to write about today's unglued generation in 30,000-50,000 words for teens and young adults in junior/senior high school before they become tomorrow's 'functional illiterates.' We are interested in publishing literature that teachers in middle and high schools can use in their Language Arts, English and Creative Writing courses. There's more to literary fare than the chit-chat Internet dialog and fantasy trips on television with cartoons or humanoids." This publisher is overstocked with juvenile books.

Fiction Young adults (ages 15-18): contemporary, humorous fictional literature for use in English courses in junior-senior high schools in U.S. Average word length: 40,000-60,000. Recently published *Surviving Sarah, the Sequel: Brown Bug & China Doll*, by Dinah Leigh (novel set in post-WWII Manhattan, ages 15-18); *The Lesson Plan*, by Irvin Gay (about an illiterate black boy who grows up to become a teacher, ages 15-18); *A Life on the Line*, by Michael Horton (about a juvenile delinquent boy who becomes a teacher, ages 15-18); *Making My Escape*, by David Lee Finkle (about a young boy who daydreams movie-making in outer space to escape unhappy family life, ages 12-18).

Nonfiction Teens: humorous. Recently published *The Runaway Game*, by Kevin Casey (a literary board game of street life in Hollywood, ages 15-18).

How to Contact/Writers Fiction: Query. Responds to queries/mss in 3 weeks. Mss returned with SASE. Publishes a book 6-12 months after acceptance.

Illustration Works with 1-2 illustrators/year. "Have enough on file for future reference." Responds only if interested. Samples returned with SASE; samples filed. Originals returned at job's completion.

Terms Pays authors royalty of 15% based on retail price; negotiable. Pays "by mutual agreement, no advances." Pays illustrators by the project (range: $75-350). Book catalog, ms guidelines free on request with SASE.

Tips "Write stories with teen narrators and activities that today's teenages can relate to. Entertain teenagers who don't, can't, won't read printed pages so your book will be useful to teachers in high schools nationwide."

DAWN PUBLICATIONS

12402 Bitney Springs Rd., Nevada City CA 95959. (530)274-7775. Fax: (530)275-7778. Web site: www.dawnpub. com. Book publisher. Co-Publishers: Muffy Weaver and Glenn J. Hovemann. **Acquisitions:** Glenn J. Hovemann. Publishes works with holistic themes dealing with nature. "Dawn Publications is dedicated to inspiring in children a deeper appreciation and understanding of nature."

Fiction Picture books exploring relationships with nature. No fantasy or legend.

Nonfiction Picture books: animal, nature/environment. Prefers "creative nonfiction."

How to Contact/Writers Query or submit complete ms. Responds to queries/mss in 3 months maximum. Publishes a book 1 year after acceptance. Will consider simultaneous submissions.

Illustration Works with 5 illustrators/year. Will review ms/illustration packages from artists. Query; send ms with dummy. Illustrations only: Query with samples, résumé.

Terms Pays authors royalty based on net sales. Offers advance. Book catalog and ms guidelines available online.

Tips Looking for "picture books expressing nature awareness with inspirational quality leading to enhanced self-awareness. Usually no animal dialogue."

DELACORTE AND DOUBLEDAY BOOKS FOR YOUNG READERS

Random House Children's Books, 1745 Broadway, Mail Drop 9-2, New York NY 10019. (212)782-9000. Web sites: www.randomhouse.com/kids, www.randomhouse.com/teens. Imprints of Random House Children's Books. 75% of books published through agents.

- Delacorte published middle-grade and young adult fiction; the Doubleday list specializes in picture books.

How to Contact/Writers Unsolicited mss are only being accepted as submissions to either the Delacorte Dell Yearling Contest for a First Middle-Grade Novel or Delacorte Press Contest for a First Young Adult Novel (contemporary). See Web site for submission guidelines. Query letters for novels are accepted when addresses to a specific editor and must be accompanied by a SASE. No e-mail queires.

Illustration Contact: Isabel Warren-Lynch, executive art and design director. Responds only if interested. Samples returned with SASE; samples filed.

Terms Pays illustrators and photographers by the project or royalties. Original artwork returned at job's completion.

🖳 DIAL BOOKS FOR YOUNG READERS

Penguin Young Readers Group, 345 Hudson St., New York NY 10014. Web site: www.penguin.com. Associate Publishers and Vice President and Publisher: Lauri Hornik. **Acquisitions:** Nancy Mercado, editor; Rebecca Waugh, editor; Liz Waniewski, associate editor; Jessica Dandino, assistant editor. **Art Director:** Lily Malcom. Publishes 35 picture books/year; 3 young readers/year; 6 middle readers/year; 9 young adult titles/year.

- Dial title *Amanda Pig and the Really Hot Day*, by Jean Van Leeuwen, illustrated by Ann Schweninger, won a 2006 Theodor Seuss Geisel Honor Award.

Fiction Picture books, young readers: adventure, animal, fantasy, folktales, history, humor, multicultural, poetry, sports. Middle readers, young adults: adventure, fantasy, folktales, history, humor, multicultural, poetry, problem novels, science fiction, sports, mystery/adventure. Published *A Year Down Yonder*, by Richard Peck (ages 10 and up); *The Sea Chest*, by Toni Buzzeo, illustrated by Mary Grand Pre (all ages, picture book); *A Penguin Pup for Pinkerton*, by Steven Kellogg (ages 3-7, picture book).

Nonfiction Will consider query letters for submissions of outstanding literary merit. Picture books, young readers, middle readers: biography, history, sports. Young adults: biography, history, sports. Recently published *A Strong Right Arm*, by Michelle Y. Green (ages 10 and up); *Dirt on their Skirts*, by Doreen Rappaport and Lyndall Callan (ages 4-8, picture book).

How to Contact/Writers "Due to the overwhelming number of unsolicited manuscripts we receive, we at Dial Books for Young Readers have had to change our submissions policy: As of August 1, 2005, Dial will no longer respond to your unsolicited submission unless interested in publishing it. Please do not include SASE with your submission. You will not hear from dial regarding the status of your submission unless we are interested, in which case you can expect a reply from us within four months. We accept entire picture book manuscripts and a maximum of 10 pages for longer works (novels, easy-to-reads). When submitting a portion of a longer work, please provide an accompanying cover letter that briefly describes your manuscript's plot, genre (i.e. easy-to-read, middle grade or YA novel), the intended age group, and your publishing credits, if any."

Illustration "Art samples should be sent to attn: Dial Design and will not be returned without SASE. Never send original art. Please do not phone, fax, or e-mail to inquire after your art submission."

Terms Pays authors and illustrators in royalties based on retail price. Average advance payment varies. Catalogue available for 9×12 envelope with four 37¢ stamps. "This is one way to become informed as to the style, subject matter, and format of our books."

Tips "Because confirmation postcards are easily separated from or hidden within the manuscript, we do not encourage you to include them with your submission. Please send only one manuscript at a time. Never send cassettes, original artwork, marketing plans, or faxes and do not send submissions by e-mail. Please know that we only keep track of requested manuscripts; we cannot track unsolicited submissions due to the volume we receive each day, so kindly refrain from calling, faxing or e-mailing to inquire after the status of an unsolicited submission as we will be unable to assist you. If you have not received a reply from us after four months, you can safely assume that we are not presently interested in publishing your work."

🅰 DK PUBLISHING, INC.

375 Hudson St., New York NY 10014. Web site: www.dk.com. **Acquisitions:** submissions editor. "DK publishes photographically illustrated nonfiction for children ages 4 and up."

- DK Publishing does not accept unagented manuscripts or proposals.

Christopher Paolini

Immersed in a world of duels, dragons, dwarves & villains

Book Publishers

Christopher Paolini is the author of the well-loved and best-selling fantasy novels *Eragon* and *Eldest,* the first two books in his Inheritance trilogy. Described by the *Seattle Post-Intelligencer* as a "fantasy wunderkind," Paolini has legions of fans eagerly awaiting the final book in his trilogy.

Paolini began writing *Eragon* at age 15. After several years of writing and revision, he and his family self-published the 600-page-plus tome. The book gained attention, and, with a little quiet intervention from Carl Hiaasen, the title was picked up by Knopf. Both *Eragon* and *Eldest* have held steady spots on *The New York Times* Best-seller List (*Eldest* at 25-weeks-and-counting at this writing), often above none other than Harry Potter.

Paolini revels in his fantasy world, takes joy in plotting ("storytelling in its purest and most magical form") and refers to editing as torture. "I discovered that editing is really another word for someone ruthlessly tearing apart your work with a big smile, all the while telling you that it will make the book so much better," he says. "And it did, though it felt like splinters of hot bamboo being driven into my tender eyeballs."

Here Paolini discusses creating the world of Alagaësia, shares his process for writing his popular fantasy novels, and talk about life after trilogy.

You've said before that clear writing is the result of clear thinking, and that you plot everything out before you start writing, which makes the writing easier. Does the creative work occur for you in the plotting, or in the writing?
Both processes require creativity, albeit in differing amounts. Before I started *Eragon,* I hammered out the trilogy's overall structure, which demanded quite a bit of my attention before I was satisfied with it. Now that I'm working on the third book, I rarely have to worry about the underlying skeleton, since the events I seek to portray were determined years ago.

I enjoy plotting my books; it allows me to move beyond the initial concept that inspired me and to experience the entire story for the first time, to view it in an idealized form and say, "Yes! *That's* what it should be!" It's storytelling in its purest and most magical form. This stage requires far less effort than the actual writing, but it's a crucial process, for if I make a mistake here, it could mean weeks or months of revisions down the road. The book might even have to be abandoned.

Still, most of the work happens when I'm staring at a blank page—electronic or otherwise—trying to coalesce sights, smells, sounds, emotions, and other intangibles into precise sentences, all the while thinking, *Is that the right word? Does it rhyme? Is it supposed to rhyme? Should it alliterate? Did I just repeat myself? Does it flow? Is that what I really want to say? Do I need more? Do I need less? . . . Does it work?*

Has there ever been a point in your writing when the plot veered off in a direction that you didn't expect? Or do you adhere pretty faithfully to your outlines?

For the most part, I'm faithful to my initial outline. However, one has to be open to change. My characters have sometimes insisted on veering from their preordained fates to do something entirely different— such as Eragon blessing the child in Book I, Saphira getting drunk in Book II, and everything about Angela the herbalist.

You were homeschooled by your parents. Do you think your creative process and your desire to write were shaped by homeschooling?

Homeschooling gave me the freedom to explore subjects that caught my interest, whether it was dinosaurs, Icelandic sagas, or Egyptian pyramids. It allowed me to work at my own pace and graduate from high school early, so I had a couple of years free to write before I had to make a decision about college. I had time to think, to daydream about adventures, to create the world of Alagaësia.

Both _Eragon_ and _Eldest_ are weighty, wonderful books. How did you discipline yourself to sit down and actually get to the business of writing, and to put all those words on the page?

Jacket art © John Jude Palencar. Reprinted with permission.

"Fantasy," says author Christopher Paolini, "is one of the oldest genres for coming-of-age stories." Paolini's _Eldest_ is the much-anticipated and weighty sequel to his best-selling fantasy novel _Eragon_, and the second book in his Inheritance trilogy. "Eragon's journey to maturity is well handled [in _Eldest_]," says _School Library Journal_. "He wrestles earnestly with definitions for good and evil, and he thoughtfully examines the question of good at what price."

I worked on _Eragon_ night and day simply because I enjoyed telling the story. Nothing brought me as much satisfaction. Then, after about a year, writing became a habit.

Writing is my job, and I treat it as such. When I get up in the morning, I grab breakfast, then write until late afternoon, when I stop to exercise. My family and I watch a movie with dinner, then, after helping with the dishes, I often write more in the evening. I follow this schedule almost every day, except during book tours.

You based _Eragon_ on the archetypal maturation plot. What about this archetypal plot stood out to you—why did it appeal to you?

I was drawn to the very thing that defines an archetypal maturation plot: the journey of a young man or woman from adolescence into adulthood. This subject fascinated me in my late preteens and early teens, as it was a transformation that I knew I would have to endure. Coming-of-age stories acted as a sort of map for me, an illustration of what I could expect and of how I should comport myself. Fantasy was just the setting that I preferred the most.

Saving the day, with a dragon at your side nonetheless, is the fantasy of many a young reader, and your books allow the readers to dream. Do you think the writing would have had the same depth if you had been older when you wrote it?
I'll be able to answer this question much better in 20 to 40 years, but the advantages to being a young author are enthusiasm and intimate knowledge of your own age group.

You're maturing as *Eragon* matures. How has this helped you to make the character more realistic? Where do you both intersect, and where do you differ?
Eragon did start as me. However, over the course of the first book, he does many things that I haven't—such as ride a dragon, fight monsters, and use magic—and these experiences conspired to differentiate him from me. In some ways the character Eragon and I have grown together, facing the greater world as public figures. But overall, we have diverged. Eragon is now his own person, similar to me in some respects, but possessing a unique history, likes, dislikes, friends, and family. I find it interesting to delve inside his mind, but his mind is no longer my own.

Why does fantasy writing appeal to you? Why not mystery or a traditional coming-of-age novel?
The Inheritance trilogy *is* a traditional coming-of-age story. What else are Wagner's Ring cycle—and the Niebelunglied upon which it is based—the Grimm folktales, the first part of the King Arthur myth, The Wizard of Oz, and many others, but dyed-in-the-wool bildungsromans? Fantasy is one of the oldest genres for coming-of-age stories.

And fantasy is perhaps the oldest form of storytelling. Mythic tales of terrible monsters and of the amazing feats of heroes and all-powerful gods and goddesses abound in folklore from around the world. Even the Homeric tales mention one-eyed giants and such. Told around campfires, whispered to children at bedtime, and chanted in castle halls, fantastic tales, perhaps based on some real events, have captured peoples' imaginations throughout the ages.

I love the exercise of pure imagination that is fantasy. It sweeps me into a world of wonder and awe, stuns me with beautiful images and phrases, has thrilling action, and gives me new insight into the minds and hearts of people.

The fantasy world you've created is complete with its own languages and history. Is there more to this world that we'll ever see in the books? That is, has the world taken on a life beyond the pages?
Most of my waking hours are spent thinking about Alagaësia. It should come as no surprise then, that the information that appears within my trilogy is only the tip of the iceberg, in regard to languages, histories, and peoples. This probably holds true for every author who does research, whether for an imaginary or real world. The challenge is to winnow the essential from the nonessential.

What came first in this fantasy world? What was the first image or character you seized upon, the one that brought the rest of the book to life?
It was the image—inspired by *Jeremy Thatcher, Dragon Hatcher*, by Bruce Coville—of a dragon egg appearing before a young man deep within a dark pinewood forest. I knew nothing beyond that, only that I empathized with that nameless youth and that I wanted to find out what happened to him next.

You've said before that you do a lot of research to make your writing more realistic. For instance, the Elven languages in the book are based on Old Norse. You've made a set of chain mail armor in the past. What other kinds of fantasy meets real-life research do you do, and why is this essential for the writing?

You can certainly write convincingly about something that you've never seen or done yourself—like murder, for example—but it sure helps to have a touchstone within your own life, something that you can relate to, in order to lend your account authenticity. I find that doing some of the same things as my characters allows me to better understand their world, as well as think of descriptions that would not otherwise occur to me.

In addition to the activities already mentioned, I've forged my own knives and swords, spun wool, camped in the Beartooth Mountains, made my own bow, built survival shelters, learned to track game, fletched arrows, felled trees, and challenged myself with other amusing ventures. However, I never allow research to interfere with my writing. If I'm in the middle of a paragraph and I need to know what a backstrap loom looks like, I'll look it up later and, in the interim, rely upon writers' most valuable tool: imagination.

How do you see the Eragon books fitting within the larger canon of fantasy writing? What unique niche do you see them occupying?

The Inheritance trilogy can easily be grouped with other epic, coming-of-age fantasy series. Beyond that, I leave it to others to place my books within the genre. My only concern is telling the best story I can.

How is work progressing on the third book in your trilogy? Any sneak peeks for avid fans?

The final novel proceeds apace, to my great joy. It continues Eragon and Saphira's adventures throughout Alagaësia and contains the usual assortment of duels, dragons, dwarves, and villains, while resolving the many issues introduced in *Eragon* and *Eldest.* Beyond that, I must beg readers' patience until the book is published, when all will be revealed.

What hopes and goals do you have for yourself as a writer once the third book is completed? Will you stay with fantasy, return to these characters, or try your hand in a new genre, or even a new creative act?

Once the Inheritance trilogy is finished, I plan to take a break and catch up on my reading. I have many other stories to tell, in fantasy and other genres. When I'm ready, I'll choose the one that inspires me the most and dive into it.

—*Meg Leder*

Book Publishers

☐ DNA PRESS, LLC

P.O. Box 572, Eagleville PA 19408. Fax: (501)694-5495. E-mail: editors@dnapress.com. Web site: www.dnapress.com. **Acquisitions:** Xela Schenk. Publishes 1 picture book/year; 2 middle readers/year; 4 young adult titles/year. 75% of books by first-time authors.

Fiction Picture books: health. Young adults: adventure, contemporary, fantasy.

Nonfiction All levels: science, investing for children, business for children.

How to Contact/Writers Fiction/nonfiction: Submit complete, disposable ms and SASE. Responds to queries in 1 month; mss in 6 weeks. Publishes book 9-12 months after acceptance.

Illustration Works with 1 illustrator/year. Uses b&w artwork only. Reviews ms/illustration packages from artists. Send ms with dummy. Illustrations only: Send Web page. Responds in 1 month. Samples not returned.

Terms Pays authors royalty of 8-15% based on net sales. Pays illustrators and photographers by the project. Sends galleys to authors; dummies to illustrators.

Tips Children's writers and illustrators should pay attention to "how-to books and books in which science knowledge is communicated to the reader. We focus on bringing science to the young reader in various forms of fiction and nonfiction books. For updates, see our Web site or the Web site of our distributor, IPG Book (www.ipgbook.com)."

DOG-EARED PUBLICATIONS

P.O. Box 620863, Middletown WI 53562-0863. (608)831-1410 or (608)831-1410. Fax: (608)831-1410. E-mail: field@dog-eared.com. Web site: www.dog-eared.com. **Art Acquisitions:** Nancy Field, publisher. Publishes 2-3 middle readers/year. 1% of books by first-time authors. "Dog-Eared Publications creates action-packed nature books for children. We aim to turn young readers into environmentally aware citizens and to foster a love for science and nature in the new generation.

Nonfiction Middle readers: activity books, animal, nature/environment, science. Average word length: varies. Recently published *Discovering Sharks and Rays*, by Nancy Field, illustrated by Michael Maydak (middle readers, activity book); *Leapfrogging Through Wetlands*, by Margaret Anderson, Nancy Field and Karen Stephenson, illustrated by Michael Maydak (middle readers, activity book); *Ancient Forests*, by Margaret Anderson, Nancy Field and Karen Stephenson, illustrated by Sharon Torvik (middle readers, activity book).

How to Contact/Writers Nonfiction: **Currently not accepting unsolicited mss**.

Illustration Works with 2-3 illustrators/year. Reviews ms/illustration packages from artists. Submit query and a few art samples. Illustrations only: Query with samples. Responds only if interested. Samples not returned; samples filed. "Interested in realistic, nature art!"

Terms Pays authors royalty based on wholesale price. Offers advances (amount varies). Pays illustrators royalty based on wholesale price. Sends galleys to authors. Originals returned to artist at job's completion. Brochure available for SASE and 1 first-class stamp or on Web site.

DUTTON CHILDREN'S BOOKS

Penguin Group (USA), 345 Hudson St., New York NY 10014-4502. (212)414-3700. Web site: www.penguin.com/youngreaders. **Acquisitions:** Stephanie Owens Lurie (picture books, middle-grade fiction); Lucia Monfried (easy-to-read, middle-grade fiction); Maureen Sullivan (middle-grade fiction, picture books); Mark McVeigh (picture books, middle-grade fiction, upper young adult fiction), Julie Strauss-Gabel (picture books, middle-grade fiction, young adult). **Art Acquisitions:** Sara Reynolds, art director. Publishes approximately 50% fiction—fewer picture books, mostly YA and mid-grade novels. 10% of books by first-time authors.

- Dutton is open to query letters only. Their title *The Schwa Was Here*, by Neal Shusterman, won a 2005 Boston Globe-Horn Book Award for fiction and poetry.

Fiction Picture books: adventure, animal, history, humor, multicultural, nature/environment, poetry, contemporary. Young readers: adventure, animal, contemporary, fantasy. Middle readers: adventure, animal, contemporary, fantasy, history, multicultural, nature/environment. Young adults: adventure, animal, contemporary, fantasy, history, multicultural, nature/environment, poetry. Recently published *The Schwa Was Here*, by Neal Shusterman (middle grade); *Skippyjon Jones*, by Juday Schachner (picture book); *Looking for Alaska*, by John Green (young adult).

Nonfiction Picture books. Recently published *With a Little Bit of Luck*, by Dennis Fradin.

How to Contact/Writers Query only. Does not accept unsolicited mss. Responds to queries in 3 months. Publishes a book 12-18 months after acceptance. Will consider simultaneous submissions.

Illustration Works with 40-60 illustrators/year. Reviews ms/illustration packages from artists. Query first. Illustrations only: Query with samples; send résumé, portfolio, slides—no original art please. Responds to art samples only if interested. Samples returned with SASE; samples filed. Original artwork returned at job's completion.

Terms Pays authors royalty of 4-10% based on retail price or outright purchase. Book catalog, ms guidelines for SAE with 8 first-class stamps. Pays illustrators royalty of 2-5% based on retail price unless jacket illustration—then pays by flat fee. Pays photographers by the project or royalty based on retail price.

Tips "Avoid topics that appear frequently. Illustrators: "We would like to see samples and portfolios from potential illustrators of picture books (full color), young novels (b&w) and jacket artists (full color)." Dutton is actively building its fiction lists, particularly upper YA titles. Humor welcome across all genres.

EDCON PUBLISHING

(formerly Imperial International), 30 Montauk Blvd., Oakdale NY 11769. (631)567-7227. Fax: (631)567-8745. E-mail: laura@edconpublishing.com. Web site: www.edconpublishing.com. **Manuscript Acquisitions:** Laura Solimene. Publishes 12 young readers/year, 12 middle readers/year, 12 young adult titles/year. 30% of books by first-time authors. Looking for workbooks in the areas of math, science, reading and history that include student activities. All classic adaptations are assigned.

Fiction Young readers, middle readers, young adult/teens: hi-lo. Average word length: young readers—4,000; middle readers—6,000; young adults—8,000. Recently published *A Midsummer Night's Dream*, adaptation by Laura Algieri; *Twelfth Night*, adaptation by Julianne Davidow; *The Merchant of Venice*, adaptation by Rachel Armington.

How to Contact/Writers Fiction and workbooks: Submit outline/synopsis and 1 sample chapter. Responds to

queries/mss in 1 month. Publishes book 6 months after acceptance. Will consider simultaneous submissions.
Illustration Works with 6 illustrators/year. Reviews ms/illustration packages from artists. Query. Illustrations only: Send postcard samples, SASE. Responds in 2 weeks. Samples returned with SASE; samples filed.
Terms Work purchased outright from authors for up to $1,000. Pays illustrators by the project (range: $250-$750). Book catalog available for 8½×11 SASE and $1.35 postage; ms and art guidelines available for SAE. Catalog available on Web site.

🖬 EDUCATORS PUBLISHING SERVICE

Imprint of Delta Education, LLC, P.O. Box 9031, Cambridge MA 02139-9031. (617)547-6706. Fax: (617)547-3805. E-mail: epsbooks@epsbooks.com. Web site: www.epsbooks.com. **Manuscript Acquisitions:** Charlie Heinle. **Art Acquisitions:** Sheila Neylon, senior editorial manager. Publishes 30-40 educational books/year. 50% of books by first-time authors.
How to Contact/Writers Responds to queries/mss in 5 weeks. Publishes book 6-12 months after acceptance. Will consider e-mail submissions, simultaneous submissions, previously published work. See Web site for submission guidelines.
Illustration Works with 12-18 illustrators/year. Reviews ms/illustration packages from artists. Query. Illustrations only: Query with samples; send promo sheet. Responds only if interested. Samples not returned; samples filed.
Photography Buys stock and assigns work. Submit cover letter, samples.
Terms Pays authors royalty of 5-12% based on retail price or work purchased outright from authors. Offers advances. Pays illustrators and photographers by the project. Sends galleys to authors. Book catalog free. All imprints included in a single catalog. Catalog available on Web site.
Tips "We accept queries from educators writing for the school market, primarily in the reading and language arts areas, grades K-8. We are interested in materials that follow certain pedagogical constraints (such as decodable texts and leveled readers) and we would consider queries and samples from authors who might be interested in working with us on ongoing or future projects."

🖬 EDUPRESS, INC.

W5527 State Road 106, Ft. Atkinson WI 53538. (920)563-9571. Fax: (920)563-7395. E-mail: edupress@highsmith.com. Web site: www.edupressinc.com. **Manuscript Acquisitions:** Liz Johnson, editor. "Our mission is to create products that make kids want to go to school!"
How to Contact/Writers Nonfiction: Submit complete ms. Responds to queries/mss in 3 months. Publishes book 1-2 years after acceptance.
Illustration Query with samples. Contact. Contact: Sandy Harris, product development manager. Responds only if interested. Samples returned with SASE.
Photography Buys stock.
Terms Work purchased outright from authors. Pays illustrators by the project. Book catalog available at no cost. Catalog available on Web site.
Tips "We are looking for unique, quality supplemental materials for Pre-K through eighth grade. We publish all subject aread in many different formats, including games. Our materials are intended for classroom and home schooling use."

EERDMAN'S BOOKS FOR YOUNG READERS

An imprint of Wm. B. Eerdmans Publishing Co., 255 Jefferson Ave. SE, Grand Rapids MI 49503. (616)459-4591. Fax: (616)776-7683. E-mail: youngreaders@eerdmans.com. Web site: www.eerdmans.com/youngreaders. We are an independent book packager/producer. **Writers contact:** Judy Zylstra, editor-in-chief. **Illustrators contact:** Gayle Brown, art director. Produces 14 picture books/year; 3 middle readers/year; 3 young adult books/year. 10% of books by first-time authors. "We seek high-quality manuscripts that explore all aspects of human experience. At one time we only published religious material but we have broadened our interest and now publish books for the school, library, and general trade markets."
Fiction Picture books: animal, concept, contemporary, folktales, history, humor, multicultural, nature/environment, poetry, religion, special needs, social issues, sports, suspense. Young readers: animal, concept, contemporary, folktales, history, humor, multicultural, poetry, religion, special needs, social issues, sports, suspense. Middle readers: adventure, contemporary, fantasy, folktales, history, humor, multicultural, nature/environment, problem novels, religion, social issues, sports, suspense. Young adults/teens: adventure, contemporary, fantasy, folktales, history, humor, multicultural, nature/environment, problem novels, religion, sports, suspense. Average word length: picture books—1,000; middle readers—15,000; young adult—45,000. Recently published *Circles of Hope*, by Karen Lynn Williams, illustrated by Linda Saport (picture book, ages 4 and up); *Going for the Record*, by Julie Swanson (novel, ages 12 and up); *Mississippi Morning*, by Ruth Vander Zee, illustrated by Floyd Cooper (picture book, ages 9 and up).
Nonfiction Middle readers: biography, history, multicultural, nature/environment, religion, science, social issues.

Young adults/teens: biography, history, multicultural, nature/environment, religion, science, social issues. Average word length: middle readers—35,000; young adult books—35,000. Recently published *Maria Mitchell*, by Beatrice Gormley (ages 10 and up, biography); *Dororthy Day*, by Deborah Kent (ages 10 and up, biography).

How to Contact/Writers Accepts international submissions. Fiction/nonfiction: Query. Responds to queries/ mss in 3-5 months. "We no longer acknowledge or respond to unsolicited manuscripts. Exceptions will be made only for exclusive submissions marked as such on outside envelope."

Illustration Accepts material from international illustrators. Works with 10-12 illustrators/year. Uses color artwork primarily. Reviews work for future assignments. If interested in illustrating future titles, send promo sheet. Submit samples to Gayle Brown, art director. Samples not returned. Samples filed.

Terms Offers advance against royalties. Author sees galleys for review. Illustrators see proofs for review. Originals returned to artist at job's completion. Catalog available for 8×10 SASE and 4 first-class stamps. Offers writer's guidelines for SASE. See Web site for writer's guidelines.

Tips "Find out who Eerdmans is before submitting a manuscript. Look at our Web site and check out our books."

ENSLOW PUBLISHERS INC.

P.O. Box 398, 40 Industrial Rd., Berkeley Heights NJ 07922-0398. Fax: (908)771-0925. E-mail: info@enslow.c om. Web site: www.enslow.com or www.myreportlinks.com. **Acquisitions:** Brian D. Enslow, vice president. Imprint: MyReportLinks.com Books. Publishes 30 young readers/year; 70 middle readers/year; 100 young adult titles/year. 30% of books by first-time authors.

- Enslow Imprint MyReportLinks.com Books produces books on animals, states, presidents, continents, countries, and a variety of other topics for middle readers and young adults, and offers links to online sources of information on topics covered in books.

Nonfiction Young readers, middle readers, young adults: animal, arts/crafts, biography, careers, geography, health, history, multicultural, nature/environment, science, social issues, sports. Middle readers, young adults: hi-lo. "Enslow is moving into the elementary (grades 3-4) level and is looking for authors who can write biography and suggest other nonfiction themes at this level." Average word length: young readers—2,000; middle readers—5,000; young adult—18,000. Published *It's About Time! Science Projects*, by Robert Gardner (grades 3-6, science); *Georgia O'Keeffe: Legendary American Painter*, by Jodie A. Shull (grades 6-12, biography); *California: A MyReportLinks.com Book*, by Jeff Savaga (grades 5-8, social studies/history).

How to Contact/Writers Nonfiction: Send for guidelines. Query. Responds to queries/mss in 2 weeks. Publishes a book 18 months after acceptance. Will not consider simultaneous submissions.

Illustration Submit résumé, business card or tearsheets to be kept on file. Responds only if interested. Samples returned with SASE only.

Terms Pays authors royalties or work purchased outright. Pays illustrators by the project. Pays photographers by the project or per photo. Sends galleys to authors. Book catalog/ms guidelines available for $3, along with an $8^1/_2 \times 11$ SAE and $2 postage or via Web site.

FACTS ON FILE

132 W. 31st St., New York NY 10001. (212)967-8800. Fax: (212)967-9196. E-mail: editorial@factsonfile.com. Web site: www.factsonfile.com. Estab. 1941. Book publisher. Editorial Director: Laurie Likoff. **Acquisitions:** Frank Darmstadt, science and technology/nature; Nicole Bowen, American history and women's studies; Jeff Soloway, language and literature; Owen Lancer, world studies; Jim Chambers, arts, health and entertainment. "We produce high-quality reference materials for the school library market and the general nonfiction trade." Publishes 25-30 young adult titles/year. 5% of books by first-time authors; 25% of books from agented writers; additional titles through book packagers, co-publishers and unagented writers.

Nonfiction Middle readers, young adults: animal, biography, careers, geography, health, history, multicultural, nature/environment, reference, religion, science, social issues and sports.

How to Contact/Writers Nonfiction: Submit outline/synopsis and sample chapters. Responds to queries in 10 weeks. Publishes a book 10-12 months after acceptance. Will consider simultaneous submissions. Sends galleys to authors. Book catalog free on request. Send SASE for submission guidelines.

Terms Submission guidelines available via Web site or with SASE.

Tips "Most projects have high reference value and fit into a series format."

FAITH KIDZ

Imprint of Cook Communications Ministries, 4050 Lee Vance View, Colorado Springs CO 80918. (719)536-0100. Fax: (719)536-3243. Web site: www.cookministries.com. **Acquisitions:** Mary McNeil, senior acquisitions editor. Publishes 3-5 picture books/year; 6-8 young readers/year; 6-12 middle readers/year. Less than 5% of books by first-time authors; 15% of books from agented authors. "All books have overt Christian values, but there is no primary theme."

- Visit Web site to see when *Faith Kidz* is accepting manuscripts.

How to Contact/Writers Only accepts online submissions (www.cookministries.com/proposals).

Illustration Works with 15 illustrators/year. "Send color material I can keep." Query with samples; send résumé, promo sheet, portfolio, tearsheets. Responds in 6 months only if interested. Samples returned with SASE; samples filed. Contact: Art Department.

Terms Pays illustrators by the project, royalty or work purchased outright. Sends dummies to illustrators. Original artwork returned at job's completion.

Tips "We're looking for writers willing to writer for fee rather than royalty to contribute stories fo Bible story books."

FARRAR, STRAUS & GIROUX INC.

19 Union Square W., New York NY 10003. (212)741-6900. Fax: (212)633-2427. Web site: www.fsgkidsbooks.com. Estab. 1946. Book publisher. Imprints: Frances Foster Books, Melanie Kroupa Books. Children's Books Editorial Director: Margaret Ferguson. **Manuscript Acquisitions:** Margaret Ferguson, editorial director; Frances Foster, Frances Foster Books; Melanie Kroupa, Melanie Kroupa Books; Beverly Reingold, executive editor; Wesley Adams, executive editor; Janine O'Malley, editor. **Art Acquisitions:** Robbin Gourley, art director, Books for Young Readers. Publishes 40 picture books/year; 15 middle readers/year; 15 young adult titles/year. 5% of books by first-time authors; 20% of books from agented writers.

- Farrar title *The Race to Save the Lord God Bird*, by Phillip Hoose (Melanie Kroupa Books), won the 2005 Boston Globe-Horn Book Award for nonfiction. Their title *That New Animal*, by Emily Jenkins, illustrated by Pierre Pratt (Frances Foster Books), won a 2005 Boston Globe-Horn Book Honor Award for picture books.

Fiction All levels: all categories. "Original and well-written material for all ages." Recently published *The Search for Bell Prater*, by Ruth White; *That New Animal*, by Emily Jenkins.

Nonfiction All levels: all categories. "We publish only literary nonfiction."

How to Contact/Writers Fiction/nonfiction: Query with outline/synopsis and sample chapters. Do not fax submissions or queries. Responds to queries/mss in 3 months. Publishes a book 18 months after acceptance. Will consider simultaneous submissions.

Illustration Works with 30-60 illustrators/year. Reviews ms/illustration packages from artists. Submit ms with 1 example of final art, remainder roughs. Do not send originals. Illustrations only: Query with tearsheets. Responds if interested in 2 months. Samples returned with SASE; samples sometimes filed.

Terms "We offer an advance against royalties for both authors and illustrators." Sends galleys to authors; dummies to illustrators. Original artwork returned at job's completion. Book catalog available for 9×12 SAE and $1.95 postage; ms guidelines for 1 first-class stamp, or can be viewed at www.fsgkidsbooks.com.

Tips "Study our catalog before submitting. We will see illustrator's portfolios by appointment. Don't ask for criticism and/or advice—it's just not possible. Never send originals. Always enclose SASE."

FIRST SECOND BOOKS

Imprint of Roaring Brook Press, 175 5th Ave., New York NY 10010. Estab. 2005. (646)307-5095. Fax: (646)307-5285. E-mail: mail@firstsecondbooks.com. Web site: www.firstsecondbooks.com. **Editorial Director:** Mark Siegel. Publishes 3 young readers/year; 3 middle readers/year; 6 young abult titles/year. "First Second aims fo high-quality, literate graphic novels for a wide range—from middle grade to young adule to adult readers."

Fiction Considers all categories. All books 96+ pages. Recently published *Sardine in Outer Space*, by Joann Sfar and Emmanuel Guibert (graphic novel, age 12 and up); *A.L.I.E.E.E.N.*, by Lewis Trondheim (graphic novel, ages 12 and up); *The Lost Colony*, by Grady Klein (graphic novel, YA).

Nonfiction Considers all categories. Recently published *Journey into Mohawk Country*, by George O'Connor (graphic novel, YA); *Kampung Boy*, by Lat (graphic novel, YA); *Missouri Boy*, by Leland Myrick (graphic novel, YA).

How to Contact/Writers Submit outline/synopsis and 1 samply chapter. Repsonds to queries/mss in 1 month. Will consider simultaneous submissions, electronic submissions and previously published work.

Illustration Works with 12 illustrators/year. Uses color artwork only. Will review ms/illustration packages from artists. Submit ms with 2-3 pieces of final art. Conact: Mark Siegel, editorial director. Illustrations only: Query with samples. Contact: Mark Siegel, editorial director. Responds in 1 month. Samples no returned.

Terms Author see galleys for review. Illustrators see dummies for review. Original artwork returned at job's completion. Book catalog available on Web site. Writer's and artist's guidelines available with SASE and on Web site.

FIVE STAR PUBLICATIONS, INC.

P.O. Box 6698, Chandler AZ 85246-6698. (480)940-8182. Fax: (480)940-8787. E-mail: info@fivestarpublications.com. Web site: www.fivestarpublications.com. **Art Acquisitions:** Sue DeFabis. Publishes 7 middle readers/year.

Nonfiction Recently published *Shakespeare for Children: The Story of Romeo & Juliet*, by Cass Foster; *The Sixty-Minute Shakespeare: Hamlet*, by Cass Foster; *The Sixty-Minute Shakespeare: Twelfth Night*, by Cass Foster.

How to Contact/Writers Nonfiction: Query.

Illustration Works with 3 illustrators/year. Reviews ms/illustration packages from artists. Query. Illustrations only: Query with samples. Responds only if interested. Samples filed.

Photography Buys stock and assigns work. Works on assignment only. Submit letter.

Terms Pays illustrators by the project. Pays photographers by the project. Sends galleys to authors; dummies to illustrators.

N FLUX

Llewellyn Worldwide, Ltd., 2143 Wooddale Drive, Woodbury MN 55125. (651)312-8613. Fax: (651)291-1908. E-mail: submissions@fluxnow.com. Web site: www.fluxnow.com. **Acquisitions Editor:** Andrew Karre. Imprint estab. 2005; Lllewelyn estab. 1901. Publishes 21 young adult titles/year. 60% of books by first-time authors. "Flux seeks to publish authors who see YA as a point of view, not a reading level. We look for books that try to capture a slice of teenage experience. We are particularly interested in books that tell the stories of young adults in unexpected or surprising situations around the globe."

Fiction Young Adults: adventure, contemporary, fantasy, history, humor, problem novels, religion, science fiction, sports, suspense. "We are not considering middle-grade manuscripts at this time. We do *not* publish picture books." Average word length: 50,000. Recently published *Blue Is for Nightmares*, by Laurie Faria Stolarz; *Riding Out the Storm*, by Claudia Jones; *How It's Done*, by Christine Kole MacLean.

How to Contact/Writers "Querying with a brief e-mail to submissions@fluxnow.com is not essential but is always appreciated. A query e-mail should briefly state what your proposed book is about, who the market is, and why you're the author to write it. An editor will respond to your query and ask for a submission if we're interested in the project." Accepts complete ms or proposal for YA (ages 12 and up) fiction of all genres. "We do not accept proposals on disk or by fax." Responds to mss in 1-3 months. Will consider simultaneous submissions and previously published work.

Terms Pays royalties of 10% based on wholesale price. Offers advance. Authors see galleys for review. Book catalog available on Web site or with 8×10 SASE. Writer's guidelines available for SASE or in Web site.

Tips "Read contemporary teen books. Be aware of what else is out there. If you don't read teen books, you probably shouldn't write them. Know your audience. Write incredibly well. Do not condescend."

FREE SPIRIT PUBLISHING

217 Fifth Ave. N., Suite 200, Minneapolis MN 55401-1299. (612)338-2068. Fax: (612)337-5050. E-mail: acquisitions@freespirit.com. Web site: www.freespirit.com. **Contact:** Acquisitions Editor. Publishes 16-22 titles/year for children and teens, teachers and parents. "Free Spirit Publishing is the home of SELF-HELP FOR KIDS® and SELF-HELP FOR TEENS® nonfiction, issue-driven, solution-focused books and materials for children and teens, and the parents and teachers who care for them."

● Free Spirit no longer accepts fiction or storybook submissions.

Nonfiction Areas of interest include emotional health, bullying and conflict resolution, tolerance and character development, social and study skills, creative learning and teaching, special needs learning, teaching, and parenting (gifted & talented and LD), family issues, healthy youth development, challenges specific to boys (including the parenting and teaching of boys), classroom activities, and innovative teaching techniques. We do not publish fiction or picture storybooks, books with animal or mythical characters, books with religious or New Age content, or single biographies, autobiographies, or memoirs. We prefer books written in a natural, friendly style, with little education/psychology jargon. We need books in our areas of emphasis and prefer titles written by specialists such as teachers, counselors, and other professionals who work with youth." Recently published *Germs Are Not for Sharing* and *Tails Are Not For Pulling*, by Elizabeth Verdick; *100 Things Guys Need to Know*, by Bill Zimmerman.

How to Contact/Writers "Submissions are accepted from prospective authors, including youth ages 16 and up, or through agents. Please review our catalog and author guidelines (both available online) before submitting proposal." Responds to queries/mss in 4-6 months. "If you'd like materials returned, enclose a SASE with sufficient postage." Write or call for catalog and submission guidelines before sending submission. Accepts queries only by e-mail. Submission guidelines available online.

Illustration Works with 5 illustrators/year. Submit samples to creative director for consideration. If appropriate, samples will be kept on file and artist will be contacted if a suitable project comes up. Enclose SASE if you'd like materials returned.

Photography Submit samples to creative director for consideration. If appropriate, samples will be kept on file and photographer will be contacted if a suitable project comes up. Enclose SASE if you'd like materials returned.

Terms Pays authors royalty based on net receipts. Offers advance. Pays illustrators by the project. Pays photographers by the project or per photo.

Tips "Free Spirit is a niche publisher known for high-quality books featuring a positive and practical focus and jargon free approach. Study our catalog, read our author guidelines, and be sure your proposal is the right 'fit' before submitting. Our preference is for books that help parents and teachers help kids [and that help kids themselves] gain personal strengths, succeed in school, stand up for themselves and others, and otherwise make a positive difference in today's world."

FREESTONE/PEACHTREE, JR.

Peachtree Publishers, 1700 Chattahooche Ave., Atlanta GA 30318-2112. (404)876-8761. Fax: (404)875-2578. E-mail: hello@peachtree-online.com. Web site: www.peachtree-online.com. **Acquisitions:** Helen Harriss. Publishes 4-8 young adult titles/year.

  ● Freestone and Peachtree, Jr. are imprints of Peachtree Publishers. See the listing for Peachtree for submission information. No e-mail or fax queries or submissions, please.

Fiction Picture books, young readers, middle readers, young adults: history, humor, multicultural, sports. Picture books: animal, folktales, nature/environment, special needs. Picture books, young readers: health. Middle readers, young adults/teens: adventure, contemporary, problem novels, suspense/mystery. Recently published *Dad, Jackie and Me*, by Myron Uhlberg, illustrated by Colin Bootman (ages 4-8, picture book); *Anna's Blizzard*, by Alison Hart, illustrated by Paul Bachem (ages 7-10; early reader); *Dog Sense*, by Sneed Collard (ages 8-12, middle reader).

Nonfiction Picture books, young readers, middle readers, young adults: history, sports. Picture books: animal, health, multicultural, nature/environment, science, social issues, special needs.

How to Contact Responds to queries/mss in 6 months.

Illustration Works with 10-20 illustrators/year. Responds only if interested. Samples not returned; samples filed. Originals returned at job's completion.

Terms Pays authors royalty. Pays illustrators by the project or royalty. Pays photographers by the project or per photo.

⚑ FRONT STREET BOOKS

Imprint of Boyds Mills Press, 862 Haywood Rd., Asheville NC 28806. (828)236-3097. Fax: (828)236-3098. E-mail: contactus@frontstreetbooks.com. Web site: www.frontstreetbooks.com. **Acquisitions:** Joy Neaves, editor. Publishes 10-15 titles/year. "We are a small independent publisher of books for children and young adults. We do not publish pablum: we try to publish books that will attract, if not addict, children to literature, and books that are a pleasure to look at and a pleasure to hold, books that will be revelations to young minds."

  ● Front Street had merged with and is now an imprint of Boyds Mills Press. See Front Street's Web site for submission guidelines and complete catalog. Front Street focuses on fiction, but will publish poetry, anthologies, nonfiction and high-end picture books. They do not accept unsolicited picture book manuscripts. Front Street title *Kalpana's Dream*, by Judith Clarke, won a 2005 Boston Globe-Horn Book Honor Award for fiction and poetry.

Fiction Recently published *The Big House*, by Carolyn Coman; *Heck*, by Martine Leavitt ; *MVP**, by Doug Evans; *Fortunes Bones*, by Marilyn Nelson.

How to Contact/Writers Fiction: Submit cover letter and complete ms if under 30 pages; submit cover letter, 1 or 2 sample chapters and plot summary if over 30 pages. Nonfiction: Submit detailed proposal and sample chapters. Poetry: Submit no more than 25 poems. Include SASE with submissions if you want them returned. "Please allow four months for a response. If no response in four months, send a status query by mail."

Illustration "Send sample illustrations."

Terms Pays royalties.

LAURA GERINGER BOOKS

Imprint of HarperCollins Publishers, 1350 Avenue of the Americas, New York NY 10019. Web site: www.haperc hildrens.com. **Manuscript and Art Acquisitions:** Laura Geringer. Publishes 6 picture books/year; 2 young readers/year; 4 middle readers/year; 3 young adult titles/year. 15% of books by first-time authors.

Fiction Picture books, young readers: adventure, folktales, humor, multicultural, poetry. Middle readers: literary, adventure, anthology, fantasy, history, humor, poetry, suspense/mystery. Young adults/teens: literary, adventure, fantasy, history, humor, suspense/mystery. Average word length: picture books—500; young readers—1,000; middle readers—25,000; young adults—40,000. Recently published *If You Take a Mouse to Party*, by Laura Numeroff, illustrated by Felicia Bond (ages 3-7); *So B.It*, by Sarah Weeks, (ages 10 and up); *Down the Rabbit Whole*, by Peter Abrahams (ages 10 and up).

How to Contact/Writers Only interested in agented material.

Illustration Works with 8 illustrators/year. Reviews ms/illustration packages from artists. Send ms with dummy and 3 pieces of final art. Illustrations only: Query with color photocopies. Contact: Laura Geringer, publisher. Responds only if interested. Samples returned with SASE.

Terms Book catalog available for 11×9 SASE and $2 postage; all imprints included in a single catalog.

GIBBS SMITH, PUBLISHER

P.O. Box 667, Layton UT 84041. (801)544-9800. Fax: (801)544-5582. E-mail: duribe@gibbs-smith.com. Web site: www.gibbs-smith.com. **Manuscript Acquisitions:** Jennifer Grillone, editor; Suzanne Taylor, vice president and editorial director (children's activity books). **Art Acquisitions:** Kurt Wahlner or Madge Baird. Book publisher; co-publisher of Sierra Club Books for Children. Imprint: Gibbs Smith. Publishes 2-3 books/year. 50% of books by first-time authors. 50% of books from agented authors. ''We accept submissions for picture books with particular interest in those with a Western (cowboy or ranch life style) theme or backdrop.''

• Gibbs Smith is not accepting fiction at this time.

Nonfiction Middle readers: activity, arts/crafts, cooking, how-to, nature/environment, science. Average word length: picture books—under 1,000 words; activity books—under 15,000 words. Recently published *Hiding in a Fort*, by G. Lawson Drinkard, illustrated by Fran Lee (ages 7-12); *Sleeping in a Sack: Camping Activities for Kids*, by Linda White, illustrated by Fran Lee (ages 7-12).

How to Contact/Writers Nonfiction: Submit an outline and writing samples for activity books; query for other types of books. Responds to queries/mss in 2 months. Publishes a book 1-2 years after acceptance. Will consider simultaneous submissions. Manuscript returned with SASE.

Illustration Works with 2 illustrators/year. Reviews ms/illustration packages from artists. Query. Submit ms with 3-5 pieces of final art. Illustrations only: Query with samples; provide résumé, promo sheet, slides (duplicate slides, not originals). Responds only if interested. Samples returned with SASE; samples filed.

Terms Pays authors royalty of 2% based on retail price or work purchased outright ($500 minimum). Offers advances (average amount: $2,000). Pays illustrators by the project or royalty of 2% based on retail price. Sends galleys to authors; color proofs to illustrators. Original artwork returned at job's completion. Book catalog available for 9×12 SAE and $2.30 postage. Manuscript guidelines available—e-mail duribe@gibbs-smith.com.

Tips ''We target ages 5-11. We do not publish young adult novels or chapter books.''

🅰 DAVID R. GODINE, PUBLISHER

9 Hamilton Place, Boston MA 02108. (617)451-9600. Fax: (617)350-0250. Web site: www.godine.com. Estab. 1970. Book publisher. Publishes 1 picture book/year; 1 young reader/year; 1 middle reader/year. 10% of books by first-time authors; 90% of books from agented writers. ''We publish books that matter for people who care.''

• This publisher is no longer considering unsolicited manuscripts of any type.

Fiction Picture books: adventure, animal, contemporary, folktales, nature/environment. Young readers: adventure, animal, contemporary, folk or fairy tales, history, nature/environment, poetry. Middle readers: adventure, animal, contemporary, folk or fairy tales, history, mystery, nature/environment, poetry. Young adults/teens: adventure, animal, contemporary, history, mystery, nature/environment, poetry. Recently published *A Cottage Garden Alphabet*, by Andrea Wisnewski (picture book); *Henrietta and the Golden Eggs*, by Hanna Johansen, illustrated by Kathi Bhend.

Nonfiction Picture books: alphabet, animal, nature/environment. Young readers: activity books, animal, history, music/dance, nature/environment. Middle readers: activity books, animal, biography, history, music/dance, nature/environment. Young adults: biography, history, music/dance, nature/environment.

How to Contact/Writers Query. Publishes a book 3 years after acceptance. Include SASE for return of material.

Illustration Only interested in agented material. Works with 4-6 illustrators/year. Reviews ms/illustration packages from artists. ''Submit roughs and one piece of finished art plus either sample chapters for very long works or whole ms for short works.'' Illustrations only: ''After query, submit slides, with one full-size blow-up of art.'' Please do not send original artwork unless solicited. ''Almost all of the children's books we accept for publication come to us with the author and illustrator already paired up. Therefore, we rarely use freelance illustrators.'' Samples returned with SASE; samples filed (if interested).

Tips ''Always enclose a SASE. Keep in mind that we do not accept unsolicited manuscripts and that we rarely use freelance illustrators.''

🅰 GOLDEN BOOKS

1745 Broadway, New York NY 10019. (212)782-9000. **Editorial Directors:** Courtney Silk, color and activity; Chris Angelilli, storybooks; Dennis Shealy, novelty. **Art Acquisitions:** Tracey Tyler, executive art director.

• See listing for Random House-Golden Books for Young Readers Group.

How to Contact/Writers Does not accept unsolicited submissions.

Fiction Publishes board books, novelty books, picture books, workbooks, series (mass market and trade).

GRAPHIA

Houghton Mifflin Company, 222 Berkeley St., Boston MA 02116. (617)351-5000. Web site: www.graphiabooks.com. **Manuscript Acquisitions:** Eden Edwards. ''Graphia publishes quality paperbacks for today's teen readers, ages 14 and up. From fiction to nonfiction, poetry to graphic novels, Graphia runs the gamut, all unified by the quality writing that is the hallmark of this new imprint.''

Fiction Young adults: adventure, contemporary, fantasy, history, humor, multicultural, poetry. Recently published: *A Certain Slant of Light*, by Laura Whitcomb; *The Rise and Fall of a 10-th Grade Social Climber*, by

Lauren Mechling and Laura Moser; *Zen in the Art of the SAT*, by Matt Bardin and Susan Fine; *48 Shade of Brown*, by Nick Earls (all novels for ages 14 and up).

Nonfiction Young adults: biography, history, multicultural, nature/environment, science, social issues.

How to Contact/Writers Query. Responds to queries/mss in 3 months. Will consider simultaneous submissions and previously published work.

Illustration Do not send original artwork or slides. Send color photocopies, tearsheets or photos to Art Dept. Include SASE if you would like your samples mailed back to you.

Terms Pays author royalties. Offers advances. Sends galleys to authors. Catalog available on Web site: (www.ho ughtonmifflin.com).

GREENE BARK PRESS

P.O. Box 1108, Bridgeport CT 06601-1108. (203)372-4861. Fax: (203)371-5856. E-mail: greenebark@aol.com. Web site: www.greenebarkpress.com. **Acquisitions:** Thomas J. Greene, publisher. Publishes 1-6 picture books/ year; majority of books by first-time or repeat authors. ''We publish quality hardcover picture books for children. Our stories are selected for originality, imagery and color. Our intention is to fire-up a child's imagination, encourage a desire to read in order to explore the world through books.''

Fiction Picture books, young readers: adventure, fantasy, humor. Average word length: picture books—650; young readers—1,400. Recently published *Edith Ellen Eddy*, by Julee Ann Granger; *Hey, There's a Gobblin Under My Throne*, by Rhett Ranson Pennell.

How to Contact/Writers Responds to queries in 2 months; mss in 6 months; must include SASE. No response without SASE. Publishes a book 18 months after acceptance. Will consider simultaneous submissions. Prefer to review complete mss with illustrations.

Illustration Works with 1-2 illustrators/year. Uses color artwork only. Reviews ms/illustration packages from artists. Submit ms with 3 pieces of final art (copies only). Illustrations only: Query with samples. Responds in 2 months only if interested. Samples returned with SASE; samples filed. Originals returned at job's completion.

Terms Pays authors royalty of 10-12% based on wholesale price. Pays illustrators by the project (range: $1,500-3,000) or 5-7% royalty based on wholesale price. No advances. Sends galleys to authors; dummies to illustrators. Book catalog available for $2, which includes mailing. All imprints included in a single catalog. Manuscript; guidelines available for SASE or per e-mail request.

Tips ''As a guide for future publications look to our latest publications, do not look to our older backlist. Please, no telephone, e-mail or fax queries.''

GREENHAVEN PRESS

Imprint of the Gale Group, 15822 Bernardo Center Drive, Suite C, San Diego CA 92127. E-mail: chandra.howard @thomas.com. Web site: www.gale.com/greenhaven. **Acquisitions:** Chandra Howard, senior acquisitions editor. Publishes 220 young adult academic reference titles/year. 50% of books by first-time authors. Greenhaven continues to print quality nonfiction anthologies for libraries and classrooms. Our well known Opposing Viewpoints series is highly respected by students and librarians in need of material on controversial social issues.

- Greenhaven accepts no unsolicited manuscripts. All writing is done on a work-for-hire basis. See also listing for Lucent Books.

Nonfiction Young adults (high school): controversial topics, history, issues.

How to Contact/Writers Send query, résumé, and list of published works by e-mail.

Terms Buys ms outright for $1,500-3,000. Sends galleys to authors. No phone calls. Short writing samples are appropriate; long unsolicited mss will not be read or returned.

Ⓐ ⓥ GREENWILLOW BOOKS

1350 Avenue of the Americas, New York NY 10019. (212)261-6500. Web site: www.harperchildrens.com. Book publisher. Imprint of HarperCollins. Vice President/Publisher: Virginia Duncan. **Art Acquisitions:** Paul Zakris, art director. Publishes 40 picture books/year; 5 middle readers/year; 5 young adult books/year. ''Greenwillow Books publishes picture books, fiction for young readers of all ages, and nonfiction primarily for children under seven years of age.''

- Greenwillow Books is currently accepting neither unsolicited manuscripts nor queries. Unsolicited mail will not be opened and will not be returned. Call (212)261-6627 for an update. Greenwillow title *Criss Cross*, by Lynne Rae Perkins, won the 2006 Newbery Medal.

Illustration Art samples (postcards only) should be sent in duplicate to Paul Zakris and Virginia Duncan.

Terms Pays authors royalty. Offers advances. Pays illustrators royalty or by the project. Sends galleys to authors.

Ⓐ GROSSET & DUNLAP PUBLISHERS

Penguin Group (USA), 345 Hudson St., New York NY 10014. Estab. 1898. **Acquisitions:** Debra Dorfman, president/publisher. Publishes 175 titles/year. ''Grosset & Dunlap publishes children's books that show children reading is fun with books that speak to their interests and are affordable so children can build a home library of their own. Focus on licensed properties, series, readers and novelty books.''

Fiction Recently published series: Camp Confidential, Flight 29 Down, Katie Kazoo, Angelina Ballerina, Darcy's Wild Life; Strawberry Shortcake (license); Dick & Jane (brand).

Nonfiction Young readers: nature/environment, science.

How to Contact/Writers Only interested in agented material.

☐ GRYPHON HOUSE

P.O. Box 207, Beltsville MD 20704-0207. (301)595-9500. Fax: (301)595-0051. E-mail: kathyc@ghbooks.com. Web site: www.gryphonhouse.com. **Acquisitions:** Kathy Charner, editor-in-chief.

Nonfiction Parent and teacher resource books—activity books, textbooks. Recently published *Reading Games*, by Jackie Silberg; *Primary Art*, by MaryAnn F. Kohl; *The Anit-Bullying and Teasing Book*, by Barbara Sprung and Merle Froschl, with Dr. Blyth Hinitz; *The Complete Resource Book for Infants*, by Pam Schiller. ''At Gryphon House, our goal is to publish books that help teachers and parents enrich the lives of children from birth through age eight. We strive to make our books useful for teachers at all levels of experience, as well as for parents, caregivers, and anyone interested in working with children.''

How to Contact/Writers Query. Submit outline/synopsis and 2 sample chapters. Responds to queries/mss in 6 months. Publishes a book 18 months after acceptance. Will consider simultaneous submissions, e-mail submissions.

Illustration Works with 4-5 illustrators/year. Uses b&w artwork only. Illustrations only: Query with samples, promo sheet. Responds in 2 months. Samples returned with SASE; samples filed.

Photography Buys photos from freelancers. Buys stock and assigns work. Submit cover letter, published samples, stock photo list.

Terms Pays authors royalty based on wholesale price. Offers advances. Pays illustrators by the project. Pays photographers by the project or per photo. Sends edited ms copy to authors. Original artwork returned at job's completion. Book catalog and ms guidelines available via Web site or with SASE.

Tips ''Send a SASE for our catalog and manuscript guidelines. Look at our books, then submit proposals that complement the books we already publish or supplement our existing books. We are looking for books of creative, participatory learning experiences that have a common conceptual theme to tie them together. The books should be on subjects that parents or teachers want to do on a daily basis.''

HACHAI PUBLISHING

762 Park Place, Brooklyn NY 11216. (718)633-0100. Fax: (718)633-0103. E-mail: info@hachai.com. Web site: www.hachai.com. **Manuscript Acquisitions:** Devorah Leah Rosenfeld, submissions editor. Publishes 4 picture books/year; 1 young reader/year; 1 middle reader/year. 75% of books published by first-time authors. ''All books have spiritual/religious themes, specifically traditional Jewish content. We're seeking books about morals and values; the Jewish experience in current and Biblical times; and Jewish observance, Sabbath and holidays.''

Fiction Picture books and young readers: contemporary, historical fiction, religion. Middle readers: adventure, contemporary, problem novels, religion. Does not want to see fantasy, animal stories, romance, problem novels depicting drug use or violence. Recently published *Let's Go Shopping*, written and illustrated by Rikki Benenfeld (ages 2-5, picture book); *What Do I Say*, by Malky Goldberg, illustrated by Patti Argoff (ages 1-2, lift-the-flap book); *Ten Tzedakah Pennies*, by Joni Klein-Higger, illustrated by Tova Leff (ages 2-5, picture book); *More Precious Than Gold*, by Evelyn Blatt (ages 7-10, short chapter book).

Nonfiction Recently published *My Jewish ABC's*, by Draizy Zelcer, illustrated by Patti Nemeroff (ages 3-6, picture book); *Shadow Play*, by Leah Pearl Shollar, illustrated by Pesach Gerber (ages 3-6, picture book); *Nine Spoons*, by Marci Stillerman, illustrated by Pesach Gerber (ages 5-8).

How to Contact/Wrtiers Fiction/nonfiction: Submit complete ms. Responds to queries/mss in 6 weeks.

Illustration Works with 4 illustrators/year. Uses primary color artwork, some b&w illustration. Reviews ms/illustration packages from authors. Submit ms with 1 piece of final art. Illustrations only: Query with samples; arrange personal portfolio review. Responds in 6 weeks. Samples returned with SASE; samples filed.

Terms Work purchased outright from authors for $800-1,000. Pays illustrators by the project (range: $2,000-3,500). Book catalog, ms/artist's guidelines available for SASE.

Tips ''Write a story that incorporates a moral, not a preachy morality tale. Originality is the key. We feel Hachai publications will appeal to a wider readership as parents become more interested in positive values for their children.''

☐ ☑ HARCOURT, INC.

15 East 26th Street, New York NY 10010. (212)592-1034. Fax: (212)592-1030. Web site: www.harcourtbooks.com. Children's Books Division includes: Harcourt Children's Books—**Editor-in-Chief:** Ms. Allyn Johnston, **Editorial Director:** Liz Van Doren; Voyager Paperbacks, Odyssey Paperbacks, Red Wagon Books. **Children's Book Publisher:** Lori Benton. **Art Director:** Scott Piehl. Publishes 50-75 picture books/year; 10-20 middle readers/

year; 25-50 young adult titles/year. 20% of books by first-time authors; 50% of books from agented writers. "Harcourt, Inc. owns some of the world's most prestigious publishing imprints—which distinguish quality products for children's educational and trade markets worldwide."

- Harcourt Children's Books no longer accepts unsolicited manuscripts, queries or illustrations. Harcourt titles *Tails*, by Matthew Van Fleet; *The Leaf Man*, by Lois Ehlert; *The Great Fuzz Frenzy*, by Janet Stevens and Susan Steven Crummel; and *How I Became a Pirate*, by Melinda Long, illustrated by David Shannon, are all New York Times bestsellers. Their title *Cowgirl Kate and Cocoa*, by Erica Silverman, illustrated by Betsy Lewin, won a 2006 Theodor Seuss Geisel Honor Award. Their title *Each Little Bird That Sings*, by Deborah Wiles, won a Golden Kite Honor Award for fiction for 2005. Their title *Baby Bear's Chairs*, illustrated by Melissa Sweet, written by Jane Yolen, won the Golden Kite Award for picture book illustration for 2005.

Fiction All levels: Considers all categories. Average word length: picture books—"varies greatly"; middle readers—20,000-50,000; young adults—35,000-65,000. See catalog or visit Web site: (www.harcourtbooks.com) for recently published titles.

Nonfiction All levels: animal, biography, concept, history, multicultural, music/dance, nature/environment, science, sports. Average word length: picture books—"varies greatly"; middle readers—20,000-50,000; young adults—35,000-65,000.

How to Contact/Writers Only interested in agented material.

Illustration Only interested in agented material.

Photography Works on assignment only.

Terms Pays authors and illustrators royalty based on retail price. Pays photographers by the project. Sends galleys to authors; dummies to illustrators. Original artwork returned at job's completion. Book catalog available for 8×10 SAE and 4 first-class stamps; ms/artist's guidelines available for business-size SASE. All imprints included in a single catalog.

ⒶＶ HARPERCOLLINS CHILDREN'S BOOKS

1350 Avenue of the Americas, New York NY 10019. (212)261-6500. Web site: www.harperchildrens.com. Book publisher. Editor-in-Chief: Kate Morgan Jackson. Editorial Director: Maria Modugno. Editorial Directors: Margaret Anastas, Barbara Lalicki, Maria Modugno, Michael Stearns, Phoebe Yeh. **Art Acquisitions:** Martha Rago or Stephanie Bart-Horvath, director. Imprints: HarperTrophy, HarperTempest, EOS, HarperFestival, Greenwillow Books, Joanna Cotler Books, Laura Geringer Books, Katherine Tegen Books.

- HarperCollins Children's Books is not accepting unsolicited and/or unagented manuscripts or queries. "Unfortunately, the volume of these submissions is so large that we cannot give them the attention they deserve. Such submissions will not be reviewed or returned." HarperCollins title *God Bless the Children*, illustrated by Jerry Pinkney, written by Billie Holiday and Arthur Herzog, Jr., won a 2005 Coretta Scott King Illustrator Honor Award. Harper title *Airborn*, by Kenneth Oppel, won a 2005 Printz Honor Award.

Fiction Publishes picture, chapter, novelty, board and TV/movie books.

How to Contact/Writers Only interested in agented material.

Illustration Art samples may be sent to Martha Rago or Stephanie Bart-Horvath. **Please do not send original art.** Works with over 100 illustrators/year. Responds only if interested. Samples returned with SASE; samples filed only if interested.

Terms Art guidelines available for SASE.

Ｄ HAYES SCHOOL PUBLISHING CO. INC.

321 Pennwood Ave., Wilkinsburg PA 15221-3398. (412)371-2373. Fax: (800)543-8771. E-mail: chayes@hayespub.com. Web site: www.hayespub.com. Estab. 1940. **Acquisitions:** Mr. Clair N. Hayes. Produces folders, workbooks, stickers, certificates. Wants to see supplementary teaching aids for grades K-12. Interested in all subject areas. Will consider simultaneous and electronic submissions.

How to Contact/Writers Query with description or complete ms. Responds in 6 weeks. SASE for return of submissions.

Illustration Works with 3-4 illustrators/year. Responds in 6 weeks. Samples returned with SASE; samples filed. Originals not returned at job's completion.

Terms Work purchased outright. Purchases all rights.

HEALTH PRESS

NA Inc., P.O. Box 37470, Albuquerque NM 87176-7479. (505)888-1394 or (877)411-0707. Fax: (505)888-1521. E-mail: goodbooks@healthpress.com. Web site: www.healthpress.com. **Acquisitions:** Editor. Publishes 4 young readers/year. 100% of books by first-time authors.

Fiction Picture books, young readers: health, special needs. Average word length: young readers—1,000-1,500; middle readers—1,000-1,500. Recently published *The Girl With No Hair*, by Elizabeth Murphy-Melas, illustrated

Tanya Lee Stone

'Write what you're excited about writing, regardless of the genre'

Book Publishers

I n a letter to readers bound in the advance galley for *A Bad Boy Can Be Good for a Girl*, Alison Meyer, assistant editor at Wendy Lamb Books, writes: "When I picked up Tanya Lee Stone's novel for the first time, I read it in one breathless sitting. I didn't get up. I didn't *look* up. I didn't care about anything else in the world."

Stone's first novel-in-verse is indeed hard to put down. Her poetry transports the reader back to high school with its I-can't-believe-he-really-*likes*-me highs and how-could-he-*do*-this-to-me lows. She tells the story through three characters, all with distinct voices, and all sharing their experiences involving the same boy, a senior with one thing on his mind. "This is not a book that will sit quietly on any shelf," says *School Library Journal* in a starred review. "It will be passed from girl to girl to girl."

While *Bad Boy* is Stone' first published novel, she's certainly not new to the world of children's publishing. She's worked as an editor (at Holt Rinehart, Macmillan, and Black-birch Press) and is a prolific nonfiction author. Her titles include *Abraham Lincoln* (DK), *Ilan Ramon: Israel's First Astronaut* (Millbrook), the Wild America series and the Wild, Wild World! series (both Blackbirch).

To learn more about Tanya Lee Stone, visit her Web site www.tanyastone.com, featuring information on her books, a good list of links, and the author's blog.

With so many nonfiction titles under your belt, why are you now delving into fiction?

I still love nonfiction and am working in new ways with it; I have new nonfiction trade books coming out in the future. But a couple of years ago, I felt tugged in a different direction. I needed to stretch. I started writing a story in the voice of Josie, the first girl in what became my first novel, and I kept on going. I love the freedom and exploratory nature of fiction.

Was it a conscious choice to write in verse for your debut YA title, *A Bad Boy Can Be Good for a Girl*, or did it just "happen"?

It definitely just happened. I am not new to poetry, though, I've been writing it since long before I was an English Major in college. Again, the catalyst was the character of Josie. I wrote in the way I heard her voice. And then I found that verse was an effective way of differentiating the voices of my three girls so that Josie, Nicolette, and Aviva all had their own sound. The rhythm of the poetry and their different voices felt real to me.

You worked on the manuscript for *Bad Boy* at Kindling Words and you have a supportive network of writer friends. Why is this important? How are retreats with other writers valuable to your process?

I love my writer friends. They "get" things that other people might tend not to. The whole "I hear voices," thing, for example. My writer friends know all about characters who talk to you, who wake you up in the middle of the night. We are also good readers for each other. Regarding retreats, I cherish my time at Kindling Words. There is a unique energy to being with other writers. I tend to go to retreats without expectations, and each time I discover I was there for a particular reason—to gain a new perspective, have a conversation that opens my eyes to something I might not have thought of, meet someone who becomes a close friend, etc. Community is especially important in a field that can feel solitary as we sit at home and type.

Bad Boy focuses on sexual choices and the impact they have on three teen girls. How do you make the jump from *B Is for Bunny* to *A Bad Boy Can Be Good for a Girl*? Were there any concerns with the sexual content of your novel as you wrote?

Jacket illustration © 2006 Gary Panter. Reprinted with permission of Wendy Lamb Books.

Well-published nonfiction author Tanya Lee Stone delved into the world of YA fiction with her debut novel *A Bad Boy Can Be Good for a Girl* published in 2006 by Wendy Lamb Books. *Bad Boy* is told in verse by three narrators, Josie, Nicolette, and Avivia, all conveying their experiences with the same boy who done them wrong. "Tanya's book drew me in because of its honesty and bravery," says editor Alison Meyer.

I wouldn't say that I had concerns about the content; but I was mindful of it. I was careful never to be gratuitous. But I wanted to really delve into the topic and embrace the pitfalls that most girls experience at one time or another. And I felt strongly that if I was going to write about sexual choices that I should keep the lights on and the topic in the forefront. In terms of jumping from *B Is for Bunny* to *Bad Boy* I think that writers write what presents itself to them in the moment. Each book is a different journey. There's no reason why you can't write something sweet and innocent one day, and serious and sultry the next.

In the acknowledgments for *Bad Boy*, you thank editor Alison Meyer for "asking the right questions without looking for the 'right' answers." What do you mean by that? Tell me about the editorial process for your first fiction project.

It was an exceptionally fun process. There were not a lot of revisions, but there were some scenes, especially given the content, that we needed to look at closely. What I meant in my acknowledgment is that Alison had a knack for pointing out a particular phrase or scene and saying something to me such as, "I know why you're doing this here, but I want you to think about how you really want to get this idea across." Or, "You might want to look at this scene from a different perspective." In this way, she would illuminate an issue that she felt needed more attention but trust me to figure it out. The process for fiction was certainly much different than for nonfiction and working with Alison Meyer and Wendy Lamb was amazing. Wendy is extremely smart and has dead-on insights.

What advantages does your editorial experience give you over writers who have only worked on one side of the desk?

I mainly edited children's nonfiction while I was an editor, so it was a natural extension for me to head in that direction when I first started writing. I had edited literally hundreds of nonfiction books for kids before I ever wrote my first one. So I definitely had an advantage in that I knew exactly how to proceed. Editors I've worked with have told me that I turn in fairly clean manuscripts, and I have no doubt it is because of my editorial background. I edit myself as I go; I don't know any other way to write.

You've written a number of series books including a 12-book series and a 30-book series. How does a writer get gigs like those?

In both instances, these were for a publisher with which I have a long history. For the 12-book series, I believe this occurred during a phone conversation in which we were brainstorming what the list needed. For the 30-book series the publisher approached me and asked me if I would do it. Both series are about animals, which I love and have an extensive knowledge base of (I did my Masters thesis on the diversity of pinnipeds). Therefore, these were fun projects for me. My son and I always play animal games—he tries to stump me with some little-known animal fact and finds it really irritating that I usually know the answer.

Why is writing nonfiction so appealing to you?

Probably because I'm just a big kid and I love finding interesting new angles for topics, or simply learning something I didn't know before. And I really love imparting the excitement I feel about a subject to kids so they want to learn more, too. My goal isn't just to get them to read my book; it's to get them excited so they'll look for other books as well.

In an interview you mentioned the importance of approaching a writing career as a business and being educated about the industry. How do you accomplish these things?

Well, it gets easier as time goes on. The learning curve can be steep. But I think it's important to go to conferences, listen to editors talk about the market, read journals in the field, visit Web sites that offer great resources about the field or keep track of editorial movement (such as www.cynthialeitichsmith.com and www.smartwriters.com or Harold Underdown's the Purple Crayon, www.underdown.org), and so on.

I always tell new writers to buy *Children's Writer's & Illustrator's Market* because it's the only book I know of that stays current on what types of books publishers buy. When I was an editor at a children's nonfiction house, you would not believe how many adult fiction and picture book manuscripts we would receive. This is a big reason why the slush piles are so large everywhere. Writers who are educated about the industry and research their own submissions increase their chances of success significantly—and help decrease slush piles—so everyone wins.

Any tips for aspiring writers about living the writing life? Getting published? Jumping genres?

It's cliché, but read, read, read. Write, write, write. It's the only thing that works. And when it comes to jumping genres, I think two things are true: (1) you have to write what you're excited about writing, regardless of the genre; and (2) in today's market it can be a real advantage to have more than one genre in which to publish.

Tell me about your upcoming projects.

I believe my next book out will be *Elizabeth Leads the Way: Elizabeth Cady Stanton and the Right to Vote* (Henry Holt, 2007). This is a picture book biography that is being illustrated by Rebecca Gibbon. I'm excited to see the artwork as she has a wonderful quirky style that really brings historical topics to life. (She did Shana Corey's *Players in Pigtails*). After that will be a Young Adult biography of Ella Fitzgerald (Viking, 2008). And I am really excited about my next YA novel I'm working on.

—Alice Pope

by Alex Hernandez (ages 8-12, picture book); *The Peanut Butter Jam*, by Elizabeth Sussman-Nassau, illustrated by Margot Ott (ages 6-12, picture book).
Nonfiction Picture books, young readers: health, special needs, social issues, self help.
How to Contact/Writers Submit complete ms. Responds in 3 month. Publishes a book 9 months after acceptance. Will consider simultaneous submissions.
Terms Pays authors royalty. Sends galleys to authors. Book catalog available.

HENDRICK-LONG PUBLISHING COMPANY

10635 Tower Oaks, Suite D, Houston TX 77070. (832)912-READ. Fax: (832)912-7353. E-mail: hendrick-long@w orldnet.att.net. **Acquisitions:** Vilma Long, vice president. Publishes 4 young readers/year; 4 middle readers/ year. 20% of books by first-time authors. Publishes fiction/nonfiction about Texas of interest to young readers through young adults/teens.
Fiction Middle readers: history books on Texas and the Southwest. No fantasy or poetry.
Nonfiction Middle, young adults: history books on Texas and the Southwest, biography, multicultural. "Would like to see more workbook-type manuscripts."
How to Contact/Writers Fiction/nonfiction: Query with outline/synopsis and sample chapter. Responds to queries in 3 months; mss in 2 months. Publishes a book 18 months after acceptance. No simultaneous submissions. Include SASE.
Illustration Works with 2-3 illustrators/year. Uses primarily b&w interior artwork; color covers only. Illustrations only: Query first. Submit résumé or promotional literature or photocopies or tearsheets—no original work sent unsolicited. No phone calls. Responds only if interested.
Terms Pays authors royalty based on selling price. Advances vary. Pays illustrators by the project or royalty. Sends galleys to authors; dummies to illustrators. Manuscript guidelines for 1 first-class stamp and #10 SAE.
Tips "Material *must* pertain to Texas or the Southwest. Check all facts about historical figures and events in both fiction and nonfiction. Be accurate."

HOLIDAY HOUSE INC.

425 Madison Ave., New York NY 10017. (212)688-0085. Fax: (212)421-6134. Web site: www.holidayhouse.com. Estab. 1935. Book publisher. Vice President/Editor-in-Chief: Regina Griffin. **Acquisitions:** Acquisitions Editor. **Art Director:** Claire Counihan. Publishes 35 picture books/year; 3 young readers/year; 15 middle readers/year; 8 young adult titles/year. 20% of books by first-time authors; 10% from agented writers. Mission Statement: "To publish high-quality books for children."
Fiction All levels: adventure, contemporary, fantasy, folktales, ghost, historical, humor, multicultural, school, suspense/mystery, sports. Recently published *Dinosaur Discoveries*, by Gail Gibbons; *The Frog Princess*, by Eric A. Kimmel, illustrated by Rosanne Litzinger; *The Naked Mole-Rat Letters*, by Mary Amato.
Nonfiction All levels: animal, biography, concept, contemporary, geography, historical, math, multicultural, music/dance, nature/environment, religion, science, social issues.
How to Contact/Writers Send queries only to editor. Responds to queries in 3 months; mss in 4 months. "If

we find your book idea suits our present needs, we will notify you by mail." Once a ms has been requested, the writers should send in the exclusive submission, with a SASE, otherwise the ms will not be returned.

Illustration Works with 35 illustrators/year. Reviews ms illustration packages from artists. Send ms with dummy. Do not submit original artwork or slides. Color photocopies or printed samples are preferred. Responds only if interested. Samples filed.

Terms Pays authors and illustrators an advance against royalties. Originals returned at job's completion. Book catalog, ms/artist's guidelines available for a SASE.

Tips "We need books with strong stories, writing and art. We do not publish board books or novelties. No easy readers."

HENRY HOLT & COMPANY

175 Fifth Ave, New York NY 10010. Unsolicited Manuscript Hotline: (646)307-5087. Web site: www.henryholtch ildrensbooks.com. Submissions Web site: www.henryholtchildrensbooks.com/submissions.htm. **Manuscript Acquisitions:** Laura Godwin, vice president and publisher of Books for Young Readers; Christy Ottaviano, executive editor; Reka Simonsen, senior editor; Kate Farrell, editor; Nina Ignatowicz, editor at large. **Art Acquisitions:** Patrick Collins, art director. Publishes 30-35 picture books/year; 6-8 chapter books/year; 10-15 middle readers/year; 8-10 young adult titles/year. 15% of books by first-time authors; 40% of books from agented writers. "Henry Holt and Company Books for Young Readers is known for publishing quality books that feature imaginative authors and illustrators. We tend to publish many new authors and illustrators each year in our effort to develop and foster new talent."

- Henry Holt title *Rosa*, illustrated by Bryan Collier, written by Nikki Giovanni, won the 2006 Coretta Scott King Illustrator Award and a 2006 Caldecott Honor Award. Their title *A Room on Lorelei Street*, by Mary E. Pearson, won the Golden Kite Award for fiction for 2005.

Fiction Picture books: animal, anthology, concept, folktales, history, humor, multicultural, nature/environment, poetry, special needs, sports. Middle readers: adventure, contemporary, history, humor, multicultural, special needs, sports, suspense/mystery. Young adults: contemporary, humor, multicultural, mystery, historical.

Nonfiction Picture books: animal, arts/crafts, biography, concept, geography, history, hobbies, multicultural, the arts, nature/environment, sports. Middle readers, young readers, young adult: biography, history, multicultural, sports.

How to Contact/Writers Fiction/nonfiction: Submit complete ms with SASE. Responds in 4-6 months only if interested, otherwise mss are not returned or responded to. Will not consider simultaneous or multiple submissions.

Illustration Works with 50-60 illustrators/year. Reviews ms/illustration packages from artists. Random samples OK. Illustrations only: Submit tearsheets, slides. Do *not* send originals. Responds to art samples only if interested. Samples filed but not returned. If accepted, original artwork returned at job's completion. Portfolios are reviewed every Monday.

Terms Pays authors/illustrators royalty based on retail price. Sends galleys to authors; proofs to illustrators.

HOUGHTON MIFFLIN CO.

Children's Trade Books, 222 Berkeley St., Boston MA 02116-3764. (617)351-5000. Fax: (617)351-1111. E-mail: childrens_books@hmco.com. Web site: www.houghtonmifflinbooks.com. **Manuscript Aquisitions:** Submissions Coordinator; Alan Smagler, publisher; Margaret Raymo, executive editor; Eden Edwards, Ann Rider, senior editors; Mary Wilcox, franchise director, Graphia senior editor; Walter Lorraine, books editor; Kate O'Sullivan, Monida Perez, editors; Erika Zappy, editorial assistant. **Art Acquisitions:** Sheila Smallwood, creative director. Imprints include Walter Lorraine Books, Clarion Books, and Graphia. Averages 60 titles/year. Publishes hardcover originals and trade paperback reprints and originals. "Houghton Mifflin gives shape to ideas that educate, inform, and above all, delight."

- Houghton Mifflin title *Song of the Water Boatman and Other Pond Poems*, illustrated by Beckie Prange, written by Joyce Sidman, won a 2006 Caldecott Honor Award. Their title *A Wreath for Emmett Till*, by Marilyn Nelson, illustrated by Phillippe Lardy, won a 2005 Boston Globe-Horn Award for fiction and poetry and a 2006 Coretta Scott King Author Honor Award. Their title *The Forbidden Schoolhouse: The True and Dramatic Story of Prudence Crandall and Her Students*, by Suzanne Jurmain, won the Golden Kite Honor Award for nonfiction for 2005.

Fiction All levels: all categories except religion. "We do not rule out any theme, though we do not publish specifically religious material." Recently published *Eddie's Kingdom*, by D.B. Johnson (ages 4-8, picture book); *Love That Baby*, by Susan Milford (ages 0-3, picture book); *Lights Out*, by Arthur Geisert (ages 4-8, picture book).

Nonfiction All levels: all categories except religion. Recently published *The Forbidden Schoolhouse: The True and Dramatic Story of Prudence Crandall and Her Students*, by Suzanne Jurmain (ages 10 and up); *Prehistoric Actual Size*, by Steve Jenkins (picture book, all ages); *Gorilla Doctors*, by Pamela S. Turner (ages 7-12).

How to Contact/Writers Fiction: Submit complete ms on unfolded white paper in a 9×12 envelope. Nonfiction: Submit outline/synopsis and sample chapters. Responds within 4 months only if interested.

Illustration Works with 60 illustrators/year. Reviews ms/illustration packages from artists. Manuscript/illustration packages or illustrations only: Query with samples (colored photocopies are fine); provide tearsheets. Responds in 4 months. Samples returned with SASE; samples filed if interested.

Terms Pays standard royalty based on retail price; offers advance. Illustrators paid by the project and royalty. Manuscript and artist's guidelines available with SASE.

HUNTER HOUSE PUBLISHERS

P.O. Box 2914, Alameda CA 94501-0914. (510)865-5282. Fax: (510)865-4295. E-mail: acquisitions@hunterhouse.com. Web site: www.hunterhouse.com. **Manuscript Acquisitions:** Jeanne Brondino. Publishes 0-1 titles for teenage women/year. 50% of books by first-time authors; 5% of books from agented writers.

Nonfiction Young adults: self help, health, multicultural, violence prevention. "We emphasize that all our books try to take multicultural experiences and concerns into account. We would be interested in a self-help book on multicultural issues." Books are therapy/personal growth-oriented. Does *not* want to see books for young children, fiction, illustrated picture books, autobiography. Published *Turning Yourself Around: Self-Help Strategies for Troubled Teens*, by Kendall Johnson, Ph.D.; *Safe Dieting for Teens*, by Linda Ojeda, Ph.D.

How to Contact/Writers Query; submit overview and chapter-by-chapter synopsis, sample chapters and statistics on your subject area, support organizations or networks and marketing ideas. "Testimonials from professionals or well-known authors are crucial." Responds to queries in 3 months; mss in 6 months. Publishes a book 18 months after acceptance. Will consider simultaneous submissions.

Terms Payment varies. Sends galleys to authors. Book catalog available for 9×12 SAE and $1.25 postage; ms guidelines for standard SAE and 1 first-class stamp.

Tips Wants teen books with solid, informative material. "We do few children's books. The ones we do are for a select, therapeutic audience. No fiction! Please, no fiction."

▲ ☑ HYPERION BOOKS FOR CHILDREN

114 Fifth Ave., New York NY 10011-5690. (212)633-4400. Fax: (212)633-4833. Web site: www.hyperionbooksforchildren.com. **Manuscript Acquisitions:** Editorial Director. **Art Director:** Anne Diebel. 10% of books by first-time authors. Publishes various categories.

- Hyperion title *The Hello, Goodbye Window*, illustrated by Chris Raschka, written by Norton Juster, won the 2006 Caldecott Medal and a 2005 Boston Globe-Horn Book Honor Award for picture books. Their title *Days of Tears: A Novel in Dialogue*, by Julius Lester, won the 2006 Coretta Scott King Author Award. Their title *Jimi & Me*, by Jaime Adoff, won the 2006 Coretta Scott King New Talent Award-Author. Their title *Dark Stones*, by Nikki Grimes, won a 2006 Coretta Scott King Author Honor Award.

Fiction Picture books, young readers, middle readers, young adults: adventure, animal, anthology (short stories), contemporary, fantasy, folktales, history, humor, multicultural, poetry, science fiction, sports, suspense/mystery. Middle readers, young adults: commercial fiction. Recently published *Emily's First 100 Days of School*, by Rosemary Wells (ages 3-6, *New York Times* best-seller); *Artemis Fowl*, by Eoin Colfer (YA novel, *New York Times* best-seller); *Dumpy The Dump Truck*, series by Julie Andrews Edwards and Emma Walton Hamilton (ages 3-7).

Nonfiction All trade subjects for all levels.

How to Contact/Writers Only interested in agented material.

Illustration Works with 100 illustrators/year. "Picture books are fully illustrated throughout. All others depend on individual project." Reviews ms/illustration packages from artists. Submit complete package. Illustrations only: Submit résumé, business card, promotional literature or tearsheets to be kept on file. Responds only if interested. Original artwork returned at job's completion.

Photography Works on assignment only. Publishes photo essays and photo concept books. Provide résumé, business card, promotional literature or tearsheets to be kept on file.

Terms Pays authors royalty based on retail price. Offers advances. Pays illustrators and photographers royalty based on retail price or a flat fee. Sends galleys to authors; dummies to illustrators. Book catalog available for 9×12 SAE and 3 first-class stamps.

ILLUMINATION ARTS

P.O. Box 1865, Bellevue WA 98009. (425)644-7185. Fax: (425)644-9274. E-mail: liteinfo@illumin.com. Web site: www.illumin.com. **Acquisitions:** Ruth Thompson, editorial director.

Fiction Word length: Prefers under 1,000, but will consider up to 1,500 words. Recently published *Am I a Color, Too?*, by Heidi Cole & Nancy Vogl, illustrated by Gerald Purnell; *Your Father Forever*, by Travis Griffith, illustrated by Raquel Abreu.

How to Contact/Writers Fiction: Submit complete ms. Responds to queries in 3 months with SASE only. No electronic or CD submissions for text or art. Publishes a book 1-2 years after acceptance. Will consider simultaneous submissions.

Illustration Works with 3-5 illustrators/year. Uses color artwork only. Reviews ms/illustration packages from artists. Query or send ms with dummy. Illustrations only: Query with color samples, résumé and promotional material to be kept on file or returned with SASE only. Responds in 3 months with SASE only. Samples returned with SASE or filed.

Terms Pays authors and illustrators royalty based on wholesale price. Book fliers available for SASE.

Tips "Read our books and follow our guidelines. Be patient. The market is competitive. We receive 2,000 submissions annually and publish 3-4 books a year. Sorry, we are unable to track unsolicited submissions."

IMPACT PUBLISHERS, INC.

P.O. Box 6016, Atascadero CA 93423-6016. (805)466-5917. Fax: (805)466-5919. E-mail: info@impactpublishers.com. Web site: www.impactpublishers.com. **Manuscript Acquisitions:** Melissa Froehner, children's editor. **Art Acquisitions:** Sharon Skinner, art director. Imprints: Little Imp Books, Rebuilding Books, The Practical Therapist Series. Publishes 1 young reader/year; 1 middle reader/year; 1 young adult title/year. 20% of books by first-time authors. "Our purpose is to make the best human services expertise available to the widest possible audience. We publish only popular psychology and self-help materials written in everyday language by professionals with advanced degrees and significant experience in the human services."

Nonfiction Young readers, middle readers, young adults: self-help. Recently published *Jigsaw Puzzle Family: The Stepkids' Guide to Fitting It Together*, by Cynthia MacGregor(ages 8-12, children's/divorce/emotions).

How to Contact/Writers Nonfiction: Query or submit complete ms, cover letter, résumé. Responds to queries in 12 weeks; mss in 3 months. Will consider simultaneous submissions or previously published work.

Illustration Works with 1 illustrator/year. Uses b&w artwork only. Reviews ms/illustration packages from artists. Query. Contact: Children's Editor. Illustrations only: Query with samples. Contact: Sharon Skinner, production manager. Responds only if interested. Samples returned with SASE; samples filed. Originals returned to artist at job's completion.

Terms Pays authors royalty of 10-12%. Offers advances. Pays illustrators by the project. Book catalog available for #10 SAE with 2 first-class stamps; ms guidelines available for SASE. All imprints included in a single catalog.

Tips "Please do not submit fiction, poetry or narratives."

▣ IPICTUREBOOKS

24 West 25th Street, 11th Floor, New York NY 10010. E-mail: info@ipicturebooks.com. Web site: www.ipicturebooks.com. **Art Director:** Matt Postawa. Online book publisher. "ipicturebooks is the #1 brand for children's e-books on the Internet. It is designed to appeal to parents, children, teachers and librarians seeking in-print, out-of-print and original enhanced e-books for use on home computers, school and library networked computers, proprietary and open hand-helds and dedicated e-book readers. It will sell e-books by individual downloaded copy, site licenses and subscription models. ipicturebooks will also introduce a variety of 'enhanced' e-books, ranging from original e-books illustrated digitally, to 'custom' e-books in which a child's name appears to 'e-pop up books' to e-books with spoken text to e-books with music and animation." See Web site for submission information for writers and illustrators, as well as sample e-books.

• ipicturebooks is temporarily closed to manuscript submissions, but is accepting illustration promo samples.

Illustration Mail or e-mail promo cards to art director at mpostawa@bpvp.com.

JEWISH LIGHTS PUBLISHING

P.O. Box 237, Rt. 4, Sunset Farm Offices, Woodstock VT 05091. (802)457-4000. Fax: (802)457-4004. E-mail: editorial@jewishlights.com. Web site: www.jewishlights.com. **Manuscript Acquisitions:** Submissions Editor. **Art Acquisitions:** Tim Holtz. Publishes 2 picture books/year; 1 young reader/year. 50% of books by first-time authors; 25% of books from agented authors. All books have spiritual/religious themes. "Jewish Lights publishes books for people of all faiths and all backgrounds who yearn for books that attract, engage, educate and spiritually inspire. Our authors are at the forefront of spiritual thought and deal with the quest for the self and for meaning in life by drawing on the Jewish wisdom tradition. Our books cover topics including history, spirituality, life cycle, children, self-help, recovery, theology and philosophy. We do *not* publish autobiography, biography, fiction, *haggadot*, poetry or cookbooks. At this point we plan to do only two books for children annually, and one will be for younger children (ages 4-10)."

Fiction Picture books, young readers, middle readers: spirituality. "We are not interested in anything other than spirituality." Recently published *God's Paintbrush*, by Sandy Eisenberg Sasso, illustrated by Annette Compton (ages 4-9).

Nonfiction Picture book, young readers, middle readers: activity books, spirituality. Recently published *When a Grandparent Dies: A Kid's Own Remembering Workbook for Dealing with Shiva and the Year Beyond*, by

Nechama Liss-Levinson, Ph.D. (ages 7-11); *Tough Questions Jews Ask: A Young Adult's Guide to Building a Jewish Life,* by Rabbi Edward Feinstein (ages 12 and up).

How to Contact/Writers Fiction/nonfiction: Query with outline/synopsis and 2 sample chapters; submit complete ms for picture books. Include SASE. Responds to queries/mss in 4 months. Publishes a book 1 year after acceptance. Will consider simultaneous submissions and previously published work.

Illustration Works with 2 illustrators/year. Reviews ms/illustration packages from artists. Query. Illustrations only: Query with samples; provide résumé. Samples returned with SASE; samples filed.

Terms Pays authors royalty of 10% of revenue received; 15% royalty for subsequent printings. Offers advances. Pays illustrators by the project or royalty. Pays photographers by the project or royalty. Sends galleys to authors; dummies to illustrators. Book catalog available for 6½×9½ SAE and 59¢ postage; ms guidelines available on Web site.

Tips "Explain in your cover letter why you're submitting your project to *us* in particular. Make sure you know what we publish."

JEWISH PUBLICATION SOCIETY

2100 Arch St., 2nd floor, Philadelphia PA 19103. (215)832-0600. Fax: (215)568-2017. Web site: www.jewishpub. org. Estab. 1888. Specializes in Judaica. **Writers contact:** Acquisitions. **Illustrators contact:** Robin Norman, production manager. Produces 1 middle reader/year; 1 young adult book/year. 50% of books by first-time authors. Jewish Publication Society's mission is "creating a shared Jewish literacy, since 1888."

Fiction Middle readers, young adults/teens: contemporary, folktales, history, short story collections, religion (Jewish). Recently published *Wise . . . and Not So Wise: 10 Tales from the Rabbis,* by Phillis Gershator, illustrated by Alexa Ginsburg (all ages).

Nonfiction Middle readers: biography (Jewish), religion. Young adults/teens: biography, religion. Recently published Kids' Catalog series (books for ages 8-12); *Ilan Ramon: Jewish Star,* by Devra Newberger Speregen.

How to Contact/Writers Accepts international submissions. Fiction: Submit outline/synopsis and 1 sample chapter. Nonfiction: Query. Responds to queries in 4 weeks; mss in 6 months. Publishes book 12-18 months after acceptance. Considers simultaneous submissions, electronic submissions, previously published work.

Illustration Accepts material from international illustrators. Works with 1 illustrator/year. Uses both color (for covers) and b&w. Reviews ms/illustration packages. For ms/illustration packages: Query. Submit ms/illustration packages to Acquisitions. Reviews work for future assignments. If interested in illustrating future titles, query with samples. Submit samples to Robin Norman.

Terms Author sees galleys for review. Originals returned to artist at job's completion. Catalog on Web site. See Web site for writer's guidelines.

Tips "We do not accept submissions for picture books for young children. While we will review all other types of children's book submissions, we are most interested in those for short story and folktale collections and for young adult novels—all with strong Jewish themes—and for new titles in our Kids' Catalog series. We generally do not acquire stories on immigrant themes or the Holocaust."

☐ KAMEHAMEHA SCHOOLS PRESS

1887 Makuakane St., Honolulu HI 96817. (808)842-8719. Fax: (808)842-8895. E-mail: kspress@ksbe.edu. Web site: kspress.ksbe.edu. **Manuscript Acquisitions:** Acquisitions Editor. "Kamehameha Schools Press publishes in the areas of Hawaiian history, Hawaiian culture, Hawaiian language and Hawaiian studies."

Fiction Young reader, middle readers, young adults: biography, history, multicultural, Hawaiian folklore.

Nonfiction Young reader, middle readers, young adults: biography, history, multicultural, Hawaiian folklore.

How to Contact/Writers Query. Responds to queries in 3 months; mss in 3 months. Publishes a book up to 2 years after acceptance.

Illustration Uses color and b&w artwork. Illustrations only: Query with samples. Responds only if interested. Samples not returned.

Terms Work purchased outright from authors or by royalty agreement. Pays illustrators by the project. Sends galleys to authors. Book catalog available (call or write for copy). All imprints included in a single catalog. Catalog available on Web site.

Tips "Writers and illustrators must be knowledgeable in Hawaiian history/culture and be able to show credentials to validate their proficiency. Greatly prefer to work with writers/illustrators available in the Honolulu area."

KAR-BEN PUBLISHING, INC.

A division of Lerner Publishing Group, 11430 Strand Drive, #2, Rockville MD 20852-4371. (301)984-8733. Fax: (301)881-9195. E-mail: karben@aol.com. Web site: www.karben.com. **Manuscript Acquisitions:** Madeline Wikler and Judye Groner, editorial directors. Publishes 10-15 books/year (mostly picture books); 20% of books by first-time authors. All of Kar-Ben Copies' books are on Jewish themes for young children and families.

• Also see listing for Lerner Publishing Group and Carolrhoda Books.

Fiction Picture books: adventures, concept, folktales, history, humor, multicultural, religion, special needs; *must be* on a Jewish theme. Average word length: picture books—1,500. Recently published *A Grandma Like Yours, A Grandpa Like Yours*, by Andrea *Warmflash Rosenbaum*, illustrated by Barb Bjornson; *It's B'Shevat*, by Edie Stoltz Zolkower, illustrated by Richard Johnson.

Nonfiction Picture books, young readers: activity books, arts/crafts, biography, careers, concept, cooking, history, how-to, multicultural, religion, social issues, special needs; must be of Jewish interest. Recently published *Paper Clips—The Making of a Children's Holocaust Memorial*, by Peter and Dagmar Schroeder (ages 8-12); *It's Purim Time*, by Latifa Berry Kropf, photos by Tod Cohen (ages 1-4); *Where Do People Go When They Die?*, by Mindy Avra Portnoy, illustrated by Shelly O. Haas (ages 5-10).

How to Contact/Writers Fiction/nonfiction: Submit complete ms. Responds to queries/mss in 6 weeks. Publishes a book 24-36 months after acceptance. Will consider simultaneous submissions.

Illustration Works with 6-8 illustrators/year. Prefers "four-color art in any medium that is scannable." Reviews ms/illustration packages from artists. Submit whole ms and sample of art (no originals). Illustrations only: Submit tearsheets, photocopies, promo sheet "which show skill in children's book illustration." Enclose SASE for response. Responds to art samples in 3-5 weeks.

Terms Pays authors royalties of 3-5% of net against advance of $500-1,000; or purchases outright (range: $2,000-3,000). Pays illustrators by the project (range: $3,000-6,000). Sends galleys to authors. Original artwork returned at job's completion. Book catalog free on request. Manuscript guidelines on Web site.

Tips Looks for "books for young children with Jewish interest and content, modern, nonsexist, not didactic. Fiction or nonfiction with a Jewish theme can be serious or humorous, life cycle, Bible story, or holiday-related. In particular, we are looking for stories that reflect the ethnic and cultural diversity of today's Jewish family.'

A KINGFISHER

Imprint of Houghton Mifflin Company, 215 Park Ave. South, New York NY 10003. (212)420-5800. Fax: (212)420-5899. Web site: www.houghtonmifflinbooks.com/kingfisher. **Contact:** Kristen McLean. Kingfisher is an award-winning publisher of nonfiction and fiction for children of all ages. They publish high-quality books with strong editorial content and world class illustration at a competitive price, offering value to parents and educators.

• Kingfisher is not currently accepting unsolicited mss. All solicitations must be made by a recognized literary agent.

Fiction Recently published *The Kingfisher Book of Family Poems*, by Belinda Hollyer.

Nonfiction Recently published *Communications*, by Richard Platt.

☒ ALFRED A. KNOPF AND CROWN BOOKS FOR YOUNG READERS

Imprint of Random House Children's Books, 1745 Broadway, New York NY 10019. (212)782-9000. Web site: www.randomhouse.com/kids. See Random House and Delacorte and Doubleday Books for Young Readers listings. Book publisher. "We publish distinguished juvenile fiction and nonfiction for ages 0-18."

• Knopf title *Traction Man is Here*, written and illustrated by Mini Grey, won the 2005 Boston Globe-Horn Book Award for picture books. Their title *Doña Flor*, by Pat Mora, illustrated by Raul Colón, won the Golden Kite Award for picture book text for 2005.

How to Contact/Writers No query letters, accompanying SASE or reply postcard. Send full picture book mss up to 25 pages plus a 1-page synopsis for longer works. "Please let us know if it is a multiple submission. If we are interested, we will reply withing 6 months of receipt of the manuscript." Address envelope to: Acquisitions Editor, Knopf & Crown/Books for Young Readers, Random House, 1745 Broadway, 9-3, New York, NY 10019.

Illustration Contact: Isabel Warren-Lynch, executive director, art & design. Responds only if interested. Samples returned with SASE; samples filed.

Terms Pays illustrators and photographers by the project or royalties. Original artwork returned at job's completion.

KRBY CREATIONS, LLC

P.O. Box 327, Bay Head NJ 08742. Fax: (815)846-0636. E-mail: info@KRBYCreations.com. Web site: www.KRBYCreations.com. Estab. 2003. Specializes in trade books, nonfiction, fiction. **Writers contact:** Kevin Burton. 40% of books by first-time authors.

Fiction Recently published *Mr. Georges and the Red Hat*, by Stephen Heigh (picture book); *Patch the Porcupine*, by Scott Nelson (picture book); *The Snowman in the Moon*, by Stephen Heigh (picture book).

How to Contact/Writers Fiction/nonfiction: Query by e-mail; request guidelines by e-mail prior to submitting mss. Responds to e-mail queries in 1 week; mss in 1-3 months. Publishes book 1 year after acceptance. Considers simultaneous submissions.

Terms Pays authors royalty of 6-15% based on wholesale price. Catalog on Web site. Offers writer's guidelines by e-mail.

Tips "Submit as professionally as possible; make your vision clear to us about what you are trying to capture. Know your market/audience and identify it in your proposal. Tell us what is new/unique with your idea. All writers submitting must first request guidelines by e-mail."

WENDY LAMB BOOKS

Imprint of Random House, 1745 Broadway, New York NY 10019. Fax: (212)782-8234. Web site: www.randomhouse.com. **Manuscript Acquisitions:** Wendy Lamb. Receives 300-400 submissions/year. Publishes 12 middle readers/year; 12 young adult titles/year. 15% of books by first-time authors and 10% unagented writers.

- Wendy Lamb Books title *Tequila Worm*, by Viola Canales, won the 2006 Pura Belpré Award.

Fiction Recently published *Eyes of the Emporer*, by Graham Salisbury; *Brian's Hunt*, by Gary Paulsen; *Bucking the Sarge*, by Christopher Paul Curtis.

How to Contact/Writers Query with SASE for reply or via e-mail. "At the moment we are not publishing picture books. A query letter should briefly describe the book you want to write, the intended age group, and your publishing credits, if any. If you like, you may send no more than 5 pages of the manuscript of shorter works (i.e. picture books) and a maximum of 10 pages for longer works (i.e. novels). *Please do not send more than the specified amount.* Also, do not send cassette tapes, videos, or other materials along with your query or excerpt. Manuscript pages sent will not be returned. Do not send original art."

Illustration Reviews ms/illustration packages from artists. Query with SASE for reply.

Terms Pays illustrators and photographers by project or royalties. Original artwork returned at job's completion.

LARK BOOKS

Sterling Publishing, 67 Broadway, Ashville NC 28801. (828)253-0467. Fax: (828)253-7952. E-mail: joe@larkbooks.com. Web site: www.larkbooks.com. Specializes in nonfiction. **Writers contact:** Joe Rhatigan, editorial director, children's books. **Illustrators contact:** Celia Naranjo, creative director. Produces 1 picture book/year; 2 young readers/year; 12 middle readers/year. 40% of books by first-time authors. "Lark Books' philisophy is to produce high-quality, content-oriented nonfiction title for ages 3-18 with a focus on art, science, nature, fun and games, crafts, and activity."

Nonfiction All levels: activity books, animal, arts/crafts, cooking, hobbies, how-to, nature/environment, self help. Recently published *The Boo Boo Book*, by Joy Masoff (ages 0-5, board book); *My Very Favorite Art Book: I Love to Draw*, by Jennifer Lipsey (ages 5-9, art instruction); *The Don't-Get-Caught Doodle Notebook*, by Susan McBride (ages 10-110, sneaky art instruction); *Pet Science: 50 Purr-Fectly Woof-Worthy Activities for You & Your Pets*, by Veronika Alice Gunter (ages 8-12, science/activity).

How to Contact/Writers Accepts international submissions. Fiction: Submit complete ms. Nonfiction: Submit outline/synopsis and 1 sample chapter. Responds to queries in 3 weeks; mss in 3 months. Publishes book 1 year after acceptance. Considers simultaneous submissions, electronic submissions, previously published work.

Illustration Accepts material from international illustrators. Works with 5-7 illustrators/year. Reviews ms/illustration packages. For ms/illustration packages: Send manuscript with dummy. Submit ms/illustration packages to Joe Rhatigan, senior editor. If interested in illustrating future titles, query with samples. Submit samples to Celia Naranjo, creative director. Samples returned with SASE.

Terms Offers advance against royalties. Author sees galleys for review. Illustrators see dummies for review. Originals not returned. Catalog on Web site. Individual catalogs for imprints. See Web site for writer's guidelines.

Tips "Study the market you're writing for. Let me know why you think now is the right time to publish your book idea. I'm always on the lookout for strong writers with an expertise in an area (science, art, etc.), and even through we publish a lot of books that appeal to teachers and parents, these books are for the kids. Our books have a lot of humor in them as well as a lot of things to do and learn."

LEE & LOW BOOKS INC.

95 Madison Ave., New York NY 10016-7801. (212)779-4400. Fax: (212) 683-1894. E-mail: info@leeandlow.com. Web site: www.leeandlow.com. **Acquisitions:** Louise May, editor-in-chief; Jennifer Fox, senior editor. Publishes 12-14 picture books/year. 25% of books by first-time authors. Lee & Low publishes only books with multicultural themes. "One of our goals is to discover new talent and produce books that reflect the multicultural society in which we live."

- Lee & Low Books is dedicated to publishing culturally authentic literature. The company makes a special effort to work with writers and artists of color and encourages new voices. See listings for their imprint Bebop Books and their New Voices Award. Their title *Brothers in Hope: The Story of the Lost Boys of Sudan*, by R. Gregory Christie, won a 2006 Coretta Scott King Illustrator Honor Award.

Fiction Picture books, young readers: anthology, contemporary, history, multicultural, poetry. "We are not considering folktales or animal stories." Picture book, middle reader: contemporary, history, multicultural, nature/environment, poetry, sports. Average word length: picture books—1,000-1,500 words. Recently pub-

Book Publishers

lished *Jazz Baby* by Carol Boston Weatherford, illustrated by Laura Freeman; *Home at Last* by Susan Middleton Elya, illustrated by Felipe Davalos.

Nonfiction Picture books: concept. Picture books, middle readers: biography, history, multicultural, science and sports. Average word length: picture books—1,500-3,000. Recently published *George Crum and the Saratoga Chip*, by Gaylia Taylor, illustrated by Frank Morrison by Lynne Barasch; *Rattlesnake Mesa*, by Ednah New Rider Weber, photographed by Richela Renkun.

How to Contact/Writers Fiction/nonfiction: Submit complete ms. No e-mail: submissions. Responds in 4 months. Publishes a book 1-2 years after acceptance. Will consider simultaneous submissions. Guidelines on Web site.

Illustration Works with 12-14 illustrators/year. Uses color artwork only. Reviews ms/illustration packages from artists. Contact: Louise May. Submit ms with dummy. Illustrations only: Query with samples, résumé, promo sheet and tearsheets. Responds only if interested. Samples returned with SASE; samples filed. Original artwork returned at job's completion.

Photography Buys photos from freelancers. Works on assignment only. Model/property releases required. Submit cover letter, résumé, promo piece and book dummy.

Terms Pays authors royalty. Offers advances against royalty. Pays illustrators royalty plus advance against royalty. Photographers paid royalty plus advance against royalty. Sends galleys to authors; proofs to illustrators. Book catalog available for 9×12 SAE and $1.75 postage; ms and art guidelines available via Web site or with SASE.

Tips ''We strongly urge writers to visit our Web site and familiarize themselves with our list before submitting. Materials will only be returned with SASE.''

LEGACY PRESS

Imprint of Rainbow Publishers, P.O. Box 70130 Richmond VA 23255. (800)323-7337. **Manuscript/Art Acquisitions:** Christy Scannell, editorial director. Publishes 3 young readers/year; 3 middle readers/year; 3 young adult titles/year. Publishes nonfiction, Bible-teaching books. ''We publish growth and development books for the evangelical Christian from a nondenominational viewpoint that may be marketed primarily through Christian bookstores.''

Nonfiction Young readers, middle readers, young adults: reference, religion. Recently published *The Christian Girl's Guide to Friendship*, by Kathy Widenhouse, illustrated by Anita DuFalla.

How to Contact/Writers Nonfiction: Submit outline/synopsis and 3-5 sample chapters. Responds to queries in 6 weeks; mss in 3 months. Publishes a book 36 months after acceptance. Will consider simultaneous submissions and previously published work.

Illustration Works with 5 illustrators/year. Reviews ms/illustration packages from artists. Submit ms with 5-10 pieces of final art. Illustrations only: Query with samples to be kept on file.

Terms Pays authors royalty or work purchased outright. Offers advances. Pays illustrators per illustration. Sends galley to authors. Book catalog available for business size SASE; ms guidelines for SASE.

Tips ''Get to know the Christian bookstore market. We are looking for innovative ways to teach and encourage children about the Christian life. No picture books please.''

LERNER PUBLISHING GROUP

241 First Ave. N., Minneapolis MN 55401. (612)332-3344. Fax: (612)332-7615. E-mail: info@lernerbooks.com. Web site: www.lernerbooks.com. **Manuscript Acquisitions:** Jennifer Zimian, nonfiction submissions editor; Zelda Wagner, fiction submissions editor. Primarily publishes books for children ages 7-18. List includes titles in geography, natural and physical science, current events, ancient and modern history, high interest, sports, world cultures, and numerous biography series.

- Lerner only accepts submissions during the month of November. See also listing for Carolrhoda Books, Inc., Kar-Ben Publishing and Millbrook Press.

How to Contact/Writers Submissions are accepted in the month of November only. Work received in any month other than November will be returned unopened. ''A SASE is required for authors who wish to have their materials returned. Please allow 8 months for a response. No phone calls please.''

Tips Lerner Publishing Group does not publish alphabet books, puzzle books, song books, textbooks, workbooks, religious subject matter or plays.

ARTHUR A. LEVINE BOOKS

Imprint of Scholastic, Inc., 557 Broadway, New York NY 10012. (212)343-4436. Fax: (212)343-4890. Web site: www.arthuralevinebooks.com. **Acquisitions:** Arthur A. Levine, editorial director. Publishes approximately 8 picture books/year; 8 full-length works for middle grade and young adult readers/year. Approximately 25% of books by first-time authors.

Fiction Recently published *The Red Bird*, by Astrid Lindgren (picture book); *Eating Up Gladys*, by Kaethe Zemach (picture book); *Stanford Wong Flunks Big Time*, by Lisa Yee (novel); *Absolutely Positively Not Gay*, by David LaRochelle (novel).

Nonfiction Recently published *A Grand Old Tree*, by Mary Newell DePalma; *Dizzy*, by Jonah Winter; *Marco Polo*, by Russell Freedman.

How to Contact/Writers Fiction/nonfiction: Accepts queries only. Responds to queries in 1 month; mss in 5 months. Publishes a book 1½ years after acceptance.

Illustration Works with 8 illustrators/year. Will review ms/illustration packages from artists. Query first. Illustrations only: Send postcard sample with tearsheets. Samples not returned.

Ⓐ LITTLE, BROWN AND COMPANY CHILDREN'S BOOKS

Time Warner Book Group Company, Time-Life Bldg., 1271 Avenue of the Americas, New York NY 10020. (212)522-8700. Fax: (212)522-7997. Web site: www.twbookmark.com/children. **Publisher:** Megan Tingley. Executive Editor: Andrea Spooner. Executive Editor: Cynthia Eagan. Senior Editor: Jennifer Hunt. **Creative Director:** Gail Doobinin. Editorial Director of Megan Tingley Books: Megan Tingley. Publishes picture books, board books, chapter books and general nonfiction and novels for middle and young adult readers.

• Little, Brown does not accept unsolicited mss or unagented material.

Fiction Picture books: adventure, animal, contemporary, folktales, history, humor, multicultural, nature/environment. Young adults: contemporary, humor, multicultural, nature/environment, suspense/mystery, chick lit. Multicultural needs include "any material by, for and about minorities." Average word length: picture books—1,000; young readers—6,000; middle readers—15,000-25,000; young adults—20,000-40,000. Recently published *Mable O'Leary*, by Mary Delaney, illustrated by Kathy Couri; *The Gift of Nothing*, by Patrick McDonnel; *Flight of the Dodo*, by Peter Brown; *How to Train Your Dragon*, by Cressida Cowell; *The Not-So-Star Spangled Life of Sunita Sen*, by Mitali Perkins.

Nonfiction Middle readers, young adults: arts/crafts, history, multicultural, nature, self help, social issues, sports, science. Average word length: middle readers—15,000-25,000; young adults—20,000-40,000. Recently published *Harlem Stomp*, by Laban Carrick Hill; *Museum 1-2-3*, by the Metropolitan Museum of Art.

How to Contact/Writers Only interested in solicited agented material. Fiction: Submit complete ms. Nonfiction: Submit cover letter, previous publications, a proposal, outline and 3 sample chapters. Do not send originals. Responds to queries in 2 weeks. Responds to mss in 2 months.

Illustration Works with 40 illustrators/year. Illustrations only: Query art director with b&w and color samples; provide résumé, promo sheet or tearsheets to be kept on file. Does not respond to art samples. Do not send originals; copies only.

Photography Works on assignment only. Model/property releases required; captions required. Publishes photo essays and photo concept books. Uses 35mm transparencies. Photographers should provide résumé, promo sheets or tearsheets to be kept on file.

Terms Pays authors royalties based on retail price. Pays illustrators and photographers by the project or royalty based on retail price. Sends galleys to authors; dummies to illustrators.

Tips "Publishers are cutting back their lists in response to a shrinking market and relying more on big names and known commodities. In order to break into the field these days, authors and illustrators should research their competition and try to come up with something outstandingly different."

Ⓒ LOLLIPOP POWER BOOKS

Imprint of Carolina Wren Press, 120 Morris Street, Durham NC 27701. (919)560-2738. Fax: (919)560-2759. E-mail: carolinawrenpress@earthlink.net. Web site: www.carolinawrenpress.org. **Manuscript Acquisitions:** Children's Book Editor. **Art Acquisitions:** Art Director. Publishes 1 picture book/year. 50% of books by first-time authors. "Carolina Wren Press and Lollipop Power specialize in children's books that counter stereotypes or debunk myths about race, gender, sexual orientation, etc. We are also interested in books that deal with health or mental health issues—our two biggest sellers are *Puzzles* (about a young girl coping with Sickle Cell Disease) and *I like it when you joke with me, I don't like it when you touch me* (about inappropriate touching). Many of our children's titles are bilingual (English/Spanish)."

Fiction Average word length: picture books—500.

How to Contact/Writers Children's lit submissions are read February through June. (Illustrators may send samples any time.) Fiction: Submit outline/synopsis and 3 sample chapters. Responds to queries/mss in 3 months. Publishes book 2 years after acceptance. Will consider simultaneous submissions.

Illustration Works with 1 illustrator/year. Reviews ms/illustration packages from artists. Submit ms with 5 pieces of final art. Illustrations only: Send photocopies, résumé, samples, SASE. Responds only if interested. Samples returned with SASE; samples filed.

Terms Pays authors royalty of 10% minimum based on retail price or work purchased outright from authors (range: $500-$2,000). Pays illustrators by the project (range: $500-$2,000). Sends galleys to authors; dummies to illustrators. Originals returned to artist at job's completion. Manuscript and art guidelines available for SASE. Catalog available on Web site.

LUCENT BOOKS

Imprint of Thomson Gale, 15822 Bernard Center Dr., Suite C, San Diego CA 92127. E-mail: chandra.howard@thomson.com. Web site: www.gale.com/lucent. **Acquisitions:** Chandra Howard. Series publisher of educational nonfiction for junior high school and library markets.

• See also listing for Greenhaven Press.

Nonfiction Young adult and academic reference: current issues, diseases, drugs, biographies, geopolitics, history. Recently launched Library of Black History. Recently published *Hurricane Katrina: Devastation on the Gulf Coast*; *Cleopatra: Egypt's Last Pharaoh*; *The Nuremberg Trials*; *The Relocation of the North American Indian*.

How to Contact/Writers E-mail query with résumé or list of publications.

Terms Work purchased outright from authors; write-for-hire, flat fee.

Tips No unsolicited manuscripts.

LUNA RISING

Imprint of Rising Moon, P.O. Box 1389, Flagstaff AZ 86002-1389. (928)774-5251. Fax: (928)774-0592. E-mail: editorial@northlandpub.com. Web site: www.lunarisingbooks.com. Estab. 2004. Published bilingual hardcover and trade paperback originals. **Writers contact:** Theresa Howell. Produces 2-4 picture books/year. 20% of books by first-time authors. "Luna Rising publishes high quality original fiction and biographies with Latino themes. Preference is given to Latino writers and illustrators."

Fiction Picture books: multicultural.

Nonfiction Picture books: biography, multicultural. Recently published *My Name is Celia: The Life of Celia Cruz*, by Monica Brown, illustrated by Rafael Lopez; *Playing Loteria*, by Rene Colato Lainez, illustrated by Jill Arena.

How to Contact/Writers Fiction/nonfiction: Submit complete ms. Responds to queries in 3 months. Publishes book 1-2 years after acceptance. Considers simultaneous submissions.

Terms Authors paid royalty or flat fee. Offers advance against royalties. Offers writer's guidelines for SASE.

Tips "We are looking for original bilingual stories and biographies of Latino role models. Call for book catalog."

MAGINATION PRESS

750 First Street, NE, Washington DC 20002-2984. (202)218-3982. Fax: (202)336-5624. Web site: www.maginationpress.com. **Acquisitions:** Darcie Conner Johnston, managing editor. Publishes 4 picture books/year; 4 young readers/year; 2 middle readers/year; 1 young adult title/year. 75% of books by first-time authors. "We publish books dealing with the psycho/therapeutic resolution of children's problems and psychological issues with a strong self-help component."

• Magination Press is an imprint of the American Psychological Association.

Fiction All levels: psychological and social issues, self-help, health, multicultural, special needs. Picture books, middle readers. Recently published *Ginny Morris and Mom's House, Dad's House*, by Mary Collins Gallagher, illustrated by Whitney Martin (ages 8-12); *Big Sister Now: A Story About Me and Our New Baby*, by Annette Sheldon, illustrated by Jackie Urbanovic (ages 4-8).

Nonfiction All levels: psychological and social issues, special needs, self help. Picture books, young readers, middle readers: activity, workbooks. Recently published *Feeling Better: A Kid's Book About Therapy*, by Rachel Rashkin, illustrated by Bonnie Adamson (ages 8-12); *What to Do When You Worry Too Much: A Kid's Guide to Overcoming Anxiety*, by Dawn Huebner, illustrated by Bonnie Matthews (ages 6-12).

How to Contact/Writers Fiction/nonfiction: Submit complete ms. Responds to queries in 1-2 months; mss in 2-6 months. Will consider simultaneous submissions. Materials returned only with a SASE. Publishes a book 18-24 months after acceptance.

Illustration Works with 10-15 illustrators/year. Reviews ms/illustration packages. Will review artwork for future assignments. Responds only if interested, or immediately if SASE or response card is included. We keep samples on file.

How to Contact/Illustrators Illustrations only: Query with samples; a few samples and Web address are best. Original artwork returned at job's completion.

Photography Buys stock.

Terms Pays authors royalty of 5-15% based on actual revenues (net). Pays illustrators by the project. Book catalog and ms guidelines on request with SASE. Catalog and ms guidelines available on Web site.

☐ MASTER BOOKS

Imprint of New Leaf Press, P.O. Box 726, Green Forest, AR 72638. (870)438-5288. Fax: (870)438-5120. E-mail: nlp@newleafpress.net. Web site: www.masterbooks.net. **Manuscript Acquisitions:** Amanda Price, acquisitions editor. **Art Acquisitions:** Brent Spurlock, art director. Publishes 2 picture books/year; 3 young readers/year; 3 middle readers/year; 2 young adult titles/year. 10% of books by first-time authors.

Nonfiction Picture books: activity books, animal, nature/environment, creation. Young readers, middle readers, young adults: activity books, animal, biography Christian, nature/environment, science, creation. Recently published *Whale of a Story*, by Buddy Davis (middle readers, Bible story); *Dinky Dinosaur*, by Darrell Wiskur (picture book, creation); *For Those Who Dare*, by John Hudson Tiner (young adult, biography).

How to Contact/Writers Nonfiction: Submit outline/synopsis and 3 sample chapters. Responds to queries/mss in 3 months. Publishes book 1 year after acceptance. Will consider simultaneous submissions.

Illustration We are not looking for illustrations.

Terms Pays authors royalty of 3-15% based on wholesale price. Sends galleys to authors. Book catalog available for 9×12 SAE and $1.85 postage; ms guidelines available for SASE. Catalog available on Web site.

Tips "All of our children's books are creation-based, including topics from the Book of Genesis. We look also for homeschool educational material that would be supplementary to a homeschool curriculum."

MARGARET K. MCELDERRY BOOKS

Imprint of Simon & Schuster Children's Publishing Division, 1230 Avenue of the Americas, New York NY 10020. (212)698-7000. Web site: www.simonsayskids.com. Vice President, Associate Publisher: Emma D. Dryden. **Acquisitions:** Karen Wojtyla, executive editor; Sarah Sevier, associate editor. **Art Acquisitions:** Ann Bobco, executive art director. Imprint of Simon & Schuster Children's Publishing Division. Publishes 15+ picture books/year; 8-10 middle readers/year; 8-10 young adult titles/year. 10% of books by first-time authors; 50% of books from agented writers. "Margaret K. McElderry Books publishes original hardcover trade books for children from preschool age through young adult. This list includes picture books, easy-to-read books, fiction for eight-to twelve-year-olds, poetry, fantasy and young adult fiction. The style and subject matter of the books we publish is almost unlimited. We do not publish textbooks, coloring and activity books, greeting cards, magazines, pamphlets, or religious publications."

- McElderry title *The Legend of Buddy Bush*, by Sheila P. Moses, won a 2005 Coretta Scott King Author Honor and was a National Book Award Finalist.

Fiction Young readers: adventure, contemporary, fantasy, history, poetry. Middle readers: adventure, contemporary, fantasy, humor, mystery. Young adults: contemporary, fantasy, mystery. "Always interested in publishing humorous picture books, original beginning reader stories, and strong poetry." Average word length: picture books—500; young readers—2,000; middle readers—10,000-20,000; young adults—45,000-50,000. Recently published *Bear Wants More*, by Karma Wilson, illustrated by Jane Chapman; *Mathmatickles*, by Betsy Franco, illustrated by Steven Salerno; *The Puppeteer's Apprentice*, by D. Anne Love; *Izzy's Place*, by Marc Kornblatt.

Nonfiction Young readers, young adult teens, biography, history. Average word length: picture books—500-1,000; young readers—1,500-3,000; middle readers—10,000-20,000; young adults—30,000-45,000. Recently published *Shout, Sister, Shout!*, by Roxane Orgill.

How to Contact/Writers Fiction/nonfiction: Submit synopsis and first 3 chapters or first 30 pages with SASE; may also include brief résumé of previous publishing credits. Send query for picture books. Responds to queries in 1 month; mss in 3-4 months. Publishes a book 20-36 months after contract signing. Will consider simultaneous submissions (only if indicated as such).

Illustration Works with 20-30 illustrators/year. Query with samples; provide promo sheet or tearsheets; arrange personal portfolio review. Contact: Ann Bobco, executive art director. Responds to art samples in 3 months. Samples returned with SASE or samples filed.

Terms Pays authors and illustrators royalty based on retail price. Pays photographers by the project. Original artwork returned at job's completion. Manuscript guidelines free on request with SASE.

Tips "We're looking for strong, original fiction, especially mysteries and middle grade humor. We are always interested in picture books for the youngest age reader."

MEADOWBROOK PRESS

5451 Smetana Dr., Minnetonka MN 55343-9012. (952)930-1100. Fax: (952)930-1940. Web site: www.meadowbrookpress.com. **Manuscript Acquisitions:** Submissions Editor. **Art Acquisitions:** Art Director. Publishes 1-2 middle readers/year. 20% of books by first-time authors; 10% of books from agented writers. Publishes children's poetry books, activity books, arts-and-crafts books and how-to books.

- Meadowbrook does not accept unsolicited children's picture books, short stories or novels. They are primarily a nonfiction press. The publisher offers specific guidelines for children's poetry. Be sure to specify the type of project you have in mind when requesting guidelines, or visit their Web site.

Nonfiction Publishes activity books, arts/crafts, how-to, poetry. Average word length: varies. Recently published *Wiggle and Giggle Busy Book*, by Trish Kuffner (activity book); *Rolling in the Aisle*, by Bruce Lansky.

How to Contact/Writers Nonfiction: See guidelines on Web site before submitting. Responds only if interested. Publishes a book 1-2 years after acceptance. Will consider simultaneous submissions.

Illustration Works with 2 illustrators/year. Reviews ms/illustration packages from artists. Submit ms with 2-3 pieces of nonreturnable samples. Responds only if interested. Samples filed.

Photography Buys photos from freelancers. Buys stock. Model/property releases required. Submit cover letter.

Audrey Couloumbis

Wresting memorable characters to the page

Book Publishers

With a string of awards including a Newbery Honor on her résumé, Audrey Couloumbis has risen to become a top novelist in the young adult genre. But before she became an established author, Couloumbis struggled to break into publishing for 10 years—until she finally decided if you can't beat 'em, join 'em.

"Over the 10 years it took me to break into the children's market, I noticed a shift in the way agents responded—they ceased to, though my writing was closer to the mark," says Couloumbis. "I needed a look at the business from the inside, so I got a job with a literary agent for children's writers."

That job proved to be just what she needed to finally make her breakthrough. "Reading the first chapter of a hundred manuscripts at a time taught me to recognize strengths and weaknesses very quickly, and I applied those lessons to my work," she says. "Less description, but more scene. Less dialogue, more conflict. I want to know right away, as the reader does, whom this book is about. What happened that made this character act out in a way that would drive a parent to the wall? I think I needed that demonstration to take my writing to the next level."

The result, *Just Before Daybreak* (St. Martin's Press), was a coming-of-age novel that deals with divorce, child abuse and violence, all told through the perspective of Allie, a precocious, strong-willed adolescent girl. That kind of protagonist has become a favorite of Couloumbis', whose subsequent novels have all had similar characters at their core. *Say Yes* (Putnam Juvenile) tells the story of 12-year-old Casey, who is abandoned by her stepmother; *Summer's End* (Putnam Juvenile) revolves around 13-year-old Grace, growing up amidst the turmoil of the Vietnam War; and the Newbery Honor-winning *Getting Near to Baby* (Puffin Books) is told by Willa Jo, a 12-year-old coping with a family tragedy. "I suppose my girls are outspoken and strong-willed because I can be," Couloumbis says. "They are not largely autobiographical, but they are very often not everybody's favorite kid. I wasn't either. So I'm sort of on their side."

As to how she creates such memorable characters, "I'd have to say my characters come to me with a life of their own, and a voice that tells the story," Couloumbis says. "Once I hear that voice, I just start writing down what it has to say." To get to know that voice a little better, Couloumbis asks herself a series of questions about the character:

- Ten observations the character would make
- Ten things he or she would fight for
- Ten decisions he or she would make
- What he or she thinks about when daydreaming
- Five sensitivities, and how they developed

- Five of their personal childhood horrors
- Five intentions they have, maybe 10
- Five reasons for something they do, or something about their appearance, that is directly related to the story

Sallie March, the main character in Couloumbis' latest novel, *The Misadventures of Maude March* (Random House), is as headstrong and unique as any of the author's earlier creations. Set in the Old West, the novel tells the tale of how Sally and her sister Maude become a pair of celebrated outlaws after fleeing from an orphanage.

A lighthearted, rollicking story, the novel is a departure from Couloumbis' earlier work. But, she says, the transition was a smooth one. "I didn't feel any particular challenge in moving from one story to another. My writing approach is eclectic by nature. I read about writing screenplays as well as novels, a lot of different kinds of fiction, I watch movies—that is, I watch them over and over to pick them apart, to figure out what made them successful or otherwise."

Couloumbis' writing approach is also influenced by advice she received from a good friend early in her career. "My friend Pauline Macmillan was once the registrar at Banks Street College, where children's books are highly respected, and so my expressed desire to write for kids did not fall on deaf ears. Her advice was always couched in the best possible way. She'd say, 'That character is really persistent, clueless, self-involved, etc., isn't she?', pinpointing something about character development that she thought I ought to look at. She would hand me books like Marilynne Robinson's *Housekeeping*, and say, 'You're going to love these people.' She got me used to thinking of my characters as people I knew. We talked about them in this over-the-back-fence way that made them come alive."

Ultimately, Couloumbis says, fictional characters are as idiosyncratic as their creator, and each writer has to find his or her own way of

Reprinted with permission.

The Misadventures of Maude March, the latest novel from Newbery Honor-winning author Audrey Couloumbis, is the Wild West tale of twice-orphaned 11-year-old tomboy Sallie and her ladylike older sister Maude. "Sallie's narration is delightful, with understatements that are laugh-out-loud hilarious," says *School Library Journal*. "While this novel at first seems a departure for Couloumbis, there are many similarities to *Getting Near to Baby* and *Say Yes*. Her strong females are memorable, largely due to her perfect pitch in conveying their unique voices."

giving their characters a voice. "However a writer wrestles that character to the page, it's a job well done. It's a matter of asking, what makes me feel like that character in someone else's book is the real thing, what do I need to be noticing, writing down? The answers are internalized while you're learning, and finally you come out on the other side, where your characters—your subconscious—will do the hard part for you."

—*Travis Adkins*

Terms Pays authors royalty of 5-7% based on retail price. Offers average advance payment of $2,000-4,000. Pays illustrators per project. Pays photographers by the project. Book catalog available for 5×11 SASE and 2 first-class stamps; ms guidelines and artists guidelines available for SASE.

Tips "Illustrators and writers should visit our Web site before submitting their work to us. Also, illustrators should take a look at the books we publish to determine whether their style is consistent with ours. Writers should also note the style and content patterns of our books. No phone calls, please—e-mail us. We work with the printed word and will respond more effectively to your questions if we have something in front of us."

MEDALLION PRESS, INC.

27825 N. Forest Garden, Wauconda IL 60084. Web site: www.medallionpress.com. Estab. 2003. Specializes in trade books, fiction. **Manuscript Acquisitions:** Wendy Burbank, acquisitions editor. Imprints: Bronze (YA), Wendy Burbank. Produces 11 young adult books/year. 80% of books by first-time authors.

Fiction Young adults/teens: adventure, contemporary, fantasy, history, humor, multicultural, nature/environment, problem novels, science fiction, special needs, sports, suspense. Average word length: young adult—55,000 minimum. Recently published *The Secret of Shabaz*, by Jennifer Macaire (ages 9 and up, YA).

How to Contact/Writers Accepts international submissions. Fiction: Submit outline/synopsis and first 3 sample chapters. Does not accept e-mail submissions and will not respond to e-mail regarding status of submissions. Responds to queries in up to 6 months; mss in up to 12 months. Publishes book up to 2 years after acceptance.

Terms Offers advance against royalties. Catalog on Web site.

Tips "We cannot stress enough how important is is that a submission packet be edited properly. You may have the best book in the world in terms of a story idea, but if the book is grammatically poor, it will be rejected. Have an unbiased editor edit your manuscript before submitting. Lead/start trends rather than follow them. We are up to our ears in YA fantasy submissions and are not currently seeking anymore. Where are the action adventure, mystery, suspense, thriller stories for young adults?"

MERIWETHER PUBLISHING LTD.

885 Elkton Dr., Colorado Springs CO 80907-3557. (719)594-9916. Fax: (719)594-9916. E-mail: merpcds@aol.com. Web site: www.meriwetherpublishing.com. **Manuscript Acquisitions:** Ted Zapel, comedy plays and educational drama; Rhonda Wray, religious drama. "We do most of our artwork in-house; we do not publish for the children's elementary market." 75% of books by first-time authors; 5% of books from agented writers. "Our niche is drama. Our books cover a wide variety of theatre subjects from play anthologies to theatrecraft. We publish books of monologs, duologs, short one-act plays, scenes for students, acting textbooks, how-to speech and theatre textbooks, improvisation and theatre games. Our Christian books cover worship on such topics as clown ministry, storytelling, banner-making, drama ministry, children's worship and more. We also publish anthologies of Christian sketches. We do not publish works of fiction or devotionals."

Fiction Middle readers, young adults: anthology, contemporary, humor, religion. "We publish plays, not prose-fiction." Our emphasis is comedy plays instead of educational themes.

Nonfiction Middle readers: activity books, how-to, religion, textbooks. Young adults: activity books, drama/theater arts, how-to church activities, religion. Average length: 250 pages. Recently published *Acting for Life*, by Jack Frakes; *Scenes Keep Happening*, by Mary Krell-Oishi; *Service with a Smile*, by Daniel Wray.

How to Contact/Writers Nonfiction: Query or submit outline/synopsis and sample chapters. Responds to queries in 3 weeks; mss in 2 months or less. Publishes a book 6-12 months after acceptance. Will consider simultaneous submissions.

Illustration Works with 2 illustrators/year. Query first. Query with samples; send résumé, promo sheet or tearsheets. Samples returned with SASE.

Terms Pays authors royalty of 10% based on retail or wholesale price. Book catalog for SAE and $2 postage; ms guidelines for SAE and 1 first-class stamp.

Tips "We are currently interested in finding unique treatments for theater arts subjects: scene books, how-to books, musical comedy scripts, monologs and short comedy plays for teens."

MILET PUBLISHING LTD.

333 N. Michigan Ave., Suite 530, Chicago IL 60601. (312)920-1828. Fax: (312)920-1829. E-mail: info@milet.com. Web site: www.milet.com. Estab. 1995. Specializes in trade books, nonfiction, fiction, multicultural material. **Writers contact:** Editorial Director. **Illustrators contact:** Editorial Director. Produces 30+ picture books, 2 middle readers/year. "Milet publishes a celebrated range of artistic and innovative children's books in English, as well as the leading range of bilingual children's books."

Fiction Picture books: adventure, animal, concept, contemporary, hi-lo, humor, multicultural, poetry. Young readers: adventure, animal, concept, contemporary, fantasy, hi-lo, multicultural, nature/environment, poetry. Middle readers: adventure, animal, contemporary, fantasy, multicultural, nature/environment, poetry, problem novels. Young adults/teens: contemporary, fantasy, multicultural, nature/environment, poetry, problem novels. Recently published *Chameleon Races*, by Laura Hambleton (ages 3 and up, picture book in English and 13 bilingual editions; *Chameleon Swims*, by Laura Hambleton (ages 3 and up, picture book in English and 13 bilingual editions; *Bella Balistica and the Indian Summer*, by Adam Guilain (ages 8-12, novel).

Nonfiction All levels: activity books, animal, arts/crafts, concept, hi-lo, multicultural, nature/environment, social issues. Recently published *Outside In: Children's Books in Translation*, ed. by Deborah Hallford & Edgardo Zaghini; *Milet Flashwords*, by Sedat Turhan & Sally Hagin (in English and 15 bilingual editions.)

How to Contact/Writers Accepts international submissions. Fiction/nonfiction: Submit outline/synopsis and 2-3 sample chapters. Responds to queries in 1 weeks; mss in 1-2 months. Publishes book 12-18 months after acceptance. Considers simultaneous submissions.

Illustration Accepts material from international illustrators. Works with 4-5 illustrators/year. Uses both color and b&w. Reviews ms/illustration packages. For ms/illustration packages: Submit ms with 2-3 pieces of final art. Reviews work for future assignments. If interested in illustrating future titles, send résumé, promo sheet, client list. Submit samples to Editorial Director. Samples returned with SASE.

Terms Authors paid all terms negotiated depending on type of project. Author sees galleys for review. Illustrators see dummies for review. Catalog on Web site. All imprints included in single catalog. See Web site for writer's, artist's guidelines.

Tips "Please check our list on our Web site to see if your work will be suitable. We are interested only in fresh, imaginative, nontraditional work."

MILKWEED EDITIONS

1011 Washington Ave. S., Suite 300, Minneapolis MN 55415-1246. (612)332-3192. Fax: (612)215-2550. E-mail: editor@milkweed.org. Web site: www.milkweed.org. **Manuscript Acquisitions:** Daniel Slager, editor-in-chief. Publishes 3-4 middle readers/year. 25% of books by first-time authors. "Milkweed Editions publishes with the intention of making a humane impact on society, in the belief that literature is a transformative art uniquely able to convey the essential experiences of the human heart and spirit. To that end, Milkweed Editions publishes distinctive voices of literary merit in handsomely designed, visually dynamic books, exploring the ethical, cultural, and esthetic issues that free societies need continually to address."

Fiction Middle readers: adventure, contemporary, fantasy, multicultural, nature/environment, suspense/mystery. Does not want to see anthologies, folktales, health, hi-lo, picture books, poetry, religion, romance, sports. Average length: middle readers—90-200 pages. Recently published *Perfect,* by Natasha Friend (contemporary); *Trudy,* by Jessica Lee Anderson (contemporary); *A Small Boat at the Bottom of the Sea*, by John Thompson (adventure).

How to Contact/Writers Fiction: Submit complete ms. Responds to mss in 6 months. Publishes a book 1 year after acceptance. Will consider simultaneous submissions.

Illustration Works with 2-4 illustrators/year. Reviews ms/illustration packages from artists. Query; submit ms with dummy. Illustrations only: Query with samples; provide résumé, promo sheet, slides, tearsheets and client list. Samples filed or returned with SASE; samples filed. Originals returned at job's completion.

Terms Pays authors royalty of 6% based on retail price. Offers advance against royalties. Illustrators' contracts are decided on an individual basis. Sends galleys to authors. Book catalog available for $1.50 to cover postage; ms guidelines available for SASE or at Web site. Must include SASE with ms submission for its return.

⬛ THE MILLBROOK PRESS

A division of Lerner Publishing Group, 241 First Avenue North Minneapolis, MN 5540. (800)328-4929. Fax: (800)332-1132. Web site: www.lernerbooks.com.

• Millbrook Press publishes supplementary series and individual titles for the K-8 School & Library market. Millbrook Press is now a division of Lerner Publishing Group, an independent publisher since 1959. See listing for Lerner for submission information.

MIRRORSTONE

Imprint of Wizards of the Coast, P.O. Box 707, Renton WA 98057. (425)254-2287. Web site: www.mirrorstonebooks. com. **Manuscript and Art Acquisitions:** Nina Hess. Publishes 12 middle readers/year; 6 young adult titles/year. 25% of books by first-time authors. "We publish series novels for young readers designed to spur the imagination."

Fiction Young readers, middle readers, young adults: fantasy. Average word length: middle readers—50-55,000; young adults—70-75,000. Recently published *Temple of the Dragonslayer*, by Tim Waggoner (ages 10 and up); *Sectret of the Spiritkeeper*, by Matt Forbeck (ages 8 and up); *Riddle in Stone*, by Ree Soesbee (ages 8 and up).

How to Contact/Writers Fiction: Query with samples, résumé. "No manuscripts, please." Responds to queries in 6-8 weeks. Publishes book 9 months after acceptance.

Illustration Works with 4 illustrators/year. Query. Illustrations only: Query with samples, résumé.

Terms Pays authors royalty of 4-6% based on retail price. Offers advances (average amount: $4,000). Pays illustrators by the project. Ms guidelines available for SASE. All imprints included in a single catalog. Catalog available on Web site.

Tips Editorial staff attended or plans to attend ALA conference.

MITCHELL LANE PUBLISHERS, INC.

P.O. Box 196, Hockessin DE 19707. (302)234-9426. Fax: (302)234-4742. E-mail: mitchelllane@mitchelllane.com. Web site: www.mitchelllane.com. **Acquisitons:** Barbara Mitchell, president. Publishes 80 young adult titles/year. "We publish nonfiction for children and young adults."

Nonfiction Young readers, middle readers, young adults: biography, multicultural. Average word length: 4,000-50,000 words. Recently published *Ashanti, Paris Hilton* (both Blue Banner Biographies); *Jamie Lynn Spears* (A Robbie Reader).

How to Contact/Writers Most assignments are work-for-hire.

Illustration Works with 2-3 illustrators/year. Reviews ms/illustration packages from artists. Query. Illustration only: Query with samples; send résumé, portfolio, slides, tearsheets. Responds only if interested. Samples not returned; samples filed.

Photography Buys stock images. Needs photos of famous and prominent minority figures. Captions required. Uses color prints or digital images. Submit cover letter, résumé, published samples, stock photo list.

Terms Work purchased outright from authors (range: $350-2,000). Pays illustrators by the project (range: $40-400). Sends galleys to authors.

Tips "Most of our assignments are work-for-hire. Submit résumé and samples of work to be considered for future assignments."

N MITTEN PRESS

Ann Arbor Media Group, 2500 S. State St., Ann Arbor MI 48104. Estab. 2005. (734)913-1302. Fax: (734)913-1249. E-mail: ljohnson@mittenpress.com. Web site: www.mittenpress.com. **Acquiring Editor:** Lynne Johnson.

Fiction Picture books: adventure, animal, folktales, history, multicultural, nature/environment, sports. Recently published: *The Far-Flung Adventure of Homer the Hummer*, by Cynthia Reynolds & Catherine McClung (ages 6-10, picture book); *The Bird in Santa's Beard*, by Jeffrey Schatzer (ages 3-10, picture book); *Pippa's First Summer*, by Catherine Badgley & Bonnie Miljour.

How to Contact/Writers Submit complete ms.

Illustration Buys 6-8 illustrations/year. Will review mss/illustration packages. Submit manuscript with 3 sample chapters to Lynne Johnson, acquisitions editor. Illustration only: Query with samples. Submit to Lynne Johnson, acquisitions editor. Responds in 4 weeks. Samples not returned; samples filed.

Terms Authors see galley for review; illustrators see dummies. Original artwork returned at job's completion. Book catalog available on Web site. All imprints included in single catalog. Writer's guidelines offered on Web site.

Tips "Think through and provide information on how your book will be marketed."

MORGAN REYNOLDS PUBLISHING

620 S. Elm St., Suite 223, Greensboro NC 27406. (336)275-1311. Fax: (336)275-1152. E-mail: editorial@morganreynolds.com. Web site: www.morganreynolds.com. **Acquisitions:** Casey Cornelius, editor. Book publisher. Publishes 30 young adult titles/year. 50% of books by first-time authors. Morgan Reynolds publishes nonfiction books for juvenile and young adult readers. "We prefer lively, well-written biographies of interesting figures for our extensive biography series. Subjects may be contemporary or historical. Books for our Great Events series should take an insightful and exciting look at pivotal periods and/or events."

Nonfiction Middle readers, young adults/teens: biography, history. Average word length: 25-35,000. Recently published *No Easy Answers: Bayard Rustin and the Civil Rights Movement*, by Calvin Craig Miller; *Empire in the East: The Story of Genghis Khan*, by Earle Rice, Jr.; *The Mail Must Go Through: The Story of the Pony Express*, by Margaret Rau; *Nikola Tesla and the Taming of Electricity*, by Lisa J. Aldrich.

How to Contact/Writers First-time authors submit entire ms. Query; submit outline/synopsis with at least 2 sample chapters and SASE. Responds to queries in 6 weeks; mss in 2 months. Publishes a book 1 year after acceptance. Will consider simultaneous submissions.

Terms Pays authors negotiated price. Offers advances and royalties. Sends galleys to authors. Manuscript guidelines available at our Web site or by mail with SASE and 1 first-class stamp. Visit Web site for complete catalog.

Tips Does not respond without SASE. "Familiarize yourself with our titles before sending a query or submission, keeping in mind that we do *not* publish fiction, poetry, memoirs, picture books. We focus on serious-minded, well-crafted, nonfiction books for young adults that will complement school curriculums, namely biographies of significant figures." Editorial staff has attended or plans to attend the following conferences: ALA, TLA.

NEW CANAAN PUBLISHING COMPANY INC.

P.O. Box 752, New Canaan CT 06840. (203)966-3408. Fax: (203)548-9072. E-mail: djm@newcanaanpublishing.com. Web site: www.newcanaanpublishing.com. Book publisher. Publishes 1 picture book/year; 1 young reader/year; 1 middle reader/year; 1 young adult title/year. 50% of books by first-time authors. "We seek books with strong educational or traditional moral content and books with Christian themes."

• To curb the number of unsolicited submissions, New Cannan Publishing only accepts: 1—books for children of military families; 2—middle readers and young adult books addressing Christian themes (e.g., devotionals, books addressing teen or preteen issues with a Christian focus, whether in a fictional context or otherwise); and 3—historical fiction.

Fiction All levels: adventure, history, religion (Christianity), suspense/mystery. Picture books: phonics readers. ''Stories about disfunctional families are not encouraged.'' Average word length: picture books—1,000-3,000; young readers—8,000-30,000; middle readers—8,000-40,000; young adults—15,000-50,000. Recently published *My Daddy Is An Airman*, by Kirk and Sharron Hilbrecht; *It's Me Again, God*, by Mary Elizabeth Anderson.

Nonfiction All levels: geography, history, how-to, reference, religion (Christian only), textbooks. Average word length: picture books—1,000-3,000; young readers—8,000-30,000; middle readers—8,000-40,000; young adults—15,000-50,000.

How to Contact/Writers Submit outline/synopsis or complete ms with biographical information and writing credentials. Does not guarantee a response unless offer to publish is forthcoming. Responds to queries in 4-6 months; mss in 6 months. Publishes a book 12-18 months after acceptance.

Illustration Works with 3-5 illustrators/year. Reviews ms/illustration packages from artists. Query or send ms with dummy. Illustrations only: Query with samples; send résumé, promo sheet. Responds in 1-2 months if need exists.

Terms Pays authors royalty of 7-12% based on wholesale price. Royalty may be shared with illustrator where relevant. Pays illustrators royalty of 4-6% as share of total royalties. Book catalog available for SAE; ms guidelines available on Web site.

Tips ''We are diligent but small, so please be patient.''

NEW VOICES PUBLISHING

Imprint of KidsTerrain, Inc., P.O. Box 560, Wilmington MA 01887. (978)658-2131. Fax: (978)988-8833. E-mail: rschiano@kidsterrain.com. Web site: www.kidsterrain.com. Estab. 2000. Specializes in fiction. **Manuscript/Art Acquisitions:** Book Editor. Publishes 2 picture books/year. 95% of books by first-time authors.

Fiction Picture books, young readers: multicultural. Average word length: picture books—500; young readers—500-1,200. Recently published *Last Night I Left Earth for Awhile*, written and illustrated by Natalie L. Brown-Douglas (ages 4-8).

How to Contact/Writers Fiction: Not accepting unsolicited manuscripts. Publishes book 12-18 months after acceptance. Will consider simultaneous submissions.

Illustration Works with 2 illustrators/year. Uses color artwork only. Reviews ms/illustration packages from artists. No queries accepted until 2007. Responds in 2 weeks. Samples returned with SASE.

Terms Pays authors royalty of 10-15% based on wholesale price. Pays illustrators by the project or royalty. Sends galleys to authors. Offers writer's guidelines for SASE.

NOMAD PRESS

2456 Christain St., White River Junction NJ 05001. (802)649-1995. Fax: (802)649-2667. E-mail: lauri@nomadpress.net. Web site: www.nomadpress.net. Estab. 2001. Specializes in nonfiction, educational material. **Contact:** Alex Kahan, publisher. Produces 6-8 young readers/year. 10% of books by first-time authors. ''We produce nonfiction children's activity books that bring a particular science or cultural topic into sharp focus.''

• Nomad Press does not accept picture books or fiction.

Nonfiction Middle readers: activity books, history, science. Average word length: middle readers—30,000. Recently published *Tools of Navigation: A Kid's Guide to the History and Science of Finding Your Way*, by Rachel Dickinson (ages 9-12, activity); *Tools of Timekeeping: A Kid's Guide to the History and Science of Telling Time*, by Linda Formichelli and Eric Martin (agest 9-12, activity/education); *Great Civil War Projects You Can Build Yourself*, by Maxine Anderson (ages 8-12, activity/education resource).

How to Contact/Writers Accepts international submissions. Nonfiction: Query or submit complete ms. Responds to queries in 1-2 months. Publishes book 1 year after acceptance.

Terms Pays authors royalty based on retail price or work purchased outright. Offers advance against royalties. Catalog on Web site. All imprints included in single catalog. See Web site for writer's guidelines.

Tips ''We publish a very specific kind of nonfiction children's activity book. Please keep this in mind when querying or submitting.''

Ⓐ NORTH-SOUTH BOOKS

350 Seventh Ave., Suite 1400, New York NY 10001. (212)706-4545. Web site: www.northsouth.com. Imprint: Night Sky. U.S. office of Nord-Siid Verlag, Switzerland. Publishes 75 titles/year.

• North-South and its imprints do not accept queries or unsolicited manuscripts.

NORTHWORD BOOKS FOR YOUNG READERS

Imprint of T&N Children's Publishing international, 11571 K-Tel Dr., Minnetonka MN 55343. (982)933-7537. Web site: www.tnkidsbooks.com. Estab. 1984. Specializes in trade books, nonfiction. **Contact:** Submissions Editor. Produces 4-6 picture books/year; 4-6 young readers/year; 6 middle readers/year. 10-20% of books by first-time authors. NorthWord's mission is "to publish books for children that encourage a love for the natural world."

Fiction Picture books: animal, concept, history, nature/environment, poetry—all nature-related. Young readers: animal, history, nature/environment, poetry—all nature-related. Average word length: picture books—500-1,000; young readers—1,000-4,000. Recently published *Good Morning Little Polar Bear*, by Carol Votaw, illustrated by Susan Banta (ages 2-5, picture book); *Traveling Babies*, by Kathryn O. Galbraith, illustrated by Jane Dippold (ages 2-5, picture book).

Nonfiction Picture books: activity books, animal, arts/crafts, biography, careers, concept, cooking, geography, history, hobbies, how-to, nature/environment, science, sports. Young readers: activity books, animal, arts/crafts, biography, careers, cooking, geography, history, hobbies, how-to, nature/environment, science, sports. Middle readers: activity books, animal, arts/crafts, biography, careers, cooking, history, hobbies, nature/environment, sports. Average word length picture books—500-1,000; young readers—1,000-4,000. Recently published *Ant Ant Ant! (An Insect Chant)*, *by April Pulley Sayre*, illustrated by Trip Park (ages 5-8, nonficiton picture book); *What Do Roots Do?*, by Kathleen V. Kudlinski, illustrated by Lindy Burnett (ages 5-8, nonfiction picure book); *Zebras*, by Jill Anderson (ages 3-6, Wild Ones series); *Animal Giants!*, by Sara Louise Kras (ages 8-11, Kids' FAQ series)

How to Contact/Writers Accepts international submissions. Submit complete mss for picture books. Nonfiction: Submit outline/synopsis. Responds to queries/mss in 3 months. Publishes book 2 years after acceptance. Considers simultaneous submissions, previously published work.

Illustration Accepts material from international illustrators. Works with 8-10 illustrators/year. Uses color artwork only. For ms/illustration packages: Send ms with dummy. Submit ms/illustration packages to Submission Editor. Reviews work for future assignments. If interested in illustrating future titles, query with samples. Submit samples to Submissions Editor. Responds in 3 months. Samples returned with SASE. Samples filed.

Photography Buys stock images. Submit photos to Submissions Editor. Looking for animal/nature photography. Model/property releases required. Photo captions required. Uses color prints. Prefers high resolution digital files. For first contact, send cover letter, client list, stock photo list, promo piece (color).

Terms Offers advance against royalties ($2,000 and up). Pays illustrators royalty based on retail price or net receipts. Pays photographers by the project (range: $100). Author sees galleys for review. Illustrators see dummies for review. Originals returned to artist at job's completion. Catalog available for 9×11 SASE and $1.29 postage. Individual catalogs for imprints. Offers writer's, artist's guidelines for SASE; see Web site for guidelines.

Tips "Know our material and mission and what we've recently published."

☐ ONSTAGE PUBLISHING

214 E. Moulton St. NE, Decatur AL 35601. (256)308-2300. (888)420-8879. Web site: www.onstagepublishing.com. **Manuscript Acquisitions:** Dianne Hamilton. Publishes 2-4 middle readers/year; 1-2 young adult titles/year. 80% of books by first-time authors.

Fiction Middle readers: adventure, contemporary, fantasy, history, nature/environment, science fiction, suspense/mystery. Young adults: adventure, contemporary, fantasy, history, humor, science fiction, suspense/mystery. Average word length: 100-1,500; middle readers—5,000 and up; young adults—25,000 and up. Recently published *The Masterpiece*, by Darren Butler (a mystery book, ages 12 and up, the Abbie Girl Spy adventures); *Saving da Vinci*, by Annie Laura Smith (historical fiction).

Nonfiction Query first; currently not producing nonfiction.

How to Contact/Writers Fiction: Send complete ms if under 20,000 words, otherwise send synopsis and first 3 chapters. Responds to queries/mss in 6 months. Publishes a book 1-2 years after acceptance. Will consider simultaneous submissions.

Illustration Reviews ms/illustration packages from artists. Submit ms with 3 pieces of final art. Contact: Dianne Hamilton, senior editor. Illustrations only: Arrange personal portfolio review. Responds in 6-8 weeks. Samples returned with SASE.

Photography Works on assignment only. Contact: Art Department. Model/property releases required; captions required. Uses color, 5×7, semigloss prints. Submit cover letter, published samples, stock photo list.

Terms Pays authors/illustrators/photographers advance plus royalties. Sends galleys to authors; dummies to illustrators. Catalog available on Web site.

Tips "Study our titles and get a sense of the kind of books we publish, so that you know whether your project is likely to be right for us."

ORCHARD BOOKS

Imprint of Scholastic, Inc., 557 Broadway, New York NY 10012. (212)343-6782. Fax: (212)343-4890. Web site: www.scholastic.com. Book publisher. Editorial Director: Ken Geist. **Manuscript Acquisitions:** Lisa A. Sandell, senior editor. **Art Acquisitions:** David Saylor, creative director. "We publish approximately 50 books yearly including fiction, poetry, picture books, and young adult novels.'' 10% of books by first-time authors.

- Orchard is not accepting unsolicited manuscripts; query letters only.

Fiction All levels: animal, contemporary, history, humor, multicultural, poetry. Recently published *Children of the Lamp: The Blue Djinn of Babylon*, by P.B. Kerr; *The Revenge of the Shadow King*, by Derek Benz and J.S. Lewis; *Beasty*, by Robert Neubecker; *A Good Night Walk*, by Elisha Cooper.

Nonfiction ''We rarely publish nonfiction.''

How to Contact/Writers Query only with SASE. Responds in 3 months.

Illustration Works with 15 illustrators/year. Art director reviews ms/illustration portfolios. Submit ''tearsheets or photocopies or Photostats of the work.'' Responds to art samples in 1 month. Samples returned with SASE. No disks or slides, please.

Terms Most commonly offers an advance against list royalties. Sends galleys to authors; dummies to illustrators. Original artwork returned at job's completion.

Tips ''Read some of our books to determine first whether your manuscript is suited to our list.''

OUR CHILD PRESS

P.O. Box 4379, Philadelphia PA 19118. Phone/fax: (610)308-8088. E-mail: ourchildpress@aol.com. Web site: www.ourchildpress.com. **Acquisitions:** Carol Perrott, president. 90% of books by first-time authors.

Fiction/Nonfiction All levels: adoption, multicultural, special needs. Published *Like Me*, written by Dawn Martelli, illustraded by Jennifer Hedy Wharton; *Is That Your Sister?*, by Catherine and Sherry Burin; *Oliver: A Story About Adoption*, by Lois Wichstrom.

How to Contact/Writers Fiction/nonfiction: Query or submit complete ms. Responds to queries/mss in 6 months. Publishes a book 6-12 months after acceptance.

Ilustration Works with 1-5 illustrators/year. Reviews ms/illustration packages from artists. Manuscript/illustration packages and illustration only: Query first. Submit résumé, tearsheets and photocopies. Responds to art samples in 2 months. Samples returned with SASE; samples kept on file.

Terms Pays authors royalty of 5-10% based on wholesale price. Pays illustrators royalty of 5-10% based on wholesale price. Original artwork returned at job's completion. Book catalog for business-size SAE and 67¢ postage.

☐ OUR SUNDAY VISITOR, INC.

200 Noll Plaza, Huntington IN 46750. (260)356-8400. Fax: (260)359-9117. Web site: www.osv.com. **Acquisitions:** Jacquelyn M. Lindsey, Michael Dubruiel, Kelly Renz. **Art Director:** Eric Schoenig. Publishes primarily religious, educational, parenting, reference and biographies. OSV is dedicated to providing books, periodicals and other products that serve the Catholic Church.

- Our Sunday Visitor, Inc., is publishing only those children's books that tie in to sacramental preparation and Catholic identity. Contact the acquisitions editor for manuscript guidelines.

Nonfiction Picture books, middle readers, young readers, young adults. Recently published *The Mass Book for Children*, by Rosemarie Gortler and Donna Piscitelli, illustrated by Mimi Sternhagen.

How to Contact/Writers Query, submit complete ms, or submit outline/synopsis and 2-3 sample chapters. Responds to queries/mss in 2 months. Publishes a book 18-24 months after acceptance. Will consider simultaneous submissions, electronic submissions via disk or modem, previously published work.

Illustration Reviews ms/illustration packages from artists. Illustration only: Query with samples. Contact: Acquisitions Editor. Responds only if interested. Samples returned with SASE; samples filed.

Photography Buys photos from freelancers. Contact: Acquisitions Editor.

Terms Pays authors royalty of 10-12% net. Pays illustrators by the project (range: $200-1,500). Sends galleys to authors; dummies to illustrators. Book catalog available for SASE; ms guidelines available for SASE.

Tips ''Stay in accordance with our guidelines.''

THE OVERMOUNTAIN PRESS

P.O. Box 1261, Johnson City TN 37605-1261. (423)926-2691. Fax: (423)929-2464. E-mail: submissions@overmtn.com. Web site: www.overmountainpress.com. **Manuscript Acquisitions:** Jason Weems, senior editor. Publishes 3 picture books/year; 2 young readers/year; 2 middle readers/year. 50% of books by first-time authors. ''We are primarily a publisher of southeastern regional history, and we have recently published several titles for children. We consider children's books about Southern Appalachia only!''

Fiction Picture books: folktales, history. Young readers, middle readers: folktales, history, suspense/mystery. Average word length: picture books—800-1,000; young readers—5,000-10,000; middle readers—20-30,000. Recently published *Bloody Mary: The Mystery of Amanda's Magic Mirror*, by Patrick Bone (young, middle reader); *Bark and Tim*, by Ellen Gidaro and Audrey Vernick; *Appalachian ABCs*, by Francie Hall, illustrated by Kent Oehm (pre-elementary, picture book).

Nonfiction Picture books, young readers, middle readers: biography (regional), history (regional). Average word

length: picture books—800-1,000; young readers—5,000-10,000; middle readers—20,000-30,000. Recently published *The Little Squash Seed*, written and illustrated by Gayla Dowdy Seale (preschool-elementary, picture book).
How to Contact/Writers Fiction/nonfiction: Submit outline/synopsis and 2 sample chapters. Responds to queries in 2 months; mss in 6 months. Publishes book 1 year after acceptance. Will consider simultaneous submissions and previously published work.
Illustration Works with 4 illustrators/year. Uses color artwork only. Reviews ms/illustration packages from artists. Send ms with dummy with at least 3 color copies of sample illustrations. Illustrations only: Send résumé. Responds only if interested. Samples not returned; samples filed.
Terms Pays authors royalty of 5-15% based on wholesale price. Pays illustrators royalty of 5-10% based on wholesale price or by author/illustrator negotiations (author pays). Sends galleys to authors; dummies to illustrators. Originals sometimes returned to artist at job's completion. Book catalog available for $8\frac{1}{2} \times 11$ SAE and 4 first-class stamps; ms guidelines available for SASE. All imprints included in a single catalog. Catalog available on Web site.
Tips "Because we are fairly new in the children's market, we will not accept a manuscript without complete illustrations. We are compiling a database of freelance illustrators which is available to interested authors. Please call if you have questions regarding the submission process or to see if your product is of interest. The children's market is huge! If the author can find a good local publisher, he or she is more likely to get published. We are currently looking for authors to represent our list in the new millennium. At this point, we are accepting regional (Southern Appalachian) manuscripts only. *Please* call if you have a question regarding this policy."

RICHARD C. OWEN PUBLISHERS, INC.
P.O. Box 585, Katonah NY 10536. (800)336-5588. Fax: (914)232-3977. Web site: www.rcowen.com. **Acquisitions:** Janice Boland, children's books editor/art director. 90% of books by first-time authors. We publish "child-focused books, with inherent instructional value, about characters and situations with which five-, six-, and seven-year-old children can identify—books that can be read for meaning, entertainment, enjoyment and information. We include multicultural stories that present minorities in a positive and natural way. Our stories show the diversity in America." Is not interested in lesson plans, or books of activities for literature studies or other content areas.
  • Due to a high volume of submissions, Richard C. Owen Publishers are currently only accepting nonfiction pieces.
Nonfiction Picture books, young readers: animals, careers, hi-lo, history, how-to, music/dance, geography, multicultural, nature/environment, science, sports. Multicultural needs include: "Good stories respectful of all heritages, races, cultural—African-American, Hispanic, American Indian." Wants lively stories. No "encyclopedic" type of information stories. Average word length: under 500 words. Recently published *The Coral Reef*.
How to Contact/Writers Fiction/nonfiction: Submit complete ms and cover letter. Responds to mss in 1 year. Publishes a book 2-3 years after acceptance. See Web site for guidelines.
Illustration Works with 20 illustrators/year. Uses color artwork only. Illustration only: Send color copies/reproductions or photos of art or provide tearsheets; do not send slides or originals. Include SASE and cover letter. Responds only if interested; samples filed.
Terms Pays authors royalty of 5% based on net price or outright purchase (range: $25-500). Offers no advances. Pays illustrators by the project (range: $100-2,500). Pays photographers by the project (range: $100-2,000) or per photo ($100-150). Original artwork returned 12-18 months after job's completion. Book brochure, ms/artists guidelines available for SASE.
Tips Seeking "authentic nonfiction that has charm, magic, impact and appeal; that children living in today's society will want to read and reread; books with strong storylines, child-appealing characters, events, language, action. Write for the ears and eyes and hearts of your readers—use an economy of words. Visit the children's room at the public library and immerse yourself in the best children's literature."

PACIFIC PRESS
P.O. Box 5353, Nampa ID 83653-5353. (208)465-2500. Fax: (208)465-2531. E-mail: booksubmissions@pacificpress.com. Web site: www.pacificpress.com/writers/books.htm. **Manuscript Acquisitions:** Tim Lale. **Art Acquisitions:** Randy Maxwell, creative director. Publishes 1 picture book/year; 2 young readers/year; 2 middle readers/year. 5% of books by first-time authors. Pacific Press brings the Bible and Christian lifestyle to children.
Fiction Picture books, young readers, middle readers, young adults: religion. Average word length: picture books—100; young readers—1,000; middle readers—15,000; young adults—40,000. Recently published *I Miss Grandpa*, by Karen Holford; *The Secret of Scarlet Cove*, by Charles Mills.
Nonfiction Picture books, young readers, middle readers, young adults: religion. Average word length: picture books—100; young readers—1,000; middle readers—15,000; young adults—40,000. Recently published *Beanie: The Horse That Wasn't a Horse*, by Heather Grovet.
How to Contact/Writers Fiction/nonfiction: Query or submit outline/synopsis and 3 sample chapters. Responds to queries in 3 months; mss in 1 year. Publishes a book 6-12 months after acceptance. Will consider e-mail submissions.

Illustration Works with 2 illustrators/year. Uses color artwork only. Query. Responds only if interested. Samples returned with SASE.

Photography Buys stock and assigns work. Model/property releases required.

Terms Pays author royalty of 6-15% based on wholesale price. Offers advances (average amount: $1,500). Pays illustrators royalty of 6-15% based on wholesale price. Pays photographers royalty of 6-15% based on wholesale price. Sends galleys to authors. Originals returned to artist at job's completion. Manuscript guidelines for SASE. Catalog available on Web site: (www.adventistbookcenter.com).

Tips Pacific Press is owned by the Seventh-day Adventist Church. The Press rejects all material that is not Bible-based.

PACIFIC VIEW PRESS

P.O. Box 2657, Berkeley CA 94702. (510)849-4213. Fax: (510)843-5835. E-mail: pvpress@sprynet.com. Web site: www.pacificviewpress.com. **Acquisitions:** Pam Zumwalt, president. Publishes 1-2 picture books/year. 50% of books by first-time authors. "We publish unique, high-quality introductions to Asian cultures and history for children 8-12, for schools, libraries and families. Our children's books focus on hardcover illustrated nonfiction. We look for titles on aspects of the history and culture of the countries and peoples of the Pacific Rim, especially China, presented in an engaging, informative and respectful manner. We are interested in books that all children will enjoy reading and using, and that parents and teachers will want to buy."

Nonfiction Young readers, middle readers: Asia-related multicultural only. Recently published *Cloud Weavers: Ancient Chinese Legends*, by Rena Krasno and Yeng-Fong Chiang (all ages); *Exploring Chinatown: A Children's Guide to Chinese Culture*, by Carol Stepanchuk (ages 8-12).

How to Contact/Writers Query with outline and sample chapter. Responds in 3 months.

Illustration Works with 2 illustrators/year. Responds only if interested. Samples returned with SASE.

Terms Pays authors royalty of 8-12% based on wholesale price. Pays illustrators by the project (range: $2,000-5,000).

Tips "We welcome proposals from persons with expertise, either academic or personal, in their area of interest. While we do accept proposals from previously unpublished authors, we would expect submitters to have considerable experience presenting their interests to children in classroom or other public settings and to have skill in writing for children."

☐ PARENTING PRESS, INC.

P.O. Box 75267, Seattle WA 98175-0267. (206)364-2900. Fax: (206)364-0702. E-mail: office@parentingpress.com. Web site: www.parentingpress.com. Estab. 1979. Book publisher. Publisher: Carolyn Threadgill. **Acquisitions:** Elizabeth Crary (parenting) and Carolyn Threadgill (children and parenting). Publishes 4-5 books/year for parents or/and children and those who work with them. 40% of books by first-time authors. "Parenting Press publishes educational books for children in story format—no straight fiction. Our company publishes books that help build competence in parents and children. We are known for practical books that teach parents and can be used successfully by parent educators, teachers, and educators who work with parents. We are interested in books that help people feel good about themselves because they gain skills needed in dealing with others. We are particularly interested in material that provides 'options' rather than 'shoulds.' "

• Parenting Press's guidelines are available on their Web site.

Fiction Picture books: concept. Publishes social skills books, problem-solving books, safety books, dealing-with-feelings books that use a "fictional" vehicle for the information. "We rarely publish straight fiction." Recently published *What About Me? 12 Ways to Get Your Parent's Attention (Without Hitting Your Sister)*, by Eileen Kennedy-Moore, illustrated by Mits Katayama (a book offering children options for getting the attention they need in positive ways).

Nonfiction Picture books: health, social skills building. Young readers: health, social skills building books. Middle readers: health, social skills building. No books on "new baby; coping with a new sibling; cookbooks; manners; books about disabilities (which we don't publish at present); animal characters in anything; books that tell children what they should do, instead of giving options." Average word length: picture books—500-800; young readers—1,000-2,000; middle readers—up to 10,000. Published *25 Things to Do When Grandpa Passes Away, Mom and Dad Get Divorced, or the Dog Dies*, by Laurie Kanyer, illustrated by Jenny Williams (ages 2-12).

How to Contact/Writers Query. Responds to queries/mss in 3 months, "after requested." Publishes a book 18 months after acceptance. Will consider simultaneous submissions.

Illustrations Works with 3-5 illustrators/year. Reviews ms/illustration packages from artists. "We do reserve the right to find our own illustrator, however." Query. Illustrations only: Submit "résumé, samples of art/drawings (no original art); photocopies or color photocopies okay." Responds only if interested. Samples returned with SASE; samples filed, if suitable.

Terms Pays authors royalty of 3-12% based on wholesale price. Pays illustrators (for text) by the project; 3-6% royalty based on wholesale price. Pays illustrators 3-6% royalty based on wholesale price, or pays by the project ($250-3,000). Sends galleys to authors; dummies to illustrators. Book catalog/ms/artist's guidelines for #10 SAE and 1 first-class stamp.

Tips "Make sure you are familiar with the unique nature of our books. All are aimed at building certain 'people' skills in adults or children. Our publishing for children follows no trend that we find appropriate. Children need nonfiction social skill-building books that help them think through problems and make their own informed decisions. The traditional illustrated story book does not *usually* fit our requirements because it does all the thinking for the child."

PAULINE BOOKS & MEDIA

50 St. Paul's Ave., Jamaica Plain MA 02130-3491. (617)522-8911. E-mail: editorial@paulinemedia.com. Web site: www.pauline.org. **Manuscript Acquisitions:** Sr. Patricia Edward Jablonski, FSP. **Art Acquisitions:** Sr. Mary Joseph Peterson, FSP, art director. Publishes 2 picture books/year; 5 young readers/year; 3-5 middle readers/year; 1-2 young adult titles/year. 20% of books by first-time authors. "We communicate the Gospel message through our lives and all available forms of media, responding to the needs and hopes of all people in the spirit of St. Paul."

Nonfiction Picture books, young readers, middle readers, young adults: religion. Average word length: picture books—150-500; young readers—8,000-10,000; middle readers—15,000-25,000. Recently published *I Pray the Rosary!*, by Margaret Rose Scarfi (ages 6-9); *Holy Friends: Thirty Saints and Blesseds of the Americas*, by Diane Amadeo (ages 9-12); *Squishy: A Book About My Five Senses*, by Cherie B. Stihler (Ages 4-7).

How to Contact/Writers Nonfiction: Submit query letter with outline/synopsis and 3 sample chapters. Responds to queries in 2 months; mss in 4 months. Publishes book 2-3 years after acceptance. Will consider simultaneous submissions, electronic submissions via disk or modem.

Illustration Works with 20-35 illustrators/year. Uses color artwork only. Illustrations only: Send résumé, promotional literature, client list or tearsheets. Responds only if interested. Samples returned with SASE only or samples filed.

Terms Varies by project. Manuscript and art guidelines available by SASE or on Web site. Catalog available on Web site.

Tips "Please be sure that all material submitted is consonant with Catholic teaching and values. We generally do not accept anthropomorphic stories, fantasy or poetry."

PAULIST PRESS

97 Macarthur Blvd., Mahwah NJ 07430. (201)825-7300. Web site: www.paulistpress.com. Acquisitions: Children's Editor. Publishes 6-8 titles/year. 40% of books by first-time authors. "Our goal is to produce books on Catholic themes."

Fiction "Virtually no picture books. Anything that we do consider in this area should be explicitly Christian, and preferably explicitly Catholic. No novels at all. No picture books on angels, adoption, grandparents, death, sharing, prejudice, September 11th, or other general themes. No retelling of Bible stories."

Nonfiction All levels: concept, social issues, Catholic doctrine, biography, prayers or customs. Recently published: *Dorothy Day*, by Elaine Murray Stone (young adult); *Child's Guide to the Seven Sacraments*, by Elizabeth Ficocelli, illustrated by Anne Catharine Blake (picture book). Publishes activity books for preschool through age 10 on specifically Catholic themes. "For these we do not want just ideas for activity books from writers or directions for arts and crafts. We want worksheets for lessons and games with a strong catechetical connection. If a book is accepted, we want printer-ready art supplied by the illustrator." Recently published activity books include *The Children's Liturgical Calendar Activity Book*, by Donece McCleary; *My Catholic School Holiday Activity Book*, by Jennifer Galvin.

How to Contact/Writers Submit complete ms for picture books; query and sample for longer works; include SASE with all submissions. "Query first on submissions for the Child's Guide series, biographies, and activity books as we already have many under development and do not want duplicate topics." Responds to queries/mss in 6 months. Publishes a book 2-3 years after acceptance.

Illustration "Overstocked on general samples right now, but would be happy to see samples of art used in catechetical settings. We tend to use artists we've used before."

Terms Pays authors royalty of 4-8% based on net sales. Average advance payment is $500. Pays illustrators by flat fee or advance and royalty, depending on the book.

Tips "When you submit, sketch out a marketing plan of your own personal, professional, and organizational contacts and strategies that would help sell your book: If we have to choose between two books, the one with a concrete hook and sales strategy is the one that will be accepted. Also we receive too many inappropriate manuscripts. Please know our books, know our market, and submit accordingly. There should be a reason why you're submitting to a Catholic publisher and not a trade house."

PEACHTREE PUBLISHERS, LTD.

1700 Chattahoochee Ave., Atlanta GA 30318-2112. (404)876-8761. Fax: (404)875-2578. E-mail: hello@peacht

Book Publishers

ree-online.com. Web site: www.peachtree-online.com. **Acquisitions:** Helen Harriss. **Art Director:** Loraine Joyner. Production Manager: Melanie McMahon Ives. Publishes 25-30 titles/year.

Fiction Picture books, young readers: adventure, animal, concept, history, nature/environment. Middle readers: adventure, animal, history, nature/environment, sports. Young adults: fiction, mystery, adventure. Does not want to see science fiction, romance.

Nonfiction Picture books: animal, history, nature/environment. Young readers, middle readers, young adults: animal, biography, nature/environment. Does not want to see religion.

How to Contact/Writers Fiction/nonfiction: Submit complete ms by postal mail only. Responds to queries/ mss in 4-6 months. Publishes a book 1-2 years after acceptance. Will consider simultaneous submissions.

Illustration Works with 8-10 illustrators/year. Illustrations only: Query production manager or art director with samples, résumé, slides, color copies to keep on file. Responds only if interested. Samples returned with SASE; samples filed.

Terms "Manuscript guidelines for SASE, visit Web site or call for a recorded message. No fax or e-mail submittals or queries please."

PELICAN PUBLISHING CO. INC.

1000 Burmaster St., Gretna LA 70053-2246. (504)368-1175. Web site: www.pelicanpub.com. **Manuscript Acquisitions:** Nina Kooij, editor-in-chief. **Art Acquisitions:** Terry Callaway, production manager. Publishes 16 young readers/year; 6 middle readers/year. 10% of books from agented writers. "Pelican publishes hardcover and trade paperback originals and reprints. Our children's books (illustrated and otherwise) include history, biography, holiday, and regional. Pelican's mission is "to publish books of quality and permanence that enrich the lives of those who read them."

Fiction Young readers: history, holiday, multicultural and regional. Middle readers: Louisiana history. Multicultural needs include stories about African-Americans, Irish-Americans, Jews, Asian-Americans, and Hispanics. Does not want animal stories, general Christmas stories, "day at school" or "accept yourself" stories. Maximum word length: young readers—1,100; middle readers—40,000. Recently published *The Warlord's Messengers*, by Virginia Walton Pelegard(ages 5-8, fiction).

Nonfiction Young readers: biography, history, multicultural. Middle readers: Louisiana history, holiday, regional. Recently published *The Pilgrims' Thanksgiving from A to Z*, by Laura Crawford (ages 5-8, holiday).

How to Contact/Writers Fiction/nonfiction: Query. Responds to queries in 1 month; mss in 3 months. Publishes a book 9-18 months after acceptance.

Illustration Works with 15 illustrators/year. Reviews ms/illustration packages from artists. Query first. Illustrations only: Query with samples (no originals). Responds only if interested. Samples returned with SASE; samples kept on file.

Terms Pays authors in royalties; buys ms outright "rarely." Sends galleys to authors. Illustrators paid by "various arrangements." Book catalog and ms guidelines available on Web site or for SASE.

Tips "No anthropomorphic stories, pet stories (fiction or nonfiction), fantasy, poetry, science fiction or romance. Writers: be as original as possible. Develop characters that lend themselves to series and always be thinking of new and interesting situations for those series. Give your story a strong hook—something that will appeal to a well-defined audience. There is a lot of competition out there for general themes. We look for stories with specific 'hooks' and audiences, and writers who actively promote their work."

PHILOMEL BOOKS

Penguin Young Readers Group (USA), 345 Hudson St., New York NY 10014. (212)414-3610. Web site: www.pen guin.com. **Manuscript Acquisitions:** submissions editor. **Art Acquisitions:** Katrina Damkoehler, design assistant. Publishes 18 picture books/year; 2 middle-grades/year; 2 young readers/year; 4 young adult titles/year. 5% of books by first-time authors; 80% of books from agented writers. "We look for beautifully written, engaging manuscripts for children and young adults."

- Philomel Books is not accepting unsolicited manuscripts. Only submissions with an SASE will be responded to.

Fiction All levels: adventure, animal, anthology, contemporary, fantasy, folktales, hi-lo, history, humor, poetry, sports, multicultural. Middle readers, young adults: problem novels, science fiction, suspense/mystery. No concept picture books, mass-market "character" books, or series. Average word length: picture books—1,000; young readers—1,500; middle readers—14,000; young adult—20,000.

Nonfiction Picture books, young readers, middle readers: hi-lo. "Creative nonfiction on any subject." Average word length: picture books—2,000; young readers—3,000; middle readers—10,000.

How to Contact/Writers Not accepting unsolicited mss. Send query letter with first chapter for Novels; complete ms with synopsis for picture books. Must include SASE for response. Responds to queries in 6 months; mss in 8 months.

Illustration Works with 20-25 illustrators/year. Reviews ms/illustration packages from artists. Query with art sample first. Illustrations only: Query with samples. Send résumé and tearsheets. Responds to art samples in 1 month. Original artwork returned at job's completion. Samples returned with SASE or kept on file.

Terms Pays authors in royalties. Average advance payment "varies." Illustrators paid by advance and in royalties. Sends galleys to authors; dummies to illustrators. Book catalog, ms guidelines free on request with SASE (9×12 envelope for catalog).

Tips Wants "unique fiction or nonfiction with a strong voice and lasting quality. Discover your own voice and own story and persevere." Looks for "something unusual, original, well-written. Fine art. The genre (fantasy, contemporary, or historical fiction) is not so important as the story itself and the spirited life the story allows its main character. We are also interested in receiving adolescent novels, current, contemporary fiction with voice."

☐ PIANO PRESS

P.O. Box 85, Del Mar CA 92014-0085. (619)884-1401. Fax: (858)755-1104. E-mail: pianopress@pianopress.com. Web site: www.pianopress.com. **Manuscript Acquisitions:** Elizabeth C. Axford, M.A, editor. "We publish music-related books, either fiction or nonfiction, coloring books, songbooks and poetry."

Fiction Picture books, young readers, middle readers, young adults: folktales, multicultural, poetry, music. Average word length: picture books—1,500-2,000. Recently published *Strum a Song of Angels*, by Linda Oatman High and Elizabeth C. Axford; *Music and Me*, by Kimberly White and Elizabeth C. Axford.

Nonfiction Picture books, young readers, middle readers, young adults: multicultural, music/dance. Average word length: picture books—1,500-2,000. Recently published *The Musical ABC*, by Dr. Phyllis J. Perry and Elizabeth C. Axford; *Merry Christmas Happy Hanukkah—A Multilingual Songbook & CD*, by Elizabeth C. Axford.

How to Contact/Writers Fiction/ nonfiction: Query. Responds to queries in 3 months; mss in 6 months. Publishes a book 1 year after acceptance. Will consider simultaneous submissions, electronic submissions via disk or modem.

Illustration Works with 1 or 2 illustrators/year. Reviews ms/illustration packages from artists. Query. Illustrations only: Query with samples. Responds in 3 months. Samples returned with SASE; samples filed.

Photography Buys stock and assigns work. Looking for music-related, multicultural. Model/property releases required. Uses glossy or flat, color or b&w prints. Submit cover letter, résumé, client list, published samples, stock photo list.

Terms Pays authors, illustrators, and photographers royalty of 5-10% based on retail price. Sends galleys to authors; dummies to illustrators. Originals returned to artist at job's completion. Book catalog available for #10 SASE and 2 first-class stamps. All imprints included in a single catalog. Catalog available on Web site.

Tips "We are looking for music-related material only for any juvenile market. Please do not send nonmusic-related materials. Query first before submitting anything."

PIÑATA BOOKS

Imprint of Arte Publico Press, University of Houston, 452 Cullen Performance Hall, Houston TX 77204-2004. (713)743-2843. Fax: (713)743-3080. Web site: www.artepublicopress.com. **Manuscript Acquisitions:** Dr. Nicholas Kanellos; Gabriela Baeza Ventura, executive editor. **Art Acquisitions:** Linda Garza, production manager. Publishes 6 picture books/year; 2 young readers/year; 5 middle readers/year; 5 young adult titles/year. 80% of books are by first-time authors. "Arte Publico's mission is the publication, promotion and dissemination of Latino literature for a variety of national and regional audiences, from early childhood to adult, through the complete gamut of delivery systems, including personal performance as well as print and electronic media."

Fiction Recently published *My Tata's Guitar/La Guitarra De Mi Tata*, by Ethriam Cash Brammer, illustrated by Daniel Lechon (ages 3-7); *Lorenzo's Revolutionary Quest*, by Lila and Rick Guzman (ages 11 and up); *Teen Angel*, by Gloria Velasquez (ages 11 and up).

Nonfiction Recently published *Cesar Chavez: The Struggle for Justice/Cesar Chavez: La Lucha Por La Justicia*, by Richard Griswold del Castillo, illustrated by Anthony Accardo (ages 3-7).

How to Contact/Writers Accepts material from U.S./Hispanic authors only (living abroad OK). Manuscripts, queries, synopses, etc. are accepted in either English or Spanish. Fiction: Submit complete ms. Nonfiction: Query. Responds to queries in 2-4 months; mss in 3-6 months. Publishes a book 2 years after acceptance. Will sometimes consider previously published work.

Illustration Works with 6 illustrators/year. Uses color artwork only. Reviews ms/illustration packages from artists. Query or send portfolio (slides, color copies). Illustrations only: Query with samples or send résumé, promo sheet, portfolio, slides, client list and tearsheets. Responds only if interested. Samples not returned; samples filed.

Terms Pays authors royalty of 10% minimum based on wholesale price. Offers advances (average amount $2,000). Pays illustrators advance and royalties of 10% based on wholesale price. Sends galleys to authors. Catalog available on Web site; ms guidelines available for SASE.

PINEAPPLE PRESS, INC.

P.O. Box 3889, Sarasota FL 34239. (941)739-2219. Fax: (941)739-2296. E-mail: info@pineapplepress.com. Web site: www.pineapplepress.com. **Manuscript Acquisitions:** June Cussen. Publishes 1 picture book/year; 1 young reader/year; 1 middle reader/year; 1 young adult title/year. 50% of books by first-time authors. "Our mission is to publish good books about Florida."

Fiction Picture books, young readers, middle readers, young adults: animal, folktales, history, nature/environment. Recently published *A Land Remembered* (Student Edition), by Patrick Smith, (ages 9 up, Florida historical fiction).

Nonfiction Picture books: animal, history, nature/environmental, science. Young readers, middle readers, young adults: animal, biography, geography, history, nature/environment, science. Recently published *Those Funny Flamingos*, by Jan Lee Wicker, illustrated by Steve Weaver (ages 5-9); *The Gopher Tortoise, A Life History*, by Ray and Patricia Ashton (ages 9 up).

How to Contact/Writers Fiction: Query or submit outline/synopsis and 3 sample chapters. Nonfiction: Query or submit outline/synopsis and intro and 3 sample chapters. Responds to queries/samples/mss in 2 months. Will consider simultaneous submissions.

Illustration Works with 2 illustrators/year. Reviews ms/illustration packages from artists. Query with nonreturnable samples. Contact: June Cussen, executive editor. Illustrations only: Query with brochure, nonreturnable samples, photocopies, résumé. Responds only if interested. Samples returned with SASE, but prefers nonreturnable; samples filed.

Terms Pays authors royalty of 10-15%. Pays illustrators royalties. Sends galleys to authors; dummies to illustrators. Originals returned to artist at job's completion. Book catalog available for 9×12 SAE with $1.06 postage; all imprints included in a single catalog. Catalog available on Web site at www.pineapplepress.com.

Tips "Learn about publishing and book marketing in general. Be familiar with the kinds of books published by the publishers to whom you are submitting."

PITSPOPANY PRESS

40 E. 78th St., #16D, New York NY 10021. (212)472-4959. Fax: (212)472-6253. E-mail: pitspop@netvision.net.il. Web site: www.pitspopany.com. Estab. 1992. Specializes in trade books, Judaica, nonfiction, fiction, multicultural material. **Manuscript Acquisitions:** Yaacov Peterseil, publisher. **Art Acquisitions:** Yaacov Peterseil, publisher. Produces 6 picture books/year; 4 young readers/year; 4 middle readers/year; 4 young adult books/year. 10% of books by first-time authors. "Pitspopany Press is dedicated to bringing quality children's books of Jewish interest into the marketplace. Our goal is to create titles that will appeal to the esthetic senses of our readers and, at the same time, offer quality Jewish content to the discerning parent, teacher, and librarian. While the people working for Pitspopany Press embody a wide spectrum of Jewish belief and opinion, we insist that our titles be respectful of the mainstream Jewish viewpoints and beliefs. Most of all, we are committed to creating books that all Jewish children can read, learn from, and enjoy."

Fiction Picture books: animal, anthology, fantasy, folktales, history, humor, multicultural, nature/environment, poetry. Young readers: adventure, animal, anthology, concept, contemporary, fantasy, folktales, health, history, humor, multicultural, nature/environment, poetry, religion, science fiction, special needs, sports, suspense. Middle readers: animal, anthology, fantasy, folktales, health, hi-lo, history, humor, multicultural, nature/environment, poetry, religion, science fiction, special needs, sports, suspense. Young adults/teens: animal, anthology, contemporary, fantasy, folktales, health, hi-lo, history, humor, multicultural, nature/environment, poetry, religion, science fiction, special needs, sports, suspense. Recently published *Hayyim's Ghost*, by Eric Kimmel, illustrated by Ari Binus (ages 6-9); *The Littlest Pair*, by Syliva Rouss, illustrated by Hally Hannan (ages 3-6); *The Converso Legacy*, by Sheldon Gardner (ages 10-14, historial fiction).

Nonfiction All levels: activity books, animal, arts/crafts, biography, careers, concept, cooking, geography, health, history, hobbies, how-to, multicultural, music/dance, nature/environment, reference, religion, science, self help, social issues, special needs, sports.

How to Contact/Writers Accepts international submissions. Fiction/nonfiction: Submit outline/synopsis. Responds to queries/mss in 6 weeks. Publishes book 9 months after acceptance. Considers simultaneous submissions, electronic submissions.

Illustration Accepts material from international illustrators. Works with 6 illustrators/year. Uses color artwork only. Reviews ms/illustration packages. For ms/illustration packages: Submit ms with 4 pieces of final art. Submit ms/illustration packages to Yaacov Peterseil, publisher. Reviews work for future assignments. If interested in illustrating future titles, send promo sheet. Submit samples to Yaacov Peterseil, publisher. Samples returned with SASE. Samples not filed.

Photography Works on assignment only. Submit photos to Yaacov Peterseil, publisher.

Terms Pays authors royalty or work purchased outright. Offers advance against royalties. Author sees galleys for review. Originals returned to artist at job's completion. Catalog on Web site. All imprints included in single catalog. Offers writer's guidelines for SASE.

☐ THE PLACE IN THE WOODS

Different Books, 3900 Glenwood Ave., Golden Valley MN 55422-5307. (763)374-2120. Fax: (952)593-5593. E-

Book Publishers

Book Publishers

mail: placewoods@aol.com. **Acquisitions:** Roger Hammer, publisher/editor. Publishes 2 elementary-age titles/year; 1 middle reader/year; 1 young adult title/year. 100% of books by first-time authors. Books feature primarily diversity/multicultural/disability themes by first-time authors and illustrators.

Fiction All levels: adventure, animal, contemporary, fantasy, folktales, hi-lo, history, humor, poetry, multicultural, special needs. Recently published *Little Horse*, by Frank Minogue, illustrated by Beth Cripe (young adult fiction); *Smile, It's OK To Be You,* by Karen Foster French, illustrated by Susan Brados (grades preschool-8, self-esteem); *Mona & Friends in Land of Joan* (series), by Dawn Rosewitz (ages 5-11, adventure).

Nonfiction All levels: hi-lo, history, multicultural, special needs. Multicultural themes must avoid negative stereotypes. ''Generally, we don't publish nonfiction, but we would look at these.'' Recently published *African America,* by Roger Hammer, illustrated by Tacoumba Aiken (ages 12 and up, history); *American Woman*, by Roger Hammer, illustrated by Christie Nelson (history); *Hispanic America*, by Roger Hammer, illustrated by Paul Moran (history).

How to Contact/Writers Fiction/nonfiction: Submit complete ms. Responds to queries/mss in 1 month with SASE. ''No multiple or simultaneous submissions. Please indicate a time frame for response.''

Illustration Works with 4 illustrators/year. Uses primarily b&w artwork only. Reviews ms/illustration packages from authors. Query; submit ms. Contact: Roger Hammer, editor. Illustration only: Query with samples. Responds in 1 month. Include SASE. ''We buy all rights.''

Photography Buys photos from freelancers on assignment only. Uses photos that appeal to children. Model/property releases required; captions required. Uses any b&w prints. Submit cover letter and samples with SASE.

Terms Manuscripts purchased outright from authors ($250). Pays illustrators by the project ($10). Pays photographers per photo (range: $10-250). For all contracts, ''initial payment repeated with each subsequent printing.'' Original artwork not returned at job's completion. Guidelines available for SASE.

Tips ''Tell me about *who* you are, *how* you've come to be *where* you are, and *what* you want to accomplish. Don't waste our time telling me how good your work is it should speak for itself.''

PLAYERS PRESS, INC.

P.O. Box 1132, Studio City CA 91614-0132. (818)789-4980. **Manuscript Acquisitions:** Robert W. Gordon, vice president/editorial director. **Art Acquisitions:** Attention: Art Director. Publishes 7-25 young readers, dramatic plays and musicals/year; 2-10 middle readers, dramatic plays and musicals/year; 4-20 young adults, dramatic plays and musicals/year. 35% of books by first-time authors; 1% of books from agented writers. Players Press philosophy: ''To create is to live life's purpose.''

Fiction All levels: plays. Recently published *Play From African Folktales*, by Carol Korty (collection of short plays); *Punch and Judy*, a play by William-Alan Landes; *Silly Soup!*, by Carol Korty (a collection of short plays with music and dance).

Nonfiction Picture books, middle readers, young readers, young adults. ''Any children's nonfiction pertaining to the entertainment industry, performing arts and how-to for the theatrical arts only.'' Needs include activity books related to theatre: arts/crafts, careers, history, how-to, music/dance, reference and textbook. Recently published *Scenery*, by J. Stell (How to Build Stage Scenery); *Monologues for Teens*, by Vernon Howard (ideal for teen performers); *Humorous Monologues*, by Vernon Howard (ideal for young performers); *Actor's Resumes*, by Richard Devin (how to prepare an acting résumé).

How to Contact/Writers Fiction/nonfiction: Submit plays or outline/synopsis and sample chapters of entertainment books. Responds to queries in 1 month; mss in 1 year. Publishes a book 10 months after acceptance. No simultaneous submissions.

Illustration Works with 2-6 new illustrators/year. Use primarily b&w artwork. Illustrations only: Submit résumé, tearsheets. Responds to art samples in 1 week only if interested. Samples returned with SASE; samples filed.

Terms Pays authors royalty based on wholesale price. Pays illustrators by the project (range: $5-1,000). Pays photographers by the project (up to $1,000); royalty varies. Sends galleys to authors; dummies to illustrators. Book catalog and ms guidelines available for 9×12 SASE.

Tips Looks for ''plays/musicals and books pertaining to the performing arts only. Illustrators: send samples that can be kept for our files.''

☐ PLAYHOUSE PUBLISHING

1566 Akron-Peninsula Rd., Akron OH 44313. (330)926-1313. Fax: (330)926-1315. E-mail: webmaster@playhousepublishing.com. Web site: www.playhousepublishing.com. **Acquisitions:** Submissions Editor. Imprints: Picture Me Books, Nibble Me Books. Publishes 10-15 novelty/board books/year. 25% of books by first-time authors. ''Playhouse Publishing is dedicated to finding imaginative new ways to inspire young minds to read, learn and grow—one book at a time.''

Fiction Picture books: adventure, animal, concept/novelty. Average word length: board books—75. Recently published *Picture Me Dancing*, by Cahty Hapka, illustrated by Monica Pritchard; *Peek-a-Boo, I See You!*, by Merry North, illustrated by Leigh Hughes; *My Halloween*, by Merry North, illustrated by Sara Misconish.

How to Contact/Writers Does not consider unsolicited mss.
Terms Catalog available online.

PLUM BLOSSOM BOOKS

Parallax Press, P.O. Box 7355, Berkeley CA 94707. (510)525-0101. Fax: (510)525-7129. E-mail: rachel@parallax. org. Web site: www.parallax.org. Estab. 1985. Specializes in nonfiction, fiction. **Writers contact:** Rachel Neuman, senior editor. Produces 2 picture books/year. 30% of books by first-time authors. ''Plum Blossom Books publishes stories for children of all ages that focus on mindfulness in daily life, Buddhism, and social justice.''
Fiction Picture books: adventure, contemporary, folktales, multicultural, nature/environment, religion. Young readers: adventure, contemporary, folktales, multicultural, nature/environment, religion. Middle readers: multicultural, nature/environment, religion. Young adults/teens: nature/environment, religion. Recently published *The Hermit and the Well*, by Thich Nhat Hanh, illustrated by Dinh Mai (ages 4-8, hardcover); *Each Breath a Smile*, by Sister Thuc Nghiem and Thich Nhat Hanh, illustrated by T. Hop (ages 2-5, paperback picture book); *Meow Said the Mouse*, by Beatrice Barbey, illustrated by Philippe Ames (ages 5-8, picture and activity book).
Nonfiction All levels: nature/environment, religion (Buddhist), Buddhist counting books.
How to Contact/Writers Accepts international submissions. Fiction/nonfiction: Query or submit complete ms. Responds to queries in 1-2 weeks. Responds to mss in 4 weeks. Publishes book 9-12 months after acceptance. Considers electronic submissions.
Illustration Accepts material from international illustrators. Works with 3 illustrators/year. Uses both color and b&w. Reviews ms/illustration packages. For ms/illustration packages: Query. Send manuscript with dummy. Reviews work for future assignments. If interested in illustrating future titles, query with samples. Responds in 4 weeks. Samples returned with SASE. Samples filed.
Photography Buys stock images and assigns work. Submit photos to Rachel Neuman, senior editor. Uses b&w prints. For first contact, send cover letter, published samples.
Terms Pays authors royalty of 20% based on wholesale price. Pays illustrators by the project. Author sees galleys for review. Illustrators see dummies for review. Originals returned to artist at job's completion. Catalog available for SASE. Offers writer's, artist's guidelines for SASE. See Web site for writer's, artist's, photographer's guidelines.
Tips ''Read our books before approaching us. We are very specifically looking for mindfulness and Buddhist messages in high-quality stories where the Buddhist message is implied rather than stated outright.''

PRICE STERN SLOAN, INC.

Penguin Group (USA), 345 Hudson St., New York NY 10014. (212)414-3590. Fax: (212)414-3396. Estab. 1963. **Acquisitions:** Debra Dorfman, president/publisher. ''Price Stern Sloan publishes quirky mass market novelty series for children's as well as licensed movie tie-in books.''
 • Price Stern Sloan does not accept unsolicited manuscripts.
Fiction Picture books, young readers: humor. ''We publish quirky, funny picture books, novelty books, and quirky full-color series.'' Recently published *Charlie & the Chocolate Factory* movie tie-in Books; Wallace & Grommit; *Napoleon Dynamite Mad Libs; Letter From Camp Mad Libs; Pretty Simple Stuff Activity Kits—Knit Now; Crazy Games—Texas Hold 'Em.*
How to Contact/Writers Query. Responds to queries in 3 weeks.
Terms Work purchased outright. Offers advance. Book catalog available for 9 × 12 SASE and 5 first-class stamps; address to Book Catalog. Manuscript guidelines available for SASE; address to Manuscript Guidelines.
Tips ''Price Stern Sloan has a unique, humorous, off the wall feel. Most of our titles are unique in concept as well as execution.''

⚓ PUFFIN BOOKS

Penguin Group (USA), Inc., 345 Hudson St., New York NY 10014-3657. (212)414-3600. Web site: www.penguin. com/youngreaders. **Acquisitions:** Sharyn November, senior editor and editorial director of Firebird. Imprints: Speak, Firebird, Sleuth. Publishes trade paperback originals (very few) and reprints. Publishes 175-200 titles/ year. Receives 600 queries and mss/year. 1% of books by first-time authors; 5% from unagented writers. ''Puffin Books publishes high-end trade paperbacks and paperback originals and reprints for preschool children, beginning and middle readers, and young adults.''
Fiction Picture books, young adult novels, middle grade and easy-to-read grades 1-3: fantasy and science fiction, graphic novels, classics. ''We publish mostly paperback reprints. We publish some original fiction and nonfiction titles.'' Recently published *Travel Team*, by Mike Lupica; *Puffin Graphics: Treasure Island*; *The Human Fly and Other Stories*, by T.C. Boyle.
Nonfiction Biography, illustrated book, young children's concept books (counting, shapes, colors). Subjects

include education (for teaching concepts and colors, not academic), women in history. "Women in history books interest us." Publishes Alloy Books series.

Illustration Reviews artwork. Send color copies.

Photography Reviews photos. Send color copies.

How to Contact/Writers Fiction: Submit 3 sample chapters with SASE. Nonfiction: Submit 5 pages of ms with SASE. "It could take up to 5 months to get response." Publishes book 1 year after acceptance. Will consider simultaneous submissions, if so noted. Does not accept unsolicited picture book mss.

Terms Pays royalty. Offers advance (varies). Book catalog for 9×12 SASE with 7 first-class stamps; send request to Marketing Department.

Ⓐ PUSH

Scholastic, 557 Broadway, New York NY 10012-3999. Web site: www.thisispush.com. Estab. 2002. Specializes in fiction. Produces 6-9 young adult books/year. 50% of books by first-time authors. PUSH publishes new voices in teen literature.

> • PUSH does not accept unsolicited manuscripts or queries, only agented or referred fiction/memoir. See Tackling Tough Topics in YA Lit to hear from PUSH editor David Levithan and PUSH author Billy Merrell.

Fiction Young adults: contemporary, multicultural, poetry. Recently published *Splintering*, by Eireann Corrigan; *Never Mind the Goldbergs*, by Matthue Roth; *Perfect World*, by Brian James.

Nonfiction Young adults: memoir. Recently published *Talking in the Dark*, by Billy Merrell; *You Remind Me of You*, by Eireann Corrigan.

How to Contact/Writers Only interested in agented material. Accepts international submissions. Fiction/nonfiction: Submit complete ms. Responds to queries in 2 months; mss in 4 months. No simultaneous, electronic, or previously published submissions.

Tips "We only publish first-time writers (and then their subsequent books), so authors who have published previously should not consider PUSH. Also, for young writers in grades 7-12, we run the PUSH novel Contest with the Scholastic Art & Writing Awards. Every year it begins in October and ends in March. Rules can be found on our Web site."

🌙 G.P. PUTNAM'S SONS

Penguin Putnam Books For Young Readers, 345 Hudson St., New York NY 10014. (212)414-3610. Web site: www.penguinputnam.com. **Manuscript Acquisitions:** Susan Kochan, assistant editorial director; John Rudolph, senior editor; Timothy Travaglini, senior editor. **Art Acquisitions:** Cecilia Yung, art director, Putnam and Philomel. Publishes 25 picture books/year; 15 middle readers/year; 5 young adult titles/year. 5% of books by first-time authors; 50% of books from agented authors.

> • G. Putnam's Sons title *Show Way*, by Jacqueline Woodson, won a 2006 Newbery Honor.

Fiction Picture books: animal, concept, contemporary, humor, multicultural. Young readers: adventure, contemporary, history, humor, multicultural, special needs, suspense/mystery. Middle readers: adventure, contemporary, history, humor, fantasy, multicultural, problem novels, special needs, sports, suspense/mystery. Young adults: contemporary, history, fantasy, problem novels, special needs. Does not want to see series. Average word length: picture books—200-1,000; middle readers—10,000-30,000; young adults—40,000-50,000. Recently published *I Wanna Iguana*, by Karen Orloff, illustrated by Dave Catrow (ages 4-8); *I Was a Nonblond Cheerleader*, by Kieran Scott (ages 12 and up).

Nonfiction Picture books: animal, biography, concept, history, nature/environment, science. Subjects must have broad appeal but inventive approach. Average word length: picture books—200-1,500. Recently published *Atlantic*, by G. Brian Karas (ages 4-8, 32 pages).

How to Contact/Writers Accepts unsolicited mss. No SASE required, as will only respond if interested. Picture books: send full mss. Fiction: Query with outline/synopsis and 10 manuscript pages. Nonfiction: Query with outline/synopsis, 10 manuscript pages, and a table of contents. Do not send art unless requested. Responds to mss within 4 months if interested. Will consider simultaneous submissions.

Illustration Write for illustrator guidelines. Works with 40 illustrators/year. Reviews ms/illustration packages from artists. Manuscript/illustration packages and illustration only: Query. Responds only if interested. Samples filed.

Terms Pays authors royalty based on retail price. Pays illustrators by the project or royalty based on retail price. Sends galleys to authors. Original artwork returned at job's completion.

Tips "Study our catalogs and get a sense of the kind of books we publish, so that you know whether your project is likely to be right for us."

RAINBOW PUBLISHERS

P.O. Box 261129, San Diego CA 92196. (858)668-3260. Web site: www.rainbowpublishers.com. **Acquisitions:** Christy Scannell, editorial director. Publishes 5 young readers/year; 5 middle readers/year; 5 young adult titles/

year. 50% of books by first-time authors. "Our mission is to publish Bible-based, teacher resource materials that contribute to and inspire spiritual growth and development in kids ages 2-12."

Nonfiction Young readers, middle readers, young adult/teens: activity books, arts/crafts, how-to, reference, religion. Does not want to see traditional puzzles. Recently published 5-Minute Sunday School Activities series, by Mary J. Davis (series of 2 books for ages 5-10).

How to Contact/Writers Nonfiction: Submit outline/synopsis and 3-5 sample chapters. Responds to queries in 6 weeks; mss in 3 months. Publishes a book 18 months after acceptance. Will consider simultaneous submissions, submissions via disk and previously published work.

Illustration Works with 2-5 illustrators/year. Reviews ms/illustration packages from artists. Submit ms with 2-5 pieces of final art. Illustrations only: Query with samples. Responds in 6 weeks. Samples returned with SASE; samples filed.

Terms For authors work purchased outright (range: $500 and up). Pays illustrators by the project (range: $300 and up). Sends galleys to authors. Book catalog available for 10 × 13 SAE and 2 first-class stamps; ms guidelines available for SASE.

Tips "Our Rainbow imprint carries reproducible books for teachers of children in Christian ministries, including crafts, activities, games and puzzles. Our Legacy imprint (new in '97) handles nonfiction titles for children in the Christian realm, such as Bible story books, devotional books, and so on. Please write for guidelines and study the market before submitting material."

🖊 🗐 🄰 RANDOM HOUSE-GOLDEN BOOKS FOR YOUNG READERS GROUP

Random House, Inc., 1745 Broadway, New York NY 10019. (212)782-9000. Estab. 1935. Book publisher. "Random House Books aims to create books that nurture the hearts and minds of children, providing and promoting quality books and a rich variety of media that entertain and educate readers from 6 months to 12 years." Publisher/Vice President: Kate Klimo. Associate Publisher/Art Director: Cathy Goldsmith. **Acquisitions:** Easy-to-Read Books (step-into-reading and picture books), color and activity books, board and novelty books, fiction and nonfiction for young and mid-grade readers: Heidi Kilgras, executive editor. Stepping Stones and middle grade fiction: Jennifer Dussling, senior editor. 100% of books published through agents; 2% of books by first-time authors.

• Random House-Golden Books does not accept unsolicited manuscripts, only agented material. They reserve the right not to return unsolicited material. Random House title *Whittington*, by Alan Armstrong, illustrated by SD Schindler, won a 2006 Newbery Honor Award.

How to Contact/Writers Only interested in agented material. Reviews ms/illustration packages from artists through agent only. Does not open or respond to unsolicited submissions.

Terms Pays authors in royalties; sometimes buys mss outright. Sends galleys to authors. Book catalog free on request.

🗐 RAVEN TREE PRESS, LLC

200 S. Washington, Suite 306, Green Bay WI 54301. (920)438-1605. Fax: (920)438-1607. E-mail: raven@raventre epress.com. Web site: www.raventreepress.com. Publishes 8-10 picture books/year. 50% of books by first-time authors. "We publish entertaining and educational bilingual materials for families."

Fiction Picture books, young readers: adventure, animal, concept, contemporary, fantasy, folktales, health, hi-lo, history, humor, multicultural, nature/environmental, poetry, science fiction, special needs, sports, suspense/mystery. No word play or rhyme. Work will be translated into Spanish by publisher. Check Web site for current needs. Average word length: 500-750.

How to Contact/Writers Check Web site for current needs, submission guidelines and deadlines.

Illustration Check Web site for current needs, submission guidelines and deadlines.

Terms Pays authors and illustrators royalty. Offers advances against royalties. Pays illustrators by the project or royalty. Originals returned to artist at job's completion. Catalog available on Web site.

Tips "Submit only based on guidelines. No e-mail or snail mail queries please. Word count is a definite issue, since we are bilingual." Staff attended or plans to attend the following conferences: BEA, NABE, IRA, ALA and SCBWI.

RED RATTLE BOOKS

Imprint of Soft Skull Press, 71 Bond St., Brooklyn NY 11217. Web site: www.softskull.com. **Manuscript/Art Acquisitions:** Richard Eoin Nash, publisher. Publishes 4-6 children's books/year. Editorial philosophy: "to satisfy the need for socially aware, nondidactic, sophisticated children's literature that's in line with the ideals of a new generation of parents."

Fiction Picture books, young adult: graphic novels, poetry. Recently published *The Saddest Little Robot*, by Brian Gage.

How to Contact/Writers Fiction: Submit cover letter with address information, phone and e-mail, outline/

synopsis and sample chapter (no more than 30 pages). Responds only if interested and SASE included. Poetry: Submit "cover letter and no more than 10 pages."

Illustration Accepts graphic novel submissions. Submit at least 5 "fully inked pages of art" with synopsis.

Tips Do not send full mss unless requested. "We do not accept phone calls or e-mail manuscripts."

☐ ☐ RENAISSANCE HOUSE

Imprint of Laredo Publishing, Beverly Hills CA 90210. (800)547-5113. Fax: (310)860-9902. E-mail: laredo@renaissancehouse.net. Web site: www.renaissancehouse.net. **Manuscript Acquisitions:** Raquel Benatar. **Art Acquisitions:** Sam Laredo. Publishes 5 picture books/year; 10 young readers/year; 10 middle readers/year; 5 young adult titles/year. 10% of books by first-time authors.

Fiction Picture books: animal, folktales, multicultural. Young readers: animal, anthology, folktales, multicultural. Middle readers, young adult/teens: anthology, folktales, multicultural, nature/environment. Recently published *Isabel Allende, Memories for a Story* (English-Spanish, age 9-12, biography); *Stories of the Americas*, a series of legends by several authors (ages 9-12, legend).

How to Contact/Writers Submit outline/synopsis. Responds to queries/mss in 3 weeks. Publishes a book 1 year after acceptance. Will consider simultaneous submissions, e-mail submissions.

Illustration Works with 25 illustrators/year. Uses color artwork only. Reviews ms/illustration packages from artists. Send ms with dummy. Contact: Sam Laredo. Illustrations only: Send tearsheets. Contact: Raquel Benatar. Responds in 3 weeks. Samples not returned; samples filed.

Terms Pays authors royalty of 5-10% based on retail price. Pays illustrators by the project. Sends galleys to authors; dummies to illustrators. Originals returned to artist at job's completion. Book catalog available for 9×12 SASE and $3 postage. All imprints included in a single catalog. Catalog available on Web site.

Ⓝ THE RGU GROUP

560 West Southern Avenue, Tempe AZ 85282. (480)736-9862. Fax: (480)736-9863. E-mail: info@theRGUgroup.com. Web site: www.theRGUgroup.com. **Manuscript/Art Acquisitions:** Laura Bofinger, Publishing Manager. Publishes 3-4 picture books/year. 50% of books by first-time authors. "The RGU Group specializes in southwestern animal-themed children's books that are entertaining and have an educational flair." For ages 4-8 years.

Fiction Picture books, board books, young readers: adventure, animal, history, humor, multicultural, nature/environment. Recently published *Life in the Slow Lane—A Desert Tortoise Tale*, by Conrad Storad, illustrated by Nathan Jensen (ages 4 and up); *Counting Little Geckos*, by Charline Profiri, illustrated by Sherry Rogers (ages 4 and up). Fiction may include nonfictional elements that complement the southwestern theme. Also will consider bilingual English/Spanish manuscripts.

How to Contact/Writers Fiction/nonfiction: Query or submit complete ms (average 500-1100 words). Responds to queries/mss in 3-4 months. Publishes book 1 year after acceptance. Will consider simultaneous submissions and previously published work.

Illustration Reviews ms/illustration packages from artists. Query or send ms with dummy. Contact: Laura Bofinger, publishing manager. Illustrations only: Query with photocopies, samples, SASE, URL. Responds in 3-4 months. Samples returned with SASE or samples filed.

Terms All contracts negotiated individually.

Tips Looking for fun and dynamic story interaction with well-crafted rising action, climax, and resolution (no flat or abrupt endings). Stories must have a southwestern element in characters and/or story setting. Give the reader a reason to care about the characters. Personify animal characters as much as possible.

RISING MOON

Imprint of Northland Publishing, Inc., P.O. Box 1389, Flagstaff AZ 86002-1389. (928)774-5251. Fax: (928)774-0592. E-mail: editorial@northlandpub.com. Web site: www.risingmoonbooks.com. Estab. 1988. **Manuscript Acquisitions:** Theresa Howell, kids editor. Publishes hardcover and trade paperback originals. Publishes 8-10 titles/year. Receives 1,000 submissions/year. 20% of books by first-time authors; 20% from unagented writers. "Rising Moon's objective is to provide children with entertaining and informative books that follow the heart and tickle the funny bone."

Fiction Rising Moon is no longer publishing middle-grade children's fiction, only fiction picture books. We are looking for exceptional fiction with wide appeal to add to our line of Southwest-themed books." Recently published *Do Princesses Wear Hiking Boots?*, by Carmela Lavigna Coyle, illustrated by Mike Gordon.

How to Contact/Writers Call for book catalog; ms guidelines online. Accepts simultaneous submissions. Responds in 3 months to queries.

Terms Pays authors royalty. Sometimes pays flat fee. Offers advance. Publishes book 1-2 years after acceptance.

Tips "Our audience is composed of regional Southwest-interest readers."

Ⓐ ROARING BROOK PRESS

143 West St., Suite W, New Milford CT 06776. (860)350-4434. **Manuscript/Art Acquisitions:** Simon Boughton,

publisher. **Executive Editor:** Deborah Brodie. Publishes approximately 40 titles/year. 1% of books by first-time authors. This publisher's goal is ''to publish distinctive high-quality children's literature for all ages. To be a great place for authors to be published. To provide personal attention and a focused and thoughtful publishing effort for every book and every author on the list.''

• Roaring Brook Press was recently purchased by Holtzbrinck Publishers, a group of companies that includes Henry Holt and Farrar, Straus & Giroux. Roaring Brook is not accepting unsolicited manuscripts.

Fiction Picture books, young readers, middle readers, young adults: adventure, animal, contemporary, fantasy, history, humor, multicultural, nature/environment, poetry, religion, science fiction, sports, suspense/mystery. Recently published *Stealing Henry*, by Carolyn MacCullough.

How to Contact/Writers Primarily interested in agented material. Not accepting unsolicited mss or queries. Will consider simultaneous agented submissions.

Illustration Primarily interested in agented material. Works with 25 illustrators/year. Illustrations only: Query with samples. Do not send original art; copies only through the mail. Samples returned with SASE.

Photography Works on assignment only.

Terms Pays authors royalty based on retail price. Pays illustrators royalty or flat fee depending on project. Sends galleys to authors; dummies to illustrators, if requested.

Tips ''You should find a reputable agent and have him/her submit your work.''

☐ RUNNING PRESS KIDS

Imprint of Running Press Book Publishers, 125 S. 22nd St., Philadelphia PA 19103-4399. (215)567-5080. Fax: (800)453-2884. Web site: www.runningpress.com. **Manuscript Acquisitions:** Submissions Editor. **Art Acquisitions:** Associate Design Director. Publishes 10 picture books/year. 20% of books by first-time authors. ''We want to publish the books and products that parents, teachers, and librarians want their kids to experience, and that kids can't wait to get their hands on.''

Fiction Picture books: adventure, animal, anthology, concept, contemporary, fantasy, folktales, health, hi-lo, history, humor, multicultural, nature/environment, poetry, suspense/mystery. Average word length: picture books—5,000. Recently published *Mice, Morals & Monkey Business*, by Christopher Wormell; *The Scary Show of Mo and Jo*, by Hanoch Piven; *Belling the Tiger*, illustrated by Pierre Pratt.

Nonfiction Picture books: activity books, animal, arts/crafts, biography, careers, concept, cooking, hi-lo, history, hobbies, how-to, science. Young readers, middle readers: activity books, animal, arts/crafts, biography, careers, concept, cooking, geography, health, hi-lo, history, hobbies, how-to, science.

How to Contact/Writers Fiction: Submit complete ms. Nonfiction: Query. Responds to queries in 1 month; mss in 2 months. Publishes book 2 years after acceptance. Will consider simultaneous submissions and previously published work.

Illustration Works with 30 illustrators/year. Reviews ms/illustration packages from artists. Send ms with dummy. Illustrations only: Send postcard sample. Responds only if interested. Samples not returned; samples filed.

Terms Pays authors royalty or work purchased outright from authors. Offers advances. Pays illustrators by the project or royalties. Sends galleys to authors; dummies to illustrators. Originals returned to artist at job's completion. Book catalog available for 9×12 SAE; ms guidelines available for SASE. All imprints included in a single catalog. Catalog available on Web site.

SALINA BOOKSHELF, INC.

1254 W. University Ave., Suite 130, Flagstaff AZ 86001. (928)773-0066. Fax: (928)526-0386. E-mail: sales@salinabookshelf.com. Web site: www.salinabookshelf.com. **Manuscript Acquisitions:** Jessie Ruffenach. **Art Acquisitions:** Art Department. Publishes 10 picture books/year; 4 young readers/year; 1 young adult title/year. 50% of books are by first-time authors.

Fiction Picture books, young readers, middle readers, young adults: adventure, animal, contemporary, folktales, multicultural.

Nonfiction Picture books: multicultural. Young readers, middle readers, young adults: biography, history, multicultural.

How to Contact/Writers Fiction/nonfiction: Query or submit complete ms. Responds to queries in 1 month; mss in 2 months. Publishes a book 1 year after acceptance. Will consider simultaneous submissions and previously published work.

Illustration Works with 8 illustrators/year. Reviews ms/illustration packages from artists. Query. Illustrations only: Query with samples. Responds in 1 month. Samples returned with SASE; samples filed.

Photography Buys stock and assigns work.

Terms Pays authors royalty based on retail price. Offers advances (average amount varies). Pays illustrators and photographers by the project. Originals returned to artist at job's completion. Catalog available for SASE or on Web site; ms guidelines available for SASE.

Tips ''Please note that all our books are Navajo-oriented.''

ⓦ SCHOLASTIC INC.

557 Broadway, New York NY 10012. (212)343-6100. Web site: www.scholastic.com. Imprints: Cartwheel Books, Orchard Books, Scholastic Press, Blue Sky Press, Scholastic Reference and Arthur A. Levine Books.

- Scholastic does not accept unsolicited manuscripts; writers may query. Scholastic title *Hitler Youth: Growing Up in Hitler's Shadow*, by Susan Campbell Bartoletti, won a 2006 Newbery Honor Award and a 2006 Sibert Honor Award. Their title *Cinderella*, by Barbara McClintock, won the Golden Kite Honor Award for picture book illustration for 2005.

Illustration Works with 50 illustrators/year. Does not review ms/illustration packages. Illustrations only: Send promo sheet and tearsheets. Responds only if interested. Samples not returned. Original artwork returned at job's completion.

Terms All contracts negotiated individually; pays royalty. Sends galleys to author; dummies to illustrators.

SCHOLASTIC LIBRARY PUBLISHING

(formerly Grolier Publishing), 90 Old Sherman Turnpike, Danbury CT 06816. (203)797-3500. Book publisher. Vice President/Publisher: Phil Friedman. **Manuscript Acquisitions:** Kate Nunn, editor-in-chief. **Art Acquisitions:** Marie O'Neil, art director. Imprints: Grolier, Children's Press, Franklin Watts. Publishes more than 400 titles/year. 5% of books by first-time authors; very few titles from agented authors. Publishes informational (nonfiction) for K-12; picture books for young readers, grades 1-3.

Fiction Publishes 1 picture book series, Rookie Readers, for grades 1-2. Does not accept unsolicited mss.

Nonfiction Photo-illustrated books for all levels: animal, arts/crafts, biography, careers, concept, geography, health, history, hobbies, how-to, multicultural, nature/environment, science, social issues, special needs, sports. Average word length: young readers—2,000; middle readers—8,000; young adult—15,000.

How to Contact/Writers Fiction: Does not accept fiction proposals. Nonfiction: Query; submit outline/synopsis, résumé and/or list of publications, and writing sample. SASE required for response. Responds in 3 months. Will consider simultaneous submissions. No phone or e-mail queries; will not respond to phone inquiries about submitted material.

Illustration Works with 15-20 illustrators/year. Uses color artwork and line drawings. Illustrations only: Query with samples or arrange personal portfolio review. Responds only if interested. Samples returned with SASE. Samples filed. Do not send originals. No phone or e-mail inquiries; contact only by mail.

Photography Contact: Caroline Anderson, photo manager. Buys stock and assigns work. Model/property releases and captions required. Uses color and b&w prints; $2\frac{1}{4} \times 2\frac{1}{4}$, 35mm transparencies, images on CD-ROM.

Terms Pays authors royalty based on net or work purchased outright. Pays illustrators at competitive rates. Photographers paid per photo. Sends galleys to authors; dummies to illustrators.

ⓦ SCHOLASTIC PRESS

557 Broadway, New York NY 10012. (212)343-6100. Web site: www.scholastic.com. **Manuscript Acquisitions:** Dianne Hess, executive editor (picture book fiction/nonfiction, 2nd-3rd grade chapter books, some middle grade fantasy that is based on reality); Lauren Thompson, senior editor (picture book fiction/nonfiction); Tracy Mack, executive editor (picture book, middle grade, YA); Leslie Budnick, editor (picture books fiction/nonfiction, middle grade); Jennifer Rees, associate editor (picture book fiction/nonfiction, middle grade, YA). **Art Acquisitions:** David Saylor, all hardcover imprints for Scholastic. Publishes 60 titles/year. 1% of books by first-time authors.

- Scholastic Press title *Zen Shorts*, by Jon J Muth, won a 2006 Caldecott Honor Award.

Fiction Looking for strong picture books, young chapter books, appealing middle grade novels (ages 8-11) and interesting and well-written young adult novels.

Nonfiction Interested in "unusual, interesting, and very appealing approaches to biography, math, history and science."

How to Contact/Writers Fiction/nonfiction: "Send query with 1 sample chapter and synopsis. Don't call! Don't e-mail!" Picture books: submission accepted from agents or previously published authors only.

Illustrations Works with 30 illustrators/year. Uses both b&w and color artwork. Illustrations only: Query with samples; send tearsheets. Responds only if interested. Samples returned with SASE. Original artwork returned at job's completion.

Terms Pays advance against royalty.

Tips "Read *currently* published children's books. Revise, rewrite, rework and find your own voice, style and subject. We are looking for authors with a strong and unique voice who can tell a great story and have the ability to evoke genuine emotion. Children's publishers are becoming more selective, looking for irresistable talent and fairly broad appeal, yet still very willing to take risks, just to keep the game interesting."

SEEDLING PUBLICATIONS

520 E. Bainbridge St., Elizabethtown PA 17022. Web site: www.SeedlingPub.com. **Acquisitions:** Josie Stewart.

20% of books by first-time authors. Publishes books for the beginning reader in English. "Natural language and predictable text are requisite to our publications. Patterned text is acceptable, but must have a unique story line. Poetry, books in rhyme and full-length picture books are not being accepted at this time. Illustrations are not necessary."

Fiction Young readers: adventure, animal, folktales, humor, multicultural, nature/environment. Multicultural needs include stories which include children from many cultures and Hispanic-centered storylines. Does not accept texts longer than 16 pages or over 150-200 words or stories in rhyme. Average word length: young readers—100. Recently published *Sherman in the Talent Show*, by Betty Erickson, illustrated by Kristine Dillard; *Moth or Butterfly?*, by Ryan Durney; *The Miller, His Son, and the Donkey*, by Lynn Salem and Josie Stewart (Legends, Fables & Folktales series).

Nonfiction Young readers: animal, arts/crafts, biography, careers, concept, multicultural, nature/environment, science. Does not accept texts longer than 16 pages or over 150-200 words. Average word length: young readers—100.

How to Contact/Writers Fiction/nonfiction: Submit complete ms. Responds in 9 months. Publishes a book 1-2 years after acceptance. Will consider simultaneous submissions. Prefers e-mail submissions from authors or illustrators outside the U.S.

Illustration Works with 8-9 illustrators/year. Uses color artwork only. Reviews ms/illustration packages from artists. Submit ms with dummy. Illustrations only: Send color copies. Responds only if interested. Samples returned with SASE only; samples filed if interested.

Photography Buys photos from freelancers. Works on assignment only. Model/property releases required. Uses color prints and 35mm transparencies. Submit cover letter and color promo piece.

Terms Work purchased outright from authors. Pays illustrators and photographers by the project. Original artwork is not returned at job's completion. Catalog available on Web site.

Tips "Study our Web site. Follow our guidelines carefully and test your story with children and educators."

SHEN'S BOOKS

40951 Fremont Blvd., Fremont CA 94538. (510)668-1898. Fax: (510)668-1057. E-mail: info@shens.com. Web site: www.shens.com. Estab. 1986. Specializes in multicultural material. **Acquisitions:** Renee Ting, president. Produces 2 picture books/year. 50% of books by first-time authors.

Fiction Picture books, young readers: folktales, multicultural. Middle readers: multicultural. Recently published *The Wishing Tree*, by Roseanne Thong, illustrated by Connie McLennan (ages 4-8); *The Magical Monkey King*, by Ji-li Jiang (ages 7-10, chapter book); *Many Ideas Open the Way*, by Randy Snook (picture books of proverbs).

Nonfiction Picture books, young readers: multicultural. Recently published *Land of Morning Calm*, by John Stickler, illustrated by Soma Han (ages 7-12, picture book).

How to Contact/Writers Accepts international submissions. Fiction/nonfiction: Submit complete ms. Responds to queries in 1-2 weeks; mss in 6-12 months. Publishes book 1 year after acceptance. Considers simultaneous submissions.

Illustration Accepts material from international illustrators. Works with 2 illustrators/year. Uses color artwork only. Reviews ms/illustration packages. For ms/illustration packages: Send ms with dummy. Submit ms/illustration packages to Renee Ting, president. Reviews work for future assignments. If interested in illustrating future titles, query with samples. Submit samples to Renee Ting, president. Samples not returned. Samples filed.

Photography Works on assignment only. Submit photos to Renee Ting, president.

Terms Authors pay negotiated by the project. Pays illustrators by the project. Pays photographers by the project. Illustrators see dummies for review. Catalog on Web site.

Tips "Be familiar with our catalog before submitting."

☐ SILVER MOON PRESS

160 Fifth Ave., New York NY 10010. (212)242-6499. Fax: (212)242-6799. E-mail: mail@silvermoonpress.com. Web site: www.silvermoonpress.com. Publisher: David Katz. Managing Editor: Hope Killcoyne. **Marketing Coordinator:** Karin Lilleb. Book publisher. Publishes 2 books for grades 4-6/year. 25% of books by first-time authors; 10% books from agented authors. Publishes mainly American historical fiction and books of educational value. Develops books which fit neatly into curriculum for grades 4-6."History comes alive when children can read about other children who lived when history was being made!"

Fiction Middle readers: historical, multicultural and mystery. Average word length: 14,000. Recently published *A Silent Witness in Harlem*, by Eve Creary; *In the Hands of the Enemy*, by Robert Sheely; *Ambush in the Wilderness*, by Kris Hemphill; *Race to Kitty Hawk*, by Edwina Raffa and Annelle Rigsby; *Brothers of the Falls*, by Joanna Emery.

How to Contact/Writers Fiction: Query. Send synopsis and/or a few chapters, along with a SASE. Responds to queries in 1 month; mss in 2 months. Publishes a book 1-2 years after acceptance. Will consider simultaneous submissions, or previously published work.

Nathan Hale

'Write about what you really want to draw'

Conventional wisdom suggests a one-niche, one-style approach to illustration. But sometimes it pays to expand your horizons. Take Nathan Hale, author and illustrator of the *The Devil You Know* (Walker). The versatile artist, who lives in Provo, Utah with his wife and son, creates humorous illustrations for children's magazines. He also specializes in scientific illustrations. But he doesn't stop there. He writes his own picture books because who knows better than he how his characters would think, act, and sound?

In this interview, Hale reveals how he conquered the magazine and book publishing markets and how he magically made his phone ring twice as often in the process.

How did you develop such detail in your illustrations?

When I was a kid I had terrible vision, I didn't get a pair of glasses until I was in the third grade. I remember leaving the optometrists with my new glasses on and being totally blown away by a tree on the other end of the parking lot. I could see every leaf—it blew my mind! So now, when I'm doing a tree I have to put every leaf in there.

I love looking at pictures that have a built in joke or narrative. Picture books seem to be made for jokes. You can set it all up one page, then turn the page for the punch line—and the punch line can be a text-free illustration.

I had been drawing weird fantasy animals long before I got into scientific illustration. The influence of my naturalistic style on my fantasy style has been amazing. My fantasy creatures look a lot wilder since they have elements of the real world in the mix.

Do you recall your very first submission?

My senior year in high school I sent out a 72-page science fiction comedy called *Tsabük* ("It's a Book"—it had umlauts over the U) about a guy in a gas mask who tries to pick a flower and ends up getting eaten, trampled or chopped up (depending on the page choices you made). It was pretty goofy, especially because the whole book was written in a fake German accent (spelled out phonetically)

I sent it to Laura Geringer's imprint at HarperCollins. The crazy thing was I got a reply! An editorial assistant called and said it was wonderfully weird, but totally inappropriate for their list. She said not to get excited, but she was sending it up to the next level. A few months later I got a form rejection letter—but I did get that phone call, which was so cool.

Illustration © 2005 Nathan Hale from *The Devil You Know* (Walker Books for Young Readers).

Illustrator Nathan Hale believes "you can draw more attention to yourself as an illustrator if you can write your own stuff." For his first picture book as an author/illustrator, *The Devil You Know* (Walker), Hale was inspired by Harry Potter hubbub, *The Exorcist* and the antics of his two-year-old son, and borrowed a bit from *Faust*. *School Library Journal* calls his book "a spirited romp [that] will appeal to readers who are not afraid of a little magic and mayhem."

Did you have a strategy when you launched your art career?

My strategy was to take any art-related job I could get. I painted kid's room murals, scenery for local theaters, and in my free time I worked on my own picture books. Scenery and murals led to diorama backgrounds and science murals for museums.

I knew I wanted to illustrate professionally, so I just went for it. In the beginning, I took a lot of work for not a lot of money. But the experience gained was invaluable. I learned there are jobs that pay well, and jobs that are great for your portfolio, but they often are not the same.

I knew I'd be getting a lot of rejection letters, so I started collecting them, and set out to wallpaper my room with them. Hey, if you're getting rejection letters, it means you're doing something. Save them, collect them, that way, when one comes in the mail, instead of being heartbroken, just add it to your collection.

Which style gets you the most assignments?

It changes every year. This year I've done mostly children's illustration and a handful of natural history jobs. They were big ones though. One was this great scene of Paleoindians butchering a Mastodon—guts all over the place, people carving off layers of fat. It required hours of research. The science-based jobs generally take longer. When it's pure fantasy, you don't have to worry about correct science.

Do you keep a reference file for nature assignments?

I do use a ton of reference but don't keep files. I like to start fresh with each project, so I don't get too hooked on an image. Google image search is great! But I always make sure to get other references too. When I do use Google, I make sure to go deep. If it's on the first few pages, chances are somebody else has used that image before. If you look at a lot of wildlife illustration, you may notice certain animals are always posed the same way. That comes from different people using the same source material. When you get into prehistoric stuff it gets really messy, because illustrators use other artist's work as reference. A lot of dinosaur poses get cloned again and again.

Science revisions are a nightmare. Scientists love to point out inaccuracies, and don't care about aesthetics—just the facts. When your art has to pass by two scientists, it gets really ugly. They rarely agree on anything.

What do magazine art directors look for in an illustrator?

Be a good reader. Go over the article several times and make notes. That will guarantee fewer revisions. You are trying to enhance the piece, so the art should fit the story. I sometimes try to fit the medium to the story. For a story that took place in the 1700s I used an etching style. Just make sure you let the art director know where you're going. Stick to the deadline no matter what. Get some caffeine. Stay up all night.

Magazine work is great. In some ways it spoiled book publishing for me. Magazines have hard, fast deadlines. You get the finished story, you do sketches, they OK them (or change them) quickly, you do the final and bang! The whole thing's done in a few weeks. Book publishing's similar, only a thousand times slower.

How did you get the idea for *The Devil You Know*?

It was my ninth or tenth picture book submission. I'd been submitting one or two manuscripts a year, and nothing was getting a response. I thought I'd send out something different, just to see what would happen.

There was this huge hubbub at the time about Harry Potter being satanic. I thought, wouldn't it be funny to do a picture book using that theme—maybe a silly version of *The Exorcist*. At the same time my two-year-old was causing all kinds of mayhem in the house, tearing through things like a little devil. The two thoughts collided and I wrote the story in a few days.

Did you send out a query letter or a dummy?

I sent out a full sketch dummy. I drew it out so editors could see where I was going with it. I did the whole book in simple line drawings with the text dropped in digitally. I did two pages as final, full color paintings, so they could see how the finished book would look. I printed eight copies and sent them out, making sure to say they were part of a small multiple submission. All eight came back—some with nice comments, some with form rejections. When all eight came back, I mailed them out again. It was in the second mailing that they found a home at Walker.

How did you feel when Walker Books for Young Readers accepted it?

I was working on a big glacier mural for the Illinois State Museum and had to climb down three levels of scaffolding to get the phone. When I finally got there I was totally out of breath. It took me a minute to understand what the guy on the phone was saying. Seeing the printed book is pretty cool, but nothing beats that first phone call.

What was the process like once your manuscript was accepted?

The wording changed a lot. My editor and I worked through several rewrites. He was really easy to work with. (In fact, he makes a cameo in the book, as one of the devils in the end papers.) The layout was virtually unchanged from my original dummy. We changed the cover at the last minute because the Marketing department didn't like our original cover idea. I must admit I like the new cover a lot more.

What advice would you give artists who seek to write their own books?

Writers always say, "Write about what you know." For author/illustrators, I say, "Write about what you really want to draw."

Having kids is a big help if you want to write a picture book. For one thing, it forces you to look at a lot of picture books. We read three a night. I get to read the books and watch what works with the kid—direct invaluable research.

Publishers love author/illustrators, if you look at the Caldecott winners over the years, the vast majority are from the individual author/illustrator. The slush piles are clogged with text-only picture book manuscripts. I know illustrators who are booked six years in advance to illustrate somebody's picture book. Illustrators, take control! Picture books are so visual, they should belong to the visual people!

Write a story, make a dummy and send it out!

Nathan Hale created this ethereal illustration to accompany a one-page poem called "Dragon's Breath" for *Cricket* magazine. "The poem ended with something like, 'We are both dragons in disguise,'" says Hale. "That was a fun painting—it was one of those lucky assignments with no revisions."

Illustration © 2004 Nathan Hale (Cricket Magazine Group).

But don't some publishers suggest artists start off illustrating other authors' manuscripts to get experience?

I think you can draw more attention to yourself as an illustrator when you write your own stuff. Once again, when you write it, you get to choose what's in the pictures. If your style is quirky, you may have to wait a long time until a publisher finds the right story for your style. Why not submit your weird illustrations attached to a weird story? Or your fluffy cute illustrations attached to a fluffy cute story? When you submit your work coupled with text you are leaping ahead, showing publishers you can work with a story. At worst, they can say, well, we like your pictures, but your story's no good. Maybe we have a story you could illustrate. And let's not forget, you double your income as an author/illustrator.

What if you have a picture book idea, but are scared to write it?

Just do it. Like Nike says. If you have a story idea, start working up character drawings, then draw a grid with 32 squares, fit the story into those 32 pages, sketch them larger and send it out. Then before you get a response, do another one. Keep the ball rolling so that when you start getting rejections it doesn't matter because the next project's already in the mail.

That was good! Got any more advice for illustrators?

Never turn down an art job. Not until you are too busy with other art jobs. Even if it's doing a flyer for somebody's band or painting cute teddy bears in somebody's nursery. All the experience adds up and you never know where a job could lead.

Be nice to everybody. Art directors are much more likely to work with you again if you are easy to deal with and friendly. Nobody wants to work with a jerk, no matter how good your portfolio is.

Always have a fresh project in the mail. Whether it's a new postcard promo, or a full dummy, make sure it's out there working for you.

Work hard. I met Wendell Minor, one of the great American illustrators. His work ethic is simple, he says he works 12 hours a day, seven days a week. I believe him. It's time consuming work!

What projects do you have cooking?

I'm in the middle of two picture books, both for Putnam. The first, *Yellowbelly and Plum,* about a character from *The Devil You Know*, will be out late 2007. The second, an Ali Baba type story about two unlucky thieves comes out in 2008. Also on the horizon is a graphic novel with Newbery Honor author Shannon Hale (no relation) due to be published by Bloomsbury in 2008.

I'd love to do concept work for films. I don't know how studios find the illustrators they hire, but can I sign up? Peter Jackson, if you're reading this, give me a call!

What is the best thing about your career?

I get to draw pictures for money!

—*Mary Cox*

Illustration Works with 2-3 illustrators/year. Reviews ms/illustration packages from artists. Query. Illustrations only: Query with samples, résumé, client list. Responds only if interested. Samples returned with SASE; samples filed. Original artwork returned at job's completion.

Photography Buys photos from freelancers. Buys stock and assigns work. Uses archival, historical, sports photos. Captions required. Uses color, b&w prints; 35mm, $2^{1}/_{4} \times 2^{1}/_{4}$, 4×5, 8×10 transparencies. Submit cover letter, résumé, published samples, client list, promo piece.

Terms Pays authors royalty or work purchased outright. Pays illustrators by the project, no royalty. Pays photographers by the project, per photo, no royalty. Sends galleys to authors; dummies to illustrators. Book catalog available for $8^{1}/_{2} \times 11$ SAE and 77¢ postage.

Tips "We do not accept biographies, poetry, or romance. We do not accept fantasy, science fiction, or historical fiction with elements of either. Submissions that fit into New York State curriculum topics such as the Revolutionary War, Colonial times, and New York State history in general stand a greater chance of acceptance than those that do not."

SIMON & SCHUSTER BOOKS FOR YOUNG READERS

1230 Avenue of the Americas, New York NY 10020. (212)698-7000. Fax: (212)698-2796. Web site: www.simonsayskids.com. **Manuscript Acquisitions:** Elizabeth Law, vice president and associate publisher; David Gale, editorial director; Kevin Lewis, executive editor; Paula Wiseman, vice president and editorial director, Paula Wiseman Books. **Art Acquisitions:** Dan Potash, creative director. Publishes 75 books/year. "We publish high-quality fiction and nonfiction for a variety of age groups and a variety of markets. Above all we strive to publish books that will offer kids a fresh perspective on their world."

- Simon & Schuster Books for Young Readers does not accept unsolicited manuscripts. Queries are accepted via mail. Simon & Schuster title *Henry and Mudge and the Great Grandpas*, by Cynthia Rylant, illustrated by Sucie Stevenson, won the 2006 Theodor Seuss Geisel Medal.

Fiction Picture books: animal, minimal text/very young readers. Middle readers, young adult: fantasy, adventure, suspense/mystery. All levels: contemporary, history, humor. Recently published *Little Quack's Bedtime*, by Lauren Thompson, illustrated by Derek Anderson (picture book, ages 3-7); *Shrimp*, by Rachel Cohn (young adult fiction, ages 13 and up).

Nonfiction Picture books: concept. All levels: narrative, current events, biography, history. "We're looking for picture book or middle grade nonfiction that have a retail potential. No photo essays." Recently published *A Is For Abigail*, by Lynne Cheney, illustrated by Robin Preiss Glasser (picture book nonfiction, all ages).

How to Contact/Writers Accepting query letters only; please note the appropriate editor. Responds to queries/mss in 3-4 months. Publishes a book 2 years after acceptance. Will consider simultaneous submissions.

Illustration Works with 70 illustrators/year. Do not submit original artwork. Editorial reviews ms/illustration packages from artists. Submit query letter to Submissions Editor. Illustrations only: Query with samples; samples filed. Provide promo sheet, tearsheets. Responds only if interested.

Terms Pays authors royalty (varies) based on retail price. Pays illustrators or photographers by the project or royalty (varies) based on retail price. Original artwork returned at job's completion. Manuscript/artist's guidelines available via Web site or free on request. Call (212)698-2707.

Tips "We're looking for picture books centered on a strong, fully-developed protagonist who grows or changes during the course of the story; YA novels that are challenging and psychologically complex; also imaginative and humorous middle-grade fiction. And we want nonfiction that is as engaging as fiction. Our imprint's slogan is 'Reading You'll Remember.' We aim to publish books that are fresh, accessible and family-oriented; we want them to have an impact on the reader."

SLEEPING BEAR PRESS

Imprint of Gale Group, 310 N. Main St., Suite 300, Chelsea MI 48118. (734)475-4411. Fax: (734)475-0787. Web site: www.sleepingbearpress.com. **Manuscript Acquisitions:** Heather Hughes. **Art Acquisitions:** Jennifer Lundahl, creative director. Publishes 30 picture books/year. 50% of books by first-time authors.

Fiction Picture books: adventure, animal, concept, folktales, history, multicultural, nature/environment, religion, sports. Young readers: adventure, animal, concept, folktales, history, humor, multicultural, nature/environment, religion, sports. Average word length: picture books—1,800. Recently published *Cosmos Moon*, by Devin Scillian, illustrated by Mark Braught (ages 4-8); *Redheaded Robbie's Christmas Story*, by Bill Luttrell, illustrated by Luc Melanson (ages 4-10); *Penny: The Forgotten Coin*, by Denise Brennan-Nelson.

Nonfiction Average word length: picture books—1,800. Recently published *The Edmund Fitzgerald*; *Mercedes and the Chocolate Pilot*; *P is for Passport*.

How to Contact/Writers Only interested in agented material. Fiction/nonfiction: Submit complete ms. Responds to queries in 1 month; mss in 2 months. Publishes book 2 years after acceptance. Will consider e-mail submissions, simultaneous submissions.

Illustration Only interested in agented material. Works with 30 illustrators/year. Uses color artwork only.

Reviews ms/illustration packages from artists. Send ms with dummy. Illustrations only: Send samples, SASE, URL. Responds in 1 month. Samples returned with SASE.

Terms Pays authors royalty. Offers advances. Pays illustrators royalty. Sends galleys to authors. Originals returned to artist at job's completion. Book catalog available. All imprints included in a single catalog. Catalog available on Web site.

Tips "Please review our book on line before sending material or calling." Editorial staff attended or plans to attend the following conferences: BEA, IRA, Regional shows, UMBE, NEBA, AASL, ALA, and numerous local conferences.

SMALLFELLOW PRESS

Imprint of Tallfellow Press, 1180 S. Beverly Dr., Suite 320, Los Angeles CA 90035. E-mail: tallfellow@pacbell.n et. Web site: www.smallfellow.com. **Manuscript/Art Acquisitions:** Claudia Sloan.

- Smallfellow no longer accepts manuscripts.

SMOOCH

Imprint of Dorchester Publishing, 200 Madison Ave., Suite 2000, New York NY 10016. Fax: (203)846-1776. Web site: www.smoochya.com. **Manuscript Acquisitions:** Kate Seaver, editor. **Art Acquisitions:** Chelsea Shriver, assistant editor. **Manuscript Acquisitions:** Brian Giblin. **Art Acquisitions:** Marcin Pilchowski. Publishes 12 picture books/year; 8 young readers/year. Soundprints publishes children's books accompanied by plush toys and read-along cassettes that deal with wildlife, history and nature. All content must be accurate and realistic and is curated by experts for veracity.

- Smooch does not accept unsolicited manuscripts.

Fiction Picture books: animal. Young readers: animal, multicultural, nature/environment. Middle readers: history, multicultural. Recently published *My Abnormal Life*, by Lee McClain; *Got Fangs?*, by Katie Maxwell.

Nonfiction Picture books: animals. Young readers: animal, multicultural, nature/environment. Middle readers: history, multicultural. Recently published *Swordfish Returns*, by Susan Korman; *Crocodile Crossing*, by Schuyler Bull; *Time to Eat, Panda*, by Ann Whitehead Nagda.

How to Contact/Writers Fiction/nonfiction: Submit published writing samples. Responds in 6-8 months. Publishes book 2 years after acceptance.

Illustration Works with 12 illustrators/year. Uses color artwork only. Query. Contact: Chelsea Shriver, assistant editor. Query with samples. Samples not returned.

Terms Work purchased outright from authors for $1,000-2,500. Pays illustrators by the project. Book catalog available for $8\frac{1}{2}\times11$ SASE; ms and art guidelines available for SASE. Catalog available on Web site.

Tips "As a small publisher with very specific guidelines for our well-defined series, we are not able to accept unsolicited manuscripts for publication. All of our authors are contracted on a 'work for hire basis,' meaning that they create manuscripts to our specifications, depending on our need. While we generally work with an established group of authors who know our needs as a publisher, we are always interested in reviewing the work of new potential authors. If you would like to submit some published writing samples, we would be happy to review them and keep them on file for future reference. Please send all writing samples to assistant editor."

N ◻ THE SPEECH BIN, INC.

1965 25th Ave., Vero Beach FL 32960. (561)770-0007. Fax: (561)770-0006. Web site: www.speechbin.com. **Acquisitions:** Jan J. Binney, senior editor. Publishes 10-12 books/year. 50% of books by first-time authors; less than 15% of books from agented writers. "Nearly all our books deal with treatment of children (as well as adults) who have communication disorders of speech or hearing or children who deal with family members who have such disorders (e.g., a grandparent with Alzheimer's disease or stroke)."

- The Speech Bin is currently overstocked with fiction.

Fiction Picture books, young readers, middle readers, young adult: special needs.

Nonfiction Picture books, young readers, middle readers, young adults: activity books, health, textbooks, special needs, communication disorders.

How to Contact/Writers Fiction/nonfiction: Query. Responds to queries in 6 weeks; mss in 3 months. Publishes a book 10-12 months after acceptance. "Will consider simultaneous submissions *only* if notified; too many authors fail to let us know if manuscript is simultaneously submitted to other publishers! We *strongly* prefer sole submissions. No electronic or faxed submissions."

Illustration Works with 4-5 illustrators/year ("usually in-house"). Reviews ms/illustration packages from artists. Manuscript/illustration packages and illustration only: "Query first!" Submit tearsheets (no original art). Responds only if interested. Samples returned with SASE. Originals returned by arrangement. No electronic or faxed submissions without prior authorization.

Photography Buys stock and assigns work. Looking for scenic shots. Model/property releases required. Uses glossy b&w prints, 35mm or 2¼×2¼ transparencies. Submit résumé, business card, promotional literature or tearsheets to be kept on file.

Terms Pays authors royalties based on selling price. Pays photographers by the project or per photo. Terms negotiable. Sends galleys to authors. Original artwork returned at job's completion. Book catalog for $1.43 postage and 9×12 SAE; ms guidelines for #10 SASE.

Tips "No calls, please. All submissions and inquiries must be in writing."

STANDARD PUBLISHING

8121 Hamilton Ave., Cincinnati OH 45231. (513)931-4050. Fax: (513)931-0950. Web site: www.standardpub.com. **Editorial Directors:** Diane Stortz, director Family Resources; Ruth Frederick, Children & Youth Ministry Resources. **Creative Services Director:** Julie Diehl. Many projects are written in-house. No young adult novels. 25-40% of books by first-time authors; 10% of books from agented writers. Publishes picture books, board books, nonfiction, devotions and resources for teachers.

 • Standard also has a listing in Greeting Card, Puzzles & Games.

Fiction Recently published *Jesus Must Be Really Special,* by Jennie Bishop, illustrated by Amy Wummer.

Nonfiction Recently published *Through the Bible Devotions,* by Mark Littleton.

How to Contact/Writers Responds in 3-6 months.

Illustration Works with 20 new illustrators/year. Illustrations only: Submit cover letter and photocopies. Responds to art samples only if interested. Samples returned with SASE; samples filed.

Terms Pays authors royalty based on net price or work purchased outright (range varies by project). Pays photographers by the photo. Sends galleys to authors on most projects. Book catalog available for $2 and 8½×11 SAE; ms guidelines available on Web site.

Tips "We look for manuscripts that help draw children into a relationship with Jesus Christ, develop insights about Bible teachings, and make reading fun."

STARSEED PRESS

Imprint of HJ Kramer in joint venture with New World Library, P.O. Box 1082, Tiburon CA 94920. (415)435-5367. Fax: (415)435-5364. Web site: www.newworldlibrary.com. **Manuscript Acquisitions:** Jan Phillips. **Art Acquisitions:** Linda Kramer, vice president. Publishes 2 picture books/year. 50% of books by first-time authors. "We publish 4-color, 32-page children's picture books dealing with self-esteem and positive values, with a non-denominational, spiritual emphasis."

Fiction Picture books: self-esteem, multicultural, nature/environment. Average word length: picture books—500-1,500. Recently published *Thank You God,* by Holly Bea, illustrated by Kim Howard (ages 3-7, picture book).

Nonfiction Picture books: multicultural, nature/environment.

How to Contact/Writers Fiction/nonfiction: Submit outline/synopsis. Responds to queries/mss in 10 weeks. Publishes a book 18 months after acceptance. Will consider simultaneous submissions, previously published work.

Illustration Works with 2 illustrators/year. Uses color artwork only. Illustrations only: Query with samples. Responds only if interested. Samples returned with SASE; samples filed.

Terms Negotiates based on publisher's net receipts. Split between author and artist. Originals returned to artist at job's completion. Book catalog available for 9×11 SAE with $1.98 postage; ms and art guidelines available for SASE. All imprints included in a single catalog.

STEMMER HOUSE PUBLISHING

4 White Brook Rd., Gilsum NH 03448. (800)345-6665 or (603)357-0236. Fax: (603)357-2073. E-mail: pbs@pathwaybook.com. Web site: www.stemmer.com. Estab. 1975. **Acquisitions:** Craig Thorn. Acquisitions Editor: Craig Thorn, Maressa Grieco. Publishes 2 picture books/year; 2 young readers/year; 1 middle reader/year. 90% of books by first-time authors.

Fiction Picture books, young readers, middle readers: animal, fantasy, folktales, nature/environment. Average word length: picture books—400; young readers—600; middle readers—800.

Nonfiction Picture books, young readers, middle readers: animal, arts/crafts, geography, history, nature/environment. Average word length: picture books—400; young readers—600; middle readers—800.

How to Contact/Writers Fiction/nonfiction: Query or submit outline/synopsis. Responds to queries in 1-2 months; mss in 4-8 weeks. Publishes book 2 years after acceptance. Will consider simultaneous submissions.

Illustration Works with 3-5 illustrators/year. Reviews ms/illustration packages from artists. Query or submit ms with 2-3 pieces of final art. Contact: Craig Thorn, editor-in-chief. Illustrations only: Query with samples, résumé, SASE, and tearsheets to be kept on file. Contact: Judith Peter. Responds only if interested. Samples returned with SASE; samples filed.

Photography Buys stock and assigns work. Uses nature, locations. Model/property releases required only upon use; captions not required. Submit cover letter and samples.

Terms Pays authors royalty of 10-15% based on wholesale price. Offers advances (average amount: $300-500). Pays illustrators and photographers royalty of 10-15% based on wholesale price. Sends galleys to authors; dummies to illustrators. Originals returned to artist at job's completion. Book catalog available for 6×9 SASE with postage.

[N] STONE ARCH BOOKS

7825 Telegraph Rd., Minneapolis MN 55438. (952)224-0514. Fax: (952)933-2410. Web site: www.stonearchbook s.com. **Acquisitions Editor:** Michael Dahl. **Art Director:** Heather Kindseth. Specialized in "high-interest, engaging fiction for struggling and reluctant reader, especially boys."

Fiction Young Readers, middle readers, young adults: adventure, contemporary, fantasy, hi-lo, humor, multicultural, science fiction, sports, suspense. Middle readers: poetry. Average word length: young readers—2,000; middle readers—5,000; young adults—7,000-10,000.

How to Contact/Writers Submit outline/synopsis and 3 sample chapters. Responds to mss in 8 weeks. Published a book 6-12 months after acceptance. Accepts e-mail submissions and simultaneous submissions.

Illustration Works with 35 illustrators/year. Used both color and b&w. Send manuscript with dummy. Contact: Heather Kindseth, art director. Samples not returned; samples filed.

Terms Work purchased outright from authors. Illustrators paid by the project. Book catalog available on Web site.

Tips "A 'high-interest' topic or activity is one that a young person would spend their free tiem on without adult direction or suggestion."

TANGLEWOOD BOOKS

P.O. Box 3009, Terre Haute IN 47803. E-mail: ptierney@tanglewoodbooks.com. Web site: www.tanglewoodboo ks.com. Estab. 2003. Specializes in trade books. **Writers contact:** Peggy Tierney, publisher. **Illustrators contact:** Peggy Tierney, publisher. Produces 2-3 picture books/year, 1-2 middle readers/year, 1-2 young adult titles/year. 20% of books by first-time authors. "Tanglewood Press strives to publishh entertaining, kid-centric books."

Fiction Picture books: adventure, animal, concept, contemporary, fantasy, humor. Average word length: picture books—800. Recently published *Mystery at Blackbeard's Cove*, by Audrey Penn, illustrated by Josh Miller and Phillip Howard (ages 8-12, adventure); *It All Began with a Bean*, by Katie McKy, illustrated by Tracy Hill (ages 4-8, humorous); *You Can't Milk a Dancing Cow*, by Tom Dunsmuir, illustrated by Brain Jones (ages 4-8, humorous).

How to Contact/Writers Accepts international submissions. Fiction: Query with 3-5 sample chapters. Responds to mss in 6-9 months. Publishes book 2 years after acceptance. Considers simultaneous submissions.

Illustration Accepts material from international illustrators. Works with 3-4 illustrators/year. Uses both color and b&w. Reviews ms/illustration packages. For ms/illustration packages: Send ms with dummy. Submit ms/ illustration packages to Peggy Tierney, publisher. If interested in illustrating future titles, query with samples. Submit samples to Peggy Tierney, publisher. Samples returned with SASE. Samples filed.

Terms Illustrators paid by the project for covers and small illustrations; royalty of 3-5% for picture books. Author sees galleys for review. Illustrators see dummies for review. Originals returned to artist at job's completion.

Tips "Please see lengthy 'Submissions' page on our Web site."

TEORA USA

2 Wisconsin Circle, #870, Chevy Chase MD 20815. (301)986-6990. Fax: (301)986-6992. E-mail: contact@teora.c om. Web site: www.teora.com. Estab. 2003. Specializes in mass market books, trade books, nonfiction, educational material. **Acquisitions:** Teora Raducanu, president. Produces 10 picture books/year, 2 young readers/ year, 1 middle reader/year.

Nonfiction All levels: activity books, animal, careers, geography, health, history, hobbies. Recently published *1000 Games for Smart Kids*; *My First Words*; *Little Rabbits Have Fur*.

How to Contact/Writers Accepts international submissions. Submit outline/synopsis and 20% of the ms. Responds to queries/mss in 6 months. Publishes book 1 year after acceptance. Considers electronic submissions, previously published work.

Illustration Accepts material from international illustrators. Uses both color and b&w. Reviews ms/illustration packages. For ms/illustration packages: Submit ms with 20% of final art. Reviews work for future assignments. If interested in illustrating future titles, query with samples. Samples not returned.

Photography Buys stock images and assigns work. Model/property releases required. Photo captions required. For first contact, send published samples, portfolio.

Terms Author sees galleys for review. Illustrators see dummies for review. Originals not returned. Catalog on Web site.

TILBURY HOUSE, PUBLISHERS

2 Mechanic St., #3, Gardiner ME 04345. (207)582-1899. Fax: (207)582-8227. E-mail: tilbury@tilburyhouse.com. Web site: www.tilburyhouse.com. **Publisher:** Jennifer Bunting. Children's Book Editor: Audrey Maynard. Publishes 1-3 young readers/year.

Fiction Picture books, young readers, middle readers: multicultural, nature/environment. Special needs include books that teach children about tolerance and honoring diversity. Recently published *Thanks to the Animals*, by Allen Sockabasin; *Playing War*, by Kathy Beckwith; *Say Something*, by Peggy Moss; *The Goat Lady*, by Jane Bregoli.

Nonfiction Picture books, young readers, middle readers: multicultural, nature/environment. Recently published *Life Under Ice*, by Mary Cerullo, with photography by Bill Curtsinger; *Saving Birds*, by Pete Salmansohn and Steve Kress.

How to Contact/Writers Fiction/ nonfiction: Submit outline/synopsis. Responds to queries/mss in 1 month. Publishes a book 1-2 years after acceptance. Will consider simultaneous submissions "with notification."

Illustration Works with 2 illustrators/year. Illustrations only: Query with samples. Responds in 1 month. Samples returned with SASE. Original artwork returned at job's completion.

Photography Buys photos from freelancers. Works on assignment only.

Terms Pays authors royalty based on wholesale price. Pays illustrators/photographers by the project; royalty based on wholesale price. Sends galleys to authors. Book catalog available for 6×9 SAE and 57¢ postage.

Tips "We are primarily interested in children's books that teach children about tolerance in a multicultural society, honor diversity, and make readers curious about the larger world. We are also interested in books that teach children about environmental issues."

A MEGAN TINGLEY BOOKS

Imprint of Little, Brown and Company, 1271 Avenue of the Americas, New York NY 10020. (212)522-8700. Fax: (212)522-7997. Web site: www.lb-kids.com, www.lb-teens.com. **Publisher:** Megan Tingley. **Manuscript Acquisitions:** Nancy Conescu, assistant editor. **Art Acquisitions:** Creative Director. Publishes 10 picture books/year; 1 middle reader/year; 2 young adult titles/year. 2% of books by first-time authors.

● Megan Tingley Books accepts agented material only.

Fiction Average word length: picture books—under 1,000 words. Recently published *You Read to Me, I'll Read to You: Very Short Fairy Tales to Read Together*, by Mary Ann Hoberman, illustrated by Michael Emberley (ages 3-6, picture book); *The Peace Book*, by Todd Parr (all ages, picture book); *Luna*, by Julie Peters (ages 12 and up); *Twilight*, by Stephanie Meyer (ages 12 and up).

Nonfiction All levels: animal, biography, history, multicultural, music/dance, nature/environment, science, self help, social issues, special needs. Recently published *Look-Alikes Christmas*, by Joan Steiner (all ages); *My New York* (revised edition), by Kathy Jakobsen; *Harlem Stomp!*, by Carrick Hill (ages 10 and up).

How to Contact/Writers Only interested in agented material. Query. Responds to mss in 2 months. Publishes a book 2 years after acceptance. Will consider simultaneous submissions, previously published work.

Illustration Works with 5 illustrators/year. Reviews ms/illustration packages from artists. Illustrations only: Query with samples. Contact: Assistant Editor. Responds only if interested. Samples not returned; samples kept on file.

Terms Pays illustrators by the project or royalty based on retail price. Sends galleys to authors. Originals returned to artist at job's completion. All imprints included in a single catalog. Responds within 2 months only if interested.

TOKYOPOP INC.

5900 Willshire Blvd., Los Angeles CA 90036. (323)692-6700. Fax: (323)692-6701. Web site: www.tokyopop.com. Estab. 1996. Specializes in trade books, fiction, multicultural material. **Manuscript Acquisitions:** Jeremy Ross, editorial director; Nicole Monsastirsky, novels; Teresa Imperato, kids books. **Art Acquisitions:** Jeremy Ross, editorial director. Produces 75 picture books/year; 6 young readers/year; 6 young adult books/year. 25% of books by first-time authors. "We are the leading Asian popculture-influenced publisher in the world. Our product lines include manga, cine-manga™, young adult novels, chapter books, and merchandise."

Fiction Young readers: adventure, contemporary, humor, science fiction, suspense. Middle readers: adventure, contemporary, fantasy, humor, problem novels, science fiction. Young adults/teens: adventure, contemporary, fantasy, humor, problem novels, science fiction, suspense. Average word length: young readers—9,000; middle readers—9,000; young adult—50,000.

Nonfiction Middle readers, young adult/teens: activity books, arts/crafts, hobbies.

How to Contact/Writers Accepts international submissions. Fiction: Submit outline/synopsis and 2 sample chapters. Responds to queries/mss in 6 months. Publishes book 18 months after acceptance.

Illustration Accepts material from international illustrators. Works with 25 illustrators/year. Uses primarily b&w artwork. Reviews ms/illustration packages. Submit ms/illustration packages to Jeremy Ross, editorial director. Reviews work for future assignments. If interested in illustrating future titles, query with samples. Submit samples to Jeremy Ross, editorial director. Responds in 3 months. Samples not returned.

Terms Pays authors royalty of 8% based on retail price. Pays illustrators by the project (range: $500-5,000). Author sees galleys for review. Illustrators see dummies for review. Originals not returned. Catalog on Web site. See Web site for artist's guidelines.

Tips "Submit cool, innovative, offbeat, cutting-edge material that captures the essence of teen pop culture."

TOMMY NELSON®

Imprint of Thomas Nelson, Inc., P.O. Box 141000, Nashville TN 37214. (615)889-9000. Fax: (615)902-2219. Web site: www.tommynelson.com.

• Tommy Nelson no longer accepts or reviews unsolicited queries, proposals, or manuscripts. Unsolicited material will be returned to sender.

TRICYCLE PRESS

Imprint of Ten Speed Press, P.O. Box 7123, Berkeley CA 94707. (510)559-1600. Web site: www.tricyclepress.c om. **Acquisitions:** Nicole Geiger, publisher. Publishes 12-14 picture books/year; 2 middle readers/year; 1 tween fiction/year; 3 board books/year. 25% of books by first-time authors. "Tricycle Press looks for something outside the mainstream; books that encourage children to look at the world from a different angle. Tricycle Press, like its parent company, Ten Speed Press, is known for its quirky, offbeat books. We publish high-quality trade books."

Fiction Board books, picture books, middle grade: animal, contemporary, fantasy, history, multicultural, nature, poetry, suspense/mystery. Picture books, young readers: concept. Middle readers: anthology, literary novels. Average word length: picture books—800-1,000. Recently published *Finklehopper Frog*, by Irene Livingston, illustrated by Brian Lies (ages 5-8 picture book); *Yesterday I Had the Blues*, by Jeron Frame, illustrated by Gregory Christie; *Don't Laugh at Me*, by Steve Seskin and Allen Shamlin, illustrated by Glin Dibley.

Nonfiction Picture books, middle readers: animal, arts/crafts, biography, careers, concept, cooking, history, how-to, multicultural, music/dance, nature/environment, science. Recently published *Q is for Quark: A Science Alphabet Book*, by David M. Schwartz (ages 9 and up, picture book); *Honest Pretzels and 64 Other Amazing Recipes for Cooks Ages 8 & Up*, by Mollie Katzen; *The Young Adventurer's Guide to Everest*, by Jonathan Chester (ages 8 and up, nonfiction picture book); *Salad People and More Real Recipes: A New Cookbook for Preschoolers and Up*, by Mollie Katzen.

How to Contact/Writers Fiction: Submit complete ms for picture books. Submit outline/synopsis and 2-3 sample chapters for chapter book. "No queries!" Nonfiction: Submit complete ms. Responds to mss in 4-6 months. Publishes a book 1-2 years after acceptance. Welcomes simultaneous submissions and previously published work. Do not send original artwork; copies only, please. No electronic or faxed submissions.

Illustration Works with 12 illustrators/year. Uses color and b&w. Reviews ms/illustration package from artists. Submit ms with dummy and/or 2-3 pieces of final art. Illustrations only: Query with samples, promo sheet, tearsheets. Responds only if interested. Samples returned with SASE; samples filed. Original artwork returned at job's completion unless work for hire.

Photography Works on assignment only. Uses 35mm transparencies or high resolution scans. Submit samples.

Terms Pays authors royalty of 7¹/₂-8¹/₂% based on net receipts. Offers advances. Pays illustrators and photographers royalty of 7¹/₂-8¹/₂% based on net receipts. Sends galleys of novels to authors. Book catalog for 9×12 SASE (3 first-class stamps). Manuscript guidelines for SASE (1 first-class stamp). Guidelines available at Web site.

Tips "We are looking for something a bit outside the mainstream and with lasting appeal (no one-shot-wonders)."

▣ TROPHY/TEMPEST/EOS PAPERBACKS

1350 Avenue of the Americas, New York NY 10019. (212)261-6500. Fax: (212)261-6668. Web site: www.harperc ollins.com and www.harperteen.com. Book publisher. Imprint of HarperCollins Children's Books Group. Publishes 20-25 chapter books/year, 70-75 middle grade titles/year, 25-30 reprint picture books/year, 10-15 teen titles/year.

• Trophy is a middle grade imprint. Tempest is a teen imprint. Eos is a fantasy/science fiction imprint. In addition to paperback reprints, Trophy and Tempest also publish a limited number of hardcover and/or paperback originals each year.

How to Contact/Writers Does not accept unsolicited or unagented mss.

TURTLE BOOKS

866 United Nations Plaza, Suite 525, New York NY 10017. (212)644-2020. Web site: www.turtlebooks.com. **Acquisitions:** John Whitman. "Turtle Books publishes only picture books for young readers. Our goal is to

publish a small, select list of quality children's books each spring and fall season. As often as possible, we will publish our books in both English and Spanish editions.''

• Turtle does a small number of books and may be slow in responding to unsolicited manuscripts.

Fiction Picture books: adventure, animal, concept, contemporary, fantasy, folktales, hi-lo, history, humor, multicultural, nature/environment, religion, sports, suspense/mystery. Recently published *The Legend of Mexicatl*, by Jo Harper, illustrated by Robert Casilla (the story of Mexicatl and the origin of the Mexican people); *Vroom, Chugga, Vroom-Vroom*, by Anne Miranda, illustrated by David Murphy (a number identification book in the form of a race car story); *The Crab Man*, by Patricia VanWest, illustrated by Cedric Lucas (the story of a young Jamaican boy who must make the difficult decision between making an income and the ethical treatment of animals); *Prairie Dog Pioneers*, by Jo and Josephine Harper, illustrated by Craig Spearing (the story of a young girl who doesn't want to move, set in 1870s Texas); *Keeper of the Swamp*, by Ann Garrett, illustrated by Karen Chandler (a dramatic coming-of-age story wherein a boy confronts his fears and learns from his ailing grandfather the secrets of the swamp); *The Lady in the Box*, by Ann McGovern, illustrated by Marni Backer (a modern story about a homeless woman named Dorrie told from the point of view of two children); *Alphabet Fiesta*, by Anne Miranda, illustrated by young schoolchildren in Madrid, Spain (an English/Spanish alphabet story).

How to Contact/Writers Send complete ms. ''Queries are a waste of time.'' Response time varies.

Illustrators Works with 6 illustrators/year. Responds to artist's queries/submissions only if interested. Samples returned with SASE only.

Terms Pays royalty. Offers advances.

TWO LIVES PUBLISHING

P.O. Box 736, Ridley Park PA 19078. (610)532-2024. Fax: (610)532-2790. E-mail: info@TwoLives.com. Web site: www.TwoLives.com. **Manuscript Acquisitions:** Bobbie Combs. Publishes 1 picture book/year; 1 middle reader/year. 100% of books by first-time authors. ''We create books for children whose parents are lesbian, gay, bisexual or transgender.''

Fiction Picture books, young readers, middle readers: contemporary.

How to Contact/Writers Fiction: Query. Responds to queries/mss in 3 weeks. Publishes book 2-3 years after acceptance. Will consider e-mail submissions, simultaneous submissions, previously published work.

Illustration Works with 2 illustrators/year. Uses color artwork only. Query ms/illustration packages. Contact: Bobbie Combs, publisher. Illustrations only: Send postcard sample with brochure, photocopies. Contact: Bobbie Combs, publisher. Responds only if interested. Samples filed.

Terms Pays authors royalty of 5-10% based on retail price. Offers advances (average amount: $250). Pays illustrators royalty of 5-10% based on retail price. Sends galleys to authors. Originals returned to artist at job's completion. Catalog available on Web site.

TWO-CAN PUBLISHING

T & N Children's Publishing, 11571 K-Tel Drive, Minnetonka MN 55343. Web site: www.two-canpublishing.com. Estab. 1990. Specializes in trade books, nonfiction. **Manuscript Acquisitions:** Jill Anderson, editorial director. Produces 10 young readers/year; 5 middle readers/year. 5% of books by first-time authors. ''Two-Can's line of nonfiction children's books feature bright, appealing designs, well-researched facts, and fun-to-read texts. Nonfiction does not have to be boring!''

Nonfiction Picture books, young readers, middle readers: animal, geography, health, history, multicultural, nature/environment, reference, science. Average word length: picture books—400-800; young readers—800-3,000; middle readers—2,500-15,000. Recently published *The Trail West*, by Ellen Galford (ages 8-11, history/art history); *My First Trip Around the World* (ages 5-8, geography/culture); *The Little Book of Dinosaurs*, by Cherie Winner (ages 4-7, animals).

How to Contact/Writers Accepts international submissions. Responds to queries/mss in 2 months. Publishes book 1-2 years after acceptance. Considers simultaneous submissions.

Illustration Works with 2 illustrators/year. Uses color artwork only. Reviews ms/illustration packages. For ms/illustration packages: Submit ms/illustration packages to Jill Anderson, editorial director. Reviews work for future assignments. If interested in illustrating future titles, query with samples, photocopies. Submit samples to Art Director. Samples not returned. Samples filed.

Photography Buys stock images; assigns work (rarely). Contact: Jill Anderson, editorial director. Photo needs ''depend on project we are working on—nature, culture, how-to—just about anything.'' Model/property releases required. Photo captions required. Uses high-res scans or color transparencies. For first contact, send cover letter, published samples, stock photo list, promo piece.

Terms Pays authors royalty based on retail price or work purchased outright. Pays illustrators by the project or royalty. Pays photographers by the project, per photo or royalty. Author sees galleys for review. Illustrators see dummies for review. See Web site for writer's and artist's guidelines.

Book Publishers

Ⓐ TYNDALE HOUSE PUBLISHERS, INC.

351 Executive Dr., P.O. Box 80, Wheaton IL 60189. (630)668-8300. Web site: www.tyndale.com. **Manuscript Acquisitions:** Jan Axford. **Art Acquisitions:** Talinda Laubach. Publishes approximately 15 Christian children's titles/year.

- Tyndale House no longer reviews unsolicited mss, only agented material.

Fiction Middle readers: adventure, religion, suspense/mystery.

Nonfiction Picture books: religion. Young readers: Bible, devotionals, Bible storybooks.

Illustration Uses full-color for book covers, b&w or color spot illustrations for some nonfiction. Illustrations only: Query with photocopies (color or b&w) of samples, résumé.

Photography Buys photos from freelancers. Works on assignment only.

Terms Pay rates for authors and illustrators vary.

Tips "All accepted manuscripts will appeal to Evangelical Christian children and parents."

UNITY HOUSE

1901 NW Blue Pkwy., Unity Village MO 64065-0001. (816)524-3550, ext. 3190. (816)251-3552. Web site: www.unityonline.org. **Manuscript Acquisitions:** Adrianne Ford. Other imprints: Wee Wisdom. Publishes 1 picture book every 2 years.

Fiction All levels: religion. Recently published *Henrietta the Homely Duckling*, by Phil Hahn (picture book).

Nonfiction All levels: religion.

How to Contact/Writers Fiction/nonfiction: Submit complete ms. Responds to queries/mss in 6 months. Publishes a book approximately 1 year after acceptance. Will consider simultaneous submissions or previously self-published work. Writer's guidelines upon request.

Illustrations Reviews ms/illustration packages from artists. Query.

Terms Pays authors royalty of 10-15% based on net receipts or work purchased outright. Offers advances (average amount: $1,000). Book catalog available.

Tips "Read our Writer's Guidelines and study our catalog before submitting. All of our publications reflect Unity's spiritual teachings, but the presentations and applications of those teachings are wide open."

URJ PRESS

633 Third Ave., New York NY 10017. (212)650-4120. Fax: (212)650-4119. E-mail: press@urj.org. Web site: www.urj.press.com. **Manuscript/Art Acquisitions:** Rabbi Hara Person, editor-in-chief. Publishes 4 picture books/year; 2 young readers/year; 2 middle readers/year; 2 young adult titles; 4 textbooks/year. "URJ publishes textbooks for the religious classroom, children's tradebooks and scholarly work of Jewish education import—no adult fiction and no YA fiction."

Fiction Picture books: religion. Average word length: picture books—1,500. Recently published *The Purim Costume*, by Peninnah Schran, illustrated by Tammy L. Keiser (ages 4-8, picture book); *A Year of Jewish Stories: 52 Tales for Children and Their Families*, by Grace Ragues Maisel and Samantha Shubert, illustrated by Tammy L. Keiser (ages 4-12, picture book).

Nonfiction Picture books, young readers, middle readers: religion. Average word length: picture books—1,500. Recently published *The Seven Species: Stories and Recipes Inspired by the Foods of the Bible*, by Matt Biers-Ariel, illustrated by Tama Goodman (story and recipe book).

How to Contact/Writers Fiction: Submit outline/synopsis and 2 sample chapters. Nonfiction: Submit complete ms. Responds to queries/mss in 4 months. Publishes a book 18-24 months after acceptance. Will consider simultaneous submissions.

Illustration Works with 5 illustrators/year. Reviews ms/illustration packages from artists. Send ms with dummy. Illustrations only: Send portfolio to be kept on file. Responds in 2 months. Samples returned with SASE. Looking specifically for Jewish themes.

Photography Buys stock and assigns work. Uses photos with Jewish content. Prefers modern settings. Submit cover letter and promo piece.

Terms Offers advances. Pays photographers by the project (range: $200-3,000) or per photo (range: $20-100). Book catalog free; ms guidelines for SASE.

Tips "Look at some of our books. Have an understanding of the Reform Jewish community. We sell mostly to Jewish congregations and day schools."

VIKING CHILDREN'S BOOKS

Penguin Group Inc., 345 Hudson St., New York NY 10014-3657. (212)414-3600. Fax: (212)414-3399. Web site: www.penguin.com. **Acquisitions:** Catherine Frank, senior editor (picture books, middle grade and young adult fiction); Tracy Gates, executive editor (picture books, middle grade, young adult fiction); Joy Peskin, senior editor (picture books, middle grade, young adult fiction); Jill Davis, senior editor (picture books, middle grade, young adult, unique nonfiction); Anne Gunton, associate editor (picture books, middle grade, young adult);

Kendra Levin, editorial assistant. **Art Acquisitions:** Denise Cronin, Viking Children's Books. Publishes hardcover originals. Publishes 60 books/year. Receives 7,500 queries/year. 25% of books from first-time authors; 33% from unagented writers. "Viking Children's Books is known for humorous, quirky picture books, in addition to more traditional fiction and publishes the highest quality trade books for children including fiction, nonfiction, and novelty books for preschoolers through young adults." Publishes book 1-2 years after acceptance of artwork. Hesitantly accepts simultaneous submissions.

- Viking Children's Books is not accepting unsolicited submissions at this time.

Fiction All levels: adventure, animal, contemporary, fantasy, hi-lo, history, humor, multicultural, nature/environment, poetry, problem novels, religion, romance, science fiction, sports, suspense/mystery. Recently published *Llama Llama Red Pajama*, by Anna Dewdney (ages 2 up, picture book); *Prom*, by Laurie Halse Anderson (ages 12 and up).

Nonfiction Picture books: animal, biography, concept. Young readers, middle readers, young adult: animal, biography, concept, geography, hi-lo, history, multicultural, music/dance, nature/environment, science, sports. Recently published *John Lennon: All I Want Is the Truth*, by Elizabeth Partridge(ages 11 up, nonfiction).

Illustration Works with 30 illustrators/year. Responds to artist's queries/submissions only if interested. Samples returned with SASE only or samples filed. Originals returned at job's completion.

Terms Pays 2-10% royalty on retail price or flat fee. Advance negotiable.

VSP BOOKS

7402-G Lockport Place, Lorton VA 22079. (703)684-8142. Fax: (703)684-7955. E-mail: mail@VSPBooks.com. Web site: www.VSPBooks.com. **Manuscript Acquisitions:** Peter Barnes. Imprints: VSP Books, Vacation Spot Publishing. Publishes 3 picture books/year. 50% of books by first-time authors. "We publish children's books about special and historic places."

Fiction Picture books: history. Average word length: picture books—1,000.

How to Contact/Writers Fiction: Query.

Illustration Works with 2-3 illustrators/year. Uses color artwork only. Reviews ms/illustration packages from artists. Query. Illustrations only: Query with photocopies. Contact: Peter Barnes, publisher. Samples not returned.

Terms Pays authors royalties based on retail price or work purchased outright. Pays illustrators by the project or royalties. Sends galleys to authors; dummies to illustrators. Originals returned to artist at job's completion. Book catalog available for SASE. Catalog available on Web site.

WALKER & COMPANY

Books for Young Readers, 104 Fifth Ave., New York NY 10011. (212)727-8300. Fax: (212)727-0984. Web site: www.walkeryoungreaders.com. **Manuscript Acquisitions:** Emily Easton, publisher; Mary Gruetzke, senior editor. Publishes 20 picture books/year; 3-5 middle readers/year; 3-5 young adult titles/year. 5% of books by first-time authors; 65% of books from agented writers.

- *The Mysterious Collection of Dr. David Harleyson*, by Jean Cassells, received a 2005 Golden Kite Award.

Fiction Picture books: adventure, history, humor. Middle readers: adventure, contemporary, history, humor, multicultural. Young adults: adventure, contemporary, humor, historical fiction, suspense/mystery. Recently published *Earth Mother*, by Ellen Jackson, illustrated by Leo and Diane Dillon (ages 3-8, picture book); *Once Upon a Cool Motorcycle Dude*, written and illustrated by Kevin O'Malley (ages 6-10, picture book); *It's a Mall World After All*, by Janette Rallison (12 and up, teen/young adult novel).

Nonfiction Picture book, middle readers: biography, history. Recently published *Blood Red Horses*, by K.M. Grant (ages 10-14); *Mutiny on the Bounty*, by Patrick O'Brien (ages 7-12, picture book history); *The Driving Book*, by Karen Gravelle (ages 15 and up). Multicultural needs include "contemporary, literary fiction and historical fiction written in an authentic voice. Also high interest nonfiction with trade appeal."

How to Contact/Writers Fiction/nonfiction: Submit outline/synopsis and sample chapters; complete ms for picture books. Responds to queries/mss in 3-4 months. Send SASE for writer's guidelines.

Illustration Works with 10-12 illustrators/year. Editorial department reviews ms/illustration packages from artists. Query or submit ms with 4-8 samples. Illustrations only: Tearsheets. "Please do not send original artwork." Responds to art samples only if interested. Samples returned with SASE.

Terms Pays authors royalty of 5-10%; pays illustrators royalty or flat fee. Offers advance payment against royalties. Original artwork returned at job's completion. Sends galleys to authors. Book catalog available for 9×12 SASE; ms guidelines for SASE.

Tips Writers: "Make sure you study our catalog before submitting. We are a small house with a tightly focused list. Illustrators: Have a well-rounded portfolio with different styles." Does not want to see folktales, ABC books, paperback series, genre fiction. "Walker and Company is committed to introducing talented new authors and illustrators to the children's book field."

WESTWINDS PRESS/ALASKA NORTHWEST BOOKS

Graphic Arts Center Publishing Company, P.O. Box 10306, Portland OR 97296-0306. (503)226-2402. Fax: (503)223-1410. E-mail: editorial@gacpc.com. Web site: www.gacpc.com. Independent book packager/producer. **Writers contact:** Tim Frew, executive editor. **Illustrators contact:** same. Produces 4 picture books/year, 1-2 young readers/year. 10% of books by first-time authors. "Graphic Arts Center Publishing Company publishes and distributes regional titles through its three imprints: Graphic Arts Books, Alaska Northwest Books and WestWinds Press. GAB is known for its excellence in publishing high-end photo-essay books. Alaska Northwest, established in 1959, is the premier publisher of nonfiction Alaska books on subjects ranging from cooking, Alaska Native culture, memoir, history, natural history, reference, biography, humor and children's books. WestWinds Press, established in 1999, echoes those themes with content that focuses on the Western States."

Fiction Picture books: animal, folktales, nature/environment. Young readers: adventure, animal, folktales, nature/environment. Average word length: picture books—1,100; young readers—9,000. Recently published *Kumak's Fish*, by Michael Bania (folktale, ages 6 and up); *Sweet Dreams, Polar Bear*, by Mindy Dwyer (3 and up); *Seldovia Sam and the Sea Otter Rescue*, by Susan Springer, illustrated by Amy Meissner (adventure, beginning chapter book).

Nonfiction Picture books: animal, nature/environment. Young readers: animal, nature/environment. Middle readers: nature/environment. Average word length: picture books—1,100; young readers—9,000. Recently published *Sharkabet*, by Ray Troll (ages 5 and up); *Winter Is*, by Anne Dixon, illustrated by Mindy Dwyer (environment/nature, ages 3-6).

How to Contact/Writers Accepts international submissions. Fiction/nonfiction: Submit complete ms. Responds to queries in 3 months; mss in 6 months. Publishes book 1-2 years after acceptance. Considers simultaneous submissions, electronic submissions, previously published work. "Please include SASE for response and return of materials."

Illustration Accepts material from international illustrators. Works with 4 illustrators/year. Uses both color and b&w. Reviews ms/illustration packages. For ms/illustration packages: Send ms with dummy. Submit ms/illustration packages to Tricia Brown, acquisitions editor. Reviews work for future assignments. If interested in illustrating future titles, query with samples. Samples returned with SASE. Samples not filed.

Photography Works on assignment only. Submit photos to Tim Frew, executive editor. Photo captions required. For first contact, send cover letter, portfolio, complete proposal, return postage.

Terms Offers advance against royalties. Originals returned to artist at job's completion. All imprints included in single catalog.

ALBERT WHITMAN & COMPANY

6340 Oakton St, Morton Grove, IL 60053-2723. (847)581-0033. Fax: (847)581-0039. Web site: www.albertwhitman.com. **Manuscript Acquisitions:** Kathleen Tucker, editor-in-chief. **Art Acquisitions:** Carol Gildar. Publishes 30 books/year. 20% of books by first-time authors; 15% off books from agented authors.

- Whitman title *Grandma's Pride*, by Becky Birtha, illustrated by Colin Bootman, won the Golden Kite Honor Award for picture book text for 2005.

Fiction Picture books, young readers, middle readers: adventure, concept (to help children deal with problems), fantasy, history, humor, multicultural, suspense. Middle readers: problem novels, suspense/mystery. "We are interested in contemporary multicultural stories—stories with holiday themes and exciting distinctive novels. We publish a wide variety of topics and are interested in stories that help children deal with their problems and concerns. Does not want to see, "religion-oriented, ABCs, pop-up, romance, counting." Recently published fiction: *Teeny Weeny Bop*, by Margaret Read MacDonald, illustrated by Diane Greenseid; *My Mom's Having a Baby!* by Dori Hillestad Butler, illustrated by Carol Thompson; *The Bully-Blockers Club*, by Teresa Bateman, illustrated by Jackie Urbanovic; *Tank Talbot' s Guide to Girls*, by Dori Hillestad Butler.

Nonfiction Picture books, young readers, middle readers: animal, arts/crafts, health, history, hobbies, multicultural, music/dance, nature/environment, science, sports, special needs. Does not want to see, "religion, any books that have to be written in, or fictionalized biographies." Recently published *Shelter Dogs*, by Peg Kehret; *Apples Here!* by Will Hubbell; *The Groundhog Day Book of Facts and Fun*, by Wendie Old, illustrated by Paige Billin-Frye.

How to Contact/Writers Fiction/Writers nonfiction: Submit query, outline, and sample chapter. For picture books send entire ms. Include cover letter. Responds to submissions in 4 months. Publishes a book 18 months after acceptance. Will consider simultaneous submissions "if notified."

Illustration "We are not accepting Illustration samples at this time. Submissions will not be returned."

Photography Publishes books illustrated with photos, but not stock photos-desires photos all taken for project. "Our books are for children and cover many topics; photos must be taken to match text. Books often show a child in a particular situation (e.g., kids being home-schooled, a sister whose brother is born prematurely)." Photographers should query with samples; send unsolicited photos by mail.

Terms Pays author's, illustrator's, and photographer's royalties. Book catalog for 8×10 SAE and 3 first-class stamps. Tips ''In both picture books and nonfiction, we are seeking stories showing life in other cultures and the variety of multicultural life in the U.S. We also want fiction and nonfiction about mentally or physically challenged children—some recent topics have been autism, stuttering, and diabetes. Look up some of our books first to be sure your submission is appropriate for Albert Whitman & Co.''

⬚ JOHN WILEY & SONS, INC.

111 River St., Hoboken NJ 07030. (201)748-6000. Web sites: www.wiley.com, www.josseybass.com. **Senior Editor:** Kate Bradford. Publishes 18 middle readers/year; 2 young adult titles/year. 10% of books by first-time authors. Publishes educational nonfiction: primarily and some history.

Nonfiction Middle readers: activity books, arts/crafts, biography, geography, health, history, hobbies, how-to, nature/environment, reference, science, self help. Young adults: activity books, arts/crafts, health, hobbies, how-to, nature/environment, reference, science, self help. Average word length: middle readers—20,000-40,000. Recently published *Myth Busters: Don't Try This at Home*, by Mary Packard (ages 8-12, science/activity—based on hit TV show on the Discovery Channel); *Have Fun with American Heroes*, by David C. King (ages 8-12, U.S. history); *Janice VanCleave's Energy for Every Kid*, by Janice VanCleave (ages 8-12, science/activity).

How to Contact/Writers Query. Submit outline/synopsis, 2 sample chapters and an author bio. Responds to queries in 1 month; mss in 3 months. Publishes a book 1 year after acceptance. Will consider simultaneous and previously published submissions.

Illustration Works with 6 illustrators/year. Uses primarily b&w artwork. Reviews ms/illustration packages from artists. Query. Illustrations only: Query with samples, résumé, client list. Responds only if interested. Samples filed. Original artwork returned at job's completion. No portfolio reviews.

Photography Buys photos from freelancers.

Terms Pays authors royalty of 10-12% based on wholesale price, or by outright purchase. Offers advances. Pays illustrators by the project. Photographers' pay negotiable. Sends galleys to authors. Book catalog available for SASE.

Tips ''We're looking for topics and writers that can really engage kids' interest, plus we're always interested in a new twist on time-tested subjects.'' Nonfiction submissions only; no picture books.

⬚ WINDWARD PUBLISHING

An imprint of the Finney Company, 3943 Meadowbrook Rd., Minneapolis MN 55426. (952)938-9330. Fax: (952)938-7353. E-mail: feedback@finney-hobar.com. Web site: www.finney-hobar.com. **Manuscript/Art Acquisitions:** Alan E. Krysan. Publishes 2 picture books/year; 4-6 young readers, middle readers, young adult titles/year. 50% of books by first-time authors.

Fiction Young readers, middle readers, young adults: adventure, animal, nature/environment. Recently published *Nightlight*, by Jeannine Anderson (ages 4-8, picture book); *Daddy Played Music for the Cows*, by Maryann Weidt (ages 4-8, picture book); *Wild Beach*, by Marion Coste (ages 4-8, picture book).

Nonfiction Young readers, middle readers, young adults: activity books, animal, careers, nature/environment, science. Young adults: textbooks. Recently published *My Little Book of Collection*, by Hope Irvin Marston (ages 4-8, introductions to the wonders of nature); *Space Station Science*, by Marianne Dyson (ages 8-13, science).

How to Contact/Writers Fiction: Query. Nonfiction: Submit outline/synopsis and 3 sample chapters. Responds to queries in 1 month; mss in 2 months. Publishes book 6-12 months after acceptance. Will consider simultaneous submissions and previously published work.

Illustration Reviews ms/illustration packages from artists. Send ms with dummy. Query with samples. Responds in 2 months. Samples returned with SASE; samples filed.

Photography Buys stock and assigns work. Photography needs depend on project—mostly ocean and beach subject matter. Uses color, 4×6, glossy prints. Submit cover letter, résumé, stock photo list.

Terms Author's payment negotiable by project. Offers advances (average amount: $500). Illustrators and photographers payment negotiable by project. Sends galleys to authors; dummies to illustrators. Originals returned to artist at job's completion. Book catalog available for 6×9 SAE and 3 first-class stamps; ms guidelines available for SASE. Catalog mostly available on Web site.

PAULA WISEMAN BOOKS

Imprint of Simon & Schuster, 1230 Sixth Ave., New York NY 10020. (212)698-7272. Fax: (212)698-2796. Web site: www.simonsays.com. Publishes 1 picture books/year; 2 middle readers/year; 2 young adult titles/year. 10% of books by first-time authors.

Fiction Considers all categories. Average word length: picture books—500; others standard length. Recently published *Double Pink*, by Kate Feiffer, illustrated by Bruce Ingman.

Nonfiction Picture books: animal, biography, concept, history, nature/environment. Young readers: animal, biography, history, multicultural, nature/environment, sports. Average word length: picture books—500; others standard length.

How to Contact/Writers Submit complete ms.

Illustration Works with 15 illustrators/year. Uses color artwork only. Will review ms/illustration packages from artists. Prefers mail for initial contact. Send manuscript with dummy.

WM KIDS

Imprint of White Mane Publishing Co., Inc., P.O. Box 708, 73 W. Burd St., Shippensburg PA 17257. (717)532-2237. Fax: (717)532-6110. E-mail: marketing@whitemane.com. Web site: www.whitemane.com. **Acquisitions:** Harold Collier, acquisitions editor. Imprints: White Mane Books, Burd Street Press, White Mane Kids, Ragged Edge Press. Publishes 10 middle readers/year. 50% of books are by first-time authors.

Fiction Middle readers, young adults: history. Average word length: middle readers—30,000. Does not publish picture books. Recently published *Lottie's Courage*, by Phyllis Haislip (historical fiction, grades 5 and up); Young Heroes of History series, by Alan Kay (grades 5 and up).

Nonfiction Middle readers, young adults: history. Average word length: middle readers—30,000. Does not publish picture books. Recently published *Slaves Who Dared: The Story of Ten African American Heroes*, by Mary Garrison (young adult).

How to Contact/Writers Fiction: Query. Nonfiction: Submit outline/synopsis and 2-3 sample chapters. Responds to queries in 1 month; mss in 3 months. Publishes a book 12-18 months after acceptance. Will consider simultaneous submissions.

Illustration Works with 3 illustrators/year. Illustrations used for cover art only. Responds only if interested. Samples returned with SASE.

Photography Buys stock and assigns work. Submit cover letter and portfolio.

Terms Pays authors royalty of 7-10%. Pays illustrators and photographers by the project. Sends galleys for review. Originals returned to artist at job's completion. Book catalog and writer's guidelines available for SASE. All imprints included in a single catalog.

☐ WORLD BOOK, INC.

233 N. Michigan Ave., Suite 2000, Chicago IL 60601. (312)729-5800. Fax: (312)729-5600. Web site: www.worldbook.com. **Manuscript Acquisitions:** Paul A. Kobasa, Editor-in-Chief. **Art Acquisitions:** Sandra Dyrland, art/design manager. World Book, Inc. (publisher of *The World Book Encyclopedia*), publishes reference sources and nonfiction series for children and young adults in the areas of science, mathematics, English-language skills, basic academic and social skills, social studies, history, and health and fitness. We publish print and nonprint material appropriate for children ages 3-14. WBT does not publish fiction, poetry, or wordless picture books.''

Nonfiction Young readers: animal, arts/crafts, careers, concept, geography, health, reference. Middle readers: animal, arts/crafts, careers, geography, health, history, hobbies, how-to, nature/environment, reference, science. Young adult: arts/crafts, careers, geography, health, history, hobbies, how-to, nature/environment, reference, science.

How to Contact/Writers Nonfiction: Submit outline/synopsis only; no mss. Responds to queries/mss in 2 months. Unsolicited mss will not be returned. Publishes a book 18 months after acceptance. Will consider simultaneous submissions.

Illustration Works with 10-30 illustrators/year. Illustrations only: Query with samples. Responds only if interested. Samples returned with SASE; samples filed ''if extra copies and if interested.''

Photography Buys stock and assigns work. Needs broad spectrum; editorial concept, specific natural, physical and social science spectrum. Model/property releases required; captions required. Uses color 8×10 glossy and matte prints, 35mm, $2\frac{1}{4} \times 2\frac{1}{4}$, 4×5, 8×10 transparencies. Submit cover letter, résumé, promo piece (color and b&w).

Terms Payment negotiated on project-by-project basis. Sends galleys to authors. Book catalog available for 9×12 SASE. Manuscript and art guidelines for SASE.

☐ THE WRIGHT GROUP/MCGRAW HILL

130 E. Randolph, 4th fl, Chicago IL 60601. (312) 233-6520. Fax: (312) 233-6605. Web site: www.wrightgroup.com. **Manuscripts Acquisitions:** Judy Sommer, vice president marketing. **Art Acquisitions:** Vicky Tripp, director of design. Publishes over 100 young readers/year, over 50 middle readers/year. ''The Wright Group is dedicated to improving literacy by providing outstanding tutorials for students and teachers.''

Fiction Picture books, young readers: adventure, animal, concept, contemporary, fantasy, folktales, hi-lo, history, humor, multicultural, nature/environment, poetry, sports, suspense/mystery. Middle readers: adventure, animal, contemporary, fantasy, folktales, hi-lo, history, humor, multicultural, nature/environment, poetry, problem novels. Average word length: young readers—50-5,000; middle readers—3,000-10,000. Recently published *Wild Crayons*, by Joy Cowley (young reader fantasy); *The Gold Dust Kids*, by Michell Dionetti (historical fiction chapter book for young readers); *Watching Josh*, by Deborah Eaton (middle reader, mystery).

Nonfiction Picture books, young readers, middle readers: animal, biography, careers, concept, geography, health, hi-lo, history, how-to, multicultural, nature/environment, science, sports. Average word length: young readers—50-3,000. Recently published *Iditarod*, by Joe Ramsey (young reader); *The Amazing Ant*, by Sara Sams (young reader); *Chameleons*, by Nic Bishop (young reader).

How to Contact/Writers Fiction/nonfiction: Submit complete ms or submit outline/synopsis and 3 sample chapters. Responds to queries in 1 month; mss in 5 months. Publishes a book 8 months after acceptance. Will consider previously published work.

Illustration Query with samples. Responds only if interested. Samples kept on file.

Photography Buys stock and assigns work. Model/property release and captions required. Uses $8\frac{1}{2} \times 11$ color prints. Submit published samples, promo pieces.

Terms Work purchased outright from authors ($500-2,400). Illustrators paid by the project. Photographers paid by the project ($3,500-5,000) or per photo ($300-350). Book catalog available online.

Tips "Much of our illustration assignments are being done by offsite developers, so our level of commission in this area is minimal."

Canadian & International Book Publishers

W hile the United States is considered the largest market in children's publishing, the children's publishing world is by no means strictly dominated by the U.S. After all, the most prestigious children's book extravaganza in the world occurs each year in Bologna, Italy, at the Bologna Children's Book Fair and some of the world's most beloved characters were born in the United Kingdom (i.e., Winnie-the-Pooh and Mr. Potter).

In this section you'll find book publishers from English-speaking countries around the world from Canada, Australia, New Zealand and the United Kingdom. The listings in this section look just like the U.S. Book Publishers section; and the publishers listed are dedicated to the same goal—publishing great books for children.

Like always, be sure to study each listing and research each publisher carefully before submitting material. Determine whether a publisher is open to U.S. or international submissions, as many publishers accept submissions only from residents of their own country. Some publishers accept illustration samples from foreign artists, but do not accept manuscripts from foreign writers. Illustrators do have a slight edge in this category as many illustrators generate commissions from all around the globe. Visit publishers' Web sites to be certain they publish the sort of work you do. Visit online bookstores to see if publishers' books are available there. Write or e-mail to request catalogs and submission guidelines.

When mailing requests or submissions out of the United States, remember that U.S. postal stamps are useless on your SASE. Always include International Reply Coupons (IRCs) with your SAE. Each IRC is good for postage for one letter. So if you want the publisher to return your manuscript or send a catalog, be sure to enclose enough IRCs to pay the postage. For more help visit the United State Postal Service Web site at www.usps.com/global. Visit www.timeanddate.com/worldclock and American Computer Resources, Inc.'s International Calling Code Directory at www.the-acr.com/codes/cntrycd.htm before calling or faxing internationally to make sure you're calling at a reasonable time and using the correct numbers.

**Useful
Web sites**

As in the rest of *Children's Writer's & Illustrator's Market*, the maple leaf 🍁 symbol identifies Canadian markets. Look for the Canadian 🍁 and International 🌐 symbols throughout *Children's Writer's & Illustrator's Market* as well. Several of the Society of Children's Book Writers and Illustrator's (SCBWI) international conferences are listed in the Conferences & Workshops section along with other events in locations around the globe. Look for more information about SCBWI's international chapters on the organization's Web site, www.scbwi.org. You'll also find international listings in Magazines and Young Writer's & Illustrator's Markets. See Useful Online Resources on page 361 for sites that offer additional international information.

Information on Canadian and international book publishers listed in the previous edition but not included in this edition of *Children's Writer's & Illustrator's Market* may be found in the General Index.

🌐 🏆 ALLEN & UNWIN

406 Albert St., East Melbourne VIC 3002 Australia. E-mail: frontdesk@allenandunwin.com. Web site: www.alle nandunwin.com. **Contact:** Children's Editor.

- Allen & Unwin was voted Publisher of the Year by Australian booksellers in 1992, 1996, 2001, 2002. They do not accept unsolicited picture book manuscripts.

Fiction Junior novels: For beginner readers ages 5-8, word length: 5,000-10,000; for confident readers ages 7-10, word length: 10,000-20,000. "Looking for fresh original storylines, strong engaging characters, a flair for language and an authentic voice." Inbetween novels: for middle readers ages 11-14, word length: 35,000-55,000. "Looking for great storytelling, popular or literary. Highly entertaining narratives avoiding heavy teenage issues preferred." Young adult novels: for teenage readers ages 13-16, word length: 40,000-60,000; for mature teenagers and older readers, ages 15+, word length: 40,000-100,000. "Need to be extremely well-written and engrossing. Looking for stories which are groundbreaking, challenging and experimental."

Nonfiction Considers nonfiction for children and teenagers "if it is imaginative, timely and authoritative."

How to Contact/Writers Fiction: Submit complete ms (5,000 words or more) and SASE "of suitable size." Nonfiction: Send proposal, detailed chapter outline and 3 sample chapters. Responds to mss in 4 months.

Tips "Do not send e-mail submissions."

🏆 ANNICK PRESS LTD.

15 Patricia Ave., Toronto ON M2M 1H9 Canada. (416)221-4802. Fax: (416)221-8400. E-mail: annickpress@annic kpress.com. Web site: www.annickpress.com. **Creative Director:** Sheryl Shapiro. Publishes 8 picture books/year; 3 young readers/year; 3 middle readers/year; 8 young adult titles/year. 25% of books by first-time authors. "Annick Press maintains a commitment to high-quality books that entertain and challenge. Our publications share fantasy and stimulate judgment and abilities."

- Annick Press does not accept unsolicited manuscripts.

Fiction No unsolicited mss. Recently published *Mimus*, by Lilli Thal (ages 12-15); *Torrie & the Pirate-Queen*, by KV Johansen (ages 9-11); *Me and My Sister*, by Ruth Ohi (ages 2-4, picture book).

Nonfiction Recently published *Evil Masters: The Frightening World of Tyrants*, by Laura Scandiffio (ages 12 and up); *Thieves!*, by Andreas Schroeder (ages 8 and up); *The Blue Jean Book: The Story Behind the Seams*, by Tanya Lloyd Kyi (ages 12 and up).

Illustration Works with 20 illustrators/year. Illustrations only: Query with samples. Contact: Creative Director. Responds in 6 months with SASE. Samples returned with SASE or kept on file.

Terms Pays authors royalty of 5-12% based on retail price. Offers advances (average amount: $3,000). Pays illustrators royalty of 5% minimum. Originals returned to artist at job's completion. Book catalog available on Web site.

🏆 BOARDWALK BOOKS

Imprint of The Dundurn Group, 3 Church St., Suite 500, Toronto ON M5E 1M2 Canada. (416)214-5544. Fax: (416)214-5556. E-mail: info@dundurn.com. Web site: www.dundurn.com. **Manuscript Acquisitions:** Barry Jowett. Boardwalk Books is the YA imprint of The Dundurn Group. Publishes 6 young adult titles/year. 25% of books by first-time authors. "We aim to publish sophisticated literary fiction for youths aged 12 to 16."

Fiction Young adults: contemporary, history, suspense/mystery. Average word length: young adults—40,000-45,000. Recently published *Sophie's Rebellion*, by Beverley Boissery (ages 12-16, fiction), *Deconstructing Dylan*, by Lesley Choyce (ages 12-16, fiction), *Viking Terror*, by Tom Henighan (ages 12-16, fiction).

How to Contact/Writers Accepts material from residents of Canada only. Fiction: Submit outline/synopsis and 3 sample chapters (or approximately 50 pages). Responds to queries/mss in 3 months. Publishes book 1 year after acceptance. Will consider simultaneous submissions.

Terms Offers advances. Sends galleys to authors. Book catalog available for 9×12 SAE with sufficient Canadian postage or international coupon. All imprints included in a single catalog. Writer's guidelines available on Web site.

Tips "Be sure your submission suits our list. We do not accept picture books."

🌐 CHILD'S PLAY (INTERNATIONAL) LTD.

Children's Play International, Ashworth Rd., Bridgeman, Swindon, Wiltshire SN5 7YD United Kingdom. (44)(179)361-6286. Fax: (44)(179)351-2795. E-mail: allday@childs-play.com. Web site: www.childs-play.com. Estab. 1972. Specializes in nonfiction, fiction, educational material, multicultural material. **Manuscript Acquisitions:** Sue Baker, Neil Burden. **Art Acquisitions:** Annie Kubler, art director. Produces 30 picture books/year;

10 young readers/year; 2 middle readers/year. 20% of books by first-time authors. "A child's early years are more important than any other. This is when children learn most about the world around them and the language they need to survive and grow. Child's Play aims to create exactly the right material for this all-important time."

Fiction Picture books: adventure, animal, concept, contemporary, folktales, multicultural, nature/environment. Young readers: adventure, animal, anthology, concept, contemporary, folktales, humor, multicultural, nature/environment, poetry. Average word length: picture books—0-1,500; young readers—2,000. Recently published *The Cockerel, the Mouse and the Little Red Hen*, by Jess Stockham (ages 3-6, fairy tale); *The Bear and Turtle and the Great Lake Race*, by A. Fusek-Peters, illustrated by Alison Edgson (ages 4-8, traditional tale); *Five Little Men in a Flying Saucer*, by Dan Crisp (ages 0-6, novelty board).

Nonfiction Picture books: activity books, animal, concept, multicultural, music/dance, nature/environment, science. Young readers: activity books, animal, concept, multicultural, music/dance, nature/environment, science. Average word length: picture books—2,000; young readers—3,000. Recently published *Little Drivers*, by Dan Crisp (ages 6 months+, novelty board); *My First Animal Signs*, by A. Kubler (ages 0-3, sign language for hearing babies); *Ocean Deep*, by R. Hatfield (ages 3-8, underwater tunnel book).

How to Contact/Writers Accepts international submissions. Fiction/nonfiction: Query or submit complete ms. Responds to queries in 10 weeks; mss in 15 weeks. Publishes book 2 years after acceptance. Considers simultaneous submissions, electronic submissions.

Illustration Accepts material from international illustrators. Works with 10 illustrators/year. Uses color artwork only. Reviews ms/illustration packages. For ms/illustration packages: Query or submit ms/illustration packages to Sue Baker, editor. Reviews work for future assignments. If interested in illustrating future titles, query with samples, CD, Web site address. Submit samples to Annie Kubler, art director. Responds in 10 weeks. Samples not returned. Samples filed.

Terms Work purchased outright from authors (range: $500-15,000). Pays illustrators by the project (range: $500-15,000). Author sees galleys for review. Originals not returned. Catalog on Web site. Offers writer's, artist's guidelines for SASE.

Tips "Look at our Web site to see the kind of work we do before sending. Do not send cartoons. We do not publish novels. We do publish lots of books with pictures of babies/toddlers."

COTEAU BOOKS LTD.

2571 Victoria Ave., Regina SK S4P 0T2 Canada. (306)777-0170. E-mail: coteau@coteaubooks.com. Web site: www.coteaubooks.com. **Acquisitions:** Barbara Sapergia, children's editor. Publishes 8-10 juvenile and/or young adult books/year; 18-20 books/year; 40% of books by first-time authors. "Coteau Books publishes the finest Canadian fiction, poetry, drama and children's literature, with an emphasis on western writers."

● Coteau Books publishes Canadian writers and illustrators only; mss from the U.S. are returned unopened.

Fiction Young readers, middle readers, young adults: adventure, contemporary, fantasy, history, humor, multicultural, nature/environment, science fiction, suspense/mystery. "No didactic, message pieces, nothing religious. No picture books. Material should reflect the diversity of culture, race, religion, creed of humankind—we're looking for fairness and balance." Recently published *Peacekeepers*, by Dianne Linden (ages 10 and up); *The Star-Glass*, by Duncan Thornton (ages 10 and up); *The Innocent Polly McDoodle*, by Mary Woodbury (ages 9 and up).

Nonfiction Young readers, middle readers, young adult/teen: biography, history, multicultural, nature/environment, social issues.

How to Contact/Writers Fiction: Submit complete ms or sample chapters to acquisitions editor. Include SASE. Responds to queries/mss in 4 months. Publishes a book 1-2 years after acceptance.

Illustration Works with 1-4 illustrators/year. Illustrations only: Submit nonreturnable samples. Responds only if interested. Samples returned with SASE; samples filed.

Photography "Very occasionally buys photos from freelancers." Buys stock and assigns work.

Terms Pays authors royalty based on retail price. Pays illustrators and photographers by the project. Sends galleys to authors; dummies to illustrators. Original artwork returned at job's completion. Book catalog free on request with 9×12 SASE.

Tips "Truthfully, the work speaks for itself! Be bold. Be creative. Be persistent! There is room, at least in the Canadian market, for quality novels for children, and at Coteau, this is a direction we will continue to take."

EMMA TREEHOUSE

Treehouse Children's Books, Little Orchard House, Mill Lane, Beckington, Somerset BA11 6SN United Kingdom. (44)(137)383-1215. Fax: (44)(137)383-1216. E-mail: sales@emmatreehouse.com. Web site: www.emmatreehouse.com. Estab. 1992. Publishes mass market books, trade books. We are an independent book packager/producer. **Manuscript Acquisitions:** David Bailey, director. **Art Acquisitions:** Richard Powell, creative director. Imprints: Treehouse Children's Books. Produces 100 young readers/year.

Fiction Picture books: adventure, animal, concept, folktales, humor.

Nonfiction Picture books: activity books, animal, concept.

How to Contact/Writers Only interested in agented material. Accepts international submissions. Fiction: Submit outline/synopsis. Nonfiction: Submit complete ms. Responds to queries in 3 weeks. No simultaneous, electronic, or previously published submissions.

Illustration Only interested in agented illustration submissions. Accepts material from international illustrators. Works with 10 illustrators/year. Uses color artwork only. Reviews ms/illustration packages. For ms/illustration packages: Send ms with dummy. Submit ms/illustration packages to Richard Powell, creative director. Reviews work for future assignments. If interested in illustrating future titles, arrange personal portfolio review. Submit samples to Richard Powell, creative director. Responds in 3 weeks. Samples returned with SASE. Samples not filed.

Terms Work purchased outright. Pays illustrators by the project. Illustrators see dummies for review. Catalog available for SASE. All imprints included in single catalog.

FABER AND FABER

3 Queen Square, London WC1N 3AU United Kingdom. Web site: www.faber.co.uk. **Contact:** The Editorial Department.

Fiction Recently published *Heir of Mystery*, by Philip Ardagh (ages 8-11, fiction); *Virtutopia*, by Russell Stannard (ages 12 and up); *Rocket Science*, by Jeanne Willis (ages 8-11).

Nonfiction Recently published *The Spy's Handbook*, by Herbie Brennan; *The Hieroglyph's Handbook*, by Philip Ardagh.

How to Contact/Writers Submit synopsis and 20 pages of sample text with SASE. Responds in 8-10 weeks.

Tips "Try to discern whether or not your work is suitable for our list by looking on our Web site or in bookshops at the types of books we publish. We do not, for example, publish in fields such as fantasy, science fiction, or photography, all of which we regularly receive."

DAVID FICKLING BOOKS

Random House Children's Books, 31 Beaumont St., Oxford OX1 2NP United Kingdom. (018)65-339000. Fax: (018)65-339009. E-mail: tburgess@randomhouse.co.uk. Web site: www.davidficklingbooks.co.uk/. Publishes 12 fiction titles/year.

Fiction Considers all categories.

How to Contact/Writers Submit 3 sample chapters. Responds to mss in 2-3 months.

Illustration Reviews ms/illustration packages from artists. Illustrations only: query with samples.

Photography Submit cover letter, résumé, promo pieces.

FITZHENRY & WHITESIDE LTD.

195 Allstate Pkwy., Markham ON L3R 4T8 Canada. (905)477-9700. Fax: (905)477-9179. E-mail: godwit@fitzhenry.ca. Web site: www.fitzhenry.ca. Book publisher. **President:** Sharon Fitzhenry; Children's Publisher: Gail Winskill; Nonfiction children's editor: Linda Biesenthal. Publishes 10 picture books/year; 5 early readers and early chapter books/year; 6 middle novels/year; 7 young adult titles/year. 10% of books by first-time authors. Publishes fiction and nonfiction—social studies, visual arts, biography, environment. Emphasis on Canadian authors and illustrators, subject or perspective.

How to Contact/Writers Fiction/nonfiction. Publishes a book 12-18 months after acceptance. No longer accepting unsolicited mss.

Illustration Works with 15 illustrators/year. Reviews ms/illustration packages from artists. Submit outline and sample illustration (copy). Illustrations only: Query with samples and promo sheet. Responds in 3 months. Samples returned with SASE; samples filed if no SASE.

Photography Buys photos from freelancers. Buys stock and assigns work. Captions required. Uses b&w 8×10 prints; 35mm and 4×5 transparencies. Submit stock photo list and promo piece.

Terms Pays authors royalty of 10%. Offers "respectable" advances for picture books, 5% to author, 5% to illustrator. Pays illustrators by the project and royalty. Pays photographers per photo. Sends galleys to authors; dummies to illustrators.

Tips "We respond to quality."

GROUNDWOOD BOOKS

110 Spadina., Suite 801, Toronto ON M5V 2K4 Canada. (416)363-4343. Fax: (416)363-1017. Web site: www.groundwoodbooks.com. **Manuscript Acquisitions:** Acquisitions Editor. **Art Acquisitions:** Art Director. Publishes 10 picture books/year; 3 young readers/year; 5 middle readers/year; 5 young adult titles/year. 10% of books by first-time authors.

Fiction Recently published *The Crazy Man*, by Pamela Porter (middle reader); *What Gloria Wants*, by Sarah Withrow (young adult); *Caramba*, by Marie-Louise Gay (picture book).

How to Contact/Writers Fiction: Submit synopsis and sample chapters. Responds to mss in 6-8 months. Will consider simultaneous submissions.

Illustration Works with 20 illustrators/year. Reviews ms/illustration packages from artists. Illustrations only: Send résumé, promo sheet, slides, color or b&w copies, and tearsheets. Responds only if interested. Samples not returned.

Terms Offers advances. Pays illustrators by the project for cover art; otherwise royalty. Sends galleys to authors; dummies to illustrators. Originals returned to artist at job's completion. Backlist available on Web site.

Tips "Try to familiarize yourself with our list before submitting to judge whether or not your work is appropriate for Groundwood. Visit our Web site for guidelines."

HYPERION PRESS LIMITED

300 Wales Ave., Winnipeg MB R2M 2S9 Canada. (204)256-9204. Fax: (204)255-7845. **Acquisitions:** Dr. M. Tutiah, editor. Publishes authentic-based, retold folktales/legends for ages 4-9. "We are interested in a good story that is well researched and how-to craft material."

Fiction Recently published *Mo & Jo*, by Katherine Ink Setter; *The Little Match Girl*, written and digitally illustrated by Helena Maria Stankiewicz; *Cossack Tales*, illustrated by Stefan Czernecki.

Nonfiction Recently published *Making Drums*, by Dennis Waring.

How to Contact/Writers Fiction/nonfiction: Query. Responds usually within 3 months.

Illustration Reviews ms/illustration packages from artists. Manuscript/illustration packages and illustration only: Query. Samples returned with SASE.

Terms Pays authors royalty. Pays illustrators by the project. Sends galleys to authors; dummies to illustrators. Book catalog available for SAE and $2 postage (Canadian).

KEY PORTER BOOKS

6 Adelaide St. E, Toronto ON M5C 1H6 Canada. (416)862-7777. Fax: (416)862-2304. E-mail: info@keyporter.com. Web site: www.keyporter.com. Book publisher. Publishes 4 picture books/year; 4 young readers/year. 30% of books by first-time authors. "Key Porter Books is the largest independent, 100% Canadian-owned trade publisher."

Fiction Picture books, young readers, middle readers, young adult: adventure, animal, anthology, fantasy, folktales, sports. Average word length: picture books—1,500; young readers—5,000. Recently published *The Goodfellows Chronicles, Book 1: The Sacred Seal, Book 2: The Messengers, Book 3: The Book of the Sage*, by J.C. Mills (young adult fiction); *Rosie in Los Angeles: Action!*, by Carol Matas (young adult); *Last Sam's Cage*, by David A. Poulson.

Nonfiction Picture books: animal, arts/crafts, cooking, geography, nature/environment, reference, science. Middle readers: animal, nature/environment, reference, science. Average word length: picture books—1,500; middle readers—15,000. Recently published *The Dinosaur Atlas*, by Don Lessem (ages 8-12); *So Cool*, by Dennis Lee; *Coyote's New Suit*, by Thomas King; *Bashful Bob and Doleful Dorinda*, by Margaret Atwood.

How to Contact/Writers Only interested in agented material; *no unsolicited mss*. "Although Key Porter Books does not review unsolicited manuscript submissions, we do try and review queries and proposals." Responds to queries/proposals in 6 months.

Photography Buys photos from freelancers. Buys stock and assigns work. Captions required. Uses 35mm transparencies. Submit cover letter, résumé, duplicate slides, stock photo list.

Tips "Please note that all proposals and accompanying materials will be discarded unless sufficient postage has been provided for their return. Please do not send any original artwork or other irreplaceable materials. We do not accept responsibility for any materials you submit."

KIDS CAN PRESS

29 Birch Ave., Toronto ON M4V 1E2 Canada. (800)265-0884. E-mail: info@kidscan.com. Web site: www.kidscanpress.com. **Manuscript Acquisitions:** Acquisitions Editor. **Art Acquisitions:** Art Director. Publishes 6-10 picture books/year; 10-15 young readers/year; 2-3 middle readers/year; 2-3 young adult titles/year. 10-15% of books by first-time authors.

• Kids Can Press is currently accepting unsolicited manuscripts from Canadian authors only.

Fiction Picture books, young readers: concept. All levels: adventure, animal, contemporary, fantasy, folktales, history, humor, multicultural, nature/environment, poetry, special needs, sports, suspense/mystery. Average word length: picture books—1,000-2,000; young readers—750-1,500; middle readers—10,000-15,000; young adults—over 15,000. Recently published *Suki's Kimono*, by Chieri Ugaki, illustrated by Stephane Jorisch (picture book); *The Mob*, by Clem Martini (novel); *Stanley's Party*, by Linda Bailey, illustrated by Bill Slavin (picture book).

Nonfiction Picture books: activity books, animal, arts/crafts, biography, careers, concept, health, history, hobbies, how-to, multicultural, nature/environment, science, social issues, special needs, sports. Young readers: activity books, animal, arts/crafts, biography, careers, concept, history, hobbies, how-to, multicultural. Middle readers: cooking, music/dance. Average word length: picture books—500-1,250; young readers—750-2,000;

middle readers—5,000-15,000. Recently published *The Kids Book of the Night Sky*, by Jane Drake and Ann Love, illustrated by Heather Collins (informational activity); *Animals at Work*, by Etta Kaner, illustrated by Pat Stephens (animal/nature); *Quilting*, by Biz Storms, illustrated by June Bradford (craft book).

How to Contact/Writers Fiction/nonfiction: Submit outline/synopsis and 2-3 sample chapters. For picture books submit complete ms. Responds in 6 months. Publishes a book 18-24 months after acceptance.

Illustration Works with 40 illustrators/year. Reviews ms/illustration packages from artists. Send color copies of illustration portfolio, cover letter outlining other experience. Contact: Art Director. Illustrations only: Send tearsheets, color photocopies. Contact: Art Director, Kids Can Press, 2250 Military Rd., Tonawanda NY 14150. Responds only if interested. Samples returned with SASE; samples filed.

🌐 KOALA BOOKS

P.O. Box 626, Mascot NSW 1460 Australia. (61)02 9667-2997. Fax: (61)02 9667-2881. E-mail: admin@koalabooks.com.au. Web site: www.koalabooks.com.au. **Manuscript Acquisitions:** Children's Editor. Art Acquisitions: Children's Designer, deb@koalabooks.com.au. "Koala Books is an independent wholly Australian-owned children's book publishing house. Our strength is providing quality books for children at competitive prices."

How to Contact/Writers Accepts material from residents of Australia only. Hard copy only. Picture books only: Submit complete ms, blurb, synopsis, brief author biography, list of author's published works. Also SASE large enough for ms return. Responds to mss in 3 months.

Illustration Accepts material from residents of Australia only. Illustrations only: Send cover letter, brief bio, list of published works and samples (color photographs or photocopies) in "an A4 folder suitable for filing." Contact: Children's Designer. Responds only if interested. Samples not returned; samples filed.

Terms Pays authors royalty of 10% based on retail price or work purchased outright occasionally (may be split with illustrator).

Tips "Take a look at our Web site to get an idea of the kinds of books we publish. A few hours research in a quality children's bookshop would be helpful when choosing a publisher."

🔲 LOBSTER PRESS

1620 Sherbrooke St. W., Suites C&D, Montreal QC H3H 1C9 Canada. (514)904-1100. Fax: (514)904-1101. E-mail: editorial@lobsterpress.com. Web site: www.lobsterpress.com. **Assistant Editor:** Meghan Nolan. Publishes picture books, young readers and YA fiction and nonfiction. "Driven by a desire to produce quality books that bring families together."

• Lobster Press is currently accepting manuscripts and queries.

Fiction Picture books, young readers, middle readers, young adults: adventure, animal, contemporary, health, history, multicultural, nature/environment, special needs, sports, suspense/mystery, science fiction, historical fiction, teen angst. Average word length: picture books—200-1,000. Recently published *The Way to Slumbertown*, by L.M Montgomery, illustrated by Rachel Bédard (picture book); *Stolen Voices*, by Ellen Dee Davidson (young adult novel).

Nonfiction Young readers, middle readers and adults/teens: animal, biography, Canadian history/culture, careers, geography, hobbies, how-to, multicultural, nature/environment, references, science, self-help, social issues, sports, travel. Average word length: middle readers—40,000. Recently published *Let's Party*, by Alison Bell, illustrated by Kun-Sung Chung.

How to Contact/Writers "Please address all submissions to Editorial, Lobster Press; e-mailed or faxed submissions will not be considered."

Illustration Works with 5 illustrators/year. Uses line drawings as well as digital and color artwork. Reviews ms/illustration packages from artists. Query with samples. Illustrations only: query with samples. Samples not returned; samples kept on file.

Terms Pays authors 5-10% royalty based on retail price. Offers advances (average amount: $2,000-4,000). Pays illustrators by the project (range: $1,000-2,000) or 2-7% royalty based on retail price. Sends galleys to authors; dummies to illustrators. Originals returned to artist at job's completion. Writer's and artist's guidelines available on Web site.

Tips "Please do not call and ask for an appointment. We do not meet with anyone unless we are going to use their work."

🌐 MANTRA LINGUA

Global House, 303 Ballards Lane, London N12 8NP United Kingdom. (44)(208)445-5123. Web site: www.mantralingua.com. **Manuscript Acquisitions:** Series Editor. Mantra Lingua "connects and transcends national differences in a way that is respectful and appreciative of local cultures."

• Mantra Lingua publishes books in English and more than 42 languages, including sign language. They are currently seeking fables, contemporary stories and folklore for picture books only.

Fiction Picture books, young readers, middle readers: folktales, multicultural, myths. Average word length:

picture books—1,000-1,500; young readers—1,000-1,500. Recently published *Little Red Hen and the Grains of Wheat*, retold by Henriette Berkow, illustrated by Jago (ages 3-7); *Ali Baba and the Forty Thieves*, by Enebor Attard, illustrated by Richard Holland (ages 6-10).

How to Contact/Writers Accepts material from residents of United Kingdom only. Fiction: Myths only. Submit outline/synopsis (250 words, describe myth, "where it is from, whether it's famous or unknown, and why it would make a great picture book.") Will consider e-mail and mail submissions. Include SASE if you'd like ms returned.

Illustration Uses 2D animations for CD-ROMs. Query with samples. Responds only if interested. Samples not returned; samples filed.

MOOSE ENTERPRISE BOOK & THEATRE PLAY PUBLISHING

Imprint of Moose Hide Books, 684 Walls Rd., Sault Ste. Marie ON P6A 5K6 Canada. E-mail: mooseenterprises@on.aibn.com. Web site: www.moosehidebooks.com. **Manuscript Acquisitions:** Edmond Alcid. Publishes 2 middle readers/year; 2 young adult titles/year. 75% of books by first-time authors. Editorial philosophy: "To assist the new writers of moral standards."

- This publisher does not offer payment for stories published in its anthologies and/or book collections. Be sure to send a SASE for guidelines.

Fiction Middle readers, young adults: adventure, fantasy, humor, suspense/mystery, story poetry. Recently published *Realm of the Golden Feather*, by C.R. Ginter (ages 12 and up, fantasy); *Tell Me a Story*, short story collection by various authors (ages 9-11, humor/adventure); *Spirits of Lost Lake*, by James Walters (ages 12 and up, adventure).

Nonfiction Middle readers, young adults: biography, history, multicultural.

How to Contact/Writers Fiction/nonfiction: Query. Responds to queries in 1 month; mss in 3 months. Publishes book 1 year after acceptance. Will consider simultaneous submissions.

Illustration Uses primarily b&w artwork. Illustrations only: Query with samples. Responds in 1 month, if interested. Samples returned with SASE; samples filed.

Terms Originals returned to artist at job's completion. Manuscript and art guidelines available for SASE.

Tips "Do not copy trends, be yourself, give me something new, something different."

NEATE PUBLISHING LTD.

33 Downside Rd., Winchester SO22 5LT United Kingdom. (44)(196)284-1479. Fax: (44)(196)284-1743. E-mail: sales@neatepublising.co.uk. Web site: www.neatepublishing.co.uk. **Art Acquisitions:** Bobbie Neate. Publishes 5 young readers/year; 5 middle readers/year; 5 young adult titles/year. 50% of books by first-time authors. "Quality nonfiction and exciting educational materials always wanted."

Nonfiction Recently published *Colours Around Us*, by Carole Roberts and Ann Langran (ages 4-7, nonfiction); *Learning How to Learn*, by Bobby Neate (ages 6-16, skill sheets); *Letters, Words and Fun*, by Tracy Spice (ages 3-6, dictionary).

How to Contact/Writers Sumbit material through postal mail, no e-mail sumbissions. Responds to queries in 1 week; mss in 1 month. Publishes book 6 months after acceptance. Will only consider e-mail submissions after initial discussion; previously published work OK.

Terms Sends galleys to authors. Catalog available on Web site.

Tips "We want adventurous and original ideas. Make sure your write for the age groups intended."

ORCA BOOK PUBLISHERS

1016 Balmoral St., Victoria BC V8T 1A8 Canada. (250)380-1229. Fax: (250)380-1892. Web site: www.orcabook.com. **Acquisitions:** Maggie deVries, children's book editor (young readers); Andrew Woolridge, editor (Orca Soundings); Bob Tyrrell, editor (teen fiction). Publishes 7 picture books/year; 16 middle readers/year; 10 young adult titles/year. 25% of books by first-time authors.

- Orca only considers authors who are Canadian or who live in Canada.

Fiction Picture books: animals, contemporary, history, nature/environment. Middle readers: contemporary, history, fantasy, nature/environment, problem novels. Young adults: adventure, contemporary, hi-lo (Orca Soundings), history, multicultural, nature/environment, problem novels, suspense/mystery. Average word length: picture books—500-1,500; middle readers—20,000-35,000; young adult—25,000-45,000; Orca Soundings—13,000-15,000. Published *Tall in the Saddle*, by Anne Carter, illustrated by David McPhail (ages 4-8, picture book); *Me and Mr. Mah*, by Andrea Spalding, illustrated by Janet Wilson (ages 5 and up, picture book); *Alone at Ninety Foot*, by Katherine Holubitsky (young adult).

How to Contact/Writers Fiction: Submit complete ms if picture book; submit outline/synopsis and 3 sample chapters. "All queries or unsolicited submissions should be accompanied by a SASE." Responds to queries in 2 months; mss in 3 months. Publishes a book 18-36 months after acceptance. Submission guidelines available online.

Illustration Works with 8-10 illustrators/year. Reviews ms/illustration packages from artists. Submit ms with

Canadian & International

3-4 pieces of final art. ''Reproductions only, no original art please.'' Illustrations only: Query with samples; provide résumé, slides. Responds in 2 months. Samples returned with SASE; samples filed.

Terms Pays authors royalty of 5% for picture books, 10% for novels, based on retail price. Offers advances (average amount: $2,000). Pays illustrators royalty of 5% minimum based on retail price and advance on royalty. Sends galleys to authors. Original artwork returned at job's completion if picture books. Book catalog available for legal or 8½×11 SAE and $2 first-class postage. Manuscript guidelines available for SASE. Art guidelines not available.

Tips ''We are not seeking seasonal stories, board books, or 'I Can Read' Books. Orca Sounding line offers high interest teen novels aimed at reluctant readers. The story should reflect the universal struggles young people face, but need not be limited to 'gritty' urban tales. Can include adventure, mystery/suspense, fantasy, etc. There's a definite need for humorous stories that appeal to boys and girls. Protagonists are between 14 and 17 years old.''

PICCADILLY PRESS

5 Castle Rd., London NW1 8PR United Kingdom. (44)(207)267-4492. Fax: (44)(207)267-4493. E-mail: books@piccadillypress.co.uk Web site: www.piccadillypress.co.uk.

Fiction Picture books: animal, contemporary, fantasy, nature/environment. Young adults: contemporary, humor, problem novels. Average word length: picture books-500-1,000; young adults-25,000-35,000. Recently published *French for Kissing*, by Sophie Parkin (young adult); *Mates, Dates and Sizzling Summers*, by Cathy Hopkins (young adult); *One Clever Creature*, by Joseph Ellis and Christyan Fox (picture book).

Nonfiction Young adults: self help (humorous). Average word length: young adults-25,000-35,000. Recently published Bringing Up Your Parents, by John Farman.

How to Contact/Writers Fiction: Submit complete ms for picture books or submit outline/synopsis and 2 sample chapters for YA. Enclose a brief cover letter and SASE for reply. Nonfiction: Submit outline/synopsis and 2 sample chapters. Responds to mss in approximately 6 weeks.

Illustration Illustrations only: Query with samples (do not send originals).

Tips ''Keep a copy of your manuscript on file.''

PIPERS' ASH LTD.

Church Rd., Christian Malford, Chippenham Wiltshire SN15 4BW United Kingdom. (44)(124)972-0563. Fax: (44)(870)056-8916. E-mail: pipersash@supamasu.com. Web site: www.supamasu.com. **Manuscript Acquisitions:** Manuscript Evaluation Desk. Publishes 1 middle reader/year; 2 young adult titles/year. 90% of books by first-time authors. Editorial philosophy is ''to discover new authors with talent and potential.''

Fiction Young readers, middle readers: adventure. Young adults: problem novels. Average word length: young readers—10,000; middle readers—20,000; young adults—30,000. Visit Web site or send for catalog for published titles.

Nonfiction Young readers: history, multicultural, nature/environment. Middle readers: biography, history, multicultural, nature/environment, sports. Young adults: self help, social issues, special needs. Average word length: young readers—10,000; middle readers—20,000; young adults—30,000.

How to Contact/Writers Fiction/nonfiction: Query. Responds to queries in 1 week; mss in 3 months. Publishes book 2 months after acceptance. Will consider e-mail submissions, previously published work.

Terms Pays authors royalty of 10% based on wholesale price. Sends galleys to authors. Book catalog available for A5 SASE. Offers ms guidelines for SASE. ''Include adequate postage for return of manuscript plus publisher's guidelines.''

Tips ''Visit our Web site—note categories open to writers and word link to pages of submission guidelines.''

PLAYNE BOOKS LIMITED

Chapel House Trefin, Haver Fordwest, Pembrokeshire SA62 5AU United Kingdom. (44)(134)883-7073. Fax: (44)(134)883-7063. E-mail: playne.books@virgin.net. Web site: www.playnebooks.com. **Manuscript Acquisitions:** Gill Davies. **Art Acquisitions:** David Playne, design and production. Publishes 2 picture books/year; 4 young readers/year.

Fiction Picture books: fantasy, early learning ''fun encapsulated in a story—and humorous.'' Young readers: early learning ''fun encapsulated in a story—and humorous.'' Recently published *A Bug is Very Little*; *One Happy Hippo*, by Gill Davies (ages 3-5, novelty/educational).

Nonfiction Picture books: activity books. Young readers: activity books, animal, nature/environment. Young adults: animal, history, theatre. Recently published *Create Your Own Stage Make-Up*, by Gill Davies (ages 13 and up, How-to achieve state make-up, step by step).

How to Contact/Writers Fiction/nonfiction: Query or submit outline/synopsis. Responds to queries in 2 weeks. Will consider e-mail submissions, simultaneous submissions.

Illustration Works with 2 illustrators/year. Reviews ms/illustration packages from artists. Query. Contact: Gill Davies, editor. Illustrations only: Query with photocopies. Responds in 2 weeks.

Photography Buys stock and assigns work. Contact: David Playne, art director. Photo captions required. Uses color, 35mm, 60×70 or 4×5 transparencies. Submit cover letter, stock photo list.

Terms Work purchased outright from authors. Pays illustrators and photographers by the project. Sends galleys to authors; dummies to illustrators. Book catalog available. All imprints included in a single catalog. Information available on Web site.

Tips "Be adaptable, persevere—keep optimistic!"

MATHEW PRICE LTD.

2 Greenhill Court, Bristol Rd., Sherborne Dorset DT94EP United Kingdom. (44)(193)581-6010. Fax: (44)(193)581-6310. E-mail: mathewp@mathewprice.com. Web site: www.mathewprice.com. **Manuscript Acquisitions:** Mathew Price, chairman. Publishes 2 picture books/year; 2 young readers/year; 3 novelties/year; 1 gift books/year. "Mathew Price Ltd. works to bring to market talented authors and artists profitably by publishing books for children that lift the hearts of people young and old all over the world."

Fiction/Nonfiction Will consider any category.

Illustration Accepts material from artists in other countries. Uses color artwork only. Reviews ms/illustration packages from artists. Send ms with dummy or submit ms with 2 pieces of final art. Nothing returned without prepaid envelope. Do not send orginals, only photocopies.

Terms Originals returned to artist at job's completion. Book catalog available. All imprints included in a single catalog. Catalog available on Web site.

Tips "Study the market, keep a copy of all your work, and include a SAE if you want materials returned."

QED PUBLISHING

Quarto Publishing plc, 226 City Road, London EC1V 2TT United Kingdom. (44)(207)812-8631. Fax: (44)(207)253-4370. E-mail: stevee@quarto.com. Web site: www.quarto.com. Estab. 2003. Specializes in trade books, educational material, multicultural material. **Manuscripts Acquisitions:** Jean Coppendale, editorial director. **Art Acquisitions:** Steve Evans, publisher. Produces 12 picture books/year; 20 young readers/year. Strives for "editorial excellence with ground-breaking design."

Fiction Average word length: picture books—500; young readers—3,000; middle readers—3,500. Recently published *Said Mouse to Mole*, by Clare Bevan, illustrated by Sanja Rescek (ages 4 and up); *Lenny's Lost Spots*, by Celia Warren, illustrated by Genny Haines (ages 2 and up); *Pet the Cat*, by Wes Magee, illustrated by Pauline Siewert (ages 5 and up, poetry).

Nonfiction Picture books: animal, arts/crafts, biography, geography, reference, science. Young readers: activity books, animal, arts/crafts, biography, geography, reference, science. Middle readers: activity books, animal, arts/crafts, biography, geography, science. Average word length: picture books—500; young readers—3,000; middle readers—3,500. Recently published *You and Your Pet Kitten*, by Jean Coppendale (ages 7 and up, animal); *Travel Through India*, by Elaine Jackson (ages 7 and up, geography); *Cartooning*, by Deri Robins (ages 7 and up, art).

How to Contact/Writers Fiction/nonfiction: Query.

Illustration Accepts material from international illustrators. Works with 25 illustrators/year. For ms/illustration packages: Submit ms with 2 pieces of final art. Submit ms/illustration packages to Zeta Davies, art director. Reviews work for future assignments. Submit samples to Jean Coppendale, editorial director. Responds in 2 weeks. Samples filed.

Photography Buys stock images and assigns work. Submit photos to Zeta Davies, art director. Uses step-by-step photos. For first contact, send CD of work or online URL.

Tips "Be persistent."

RAINCOAST BOOKS

9050 Shaughnessy St., Vancouver BC V6P 6E5 Canada. (604)323-7100. Fax: (604)323-2600. E-mail: info@raincoast.com. Web site: www.raincoast.com. **Manuscript Acquisitions:** Editorial Department. Imprints: Polestar. Publishes 4 picture books/year; 4 young adult titles/year.

- Raincoast Books does not accept unsolicited manuscripts or e-mail: queries. They accept material from Canadian residents only.

Fiction Picture books, young readers, young adults: contemporary, history. Recently published *Greztky's Game*, by Mike Leonetti; *The Freedom of Jenny*, by Julie Burtinshaw; *The Cure for Crushes*, by Karen Rivers.

Nonfiction Picture books, young readers: science, sports, natural history. Recently published *Albertosaurus Death of a Predator*, by Monique Keiran; *Sensational Scientists*, by Barry Shell.

How to Contact/Writers Fiction/nonfiction: query letter with "details about the work including word count, subject matter and your publication history for picture books and young readers." For young adult fiction submit query letter with list of publication credits plus 1-page outline of the plot. Responds to queries in 4 months. Will consider simultaneous submissions (indicate in query letter).

Illustration Illustrations only: Query with samples; "no more than 10, nonreturnable color photocopies. Do not send original artwork or slides. Submit new samples to us as they become available." Contact: Creative Director. Responds only if interested. Samples not returned.

Terms Book catalog available online.

Tips "For older (teen readers) we're looking for subject matter that pushes the boundaries a little. For children's illustrative work, we are interested in illustrators who can successfully convey an artistic, painterly, whimsical style. Please refer to our catalogue for examples."

🌐 RANDOM HOUSE CHILDREN'S BOOKS

61-63 Uxbridge Rd., London W5 5SA England. (44)(208)231-6000. Fax: (44)(208)231-6737. E-mail: enquiries@r andomhouse.co.uk. Web site: www.kidsatrandomhouse.co.uk. Book publisher. **Manuscript Acquisitions:** Philippa Dickinson, managing director. Imprints: Doubleday, Corgi, Johnathan Cape, Hutchinson, Bodley Head, Red Fox, David Fickling Books. Publishes 120 picture books/year; 120 fiction titles/year.

Fiction Picture books: adventure, animal, anthology, contemporary, fantasy, folktales, humor, multicultural, nature/environment, poetry, suspense/mystery. Young readers: adventure, animal, anthology, contemporary, fantasy, folktales, humor, multicultural, nature/environment, poetry, sports, suspense/mystery. Middle readers: adventure, animal, anthology, contemporary, fantasy, folktales, humor, multicultural, nature/environment, problem novels, romance, sports, suspense/mystery. Young adults: adventure, contemporary, fantasy, humor, multicultural, nature/environment, problem novels, romance, science fiction, suspense/mystery. Average word length: picture books—800; young readers—1,500-6,000; middle readers—10,000-15,000; young adults— 20,000-45,000.

How to Contact/Writers Only interested in agented material. No unsolicited mss.

Illustration Works with 50 illustrators/year. Reviews ms/illustration packages from artists. Query with samples. Contact: Hannah Featherstone. Samples are returned with SASE (IRC).

Photography Buys photos from freelancers. Contact: Alison Gadsby. Photo captions required. Uses color or b&w prints. Submit cover letter, published samples.

Terms Pays authors royalty. Offers advances. Pays illustrators by the project or royalty. Pays photographers by the project or per photo.

Tips "Although Random House is a big publisher, each imprint only publishes a small number of books each year. Our lists for the next few years are already full. Any book we take on from a previously unpublished author has to be truly exceptional. Manuscripts should be sent to us via literary agents."

🔲 RED DEER PRESS

Rm. 813, MacKimmie Library Tower, 2500 University Dr. NW, Calgary AB T2N 1N4 Canada. (403)220-4334. Fax: (403)210-8191. E-mail: rdp@reddeerpress.com. Web site: www.reddeerpress.com. **Manuscript/Art Acquisitions:** Peter Carver, children's editor. Publishes 3 picture books/year; 4 young adult titles/year. 20% of books by first-time authors. Red Deer Press is known for their "high-quality international children's program that tackles risky and/or serious issues for kids."

- Red Deer only publishes books written and illustrated by Canadians and books that are about or of interest to Canadians.

Fiction Picture books, young readers: adventure, contemporary, fantasy, folktales, history, humor, multicultural, nature/environment, poetry. Middle readers, young adult/teens: adventure, contemporary, fantasy, folktales, hi-lo, history, humor, multicultural, nature/environment, problem novels, suspense/mystery. Recently published *Courage to Fly*, by Troon Harrison, illustrated by Zhong-Yang Huung (ages 4-7, picture book); *Amber Waiting*, by Nan Gregory, illustrated by Macdonald Denton (ages 4-7, picture book); *Tom Finder*, by Martine Leavitt (ages 14 and up).

How to Contact/Writers Fiction/nonfiction: Query or submit outline/synopsis. Responds to queries in 6 months; mss in 8 months. Publishes a book 18 months after acceptance. Will consider simultaneous submissions.

Illustration Works with 4-6 illustrators/year. Illustrations only: Query with samples. Responds only if interested. Samples not returned; samples filed for six months. Canadian illustrators only.

Photography Buys stock and assigns work. Model/property releases required. Submit cover letter, résumé and color promo piece.

Terms Pays authors royalty (negotiated). Occasionally offers advances (negotiated). Pays illustrators and photographers by the project or royalty (depends on the project). Sends galleys to authors. Originals returned to artist at job's completion. Guidelines not available.

Tips "Our publishing program is full for the next several years in the children's picture book, juvenile and teen fiction categories, thus we are only accepting manuscripts with exceptional potential. Writers, illustrators, and photographers should familiarize themselves with Red Deer Press's children's publishing program."

RONSDALE PRESS

3350 W. 21st Ave., Vancouver BC V6S 1G7 Canada. (604)738-4688. Fax: (604)731-4548. E-mail: ronsdale@shaw .com. Web site: ronsdalepress.com. Estab. 1988. Book publisher. **Manuscript/Art Acquisitions:** Veronica Hatch, children's editor. Publishes 2 children's books/year. 40% of titles by first-time authors. "Ronsdale Press is a Canadian literary publishing house that publishes 8-10 books each year, two of which are children's titles. Of particular interest are books involving children exploring and discovering new aspects of Canadian history."

Fiction Young adults: Canadian historical novels. Average word length: middle readers and young adults— 50,000. Recently published *Red Goodwin*, by John Wilson (ages 10-14); *The Tenth Pupil*, by Constance Horne (ages 10-14); *Dark Times*, edited by Ann Walsh (anthology of short stories, ages 10 and up); *Rosie's Dream Cape*, by Zelsa Freedman (ages 8-14); *Hurricanes over London*, by Charles Reid (ages 10-14).

Nonfiction Middle readers, young adults: animal, biography, history, multicultural, social issues. Average word length: young readers—90; middle readers—90.

How to Contact/Writers Accepts material from residents of Canada only. Fiction/nonfiction: Submit complete ms. Responds to queries in 2 weeks; mss in 2 months. Publishes a book 1 year after acceptance. Will consider simultaneous submissions.

Illustrations Works with 2 illustrators/year. Reviews ms/illustration packages from artists. Requires only cover art. Responds in 2 weeks. Samples returned with SASE. Originals returned to artist at job's completion.

Terms Pays authors royalty of 10% based on retail price. Pays illustrators by the project $800-1,200. Sends galleys to authors. Book catalog available for 8½×11 SAE and $1 postage; ms and art guidelines available for SASE.

Tips "Ronsdale Press publishes well-written books that have a new slant on things and that can take an age-old story and give it a new spin. We are particularly interested in novels for young adults with a historical component that offers new insights into a part of Canada's history. We publish only Canadian authors."

SCHOLASTIC AUSTRALIA

Scholastic Press and Margaret Hamilton Books, P.O. Box 579, Lindfield NSW 2070 Australia. Web site: www.sch olastic.com.au. **Manuscript Acquisitions:** Megan Fauvet, publishing secretary, Scholastic Press and Margaret Hamilton Books; Dyan Blacklock, publisher Omnibus Books. **Art Acquisitions:** Megan Fauvet, publishing secretary, Scholastic Press and Margaret Hamilton Books; Dyan Blacklock, publisher, Omnibus Books. Imprints: Scholastic Press (Margrete Lamond, acquisitions editor); Margaret Hamilton Books (Margrete Lamond, acquisitions editor); Omnibus Books (Dyan Blacklock). "Communicating with children around the world."

● Scholastic Australia accepts material from residents of Australia only.

Fiction Picture books, young readers. Recently published *After Alice*, by Jane Carroll (ages 8-12, fiction); *Amelia Ellicott's Garden*, by Lilianna Stafford, illustrated by Stephen Michael King (ages 5-7, picture book); *An Ordinary Day*, by Libby Gleeson, illustrated by Armin Greder (ages 5-15, picture book).

Nonfiction Omnibus and Scholastic Press will consider nonfiction. Recently published *Bass and Flinders*, by Cathy Dodson, illustrated by Roland Harvey (ages 9-12, history); *The Cartoon Faces Book*, by Robert Ainsworth (ages 7-14, art & craft); *Excuse Me, Captain Cook, Who Did Discover Australia?*, by Michael Salmon (ages 7-12, history).

How to Contact/Writers Fiction/nonfiction: Submit complete ms. For picture books, submit only ms, no art. Responds to mss in 2 months.

Illustration Illustrations only: Send portfolio. Contact appropriate office for more information on what to include with portfolio.

Tips "Scholastic Australia publishes books for children under three publishing imprints—Scholastic Press, Omnibus Books and Margaret Hamilton Books. To get a more specific idea of the flavor of each list, you will need to visit your local bookstore. Don't be too surprised or disappointed if your first attempts are not successful. Children's book publishing is a highly competitive field, and writing children's books is not quite as easy as some might imagine. But we are always ready to find the next Harry Potter or Paddington Bear, so if you believe you can write it, we're ready to hear from you."

SCHOLASTIC CANADA LTD.

604 King St. West, ON M5V 1E1 Canada. (905)887-READ. Fax: (905)887-1131. Web site: www.scholastic.ca; for ms/artist guidelines: www.scholastic.ca. **Acquisitions:** Editor, children's books. Publishes hardcover and trade paperback originals. Imprints: Scholastic Canada; North Winds Press; Les Editions Scholastic. Publishes 30 titles/year; imprint publishes 4 titles/year. 3% of books from first-time authors; 50% from unagented writers. Canadian authors, theme or setting required.

● At presstime Scholastic Canada was not accepting unsolicited manuscripts. For up-to-date information on their current submission policy, call their publishing status line at (905)887-7323, ext. 4308 or view their submission guidelines on their Web site.

Canadian & International

Fiction Picture books, young readers, young adult. Average word length: picture books—under 1,000; young readers—7,000-10,000; young adult—25,000-40,000.

Nonfiction Animals, biography, history, hobbies, nature, recreation, science, sports. Reviews artwork/photos as part of ms package. Send photocopies.

How to Contact/Writers Query with synopsis, 3 sample chapters and SASE. Nonfiction: Query with outline, 1-2 sample chapters and SASE (IRC or Canadian stamps only). Responds in 3 months. Publishes book 1 year after acceptance.

Illustration Illustrations only: Query with samples; send résumé. Never send originals. Contact: Ms. Yuksel Hassan.

Terms Pays authors royalty of 5-10% based on retail price. Offers advances (range: $1,000-5,000, Canadian). Book catalog for $8^{1}/_{2} \times 11$ SAE with $2.05 postage stamps (IRC or Canadian stamps only).

SCHOLASTIC CHILDREN'S BOOKS UK

Euston House, 24 Eversholt St., London NW1 1DB United Kingdom. Web site: www.scholastic.co.uk. **Submissions:** The Editorial Department.

● Scholastic UK accepts material from residents of United Kingdom only.

Fiction Recently published *A Darkling Plain*, by Philip Reeve; *Storm Thief*, by Chris Wooding; *Looking for JJ*, by Anne Cassidy.

Nonfiction Recently published *The Stunning Science of Everything*, by Nick Arnold and Tony de Saulles; *Horrible Histories: Dublin*, by Terry Deary.

How to Contact/Writers Fiction/nonfiction: Query or submit complete ms and SASE. Responds to queries/mss in 6 months. Does not accept electronic submissions.

Tip "Do not be depressed if your work is not accepted. Getting work published can be a frustrating process, and it's often best to be prepared for disappointment."

SECOND STORY PRESS

20 Maud St., Suite 401, Toronto ON M5V 2M5 Canada. (416)537-7850. Fax: (416)537-0588. E-mail: info@second storypress.ca. Web site: www.secondstorypress.on.ca.

Fiction Considers nonsexist, nonracist, and nonviolent stories, as well as historical fiction, chapter books, picture books. Recently published *Mom and Mum Are Getting Married!*, by Ken Setterington.

Nonfiction Picture books: biography. Recently published *The Underground Reporters: A True Story*, by Kathy Kacer (a new addition to our Holocaust remembrance series for young readers).

How to Contact/Writers Accepts appropriate material from residents of Canada only. Fiction and nonfiction: Submit complete ms or submit outline and sample chapters by postal mail only. No electronic submissions or queries.

TAFELBERG PUBLISHERS

Imprint of NB Publishers, 40 Heerengracht, Cape Town, Western Cape 8001 South Africa. (27)(21)406-3033. Fax: (27)(21)406-3812. E-mail: lsteyn@tafelberg.com. Web site: www.tafelberg.com. **Manuscript Acquisitions:** Louise Steyn, publisher. Publishes 3 picture books/year; 2 young readers/year; 2 middle readers/year; 4 young adult titles/year. 40% of books by first-time authors.

Fiction Picture books, young readers: animal, anthology, contemporary, fantasy, folktales, hi-lo, humor, multicultural, nature/environment, scient fiction, special needs. Middle readers, young adults: animal (middle reader only), contemporary, fantasy, hi-lo, humor, multicultural, nature/environment, problem novels, science fiction, special needs, sports, suspense/mystery. Average word length: picture books—1,500-7,500; young readers—25,000; middle readers—15,000; young adults—40,000. Recently published *Because Pula Means Rain*, by Jenny Robson (ages 12-15, realism); *BreinBliksem*, by Fanie Viljoen (ages 13-18, realism); *SuperZero*, by Darrel Bristow-Bovey (ages 9-12, realism/humor).

How to Contact/Writers Fiction: Query or submit complete ms. Responds to queries in 2 weeks; mss in 2-6 months. Publishes book 1 year after acceptance. Will consider e-mail submissions.

Illustration Works with 2-3 illustrators/year. Reviews ms/illustration packages from artists. Send ms with dummy or e-mail and jpegs. Contact: Louise Steyn, publisher. Illustrations only: Query with brochure, photocopies, résumé, URL, JPEGs. Responds only if interested. Samples not returned.

Terms Pays authors royalty of 15-18% based on wholesale price. Pays illustrators by the project or royalty of $7^{1}/_{2}$% based on wholesale price. Sends galleys to authors. Originals returned to artist at job's completion.

Tips "Writers: Story needs to have a South African or African style. Illustrators: I'd like to look, but the chances of getting commissioned are slim. The market is small and difficult. Do not expect huge advances. Editorial staff attended or plans to attend the following conferences: IBBY, Frankfurt, SCBWI Bologna."

THISTLEDOWN PRESS LTD.

633 Main St., Saskatoon SK S7H 0J8 Canada. (306)244-1722. Fax: (306)244-1762. E-mail: tdpress@thistledown.s

k.ca. Web site: www.thistledown.sk.ca. **Acquisitions:** Allan Forrie, publisher. Publishes numerous middle reader and young adult titles/year. "Thistledown originates books by Canadian authors only, although we have co-published titles by authors outside Canada. We do not publish children's picture books."

• Thistledown publishes books by Canadian authors only.

Fiction Middle readers, young adults: adventure, anthology, contemporary, fantasy, humor, poetry, romance, science fiction, suspense/mystery, short stories. Average word length: young adults—40,000. Recently published *Up All Night*, edited by R.P. MacIntyre (young adult, anthology); *Offside*, by Cathy Beveridge (young adult, novel); *Cheeseburger Subversive*, by Richard Scarsbrook; *The Alchemist's Daughter*, by Eileen Kernaghan.

How to Contact/Writers Submit outline/synopsis and sample chapters. "We do not accept unsolicted full-length manuscripts. These will be returned." Responds to queries in 4 months. Publishes a book about 1 year after acceptance. No simultaneous submissions.

Illustration Prefers agented illustrators but "not mandatory." Works with few illustrators. Illustrations only: Query with samples, promo sheet, slides, tearsheets. Responds only if interested. Samples returned with SASE; samples filed.

Terms Pays authors royalty of 10-12% based on retail price. Pays illustrators and photographers by the project (range: $250-750). Sends galleys to authors. Original artwork returned at job's completion. Book catalog free on request. Manuscript guidelines for #10 envelope and IRC.

Tips "Send cover letter including publishing history and SASE."

TORMONT PUBLICATIONS

338 Saint Antoine St. E., Montreal QC H2Y 1A3 Canada. E-mail: info@tormont.ca. Estab. 1984. **Manuscript Acquisitions:** Diane Mineau, director, editorial and art. "We specialize in children's mass market books as well as novelty books, games, and activity kits."

Fiction Considers mass market books.

Nonfiction Picture books, young readers, middle readers, young adults: activity books. Considers novelty books, games.

How to Contact/Writers Accepts material from residents of Canada only. Fiction/nonfiction: Submit complete ms. Responds to mss in 2 months.

Illustration Illustrations only: Send portfolio. Responds in 2 months. Samples returned with SASE.

Tips "Work submitted should be of the highest quality and the subject matter should 'travel well, ' that is, it should be of broad interest and relevance to the world children's market, since we publish internationally in well over a dozen languages. Please do not send any originals of your manuscripts, illustrations or prototypes, since we cannot be held responsible for lost or damaged materials. Send only photocopies. For U.S. and international/submissions, include a Universal Postal Order for the cost of return postage."

USBORNE PUBLISHING

83-85 Saffron Hill, London EC1N 8RT United Kingdom. Fax: (44)(20)743-1562. Web site: www.usborne.com. **Manuscript Acquisitions:** Fiction Editorial Director. **Art Acquisitions:** Usborne Art Department. "Usborne Publishing is a multiple-award winning, world-wide children's publishing company specializing in superbly researched and produced information books with a unique appeal to young readers."

Fiction Young readers, middle readers: adventure, contemporary, fantasy, history, humor, multicultural, nature/environment, science fiction, suspense/mystery. Average word length: young readers—3,500-8,000; middle readers—10,000-30,000. Recently published *Lift-the-Flap Dinosaurs*, by Alastair Smith (preschool); Fame School Series, by Cindy Jefferies (ages 8 and up).

How to Contact/Writers Refer to guidelines on Web site or request from above address. Fiction: Submit 3 sample chapters and a full synopsis with SASE. Does not accept submissions for nonfiction. Responds to queries in 1 month; mss in 4 months.

Illustration Works with 30 illustrators per year. Illustrations only: Query with samples. Samples not returned; samples filed.

PhotographyContact: Usbourne Art Department. Submit samples.

Terms Pays authors royalty of 7½-10% based on retail price.

Tips "Do not send any original work and, sorry, but we cannot guarantee a reply."

Magazines

C hildren's magazines are a great place for unpublished writers and illustrators to break into the market. Writers, illustrators and photographers alike may find it easier to get book assignments if they have tearsheets from magazines. Having magazine work under your belt shows you're professional and have experience working with editors and art directors and meeting deadlines.

But magazines aren't merely a breaking-in point. Writing, illustration and photo assignments for magazines let you see your work in print quickly, and the magazine market can offer steady work and regular paychecks (a number of them pay on acceptance). Book authors and illustrators may have to wait a year or two before receiving royalties from a project. The magazine market is also a good place to use research material that didn't make it into a book project you're working on. You may even work on a magazine idea that blossoms into a book project.

TARGETING YOUR SUBMISSIONS

It's important to know the topics typically covered by different children's magazines. To help you match your work with the right publications, we've included several indexes in the back of this book. The **Subject Index** lists both book and magazine publishers by the fiction and nonfiction subjects they're seeking.

If you're a writer, use the Subject Index in conjunction with the **Age-Level Index** to narrow your list of markets. Targeting the correct age group with your submission is an important consideration. Many rejection slips are sent because a writer has not targeted a manuscript to the correct age. Few magazines are aimed at children of all ages, so you must be certain your manuscript is written for the audience level of the particular magazine you're submitting to. Magazines for children (just as magazines for adults) may also target a specific gender.

If you're a poet, refer to the **Poetry Index** to find which magazines publish poems.

Each magazine has a different editorial philosophy. Language usage also varies between periodicals, as does the length of feature articles and the use of artwork and photographs. Reading magazines *before* submitting is the best way to determine if your material is appropriate. Also, because magazines targeted to specific age groups have a natural turnover in readership every few years, old topics (with a new slant) can be recycled.

If you're a photographer, the **Photography Index** lists children's magazines that use photos from freelancers. Using it in combination with the subject index can narrow your search. For instance, if you photograph sports, compare the Magazine list in the Photography Index with the list under Sports in the Subject Index. Highlight the markets that appear on both lists, then read those listings to decide which magazines might be best for your work.

Since many kids' magazines sell subscriptions through direct mail or schools, you may not be able to find a particular publication at bookstores or newsstands. Check your local library, or send for copies of the magazines you're interested in. Most magazines in this section have sample copies available and will send them for a SASE or small fee.

Also, many magazines have submission guidelines and theme lists available for a SASE. Check magazines' Web sites, too. Many offer excerpts of articles, submission guidelines, and theme lists and will give you a feel for the editorial focus of the publication.

Watch for the Canadian ⚏ and International 🌐 symbols. These publications' needs and requirements may differ from their U.S. counterparts.

Information on magazines listed in the previous edition but not included in this edition of *Children's Writer's & Illustrator's Market* may be found in the General Index.

ADVENTURES

WordAction Publishing Company, 6401 The Paseo, Kansas City MO 64131. (816)333-7000. Fax: (816)333-4439. E-mail: jjsmith@nazarene.org. **Articles Editor:** Julie J. Smith. Weekly magazine. "Adventures is a full-color story paper for first and second graders. It is designed to connect Sunday School learning with the daily living experiences of the early elementary child. The reading level should be beginning. The intent of Adventures is to provide a life-related paper that will promote Christian values, encouraging good choices and providing reinforcement for biblical concepts taught in Faith Connections curriculum published by WordAction Publishing." Entire publication aimed at juvenile market.
  • Adventures is not accepting new submissions until September 2006.

ADVOCATE, PKA'S PUBLICATION

PKA Publication, 1881 Little Westkill Rd., Prattsville NY 12468. (518)299-3103. **Publisher:** Patricia Keller. Bimonthly tabloid. Estab. 1987. Circ. 12,000. "*Advocate* advocates good writers and quality writings. We publish art, fiction, photos and poetry. *Advocate*'s submitters are talented people of all ages who do not earn their livings as writers. We wish to promote the arts and to give those we publish the opportunity to be published."
  • Gaited Horse Association newsletter is included in this publication. Horse-oriented stories, poetry, art and photos are currently needed.
Fiction Middle readers, young adults/teens: adventure, animal, contemporary, fantasy, folktales, health, humorous, nature/environment, problem-solving, romance, science fiction, sports, suspense/mystery. Looks for "well written, entertaining work, whether fiction or nonfiction." Buys approximately 42 mss/year. Prose pieces should not exceed 1,500 words. Byline given. Wants to see more humorous material, nature/environment and romantic comedy.
Nonfiction Middle readers, young adults/teens: animal, arts/crafts, biography, careers, concept, cooking, fashion, games/puzzles, geography, history, hobbies, how-to, humorous, interview/profile, nature/environment, problem-solving, science, social issues, sports, travel. Buys 10 mss/year. Prose pieces should not exceed 1,500 words. Byline given.
Poetry Reviews poetry any length.
How to Contact/Writers Fiction/nonfiction: send complete ms. Responds to queries in 6 weeks; mss in 2 months. Publishes ms 2-18 months after acceptance.
Illustration Uses b&w artwork only. Uses cartoons. Reviews ms/illustration packages from artists. Submit a photo print (b&w or color), an excellent copy of work (no larger than 8×10) or original. Illustrations only: "Send previous unpublished art with SASE, please." Responds in 2 months. Samples returned with SASE; samples not filed. Credit line given.
Photography Buys photos from freelancers. Model/property releases required. Uses color and b&w prints (no slides). Send unsolicited photos by mail with SASE. Responds in 2 months. Wants nature, artistic and humorous photos.
Terms Pays on publication with contributor's copies. Acquires first rights for mss, artwork and photographs. Pays in copies. Original work returned upon job's completion. Sample copies for $4. Writer's/illustrator/photo guidelines with sample copy.
Tips " Please, no simultaneous submissions, work that has appeared on the Internet, po rnography, overt religiousity, anti-environmentalism or gratuitous violence. Artists and photographers should keep in mind that we are a b&w paper. Please do not send postcards. Use envelope with SASE."

AIM MAGAZINE, America's Intercultural Magazine

P.O. Box 1174, Maywood IL 60153-8174. Web site: www.aimmagazine.org. **Contact:** Ruth Apilado, associate editor. Quarterly magazine. Circ. 8,000. "Readers are high school and college students, teachers, adults inter-

ested in helping to purge racism from the human blood stream by the way of the written word—that is our goal!'' 15% of material aimed at juvenile audience.
Fiction Young adults/teens: adventure, folktales, humorous, history, multicultural, ''stories with social significance.'' Wants stories that teach children that people are more alike than they are different. Does not want to see religious fiction. Buys 20 mss/year. Average word length: 1,000-4,000. Byline given.
Nonfiction Young adults/teens: biography, interview/profile, multicultural, ''stuff with social significance.'' Does not want to see religious nonfiction. Buys 20 mss/year. Average word length: 500-2,000. Byline given.
How to Contact/Writers Fiction: Send complete ms. Nonfiction: Query with published clips. Responds to queries/mss in 1 month. Will consider simultaneous submissions.
Illustration Buys 6 illustrations/issue. Preferred theme: Overcoming social injustices through nonviolent means. Reviews ms/illustration packages from artists. Query first. Illustrations only: Query with tearsheets. Responds to art samples in 1 month. Samples filed. Original artwork returned at job's completion ''if desired.'' Credit line given.
Photography Wants ''photos of activists who are trying to contribute to social improvement.''
Terms Pays on acceptance. Buys first North American serial rights. Pays $15-25 for stories/articles. Pays in contributor copies if copies are requested. Pays $25 for b&w cover illustration. Photographers paid by the project. Sample copies for $5.
Tips ''Write about what you know.''

AMERICAN CAREERS

Career Communications, Inc., 6701 W. 64th St., Overland Park KS 66202. (913)362-7788. Fax: (913)362-4864. Web site: www.carcom.com. **Articles Editor:** Mary Pitchford. **Art Director:** Jerry Kanabel. Published 1 time/year. Estab. 1990. Circ. 400,000. Publishes career and education information for students in grades 8-10.
Nonfiction Buys 20 mss/year. Average word length: 300-800. Byline given.
How to Contact/Writers Nonfiction: Query with résumé and published clips. Acknowledges queries within 30 days. Keeps queries on file up to 2 years. Accepts simultaneous submissions with notification.
Terms Pays on acceptance. Pays writers variable amount.
Tips Send a query in writing with résumé and clips.

AMERICAN CHEERLEADER

Lifestyle Ventures LLC, 250 W. 57th St., Suite 420, New York NY 10107. (212)265-8890. Fax: (212)265-8908. E-mail: editors@americancheerleader.com. Web site: www.americancheerleader.com. **Editorial Director:** Sheila Noone. **Managing Editor:** Marisa Walker. Bimonthly magazine. Estab. 1995. Circ. 200,000. Special interest teen magazine for kids who cheer.
Nonfiction Young adults: biography, interview/profile (sports personalities), careers, fashion, beauty, health, how-to (cheering techniques, routines, pep songs, etc.), problem-solving, sports, cheerleading specific material. ''We're looking for authors who know cheerleading.'' Buys 20 mss/year. Average word length: 750-2,000. Byline given.
How to Contact/Writers Query with published clips. Responds to queries/mss in 3 months. Publishes ms 3 months after acceptance. Will consider electronic submission via disk or e-mail.
Illustration Buys 2 illustrations/issue; 12-20 illustrations/year. Works on assignment only. Reviews ms/illustration packages from artists. Illustrations only: Query with samples; arrange portfolio review. Responds only if interested. Samples filed. Originals not returned at job's completion. Credit line given.
Photography Buys photos from freelancers. Looking for cheerleading at different sports games, events, etc. Uses 35mm, 2¼×2¼ transparencies and 5×7 prints. Query with samples; provide résumé, business card, tearsheets to be kept on file. ''After sending query, we'll set up an interview.'' Responds only if interested.
Terms Pays on publication. Buys all rights for mss, artwork and photographs. Pays $100-500 for stories. Pays illustrators $50-200 for b&w inside, $100-300 for color inside. Pays photographers by the project $300-750; per photo (range: $25-100). Sample copies for $4.
Tips ''Authors: We invite proposals from freelance writers who are involved in or have been involved in cheerleading—i.e. coaches, sponsors or cheerleaders. Our writing style is upbeat, and 'sporty' to catch and hold the attention of our teen readers. Articles should be broken down into lots of sidebars, bulleted lists, etc. Photographers and illustrators must have teen magazine experience or high profile experience.''

AMERICAN GIRL, INC.

8400 Fairway Place, Middleton WI 53562-0984. (608)836-4848. Web site: www.americangirl.com. **Contact:** Editorial Dept. Assistant. Bimonthly magazine. Estab. 1992. Circ. 750,000. ''For girls ages 8-12. We use fiction and nonfiction.''
Fiction Middle readers: contemporary, multicultural, suspense/mystery, good fiction about anything. No romance, science fiction or fantasy. No preachy, moralistic tales or stories with animals as protagonists. Only girl characters—no boys. Buys approximately 2 mss/year. Average word length: 2,300. Byline given.
Nonfiction How-to, interview/profile, history. Any articles aimed at girls ages 8-12. Buys 3-10 mss/year. Average

word length: 600. Byline sometimes given. No historical profiles about obvious female heroines—Annie Oakley, Amelia Earhart; no romance or dating.

How to Contact/Writers Fiction: Query with published clips. Nonfiction: Query. Responds to queries/mss in 3 months. Will consider simultaneous submissions.

Illustration Works on assignment only.

Terms Pays on acceptance. Buys first North American serial rights. Pays $500 minimum for stories; $300 minimum for articles. Sample copies for $3.95 and 9×12 SAE with $1.93 in postage (send to Magazine Department Assistant). Writer's guidelines free for SASE.

Tips "Keep (stories and articles) simple but interesting. Kids are discriminating readers, too. They won't read a boring or pretentious story. We're looking for short (maximum 175 words) how-to stories and short profiles of girls for 'Girls Express' section, as well as word games, puzzles and mazes."

APPLESEEDS, The Magazine for Young Readers

Cobblestone Publishing, A Division of Carus Publishing, 140 E. 83rd St., New York NY 10028. E-mail (for writers queries): swbuc@aol.com. Web site: www.cobblestonepub.com. **Editor:** Susan Buckley. Magazine published monthly except June, July and August. *AppleSeeds* is a 36-page, multidisciplinary, nonfiction social studies magazine from Cobblestone Publishing for ages 8-10. Published 9 times/year.

- Above address is for *AppleSeeds* editorial submissions only. Cobblestone address is: 30 Grove St., Petersborough NH 03458. Requests for sample issues should be mailed to Cobblestone directly. *AppleSeeds* is aimed toward readers ages 8-10. See Web site for current theme list.

How to Contact/Writers Nonfiction: Query only. Send all queries to Susan Buckley. See Web site for submission guidelines and theme list. E-mail queries are preferred. See Web site for editorial guidelines.

Illustration Contact Ann Dillon. See Web site for illustration guidelines.

Tips "Submit queries specifically focused on the theme of an upcoming issue. We generally work 6 months ahead on themes. We look for unusual perspectives, original ideas, and excellent scholarship. We accept **no unsolicited manuscripts**. Writers should check our Web site at cobblestonepub.com/pages/writersAPPguides/html for current guidelines, topics, and query deadlines. We use very little fiction. Illustrators should not submit unsolicited art."

🌐 AQUILA

New Leaf Publishing, P.O. Box 2518, Eastbourne BN22 8AP United Kingdom. (44)(132)343-1313. Fax: (44)(132)373-1136. E-mail: info@aquila.co.uk. Web site: www.aquila.co.uk. **Submissions Editor:** Jackie Berry and Karen Lutener. Monthly magazine. Estab. 1993. "Aquila is an educational magazine for readers ages 8-13 including factual articles (no pop/celebrity material), arts/crafts and puzzles." Entire publication aimed at juvenile market.

Fiction Young Readers: animal, contemporary, fantasy, folktales, health, history, humorous, multicultural, nature/environment, problem solving, religious, science fiction, sports, suspense/mystery. Middle Readers: animal, contemporary, fantasy, folktales, health, history, humorous, multicultural, nature/environment, problem solving, religious, romance, science fiction, sports, suspense/mystery. Buys 6-8 mss/year. Byline given.

Nonfiction Considers Young Readers: animal, arts/crafts, concept, cooking, games/puzzles, health, history, how-to, interview/profile, math, nature/environment, science, sports. Middle Readers: animal, arts/crafts, concept, cooking, games/puzzles, health, history, interview/profile, math, nature/environment, science, sports. Buys 48 mss/year. Average word length: 350-750.

How To Contact/Writers Fiction: Query with published clips. Nonfiction: Query with published clips. Responds to queries in 6-8 weeks.Publishes ms 1 year after acceptance. Considers electronic submissions via disk or e-mail, previously published work.

Illustration Color artwork only.Works on assignment only. For first contact, query with samples. Submit samples to Jackie Berry, Editor. Responds only if interested. Samples not returned. Samples filed.

Terms Buys exclusive magazine rights. Buys exclusive magazine rights rights for artwork. Pays 150-200 for stories; 50-100 for articles. Additional payment for ms/illustration packages. Additional payment for ms/photo packages. Pays illustrators $130-150 for color cover. Sample copies free for SASE. Writer's guidelines free for SASE. Publishes work by children.

Tips "We only accept a high level of educational material for children ages 8-13 with a good standard of literacy and ability."

ASK, Arts and Sciences for Kids

Carus Publishing, 140 S. Dearborn, Suite 1450, Chicago IL 60603. (312)701-1720. E-mail: ask@caruspub.com. Web site: www.cricketmag.com. **Editor:** Lonnie Plecha. **Art Director:** Karen Kohn. Magazine published 9 times/year. Estab. 2002. "*ASK* encourages children between the ages of 7 and 10 to inquire about the world around them."

Nonfiction Young readers, middle readers: animal, history, nature/environment, science. Average word length: 150-1,500. Byline given.

How to Contact/Writers *Ask* does not accept unsolicited mss or queries. All articles are commissioned. To be considered for assignments, experienced science writers may send a résumé and 3 published clips.

Illustration Buys 10 illustrations/issue; 60 illustrations/year. Works on assignment only. Illustrations only: Query with samples.

BABAGANEWZ

Jewish Family & Life, 11141 Georgia Ave. #406, Wheaton MD 20902. (301)962-9636. Fax: (301)962-9635. Web site: www.babaganewz.com. **Articles Editor:** Mark Levine. **Production Editor:** Aviva Werner. Monthly magazine. Estab. 2001. Circ. 40,000. "*BabagaNewz* helps middle school students explore Jewish values that are at the core of Jewish beliefs and practices."

Fiction Middle readers: religious, Jewish themes. Buys 1 ms/year. Average word length: 1,000-1,500. Byline given.

Nonfiction Middle readers: arts/crafts, concept, games/puzzles, geography, history, humorous, interview/profile, nature/environment, religion, science, social issues. Most articles are written by assignment. Average word length: 350-1,000. Byline given.

How to Contact/Writers Queries only for fiction; queries preferred for nonfiction. **No unsolicited manuscripts**.

Illustration Uses color artwork only. Works on assignment only. Illustrations only: Send postcard sample with promo sheet, résumé, URL. Responds only if interested. Credit line given.

Photography Photos by assigment.

Terms Pays on acceptance. Usually buys all rights for mss. Original artwork returned at job's completion. Sample copies free for SAE 9×12 and 4 first-class stamps.

Tips "Most work is done on assignment. We are looking for freelance writers with experience writing nonfiction for 9- to 13-year-olds, especially on Jewish-related themes. No unsolicited manuscripts."

BABYBUG

Carus Publishing Company, 140 S. Dearborn, Suite 1450, Chicago IL 60603. **Editor:** Paula Morrow. **Art Director:** Suzanne Beck. Published 10 times/year (monthly except for combined May/June and July/August issues). Estab. 1994. "A listening and looking magazine for infants and toddlers ages 6 to 24 months, *Babybug* is 6×7, 24 pages long, printed in large type on high-quality cardboard stock with rounded corners and no staples."

Fiction Looking for very simple and concrete stories, 4-6 short sentences maximum.

Nonfiction Must use very basic words and concepts, 10 words maximum.

Poetry Maximum length 8 lines. Looking for rhythmic, rhyming poems.

How to Contact/Writers "Please do not query first." Send complete ms with SASE. "Submissions without SASE will be discarded." Responds in 3 months.

Illustration Uses color artwork only. Works on assignment only. Reviews ms/illustration packages from artists. "The manuscripts will be evaluated for quality of concept and text before the art is considered." Contact: Suzanne Beck. Illustrations only: Send tearsheets or photo prints/photocopies with SASE. "Submissions without SASE will be discarded." Responds in 3 months. Samples filed.

Terms Pays on publication for mss; after delivery of completed assignment for illustrators. Rights purchased vary. Original artwork returned at job's completion. Rates vary ($25 minimum for mss; $250 minimum for art). Sample copy for $5. Guidelines free for SASE or available on Web site, FAQ at www.cricketmag.com.

Tips "*Babybug* would like to reach as many children's authors and artists as possible for original contributions, but our standards are very high, and we will accept only top-quality material. Before attempting to write for *Babybug*, be sure to familiarize yourself with this age child."

BOYS' LIFE

Boy Scouts of America, 1325 W. Walnut Hill Lane, Irving TX 75015-2079. (972)580-2366. Fax: (972)580-2079. Web site: www.boyslife.org. **Managing Editor:** W. Butterworth, IV. **Senior Editor:** Michael Goldman. **Fiction Editor:** Paula Murphey. **Director of Design:** Scott Feaster. Monthly magazine. Estab. 1911. Circ. 1,300,000. *Boys' Life* is "a 4-color general interest magazine for boys 8 to 18 who are members of the Cub Scouts, Boy Scouts or Venturers."

Fiction Young readers, middle readers, young adults: adventure, animal, contemporary, history, humor, multicultural, nature/environment, problem-solving, sports, science fiction, spy/mystery. Does not want to see "talking animals and adult reminiscence." Buys only 12-16 mss/year. Average word length: 1,000-1,500. Byline given.

Nonfiction Young readers, middle readers, young adult: animal, arts/crafts, biography, careers (middle readers and young adults only), cooking, health, history, hobbies, how-to, interview/profile, multicultural, nature/environment, problem-solving, science, sports. "Subject matter is broad. We cover everything from professional sports to American history to how to pack a canoe. A look at a current list of the BSA's more than 100 merit badge pamphlets gives an idea of the wide range of subjects possible. Even better, look at a year's worth of recent issues. Column subjects are science, nature, earth, health, sports, space and aviation, cars, computers, entertainment, pets, history, music and others.'' Average word length: 500-1,500. Columns 300-750 words. Byline given.

How to Contact/Writers Fiction: Send complete ms with cover letter and SASE to fiction editor. Nonfiction: Major articles query senior editor. Columns query associate editor with SASE for response. Responds to queries/mss in 2 months.

Illustration Buys 10-12 illustrations/issue; 100-125 illustrations/year. Works on assignment only. Reviews ms/illustration packages from artists. ''Query first.'' Illustrations only: Send tearsheets. Responds to art samples only if interested. Samples returned with SASE. Original artwork returned at job's completion. Credit line given.

Terms Pays on acceptance. Buys first rights. Pays $750 and up for fiction; $400-1,500 for major articles; $150-400 for columns; $250-300 for how-to features. Pays illustrators $1,500-3,000 for color cover; $100-1,500 color inside. Pays photographers by the project. Sample copies for $3.60 plus 9×12 SASE. Writer's/illustrator's/photo guidelines available for SASE.

Tips ''We strongly urge you to study at least a year's issues to better understand the type of material published. Articles for *Boys' Life* must interest and entertain boys ages 8 to 18. Write for a boy you know who is 12. Our readers demand crisp, punchy writing in relatively short, straightforward sentences. The editors demand well-reported articles that demonstrate high standards of journalism. We follow *The New York Times* manual of style and usage. All submissions must be accompanied by SASE with adequate postage.''

BOYS' QUEST

P.O. Box 227, Bluffton OH 45817-0227. (419)358-4610. Fax: (419)358-5027. Web site: www.boysquest.com. **Articles Editor:** Marilyn Edwards. Bimonthly magazine. Estab. 1995. ''*Boys' Quest* is a magazine created for boys from 6 to 13 years, with youngsters 8, 9 and 10 the specific target age. Our point of view is that every young boy deserves the right to be a young boy for a number of years before he becomes a young adult. As a result, *Boys' Quest* looks for articles, fiction, nonfiction, and poetry that deal with timeless topics, such as pets, nature, hobbies, science, games, sports, careers, simple cooking, and anything else likely to interest a young boy.''

Fiction Picture-oriented material, young readers, middle readers: adventure, animal, history, humorous, multicultural, nature/environment, problem-solving, sports. Does not want to see violence, teenage themes. Buys 30 mss/year. Average word length: 200-500. Byline given.

Nonfiction Picture-oriented material, young readers, middle readers: animal, arts/crafts, cooking, games/puzzles, history, hobbies, how-to, humorous, math, problem-solving, sports. Prefer photo support with nonfiction. Buys 30 mss/year. Average word length: 200-500. Byline given.

Poetry Reviews poetry. Maximum length: 21 lines. Limit submissions to 6 poems.

How to Contact/Writers All writers should consult the theme list before sending in articles. To receive current theme list, send a SASE. Fiction/Nonfiction: Query or send complete ms (preferred). Send SASE with correct postage. No faxed or e-mailed material. Responds to queries in 2 weeks; mss in 2 weeks (if rejected); 5 weeks (if scheduled). Publishes ms 3 months-3 years after acceptance. Will consider simultaneous submissions and previously published work.

Illustration Buys 10 illustrations/issue; 60-70 illustrations/year. Uses b&w artwork only. Works on assignment only. Reviews ms/illustration packages from artists. Illustrations only: Query with samples, tearsheets. Responds in 1 month only if interested and a SASE. Samples returned with SASE; samples filed. Credit line given.

Photography Photos used for support of nonfiction. ''Excellent photographs included with a nonfiction story is considered very seriously.'' Model/property releases required. Uses b&w, 5×7 or 3×5 prints. Query with samples; send unsolicited photos by mail. Responds in 3 weeks.

Terms Pays on publication. Buys first North American serial rights for mss. Buys first rights for artwork. Pays 5/word for stories and articles. Additional payment for ms/illustration packages and for photos accompanying articles. Pays $150-200 for color cover; $25-35 for b&w inside. Pays photographers per photo (range: $5-10). Originals returned to artist at job's completion. Sample copies for $5 (includes postage); $6 outside U.S. Writer's/illustrator's/photographer's guidelines and theme list are free for SASE.

Tips ''First be familiar with our magazines. We are looking for lively writing, most of it from a young boy's point of view—with the boy or boys directly involved in an activity that is both wholesome and unusual. We need nonfiction with photos and fiction stories—around 500 words—puzzles, poems, cooking, carpentry projects, jokes and riddles. Nonfiction pieces that are accompanied by black and white photos are far more likely to be accepted than those that need illustrations. We will entertain simultaneous submissions as long as that fact is noted on the manuscript.''

BREAD FOR GOD'S CHILDREN

Bread Ministries, Inc., P.O. Box 1017, Arcadia FL 34265-1017. (863)494-6214. Fax: (863)993-0154. E-mail: bread@sunline.net. Web site: www.breadministries.org. **Editor:** Judith M. Gibbs. Bimonthly magazine. Estab. 1972. Circ. 10,000 (U.S. and Canada). ''*Bread* is designed as a teaching tool for Christian families.'' 85% of publication aimed at juvenile market.

Fiction Young readers, middle readers, young adult/teen: adventure, religious, problem-solving, sports. Looks for "teaching stories that portray Christian lifestyles without preaching." Buys approximately 20 mss/year. Average word length: 900-1,500 (for teens); 600-900 (for young children). Byline given.

Nonfiction All levels: how-to. "We do not want anything detrimental to solid family values. Most topics will fit if they are slanted to our basic needs." Buys 3-4 mss/year. Average word length: 500-800. Byline given.

Illustration "The only illustrations we purchase are those occasional good ones accompanying an accepted story."

How to Contact/Writers Fiction/nonfiction: Send complete ms. Responds to mss in 6 months "if considered for use." Will consider simultaneous submissions and previously published work.

Terms Pays on publication. Pays $30-50 for stories; $30 for articles. Sample copies free for 9 × 12 SAE and 5 first-class stamps (for 2 copies).

Tips "We want stories or articles that illustrate overcoming obstacles by faith and living solid, Christian lives. Know our publication and what we have used in the past. Know the readership and publisher's guidelines. Stories should teach the value of morality and honesty without preaching. Edit carefully for content and grammar."

BRILLIANT STAR

National Spiritual Assembly of the Bahá'ís of the U.S., 1233 Central St., Evanston IL 60201. (847)853-2354. Fax: (847)256-1372. E-mail: brilliantstar@usbnc.org. Web site: www.brilliantstar.org. **Associate Editor:** Susan Engle. **Art Director:** Amethel Parel-Sewell. Publishes 6 issues/year. Estab. 1969. "Our magazine is designed for children ages 8-12. *Brilliant Star* presents Bahá'í history and principles through fiction, nonfiction, activities, interviews, puzzles, cartoons, games, music, and art. Universal values of good character, such as kindness, courage, creativity, and helpfulness are incorporated into the magazine.

Fiction Middle readers: contemporary, fantasy, folktale, multicultural, nature/environment, problem-solving, religious. Average word length: 700-1,400. Byline given.

Nonfiction Middle readers: arts/crafts, games/puzzles, geography, how-to, humorous, multicultural, nature/environment, religion, social issues. Buys 6 mss/year. Average word length: 300-700. Byline given.

Poetry "We only publish poetry written by children at the moment."

How to Contact/Writers Fiction: Send complete ms. Nonfiction: Query. Responds to queries/mss in 6 weeks. Publishes ms 6 months-1 year after acceptance. Will consider e-mail submissions.

Illustration Works on assignment only. Reviews ms/illustration packages from artists. Illustrations only: Query with samples. Contact: Aaron Kreader, graphic designer. Responds only if interested. Samples kept on file. Credit line given.

Photography Buys photos with accompanying ms only. Model/property release required; captions required. Responds only if interested.

Terms Pays 2 copies of issue. Buys first rights and reprint rights for mss. Buys first rights and reprint rights for artwork; first rights and reprint rights for photos. Sample copies for $3. Writer's/illustrator's/photo guidelines for SASE.

Tips "*Brilliant Star's* content is developed with a focus on children in their 'tween' years, ages 8-12. This is a period of intense emotional, physical, and psychological development. Familiarize yourself with the interests and challenges of children in this age range. Protaganists in our fiction are usually in the upper part of our age-range: 10-12 years old. They solve their problems without adult intervention. We appreciate seeing a sense of humor but not related to bodily functions or put-downs. Keep your language and concepts age-appropriate. Use short words, sentences, and paragraphs. Activities and games may be submitted in rough or final form. Send us a description of your activity along with short, simple instructions. We avoid long, complicated activities that require adult supervision. If you think they will be helpful, please try to provide step-by-step rough sketches of the instructions. You may also submit photographs to illustrate the activity."

CADET QUEST

Calvinist Cadet Corps, P.O. Box 7259, Grand Rapids MI 49510. (616)241-5616. E-mail: submissions@calvinistcadets.org. Web site: www.calvinistcadets.org. **Editor:** G. Richard Broene. Magazine published 7 times/year. Circ. 10,000. "Our magazine is for members of the Calvinist Cadet Corps—boys aged 9-14. Our purpose is to show how God is at work in their lives and in the world around them. Our magazine offers nonfiction articles and fast-moving fiction—everything to appeal to the interests and concerns of boys and teach Christian values."

Fiction Middle readers, boys/early teens: adventure, humorous, multicultural, problem-solving, religious, sports. Buys 12 mss/year. Average word length: 900-1,500.

Nonfiction Middle readers, boys/early teens: arts/crafts, games/puzzles, hobbies, how-to, humorous, interview/profile, problem-solving, science, sports. Buys 6 mss/year. Average word length: 400-900.

How to Contact/Writers Fiction/nonfiction: Send complete ms by mail with SASE or by e-mail. "Please note: e-mail submissions must have material in the body of the e-mail. We do not open attachments." Responds to queries in 1 month; mss in 2 months. Will consider simultaneous submissions.

Illustration Buys 2 illustration/issue; buys 12 illustrations/year. Works on assignment only. Reviews ms/illustration packages from artists. Responds in 5 weeks. Samples returned with SASE. Originals returned to artist at job's completion. Credit line given.

Photography Buys photos from freelancers. Wants nature photos and photos of boys.

Terms Pays on acceptance. Buys first North American serial rights; reprint rights. Pays 4-5$\frac{1}{2}$¢/word for stories/articles. Pays illustrators $50-200 for b&w/color cover or b&w/color inside. Sample copy free with 9×12 SAE and 4 first-class stamps.

Tips "Our publication is mostly open to fiction; look for new themes at our Web site. We use mostly fast-moving fiction that appeals to a boy's sense of adventure or sense of humor. Avoid preachiness, simplistic answers to complicated problems and long dialogue with little action. Articles on sports, outdoor activities, science, crafts, etc. should emphasize a Christian perspective."

CALLIOPE, Exploring World History

Cobblestone Publishing Company, 30 Grove St., Peterborough NH 03458. (603)924-7209. Fax: (603)924-7380. Web site: www.cobblestonepub.com. **Editorial Director:** Lou Waryncia. **Co-editors:** Rosalie Baker and Charles Baker. **Art Director:** Ann Dillon. Magazine published 9 times/year. "*Calliope* covers world history (East/West), and lively, original approaches to the subject are the primary concerns of the editors in choosing material."

> • *Calliope* themes for 2005-2006 include the Aztecs, Medieval Japan, the Spice Trade, Rembrandt, the Irish Potato Famine, Charles Dickens. For additional themes and time frames, visit their Web site.

Fiction Middle readers and young adults: adventure, folktales, plays, history, biographical fiction. Material must relate to forthcoming themes. Word length: up to 800.

Nonfiction Middle readers and young adults: arts/crafts, biography, cooking, games/puzzles, history. Material must relate to forthcoming themes. Word length: 300-1,000.

How to Contact/Writers "A query must consist of the following to be considered (please use nonerasable paper): a brief cover letter stating subject and word length of the proposed article; a detailed one-page outline explaining the information to be presented in the article; an bibliography of materials the author intends to use in preparing the article; a self-addressed stamped envelope. Writers new to *Calliope* should send a writing sample with query. In all correspondence, please include your complete address as well as a telephone number where you can be reached. A writer may send as many queries for one issue as he or she wishes, but each query must have a separate cover letter, outline, bibliography and SASE. Telephone and e-mail queries are not accepted. Handwritten queries will not be considered. Queries may be submitted at any time, but queries sent well in advance of deadline *may not be answered for several months*. Go-aheads requesting material proposed in queries are usually sent five months prior to publication date. Unused queries will be returned approximately three to four months prior to publication date."

Illustration Illustrations only: Send tearsheets, photocopies. Original work returned upon job's completion (upon written request).

Photography Buys photos from freelancers. Wants photos pertaining to any forthcoming themes. Uses b&w/color prints, 35mm transparencies. Send unsolicited photos by mail (on speculation).

Terms Buys all rights for mss and artwork. Pays 20-25¢/word for stories/articles. Pays on an individual basis for poetry, activities, games/puzzles. "Covers are assigned and paid on an individual basis." Pays photographers per photo ($15-100 for b&w; $25-100 for color). Sample copy for $5.95 and SAE with $2 postage. Writer's/illustrator's/photo guidelines for SASE.

CAMPUS LIFE'S IGNITE YOUR FAITH

(formerly *Campus Life*), Christianity Today, International, 465 Gundersen Dr., Carol Stream IL 60188. (630)260-6200. Fax: (630)260-0114. E-mail: iyf@igniteyourfaith.com. Web site: www.igniteyourfaith.com. **Articles and Fiction Editor:** Chris Lutes. Bimonthly magazine. Estab. 1944. Circ. 100,000. "Our purpose is to creatively engage and empower Christian teens to become fully devoted followers of Jesus Christ."

Fiction Young adults: humorous, problem-solving. Buys 5-6 mss/year. Byline given.

Poetry Reviews poetry.

How to Contact/Writers Fiction/nonfiction: Query only.

Terms Pays on acceptance. Writer's guidelines available on Web site.

CAREER WORLD

Weekly Reader Corp., 200 First Stamford Place, P.O. Box 120023, Stamford CT 06912-0023. E-mail: careerworld @weeklyreader.com. **Articles Editor:** Anne Flounders. **Art Director:** Kimberly Shake. Monthly (school year) magazine. Estab. 1972. A guide to careers, for students grades 6-12.

Nonfiction Young adults/teens: education, how-to, interview/profile, career awareness and development. Byline given.

How to Contact/Writers Nonfiction: Query with published clips and résumé. "We do not want any unsolicited manuscripts." Responds to queries in 2 weeks.

Illustration Buys 5-10 illustrations/year. Works on assignment only. Reviews ms/illustration packages from artists. Manuscript/illustration packages and illustration only: Query; send promo sheet and tearsheets. Credit line given.

Photography Purchases photos from freelancers.

Terms Pays on publication. Buys all rights for mss. Pays $150 and up for articles. Pays illustrators by the project. Writer's guidelines free, but only on assignment.

CAREERS AND COLLEGES

A division of Alloy Education, an Alloy Media + Marketing Company, 10 Abeel Road, Cranbury NJ 08512. (609)619-8739. Web site: www.careersandcolleges.com. **SVP/Managing Director:** Jayne Pennington. Editor: Don Rauf. Magazine published 4 times during school year (September, November, January, March). Audited circulation: 750,000. Distributed to 10,000 high schools. *Careers and Colleges* magazine provides juniors and seniors in high school with editorial, tips, trends, and Web sites to assist them in the transition to college, career, young adulthood, and independence.

Nonfiction Young adults/teens: careers, college, health, how-to, humorous, interview/profile, personal development, problem-solving, social issues, sports, travel. Buys 10-20 mss/year. Average word length: 1,000-1,500. Byline given.

How to Contact/Writers Nonfiction: Query. Responds to queries in 6 weeks. Will consider electronic submissions.

Illustration Buys 2 illustrations/issue; buys 8 illustrations/year. Works on assignment only. Reviews samples online. Query first. Credit line given.

Terms Pays on acceptance plus 45 days. Buys all rights. Pays $100-600 for assigned/unsolicited articles. Additional payment for ms/illustration packages "must be negotiated." Pays $300-1,000 for color illustration; $200-700 for b&w/color inside illustration. Pays photographers by the project. Sample copy $5. Contributor's Guidelines are available electronically.

Tips "Articles with great quotes, good reporting, good writing. Rich with examples and anecdotes. Must tie in with the objective to help teenaged readers plan for their futures. Current trends, policy changes and information regarding college admissions, financial aid, and career opportunities."

CARUS PUBLISHING COMPANY

P.O. Box 300, Peru IL 61354.

- See listings for *Babybug, Cicada, Click, Cricket, Ladybug, Muse, Spider* and *ASK*. Carus Publishing owns Cobblestone Publishing, publisher of *AppleSeeds, Calliope, Cobblestone, Dig, Faces* and *Odyssey*.

CATHOLIC FORESTER

Catholic Order of Foresters, P.O. Box 3012, 355 Shuman Blvd., Naperville IL 60566-7012. (630)983-4900. E-mail: magazine@CatholicForester.com. Web site: www.chatholicforester.com. **Articles Editor:** Patricia Baron. **Assistant V.P. Communication:** Mary Ann File. **Art Director:** Keith Halla. Quarterly magazine. Estab. 1883. Circ. 85,000. Targets members of the Catholic Order of Foresters. In addition to the organization's news, it offers general interest pieces on health, finance, family life. Also use inspirational and humorous fiction.

Fiction Buys 6-10 mss/year. Average word length: 500-1,500.

How to Contact/Writers Fiction: Submit complete ms. Responds in 4 months. Will consider previously published work.

Illustration Buys 2-4 illustrations/issue. Uses color artwork only. Works on assignment only.

Photography Buys photos with accompanying ms only.

Terms Pays on acceptance. Buys first North American serial rights, reprint rights, one-time rights. Sample copies for 9×12 SASE with 3 first-class stamps. Writer's guidelines free for SASE.

CELEBRATE

Word Action Publishing Co., Church of the Nazarene, 6401 The Paseo, Kansas City MO 64131. (816)333-7000, ext. 2487. Fax: (816)333-4439. E-mail: dwillemin@nazarene.org. Web site: www.wordaction.com. **Editor:** Pam Asher. **Assistant Editor:** Denise Willemin. Weekly publication. Estab. 2001. Circ. 30,000. "This weekly take-home paper connects Sunday School learning to life for preschoolers (age 3 and 4), kindergartners (age 5 and 6) and their families." 75% of publication aimed at juvenile market; 25% parents.

Nonfiction Picture-oriented material: arts/crafts, cooking, poems, action rhymes, piggyback songs (theme based). 50% of mss nonfiction. Byline given.

Poetry Reviews poetry. Maximum length: 4-8 lines. Unlimited submissions.

How to Contact/Writers Nonfiction: query. Responds to queries in 1 month. Responds to mss in 6 weeks. Publishes ms 1 year after acceptance. Will accept electronic submission via e-mail.

Terms Pays on acceptance. Buys all rights, multi-use rights. Pays a minimum of $2 for songs and rhymes; 25¢/line

for poetry; $15 for activities, crafts, recipes. Compensation includes 2 contributor copies. Sample copy for SASE.
Tips "We are accepting submissions at this time."

🌐 CHALLENGE

Pearson Education Australia, P.O. Box 1024, South Melbourne VIC 3205 Australia. (61)03 9811 2800. Fax: (61)03 981 2999. E-mail: magazines@pearsoned.com.au. Web site: www.pearsoned.com.au/schools. **Articles Editor:** Petra Poupa. **Fiction Editor:** Meredith Costain. Quarterly Magazine. Circ. 20,000. "Magazines are educational and fun. We publish mainly nonfiction articles in a variety of genres and text types. They must be appropriate, factually correct, and of high interest. We publish interviews, recounts, informational and argumentative articles."

- *Challenge* is a theme-based publication geared to ages 11-14. Check the Web site to see upcoming themes and deadlines.

Fiction Middle readers, young adults: adventure, animal, contemporary, fantasy, folktale, humorous, multicultural, problem-solving, science fiction, sports, suspense/mystery. Buys 12 mss/year. Average word length: 400-1,000. Byline given.

Nonfiction Middle readers, young adults: animal, arts/crafts, biography, careers, cooking, fashion, geography, health, history, hobbies, how-to, humorous, interview/profile, math, multicultural, nature/environment, problem-solving, science, social issues, sports, travel (depends on theme of issue). Buys 100 ms/year. Average word length: 200-600. Byline given.

Poetry Reviews poetry.

How to Contact/Writers Fiction/nonfiction: Send complete ms. Responds to queries in 4-5 months; mss in 3 months. Publishes ms 3 months after acceptance. Will consider simultaneous submissions and electronic submissions via disk or e-mail.

Photography Looking for photos to suit various themes; photos needed depend on stories. Model/property release required; captions required. Uses color, standard sized, prints, high resolution digital images and 35mm transparencies. Provide résumé, business card, promotional literature and tearsheets to be kept on file.

Terms Pays on publication. Buys first Australian serial rights. Pays $80-200 (Australian) for stories; $100-220 (Australian) for articles.

Tips "Check out our Web site for information about our publications." Also see listings for *Comet* and *Explore*.

📷 CHEMMATTERS

American Chemical Society, 1155 16th Street, NW, Washington DC 20036. (202)872-6164. Fax: (202)833-7732. E-mail: chemmatters@acs.org. Web site: www.chemistry.org/education/chemmatters.html. **Articles Editor:** Kevin McCue. **Art Director:** Cornithia Harris. Quarterly magazine. Estab. 1983. Circ. 35,000. "*ChemMatters* is a magazine for connecting high school readers with the fascinating chemistry of their everyday lives."

- *ChemMatters* only accepts e-mail submissions.

Nonfiction Young adults: biography, health, history, nature/environment, problem-solving, science. Must be related to chemistry. Buys 20 mss/year. Average word length: 1,400-2,100. Byline given.

How to Contact/Writers Nonfiction: Query with published clips. Only e-mail submissions will be considered. Responds to queries/mss in 2 weeks. Publishes ms 6 months after acceptance. Will consider simultaneous submissions, e-mail submissions.

Illustration Buys 3 illustrations/issue; 12 illustrations/year. Uses color artwork only. Works on assignment only. Reviews ms/illustration packages from artists. Query. Contact: Cornithia Harris, art director *ChemMatters*. Illustrations only: Query with promo sheet, résumé. Responds in 2 weeks. Samples returned with SASE; samples not filed. Credit line given.

Photography Looking for photos of high school students engaged in science-related activities. Model/property release required; captions required. Uses color prints, but prefers high-res PDFs. Query with samples. Responds in 2 weeks.

Terms Pays on acceptance. Minimally buys first North American serial rights, but prefers to buy all rights, reprint rights, electronic rights for mss. Buys all rights for artwork; non-exclusive first rights for photos. Pays $500-$1,000 for articles. Additional payment for ms/illustration packages and for photos accompanying articles. Sample copies free for SAE 10×13 and 3 first-class stamps. Writer's guidelines free for SASE (available as e-mail attachment upon request).

Tips "Be aware of the content covered in a standard high school chemistry textbook. Choose themes and topics that are timely, interesting, fun, mystifying, *and* that relate to the content and concepts of the first-year chemistry course. Articles should describe real people involved with real science. Best articles feature young people making a difference or solving a problem."

CHILDREN'S BETTER HEALTH INSTITUTE

1100 Waterway Blvd., P.O. Box 567, Indianapolis IN 46206. See listings for *Children's Digest, Children's Playmate, Humpty Dumpty's Magazine, Jack and Jill, Turtle* and *U*S* Kids*.

CHILDREN'S DIGEST

Children's Better Health Institute, 1100 Waterway Blvd., P.O. Box 567, Indianapolis IN 46206. (317)634-1100. Fax: (317)684-8094. Web site: www.childrensdigestmag.org. For children ages 10-12.
• See Web site for submission guidelines.

CHILDREN'S PLAYMATE

Children's Better Health Institute, 1100 Waterway Blvd., Box 567, Indianapolis IN 46206. (317)634-1100. Fax: (317)684-8094. Web site: www.childrensplaymatemag.org. **Editor:** Terry Harshman. **Art Director:** Rob Falco. Magazine published 6 times/year. Estab. 1929. Circ. 135,000. For children ages 6-8 years; approximately 50% of content is health-related.
Fiction Average word length: 100-300. Byline given. Sample copies $2.95.
Nonfiction Young readers: easy recipes, games/puzzles, health, medicine, safety, science. Buys 16-20 mss/year. Average word length: 300-500. Byline given.
Poetry Maximum length: 20-25 lines.
How to Contact/Writers Fiction/nonfiction: Send complete ms. Responds to mss in 3 months. Do not send queries.
Illustration Works on assignment only. Reviews ms/illustration packages from artists. Query first.
Terms Pays on publication for illustrators and writers. Buys all rights for mss and artwork. Pays 17¢/word for stories. Pays minimum $25 for poems. Pays $275 for color cover illustration; $90 for b&w inside; $70-155 for color inside. Sample copy $1.75. Writer's/illustrator's guidelines for SASE.

CICADA

Carus Publishing Company, P.O. Box 300, 315 Fifth St., Peru IL 61354. (815)224-5803, ext. 656. Fax: (815)224-6615. E-mail: cicada@caruspub.com. Web site: www.cricketmag.com. **Editor-in-Chief:** Marianne Carus. **Executive Editor:** Deborah Vetter. **Senior Editor:** Tracy C. Schoenle. **Senior Art Director:** Ron McCutchan. Bimonthly magazine. Estab. 1998. *Cicada* publishes fiction and poetry with a genuine teen sensibility, aimed at the high school and college-age market. The editors are looking for stories and poems that are thought-provoking but entertaining.
Fiction Young adults: adventure, animal, contemporary, fantasy, history, humorous, multicultural, nature/environment, romance, science fiction, sports, suspense/mystery, stories that will adapt themselves to a sophisticated cartoon, or graphic novel format. Buys up to 60 mss/year. Average word length: about 5,000 words for short stories; up to 15,000 for novellas (one novella per issue).
Nonfiction Young adults: first-person, coming-of-age experiences that are relevant to teens and young adults (example: life in the Peace Corps). Buys 6 mss/year. Average word length: about 5,000 words. Byline given.
Poetry Reviews serious, humorous, free verse, rhyming (if done well) poetry. Maximum length: up to 25 lines. Limit submissions to 5 poems.
How to Contact/Writers Fiction/nonfiction: send complete ms. Responds to mss in 3 months. Publishes ms 1-2 years after acceptance. Will consider simultaneous submissions if author lets us know.
Illustration Buys 20 illustrations/issue; 120 illustrations/year. Uses color artwork for cover; b&w for interior. Works on assignment only. Reviews ms/illustration packages from artists. Send ms with 1-2 sketches and samples of other finished art. Illustrations only: Query with samples. Responds in 6 weeks. Samples returned with SASE; samples filed. Credit line given.
Photography Wants documentary photos (clear shots that illustrate specific artifacts, persons, locations, phenomena, etc., cited in the text) and "art" shots of teens in photo montage/lighting effects etc. Uses b&w 4×5 glossy prints. Submit portfolio for review. Responds in 6 weeks.
Terms Pays on publication. Rights purchased vary. Pays up to 25¢/word for mss; up to $3/line for poetry. Pays illustrators $750 for color cover; $50-150 for b&w inside. Pays photographers per photo (range: $50-150). Sample copies for $8.50. Writer's/illustrator's/photo guidelines for SASE.
Tips "Please don't write for a junior high audience. We're looking for complex character development, strong plots, and thought-provoking themes for young people in high school and college. Don't forget humor and romance! We're getting too many cancer-related stories and too much depressing fiction in general. We're getting too many cancer-related stories and too much depressing fiction in general. We'd like to publish more nonfiction first-person experiences. Please note that this is a separate category from the shorter, teen-written 'expressions' feature."

THE CLAREMONT REVIEW

4980 Wesley Road, Victoria BC V8Y 1Y9 Canada. (250)685-5221. Fax: (250)658-5387. E-mail: editor@theClaremontReview.ca. Web site: www.theClaremontReview.ca. Magazine 2 times/year. Estab. 1992. Circ. 500. "Publish quality fiction and poetry of emerging writers aged 13 to 19."
Fiction Young adults: multicultural, problem-solving, social issues, relationships. Average word length: 1,500-3,000.

Poetry Maximum length: 60 lines. No limit on submissions.

How to Contact/Writers Fiction: Send complete ms. Responds to queries in 2 weeks; mss in 2 months. Publishes ms 6 months after acceptance.

Illustration Illustrations only: Send postcard sample with samples, SASE. Contact: Janice McCachen, editor. Responds in 2 months. Samples returned with SASE. Credit line given.

Terms Buys first North American rights for mss. Pays contributor's copies when published. Sample copies for $8.00. Writer's guidelines for SASE.

Tips "Looking for good, concrete narratives with credible dialogue and solid use of original detail. It must be unique, honest and have a glimpse of some truth. Send an error-free final draft with a short covering letter and bio. Read our magazine first to familiarize yourself with what we publish."

CLICK

140 S. Dearborn, Suite 1450, Chicago IL 60603. (312)701-1720. Fax: (312)701-1728. E-mail: click@caruspub.c om. Web site: www.cricketmag.com. **Editor:** Lonnie Plecha. **Art Director:** Deb Porter. 9 issues/year. Estab. 1998. "*Click* is a science and exploration magazine for children ages 3 to 7. Designed and written with the idea that it's never too early to encourage a

child's natural curiosity about the world, *Click*'s 40 full-color pages are filled with amazing photographs, beautiful illustrations, and stories and articles that are both entertaining and thought-provoking."

Nonfiction Young readers: animals, nature/environment, science. Average word length: 300-1000. Byline given.

How to Contact Writers *Click* does not accept unsolicited manuscripts or queries. All articles are commissioned. To be considered for assignments, experienced science writers may send a résumé and three published clips.

Illustration Buys 10 illustrations/issue; 60 illustrations/year. Works on assignment only. Query with samples. Responds only if interested. Credit line given.

COBBLESTONE: Discover American History

Cobblestone Publishing, 30 Grove St., Suite C, Peterborough NH 03458. (603)924-7209. Fax: (603)924-7380. Web site: www.cobblestonepub.com. **Editor:** Meg Chorlian. **Art Director:** Ann Dillon. **Editorial Director:** Lou Waryncia. Magazine published 9 times/year. Circ. 30,000. "*Cobblestone* is theme-related. Writers should request editorial guidelines which explain procedure and list upcoming themes. Queries must relate to an upcoming theme. It is recommended that writers become familiar with the magazine (sample copies available)."

• *Cobblestone* themes and deadline are available on Web site or with SASE.

Fiction Middle readers, young adults: folktales, history, multicultural.

Nonfiction Middle readers (school ages 8-14): arts/crafts, biography, geography, history (world and American), multicultural, social issues. All articles must relate to the issue's theme. Buys 120 mss/year. Average word length: 600-800. Byline given.

Poetry Up to 100 lines. "Clear, objective imagery. Serious and light verse considered." Pays on an individual basis. Must relate to theme.

How to Contact/Writers Fiction/nonfiction: Query. "A query must consist of all of the following to be considered: a brief cover letter stating the subject and word length of the proposed article, a detailed one-page outline explaining the information to be presented in the article, an extensive bibliography of materials the author intends to use in preparing the article, a SASE. Writers new to *Cobblestone* should send a writing sample with query. If you would like to know if your query has been received, please also include a stamped postcard that requests acknowledgment of receipt. In all correspondence, please include your complete address as well as a telephone number where you can be reached. A writer may send as many queries for one issue as he or she wishes, but each query must have a separate cover letter, outline, bibliography and SASE. Telephone queries are not accepted. Handwritten queries will not be considered. Queries may be submitted at any time, but queries sent well in advance of deadline *may not be answered for several months*. Go-aheads requesting material proposed in queries are usually sent five months prior to publication date. Unused queries will be returned approximately three to four months prior to publication date."

Illustration Buys 5 color illustrations/issue; 45 illustrations/year. Preferred theme or style: Material that is simple, clear and accurate but not too juvenile. Sophisticated sources are a must. Works on assignment only. Reviews ms/illustration packages from artists. Query. Illustrations only: Send photocopies, tearsheets, or other nonreturnable samples. "Illustrators should consult issues of *Cobblestone* to familiarize themselves with our needs." Responds to art samples in 1 month. Samples are not returned; samples filed. Original artwork returned at job's completion (upon written request). Credit line given.

Photography Photos must relate to upcoming themes. Send transparencies and/or color prints. Submit on speculation.

Terms Pays on publication. Buys all rights to articles and artwork. Pays 20-25¢/word for articles/stories. Pays on an individual basis for poetry, activities, games/puzzles. Pays photographers per photo ($50-100 for color).

Sample copy $5.95 with 9×12 SAE and 4 first-class stamps; writer's/illustrator's/photo guidelines free with SAE and 1 first-class stamp.

Tips Writers: "Submit detailed queries which show attention to historical accuracy and which offer interesting and entertaining information. Study past issues to know what we look for. All feature articles, recipes, activities, fiction and supplemental nonfiction are freelance contributions." Illustrators: "Submit color samples, not too juvenile. Study past issues to know what we look for. The illustration we use is generally for stories, recipes and activities." (See listings for *AppleSeeds*, *Calliope*, *Dig*, *Faces*, *Footsteps*, and *Odyssey*.)

COLLEGEBOUND TEEN MAGAZINE

Ramholtz Publishing, Inc., 1200 South Ave., Suite 202, Staten Island NY 10314. (718)761-4800. Fax: (718)761-3300. E-mail: editorial@collegebound.net. Web site: www.collegebound.net. **Articles Editor:** Gina LaGuardia. **Art Director:** Suzanne Vidal. Monthly magazine and Web site. Estab. 1987. Circ. 75,000 (regionals); 725,000 (nationals). *CollegeBound Teen Magazine* is written by college students (and those "young at heart") for high school juniors and seniors. It is designed to provide an inside view of college life, with college students from around the country serving as correspondents. The magazine's editorial content offers its teen readership personal accounts on all aspects of college, from living with a roommate, choosing a major, and joining a fraternity or sorority, to college dating, interesting courses, beating the financial aid fuss, and other college-bound concerns. *CollegeBound Teen Magazine* is published six times regionally throughout the tri-state area. Special issues include the National Editions (published each September and February) and Spring and Fall California, Illinois, Texas, Florida and New England issues. The magazine offers award-winning World Wide Web affiliates starting at *CollegeBound.NET*, at www.collegebound.net.

Nonfiction Young adults: careers, college prep, fashion, health, how-to, interview/profile, problem-solving, social issues, college life. Buys 70 mss/year. Average word length: 800-1,100 words. Byline given.

How to Contact/Writers Nonfiction: Query with published clips. Responds to queries in 2 months; mss in 10 weeks. Publishes ms 3-4 months after acceptance. Will consider electronic submission via disk or modem, previously published work (as long as not a competitor title).

Illustration Buys 2-3 illustrations/issue. Uses color artwork only. Works on assignment only. Reviews ms/illustration packages from artists. Query. Illustrations only: Query with samples. Responds in 2 months. Samples kept on file. Credit line given.

Terms Pays on publication. Buys first North American serial rights, all rights or reprint rights for mss. Buys first rights for artwork. Originals returned if requested, with SASE. Pays $25-100 for articles 30 days upon publication. All contributors receive 2 issues with payment. Pays illustrators $25-125 for color inside. Sample copies free for #10 SASE and $3 postage. Writer's guidelines for SASE.

Tips "Review the sample issue and get a good feel for the types of articles we accept and our tone and purpose."

🌐 COMET

Pearson Education Australia, 95 Coventry St., South Melbourne VIC Australia. (61)03 9697 0666. Fax: (61)03 9699 2041. E-mail: magazines@pearsoned.com.au. Web site: www.pearsoned.com.au/schools. **Articles Editor:** Petra Poupa. **Fiction Editor:** Meredith Costain. Quarterly Magazine. Circ. 20,000. "Magazines are educational and fun. We publish mainly nonfiction articles in a variety of genres and text types. They must be appropriate, factually correct, and of high interest. We publish interviews, recounts, informational and argumentative articles."

• *Comet* is a theme based publication. Check their Web site to see upcoming themes and deadlines.

Fiction Picture-oriented material, young readers: adventure, animal, contemporary, folktale, multicultural, nature/environment, problem solving. Young readers: fantasy, humorous, suspense/mystery. Average word length: 400-1,000. Byline given.

Nonfiction Picture-oriented material, young readers: animal, arts/crafts, biography, careers, cooking, health, hobbies, how-to, interview/profile, math, multicultural, nature/environment, problem-solving, science, social issues, sports, travel. Picture-oriented material: geography. Young readers: games/puzzles, humorous. Average word length: 200-600. Byline given.

Poetry Reviews poetry.

How to Contact/Writers Fiction/nonfiction: Send complete ms. Responds to queries in 1 month; mss in 3 months. Publishes ms 3 months after acceptance. Will consider simultaneous submissions and electronic submissions via disk or e-mail.

Photography Looking for photos to suit various themes; photos needed depend on stories. Model/property release required; captions required. Uses color, standard sized, prints, high resolution digital images and 35mm transparencies. Provide résumé, business card, promotional literature and tearsheets to be kept on file.

Terms Pays on publication. Buys first Australian rights. Pays $80-200 (Australian) for stories; $100-220 (Australian) for articles.

Tips "Check out our Web site for information about our publications." Also see listings for *Challenge* and *Explore*.

CRICKET

Carus Publishing Company, P.O. Box 300, Peru IL 61354. (815)224-5803, ext. 656. Web site: www.cricketmag.c om. **Editor-in-Chief:** Marianne Carus. **Executive Editor:** Deborah Vetter. **Senior Editor:** Tracy Schoenle. **Assistant Editor:** Adam Oldaker. **Senior Art Director:** Ron McCutchan. Monthly magazine. Estab. 1973. Circ. 72,000. Children's literary magazine for ages 9-14.

Fiction Middle readers, young adults/teens: contemporary, fantasy, folk and fairy tales, history, humorous, science fiction, suspense/mystery. Buys 140 mss/year. Maximum word length: 2,000. Byline given.

Nonfiction Middle readers, young adults/teens: adventure, architecture, archaeology, biography, foreign culture, games/puzzles, geography, natural history, science and technology, social science, sports, travel. Multicultural needs include articles on customs and cultures. Requests bibliography with submissions. Buys 40 mss/year. Average word length: 200-1,500. Byline given.

Poetry Reviews poems, 1-page maximum length. Limit submission to 5 poems or less.

How to Contact/Writers Send complete ms. Do not query first. Responds to mss in 3 months. Does not like but will consider simultaneous submissions. SASE required for response.

Illustration Buys 35 illustrations (14 separate commissions)/issue; 425 illustrations/year. Preferred theme for style: "strong realism; strong people, especially kids; good action illustration; no cartoons. All media, but prefer other than pencil." Reviews ms/illustration packages from artists, "but reserves option to re-illustrate." Send complete ms with sample and query. Illustrations only: Provide tearsheets or good quality photocopies to be kept on file. SASE required for response/return of samples. Responds to art samples in 2 months.

Photography Purchases photos with accompanying ms only. Model/property releases required. Uses color transparencies, b&w glossy prints.

Terms Pays on publication. Rights purchased vary. Do not send original artwork. Pays up to 25¢/word for unsolicited articles; up to $3/line for poetry. Pays $750 for color cover; $75-150 for b&w, $150-250 for color inside. Writer's/illustrator's guidelines for SASE.

Tips Writers: "Read copies of back issues and current issues. Adhere to specified word limits. *Please* do not query." Illustrators: "Edit your samples. Send only your best work and be able to reproduce that quality in assignments. Put name and address on *all* samples. Know a publication before you submitis your style appropriate?"

CURRENT SCIENCE

Weekly Reader Corp., 200 First Stanford Place, Stanford CT 06912-0034. (203)705-3500. Fax: (203)705-1661. E-mail: science@weeklyreader.com. Web site: www.weeklyreader.com. **Managing Editor:** Hugh Westrup. 16 times/year magazine. Estab. 1927. "*Current Science*uses today's new to make science relevant to students in grades 6-10. Each issue covers every area of the science curriculum—life, earth, and physical science, plus health and technology."

● *Current Science* is no longer accepting unsolicited submissions.

DANCE MAGAZINE

333 Seventh Ave., 11th Floor, New York NY 10001. (212)979-4803. Fax: (646)674-0102. Web site: www.dancem agazine.com. **Editor-in-Chief:** Wendy Perron. **Art Director:** Ragnar Johnson. Monthly magazine. Estab. 1927. Circ. 45,000. Covers "all things dance—features, news, reviews, calendar."

● Also publishers *Young Dancer* magazine. See Web site for more information.

How to Contact Query with published clips.

Photography Uses dance photos.

Terms Pays on publication. Buys first rights. Additional payment for ms/illustration packages and for photos accompanying articles. Pays photographers per photo. Byline given. Sample copies for $4.95. (Go to Web site and click on subscription services.)

Tips "Study the magazine for style."

DAVEY AND GOLIATH'S DEVOTIONS

Augsburg Fortress, 100 S. Fifth St., Suite 700, Minneapolis MN 55440. E-mail: cllsub@augsburgfortress.org. Web site: www.augsburgfortress.org. **Editor:** Pamela Foster. Quarterly magazine. Circ. approximately 50,000. This is a booklet of interactive conversations and activities related to weekly devotional material. Used primarily by Lutheran families with elementary school-aged children."Davey and Goliath is a magazine with concrete ideas that families can use to build biblical literacy and share faith. It included bible stories, family activities, crafts, games, and a section of puzzles, mazes, and other kid-stuff."

How to Contact/Writers Visit www.augsburgfortress.org/company/downloads/FamilyDevotionalSampleBriefi ng.doc to view sample briefing. Follow instructions in briefing if interested in submitting a sample for the devotional. Published material is 100% assigned.

Terms Pays on acceptance of final ms assignment. Buys all rights. Pays $40/printed page on assignment. Free sample and information for prospective writers. Include 6×9 SAE and postage.

Tips "Pay attention to details in the sample devotional. Follow the process laid out in the information for prospective writers. Ability to interpret Bible texts appropriately for children is required."

DIG

Cobblestone Publishing, 30 Grove St., Suite C, Peterborough NH 03450. (603)924-7209. Fax: (603)924-7380. E-mail: cfbakeriii@meganet.net. Web site: www.digonsite.com. **Editor:** Rosalie Baker. **Editorial Director:** Lou Waryncia. **Art Director:** Ann Dillon. Magazine published 9 times/year. Estab. 1999. Circ. 20,000. An archaeology magazine for kids ages 8-14. Publishes entertaining and educational stories about discoveries, artifacts, archaeologists.

- *Dig* was purchased by Cobblestone Publishing, a division of Carus Publishing.

Nonfiction Middle readers, young adults: biography, games/puzzles, history, science, archaeology. Buys 50 mss/year. Average word length: 400-800. Byline given.

How to Contact/Writers Fiction/nonfiction: Query. "A query must consist of all of the following to be considered: a brief cover letter stating the subject and word length of the proposed article, a detailed one-page outline explaining the information to be presented in the article, a bibliography of materials the author intends to use in preparing the article, and a SASE. Writers new to *Dig* should send a writing sample with query. If you would like to know if a query has been received, include a stamped postcard that requests acknowledgement of receipt." Multiple queries accepted (include separate cover letter, outline, bibliography, SASE) may not be answered for many months. Go-aheads requesting material proposed in queries are usually sent 5 months prior to publication date. Unused queries will be returned approximately 3-4 months prior to publication date.

Illustration Buys 10-15 illustrations/issue; 60-75 illustrations/year. Prefers color artwork. Works on assignment only. Reviews ms/illustration packages from artists. Query. Illustrations only: Query with samples. Arrange portfolio review. Send tearsheets. Responds in 2 months only if interested. Samples not returned; samples filed. Credit line given.

Photography Uses anything related to archaeology, history, artifacts, and current archaeological events that relate to kids. Uses color prints and 35mm transparencies. Provide résumé, promotional literature or tearsheets to be kept on file. Responds only if interested.

Terms Pays on publication. Buys all rights for mss. Buys first North American rights for photos. Original artwork returned at job's completion. Pays 20-25¢/word. Additional payment for ms/illustration packages and for photos accompanying articles. Pays per photo.

Tips "We are looking for writers who can communicate archaeological concepts in a conversational, interesting, informative and *accurate* style for kids. Writers should have some idea where photography can be located to support their work."

DISCOVERIES

Children's Ministries, Sunday School Curriculum, 6401 The Paseo, Kansas City MO 64131. (816)333-7000. Fax: (816)333-4439. E-mail: vfolsom@nazarene.org. **Editor:** Virginia L. Folsom. **Executive Editor:** Donna L. Fillmore. **Assistant Editor:** Sarah Weatherwax. Take-home paper. "*Discoveries* is a leisure-reading piece for third- and fourth-graders. It is published weekly by WordAction Publishing. The major purpose of the magazine is to provide a leisure-reading piece which will build Christian behavior and values and provide reinforcement for Biblical concepts taught in the Sunday School curriculum. The focus of the reinforcement will be life-related, with some historical appreciation. *Discoveries'* target audience is children ages eight to ten in grades three and four. The readability goal is third to fourth grade."

- *Discoveries* is not accepting submissions at this time. They are in the process of creating new guidelines that will be available near the beginning of 2007.

DRAMATICS MAGAZINE

Educational Theatre Association, 2343 Auburn Ave., Cincinnati OH 45219. (513)421-3900. E-mail: dcorathers@edta.org. Web site: www.edta.org. **Articles Editor:** Don Corathers. **Art Director:** William Johnston. Published monthly September-May. Estab. 1929. Circ. 35,000. "Dramatics is for students (mainly high school age) and teachers of theater. Mix includes how-to (tech theater, acting, directing, etc.), informational, interview, photo feature, humorous, profile, technical. We want our student readers to grow as theater artists and become a more discerning and appreciative audience. Material is directed to both theater students and their teachers, with strong student slant."

Fiction Young adults: drama (one-act and full-length plays). Does not want to see plays that show no understanding of the conventions of the theater. No plays for children, no Christmas or didactic "message" plays. "We prefer unpublished scripts that have been produced at least once." Buys 5-9 plays/year. Emerging playwrights have better chances with résumé of credits.

Nonfiction Young adults: arts/crafts, careers, how-to, interview/profile, multicultural (all theater-related). "We try to portray the theater community in all its diversity." Does not want to see academic treatises. Buys 50 mss/year. Average word length: 750-3,000. Byline given.

How to Contact/Writers Send complete ms. Responds in 3 months (longer for plays). Published ms 3 months after acceptance. Will consider simultaneous submissions and previously published work occasionally.

Illustration Buys 0-2 illustrations/year. Works on assignment only. Arrange portfolio review; send résumé, promo sheets and tearsheets. Responds only if interested. Samples returned with SASE; sample not filed. Credit line given.

Photography Buys photos with accompanying ms only. Looking for "good-quality production or candid photography to accompany article. We very occasionally publish photo essays." Model/property release and captions required. Uses 5×7 or 8×10 b&w glossy prints and 35mm transparencies. Also uses high resolution digital files or Zip disk or CD (JPEG or TIFF files). Query with résumé of credits. Responds only if interested.

Terms Pays on acceptance. Buys one-time print and short term Web rights. Buys one-time rights for artwork and photos. Original artwork returned at job's completion. Pays $100-500 for plays; $50-500 for articles; up to $100 for illustrations. Pays photographers by the project or per photo. Sometimes offers additional payment for ms/illustration packages and photos accompanying a ms. Sample copy available for 9×12 SAE with 4 ounces first-class postage. Writer's and photo guidelines available for SASE or via Web site.

Tips "Obtain our writer's guidelines and look at recent back issues. The best way to break in is to know our audience—drama students, teachers and others interested in theater—and write for them. Writers who have some practical experience in theater, especially in technical areas, have an advantage, but we'll work with anybody who has a good idea. Some freelancers have become regular contributors."

DYNAMATH

Scholastic Inc., 557 Broadway, Room 4052, New York NY 10012-3999. (212)343-6458. Fax: (212)343-4459. E-mail: dynamath@scholastic.com. Web site: www.scholastic.com/dynamath. **Editor:** Matt Friedman. **Art Director:** Vanessa Frazier. Monthly magazine. Estab. 1982. Circ. 200,000. Purpose is "to make learning math fun, challenging and uncomplicated for young minds in a very complex world."

Nonfiction Middle readers: animal, arts/crafts, cooking, fashion, games/puzzles, health, history, hobbies, how-to, humorous, math, multicultural, nature/environment, problem-solving, science, social issues, sports—all must relate to math and science topics and end with a 5 question math or science activity. Average length: 600 words.

How to Contact/Writers Nonfiction: Query with published clips, send ms. Responds to queries in 1 month; mss in 6 weeks. Publishes ms 4 months after acceptance. Will consider simultaneous submissions.

Illustration Buys 4 illustrations/issue. Illustration only: Query first; send résumé and tearsheets. Responds on submissions only if interested. Credit line given.

Terms Pays on acceptance. Buys all rights for mss, artwork, photographs. Originals returned to artist at job's completion. Pays $50-450 for stories.

EXPLORE

Pearson Education Australia, P.O. Box 1024 South Melbourne VIC 3205 Australia. (61)03 9811 2800. Fax: (61)03 9811 2999. E-mail: magazines@pearsoned.com.au. Web site: www.pearsoned.com.au/schools. Quarterly Magazine. Circ. 20,000. Pearson Education publishes "educational magazines that include a variety of nonfiction articles in a variety of genres and text types (interviews, diary, informational, recount, argumentative, etc.). They must be appropriate, factually correct and of high interest.

- *Explore* is a theme based publication. Check the Web site to see upcoming themes and deadlines.

Fiction Young readers, middle readers: adventure, animal, contemporary, fantasy, folktale, humorous, multicultural, nature/environment, problem-solving, suspense/mystery. Middle readers: science fiction, sports. Average word length: 400-1,000. Byline given.

Nonfiction Young readers, middle readers: animal, arts/crafts, biography, careers, cooking, health, history, hobbies, how-to, interview/profile, math, multicultural, nature/environment, problem-solving, science, social issues, sports, travel. Young readers: games/puzzles. Middle readers: concept, fashion, geography. Average word length: 200-600. Byline given.

Poetry Reviews poetry.

How to Contact/Writers Fiction/nonfiction: Send complete ms. Responds to queries in 1 month; mss in 3 months. Publishes ms 3 months after acceptance. Will consider simultaneous submissions and electronic submissions via disk or e-mail.

Photography Looking for photos to suit various themes; photos needed depend on stories. Model/property release required; captions required. Uses color, standard sized, prints, high resolution digital images and 35mm transparencies. Provide résumé, business card, promotional literature and tearsheets to be kept on file.

Terms Pays on publication. Buys first Australian rights. Pays $80-200 (Australian) for stories; $100-220 (Australian) for articles.

Tips "Check out our Web site for information about our publications." Also see listings for *Challenge* and *Comet*.

FACES, People, Places & Cultures

Cobblestone Publishing Company, 30 Grove St., Peterborough NH 03458. (603)924-7209. Fax: (603)924-7380. E-mail: facesmag@yahoo.com. Web site: www.cobblestonepub.com. **Editor:** Elizabeth Crooker Carpentiere. **Editorial Director:** Lou Warnycia. **Art Director:** Ann Dillon. Magazine published 9 times/year (September-May). Circ. 15,000. *Faces* is a theme-related magazine; writers should send for theme list before submitting ideas/queries. Each month a different world culture is featured through the use of feature articles, activities and photographs and illustrations.

• See Web site for 2006-2007 theme list for *Faces*.

Fiction Middle readers, young adults/teens: adventure, folktales, history, multicultural, plays, religious, travel. Does not want to see material that does not relate to a specific upcoming theme. Buys 9 mss/year. Maximum word length: 800. Byline given.

Nonfiction Middle readers and young adults/teens: animal, anthropology, arts/crafts, biography, cooking, fashion, games/puzzles, geography, history, how-to, humorous, interview/profile, nature/environment, religious, social issues, sports, travel. Does not want to see material not related to a specific upcoming theme. Buys 63 mss/year. Average word length: 300-600. Byline given.

Poetry Clear, objective imagery; up to 100 lines. Must relate to theme.

How to Contact/Writers Fiction/nonfiction: Query with published clips and 2-3 line biographical sketch. "Ideas should be submitted six to nine months prior to the publication date. Responses to ideas are usually sent approximately four months before the publication date." Guidelines on Web site.

Illustration Buys 3 illustrations/issue; buys 27 illustrations/year. Preferred theme or style: Material that is meticulously researched (most articles are written by professional anthropologists); simple, direct style preferred, but not too juvenile. Works on assignment only. Roughs required. Reviews ms/illustration packages from artists. Illustrations only: Send samples of b&w work. "Illustrators should consult issues of *Faces* to familiarize themselves with our needs." Responds to art samples only if interested. Samples returned with SASE. Original artwork returned at job's completion (upon written request). Credit line given.

Photography Wants photos relating to forthcoming themes.

Terms Pays on publication. Buys all rights for mss and artwork. Pays 20-25¢/word for articles/stories. Pays on an individual basis for poetry. Covers are assigned and paid on an individual basis. Pays illustrators $50-300 for color inside. Pays photographers per photo ($25-100 for color). Sample copy $4.95 with 7½ × 10½ SAE and 5 first-class stamps. Writer's/illustrator's/photo guidelines via Web site or free with SAE and 1 first-class stamp.

Tips "Writers are encouraged to study past issues of the magazine to become familiar with our style and content. Writers with anthropological and/or travel experience are particularly encouraged; *Faces* is about world cultures. All feature articles, recipes and activities are freelance contributions." Illustrators: "Submit b&w samples, not too juvenile. Study past issues to know what we look for. The illustration we use is generally for retold legends, recipes and activities."

THE FRIEND MAGAZINE

The Church of Jesus Christ of Latter-day Saints, 50 E. North Temple, Salt Lake City UT 84150-3226. (801)240-2210. **Editor:** Vivian Paulsen. **Art Director:** Mark Robison. Monthly magazine for 3-11 year olds. Estab. 1971. Circ. 275,000.

Nonfiction Publishes children's/true stories—adventure, ethnic, some historical, humor, mainstream, religious/inspirational, nature. Length: 1,000 words maximum.

Poetry Reviews poetry. Maximum length: 20 lines.

How to Contact/Writers Send complete ms. Responds to mss in 2 months.

Illustration Illustrations only: Query with samples; arrange personal interview to show portfolio; provide résumé and tearsheets for files.

Terms Pays on acceptance. Buys all rights for mss. Pays $100-250 (400 words and up) for stories; $250 for 400 words and up; $50 for poems; $15 for recipes, activities and games. Contributors are encouraged to send for sample copy for $1.50, 9 × 11 envelope and four 37-cent stamps. Free writer's guidelines.

Tips "*The Friend* is published by The Church of Jesus Christ of Latter-day Saints for boys and girls up to eleven years of age. All submissions are carefully read by the *Friend* staff, and those not accepted are returned within two months for SASE. Submit seasonal material at least one year in advance. Query letters and simultaneous submissions are not encouraged. Authors may request rights to have their work reprinted after their manuscript is published."

FUN FOR KIDZ

P.O. Box 227, Bluffton OH 45817-0227. (419)358-4610. Fax: (419)358-5027. Web site: www.funforkidz.com. **Articles Editor:** Marilyn Edwards. Bimonthly magazine. Estab. 2002. "*Fun for Kidz* is a magazine created for boys and girls ages 6-13, with youngsters 8, 9, and 10 the specific target age. The magazine is designed as an activity publication to be enjoyed by both boys and girls on the alternative months of *Hopscotch* and *Boys' Quest* magazines.''

• *Fun for Kidz* is theme-oriented. Send SASE for theme list and writer's guidelines.

Fiction Picture-oriented material, young readers, middle readers: adventure, animal, history, humorous, problem-solving, multicultural, nature/environment, sports. Average word length: 300-700.

Nonfiction Picture-oriented material, young readers, middle readers: animal, arts/crafts, cooking, games/puzzles, history, hobbies, how-to, humorous, problem-solving, sports, carpentry projects. Average word length: 300-700. Byline given.

Poetry Reviews poetry.

How to Contact/Writers Fiction/nonfiction: Send complete ms. Responds to queries in 2 weeks; mss in 5 weeks. Will consider simultaneous submissions. ''Will not respond to faxed/e-mailed queries, mss, etc.''

Illustration Works on assignment mostly. ''We are anxious to find artists capable of illustrating stories and features. Our inside art is pen & ink.'' Query with samples. Samples kept on file.

Photography ''We use a number of back & white photos inside the magazine; most support the articles used.''

Terms Pays on publication. Buys first American serial rights. Buys first American serial rights and photos for artwork. Pays 5/word; $10/poem or puzzle; $35 for art (full page); $25 for art (partial page). Pays illustrators $5-10 for b&w photos. Sample copies available for $5 (includes postage); $6 outside U.S.

Tips ''Our point of view is that every child deserves the right to be a child for a number of years before he or she becomes a young adult. As a result, *Fun for Kidz* looks for activities that deal with timeless topics, such as pets, nature, hobbies, science, games, sports, careers, simple cooking, and anything else likely to interest a child.''

GIRLS' LIFE

Monarch, 4517 Harford Rd., Baltimore MD 21214. (410)426-9600. Fax: (410)254-0991. E-mail: lizzie@girlslife.com. Web site: www.girlslife.com. **Associate Editor:** Lizzie Skurnick. Bimonthly magazine. Estab. 1994. General interest magazine for girls, ages 10-15.

Fiction Teen and 'tween.

Nonfiction Arts/crafts, fashion, interview/profile, social issues, sports, travel, hobbies, relationships. Buys appoximately 25 mss/year. Word length varies. Byline given.

How to Contact/Writers Nonfiction: Query with descriptive story ideas, résumé and published writing samples. Responds in 6 weeks. Publishes ms 3 months after acceptance. Will consider simultaneous submissions. No phone calls. No e-mails.

Illustration Uses color artwork only. Works on assignment only. Reviews ms/illustration packages from artists. Send ms with dummy. Illustration only: Query with samples; send tearsheets. Contact: Chun Kim, creative director. Responds only if interested. Samples returned with SASE; samples filed. Credit line given.

Photography Hires photographers. Send portfolio. Responds only if interested.

Terms Pays on publication. Original artwork returned at job's completion. Pays $500-800 for features; $150-350 for departments. Sample copies available for $5. Writer's guidelines for SASE or via Web site.

Tips ''Don't call with queries. Make query short and punchy.''

GUIDE MAGAZINE

Review and Herald Publishing Association, 55 W. Oak Ridge Dr., Hagerstown MD 21740. (301)393-4037. Fax: (301)393-4055. E-mail: guide@rhpa.org. Web site: www.guidemagazine.org. **Editor:** Randy Fishell. **Designer:** Brandon Reese. Weekly magazine. Estab. 1953. Circ. 32,000. ''Ours is a weekly Christian journal written for middle readers and young teens (ages 10-14), presenting true stories relevant to the needs of today's young person, emphasizing positive aspects of Christian living.''

Nonfiction Middle readers, young adults/teens: adventure, animal, character-building, contemporary, games/puzzles, humorous, multicultural, problem-solving, religious. ''We need true, or based on true, happenings, not merely true-to-life. Our stories and puzzles must have a spiritual emphasis.'' No violence. No articles. ''We always need humor and adventure stories.'' Buys 150 mss/year. Average word length: 500-600 minimum, 1,200-1,300 maximum. Byline given.

How to Contact/Writers Nonfiction: Send complete ms. Responds in 6 weeks. Will consider simultaneous submissions. ''We can pay half of the regular amount for reprints.'' Responds to queries/mss in 6 weeks. Credit line given. ''We encourage e-mail submissions.''

Terms Pays on acceptance. Buys first North American serial rights; first rights; one-time rights; second serial (reprint rights); simultaneous rights. Pays 6-12¢/word for stories and articles. ''Writer receives several complimentary copies of issue in which work appears.'' Sample copy free with 6×9 SAE and 2 first-class stamps. Writer's guidelines for SASE.

Tips ''Children's magazines want mystery, action, discovery, suspense and humor—no matter what the topic. For us, truth is stronger than fiction.''

GUIDEPOSTS FOR KIDS

1050 Broadway, Suite 6, Chesterton IN 46304. Fax: (219)926-3839. E-mail: gp4k@guideposts.org. Web site: www.gp4k.com. **Editor-in-Chief:** Mary Lou Carney. **Managing Editor:** Rosanne Tolin. **Art Coordinator:** Rose Pomeroy. Electronic magazine. Estab. 1998. 95,000 plus unique visitors/month. *"Guideposts for Kids* online by Guideposts for kids 6-13 years old (emphasis on upper end of that age bracket). It is a value-centered, electronic magazine that is *fun* to visit. The site hosts a long list of interactive and editorial features including games, puzzles, how-tos, stories, poems, facts and trivia.

• *Guideposts for Kids* is online only.

Fiction Middle readers: adventure, animal, contemporary, fantasy, folktales, historical, humorous, multicultural, nature/environment, problem-solving, science fiction, sports, suspense/mystery. Multicultural needs include: Kids in other cultures—school, sports, families. Does not want to see preachy fiction. "We want real stories about real kids doing real things—conflicts our readers will respect; resolutions our readers will accept. Problematic. Tight. Filled with realistic dialogue and sharp imagery. No stories about 'good' children always making the right decision. If present at all, adults are minor characters and *do not* solve kids' problems for them." Buys approximately 25 mss/year. Average word length: 200-900. Byline given.

Nonfiction Middle readers: animal, current events, games/puzzles, history, how-to, humorous, interview/profile, multicultural, nature/environment, problem-solving, profiles of kids, science, seasonal, social issues, sports. "Make nonfiction issue-oriented, controversial, thought-provoking. Something kids not only *need* to know but *want* to know as well." Buys 20 mss/year. Average word length: 200-1,300. Byline usually given.

How to Contact/Writers Fiction: Send complete ms. Nonfiction: Query or send ms. Responds to queries/mss in 6 weeks.

Photography Looks for "spontaneous, *real* kids in action shots."

Terms Pays on acceptance. Buys electronic and nonexclusive print rights. "Features range in payment from $50-200; fiction from $75-250. We pay higher rates for stories exceptionally well-written or well-researched. Regular contributors get bigger bucks, too." Writer's guidelines free for SASE.

Tips "Make your manuscript good, relevant and playful. No preachy stories about Bible-toting children. *Guideposts for Kids* is not a beginner's market. Study our e-zine magazine. (Sure, you've heard that before—but it's *necessary!*) Neatness *does* count. So do creativity and professionalism. SASE essential if sending a query by snail mail."

GUIDEPOSTS SWEET 16

1050 Broadway, Suite 6, Chesterton IN 46304. (219)929-4429. Fax: (219)926-3839. E-mail: gp4t@guideposts.org. Web site: www.gp4teens.com. E-mail: writers@sweet16mag.com. Web site: www.sweet16mag.com. **Editor-in-Chief:** Mary Lou Carney. **Art Director:** Meghan McPhail. **Art Coordinator:** Rose Pomeroy. Bimonthly magazine. Estab. 1998. *"Guideposts Sweet 16* is a general-interest magazine for teenage girls, ages 11-17. We are an inspirational publication that offers true, first-person stories about real teens. Our watchwords are 'wholesome,' 'current,' 'fun,' and 'inspiring.' We also publish shorter pieces on fashion, beauty, celebrity, boys, embarrassing moments, and advice columns."

Nonfiction Young adults: quizzes, DIYs, celebrity interviews, true stories, fashion and beauty. Average word length: 200-1,500. Byline sometimes given.

How to Contact/Writers Nonfiction: Query. Responds to queries/mss in 6 weeks. Will consider simultaneous submissions or electronic submission via e-mail. Send SASE for writer's guidelines.

Illustration Uses color artwork only. Works on assignment only. Reviews ms/illustration packages from artists. Query. Contact: Rose Pomeroy, art coordinator. Illustrations only: Query with samples. Responds only if interested. Samples kept on file. Credit line given.

Photography Buys photos separately. Wants location photography and stock; digital OK. Uses color prints and 35mm, $2\frac{1}{4} \times 2\frac{1}{4}$, or 8×10 transparencies. Query with samples; provide Web address. Responds only if interested.

Terms Pays on acceptance. Buys all rights for mss. Buys one-time rights for artwork. Original artwork returned at job's completion. Pays $300-500 for true stories; $100-300 for articles. Additional payment for photos accompanying articles. Pays illustrators $125-1,500 for color inside (depends on size). Pays photographers by the project (range: $100-1,000). Sample copies for $4.50 from: Guideposts, 39 Seminary Hill Rd., Carmel NY 10512. Attn: Special Handling.

Tips "Study our magazine! Language and subject matter should be current and teen-friendly. No preaching, please! (Your 'takeaway' should be inherent.) We are most in need of inspirational action/adventure, and relationship stories written in first-person and narrated by teenage girls. We need 'light' stories about finding a date and learning to drive, as well as catch-in-the-throat stories. We also need short (250-word) true stories with a miracle/'aha' ending for our 'Mysterious Moments' department. For illustrators: We get illustrators from two basic sources: submissions by mail and submissions by Internet. We also consult major illustrator reference books. We prefer color illustrations, 'on-the-edge' style. We accept art in almost any digital or reflective format."

HIGH ADVENTURE

Assemblies of God, 1445 N. Boonville Ave., Springfield MO 65802. (417)862-2781, ext. 4181. E-mail: rangers@ag .org. Web site: www.royalrangers.ag.org . **Editor:** John Hicks. Quarterly magazine, circulation aprox. 100,000, established 1971. Magazine is designed to provide boys ages 12-18 with interesting informative technical reading on subjects pertaining to sporting or outdoor activities such as camping, hiking, backpacking, wilderness survival, hunting, canoeing, or other similar topics. Preference given to informational/instructional articles or accounts of actual high-adventure events or activities. Items of historical or patriotic significance are also accepted.

Fiction Adventure, humorous, problem solving, religious, sports, travel. Maximum word length: 1,000.

Nonfiction Christian living, devotional, Holy Spirit, salvation, self-help, biography, missionary stories, news items, testimonies, inspirational stories based on true-life experiences, health, how-to, humorous, nature/environment, problem-solving, sports, travel.

How to Contact Send complete manuscript. Will consider simultaneous submissions. Samples returned with SASE by request. Prefer hardcopy and media (3.5, CD or via e-mail).

Terms Pays on publication. Buys first or all rights. Pays 6 cents per word for articles (typically $30-35 for one page; $60-65 for two pages); $25-30 for cartoons; $15 for puzzles, $5 for jokes. Sample copy free with 9×12 SASE. Free writer's/illustrator's guidelines with SASE.

HIGHLIGHTS FOR CHILDREN

803 Church St., Honesdale PA 18431. (570)253-1080. E-mail: eds@highlights-corp.com. Web site: www.highlig hts.com. **Contact:** Manuscript Coordinator. Editor: Christine French Clark. **Art Director:** Cindy Smith. Monthly magazine. Estab. 1946. Circ. 2.5 million. "Our motto is 'Fun With a Purpose.' We are looking for quality fiction and nonfiction that appeals to children, encourages them to read, and reinforces positive values. All art is done on assignment."

Fiction Picture-oriented material, young readers, middle readers: adventure, animal, contemporary, fantasy, folktales, history, humorous, multicultural, problem-solving, sports. Multicultural needs include first person accounts of children from other cultures and first-person accounts of children from other countries. Does not want to see war, crime, violence. "We see too many stories with overt morals." Would like to see more contemporary, multicultural and world culture fiction, mystery stories, action/adventure stories, humorous stories, and fiction for younger readers. Buys 150 mss/year. Average word length: 500-800. Byline given.

Nonfiction Picture-oriented material, young readers, middle readers: animal, arts/crafts, biography, careers, games/puzzles, geography, health, history, hobbies, how-to, interview/profile, multicultural, nature/environment, problem-solving, science, sports. Multicultural needs include articles set in a country *about* the people of the country. Does not want to see trendy topics, fads, personalities who would not be good role models for children, guns, war, crime, violence. "We'd like to see more nonfiction for younger readers—maximum of 500 words. We still need older-reader material, too—500-800 words." Buys 200 mss/year. Maximum word length: 800. Byline given.

How to Contact/Writers Send complete ms. Responds to queries in 1 month; mss in 6 weeks.

Illustration Buys 25-30 illustrations/issue. Preferred theme or style: Realistic, some stylization. Works on assignment only. Reviews ms/illustration packages from artists. Illustrations only: photocopies, promo sheet, tearsheets, or slides. Résumé optional. Portfolio only if requested. Contact: Art Director. Responds to art samples in 2 months. Samples returned with SASE; samples filed. Credit line given.

Terms Pays on acceptance. Buys all rights for mss. Pays $50 and up for unsolicited articles. Pays illustrators $1,000 for color cover; $25-200 for b&w inside, $100-500 for color inside. Sample copies $3.95 and 9×11 SASE with 4 first-class stamps. Writer's/illustrator's guidelines free with SASE and on Web site.

Tips "Know the magazine's style before submitting. Send for guidelines and sample issue if necessary." Writers: "At *Highlights* we're paying closer attention to acquiring more nonfiction for young readers than we have in the past. We're also looking for more material for kids ages 2-6." Illustrators: "Fresh, imaginative work encouraged. Flexibility in working relationships a plus. Illustrators presenting their work need not confine themselves to just children's illustrations as long as work can translate to our needs. We also use animal illustrations, real and imaginary. We need crafts, puzzles and any activity that will stimulate children mentally and creatively. We are always looking for imaginative cover subjects. Know our publication's standards and content by reading sample issues, not just the guidelines. Avoid tired themes, or put a fresh twist on an old theme so that its style is fun and lively. We'd like to see stories with subtle messages, but the fun of the story should come first. Write what inspires you, not what you think the market needs."

HOPSCOTCH, The Magazine for Girls

The Bluffton News Publishing and Printing Company, P.O. Box 164, Bluffton OH 45817-0164. (419)358-4610. Fax: (419)358-5027. Web site: hopscotchmagazine.com. **Editor:** Marilyn Edwards. Editorial Assistant: Brigette Hoff. Bimonthly magazine. Estab. 1989. Circ. 14,000. For girls from ages 6-12, featuring traditional subjects—

pets, games, hobbies, nature, science, sports, etc.—with an emphasis on articles that show girls actively involved in unusual and/or worthwhile activities.''

Fiction Picture-oriented material, young readers, middle readers: adventure, animal, history, humorous, nature/environment, sports, suspense/mystery. Does not want to see stories dealing with dating, sex, fashion, hard rock music. Buys 30 mss/year. Average word length: 300-700. Byline given.

Nonfiction Picture-oriented material, young readers, middle readers: animal, arts/crafts, biography, cooking, games/puzzles, geography, hobbies, how-to, humorous, math, nature/environment, science. Does not want to see pieces dealing with dating, sex, fashion, hard rock music. ''Need more nonfiction with quality photos about a *Hopscotch*-age girl involved in a worthwhile activity.'' Buys 46 mss/year. Average word length: 400-700. Byline given.

Poetry Reviews traditional, wholesome, humorous poems. Maximum word length: 300; maximum line length: 20. Will accept 6 submissions/author.

How to Contact/Writers All writers should consult the theme list before sending in articles. To receive a current theme list, send a SASE. Fiction: Send complete ms. Nonfiction: Query or send complete ms. Responds to queries in 2 weeks; mss in 5 weeks. Will consider simultaneous submissions.

Illustration Buys approximately 10 illustrations/issue; buys 60-70 articles/year. ''Generally, the illustrations are assigned after we have purchased a piece (usually fiction). Occasionally, we will use a painting—in any given medium—for the cover, and these are usually seasonal.'' Uses b&w artwork only for inside; color for cover. Reviews ms/illustration packages from artists. Query first or send complete ms with final art. Illustrations only: Send résumé, portfolio, client list and tearsheets. Responds to art samples only if interested and SASE in 1 month. Samples returned with SASE. Credit line given.

Photography Purchases photos separately (cover only) and with accompanying ms only. Looking for photos to accompany article. Model/property releases required. Uses 5×7, b&w prints; 35mm transparencies. Black & white photos should go with ms. Should show girl or girls ages 6-12.

Terms For mss: pays on publication. For mss, artwork and photos, buys first North American serial rights; second serial (reprint rights). Original artwork returned at job's completion. Pays 5¢/word and $5-10/photo. ''We always send a copy of the issue to the writer or illustrator.'' Text and art are treated separately. Pays $200 maximum for color cover; $25-35 for b&w inside. Sample copy for $5 and 8×12 SASE. Writer's/illustrator's/photo guidelines, theme list free for #10 SASE.

Tips ''Remember we publish only six issues a year, which means our editorial needs are extremely limited. Please look at our guidelines and our magazine . . . and remember, we use far more nonfiction than fiction. Guidelines and current theme list can be downloaded from our Web site. If decent photos accompany the piece, it stands an even better chance of being accepted. We believe it is the responsibility of the contributor to come up with photos. Please remember, our readers are 6-12 years—most are 8-10—and your text should reflect that. Many magazines try to entertain first and educate second. We try to do the reverse. Our magazine is more simplistic, like a book to be read from cover to cover. We are looking for wholesome, non-dated material.''

HORSEPOWER, Magazine for Young Horse Lovers

Horse Publications Group, Magazine for Young Horse Lovers, P.O. Box 670, Aurora ON L4G 4J9 Canada. (800)505-7428. Fax: (905)841-1530. E-mail: info@horse-canada.com. Web site: www.horse-canada.com. **Editor:** Susan Stafford. Bimonthly 16-page magazine, bound into Horse Canada, a bimonthly family horse magazine. Estab. 1988. Circ. 17,000. ''*Horsepower* offers how-to articles and stories relating to horse care for kids ages 6-16, with a focus on safety.''

  • *Horsepower* no longer accepts fiction.

Nonfiction Middle readers, young adults: arts/crafts, biography, careers, fashion, games/puzzles, health, history, hobbies, how-to, humorous, interview/profile, problem-solving, travel. Buys 6-10 mss/year. Average word length: 500-1,200. Byline given.

How to Contact/Writers Fiction: query. Nonfiction: send complete ms. Responds to queries in 6 months; mss in 3 months. Publishes ms 6 months after acceptance. Will consider simultaneous submissions, electronic submission via disk or e-mail, previously published work.

Illustration Buys 3 illustrations/year. Reviews ms/illustration packages from artists. Contact: Editor. Query with samples. Responds only if interested. Samples returned with SASE; samples kept on file. Credit line given.

Photography Look for photos of kids and horses, instructional/educational, relating to riding or horse care. Uses b&w and color 4×6, 5×7, matte or glossy prints. Query with samples. Responds only if interested. Accepts TIFF or JPEG 300 dpi, disk or e-mail. Children on horseback must be wearing riding helmets of photos cannot be published.

Terms Pays on publication. Buys one-time rights for mss. Original artwork returned at job's completion if SASE provided. Pays $50-75 for stories. Additional payment for ms/illustration packages and for photos accompanying articles. Pays illustrators $25-50 for color inside. Pays photographers per photo (range: $10-15). Sample copies for $4.50. Writer's/illustrator's/photo guidelines for SASE.

Tips ''Articles must be easy to understand, yet detailed and accurate. How-to or other educational features must be written by, or in conjunction with, a riding/teaching professional. Fiction is not encouraged, unless it is outstanding and teaches a moral or practical lesson. Note: preference will be given to Canadian writers and photographers due to Canadian content laws. Non-Canadian contributors accepted on a very limited basis.''

HUMPTY DUMPTY'S MAGAZINE

Children's Better Health Institute, 1100 Waterway Blvd., Indianapolis IN 46206. (317)636-8881. Fax: (317)684-8094. Web site: www.humptydumptymag.org. **Editor/Art Director:** Phyllis Lybarger. Magazine published 6 times/year. *HDM* is edited for children ages 4-6. It includes fiction (easy-to-reads; read alouds; rhyming stories; rebus stories), nonfiction articles (some with photo illustrations), poems, crafts, recipes, and puzzles. Content encourages development of better health habits.

- *Humpty Dumpty's* publishes material promoting health and fitness with emphasis on simple activities, poems and fiction.

Fiction Picture-oriented stories: adventure, animal, contemporary, fantasy, folktales, health, humorous, multicultural, nature/environment, problem-solving, science fiction, sports. Also, talking inanimate objects are very difficult to do well. Beginners (and maybe everyone) should avoid these.'' Buys 8-10 mss/year. Maximum word length: 300. Byline given.

Nonfiction Picture-oriented articles: animal, arts/crafts, concept, games/puzzles, health, how-to, humorous, nature/environment, no-cook recipes, science, social issues, sports. Buys 6-10 mss/year. Prefers very short nonfiction pieces—200 words maximum. Byline given. Send ms with SASE if you want ms returned.

How to Contact/Writers Send complete ms. Nonfiction: Send complete ms with bibliography if applicable. ''No queries, please!'' Responds to mss in 3 months. Send seasonal material at least 8 months in advance.

Illustration Buys 5-8 illustrations/issue; 30-48 illustrations/year. Preferred theme or style: Realistic or cartoon. Works on assignment only. Illustrations only. Query with slides, printed pieces or photocopies. Samples are not returned; samples filed. Responds to art samples only if interested. Credit line given.

Terms Writers: Pays on publication. Artists: Pays within 2 months. Buys all rights. ''One-time book rights may be returned if author can provide name of interested book publisher and tentative date of publication.'' Pays up to 22¢/word for stories/articles; payment varies for poems and activities. 10 complimentary issues are provided to author with check. Pays $275 for color cover illustration; $35-90 per page b&w inside; $70-155 for color inside. Sample copies for $1.75. Writer's/illustrator's guidelines free with SASE.

I.D.

Cook Communications Ministries, 4050 Lee Vance View, Colorado Springs CO 80918-7102. (719)536-0100. Fax: (719)536-3296. Web site: www.cookministries.org. **Editor:** Gail Rohlfing. **Designer:** Kelly Robinson. Weekly magazine. Estab. 1991. Circ. 100,000. ''*I.D.* is a class-and-home paper for senior high Sunday school students. Stories relate to Bible study.''

Fiction Young adults: religious.

How to Contact/Writers Currently not accepting new submissions.

Illustrations Buys 5 illustrations/year. Uses b&w and color artwork. Illustrations only: Query. Works on assignment only. Responds in 6 months.

Terms Pays on acceptance. Pays $50-300 for stories and articles.

Tips ''Sample copies of product are not available. *I.D.* is sold in Christian bookstores.''

INSIGHT

Because Life is Full of Decisions, 55 W. Oak Ridge Dr., Hagerstown MD 21740. (301)393-4038. Fax: (301)393-4055. E-mail: insight@rhpa.org. Web site: www.insightmagazine.org. **Contact:** Dwain Nielson Esmond. Weekly magazine. Estab. 1970. Circ. 14,000. ''Our readers crave true stories written by teens or written about teens that convey a strong spiritual point or portray a spiritual truth.'' 100% of publication aimed at teen market.

Nonfiction Young adults: animal, biography, fashion, health, humorous, interview/profile, multicultural, nature/environment, problem-solving, social issues, sports, travel: first-person accounts preferred. Buys 200 mss/year. Average word length: 500-1,500. Byline given.

Poetry Publishes poems written by teens. Maximum length: 250-500 words.

How to Contact/Writers Nonfiction: Send complete ms. Responds to queries in 2 months. Publishes ms 6-12 months after acceptance. Will consider simultaneous submissions, electronic submission via disk or modem, previously published work.

Illustration Works on assignment only. Reviews ms/illustration packages from artists. Query. Illustrations only: Query with samples. Samples kept on file. Credit line given.

Photography Looking for photos that will catch a young person's eye with unique elements such as juxtaposition. Model/property release required; captions not required but helpful. Uses color prints and 35mm, $2\frac{1}{4} \times 2\frac{1}{4}$,

4×5, 8×10 transparencies. Query with samples; provide business card, promotional literature or tearsheets to be kept on file. Responds only if interested.

Terms Pays on publication. Buys first North American serial rights for mss. Buys one-time rights for artwork and photos. Original artwork returned at job's completion. Pays $10-100 for stories/articles. Pays illustrators $100-300 for b&w (cover), color cover, b&w (inside), or color inside. Pays photographers by the project. Sample copies for 9×14 SAE and 4 first-class stamps.

Tips "Do your best to make your work look 'hip,' 'cool,' appealing to young people."

INSPIRATIONSTATION MAGAZINE

1119 S. Despelder #6, Grand Haven MI 49417. (616)846-7283. E-mail: kevinscottcollier@hotmail.com. Web site: www.inspirationstation.faithweb.com. **Editor and Art Director:** Kevin Scott Collier. Quarterly online magazine. Estab. 2005. Circ. 1,500 hits/issue. Magazine offers "Christian Children's fiction and original series characters created and written by Christian children's writers presented with illustrations meant to entertain and inspire kid." 100% of publication aimed at juvenile market.

Fiction Picture-oriented material: adventure, animal, fantasy, humorous, problem-solving, religious. Average word length: 500-1,000. Byline given.

How to Contact/Writers Query. Responds to queries in 1 week. Publishes ms 2 months after acceptance. Will consider submissions by disk or e-mail.

Terms Offers publication only. "No pay, all volunteer. Writers keep all rights to their works."

Tips Currently accepting very few submissions.

JACK AND JILL

Children's Better Health Institute, 1100 Waterway Blvd., P.O. Box 567, Indianapolis IN 46202. (317)634-1100. Fax: (317)684-8094. Web site: www.cbhi.org/magazines/jackandjill/index.shtml. **Editor:** Daniel Lee. **Art Director:** Jennifer Webber. Magazine for children ages 7-10, published 6 times/year. Estab. 1938. Circ. 360,000. "Write entertaining and imaginative stories *for* kids, not just *about* them. Writers should understand what is funny to kids, what's important to them, what excites them. Don't write from an adult 'kids are so cute' perspective. We're also looking for health and healthful lifestyle stories and articles, but don't be preachy."

Fiction Young readers and middle readers: adventure, contemporary, folktales, health, history, humorous, nature, sports. Buys 30-35 mss/year. Average word length: 700. Byline given.

Nonfiction Young readers, middle readers: animal, arts/crafts, cooking, games/puzzles, history, hobbies, how-to, humorous, interview/profile, nature, science, sports. Buys 8-10 mss/year. Average word length: 500. Byline given.

Poetry Reviews poetry.

How to Contact/Writers Fiction/nonfiction: Send complete ms. Queries not accepted. Responds to mss in 3 months. Guidelines by request with a #10 SASE.

Illustration Buys 15 illustrations/issue; 90 illustrations/year. Responds only if interested. Samples not returned; samples filed. Credit line given.

Terms Pays on publication; up to 17¢/word. Pays illustrators $275 for color cover; $35-90 for b&w, $70-155 for color inside. Pays photographers negotiated rate. Sample copies $1.25. Buys all rights to mss and one-time rights to photos.

Tips Publishes writing/art/photos by children.

KEYS FOR KIDS

CBH Ministries, Box 1001, Grand Rapids MI 49501-1001. (616)647-4971. Fax: (616)647-4950. E-mail: hazel@cbh ministries.org. Web site: www.cbhministries.org. **Fiction Editor:** Hazel Marett. Bimonthly devotional booklet. Estab. 1982. "This is a devotional booklet for children and is also widely used for family devotions."

Fiction Young readers, middle readers: religious. Buys 60 mss/year. Average word length: 400.

How to Contact/Writers Fiction: Send complete ms. Will consider simultaneous submissions, E-mail: submissio ns, previously published work.

Terms Pays on acceptance. Buys reprint rights or first rights for mss. Pays $25 for stories. Sample copies free for SAE 6×9 and 3 first-class stamps. Writer's guidelines for SASE.

Tips "Be sure to *follow* guidelines after studying sample copy of the publication."

KID ZONE

Scott Publications, LLC, 801 W. Norton Ave., Suite 200, Muskegon, MI 49441. (616)475-0414. Fax: (616)475-0411. E-mail: ahuizenga@scottpublications.com. Web site: www.scottpublications.com. **Articles Editor:** Anne Huizenga. Bi-monthly magazine. Estab. 2000. Circ. 65,000. Kid Zone is a crafts and activities magazine for 4-12 year olds. "We publish projects, trivia, recipes, games, puzzles, and kid-friendly features on a variety of topics."

Magazines

Nonfiction Picture-oriented material, middle readers: animal, arts/crafts, cooking, how-to, multicultural, nature/environment, science. Buys 20 mss/year. Average word length: 300-700. Byline given.

How to Contact/Writers Nonfiction: Send complete ms. Publishes ms 6-12 months after acceptance. Will consider simultaneous submissions, e-mail submissions.

Illustration Buys 6 illustrations/issue. Uses color artwork only. Works on assignment only. Illustrations only: Send postcard sample. Contact: Anne Huizenga, editor. Responds only if interested. Samples filed. Credit line sometimes given.

Photography Uses photos with accompanying ms only. Model/property release required. Uses color prints or digital images. Responds only if interested.

Terms Pays on publication. Buys world rights for mss. Buys first world rights for artwork. Pays $10-$50 for stories. Sample copies for $4.95 plus SASE. Writer's guidelines for SASE.

Tips ''Nonfiction writers who can provide extras to coincide with their submission (photos, games, project ideas, recipes) are more likely to be selected also make sure that you have actually looked at our magazine.''

▣ THE KIDS HALL OF FAME NEWS

The Kids Hall of Fame, 3 Ibsen Court, Dix Hills NY 11746. (631)242-9105. Fax: (631)242-8101. E-mail: VictoriaNesnick@TheKidsHallofFame.com. Web site: www.TheKidsHallofFame.com. **Publisher:** Victoria Nesnick. **Art/Photo Editor:** Amy Gilvary. Online publication. Estab. 1998. ''We spotlight and archive extraordinary positive achievements of contemporary and historical kids internationally under age 20. These inspirational stories are intended to provide positive peer role models and empower others to say, 'If that kid can do it, so can I,' or 'I can do better.' Our magazine is the prelude to The Kids Hall of Fame set of books (one volume per age) and museum.''

How to Contact/Writers Query with published clips or send complete mss with SASE for response. Go to Web site for sample stories and for The Kids Hall of Fame nomination form.

Tips ''Nomination stories must be positive and inspirational, and whenever possible, address the 7 items listed in the 'Your Story and Photo' page of our Web site. Request writers' guidelines and list of suggested nominees. Day and evening telephone queries acceptable.''

LADYBUG, The Magazine for Young Children

140 S. Dearborn, Suite 1450, Chicago IL 60603. (312)701-1720. **Editor:** Paula Morrow. **Art Director:** Suzanne Beck. Monthly magazine. Estab. 1990. Circ. 130,000. Literary magazine for children 2-6, with stories, poems, activities, songs and picture stories.

Fiction Picture-oriented material: adventure, animal, fantasy, folktales, humorous, multicultural, nature/environment, problem-solving, science fiction, sports, suspense/mystery. ''Open to any easy fiction stories.'' Buys 50 mss/year. Story length: limit 800 words. Byline given.

Nonfiction Picture-oriented material: activities, animal, arts/crafts, concept, cooking, humorous, math, nature/environment, problem-solving, science. Buys 35 mss/year. Story length: limit 800 words.

Poetry Reviews poems, 20-line maximum length; limit submissions to 5 poems. Uses lyrical, humorous, simple language.

How to Contact/Writers Fiction/nonfiction: Send complete ms. Queries not accepted. Responds to mss in 3 months. Publishes ms up to 3 years after acceptance. Will consider simultaneous submissions if informed. Submissions without SASE will be discarded.

Illustration Buys 12 illustrations/issue; 145 illustrations/year. Prefers ''bright colors; all media, but use watercolor and acrylics most often; same size as magazine is preferred but not required.'' To be considered for future assignments: Submit promo sheet, slides, tearsheets, color and b&w photocopies. Responds to art samples in 3 months. Submissions without SASE will be discarded.

Terms Pays on publication for mss; after delivery of completed assignment for illustrators. Rights purchased vary. Original artwork returned at job's completion. Pays 25¢/word for prose; $3/line for poetry. Pays $750 for color (cover) illustration, $50-100 for b&w (inside) illustration, $250/page for color (inside). Sample copy for $5. Writer's/illustrator's guidelines free for SASE or available on Web site, FAQ at www.cricketmag.com.

Tips Writers: ''Get to know several young children on an individual basis. Respect your audience. We want less cute, condescending or 'preachy-teachy' material. Less gratuitous anthropomorphism. More rich, evocative language, sense of joy or wonder. Keep in mind that people come in all colors, sizes, physical conditions. Be inclusive in creating characters. Set your manuscript aside for at least a month, then reread critically.'' Illustrators: ''Include examples, where possible, of children, animals, and—most important—action and narrative (i.e., several scenes from a story, showing continuity and an ability to maintain interest).'' (See listings for *Babybug*, *Cicada*, *Cricket*, *Muse* and *Spider*.)

LEADING EDGE

4198 JFSB, Provo UT 84602. (801)378-3553. E-mail: poetry@leadingedgemagazine.com. Web site: www.leading

Magazines

edgemagazine.com. **Nonfiction Director:** Greg Baum. **Fiction Director:** Tammy Whitfield. **Art Director:** Amanda Wallace. Twice yearly magazine. Estab. 1981. Circ. 500. ''We general publish fantasy and science fiction.'' 20% of publication aimed at juvenile market.

Fiction Young adults: fantasy, science fiction. Buys 16 mss/year. Average word length: up to 17,000. Byline given.

Nonfiction Young adults: science. Buys 2-3 mss/year. Average word length: up to 17,000. Byline given.

How to Contact/Writers Fiction/Nonfiction: Send complete ms. Responds to queries/mss in 4 months. Publishes ms 2-6 months after acceptance.

Illustration Buys 24 illustrations/issue; 48 illustrations/year. Uses b&w artwork only. Works on assignment only. Send manuscript with dummy. Contact: Amanda Wallace, art director. Illustrations only: Send postcard sample with portfolio, samples, SASE, URL. Responds only if interested. Samples returned with SASE; samples filed. Credit line given.

Terms Pays on publication. Buys first North American serial rights for mss. Buys first North American serial rights for artwork. Original artwork returned at job's completion. Pays $10-$100 for stories. Additional payment for ms/illustration packages. Pays illustrators $50 for color cover, $30 for b&w inside. Sample copies for $4.95. Writer's/illustrator's guidelines for SASE.

LISTEN, Drug-Free Possibilities for Teens

The Health Connection, 55 West Oak Ridge Dr., Hagerstown MD 21740. (301)393-4019. Fax: (301)393-3294. E-mail: listen@healthconnection.org. **Editor:** Céleste Perrino-Walker. Monthly magazine, 9 issues. Estab. 1948. Circ. 50,000. ''*Listen* offers positive alternatives to drug use for its teenage readers. Helps them have a happy and productive life by making the right choices.''

Nonfiction How-to, health, humorous, life skills, problem-solving, social issues, true stories, drug facts, drug-free living. Wants to see more factual articles on drug abuse. Buys 50 mss/year. Average word length: 800. Byline given.

How to Contact/Writers Fiction/nonfiction: Query. Responds to queries in 6 weeks; mss in 2 months. Will consider simultaneous submissions, e-mail and previously published work.

Illustration Buys 3-6 illustrations/issue; 50 illustrators/year. Reviews ms/illustration packages from artists. Manuscript/illustration packages and illustration only: Query. Contact: Ron J. Pride, designer. Responds only if interested. Originals returned at job's completion. Samples returned with SASE. Credit line given.

Photography Purchases photos from freelancers. Photos purchased with accompanying ms only. Uses color and b&w photos; digital, 35mm, transparencies or prints. Query with samples. Looks for ''youth oriented— action (sports, outdoors), personality photos.''

Terms Pays on acceptance. Buys exclusive magazine rights for mss. Buys one-time rights for artwork and photographs. Pays $80-100 for stories/articles. Pays illustrators $500 for color cover; $75-225 for b&w inside; $135-450 for color inside. Pays photographers by the project (range: $125-500); pays per photo (range: $125-500). Additional payment for ms/illustration packages and photos accompanying articles. Sample copy for $2 and 9×12 SASE and 2 first class stamps. Writer's guidelines free with SASE.

Tips ''*Listen* is a magazine for teenagers. It encourages development of good habits and high ideals of physical, social and mental health. It bases its editorial philosophy of primary drug prevention on total abstinence from tobacco, alcohol, and other drugs. Because it is used extensively in public high school classes, it does not accept articles and stories with overt religious emphasis. Four specific purposes guide the editors in selecting materials for *Listen*: (1) To portray a positive lifestyle and to foster skills and values that will help teenagers deal with contemporary problems, including smoking, drinking, and using drugs. This is *Listen*'s primary purpose. (2) To offer positive alternatives to a lifestyle of drug use of any kind. (3) To present scientifically accurate information about the nature and effects of tobacco, alcohol, and other drugs. (4) To report medical research, community programs, and educational efforts which are solving problems connected with smoking, alcohol, and other drugs. Articles should offer their readers activities that increase one's sense of self-worth through achievement and/or involvement in helping others. They are often categorized by three kinds of focus: (1) Hobbies. (2) Recreation. (3) Community Service.''

MUSE

Carus Publishing, 140 S. Dearborn St., Suite 1450, Chicago IL 60603. (312)701-1720. Fax: (312)701-1728. E-mail: muse@caruspub.com. Web site: www.cricketmag.com. **Editor:** Diana Lutz. **Art Director:** Karen Kohn. **Photo Editor:** Carol Parden. Estab. 1996. Circ. 50,000. ''The goal of *Muse* is to give as many children as possible access to the most important ideas and concepts underlying the principal areas of human knowledge. Articles should meet the highest possible standards of clarity and transparency aided, wherever possible, by a tone of skepticism, humor, and irreverence.''

Nonfiction Middle readers, young adult: animal, arts, history, math, nature/environment, problem-solving, science, social issues.

How to Contact/Writers *Muse* is not accepting unsolicited mss or queries. All articles are commissioned. To be considered for assignments, experienced science writers may send a résumé and 3 published clips.

Illustration Buys 6 illustrations/issue; 40 illustrations/year. Uses color artwork only. Works on assignment only. Responds only if interested. Samples returned with SASE. Credit line given.

Photography Needs vary. Query with samples to photo editor.

MY FRIEND, The Catholic Magazine for Kids

Pauline Books & Media, 50 Saint Pauls Ave., Boston MA 02130-3491. (617)522-8911. Fax: (617)541-9805. E-mail: myfriend@pauline media.org. Web site: www.myfriendmagazine.org. **Editor:** Sister Maria Grace Dateno, FSP. Monthly magazine (not published in July and August). Estab. 1979. Circ. 8,000. *"My Friend, The Catholic Magazine for Kids*, is a 32-page monthly Catholic magazine for boys and girls ages 7-12, designed to reinforce the growth of the child's faith and friendship with Jesus. Its pages are packed with true and fictional stories, puzzles, crafts, comics, contests, etc. Together with its Web page, *My Friend* provided kids with a fun way to receive a solid grounding in the faith and values that are most important for life and for eternity."

Fiction Young readers, middle readers: adventure, Christmas, contemporary, humorous, multicultural, nature/environment, problem-solving, religious, sports. Buys 30 mss/year. Average word length: 750-1,100. Byline given.

Nonfiction Young readers, middle readers: humorous, interview/profile, media literacy, problem-solving, religious, multicultural, social issues. Does not want to see material that is not compatible with Catholic values. Staff writes doctrinal articles and prepares puzzles. Buys 10 mss/year. Average word length: 450-750. Byline given.

How to Contact/Writers Fiction/nonfiction: Send complete ms. Responds to mss in 2 months. See complete writers' guidelines and theme list on Web site. Click on "For Contributors" at the botten of the page.

Terms Pays on acceptance for mss. Buys first rights for mss; variable for artwork. Original artwork returned at job's completion. Pays $80-150 for stories/articles. Sample copy $2 with 9 × 12 SAE and 4 first-class stamps. Writer's guidelines and theme list free with SASE.

Tips Writers: "We are looking for stories that immediately grab the imagination of the reader. Good dialogue, realistic character development, and current lingo are necessary. Not all the stories of each issue have to be directly related to the theme. We continue to need stories that are simply fun and humorous."

NATIONAL GEOGRAPHIC KIDS

National Geographic Society, 1145 17th St. NW, Washington DC 20036-4688. (202)857-7000. Fax: (202)775-6112. Web site: www.nationalgeographic.com/ngkids. **Editor:** Melina Bellows. **Art Director:** Jonathan Halling. **Photo Director:** Jay Sumner. Monthly magazine. Estab. 1975. Circ. 900,000.

NATURE FRIEND MAGAZINE

2673 Twp. Rd., Sugarcreek OH 44681. (330)852-1900. Fax: (330)852-3285. **Articles Editor:** Marvin Wengerd. Monthly magazine. Estab. 1983. Circ. 13,000.

Fiction Picture-oriented material, conversational, no talking animal stories.

Nonfiction Picture-oriented material: animal, how-to, nature, photo-essays. No talking animal stories. No evolutionary material. Buys 50 mss/year. Average word length: 500. Byline given.

Photography Pays $75 for front cover, $50 for back cover, $75 for centerfold, $15-30 for text photos. Submit on CD with color printout. Photo guidelines free with SASE.

Terms Pays on publication. Buys one-time rights. Pays $15 minimum. Payment for illustrations: $15-80/b&w, $50-100/color inside. Two sample copies and writer's guidelines for $5 with 9 × 12 SAE and $2 postage.

Tips Needs stories about unique animals or nature phenomena. "Please examine samples and writer's guide before submitting." Current needs: science and nature experiments (for ages 8-12) with art of photographs for the Learning by Doing feature; hands-on material.

NEW MOON: The Magazine for Girls & Their Dreams

New Moon Publishing, Inc., 2W. First St., #101, Duluth MN 55802. (218)728-5507. Fax: (218)728-0314. E-mail: girl@newmoon.org. Web site: www.newmoon.org. **Managing Editor:** Kate Freeborn. Bimonthly magazine. Estab. 1992. Circ. 30,000. *"New Moon* is for every girl who wants her voice heard and her dreams taken seriously. *New Moon* portrays strong female role models of all ages, backgrounds and cultures now and in the past."

Fiction Middle readers, young adults: adventure, contemporary, fantasy, folktales, history, humorous, multicultural, nature/environment, problem-solving, religious, science fiction, sports, suspense/mystery, travel. Buys 6 mss/year. Average word length: 1,200-1,600. Byline given.

Nonfiction Middle readers, young adults: animal, arts/crafts, biography, careers, cooking, games/puzzles, health, history, hobbies, humorous, interview/profile, math, multicultural, nature/environment, problem-solving, science, social issues, sports, travel, stories about real girls. Does not want to see how-to stories. Wants

Magazines

more stories about real girls doing real things written *by girls*. Buys 6-12 adult-written mss/year; 30 girl-written mss/year. Average word length: 600. Byline given.

How to Contact/Writers Fiction/Nonfiction: Does not return or acknowledge unsolicited mss. Send copies only. Responds only if interested. Will consider simultaneous and e-mail submissions.

Illustration Buys 6-12 illustrations/year from freelancers. *New Moon* seeks 4-color cover illustrations. Reviews ms/illustrations packages from artists. Query. Submit ms with rough sketches. Illustration only: Query; send portfolio and tearsheets. Samples not returned; samples filed. Responds in 6 months only if interested. Credit line given.

Terms Pays on publication. Buys all rights for mss. Buys one-time rights, reprint rights, for artwork. Original artwork returned at job's completion. Pays 6-12¢/word for stories and articles. Pays in contributor's copies. Pays illustrators $400 for color cover; $50-300 for color inside. Sample copies for $6.50. Writer's/cover art guidelines for SASE or available on Web site.

Tips "Please refer to a copy of *New Moon* to understand the style and philosophy of the magazine. Writers and artists who understand our goals have the best chance of publication. We're looking for stories about real girls, women's careers, and historical profiles. We publish girl's and women's writing only." Publishes writing/art/photos by girls.

NICK JR. FAMILY MAGAZINE

Nickelodeon Magazine Group, 1633 Broadway, 7th Floor, New York NY 10019. (212)654-7707. Fax: (212)654-4840. Web site: www.nickjr.com/magazine. **Deputy Editor:** Wendy Smolen. **Creative Director:** Don Morris. Published 9 times/year. Estab. 1999. Circ. 1,100,000. A magazine where kids play to learn and parents learn to play. 30% of publication aimed at juvenile market.

Fiction Picture-oriented material: adventure, animal, contemporary, humorous, multicultural, nature/environment, problem-solving, sports. Byline sometimes given.

Nonfiction Picture-oriented material: animal, arts/crafts, concept, cooking, games/puzzles, hobbies, how-to, humorous, math, multicultural, nature/environment, problem-solving, science, social issues, sports. Byline sometimes given.

How to Contact/Writers Fiction/nonfiction: Query or submit complete ms. Responds to queries/mss in 3-12 weeks.

Illustration Only interested in agented material. Works on assignment only. Reviews ms/illustration packages from artists. Query or send ms with dummy. Contact: Don Morris, creative director. Illustrations only: arrange portfolio review; send résumé, promo sheet and portfolio. Responds only if interested. Samples not returned; samples kept on file. Credit line sometimes given.

Tips "Writers should study the magazine before submitting stories. Read-Together Stories must include an interactive element that invited children to participate in telling the story: a repeating line, a fill-in-the-blank rhyme, or rebus pictures."

ODYSSEY, Adventures in Science

Cobblestone Publishing Company, 30 Grove St., Suite C, Peterborough NH 03458. (603)924-7209. Fax: (603)924-7380. E-mail: odyssey@cobblestone.mv.com. Web site: www.odysseymagazine.com. **Editor:** Elizabeth E. Lindstrom. **Executive Director:** Lou Waryncia. **Art Director:** Ann Dillon. Magazine published 9 times/year. Estab. 1979. Circ. 22,000. Magazine covers earth, general science and technology, astronomy and space exploration for children ages 10-16. All material must relate to the theme of a specific upcoming issue in order to be considered.

• *Odyssey* themes can be found on Web site: www.odysseymagazine.com.

Fiction Middle readers and young adults/teens: science fiction, science, astronomy. Does not want to see anything not theme-related. Average word length: 900-1,200 words.

Nonfiction Middle readers and young adults/teens: interiors, activities. Don't send anything not theme-related. Average word length: 750-1,200, depending on section article is used in.

How to Contact/Writers Prefers hard copy queries to e-mail. "A query must consist of all of the following to be considered (please use nonerasable paper): a brief cover letter stating the subject and word length of the proposed article; a detailed one-page outline explaining the information to be presented in the article; an extensive bibliography of materials/interviews the author intends to use in preparing the article; a SASE. Writers new to *Odyssey* should send a writing sample with query. If you would like to know if your query has been received, please also include a stamped postcard that requests acknowledgment of receipt. In all correspondence, please include your complete address as well as a telephone number and e-mail address where you can be reached. A writer may send as many queries for one issue as he or she wishes, but each query must have a separate cover letter, outline, bibliography, and SASE. Telephone queries are not accepted. Handwritten queries will not be considered. Queries may be submitted at any time."

Illustration Buys 3 illustrations/issue; 27 illustrations/year. Works on assignment only. Reviews ms/illustration

Magazines

packages from artists. Query. Contact: Beth Lindstrom, editor. Illustration only: Query with samples. Send tearsheets, photocopies. Responds in 2 weeks. Samples returned with SASE; samples not filed. Original artwork returned upon job's completion (upon written request).

Photography Wants photos pertaining to any of our forthcoming themes. Uses color prints; 35mm transparencies, digital images. Photographers should send unsolicited photos by mail on speculation.

Terms Pays on publication. Buys all rights for mss and artwork. Pays 20-25¢/word for stories/articles. Covers are assigned and paid on an individual basis. Pays photographers per photo ($15-100 for b&w; $25-100 for color). Sample copy for $4.95 and SASE with $2 postage. Writer's/illustrator's/photo guidelines for SASE. (See listings for *AppleSeeds*, *Calliope*, *Cobblestone*, *Dig*, and *Faces*.)

ON COURSE, A Magazine for Teens

General Council of the Assemblies of God, 1445 Boonville Ave., Springfield MO 65802-1894. (417)862-2781. Fax: (417)862-1693. E-mail: oncourse@ag.org. Web site: www.oncourse.ag.org. **Editor:** Amber Weigand-Buckley. **Art Director:** James Gerhold. Quarterly magazine. Estab. 1991. Circ. 160,000. *On Course* is a magazine to empower students to grow in a real-life relationship with Christ.

   • *On Course* no longer uses illustrations, only photos.

Fiction Young adults: Christian discipleship, contemporary, humorous, multicultural, problem-solving, sports. Average word length: 800. Byline given.

Nonfiction Young adults: careers, interview/profile, multicultural, religion, social issues, college life, Christian discipleship.

How to Contact/Writers Works on assignment basis only. Resumes and writing samples will be considered for inclusion in Writer's File to receive story assignments.

Photography Buys photos from freelancers. "Teen life, church life, college life; unposed; often used for illustrative purposes." Model/property releases required. Uses color glossy prints and 35mm or 2¼×2¼ transparencies. Query with samples; send business card, promotional literature, tearsheets or catalog. Responds only if interested.

Terms Pays on acceptance. Buys first or reprint rights for mss. Buys one-time rights for photographs. Pays 10¢/word for stories/articles. Pays illustrators and photographers "as negotiated." Sample copies free for 9×11 SAE. Writer's guidelines for SASE.

PASSPORT

Sunday School Curriculum, 6401 The Paseo, Kansas City MO 64131-1284. (816)333-7000. Fax: (816)333-4439. E-mail: sweatherwax@nazarene.org. Web site: www.nazarene.org. **Editor:** Mike Wonch. Weekly take-home paper. "*Passport* looks for a casual, witty approach to Christian themes. We want hot topics relevant to pre-teens."

   • Not accepting submissions at this time.

POCKETS, Devotional Magazine for Children

The Upper Room, 1908 Grand Ave., P.O. Box 340004, Nashville TN 37203-0004. (615)340-7333. Fax: (615)340-7267. E-mail: pockets@upperroom.org. Web site: www.pockets.org. **Articles/Fiction Editor:** Lynn W. Gilliam. **Art Director:** Chris Schechner, 408 Inglewood Dr., Richardson TX 75080. Magazine published 11 times/year. Estab. 1981. Circ. 99,000. "*Pockets* is a Christian devotional magazine for children ages 6-11. Stories should help children experience a Christian lifestyle that is not always a neatly wrapped moral package but is open to the continuing revelation of God's will."

Fiction Picture-oriented, young readers, middle readers: adventure, contemporary, occasional folktales, multicultural, nature/environment, problem-solving, religious. Does not accept violence or talking animal stories. Buys 25-30 mss/year. Average word length: 600-1,400. Byline given. *Pockets* also accepts short-short stories (no more than 600 words) for children 5-7. Buys 11 mss/year.

Nonfiction Picture-oriented, young readers, middle readers: cooking, games/puzzles. "*Pockets* seeks biographical sketches of persons, famous or unknown, whose lives reflect their Christian commitment, written in a way that appeals to children." Does not accept how-to articles. "Our nonfiction reads like a story." Multicultural needs include: stories that feature children of various racial/ethnic groups and do so in a way that is true to those depicted. Buys 10 mss/year. Average word length: 400-1,000. Byline given.

How to Contact/Writers Fiction/nonfiction: Send complete ms. "Do not accept queries." Responds to mss in 6 weeks. Will consider simultaneous submissions.

Illustration Buys 40-50 illustrations/issue. Preferred theme or style: varied; both 4-color. Works on assignment only. Illustrations only: Send promo sheet, tearsheets.

POGO STICK

Stone Lightning Press, 1300 Kicker Rd., Tuscaloosa AL 35404. (205)553-2284. E-mail: lillskm@gmail.com.

Magazines

Articles Editor: Lillian Kopaska-Merkel. **Art Director:** Rain Kennedy. Quarterly digest-sized with saddle stitching. Estab. 2004. Publishes "fantasy and realistic fiction, poems, short stories, jokes, riddles, and art for and by kids under 17." Entire publication aimed at juvenile market.

Fiction Young Readers: adventure, animal, fantasy, humorous, multicultural, nature/environment, problem-solving, suspense/mystery. Middle Readers: adventure, animal, fantasy, humorous, multicultural, nature/environment, suspense/mystery. Young Adults/Teens: adventure, animal, fantasy, humorous, multicultural, nature/environment, suspense/mystery. Average word length: 50-2,000. Byline given.

Nonfiction Young readers, middle readers, young adults/teens: arts/crafts, games/puzzles.

Poetry Seeks fantasy, child-appropriate poetry. Max length: 100 words. Max of 6 poems/submission.

How To Contact/Writers Fiction: Send complete ms. Responds to queries in 2 months. Considers simultaneous submissions.

Illustration Black & white artwork only. For first contact, query with samples. Contact: Rain Kennedy, art director. Responds in 2 months. Samples returned with SASE. Credit line given.

Terms Pays on publication. Buys first North American serial rights.Pays with contributor copies. Sample copies available for $3.50. Writer's guidelines free for SASE. Illustrator's guidelines free for SASE. Publishes work by children.

Tips "Always read guidelines first."

ꭴ POSITIVE TEENS

Accentuating the Positive in Today's Teens, P.O. Box 301126, Boston MA 02130-0010. (617)522-2961. Fax: (617)522-2961. E-mail: info@positiveteensmag.com. Web site: www.positiveteensmag.com. **Manuscript Acquisition:** Susan Manning, publisher/editor-in-chief. **Art Acquisition:** Sean Collins. Bimonthly magazine. Estab. 1997. Circ. 60,000. "*Positive Teens* magazine uses its pages to accentuate the positive in the talents, lives, skill and voices of the youth of today. *Positive Teens* encourages young adults from 12-21 to take an interest in issues directly or indirectly affecting their schools and community, their future and the world. *Positive Teens* magazine is inclusive of all youth, male and female, of all ethnic, racial and religious groups, of all sexual orientations and all physical abilities."

Fiction Buys 2-5 mss/year. 1,200 words max.

Nonfiction Young adults/teens: biography, careers, games/puzzles, health, history, hobbies, how-to, interview/profile, multicultural, problem-solving, social issues, sports, travel. Buys 3-10 mss/year from freelancers. Average word length/articles: 500-1,200. Byline given.

Poetry No length requirements. Limit submissions to 6-8 poems.

How to Contact/Writers Fiction: query; nonfiction: Send complete mss. Responds to queries/mss in 2-3 months. Publishes ms 1-3 months after acceptance. Will consider simultaneous submission and e-mail submissions.

Illustration Buys 2-4 illustrations/year. Review ms/illustration packages from youth only. Send ms with dummy to Susan Manning, publisher. Responds in 1-2 months only if interested. Samples returned with SASE; samples filed. Credit line given.

Photography Uses photos relating to teen and young adult interests. Model/property release required; captions required. Uses 4×6 and 8¾×11½ prints. Send unsolicited photos by mail. Responds in 1-2 months only if interested.

Terms Pays on publication. Buys reprint rights, exclusive for 18 months. Originals returned at job's completion with SASE. Pays $5-35 for stories/articles. Pays illustrators $5-25 for b&w color/insider. Pays photographers $5-25. Sample $3 for back issues; $4.50 for new issues plus $1.35 postage. Writer's/illustrator's/photographer's guidelines for SASE.

Tips "Adult writers (those over the age of 25) should understand that the audience *Positive Teens* is targeting is teens and young adults, not children. Articles that we receive with a child's theme would never be considered for publication. Also, we prefer nonfiction article from adult writers—interviews, lifestyle, sports, etc. *Positive Teens* magazine featured artwork created by teenagers and young adults, but we would consider illustrations or photographs that would be an accompaniment to a written article."

PRIMARY STREET

Urban Ministries, Inc., 1551 Regency Ct., Columet City IL 60409. (708)868-7100. Web site: www.urbanministries .com. **Articles Editor:** Judith St. Clair Hull, Ph.D. Quarterly. Estab. 1975. Circ. 50,000. "We are looking for Sunday school curriculum that is relevant for African American children."

Fiction Young readers: religious.

Nonfiction Young readers: religious. Buys 12 lesson mss/year. Average length: 5,800 characters-5,900 characters.

How to Contact/Writers Nonfiction: Query with published clips. Responds to queries in 3 months. Publishes ms 1 year after acceptance.

Terms Pays on acceptance. Buys all rights for mss.

Tips "We are looking for born again African-American writers who are able to convey the way of salvation to children."

RANGER RICK

National Wildlife Federation, 11100 Wildlife Center Dr., Reston VA 20190. (703)438-6000. Web site: www.nwf. org/rangerrick. **Editor:** Gerald Bishop. **Design Director:** Donna Miller. Monthly magazine. Circ. 600,000. ''Our audience ranges from ages 7 to 12, though we aim the reading level of most material at 9-year-olds or fourth graders.''

● Ranger Rick does not accept submissions or queries.

Fiction Middle readers: animal (wildlife), fables, fantasy, humorous, multicultural, plays, science fiction. Average word length: 900. Byline given.

Nonfiction Middle readers: animal (wildlife), conservation, humorous, nature/environment, outdoor adventure, travel. Buys 15-20 mss/year. Average word length: 900. Byline given.

How to Contact/Writers No longer accepting unsolicited queries/mss.

Illustration Buys 5-7 illustrations/issue. Preferred theme: nature, wildlife. Works on assignment only. Illustrations only: Send résumé, tearsheets. Responds to art samples in 2 months.

Terms Pays on acceptance. Buys exclusive first-time worldwide rights and non-exclusive worldwide rights thereafter to reprint, transmit, and distribute the work in any form or medium. Original artwork returned at job's completion. Pays up to $700 for full-length of best quality. For illustrations, buys one-time rights. Pays $150-250 for b&w; $250-1,200 for color (inside, per page) illustration. Sample copies for $2.15 plus a 9×12 SASE.

READ

Weekly Reader Corporation, 200 First Stamford Place, P.O. Box 120023, Stamford CT 06912-0023. Fax: (203)705-1661. Web site: www.weeklyreader.com. **Editor:** Melanie Milgram. **Senior Editor:** Debra Nevins. Magazine published 18 times during the school year. Language arts periodical for use in classrooms for students ages 12-16; motivates students to read and teaches skills in listening, comprehension, speaking, writing and critical thinking.

Fiction Wants short stories, narratives and plays to be used for classroom reading and discussions. Middle readers, young adult/teens: adventure, animal, contemporary, fantasy, folktales, history, humorous, multicultural, nature/environment, sports. Average word length: 1,000-2,500.

Nonfiction Middle readers, young adult/teen: animal, games/puzzles, history, humorous, problem solving, social issues.

How to Contact Responds to queries in 6 weeks. ''*READ* magazine is currently not accepting unsolicited manuscripts in any category.''

Tips ''We especially like plot twists and surprise endings. Stories should be relevant to teens and contain realistic conflicts and dialogue. Plays should have at least 12 speaking parts for classroom reading. Avoid formula plots, trite themes, underage material, stilted or profane language, and sexual suggestion. Get to know the style of our magazine as well as our teen audience. They are very demanding and require an engaging and engrossing read. Grab their attention, keep the pace and action lively, build to a great climax, and make the ending satisfying and/or surprising. Make sure characters and dialogue are realistic. Do not use cliché. Make the writing fresh—simple, yet original. Obtain guidelines first. Be sure submissions are relevant.''

SCIENCE WEEKLY

Science Weekly Inc., P.O. Box 70638, Chevy Chase MD 20813. (301)680-8804. Fax: (301)680-9240. E-mail: scienceweekly@erols.com. Web site: www.scienceweekly.com. **Publisher:** Dr. Claude Mayberry. Magazine published 14 times/year. Estab. 1984. Circ. 200,000.

● *Science Weekly* uses freelance writers to develop and write an entire issue on a single science topic. Send résumé only, not submissions. Authors must be within the greater D.C., Virginia, Maryland area. *Science Weekly* works on assignment only.

Nonfiction Young readers, middle readers, (K-6th grade): science/math education, education, problem-solving.

Terms Pays on publication. Prefers people with education, science and children's writing background. *Send résumé only.* Samples copies free with SAE and 3 first-class stamps.

SCIENCE WORLD

Scholastic Inc., 557 Broadway, New York NY 10012-3999. (212)343-6100. Fax: (212)343-6945. E-mail: scienceworl d@scholastic.com. **Editor:** Patty Janes. **Art Director:** Felix Batcup. Magazine published biweekly during the school year. Estab. 1959. Circ. 400,000. Publishes articles in Life Science/Health, Physical Science/Technology, Earth Science/Environment/Astronomy for students in grades 7-10. The goal is to make science relevant for teens.

● *Science World* publishes a separate teacher's edition with lesson plans and skills pages to accompany feature articles.

Nonfiction Young adults/teens: animal, concept, geography, health, nature/environment, science. Multicultural needs include: minority scientists as role models. Does not want to see stories without a clear news hook. Buys

20 mss/year. Average word length: 800-1,000. Byline given. Currently does not accept unsolicited mss.
How to Contact/Writers Nonfiction: Query with published clips and/or brief summaries of article ideas. Responds only if interested. No unsolicited mss.
Illustration Buys 2 illustrations/issue; 28 illustrations/year. Works on assignment only. Illustration only: Query with samples, tearsheets. Responds only if interested. Samples returned with SASE; samples filed ''if we use them.'' Credit line given.
Photography Model/property releases required; captions required including background information. Provide résumé, business card, promotional literature or tearsheets to be kept on file. Responds only if interested.
Terms Pays on acceptance. Buys all rights for mss/artwork. Originals returned to artist at job's completion. For stories/articles, pays $200. Pays photographers per photo.

Ⓐ SEVENTEEN MAGAZINE
Hearst Magazines, 1440 Broadway, 13th Floor, New York NY 10018. (917)934-6500. Fax: (917)934-6574. Web site: www.seventeen.com. Monthly magazine. Estab. 1944. ''We reach 14.5 million girls each month. Over the past five decades, *Seventeen* has helped shape teenage life in America. We represent an important rite of passage, helping to define, socialize and empower young women. We create notions of beauty and style, proclaim what's hot in popular culture and identify social issues.''
Nonfiction Young adults: careers, cooking, hobbies, how-to, humorous, interview/profile, multicultural, social issues. Buys 7-12 mss/year. Word length: Varies from 200-2,000 words for articles. Byline sometimes given.
Illustration Only interested in agented material. Buys 10 illustrations/issue; 120 illustrations/year. Works on assignment only. Reviews ms/illustration packages. Illustrations only: Query with samples. Responds only if interested. Samples not returned; samples filed. Credit line given.
Photography Looking for photos to match current stories. Model/property releases required; captions required. Uses color, 8×10 prints; 35mm, 2¼×2¼, 4×5 or 8×10 transparencies. Query with samples or résumé of credits, or submit portfolio for review. Responds only if interested.
Terms Pays on publication. Buys first North American serial rights, first rights or all rights for mss. Buys exclusive rights for 3 months; online rights for photos. Original artwork returned at job's completion. Pays $1/word for articles/stories (varies by experience). Additional payment for photos accompanying articles. Pays illustrators/photographers $150-500. Sample copies not available. Writer's guidelines for SASE.
Tips Send for guidelines before submitting.

SHARING THE VICTORY, Fellowship of Christian Athletes
8701 Leeds, Kansas City MO 64129. (816)921-0909. Fax: (816)921-8755. Web site: www.sharingthevictory.com. **Articles/Photo Editor:** Jill Ewert. **Art Director:** Cameron Thorp. Magazine published 9 times a year. Estab. 1982. Circ. 80,000. Purpose is to serve as a ministry tool of the Fellowship of Christian Athletes (FCA) by aligning with its mission to present to athletes and coaches and all whom they influence, the challenge and adventure of receiving Jesus Christ as Savior and Lord.
Nonfiction Young adults/teens: religion, sports. Buys 10 mss/year. Average word length: 700-1,200. Byline given.
How to Contact/Writers Nonfiction: Query with published clips. Publishes ms 3 months after acceptance. Will consider electronic submissions via e-mail.
Photography Purchases photos separately. Looking for photos of sports action. Uses color prints and high resolution electronic files of 300 dpi or higher.
Terms Pays on publication. Buys first rights and second serial (reprint) rights. Pays $150-400 for assigned and unsolicited articles. Photographers paid per photo. Sample copies for 9×12 SASE and $1. Writer's/photo guidelines for SASE.
Tips ''All stories must be tied to FCA ministry.''

SHINE brightly
GEMS Girls' Clubs, P.O. Box 7259, Grand Rapids MI 49510. (616)241-5616. Fax: (616)241-5558. E-mail: christina@gemsgc.org. Web site: www.gems.org. **Editor:** Jan Boone. **Managing Editor:** Christina Malone. Monthly (with combined June/July/August summer issue) magazine. Circ. 15,000. ''*SHINE brightly* is designed to help girls ages 9-14 see how God is at work in their lives and in the world around them.''
Fiction Middle readers: adventure, animal, contemporary, health, history, humorous, multicultural, nature/environment, problem-solving, religious, sports. Does not want to see unrealistic stories and those with trite, easy endings. Buys 30 mss/year. Average word length: 400-900. Byline given.
Nonfiction Middle readers: animal, arts/crafts, careers, cooking, fashion, games/puzzles, health, hobbies, how-to, humorous, nature/environment, multicultural, problem-solving, religious, service projects, social issues, sports, travel, also movies, music and musicians, famous people, interacting with family and friends. Buys 9 mss/year. Average word length: 100-800. Byline given.

How to Contact/Writers Send for annual update for publication themes. Fiction/nonfiction: Send complete ms. Responds to mss in 1 month. Will consider simultaneous submissions. Guidelines on Web site.

Illustration Buys 3 illustrations/year. Prefers ms/illustration packages. Works on assignment only. Responds to submissions in 1 month. Samples returned with SASE. Credit line given.

Terms Pays on publication. Buys first North American serial rights, first rights, second serial (reprint rights) or simultaneous rights. Original artwork not returned at job's completion. Pays 3-5¢/word, up to $35 for stories, assigned articles and unsolicited articles. Poetry is $5-15. Games and Puzzles are $5-10. "We send complimentary copies in addition to pay." Pays up to $125 for color cover illustration; $25-50 for color inside illustration. Pays photographers by the project ($20-50 per photo). Writer's guidelines for SASE.

Tips Writers: "The stories should be current, deal with pre-adolescent problems and joys, and help girls see God at work in their lives through humor as well as problem-solving."

⚡ SKIPPING STONES

A Multicultural Children's Magazine, P.O. Box 3939, Eugene OR 97403. (541)342-4956. E-mail: editor@skipping stones.org. Web site: www.skippingstones.org. **Articles/Photo/Fiction Editor:** Arun N. Toke. Bimonthly magazine. Estab. 1988. Circ. 2,500. "*Skipping Stones* is an award-winning multicultural, nonprofit children's magazine designed to encourage cooperation, creativity and celebration of cultural and ecological richness. We encourage submissions by minorities and under-represented populations."

• Send SASE for *Skipping Stones* guidelines and theme list for detailed descriptions of the topics they want. *Skipping Stones*, now in it's 18th year, has won EDPRESS, N.A.M.E. (National Association for Multicultural Education) and Parent's Choice Awards.

Fiction Middle readers, young adult/teens: contemporary, meaningful, humorous. All levels: folktales, multicultural, nature/environment. Multicultural needs include: bilingual or multilingual pieces; use of words from other languages; settings in other countries, cultures or multi-ethnic communities.

Nonfiction All levels: animal, biography, cooking, games/puzzles, history, humorous, interview/profile, multicultural, nature/environment, creative problem-solving, religion and cultural celebrations, sports, travel, social and international awareness. Does not want to see preaching, violence or abusive language; no poems by authors over 18 years old; no suspense or romance stories. Average word length: 500-750. Byline given.

How to Contact/Writers Fiction: Query. Nonfiction: Send complete ms. Responds to queries in 1 month; mss in 4 months. Will consider simultaneous submissions; reviews artwork for future assignments. Please include your name on each page.

Illustration Prefers illustrations by teenagers and young adults. Will consider all illustration packages. Manuscript/illustration packages: Query; submit complete ms with final art; submit tearsheets. Responds in 4 months. Credit line given.

Photography Black & white photos preferred, but color photos with good contrast are welcome. Needs: youth 7-17, international, nature, celebration.

Terms Acquires first and reprint rights for mss and photographs. Pays in copies for authors, photographers and illustrators. Sample copies for $5 with SAE and 4 first-class stamps. Writer's/illustrator's guidelines for 4×9 SASE.

Tips "We want material meant for children and young adults/teenagers with multicultural or ecological awareness themes. Think, live and write as if you were a child, 'tween or teen." Wants "material that gives insight to cultural celebrations, lifestyle, custom and tradition, glimpse of daily life in other countries and cultures. Photos, songs, artwork are most welcome if they illustrate/highlight the points. Translations are invited if your submission is in a language other than English. Upcoming themes will include cultural celebrations, living abroad, disability, hospitality customs of various cultures, cross-cultural understanding, African, Asian and Latin American cultures, humor, international, turning points and magical moments in life, caring for the earth, spirituality, and Multicutural Awareness."

SPARKLE

GEMS Girls' Clubs, P.O. Box 7259, Grand Rapids MI 49510. (616)241-5616. Fax: (616)241-5558. E-mail: sarahv@gemsgc.org. Web site: www.gemsgc.org. **Articles/Fiction Editor:** Sarah Vanderaa. **Art Director/Photo Editor:** Jamie Brokus. Magazine published 3 times/year. Estab. 2002. "We are a Christian magazine geared toward girls in the 1st-3rd grades. *Sparkle* prints stories, articles, crafts, recipes, games and more. The magazine is based on an annual theme."

Fiction Young readers: adventure, animal, contemporary, health, humorous, multicultural, music and musicians, nature/environment, problem-solving, puzzles, religious, recipes, service project, sports, suspense/mystery, interacting with family and friends. Buys 8 mss/year. Average word length: 100-400. Byline given.

Nonfiction Young readers, middle readers: animal, arts/crafts, biography, careers, cooking, concept, fashion, games/puzzles, geography, health, history, hobbies, how-to, interview/profile, math, multicultural, nature/

Magazines

environment, problem-solving, quizzes, science, social issues, sports, travel, famous people, interacting with family and friends. Average word length: 100-400. Byline given.

How to Contact/Writers Fiction/nonfiction: Send complete ms. Responds to ms in 1 month. Publishes ms 4-6 months after acceptance. Will consider previously published work.

Illustration Buys 2 illustrations/issue; 6 illustrations/year. Uses color artwork only. Works on assignment only. Reviews ms/illustration packages from artists. Send ms with dummy. Contact: Sarah Vanderaa, managing editor. Illustrations only: send promo sheet. Responds only if interested. Samples returned with SASE; samples filed. Credit line given.

Photography Looking for close-up photos of girls, grades 1-3. Uses color prints. Send unsolicited photos by mail. Responds only if interested.

Terms Pays on publication. Buys first North American serial rights, first rights, second serial (reprint rights) or simltaneous rights for mss, artwork and photos. Pays $20 minimum for stories and articles. Pays illustrators $50-100 for color cover; $25-100 for color inside. Pays photographers per photo (range: $25-100). Additional payment for ms/illustration packages and for photos accompanying articles. Orginal artwork not returned at job's completion. Sample copies for $1. Writer's/illustrator/photo guidelines free for SASE.

SPIDER, The Magazine for Children

Carus Publishing Company, 140 S. Dearborn, Suite 1450, Chicago IL 60603. (312)701-1720. Web site: www.cricketm ag.com. **Editor-in-Chief:** Marianne Carus. **Editor:** Heather Delabre. **Art Director:** Sue Beck. Monthly magazine. Estab. 1994. Circ. 70,000. *Spider* publishes high-quality literature for beginning readers, primarily ages 6-9.

Fiction Young readers: adventure, contemporary, fantasy, folktales, science fiction. "Authentic, well-researched stories from all cultures are welcome. No didactic, religious, or violent stories, or anything that talks down to children." Average word length: 300-1,000. Byline given.

Nonfiction Young readers: animal, arts/crafts, cooking, games/puzzles, geography, history, math, multicultural, nature/environment, problem-solving, science. "Well-researched articles on all cultures are welcome. Would like to see more games, puzzles and activities, especially ones adaptable to *Spider*'s takeout pages. No encyclope-dic or overtly educational articles." Average word length: 300-800. Byline given.

Poetry Serious, humorous. Maximum length: 20 lines.

How to Contact/Writers Fiction/nonfiction: Send complete ms with SASE. Do not query. Responds to mss in 3 months. Publishes ms 2-3 years after acceptance. Will consider simultaneous submissions and previously published work.

Illustration Buys 20 illustrations/issue; 240 illustrations/year. Uses color artwork only. "Any medium—prefera-bly one that can wrap on a laser scanner—no larger than 20×24. We use more realism than cartoon-style art." Works on assignment only. Reviews ms/illustration packages from artists. Illustrations only: Send promo sheet and tearsheets. Responds in 6 weeks. Samples returned with SASE; samples filed. Credit line given.

Photography Buys photos from freelancers. Buys photos with accompanying ms only. Model/property releases and captions required. Uses 35mm or $2\frac{1}{4} \times 2\frac{1}{4}$ transparencies. Send unsolicited photos by mail; provide résumé and tearsheets. Responds in 6 weeks.

Terms Pays on publication for text; within 45 days from acceptance for art. Rights purchased vary. Buys first and promotional rights for artwork; one-time rights for photographs. Original artwork returned at job's completion. Pays up to 25¢/word for previously unpublished stories/articles. Authors also receive 2 complimen-tary copies of the issue in which work appears. Additional payment for ms/illustration packages and for photos accompanying articles. Pays illustrators $750 for color cover; $200-300 for color inside. Pays photographers per photo (range: $25-75). Sample copies for $5. Writer's/illustrator's guidelines for SASE.

Tips Writers: "Read back issues before submitting." (See listings for *Babybug, Cicada, Cricket, Muse, Ladybug* and *ASK*.)

TEEN MAGAZINE

Hearst Magazines, 3000 Ocean Park Blvd., Suite 3048, Santa Monica CA 90405. (310)664-2950. Fax: (310)664-2959. Web site: www.teenmag.com. **Contact:** Jane Fort, editor-in-chief (fashion, beauty, TeenPROM); Kelly Bryant, deputy editor (entertainment, movies, TV, music, books, covers, photo editor); Heather Hewitt, manag-ing editor (manufacturing, advertising, new products, what's hot, intern coordinator). Quarterly magazine. Estab. 1957. "We are a pure junior high school female (ages 10-15) audience. *TEEN*'s audience is upbeat and wants to be informed."

Fiction Young adults: romance. Does not want to see "that which does not apply to our market , i.e., science fiction, history, religious, adult-oriented."

Nonfiction Young adults: how-to, arts/crafts, fashion, interview/profile, games/puzzles. Does not want to see adult-oriented, adult point of view.

How to Contact/Writers No unsolicited materials accepted.

Illustration Buys 10 illustrations/issues; 50 illustrations/year. Uses various styles. "Light, upbeat." Illustrations only: "Want to see samples whether it be tearsheets, slides, finished pieces showing the style." Responds only if interested. Credit line given.

Terms Pays on acceptance. Buys all rights. Pays $ 500-1,000 for illustrations.

Tips Illustrators: "Present professional finished work. Get familiar with our magazine and send samples that would be compatible with the style of publication." There is a need for artwork with "fiction/specialty articles. Send samples or promotional materials on a regular basis."

THREE LEAPING FROGS, (Northern Nevada's Fun Newspaper for Kids)

Juniper Creek Publishing Inc., P.O. Box 2205, Carson City NV 89702. (775)849-1637. Fax: (775)849-1707. Web site: www.goshawkroad.com. **Articles/Fiction Editor:** Ellen Hopkins. Bimonthly tabloid. Estab. 2001. Circ. 30,000. "Three Leaping Frogs is a regional, themed publication. All articles/stories should be aimed at children ages 8-13 and adhere to our themes."

Fiction Middle readers, young adults: adventure, animal, contemporary, folktale, health, history, humorous, multicultural, nature/environment, problem-solving, sports (middle reader only). Buys 5 mss/year. Average word length: 300-600. Byline given.

Nonfiction Middle readers: animal, art/crafts, biography, cooking, games/puzzles, geography, health, history, how-to, humorous, interview/profile, math, multicultural, nature/environment, problem-solving, science, social issues, sports. Buys 50 mss/year. Average word length: 350-600. Byline given.

Poetry Maximum length: 20 lines. Limit submissions to 5 poems.

How to Contact/Writers Fiction/Nonfiction: Send complete by e-mail. Responds to queries/mss in 6 weeks or less. Publishes ms 3 months after acceptance. Will consider simultaneous submissions, e-mail submissions, previously published work.

Photography Buys photos with accompanying ms only. Model/property release required. "Digital images only."

Terms Pays on publication. Buys one-time rights for mss. Buys one-time rights for photos. Pays copies—$25 for stories and articles. Additional payment for ms/illustration packages and for photos accompanying articles. Pays writers with contributor's copies in lieu of cash for games, crafts, and puzzles. Sample copies for $1.00. Writer's guidelines for SASE.

Tips "Three Leaping Frogs is a regional publication. Please review guidelines before submitting. E-mail submissions strongly preferred."

TURTLE MAGAZINE, For Preschool Kids

Children's Better Health Institute, 1100 Waterway Blvd., Indianapolis IN 46206-0567. (317)636-8881. Fax: (317)684-8094. Web site: www.turtlemag.org. **Editor:** Terry Harshman. **Art Director:** Bart Rivers. Monthly/bimonthly magazine published 6 times/year. Circ. 300,000. *Turtle* uses read-aloud stories, especially suitable for bedtime or naptime reading, for children ages 2-5. Also uses poems, simple science experiments, easy recipes and health-related articles.

Fiction Picture-oriented material: health-related, medical, history, humorous, multicultural, nature/environment, problem-solving, sports, recipes, simple science experiments. Avoid stories in which the characters indulge in unhealthy activities. Buys 20 mss/year. Average word length: 150-300. Byline given. Currently accepting submissions for Rebus stories only.

Nonfiction Picture-oriented material: cooking, health, sports, simple science. "We use very simple experiments illustrating basic science concepts. These should be pretested. We also publish simple, healthful recipes." Buys 24 mss/year. Average word length: 100-300. Byline given.

Poetry "We're especially looking for short poems (4-8 lines) and slightly longer action rhymes to foster creative movement in preschoolers. We also use short verse on our inside front cover and back cover."

How to Contact/Writers Fiction/nonfiction: Send complete mss. Queries are not accepted. Responds to mss in 3 months.

Terms Pays on publication. Buys all rights for mss. Pays up to 22¢/word for stories and articles (depending upon length and quality) and 10 complimentary copies. Pays $25 minimum for poems. Sample copy $1.75. Writer's guidelines free with SASE and on Web site.

Tips "Our need for health-related material, especially features that encourage fitness, is ongoing. Health subjects must be age-appropriate. When writing about them, think creatively and lighten up! Always keep in mind that in order for a story or article to educate preschoolers, it first must be entertaining—warm and engaging, exciting, or genuinely funny. Here the trend is toward leaner, lighter writing. There will be a growing need for interactive activities. Writers might want to consider developing an activity to accompany their concise manuscripts." (See listings for *Child Life, Children's Digest, Children's Playmate, Humpty Dumpty's Magazine, Jack and Jill* and *U*S* Kids*.)

U*S* KIDS

Children's Better Health Institute, 1100 Waterway Blvd., P.O. Box 567, Indianapolis IN 46202. (317)636-8881.

Web site: www.uskidsmag.org. **Editor:** Daniel Lee. **Art Director:** Greg Vanzo. Magazine for children ages 6-11, published 6 times a year. Estab. 1987. Circ. 230,000.

Fiction Young readers: adventure, animal, contemporary, health, history, humorous, multicultural, nature/environment, problem-solving, sports, suspense/mystery. Buys limited number of stories/year. Query first. Average word length: 500-800. Byline given.

Nonfiction Young readers: animal, arts/crafts, cooking, games/puzzles, health, history, hobbies, how-to, humorous, interview/profile, multicultural, nature/environment, science, social issues, sports, travel. Wants to see interviews with kids ages 5-10, who have done something unusual or different. Buys 30-40 mss/year. Average word length: 400. Byline given.

Poetry Maximum length: 8-24 lines.

How to Contact/Writers Fiction: Send complete ms. Responds to queries and mss in 3 months.

Illustration Buys 8 illustrations/issue; 70 illustrations/year. Color artwork only. Works on assignment only. Reviews ms/illustration packages from artists. Query. Illustrations only: Send résumé and tearsheets. Responds only if interested. Samples returned with SASE; samples kept on file. Does not return originals. Credit line given.

Photography Purchases photography from freelancers. Looking for photos that pertain to children ages 5-10. Model/property release required. Uses color and b&w prints; 35mm, $2\frac{1}{4} \times 2\frac{1}{4}$, 4×5 and 8×10 transparencies. Photographers should provide résumé, business card, promotional literature or tearsheets to be kept on file. Responds only if interested.

Terms Pays on publication. Buys all rights for mss. Purchases all rights for artwork. Purchases one-time rights for photographs. Pays 17¢/word minimum. Additional payment for ms/illustration packages. Pays illustrators $155/page for color inside. Photographers paid by the project or per photo (negotiable). Sample copies for $2.95. Writer's/illustrator/photo guidelines for #10 SASE.

Tips "Write clearly and concisely without preaching or being obvious." (See listings for *Child Life*, *Children's Digest*, *Children's Playmate*, *Humpty Dumpty's Magazine*, *Jack and Jill* and *Turtle Magazine*.)

▣ WEE ONES E-MAGAZINE

1011 Main St., Darlington MD 21034. E-mail: submissions@weeonesmag.com. Web site: www.weeonesmag.com. **Editor:** Jennifer Reed. **Poetry Editor:** Kim Hutmacher. Online magazine. Estab. 2001. "We are an online children's magazine for children ages 5-10. Our mission is to use the Internet to encourage kids to read. We promote literacy and family unity." 100% of publication aimed at juvenile market.

Fiction Picture-oriented material: adventure, contemporary, health, history, humorous, multicultural, nature/environment, problem-solving, sports, rebus with illustrations. Buys 40 mss/year. Average word length: up to 500. Byline given.

Nonfiction Picture-oriented material: animal, arts/crafts, biography, concept, cooking, games/puzzles, geography, health, history, hobbies, how-to, humorous, multicultural, nature/environment, problem-solving, science, sports, travel. Buys over 60 mss/year. Average word length: up to 600. Byline given.

Poetry Uses all types of poetry. Limit submissions to 3 poems, up to 20 lines.

How to Contact/Writers Fiction/nonfiction: Send complete ms via e-mail. Responds to mss in 1-2 months. Publishes ms 6-12 months after acceptance. Will consider simultaneous submissions, electronic submissions via e-mail. No attachments please!

Illustration Buys 6 illustrations/issue. Works on assignment only. Reviews ms/illustration packages from artists. Query. Illustrations only: Query with samples. Contact: Jeff Reed, art editor. Responds only if interested. Samples returned with SASE or kept on file. Credit line given.

Terms Pays on publication. Buys nonexclusive worldwide electronic and reprint rights for mss, artwork and photos. Pays 5¢/word for stories and articles. Additional payment for ms/illustration packages and for photos accompanying articles. Pays $5-20 for b&w and color inside. Pays photographers per photo (range: $3). Writer's/illustrator's/photo guidelines for SASE.

Tips "*Wee Ones* is a growing online children's magazine. We are also available on CD. We reach over 90 countries and receive 50,000 hits per month. Study our magazine before submitting. Our guidelines are located on our site. Your chance for acceptance depends widely on how well you know our magazine and follow our guidelines. We do not publish sci-fi or fantasy stories with monsters or stories with witches, ghosts or Halloween themes."

◪ WHAT IF?, Canada's Fiction Magazine for Teens

What If Publications, 19 Lynwood Place, Guelph ON N1G 2V9 Canada. (519)823-2941. Fax: (519)823-8081. E-mail: editor@whatifmagazine.com. Web site: www.whatifmagazine.com. **Articles/Fiction Editor:** Mike Leslie. **Art Director:** Jean Leslie. Bimonthly magazine. Estab. 2003. Circ. 25,000. "The goal of *What If?* is to help young adults get published for the first time in a quality literary setting."

Fiction Young adults: adventure, contemporary, fantasy, folktale, health, humorous, multicultural, nature/

environment, problem-solving, science fiction, sports, suspense/mystery. Buys 48 mss/year. Average word length: 500-3,000. Byline given.

Nonfiction Young adults: editorial. "We publish editorial content from young adult writers only—similar to material seen on newspapers op-ed page." Average word length: 500. Byline given.

Poetry Reviews poetry: all styles. Maximum length: 20 lines. Limit submissions to 4 poems.

How to Contact/Writers Fiction/Nonfiction: Send complete ms. Responds to mss in 3 months. Publishes ms 4 months after acceptance. Will consider e-mail submissions, previously published work if the author owns all rights.

Illustration Buys approximately 150 illustrations/year. Reviews ms/illustration packages from young adult artists. Send ms with dummy. Query with samples. Contact: Jean Leslie, production manager. Responds in 2 months. Samples returned with SASE. Credit line given.

Terms Pays on publication. Acquires first rights for mss and artwork. Original artwork returned at job's completion. Pays 3 copies for stories; 1 copy for articles; 3 copies for illustration. Sample copies for $7.50. Writer's/illustrator's guidelines for SASE or available by e-mail.

Tips "Read our magazine. The majority of the material we publish (90%) is by Canadian young adults. Another 10% is staff written. We are currently accepting material from Canadian teens only."

⚡ WHAT'S HERS/PARK & PIPE

(formerly *What's Hers/What's His*), What! Publishers Inc., 03-212 Henderson Hwy., Suite 328, Winnepeg MB R2L 1L8 Canada. (204)985-8160. Fax: (204)957-5638. E-mail: letters@whatshers.com; info@parkandpipemagazine.com. Web site: www.whatshers.com; www.parkandpipemagazine.com. **Editor-in-Chief:** Twila Driedger. Magazine published 4 times/year. Estab. 1987. Circ. 180,000, *What's Hers*; 200,000, *Park & Pipe*. "Informative and entertaining teen magazine for both genders ages 13-19. Articles deal with issues and ideas of relevance to Canadian teens. Articles must include Canadian references. The magazine is distributed through schools so we aim to be cool and responsible at the same time."

Nonfiction Young adults (13 and up): biography, careers, concept, health, how-to, humorous, interview/profile, nature/environment, science, social issues, sports. "No cliché teen stuff. Absolutely no fiction. Also, we're getting too many heavy pitches lately on teen pregnancy, AIDS, etc." Buys 8 mss/year. Average word length: 400-1,800. Byline given.

How to Contact/Writers Nonfiction: Query with published clips. Responds to queries/mss in 2 months. Publishes ms 2 months after acceptance.

Terms Pays on publication plus 30 days. Buys first rights for mss. Pays $100-300 (Canadian) for articles. Sample copies available for 9×12 SASE and $1.45 (Canadian). Writer's guidelines free for SASE or my e-mail.

Tips "Teens are smarter today than ever before. Respect that intelligence in queries and articles. Aim for the older end of our age-range (14-19) and avoid cliché. Humor works for us almost all the time."

WINNER

The Health Connection, 55 W. Oak Ridge Dr., Hagerstown MD 21740. (301)393-4017. Fax: (301)393-3294. E-mail: jschleifer@rhpa.org. Web site: www.winnermagazine.org. **Editor:** Jan Schleifer. **Art Director:** Madelyn Gatz. Monthly magazine (September-May). Estab. 1958. Publishes articles that will promote children in grades 4-6 choosing a positive lifestyle and choosing to be drug-free.

Fiction Young readers, middle readers: contemporary, health, nature/environment, problem-solving, anti tobacco, alcohol, and drugs. Byline given.

Nonfiction Young readers, middle readers: positive role model personality features, health. Buys 10-15 mss/year. Average word length: 600-650 (in addition, needs 3 related thought questions and one puzzle/activity). Byline given.

How to Contact/Writers Fiction/nonfiction: Send complete ms; prefers e-mail submissions. Responds in 2 months. Publishes ms 6-12 months after acceptance. Will consider simultaneous.

Illustration Buys up to 3 illustrations/issue; up to 30 illustrations/year. Uses color artwork only. Works on assignment only. Reviews ms/illustration packages from artists. Send ms with dummy. Responds only if interested. Samples returned with SASE.

Terms Pays on acceptance. Buys first rights for mss. Original artwork returned at job's completion. Additional payment for ms/illustration packages. Sometimes additional payment when photos accompany articles. Pays $300 for color inside. Writer's guidelines for SASE. Sample magazine $2; include 9×12 envelope with 2 first-class stamps.

Tips "Keep material upbeat and positive for elementary age children."

WITH, The Magazine for Radical Christian Youth

Faith & Life Resources, 722 Main, Newton KS 67114. Fax: (620)367-8218. E-mail: carold@mennoniteusa.org. Web site: www.withonline.org. **Editor:** Carol Duerksen. Published 6 times a year. Circ. 3,000. Magazine published for Christian teenagers, ages 15-18. "We deal with issues affecting teens and try to help them make choices reflecting a radical Christian faith."

Fiction Young adults/teens: contemporary, fantasy, humorous, multicultural, problem-solving, religious, romance. Multicultural needs include race relations, first-person stories featuring teens of ethnic minorities. Buys 15 mss/year. Average word length: 1,000. Byline given.

Nonfiction Young adults/teens: first-person teen experience (as-told-to), how-to, humorous, multicultural, problem-solving, religion, social issues. Buys 15-20 mss/year. Average word length: 1,000. Byline given.

Poetry Wants to see religious, humorous, nature. "Buys 1-2 poems/year." Maximum length: 50 lines.

How to Contact/Writers Send complete ms. Query on first-person teen experience stories and how-to articles. (Detailed guidelines for first-person stories, how-tos, and fiction available for SASE.) Responds to queries in 3 weeks; mss in 6 weeks. Will consider simultaneous submissions.

Illustration Buys 6-8 assigned illustrations/issue; buys 64 assigned illustrations/year. Uses b&w and 2-color artwork only. Preferred theme or style: candids/interracial. Reviews ms/illustration packages from artists. Query first. Illustrations only: Query with portfolio (photocopies only) or tearsheets. Responds only if interested. Credit line given.

Photography Buys photos from freelancers. Looking for candid photos of teens (ages 15-18), especially ethnic minorities. Uses 8×10 b&w glossy prints. Photographers should send unsolicited photos by mail.

Terms Pays on acceptance. For mss buys first rights, one-time rights; second serial (reprint rights). Buys one-time rights for artwork and photos. Original artwork returned at job's completion upon request. Pays 6¢/word for unpublished mss; 4¢/word for reprints. Will pay more for assigned as-told-to stories. Pays $10-25 for poetry. Pays $50-60 for b&w cover illustration and b&w inside illustration. Pays photographers per project (range: $120-180). Sample copy for 9×12 SAE and 4 first-class stamps. Writer's/illustrator's guidelines for SASE.

Tips "We want stories, fiction or nonfiction, in which high-school-age youth of various cultures/ethnic groups are the protaganists. Stories may or may not focus on cross-cultural relationships. We're hungry for stuff that makes teens laugh—fiction, nonfiction and cartoons. It doesn't have to be religious, but must be wholesome. Most of our stories would not be accepted by other Christian youth magazines. They would be considered too gritty, too controversial, or too painful. Our regular writers are on the *With* wavelength. Most writers for Christian youth magazines aren't. Fiction and humor are the best places to break in. Send SASE and request guidelines and theme list." For photographers: "If you're willing to line up models and shoot to illustrate specific story scenes, send us a letter of introduction and some samples of your work."

⚡ YES MAG, Canada's Science Magazine for Kids

Peter Piper Publishing Inc., 3968 Long Gun Place, Victoria BC V8N 3A9 Canada. Fax: (250)477-5390. E-mail: editor@yesmag.ca. Web site: www.yesmag.ca. **Editor:** Shannon Hunt. **Art/Photo Director:** David Garrison. Managing Editor: Jude Isabella. Bimonthly magazine. Estab. 1996. Circ. 22,000. "*YES Mag* is designed to make science accessible, interesting, exciting, and fun. Written for children ages 9 to 14, *YES Mag* covers a range of topics including science and technology news, environmental updates, do-at-home projects and articles about Canadian s cience and scientists."

Nonfiction Middle readers: all the sciences—math, engineering, biology, physics, chemistry, etc. Buys 70 mss/year. Average word length: 250-1,250. Byline given.

How to Contact/Writers Nonfiction: Query with published clips. "We prefer e-mail queries." Responds to queries/mss in 6 weeks. Generally publishes ms 3 months after acceptance. Will consider simultaneous submissions, previously published work.

Illustration Buys 2 illustrations/issue; 10 illustrations/year. Uses color artwork only. Works on assignment only. Reviews ms/illustration packages from artists. Query. Illustration only: Query with samples. Responds in 6 weeks. Samples filed. Credit line given.

Photography "Looking for science, technology, nature/environment photos based on current editorial needs." Photo captions required. Uses color prints. Provide résumé, business card, promotional literature, tearsheets if possible. Responds in 3 weeks.

Terms Pays on publication. Buys one-time rights for mss. Buys one-time rights for artwork/photos. Original artwork returned at job's completion. Pays $70-200 for stories and articles. Sample copies for $4. E-mail for writer's guidelines.

Tips "We do not publish fiction or science fiction. Visit our Web site for more information and sample articles. Articles relating to the physical sciences and mathematics are encouraged."

YOUNG & ALIVE

P.O. Box 6097, Lincoln NE 68506. (402)488-0981. Fax: (402)488-7582. E-mail: editorial@christianrecord.org. Web site: www.christianrecord.org. **Articles Editor:** Ms. Gaylena Gibson. Quarterly magazine. Estab. 1976.

Circ. 28,000. "We seek to provide wholesome, entertaining material for young adults ages 12 through age 25."
- *Young & Alive* is not accepting submissions until 2009.

YOUNG RIDER, The Magazine for Horse and Pony Lovers
Fancy Publications, P.O. Box 8237, Lexington KY 40533. (859)260-9800. Fax: (859)260-9814. Web site: www.yo ungrider.com. **Editor:** Lesley Ward. Bimonthly magazine. Estab. 1994. "*Young Rider* magazine teaches young people, in an easy-to-read and entertaining way, how to look after their horses properly, and how to improve their riding skills safely."

Fiction Young adults: adventure, animal, horses, horse celebrities, famous equestrians. Buys 10 mss/year. Average word length: 1,500 maximum. Byline given.

Nonfiction Young adults: animal, careers, health (horse), sports, riding. Buys 20-30 mss/year. Average word length: 1,000 maximum. Byline given.

How to Contact/Writers Fiction/nonfiction: Query with published clips. Responds to queries in 2 weeks. Publishes ms 6-12 months after acceptance. Will consider simultaneous submissions, electronic submissions via disk or modem, previously published work.

Illustration Buys 2 illustrations/issue; 10 illustrations/year. Works on assignment only. Reviews ms/illustration packages from artists. Query. Contact: Lesley Ward, editor. Illustrations only: Query with samples. Contact: Lesley Ward, editor. Responds in 2 weeks. Samples returned with SASE. Credit line given.

Photography Buys photos with accompanying ms only. Uses color, slides, photos—in focus, good light. Model/ property release required; captions required. Uses color 4×6 prints, 35mm transparencies. Query with samples. Responds in 2 weeks. Digital images must be high-res.

Terms Pays on publication. Buys first North American serial rights for mss, artwork, photos. Original artwork returned at job's completion. Pays $150 maximum for stories; $250 maximum for articles. Additional payment for ms/illustration packages and for photos accompanying articles. Pays $70-140 for color inside. Pays photographers per photo (range: $65-155). Sample copies for $3.50. Writer's/illustrator's/photo guidelines for SASE.

Tips "Fiction must be in third person. Read magazine before sending in a query. No 'true story from when I was a youngster.' No moralistic stories. Fiction must be up-to-date and humorous, teen-oriented. Need horsey interest or celebrity rider features. No practical or how-to articles—all done in-house."

YOUNG SALVATIONIST
The Salvation Army, 615 Slaters Lane, Alexandria VA 22314-1112. (703)684-5500. Fax: (703)684-5534. E-mail: ys@usn.salvationarmy.org. Web site: www.salpubs.com. **Editor-in-Chief:** Maj. Ed Forster. **Editor:** Capt. Curtis Hartley. "We accept material with clear Christian content written for teens and collage-age young adults. *Young Salvationist* is published for teenage members of The Salvation Army, an evangelical part of the Christian Church that focuses on living the Christian life."

Fiction Young adults/teens: contemporary, humorous, problem-solving, religious. Buys 10-11 mss/year. Average word length: 750-1,200. Byline given.

Nonfiction Young adults/teens: religious—careers, concept, interview/profile, how-to, humorous, multicultural, problem-solving, social issues, sports. Buys 40-50 mss/year. Average word length: 750-1,200. Byline given.

How to Contact/Writers Fiction/nonfiction: Query with published clips or send complete ms. Responds to queries/mss in 1 month. Will consider simultaneous submissions.

Illustrations Buys 3-5 illustrations/issue; 20-30 illustrations/year. Reviews ms/illustration packages from artists. Send ms with art. Illustrations only: Query; send résumé, promo sheet, portfolio, tearsheets. Responds only if interested. Samples returned with SASE; samples filed. Credit line given.

Photography Purchases photography from freelancers. Looking for teens in action.

Terms Pays on acceptance. Buys first North American serial rights, first rights, one-time rights or second serial (reprint) rights for mss. Purchases one-time rights for artwork and photographs. Original artwork returned at job's completion "if requested." For mss, pays 10-15¢/word; 10¢/word for reprints. Pays $60-150 color (cover) illustration; $60-150 b&w (inside) illustration; $60-150 color (inside) illustration. Pays photographers per photo (range: $60-150). Sample copy for 9×12 SAE and 4 first-class stamps. Writer's guidelines for #10 SASE.

Tips "Ask for theme list/sample copy! Write 'up,' not down to teens. Aim at young *adults*, not children." Wants "less fiction, more 'journalistic' nonfiction."

Greeting Cards, Puzzles & Games

In this section you'll find companies that produce puzzles, games, greeting cards, and other items (like coloring books, stickers, and giftwrap) especially for kids. These are items you'll find in children's sections of bookstores, toy stores, department stores, and card shops.

Because these markets create an array of products, their needs vary greatly. Some may need the service of freelance writers for greeting card copy or slogans for buttons and stickers. Others are in need of illustrators for coloring books or photographers for puzzles. Artists should send copies of their work that art directors can keep on file—never originals. Carefully read through the listings to find companies' needs, and send for guidelines and catalogs if they're available, just as you would for book or magazine publishers.

If you'd like to find out more about the greeting card industry beyond the market for children, there are a number of resources to help you. The Greeting Card Association is a national trade organization for the industry. For membership information, contact the GCA at 1156 15th St. NW, Suite 900, Washington DC 20005, (202)393-1778, info@greetingcard.org, www.greetingcard.org. *Greetings Etc.* (Edgel Communications), a quarterly trade magazine covering the greeting card industry, is the official publication of the Greeting Card Association. For information call (973)252-0100 or visit www.greetingsmagazine.com. For a complete list of companies, consult the latest edition of *Artist's & Graphic Designer's Market* (Writer's Digest Books). Writers should see *You Can Write Greeting Cards*, by Karen Ann Moore (Writer's Digest Books).

Information on greeting card, puzzle, and game companies listed in the previous edition but not included in this edition of *Children's Writer's & Illustrator's Market* may be found in the General Index.

Greeting Cards

ABBY LOU ENTERTAINMENT

1411 Edgehill Place, Pasadena CA 91103. (612)795-7334. Fax: (626)795-4013. E-mail: ale@full-moon.com. **President:** George LeFave. Estab. 1985. Animation production company and book publisher. "We are looking for top creative children's illustrators with classic artwork. We are a children's book publisher moving into greeting cards—nature illustrations with characters." Publishes greeting cards (Whispering Gardens), coloring books, puzzles, games, posters, calendars, books (Adventures in Whispering Gardens). 100% of products are made for kids or have kid's themes.

Writing Needs freelance writing for children's greeting cards and other children's products. Makes 6 writing assignments/year. For greeting cards, accepts both rhymed and unrhymed verse ideas. Other needs for freelance writing include the theme of "Listen to your heart and you will hear the whispers." To contact, send cover letter, résumé, client list, writing samples. Responds in 2 weeks. Materials not returned; materials filed. For greeting cards, pays flat fee of $500, royalty of 3-10%; negotiable or negotiable advance against royalty. For other writing, payment is negotiated. Pays on acceptance. Buys one-time rights; negotiable. Credit line given.

Illustration Need freelance illustration for children's greeting cards, posters and TV related property. Makes 12 illustration assignments/year. Prefers a "classical look—property that needs illustration is Adventures in Whispering Gardens and multidimentional entertainment." Uses color artwork only. To contact send cover letter, published samples, slides, color photocopies and color promo pieces. Materials not returned; materials filed. For greeting cards and other artwork, payment is negotiable. Pays on acceptance or publication. Rights purchased are negotiable. Credit line given.

Tips "Give clear vision of what you want to do in the business and produce top quality, creative work."

AVONLEA TRADITIONS, INC.

17075 Leslie St., Units 12-15, Newmarket ON L3Y 8E1 Canada. (905)853-1777. Fax: (905)853-1763. Web site: www.avonlea-traditions.com and www.maplelea.com. **President:** Kathryn Morton. Estab. 1988. Giftware and doll designer, importer and distributor. Creators of the new Maplelea Girls™, 18-inch vinyl doll play system which includes chapter books, journals, and accessories. Designs, imports and distributes products related to Canada's famous storybook, *Anne of Green Gables*, and other Canadian themes.

Writing (Girls) fiction.

Illustration Needs freelance illustration for books, stationery and packaging. Makes 2-3 illustration assignments/ month; 24/year. Prefers realistic style of artwork for chapter books. Also uses other youthful artwork styles. To contact, send color photocopies and promo pieces. Responds only if interested. Materials not returned; materials filed. For other artwork, pays by the hour (range: $20-30). Pays on publication. Buys all rights. Credit line sometimes given.

Photography Sometimes uses stock photography of Canadian people and places.

Tips "We only use artists/writers who are Canadian."

THE BEISTLE COMPANY

P.O. Box 10, Shippensburg PA 17257. (717)532-2131. Fax: (717)532-7789. E-mail: sales@beistle.com. Web site: www.beistle.com. **Contact:** Rick Buterbaugh, art director. Estab. 1900. Paper products company. Produces decorations and party goods, posters—baby, baptism, birthday, holidays, educational, wedding/anniversary, graduation, ethnic themes, and New Year parties. 50% of products are made for kids or have kids' themes.

Illustration Needs freelance illustration for decorations, party goods, school supplies, point-of-purchase display materials and gift wrap. Makes 100 illustration assignments/year. Prefers fanciful style, cute 4- to 5-color illustration, Illustrator or Photoshop computer illustration. To contact, send cover letter, résumé, client list, promo piece. To query with specific ideas, phone, write or fax. Responds only if interested. Materials returned with SASE; materials filed. Pays by the project or by contractual agreement; price varies according to type of project. Pays on acceptance. Buys all rights. Artist's guidelines available for SASE.

Tips Submit seasonal material 6 months in advance.

COURAGE CARDS

3915 Golden Valley Rd., Minneapolis MN 55422. (763)520-0211. Fax: (763)520-0299. E-mail: artsearch@courag e.org. Web site: www.couragecards.org. **Art and Production:** Laura Brooks. Estab. 1959. Not-for-profit greeting card company. Courage Cards helps support Courage Center, a not-for-profit provider of rehabilitation and independent living services for children and adults with disabilities. Publishes holiday greeting cards.

Illustration Needs freelance illustration for holiday greeting cards. Makes 40 illustration assignments/year. Prefers colorful traditional Christmas, peace, international and fall/winter seasonal art for holiday cards. Uses color artwork only. To contact, download guidelines from Web site or request via e-mail or phone. Responds to submissions in 6 months. Returns materials if accompanied by SASE. For greeting cards, pays flat fee of $400. Pays on publication. Buys reprint rights. Artist photo and promotion on the back of every card; credit line given for artists. Guidelines and application for the annual art search available on Web site.

Tips ''We encourage artists to send in art entries through the art search. Please contact us for specific guidelines.''

DESIGN DESIGN INC.

P.O. Box 2266, Grand Rapids MI 49501. (616)774-2448. Fax: (616)774-4020. **Creative Director:** Tom Vituj. Estab. 1986. Greeting card company. 5% of products are made for kids or have kids themes.

Writing Needs freelance writing for children's greeting cards. Prefers both rhymed and unrhymed verse ideas. To contact, send cover letter and writing samples. Materials returned with SASE; materials not filed. For greeting cards, pays flat fee. Buys all rights or exclusive product rights; negotiable. No credit line given. Writer's guidelines for SASE.

Illustration Needs freelance illustration for children's greeting cards and related products. To contact, send cover letter, published samples, color or b&w photocopies, color or b&w promo pieces or portfolio. Returns materials with SASE. Pays by royalty. Buys all rights or exclusive product rights; negotiable. Artist's guidelines available for SASE. Do not send original art.

Photography Buys stock and assigns work. Looking for the following subject matter: babies, animals, dog, cats, humorous situations. Uses 4×5 transparencies or high quality 35mm slides. To contact, send cover letter with slides, stock photo list, color copies, published samples and promo piece. Materials returned with SASE; materials not filed. Pays royalties. Buys all rights or exclusive product rights; negotiable. Photographer's guidelines for SASE. Do not send original photography.

Tips Seasonal material must be submitted 1 year in advance.

GALLERY GRAPHICS, INC.

P.O. Box 502, 20136 State Hwy. 59, Noel MO 64854-0502. (417)475-6191. Fax: (417)475-6494. E-mail: jacob@gallerygraphics.com. Web site: www.gallerygraphics.com. **Marketing Director:** Olivia Jacob. Estab. 1979. Greeting card, paper products company. Specializes in products including prints, cards, calendars, stationery, magnets, framed items, books, flue covers and sachets. We market towards all age groups. Publishes reproductions of children's books from the 1800s. 10% of products are made for kids or have kid's themes.

Illustration Needs freelance illustration for children's greeting cards, & other children's products. Makes 8 illustration assignments/year. Prefers children, angels, animals in any medium. Uses color artwork only. To contact, send cover letter, published samples, photocopies (prefer color), promo pieces. Responds in 3 weeks. ''We'll return materials if a SASE is included. If artist can send something we can file, that would be ideal.'' Pays on sales. Buys exclusive product rights. Credit line sometimes given.

Tips ''We've significantly increased our licensing over the last year. Most of these are set up on a 5% royalty basis. Submit various art subjects.''

GLOBAL GRAPHICS & GIFTS, LCC

16781 Chagrin Blvd. #333, Cleveland OH 44120. E-mail: fredw@globalgraphics-gifts.com. Web site: www.globalgraphics-gifts.com. **Contact:** Fred Willingham, president. Estab. 1995. Greeting card company. ''Products include cards, gift bags, wrapping paper, party supplies, and stationery products.'' Produces greeting cards. 15% products for kids.

Writing Needs freelancers for children's greeting cards. For greeting cards, uses rhymed and unrhymed verse. For first contact, send cover letter, writing samples. Does not return materials. Samples filed. For children's greeting cards, pays writers flat fee of $25. For other assignments, pays by the project $25. Pays on acceptance. Buys all rights. Credit line sometimes given. Writer's guidelines on Web site.

Illustration Needs freelance illustration for children's greeting cards. Gives varied number of assignments/year. ''We only accept wholesome subjects and themes. We like fun, loose and colorful styles. Animals always work well. Also, animals with human characteristics.'' Uses color artwork only. For first contact, send published samples, color photocopies, color promo pieces, unpublished samples. Responds only if interested. Does not return materials. Samples filed. For children's greeting card art, pays flat fee of $150-$400. For artwork for children's products, pays by the project: $150-$400. Pays on acceptance. Buys all rights. Sometimes gives credit line. Artist's guidelines on Web site.

Photography Buys stock and assigns work. Buys varied amount of stock images/year. Gives varied amount of assignments/year. ''Seeking photos of animals and children, humorous, cute. Wholesome only. Images should tell a story.'' Accepts 4×5 transparencies. For first contact, send cover letter, résumé, stock photo list. Responds only if interested. Does not return materials. Promo materials filed. Pays by the project, a minimum of $150. Pays on acceptance. Buys all rights. Credit line sometimes given. Guidelines on Web site. Submit seasonal material 12 months in advance.

GREAT AMERICAN PUZZLE FACTORY, INC.

16 S. Main St., Norwalk CT 06854. (203)838-4240. Fax: (203)866-9601. E-mail: info@greatamericanpuzzle.com.

Web site: www.greatamericanpuzzle.com. **Contact:** Art Director. Estab. 1976. Produces puzzles and games. 50% of products are made for kids or have kids' themes.

Illustration Needs freelance illustration for puzzles. Makes over 20 freelance assignments/year. To contact, send cover letter, color photocopies and color promo pieces (no slides or original art) with SASE. Responds in 1-2 months. Artists guidelines available for SASE. Rights purchased vary. Buys all rights to puzzles. Pays on publication. Payment varies. Also can contact via e-mail with Web site address or samples.

Photography Needs local cityscapes for regional puzzles. "Photos that we have used have been of wildlife. We do occasionally use city skylines. These are only for custom jobs, though, and must be 4×5 or larger format."

Tips Targets ages 4-12 and adult. "Go to a toy store and look at puzzles. See what is appropriate. No slides. Send color copies (3-4) for style. Looking for whimsical, fantasy and animal themes with a bright, contemporary style. Not too washy or cute. No people, babies, abstracts, landscapes or still life. We often buy reprint rights to existing work." Submit seasonal material 1 year in advance.

INTERCONTINENTAL GREETINGS LTD.

176 Madison Ave., New York NY 10016. (212)683-5830. Fax: (212)779-8564. Web site: www.intercontinental-ltd.com. **Art Director:** Thea Groene. Estab. 1964. 100% of material freelance written and illustrated. Intended for greeting cards, scholastic products (notebook covers, pencil cases), novelties (gift bags, mugs), tin gift boxes, shower and bedding curtains. 30-40% of products are made for kids or have kids' themes.

Illustration Needs illustrations for children's greeting cards, notebook covers, photo albums, gift products. Prefers primarily greeting card subjects, suitable for gift industry. To contact, send cover letter, client list and published samples (if available), photocopies, slides and/or CDs with SASE. Pays percentage on publication. Clients purchase temporary exclusive product rights for contract period of 3 years. Credit line sometimes given.

Photography Needs stylized and interesting still lifes, studio florals, all themed toward the paper and gift industry. Guidelines available for SASE.

Tips Target group for juvenile cards: ages 1-10. Illustrators: Use clean colors, not muddy or dark. Send a neat, concise sampling of your work. Include a SASE to issue return of your samples if wanted.

INTERNATIONAL PLAYTHINGS, INC.

75D Lackawanna Ave., Parsippany NJ 07054-1712. (973)316-2500. Fax: (973)316-5883. E-mail: info@intplay.com. Web site: www.intplay.com. Estab. 1968. Toy/game company. Distributes and markets children's toys, games in specialty toy markets. 100% of products are made for kids or have kids' themes.

Illustration Needs freelance illustration for children's puzzles and games. Makes 10-20 illustration assignments/year. Prefers fine-quality, original illustration for children's puzzles. Uses color artwork only. To contact, send published samples, slides, portfolio, color photocopies or promo pieces. Responds in 1 month only if interested. Materials filed. For artwork, pays by the project (range: $500-2,000). Pays on publication. Buys one-time rights, negotiable.

Tips "Mail correspondence only, please. Sent to the attention of the Art Director. No phone calls. Send child-themed art, not cartoon-y. Use up-to-date themes and colors."

JILLSON & ROBERTS

3300 W. Castor St., Santa Ana CA 92704-3908. (714)424-0111. Fax: (714)424-0054. Web site: www.jillsonroberts.com. **Art Director:** Shawn Doll. Estab. 1973. Paper products company. Makes gift wrap/gift bags. 20% of products are made for kids or have kids' themes.

Illustration Needs freelance illustration for children's gift wrap. Makes 6-12 illustration assignments/year. Wants children/baby/juvenile themes. To contact, send cover letter. Responds in 1 month. For wrap and bag designs, pays flat fee (varies). Pays on publication. Rights negotiable. Artist's guidelines for SASE.

Tips Seasonal material should be submitted up to $3\frac{1}{2}$ months in advance. "We produce two lines of gift wrap per year: one everyday line and one Christmas line. The closing date for everyday is July 1 and Christmas is September 1."

☐ MINDWARE

2100 County Road C West, Roseville MN 55113. (651)582-0555. Fax: (651)582-0556. E-mail: ddavern@mindwareonline.com. Web site: www.mindwareonline.com. **New Product Development Manager:** Dawn Davern. Estab. 1990. Educational game and puzzle company. "Mind Ware creates and sells brainy toys for kids of all ages. Our coloring books and Squzzle Puzzles are beautifully illustrated and visually stimulating. Publishes educational toys, brainteasers, coloring books, puzzles, games, picture books (4/year), maze books, nonfiction and reference, whodunit mysteries.

Illustration Needs freelance illustration for children's products. Makes 8-10 illustration assignments/year. To contact, send cover letter and URL. Materials returned with SASE; materials filed.

NOVO CARD PUBLISHERS, INC.
3630 W. Pratt Ave., Lincolnwood IL 60712. (847)763-0077. Fax: (847)763-0020. E-mail: art@novocard.net. Web site: www.novocard.net. **Contact:** Art Department. Estab. 1926. Greeting card company. Company publishes greeting cards, note/invitation packs and gift envelopes for middle market. Publishes greeting cards (Novo Card/Cloud-9). 40% of products are made for kids or have kids' themes.
Writing Needs freelance writing for children's greeting cards. Makes 400 writing assignments/year. Other needs for freelance writing include invitation notes. To contact, send writing samples. Responds in approximately 1 month only if interested. Materials returned only for SASE. For greeting cards, pays flat fee of $2/line. Pays on acceptance. Buys all rights. No royalties. Credit line sometimes given. Writer's guidelines available for SASE.
Illustration Needs freelance illustration for children's greeting cards. Makes 500 illustration assignments/year. Prefers just about all types: traditional, humor, contemporary, etc. To contact, send published samples, slides and color photocopies. Responds in approximately 2 months if interested. Materials returned with SASE. For greeting cards, payment negotiable. Pays on acceptance. Buys all greeting card and stationery rights. Credit line sometimes given. Artist's guidelines available for SASE.
Photography Buys stock and assigns work. Buys more than 100 stock images/year. Wants all types. Uses color and b&w prints; 35mm transparencies. To contact, send slides, stock photo list, published samples, paper copies acceptable. Responds in approximately 2 months. Materials returned with SASE. Pays negotiable rate. Pays on acceptance. Buys all greeting card and stationery rights. Credit line sometimes given. Guidelines for SASE.
Tips Submit seasonal material 10-12 months in advance. ''Novo has extensive lines of greeting cards: everyday, seasonal (all) and alternative lines (over 24 separate lines of note card packs and gift enclosures). Our lines encompass all types of styles and images.''

P.S. GREETINGS/FANTUS PAPER PRODUCTS
5730 North Tripp Ave., Chicago IL 60646. (773)267-6069. Fax: (773)267-6055. Web site: www.psgreetings.com. **Contact:** Design Director. Greeting card company. Publishes boxed and individual counter greeting cards. Seasons include: Christmas, every major holiday and everyday. 20% of products are made for kids or have kid's themes. No phone calls please.
Writing Needs freelance writing for children's greeting cards. Makes 10-20 writing assignments/year. To contact, send writing samples. Responds in 1 month. Material returned only if accompanied with SASE. For greeting cards, pays flat fee/line. Pays on acceptance. Buys exclusive greeting card rights. Writer's guidelines free for SASE.
Illustration Needs freelance illustration for children's greeting cards. Makes about 30-50 illustration assignments/year. Open to all mediums, all themes. Uses primarily commissioned artwork. To contact, send published samples, color promo pieces and color photocopies only. Responds in 1 month. Material returned only if accompanied with SASE. Pays flat fee upon acceptance. Buys exclusive greeting card rights. Artist's guidelines free for SASE (speculative and on assignment).
Photography Buys photography from freelancers. Speculative and on assignment. Prefers finished digital files. To contact, send slides or CD of work. Responds in 1 month. Materials returned only for SASE; materials filed. Pays flat fee upon acceptance. Buys exclusive greeting card rights. Photographer's guidelines free for SASE.
Tips Seasonal material should be submitted 8 months in advance.

RECO INTERNATIONAL CORP.
706 Woodlawn Ave., Cambridge OH 43725. Fax: (740)432-8811. E-mail: info@reco.com. Web site: www.reco.com. **President:** Heio W. Reich. Estab. 1967. Collector's plate, giftware producer. 60% of products are made for kids or have kids' themes.
Illustration Needs freelance illustration for collector's plates—children's subjects mainly, but also western, Indian, flowers, animals, fantasy and mystical. Makes 40 assignments/year. Uses color artwork only. To contact, send portfolio. Submit specific ideas. Responds in 1 month. Materials returned with SASE; materials filed. For greeting art licensed, pays flat fee and royalty. For other artwork, pays royalty and advance. Pays on acceptance. Buys exclusive product rights.
Photography Buys photos at times. Wants good art photos.
Tips Submit seasonal material 12-18 months in advance (although rarely uses seasonal work).

STANDARD PUBLISHING
8121 Hamilton Ave., Cincinnati OH 45231. (513)931-4050. Fax: (513)931-0950. E-mail: tneunschwander@standardpub.com. Web site: www.standardpub.com. **Editorial Directors:** Dianne Stortz, Family Resources; Ruth Frederick, Children & Youth Ministry Resources. **Creative Services Director:** Julie Diehl. Estab. 1866. Publishes children's books and teacher helps for the religious market. 75% of products are made for kids or have kids' themes.

• Standard also has a listing in Book Publishers.

Writing Responds in 3 months. Payment method varies. Credit line given.

Illustration Needs freelance illustration for puzzle, activity books, teacher guides. Makes 6-10 illustration assignments/year. To contact, send cover letter and photocopies. Responds in 3 months if interested. Payment method varies. Credit line given.

Photography Buys a limited amount of photos from freelancers. Wants mature, scenic and Christian themes.

Tips "Many of our projects are developed in-house and assigned. Study our catalog and products; visit Christian bookstores. We are currently looking for Bible-based word puzzles and activities."

WARNER PRESS

P.O. Box 2499, Anderson IN 46018-9988. Fax: (765)640-8005. E-mail: krhodes@warnerpress.org. Web site: www.warnerpress.com. **Senior Editor:** Karen Rhodes. **Creative Director:** Curtis Corzine. Estab. 1880. Publishes church resources, coloring and activity books and children's supplies, all religious-oriented. 15% of products are made for kids.

Writing To contact, request guidelines first with SASE. ("We do not respond if SASE is not included.") Contact: Karen Rhodes, senior editor. Responds in 2 months. Limited purchases of children's material right now. Materials may be kept on file for future use. Pays on acceptance. Buys all rights. Credit line sometimes given. E-mail for writer's guidelines or send SASE.

Illustration We purchase a very limited amount of freelance art at this time, but we are always looking for excellent coloring/activity book illustrators.

Photography Buys photography from freelancers for church bulletin covers. Contact: Curtis Corzine, creative director.

Tips "Writers request guidelines for church resource products before submitting. No guidelines available for children's products at present. We purchase a very limited amount of children's material, but we may grow into more children's products and opportunities. Make sure to include SASE. Solicited material will not be returned without SASE. Unsolicited material that does not follow guidelines will not be reviewed."

Play Publishers & Producers

Writing plays for children and family audiences is a special challenge. Whether creating an original work or adapting a classic, plays for children must hold the attention of audiences that often include children and adults. Using rhythm, repetition, and dramatic action are effective ways of holding the attention of kids. Pick subjects children can relate to, and never talk down to them.

Theater companies often have limited budgets so plays with elaborate staging and costumes often can't be produced. Touring companies want simple sets that can be moved easily. Keep in mind that they may have as few as three actors, so roles may have to be doubled up.

Many of the companies listed here produce plays with roles for adults and children, so check the percentage of plays written for adult and children's roles. Most importantly, study the types of plays a theater wants and doesn't want. Many name plays they've recently published or produced, and some have additional guidelines or information available. Be sure to check theaters' Web sites if they're given. For more listings of theaters open to submissions of children's and adult material and information on contests and organizations for playwrights, consult *Dramatists Sourcebook* (Theatre Communications Group, Inc.).

Information on play publishers listed in the previous edition but not included in this edition of *Children's Writer's & Illustrator's Market* may be found in the General Index.

Play Publishers

AMERICAN STAGE

P.O. Box 1560, St. Petersburg FL 33731-1560. (727)823-1600. Fax: (727)821-2444. E-mail: info@americanstage.o
rg. Web site: www.americanstage.org. **Producing Artistic Director:** Todd Olson. Estab. 1977. Produces 1 children's plays/year. Produces children's plays for mainstage, school tours.

Needs Limited by "Small mainstage venue, 1 touring production conducive to small cast, light technical pieces."
Subject matter: classics and original work for children (ages K-12) and families. Recently produced plays: *King Island Christmas* for the Mainstage and *Alexander and the Terrible, Horrible, No Good Very Bad Day* for the School Tour and Mainstage.

How to Contact Query with synopsis, character breakdown and set description. Will consider simultaneous submissions and previously performed work.

Terms Purchases "professional rights." Pays writers in royalties (6-8%); $25-35/performance. SASE for return of submission.

Tips Sees a move in plays toward basic human values, relationships and multicultural communities.

ANCHORAGE PRESS PLAYS, INC.

P.O. Box 2901, Louisville KY 40201-2901. Phone/fax: (502)583-2288. E-mail: applays@bellsouth.net. Web site: www.applays.com. **Publisher:** Marilee Miller. Estab. 1935. Publishes 4-6 plays/year.

Needs Seeking theatrical play scripts suitable for K-12 audience and family audience with timeless themes and well told stories. We publish plays and plays with music. Recently produced plays: *The Rose of Treason*, by James Devita; *The Pied Piper of Hamelin*, by Tim Wright; *Bless Cricket, Crest Toothpaste and Tommy Tune*, by Linda Daugerty; *Hey Diddle Diddle!*, by Marilee Hebert Miller.

How to Contact Query for guidelines first. Will consider simultaneous submissions and previously performed work "essential to be proven." Responds in 1 year.

Terms Buys all stage rights. Pays royalty (varies extensively from 50% minimum to 75%). Submissions returned with SASE.

Tips "The plays we publish are chosen for their suitability to be produced for a youth or family audience. We are less interested in classroom teaching aids."

APPLE TREE THEATRE

595 Elm Place, Suite 210, Highland Park IL 60035. (847)432-8223. Fax: (847)432-5214. E-mail: msage@appletreeth eatre.com. Web site: www.appletreetheatre.com. **Contact:** Education Director. Produces 3 children's plays/year.

Needs Produces professional, daytime and educational outreach programs for grades 4-9. 98% of plays written for adult roles; 2% for juvenile roles. Uses a unit set and limited to 9 actors. No musicals. Straight plays only. Does not want to see: "children's theater," i.e. Peter Rabbit, Snow White. Material *must* be based in social issues. Recently produced plays: *Diary of Anne Frank*, by Frances Goodrich and Albert Hackett (about the Holocaust, ages 10-up); *Roll of Thunder, Hear My Cry*, adapted from the novel by Mildred Taylor (about civil rights, racial discrimination in Mississippi in 1930s, ages 10-up).

How to Contact Query for guidelines first. Query with synopsis, character breakdown and set description. Will consider simultaneous submissions and previously performed work. Responds in 2 months.

Terms Payment negotiated per contract. Submissions returned with SASE.

Tips "Never send an unsolicited manuscript. Include reply postcard for queries."

BAKER'S PLAYS

P.O. Box 699222, Quincy MA 02269-9222. (617)745-0805. Fax: (617)745-9891. E-mail: info@bakersplays.com. Web site: www.bakersplays.com. **Managing Director:** Deirdre Shaw. Estab. 1845. Publishes 20 plays/year; 2 musicals/year.

Needs Adaptations of both popular and lesser known folktales. Subject matter: "full lengths for family audience and full lengths and one act plays for teens." Recently published plays: *Fairy Tale Courtroom*, by Dana Proulx; *More Aesop's (oh so slightly) Updated Fables*, by Kim Esop-Wylie.

How to Contact Submit complete ms, score and tape or CD of songs. Responds in approximately 8 months.

Terms Obtains worldwide rights. Pays writers in production royalties (amount varies) and book royalties.

Tips "Know the audience you're writing for before you submit your play anywhere. 90% of the plays we reject are not written for our market. When writing for children, never be afraid to experiment with language, characters or story. They are fertile soil for fresh, new ideas."

BARTER THEATRE EDUCATION WING

P.O. Box 867, Abingdon VA 24212. (276)628-2281, ext. 318. Fax: (276)619-3335. E-mail: education@bartertheat re.com. Web site: www.bartertheatre.com. **Artistic Director:** Richard Rose. **Education Director:** Katy Brown. Estab. 1933. Produces 7-10 children's plays/year.

Needs "We produce professional children's productions. 5-10% of plays/musicals written for adult roles; 90% written for juvenile roles. Recently produced plays: *Miss Nelson is Missing* (musical).

How to Contact Query with synopsis, character breakdown and set description. Will consider simultaneous submissions and previously performed work. Responds only if interested.

Terms Pays for performance ($20-60). Submissions returned with SASE.

Tips "Find creative, interesting material for children K-12. Don't talk below the audience."

CALIFORNIA THEATRE CENTER

P.O. Box 2007, Sunnyvale CA 94087. Fax: (408)245-0235. E-mail: resdir@ctcinc.org. Web site: www.ctcinc.org. **Resident Director:** Will Huddleston. Estab. 1975. Produces 15 children's plays and 1 musical for professional productions.

Needs 75% of plays/musicals written for adult roles; 20% for juvenile roles. Prefers material suitable for professional tours and repertory performance; one-hour time limit, limited technical facilities. Recently produced *Brave Irene*, adapted by Joan Cushing (children's lit, for grades K and up); *Dear Mr. Henshaw*, adapted by Gayle Cornelison from Beverley Cleary (children's classic, for greades 2 and up).

How to Contact Query with synopsis, character breakdown and set description. Send to: Will Huddleston. Will consider previously performed work. Responds in 6-12 months.

Terms Rights negotiable. Pays writers royalties; pays $35-50/performance. Submissions returned with SASE.

Tips "We sell to schools, so the title and material must appeal to teachers who look for things familiar to them. We look for good themes, universality. We also do a summer conservatory that requires plays with casts of 15-30 student actors."

CIRCA '21 DINNER THEATRE

P.O. Box 3784, Rock Island IL 61204-3784. (309)786-2667. Fax: (309)786-4119. Web site: http://circa21.com. **Producer:** Dennis Hitchcock. Estab. 1977. Produces 3 children's musicals/year.

Needs Produces children's plays for professional productions. 95% of musicals written for adult roles; 5% written for juvenile roles. "Prefer a cast of four to eight—no larger than ten. Plays are produced on mainstage sets." Recently produced plays: *Little Red Riding Hood's Big Adventure*, by Marc Pence (ages 4-adult); *Cinderella*, by Prince Street Players (ages 4-adult).

How to Contact Send complete script with audiotape of music. Responds in 3 months.

Terms Payment negotiable.

COLUMBIA ENTERTAINMENT COMPANY

% Betsy Phillips, 309 Parkade, Columbia MO 65202-1447. (573)874-5628. E-mail: bybetsy@yahoo.com. Web site: www.cectheatre.org. **Contest Director:** Betsy Phillips. Estab. 1988. Produces 0-2 children's plays/year; 0-1 children's musicals/year.

How to Contact Plays: Submit complete ms; use SASE to get form. Musicals: Submit complete ms and lead sheets. Score required if play is produced. CD or tape of music must be included, use SASE to get entry form. Will consider simultaneous submissions and previously performed work. Responds within 3 months of June 1st deadline. All scripts are read by a minimum of 3 readers. The authors will receive a written evaluation of the strengths and weaknesses of the play.

Terms "We have production rights sans royalties for one production. Production rights remain with author." Pays $500 1st prize. Submissions returned with SASE.

Tips "Please write a play/musical that appeals to all ages. We like plays that audiences of all ages will enjoy. We always need lots of parts, especially for girls."

COLUMBUS CHILDREN'S THEATRE

372 W. Nationwide Blvd., Columbus OH 43215. (614)224-6672. Fax: (614)224-8844. E-mail: bgshows@aol.com. Web site: www.colschildrenstheatre.org. **Artistic Director:** William Goldsmith. Estab. 1963. Produces 14 children's plays/year; 2-4 children's musicals/year.

Needs Produces Semi-Professional Children's Theatre Series, professional touring company (4 actors), Academy summer productions for ages 10-16 and ages 16-21. 60% of plays/musicals written for adult roles; 40% for juvenile roles. "Have some scenic limitations—a 175 seat thrust stage, very little backstage." Musical needs: "Always looking for a new holiday show." Recently produced plays: *Ebenzer!*, book by William Goldsmith, music and lyrics by Janet Vogt and Mark Friedman (world premiere musical for ages 4 and up); *The Forgiving Harvest*, by Y. York; *The Wright Brothers*, by William Godsmith (play for 4 actors performed by CCT Touring Company).

How to Contact Plays/musicals: Query with synopsis, character breakdown and set description. Will consider simultaneous submissions, e-mail submissions, previously performed work. Responds in 4-6 months.

Terms Rights on mss and scores negotiable. Pays 8% royalties; pays $35-$80/performance. Submissions returned with SASE.

Play Publishers

Tips "Be careful of 'dark' stories. No matter how good they are, parents do not want to bring their 4- or 5-year-olds to watch a play about a child dying. They can have serious subjects, but don't treat them darkly."

CONTEMPORARY DRAMA SERVICE

Division of Meriwether Publishing Ltd., 885 Elkton Dr., Colorado Springs CO 80907-3557. (719)594-4422. Fax: (719)594-9916. E-mail: merpcds@aol.com. Web site: www.meriwether.com. **Associate Editor:** Arthur L. Zapel. Estab. 1979. Publishes 60 children's plays/year; 15 children's musicals/year.

Needs Prefer shows with a large cast. 50% of plays/musicals written for adult roles; 50% for juvenile roles. Recently published plays: *Pecos Bill, Slue Foot Sue and the Wing Dang Doo!*, by Arthur Zapel and Bill Francoeur (a musical); *Cinderella*, by Kirk Buis (a comedy spoof); *The Night the Animals Sang*, by Katherine Babb (a Christmas play). "We publish church plays for elementary level for Christmas and Easter. Most of our secular plays are for teens or college level." Does not want to see "full-length, three-act plays unless they are adaptations of classic works or have unique comedy appeal."

How to Contact Query with synopsis, character breakdown and set description; "query first if a musical." Will consider simultaneous submissions or previously performed work. Responds in 1 month.

Terms Purchases first rights. Pays writers royalty (10%) or buys material outright for $200-1,000. SASE for return of submission.

Tips "If the writer is submitting a musical play, a CD of the music should be sent. We prefer plays with humorous action. We like comedies, spoofs, satires and parodies of known works. A writer should provide credentials of plays published and produced. Writers should not submit items for the elementary age level."

DALLAS CHILDREN'S THEATER

5938 Skillman, Dallas TX 75231-7608. Fax: (214)978-0118. E-mail: family@dct.org. Web site: www.dct.org. **Artistic Associate:** Artie Olaisen. Estab. 1984. Produces 8-10 youth/family plays/year. Produces 1-2 youth/family musicals/year.

Needs Produces children's plays for professional theater. 80% of plays/musicals written for adult roles; 20% for juvenile roles. Prefer cast size between 8-12. Musical needs: "We do produce musical works, but prefer nonmusical. Availability of music tracks is a plus." Does not want to see: anything not appropriate for a youth/family audience. Recently produced plays: *Holes*, by Louis Sachar (based on popular book, darkly humorous tale of crime, punishment and redemption for ages 8 and older); *Coyote Tales*, by Linda Daugherty (lively telling of traditional folk stories of Mexico for all ages). Does not accept unsolicited manuscripts.

How to Contact Plays and musicals: Query with synopsis, character breakdown and set description. Will consider previously performed work. Responds in up to 1 year. Please, no phone calls; no unsolicited scripts.

Terms Rights and payment are negotiable. Submissions returned with SASE. All scripts should be sent to the attention of Artie Olaisen.

Tips "We are only interested in full-length substantive works. Please no classroom pieces. Our mainstage season serves a multi-generational family audience."

DRAMATIC PUBLISHING, INC.

311 Washington St., Woodstock IL 60098. (815)338-7170. Fax: (815)338-8981. E-mail: plays@dramaticpublishing.com. Web site: www.dramaticpublishing.com. **Acquisitions Editor:** Linda Habjan. Estab. 1885. Publishes 10-15 children's plays/year; 4-6 children's musicals.

Needs Recently published: *Redwall: The Legend of Redwall Abbey*, by Evelyn Swensson, based on the book by Brian Jacques. *Gooney Bird Green and Her True-Life Adventures*, adapted by Kent R. Brown from the book by Lois Lowry; *Anastasia Krupnik*, by Meryl Friedman, based on the book by Lois Lowry; *A Village Fable*, by James Still, adapted from *In the Suicide Mountain*, by John Gardner; *The Little Prince*, adapted by Rick Cummins and John Scoullar.

How to Contact Submit complete ms/score and CD/videotape (if a musical); include SASE if materials are to be returned. Responds in 3 months. Pays writers in royalties.

Tips "Original plays dealing with hopes, joys and fears of today's children are preferred to adaptations of old classics. No more adapted fairytales."

DRAMATICS MAGAZINE

2343 Auburn Ave., Cincinnati OH 45219-2815. (513)421-3900. Fax: (513)421-7077. Web site: www.edta.org. **Editor:** Don Corathers. Publishes 7 young adult plays/year.

Needs Most of plays written for high school actors. 14-18 years old (grades 9-12) appropriate for high school production and study. "We prefer not to receive plays geared for young children." Recently produced plays: *Korczak's Children*, by Jeffrey Hatcher (about the final days of the orphanage in the Warsaw Ghetto); *Governing Alice*, by C. Denby Swanson (a young woman breaks all the rules to honor her brother, who was killed in a botched holdup of a conveneince store, ages 15 and up).

How to Contact Plays: Submit complete ms. Musicals: Not accepted. Will consider simultaneous submissions, electronic submissions via disk/modem, previously performed work. Responds in 6 months.
Terms Buys one-time publication rights. Payment varies. Submissions returned with SASE.
Tips Our readers are savvy theater makers. Give them more than stereotypes and fairy tales to work with.

ELDRIDGE PUBLISHING CO. INC.

P.O. Box 14367, Tallahassee FL 32317. (800)447-8243. Fax: (800)453-5179. E-mail: info@histage.com. Web site: www.histage.com or www.95church.com. **Editor:** Nancy Vorhis. Estab. 1906. Publishes approximately 25 children's plays/year; 2-3 children's musicals/year.
Needs "We publish for junior and senior high school, community theater and children's theater (adults performing for children), all genres, also religious plays." Recently published plays: *A Midsummer Night's Dream—A Musical*, adapted by Wade Bradford with music by Rachel Greenlee. Prefers work which has been performed or at least had a staged reading.
How to Contact Submit complete ms, sample or score and tape or CD of songs (if a musical). Will consider simultaneous submissions if noted. Responds in 3 months.
Terms Purchases all dramatic rights. Pays writers royalties of 50%; 10% copy sales; buys material outright for religious market.
Tips "Try to have your work performed, if at all possible, before submitting. We're always on the lookout for comedies which provide a lot of fun for our customers. But other more serious topics that concern teens, as well as intriguing mysteries and children's theater programs are of interest to us as well. We know there are many new talented playwrights out there, and we look forward to reading their fresh scripts."

ENCORE PERFORMANCE PUBLISHING

P.O. Box 95567, South Jordan UT 84095. (801)282-8159. Fax: (801)282-1701. E-mail: encoreplay@aol.com. Web site: www.encoreplay.com. **Contact:** Mike Perry. Estab. 1978. Publishes 20-30 children's plays/year; 10-20 children's musicals/year.
Needs Prefers close to equal male/female ratio if possible. Adaptations for K-12 and older. 60% of plays written for adult roles; 40% for juvenile roles. Recently published plays: *Boy Who Knew No Fear*, by G. Riley Mills/Mark Levenson (adaptation of fairy tale, ages 8-16); *Two Chains*, by Paul Burton (about drug abuse, ages 11-18).
How to Contact Query first with synopsis, character breakdown, set description, production history, and song list if musical. Will only consider previously performed work. Responds in 2 months.
Terms Purchases all publication and production rights. Author retains copyright. Pays writers in royalties (50%). SASE for return of submission.
Tips "Give us issue and substance, be controversial without offense. Use a laser printer! Don't send an old manuscript. Make yours look the most professional."

FLORIDA STUDIO THEATRE

1241 N. Palm Ave., Sarasota FL 34236. (941)366-9017. Fax: (941)955-4137. E-mail: james@fst2000.org. Web site: www.fst2000.org. **Artistic Director:** Richard Hopkins. **Casting and Literary Coordinator:** James Ashford. Estab. 1973. Produces 3 children's plays/year.
Needs Produces children's plays for professional productions. "Prefer small cast plays (5-8 characters) that use imagination more than heavy scenery." Will consider new plays and previously performed work.
How to Contact Query with synopsis, character breakdown, 5 pages of sample dialogue; Attn: James Ashford. Responds in 1 month to queries. Rights negotiable. Payment negotiable. Submissions returned with SASE.
Tips "Children are a tremendously sophisticated audience. The material should respect this."

THE FREELANCE PRESS

P.O. Box 548, Dover MA 02030. (508)785-8250. **Managing Editor:** Narcissa Campion. Estab. 1979.
Needs Casts are comprised of young people, ages 8-15, and number 25-30. "We publish original musicals on contemporary topics for children and adaptations of children's classics (e.g., Rip Van Winkle)." Published plays: *The Tortoise and the Hare* (based on story of same name, for ages 8-12); *Monopoly*, (3 young people walk through board game, for ages 11-15).
  • The Freelance Press does not accept plays for adult performers.
How to Contact Submit complete ms and score with SASE. Will consider simultaneous submissions and previously performed work. Responds in 3 months.
Terms Pays writers 10% royalties on book sales, plus performance royalties. SASE for return of submission.

SAMUEL FRENCH, INC.

45 W. 25th St., New York NY 10010. (212)206-8990. Fax: (212)206-1429. **Senior Editor:** Lawrence Harbison. Estab. 1830. Publishes very few children's plays/year; "variable number of musicals."
Needs Subject matter: "all genres, all ages. No puppet plays. No adaptations of any of those old 'fairy tales.' No 'Once upon a time, long ago and far away.' No kings, princesses, fairies, trolls, etc."

How to Contact Submit complete ms and demo tape (if a musical). Responds in "minimum of 2 months."

Terms Purchases "publication rights, amateur and professional production rights, option to publish next 3 plays." Pays writers "book royalty of 10%; variable royalty for professional and amateur productions. SASE for return of submissions.

Tips "Most of our recent children's plays have been published by our London affiliate, Samuel French, Ltd., or by our subsidiary, Baker's Plays."

HANGAR THEATRE

P.O. Box 205, Ithaca NY 14851. (607)273-8588. Fax: (607)273-4516. E-mail: playwrights@hangartheatre.org. Web site: www.hangartheatre.org. **Artistic Director:** Kevin Moriarty. Estab. 1975. Produces 7 children's plays/year; 2 children's musicals/year.

Needs Produces summer season of children's plays performed by the Lab Company. 100% of plays/musicals written for adult roles. Musical needs: "No new musicals accepted." Recently produced plays: *Jack and the Beanstalk*, by Marjorie Sokoloff (play about a boy's coming of age including deaf and hearing actors for ages 5-10); *Pinocchio, A Musical About Adoption*, by Susan DiLallo and Jeffrey Harris (ages 4-10).

How to Contact Plays: Submit complete ms. Responds only if interested.

Terms Royalties negotiable. Submissions returned with SASE.

Tips "Children's plays should be 60 minutes, with a recognizable title, character, or theme, and have less than 10 characters."

HEUER PUBLISHING COMPANY

P.O. Box 248, Cedar Rapids IA 52406. (319)368-8008. Fax: (319)368-8011. E-mail: editor@hitplays.com. Web site: www.heuerpublishing.com. Estab. 1928. **Editor in Chief:** Geri Albrecht. Publishes 30+ plays/year. 5+ musicals/year. Serves the educational and community theater markets.

Needs Heuer is a pioneer in commissioning and publishing unique works from a broad range of playwrights and composers for schools and community theatres. We are interested in shows that are entertaining, yet thought-provoking, family appropriate yet edgy. Our new genre of plays and musicals address such areas as Multi-Cultural Awareness, Interactive Plays, Creative Dramatics and dramas that address a broad range of social challenges in the Social Scene. Recently published plays/musicals: *Hush, Little Baby*, by Craig Sodaro (a luminous drama about the destructive chain of child abuse); *The Gilded Turkey*, by T.A. Powell (a romantic comedy); *Mye and the Sandpeople*, by Celeste Bonfanti (a fantastical interactive fairy tale); *Romeo and Beatrice and Toto, Too*, by Claudia Haas (a backstage comedy).

How to Contact Submissions accepted online at www.heuerpublishing.com or through the mail. Will consider simultaneous submissions and welcomes previously performed work. Responds in 2 months.

Terms Contracts amateur and professional rights. Pays royalty or purchases work outright. Submissions returned with SASE.

Tips "We will continue to broaden our product offering and will expand our thematic areas of interest in 2005-2006 to include ten-minute plays, children' s theatre with flexibility for child or adult actors, classic literature, Shakespeare with a twist, operas/operettas, radio theater, world theatre, curriculum-based plays and duets."

MU PERFORMING ARTS

2700 NE Winter St. #1A, Minneapolis MN 55413. (612)824-4804. Fax: (612)824-3396. E-mail: ricks@muperformingarts.org. Web site: www.muperformingarts.org. **Artistic Director:** Rick Shiomi. Estab. 1992. Produces 1 children's play/year.

Needs Produces professional (nonequity) regular seasons of 4 productions per year plus various development festivals. 90% of plays/musicals written for adult roles; 10% for juvenile roles. Musical needs: and Asian American subject matter." Recently produced plays: *Tiger Tales: Hmong Folktales*, by R.A. Shiomi Cha Yang (play of Hmong folktales about tigers for elementary thr ough middle school); *The Magic Bus to Asian Folktales*, by R.A. Shiomi, Cha Yang Jaz Canlas (play about Asian folktales told by school bus driver for ages elementary thr ough middle school).

How to Contact Plays: Query with synopsis, character breakdown and set description; submit complete ms. Musicals: Query with synopsis, character breakdown and set description. Will consider simultaneous submissions, previously performed work. Responds only if interested.

Terms Buys all rights on manuscripts, production, and scores. Pays royalties; pays/performance.

Tips "Send synopsis and script and if you hear from us, we are interested."

THE NEW CONSERVATORY THEATRE CENTER

25 Van Ness Ave., San Francisco CA 94102-6033. (415)861-4914. Fax: (415)861-6988. E-mail: e-mail@nctcsf.org. Web site: www.nctcsf.org. **Executive Director:** Ed Decker. Estab. 1981. Produces 3-5 children's plays/year; 1 children's musical/year.

Needs Limited budget and small casts only. Produces children's plays as part of ''a professional theater arts training program for youths ages 8-19 during the school year and 2 summer sessions. The New Conservatory also produces educational plays for its touring company. We do not want to see any preachy or didactic material.'' Recently produced plays: *Really Rosie* (ages 5-8); *And Then They Came For Me: Remembering the World of Anne Frank*, by James Still (ages 12 and up).

How to Contact Query with synopsis, character breakdown and set description, or submit complete ms and score. Responds in 3 months.

Terms Rights purchased negotiable. Pays writers in royalties. SASE for return of submission.

Tips ''Wants plays with name recognition, i.e., *The Lion, the Witch and the Wardrobe* as well as socially relevant issues. Plays should be under 50 minutes in length.''

NEW PLAYS INCORPORATED

P.O. Box 5074, Charlottesville VA 22905-0074. (434)823-7555. E-mail: patwhitton@aol.com. Web site: www.newplaysforchildren.com. **Publisher:** Patricia Whitton Forrest. Estab. 1964. Publishes 3-4 plays/year; 1 or 2 children's musicals/year.

Needs Publishes ''generally material for kindergarten through junior high.'' Recently published: *Everyman in the Circus of Life*, by Travis Tyre (contemporary adaptation of the medieval classic); *Buried Treasure*, by Tom Ballmar (adventure play for upper elementary/junior high).

How to Contact Submit complete ms and score. Will consider simultaneous submissions and previously performed work. Responds in 2 months (usually).

Terms Purchases exclusive rights to sell acting scripts. Pays writers in royalties (50% of production royalties; 10% of script sales). SASE for return of submission.

Tips ''Write the play you really want to write (not what you think will sell) and find a director to put it on.''

NEW YORK STATE THEATRE INSTITUTE

37 First St., Troy NY 12180. (518)274-3200. Fax: (518)274-3815. E-mail: nysti@capital.net. Web site: www.nysti.org. **Producing Artistic Director:** Patricia B. Snyder. Estab. 1976. Produces 5 children's plays/year; 1-2 children's musicals/year.

Needs Produces full-length family plays for professional theater. 90% of plays/musicals are written for adult roles; 10% for juvenile roles. Does not want to see plays for children only. Produced plays: *A Tale of Cinderella*, by Will Severin, W.A. Frankonis and George David Weiss (all ages); *Miracle On 34th Street*, by Valentine Davies; more than 3 dozen premieres.

How to Contact Query with synopsis, character breakdown and set description; submit tape of songs (if a musical). Will consider simultaneous submissions and previously performed work. Responds in 6 weeks for queries. SASE for return of submission.

Tips Writers should be mindful of ''audience *sophistication*. We do not wish to see material that is childish. Writers should submit work that is respectful of young people's intelligence and perception—work that is appropriate for families, but that is also challenging and provocative.''

THE OPEN EYE THEATER

P.O. Box 959, Margaretville NY 12455. Phone/fax: (845)586-1660. E-mail: openeye@catskill.net. Web site: www.theopeneye.org. **Producing Artistic Director:** Amie Brockway. Estab. 1972 (theater). Produces 3 plays/year for a family audience. Most productions include music but are not musicals.

Needs ''Casts of various sizes. Technical requirements are kept to a minimum.'' Produces professional productions combining professional artists and artists-in-training (actors of all ages). Recently produced plays: *Freddy, The King of Detectives*, by Sandra Fenichel Asher, with music by Robert Cucinnota; *John Chapman and the Devil*, by Mary Barile; *The Wide Awake Princess*, by David Paterson, music by Steve Liebman; *Pixies, Kings and Magical Things*, by Ric Averil.

How to Contact ''No videos or cassettes. Letter of inquiry only. Will consider previously performed work. '' Responds in 6 months.

Terms Rights agreement negotiated with author. Pays writers one-time fee or royalty negotiated with publisher. SASE for return of submission.

Tips ''Send letter of inquiry only. We are interested in plays for a multigenerational audience (8-adult).''

PIONEER DRAMA SERVICE

P.O. Box 4267, Englewood CO 80155-4267. (303)779-4035. Fax: (303)779-4315. E-mail: editors@pioneerdrama.com. Web site: www.pioneerdrama.com. **Submissions Editor:** Lori Conary. **Publisher:** Steven Fendrich. Estab. 1960. Publishes more than 10 new plays and musicals/year.

Needs ''We are looking for plays no longer than 90 minutes long, large ensemble casts with plenty of female and/or flexible roles and simple sets.'' Publishes plays for ages upper elementary school through high school, children's and community theatre. Recently published plays/musicals: *No Strings Attached*, by Patrick Rainville Dorn, music and lyrics by Bill Francoeur; *Comic Book Artist*, by Pat Lydersen. Wants to see "script, CD/tape of music, proof of production and reviews."

How to Contact Query with synopsis, character breakdown, running time and set description or submit complete ms and CD/cassette of music (if a musical) with SASE. Will consider simultaneous submissions, e-mail submissions, previously performed work. Contact submissions editor. Responds in 4-6 months. Send SASE for writer's guidelines.

Terms Purchases all rights. Pays writers in royalties (10% on sales, 50% royalties on productions). Research Pioneer through catalog and Web site.

Tips "Research the company. Include a cover letter and a SASE."

PLAYERS PRESS, INC.

P.O. Box 1132, Studio City CA 91614-0132. (818)789-4980. **Vice President:** R.W. Gordon. Estab. 1965. Publishes 10-20 children's plays/year; 3-12 children's musicals/year.

Needs Subject matter: "We publish for all age groups." Recently published: *African Folk Tales*, by Carol Korty (for ages 10-14).

How to Contact Query with synopsis, character breakdown and set description; include #10 SASE with query. Considers previously performed work only. Responds to query in 1 month; submissions in 1 year.

Terms Purchases stage, screen, TV rights. Payment varies; work purchased possibly outright upon written request. Submissions returned with SASE.

Tips "Submit as requested—query first and send only previously produced material. Entertainment quality is on the upswing and needs to be directed at the world, no longer just the U.S. Please submit with two #10 SASEs plus manuscript-size SASE. Please do not call."

PLAYS, The Drama Magazine for Young People

P.O. Box 600160, Newton MA 02460. E-mail: lpreston@playsmag.com. Web site: www.playsmag.com. **Editor:** Elizabeth Preston. Estab. 1941. Publishes 70-75 children's plays/year.

Needs "Props and staging should not be overly elaborate or costly. There is little call among our subscribers for plays with only a few characters; ten or more (to allow all students in a class to participate, for instance) is preferred. We're especially in need of play for high school that have roles for 15-20 actors. Our plays are performed by children in school from lower elementary grades through middle school and high school." 100% of plays written for juvenile roles. Subject matter: Audience is lower grades through high school. Recently published plays: Critic's Choice, by Craig Sodaro (when three women stranded in a snowstorm come upon an abandoned cabin, their initial relief turns to high anxiety as they realize they're not alone); *The Booth Who Saved Lincoln*, by Renee C. Rebman (a bizarre turn of events forever connects two famous names in history); *The Bully of Barksdale Street*, by Eric Alter (Josh outsmarts the neighborhood tough guy—a tribute to best friends and baseball card collectors everywhere); *Tales of the Tangled Tresses*, by Christina Hamlett (fairy tale characters get major makeovers at the Fabulous Frills Salon); *The Pie That Changed History*, by Maureen Crane Wartski (a favorite family recipe inspires Joel to honor ancestors who helped slaves find their way on the Underground Railroad). "Send nothing downbeat—no plays about drugs, sex or other 'heavy' topics."

How to Contact Query first on adaptations of folktales and classics; otherwise submit complete ms. Responds in 2 weeks to queries, 4 weeks to mss.

Terms Buys all rights. Pay rates vary. Guidelines available; send SASE. For sample copy, send 6×9 SAE with 87¢ postage.

Tips "Get your play underway quickly. Keep it wholesome and entertaining. No preachiness, heavy moral or educational message. Any 'lesson' should be imparted through the actions of the characters, not through unbelievable dialogue. Use realistic situations and settings without getting into downbeat, depressing topics. No sex, drugs, violence, alcohol."

RIVERSIDE CHILDREN'S THEATRE

3280 Riverside Park Dr., Vero Beach FL 32963. (772)234-8052. Fax: (772)234-4407. E-mail: rct@riversidetheatre.com. Web site: www.riversidetheatre.com. **Education Director:** Linda Downey. Estab. 1980. Produces 4 children's plays/year; 2 children's musicals/year.

Needs Produces amateur youth productions. 100% of plays/musicals written for juvenile roles. Musical needs: for children ages 6-18. Produced plays: *The Beloved Dearly*, by Dory Cooney (pet bereavement, general); *Taming of the Shrew*, by Shakespeare (general).

How to Contact Plays/musicals: Query with synopsis, character breakdown and set description. Will consider simultaneous submissions, electronic submissions via disk/modem and previously performed work. Responds only if interested.

Terms Pays royalty or $40-60 per performance. Submissions returned with SASE.
Tips ''Interested in youth theatre for children ages 6-18 to perform.''

SEATTLE CHILDREN'S THEATRE

201 Thomas St., Seattle WA 98109. Fax: (206)443-0442. Web site: www.sct.org. **Literary Manager:** Torrie McDonald. Estab. 1975. Produces 7 full-length children's plays/year; 1 full-length children's musical/year. Produces children's plays for professional productions (September-June).
Needs ''We generally use adult actors even for juvenile roles.'' Recenlty produced plays: *Bunniculam*, by James and Deborah Howe; *Pink and Say*, by Oyamo (adaptation from Patricia Polacco 's book); *Holes*, by Louis Sacher. Does not want to see anything that condescends to young people—anything overly broad in style.
How to Contact Accepts agented scripts or those accompanied by a professional letter of recommendation (director or dramaturg). Responds in 1 year.
Terms Rights vary. Payment method varies. Submissions returned with SASE.
Tips ''Please *do not* send unsolicited manuscripts. We prefer sophisticated material (our weekend performances have an audience that is half adults).''

TADA!

15 W. 28th St., 3rd Floor, New York NY 10001. (212)252-1619. Fax: (212)252-8763. E-mail: jgreer@tadatheater.com. Web site: www.tadatheater.com. **Associate Artistic Director:** Joanna Greer. Estab. 1984. Produces 4 staged readings of children's plays and 3 musicals/year.
Needs ''All actors are children, ages 8-17.'' Produces children's plays for professional, year-round theater. 100% of plays/musicals written for juvenile roles. Recently produced musicals: *Sleepover*, by Phillip Freedman and James Belloff (peer acceptance, for ages 3 and up); *The Little House of Cookies*, by Janine Nina Trevens and Joel Gelpe (international communication and friendship). Does not want to see fairy tales or material that talks down to children.
How to Contact Query with synopsis, character breakdown and set description; submit complete ms, score and tape of songs (if a musical). Responds in 1 year ''or in October following the August deadline for our Annual Playwriting Competition. (Send two copies of manuscript if for competition).''
Terms Rights purchased ''depend on the piece.'' Pays writers in royalties of 6% and/or pays commissioning fee. SASE a must for return of submissions.
Tips ''For plays for our Annual One Act Playwriting Competition, submit before early January (January 9 for 2006 competition). We're looking for plays with current topics that specific age ranges can identify with, with a small cast of children and one or two adults. Our company is multiracial and city-oriented. We are not interested in fairy tales. We like to produce material that kids relate to and that touches their lives today.''

THEATRE FOR YOUNG AMERICA

P.O. Box 356, Mission KS 66202. (913)831-2131. **Artistic Director:** Gene Mackey. Estab. 1974. Produces 9 children's plays/year; 3-5 children's musicals/year.
Needs ''We use a small cast (4-7), open thrust stage.'' Theatre for Young America is a professional equity company. 90% of plays/musicals written for adult roles; 10% for juvenile roles. Produced plays: *The Wizard of Oz*, by Jim Eiler and Jeanne Bargy (for ages 6 and up); *A Partridge in a Pear Tree*, by Lowell Swortzell (deals with the 12 days of Christmas, for ages 6 and up); *Three Billy Goats Gruff*, by Gene Mackey and Molly Jessup (Norwegian folk tales, for ages 6 and up).
How to Contact Query with synopsis, character breakdown and set description. Will consider simultaneous submissions and previously performed work. Responds in 2 months.
Terms Purchases production rights, tour rights in local area. Pays writers in royalties or $10-50/performance.
Tips Looking for ''cross-cultural material that respects the intelligence, sensitivity and taste of the child audience.''

THEATREWORKS/USA

151 W. 26th, 7th Floor, New York NY 10001. (212)647-1100. Fax: (212)924-5377. E-mail: info@theatreworksusa.org. Web site: www.theatreworks.org. **Artistic Director:** Barbara Pasternack. **Associate Artistic Director:** Michael Alltop. Estab. 1960. Produces 3-4 children's plays and musicals/year.
Needs Cast of 5 or 6 actors. Play should be 1 hour long, tourable. Professional children's theatre comprised of adult equity actors. 100% of shows are written for adult roles. Produced plays: *Junie B. Jones*, by Marcie Heisler and Zina Goldrich; *Sarah, Plain and Tall*, by Larry O'Keefe, Nell Benjamin and Julia Jordan; *Henry and Mudge*, by Brian Lowdermilk and Kait Kerrigan.
How to Contact Currently not accepting submissions.
Terms Pays writers royalties of 6%. SASE for return of submission.
Tips ''Plays should be not only entertaining, but 'about something.' They should touch the heart and the mind. They should not condescend to children.''

Young Writer's & Illustrator's Markets

The listings in this section are special because they publish work of young writers and artists (under age 18). Some of the magazines listed exclusively feature the work of young people. Others are adult magazines with special sections for the work of young writers. There are also a few book publishers listed that exclusively publish the work of young writers and artists. Many of the magazines and publishers listed here pay only in copies, meaning authors and illustrators receive one or more free copies of the magazine or book to which they contributed.

As with adult markets, markets for children expect writers to be familiar with their editorial needs before submitting. Many of the markets listed will send guidelines to writers. Guidelines state exactly what a publisher accepts and how to submit it. You can often get these by sending a request with a self-addressed, stamped envelope (SASE) to the magazine or publisher, or by checking a publication's Web site (a number of listings include Web addresses). In addition to obtaining guidelines, read through a few copies of any magazines you'd like to submit to—this is the best way to determine if your work is right for them.

A number of kids' magazines are available on newsstands or in libraries. Others are distributed only through schools, churches or home subscriptions. If you can't find a magazine you'd like to see, most editors will send sample copies for a small fee.

Before you submit your material to editors, take a few minutes to read Before Your First Sale on page 7 for more information on proper submission procedures. You may also want to check out two other sections—Contests, Awards & Grants and Conferences & Workshops. Some listings in these sections are open to students (some exclusively)—look for the phrase **Open to students** in bold. Additional opportunities and advice for young writers can be found in *The Young Writers Guide to Getting Published* (Writer's Digest Books) and *A Teen's Guide to Getting Published: the only writer's guide written by teens for teens*, by Danielle and Jessica Dunn (Prufrock Press). More information on these books are given in the Helpful Books & Publications section in the back of this book.

Information on companies listed in the previous edition but not included in this edition of *Children's Writer's & Illustrator's Market* may be found in the General Index.

THE ACORN

1530 Seventh St., Rock Island IL 61201. (309)788-3980. **Editor:** Betty Mowery. Audience consists of "teachers, parents, young authors." Purpose in publishing works of children: "to provide a showcase for young authors. We hope to publish material other publications won't." Children must be K-12 (put name, address, grade on mss). Guidelines and contest rules available for SASE.

Magazines 100% of magazine written by children. Uses 6 fiction pieces (500 words); 20 pieces of poetry (32 lines). No personal essays. No payment; purchase of a copy isn't necessary to be printed. Sample copy $3. Subscription $10 for 4 issues. Submit mss to Betty Mowery, editor. Send complete ms. Will accept typewritten, legibly handwritten and/or computer printout. Include SASE. Responds in 1 week. Will not respond without SASE.

Artwork Publishes artwork by children. Looks for "all types; size 4×5. Use black ink in artwork." No cash payment or copy. Submit artwork either with ms or separately to Betty Mowery. Include SASE. Responds in 1 week.

Tips "Always include SASE and put name on manuscripts. When submitting to contests send SASE plus entry fee of six 37¢ stamps." Also publishes *The Shepherd*, and inspirational publication.

AMERICAN GIRL

8400 Fairway Place, Middleton WI 53562. (608)836-4848. Fax: (608)831-7089. Web site: www.americangirl.com. **Contact:** Magazine Department Assistant. Bimonthly magazine. Audience consists of girls ages 8-12 who are joyful about being girls. Purpose in publishing works by young people: "self-esteem boost and entertainment for readers. *American Girl* values girls' opinions and ideas. By publishing their work in the magazine, girls can share their thoughts with other girls! Young writers should be 8-12 years old. We don't have writer's guidelines for children's submissions. Instruction for specific solicitations appears in the magazine."

Magazines 20% of magazine written by young people. "A few pages of each issue feature articles that include children's answers to questions or requests that have appeared in a previous issue of *American Girl*." Pays in copies. Submit to address listed in magazine. Will accept legibly handwritten mss. Include SASE. Responds in 3 months.

Tips "Please, no stories, poems, etc. about American Girls Collection Characters (Felicity, Samantha, Molly, Kirsten, Addy, Josefina or Kit). Inside *American Girl*, there are several departments that call for submissions. Read the magazine carefully and submit your ideas based on what we ask for."

CHILD LIFE

Children's Better Health Institute, P.O. Box 567, Indianapolis IN 46206. Parcels and packages: please send to 1100 Waterway Blvd., Indianpolis IN 46202. (317)634-1100. Fax: (317)684-8094. Web site: www.childlifemag.org. **Editor:** Jack Gramling. **Art Director:** Rob Falco. Magazine published 6 times/year. Estab. 1921. Circ. 30,000. Targeted toward kids ages 9-11. Focuses on health, sports, fitness, nutrition, safety, academic excellence, general interests, and the nostalgia of *Child Life's* early days. "We publish jokes, riddles and poems by children." Kids should include name, address, phone number (for office use) and school photo. "No mass duplicated, multiple submissions."

• Child Life is no longer accepting manuscripts for publication. "We use submissions from kids ages 9-11. Those older or younger should try one of our sister publications: *Children's Digest, Children's Playmate, Humpty Dumpty's Magazine, Jack and Jill, Turtle Magazine, U*S*Kids*."

CHIXLIT, the literary 'zine by and for chicks ages 7 to 17

P.O. Box 12051, Orange CA 92859. E-mail: submit@chixlit.com. Web site: www.chixlit.com. Bimonthly 'zine is a place for girls ages 7-17 to express themselves. "We coax emerging talent and emotions; share writing techniques and feelings; and let each other know we are not alone. Writers must be female and age 7-17. From anywhere in the world is OK, if writing in English. We like a parent or adult guardian to tap with us and let us know it's honest work and OK to print. Writer's guidelines available on request and on Web site. Our audience is also teachers, librarians and scout leaders who want to encourage writing and confidence-building, as well as children's book authors who want to know what's going on in our heads!"

Magazines 95% written by young people. "We publish poems, short stories, reviews, rants, raves, love letters, song lyrics, journal entries and more. Always looking for regular contributors, critics, editors." Pays 1 free copy of the 'zine and discount on subscription rate. Prizes for contests. Submit complete ms. Will accept typewritten form. Accepts e-mail submissions "in the body of an e-mail (no attachments). Must be in English. We plan a bilingual-Spanish-language edition for late 2006." Include SASE if you want your submission back or an answer by snail mail (but we prefer e-mail). Responds in 4 weeks, usually faster; include your contact info!

Artwork Publishes artwork and photography by girls ages 7-17 or of girls in that age range. Looks for "iconic images of chix, things chix like, or whatever makes you think of chix. Must be flat and scannable and look decent in b&w." Pays 1 free issue for artwork used and a small gift if chosen for the cover. "We prefer submission of work (original or a good color or b&w copy) in a flat envelope (not rolled) and sent to our P.O. box (so not too big)."

Tips "We dare you to dare. Our motto is, 'Words are powerful, and they can make you powerful too.' Buy a subscription or back issues to see what we're about and what other chix are up to."

CICADA

Carus Publishing Company, P.O. Box 300, 315 Fifth St., Peru IL 61354. (815)224-5803, ext. 656. Fax: (815)224-6615. Web site: www.cricketmag.com. **Editor-in-Chief:** Marianne Carus. **Executive Editor:** Deborah Vetter. **Associate Editor:** Tracy Schoenle. Senior Art Director: Ron McCutchan. Bimonthly magazine.

- *Cicada* publishes work of writers and artists of high-school age (must be at least 14 years old). See the *Cicada* listing in the magazines section for more information, or check their Web site or copies of the magazine.

⚙ THE CLAREMONT REVIEW

4980 Wesley Rd., Victoria BC V8Y 1Y9 Canada. (250)658-5221. Fax: (250)658-5387. E-mail: susan_field@sd63.bc.ca. Web site: www.theClaremontReview.ca. Magazine. Publishes 2 books/year by young adults. Publishes poetry and fiction with literary value by students aged 13-19 anywhere in English-speaking world. Purpose in publishing work by young people: to provide a literary venue. Sponsors annual writing contest with March 15 deadline.

Magazines Uses 10-12 fiction stories (200-2,500 words); 30-40 poems. Pays in copies. Submit mss to editors. Submit complete ms. Will accept typewritten mss. SASE. Responds in 6 weeks (except during the summer).

Artwork Publishes artwork by young adults. Looks for b&w copies of imaginative art. Pays in copies. Send picture for review. Negative may be requested. Submit art and photographs to editors. SASE. Responds in 6 weeks.

Tips "Read us first—it saves disappointment. Know who we are and what we publish. We're closed July and August. SASE a must. American students send I.R.C.'s as American stamps *do not* work in Canada."

CREATIVE KIDS

P.O. Box 8813, Waco TX 76714-8813. (800)998-2208. Fax: (254)756-3339. E-mail: ck@prufrock.com. Web site: www.prufrock.com. **Editor:** Jenny Robins. Magazine published 4 times/year. Estab. 1979. "All material is by children, for children." Purpose in publishing works by children: "to create a product that provides children with an authentic experience and to offer an opportunity for children to see their work in print. *Creative Kids* contains the best stories, poetry, opinion, artwork, games and photography by kids ages 8-14." Writers ages 8-14 must have statement by teacher or parent verifying originality. Writer's guidelines available on request with SASE.

Magazines Uses fiction and nonfiction stories (800-900 words), poetry, plays, ideas to share (200-750 words) per issue. Pays "free magazine." Submit mss to submissions editor. Will accept typewritten mss. Include SASE. Responds in 1 month.

Artwork/Photography Publishes artwork and photos by children. Looks for "any kind of drawing, cartoon, or painting." Pays "free magazine." Send color copy of the work to submissions editor. Include SASE. Responds in 1 month.

Tips "*Creative Kids* is a magazine by kids, for kids. The work represents children's ideas, questions, fears, concerns and pleasures. The material never contains racist, sexist, or violent expression. A person may submit one piece of work per envelope. Each piece must be labeled with the student's name, birth date, grade, school, home address and school address. Material submitted to *Creative Kids* must not be under consideration by any other publication. Items should be carefully prepared, proofread and double checked (perhaps also by a parent or teacher). All activities requiring solutions must be accompanied by the correct answers. Young writers and artists should always write for guidelines and then follow them."

CREATIVE WITH WORDS, Thematic anthologies

Creative with Words Publications, P.O. Box 223226, Carmel CA 93922. Fax: (831)655-8627. E-mail: cwwpub@us a.net. Web site: http://members.tripod.com/CreativeWithWords. **Editor:** Brigitta Geltrich. **Nature Editor:** Bert Hower. Publishes 10 anthologies/year. Estab. 1975. "We publish the creative writing of children (2 anthologies written by children; 2 anthologies written by adults; 6-8 anthologies written by all ages)." Audience consists of children, families, schools, libraries, adults, reading programs. Purpose in publishing works by children: to offer them an opportunity to get started in publishing. "Work must be of quality, typed, original, unedited, and not published before; age must be given (up to 19 years old) and home address." SASE must be enclosed with all correspondence and mss. Writer's guidelines and theme list available on request with SASE, via e-mail or on Web site.

Books Considers all categories except those dealing with sensationalism, death, violence, pornography and overtly religious themes. Uses fairy tales, folklore items (up to 800 words) and poetry (not to exceed 20 lines, 46 characters across). Published Folklore and Nature Series: Seasons, Nature, School, Love and Relationships (all children and adults). Offers 20% discount on each copy of publication in which fiction or poetry by children appears. Submit mss to editor. Query; child, teacher or parent can submit; teacher and/or parents must verify originality of writing. Will accept typewritten and/or legibly handwritten mss sent with SASE. ''Will not go through agents or over-protective 'stage mothers.''' Responds in 1 month after deadline of any theme.

Artwork/Photography Publishes b&w artwork, b&w photos and computer artwork created by children (language art work). No already existing computer artwork. Offers 20% discount on every copy of publication in which work by children appears. Submit artwork to editor, and request info on payment.

Tips ''Enjoy the English language, life and the world around you. Look at everything from a different perspective. Look at the greatness inside all of us. Be less descriptive and use words wisely. Let the reader experience a story through a viewpoint character, don't be overly dramatic. Match illustrations/photos to the meaning of the story or poem.''

HIGH SCHOOL WRITER

P.O. Box 718, Grand Rapids MN 55744-0718. (218)326-8025. Fax: (218)326-8025. E-mail: writer@mx3.com. **Editor:** Emily Benes. Magazine published 6 times during the school year. ''The *High School Writer* is a magazine written *by* students *for* students. All submissions must exceed contemporary standards of decency.'' Purpose in publishing works by young people: to provide a real audience for student writers—and text for study. Submissions by junior high and middle school students accepted for our junior edition. Senior high students' works are accepted for our senior high edition. Students attending schools that subscribe to our publication are eligible to submit their work.'' Writer's guidelines available on request.

Magazines Uses fiction, nonfiction (2,000 words maximum) and poetry. Submit mss to editor. Submit complete ms (teacher must submit). Will accept typewritten, computer-generated (good quality) mss.

Tips ''Submissions should not be sent without first obtaining a copy of our guidelines (see page 2 of every issue). Also, submissions will not be considered unless student's school subscribes.''

HIGHLIGHTS FOR CHILDREN

803 Church St., Honesdale PA 18431. (570)253-1080. Magazine. Published monthly. ''We strive to provide wholesome, stimulating, entertaining material that will encourage children to read. Our audience is children ages 2-12.'' Purpose in publishing works by young people: to encourage children's creative expression.

Magazines 15-20% of magazine written by children. Uses stories and poems. Also uses jokes, riddles, tongue twisters. Features that occur occasionally: ''What Are Your Favorite Books?'' (8-10/year), Recipes (8-10/year), ''Science Letters'' (15-20/year). Special features that invite children's submissions on a specific topic occur several times per year. Recent examples include ''Pet Stories,'' ''Best Costume Ever,'' ''Your Dream Job,'' and ''Help the Cartoonists.'' Pays in copies. Submit complete ms to the editor. Will accept typewritten, legibly handwritten and computer printout mss. Responds in 6 weeks.

Artwork Publishes artwork by children. Pays in copies. No cartoon or comic book characters. No commercial products. Submit b&w or color artwork on unlined paper for ''Your Own Pages.'' Features include ''Creatures Nobody Has Ever Seen'' (5-8/year) and ''You Illustrate the Story'' (18-20/year). Responds in 6 weeks.

Tips ''Remember to keep a photocopy of your work because we cannot return it. When submitting your work, please include your name, age, and full address.''

KWIL KIDS PUBLISHING, The Little Publishing Company That Kwil Built

Kwilville, P.O. Box 29556, Maple Ridge BC V2X 2V0 Canada. E-mail: kwilville@shaw.ca. Publishes weekly column in local paper, four quarterly newsletters. ''*Kwil Kids* come in all ages, shapes and sizes—from 4-64 and a whole lot more! Kwil does not pay for the creative work of children but provides opportunity/encouragement. We promote literacy, creativity and creative 'connections' through written and artistic expression and publish autobiographical, inspirational, stories of gentleness, compassion, truth and beauty. Our purpose is to foster a sense of pride and enthusiasm in young writers and artists, to celebrate the voice of youth and to encourage growth through joy-filled practice and cheerleading, not criticism.'' Must include name, age, address and parent signature (if a minor). Will send guidelines upon request.''

Books Publishes autobiographical, inspirational, creative stories (alliterative, rhyming refrains, juicy words), short rhyming and nonrhyming poems (creative, fun, original, expressive). Length: 500 words for fiction; 8-16 lines for poetry. No payments; self-published and sold ''at cost'' only (1 free copy). Submit mss to Kwil or Mr. Marquis. Submit complete ms. Send copy only; expect a reply but will not return ms. Will accept typewritten and legibly handwritten mss and e-mail. Include SASE or enclose IRC or $1 for postage, as US stamps may not be used from Canada. Responds in April, August and December.

Newsletter 95% of newsletter written by young people. Uses 15 short stories, poems (20-100 words). No

Young Writer's

payment; free newsletters only. Submit complete ms. Will accept typewritten and legibly handwritten mss and e-mail. Kwil answers every letter in verse. Responds in April, August and December.

Artwork Publishes artwork and photography by children with writing. Looks for black ink sketches to go with writing and photos to go with writing. Submit by postal mail only; white background for sketches. Submit artwork/photos to Kwil publisher. Submit holiday/seasonal work 4 months in advance. Include SASE. Responds in 3 months.

Tips "We love stories that teach a lesson or encourage peace, love and a fresh, new understanding. Just be who you are and do what you do. Then all of life's treasures will come to you."

NATIONAL GEOGRAPHIC KIDS

1145 17th St. NW, Washington DC 20036-4688. (202)857-7000. Fax: (202)775-6112. Web site: www.nationalgeo graphic.com/ngkids. Magazine published 10 times/year. Photo-driven magazine for ages 8-14. Purpose in publishing work for young people: to entertain while educating and exciting them about their world.

 • *National Geographic Kids* does not accept unsolicited manuscripts.

Tips Publishes children's artwork in the art department section, jokes in the just-joking section, and captions in the back talk section regarding the pictures appearing in previous issues. No payment given. Send by mail to: Submissions Committee. "Sorry, but we cannot acknowledge or return your contributions."

NEW MOON: The Magazine for Girls & Their Dreams

New Moon Publishing, Inc., 2 W. First St., #101, Duluth MN 55802. (218)728-5507. Fax: (218)728-0314. E-mail: girl@newmoon.org. Web site: www.newmoon.org. **Managing Editor:** Kate Freeborn. Bimonthly magazine. *New Moon*'s primary audience is girls ages 8-14. "We publish a magazine that listens to girls." More than 70% of *New Moon* is written by girls. Purpose in publishing work by children/teens: "We want girls' voices to be heard. *New Moon* wants girls to see that their opinions, dreams, thoughts and ideas count." Writer's guidelines available for SASE or online.

 • See *New Moon*'s listing in Magazines section.

Magazine Buys 6 fiction mss/year (1,200-1,600 words); 30 nonfiction mss/year (600 words). Submit to Editorial Department. Submit query or complete mss for nonfiction; complete ms only for fiction. "We do not return or acknowledge unsolicited material. Do not send originals—we will not return any materials." Responds in 6 months if interested.

Artwork/Photography Publishes artwork and photography by girls. "We do not return unsolicited material."

Tips "Read *New Moon* to completely understand our needs."

POTLUCK CHILDREN'S LITERARY MAGAZINE

P.O. Box 546, Deerfield IL 60015. (847)948-1139. Fax: (847)317-9492. E-mail: submissions@potluckmagazine.o rg. Web site: www.potluckmagazine.org. A not-for-profit quarterly magazine for and by writers/artists ages 8-16. "We look for works with imagery, humor and human truths. Editors are available to answer any questions the writer may have concerning his or her work. The purpose of *Potluck* is to educate today's young writers, to encourage creative expression and to provide a professional forum in which their voices can be heard. *Potluck* includes educational articles to help expand writing skills and the 'business' of writing. *Potluck* wants each writer's experience to be full of new accomplishments and new understandings." Writer's guidelines available on request with a SASE, within the magazine, or online.

Magazines 99% of magazine written by young people. Uses fiction (1,500 words); nonfiction (1,500 words); poetry (30 lines); book reviews (250 words). Pays with copy. Submit mss to Susan Napoli Picchietti, editor-in-chief. Submit complete ms; teacher may send en masse, but must review all work to ensure it complies with guidelines. Include a SASE for reply. Will accept typewritten and e-mailed mss (no attachments—place work within body of e-mail). Include SASE. Responds 6 weeks after deadline.

Artwork/Photography Publishes artwork by young artists. Looks for all types of artwork—no textured works. $8^{1}/_{2} \times 11$ preferred. Pays in copies. Do not fold submissions. Include proper postage and envelope for return of original artwork. Color photo copy accepted. Submit artwork to Susan Napoli Picchietti, editor-in-chief. Include SASE. Responds in 6 weeks after deadline.

Tips "Relax, observe and acknowledge all that is around you. Life gives us a lot to draw on. Don't get carried away with, 'style' let your words speak for themselves. If you want to be taken seriously as a writer, you must take yourself seriously. The rest will follow. Enjoy yourself and take pride in every piece, even the bad ones, because they keep you humble."

THE SHEPHERD

1530 7th St., Rock Island IL 61201. (309)788-3980. Magazine. **Editor:** Betty Mowery. "An inspirational publication including work by children K-12." 50% of material written by children.

Magazines Publishes fiction up to 500 words and poetry up to 35 lines. No payment offered. Manuscripts: SASE must be included.

Tips "Guidelines and contest rules are available with SASE. A sample copy is available for $3. Also publishes *The Acorn.*"

SKIPPING STONES

Multicultural Children's Magazine, P.O. Box 3939, Eugene OR 97403-0939. (541)342-4956. E-mail: editor@Skipp ingStones.org. Web site: www.SkippingStones.org. **Articles/Poems/Fiction Editor:** Arun N. Toke. 5 issues a year. Estab. 1988. Circulation 2,500. "*Skipping Stones* is a multicultural, nonprofit, children's magazine to encourage cooperation, creativity and celebration of cultural and environmental richness. It offers itself as a creative forum for communication among children from different lands and backgrounds. We prefer work by children under 18 years old. International, minorities and under-represented populations receive priority, multilingual submissions are encouraged." Guidelines for children's work available on request with SASE.

- *Skipping Stones'* theme for the Youth Honor Awards is multicultural/international understanding and nature awareness. Send SASE for guidelines and more information on the awards. *Skipping Stones*, now in it's 18th year, is winner of the N.A.M.E., Parents' Choice, and EDPRESS awards.

Magazines 70% written by children and teenagers. Uses 5-10 fiction short stories and plays (500-750 words); 5-10 nonfiction articles, interviews, letters, history, descriptions of celebrations (500-750 words); 15-20 poems, jokes, riddles, proverbs (250 words or less) per issue. Pays in contributor's copies. Submit mss to editor. Submit complete ms for fiction or nonfiction work; teachers and parents can also submit their contributions. Submissions should include "cover letter with name, age, address, school, cultural background, inspiration piece, dreams for future." Will accept typewritten, legibly handwritten and computer/word processor mss. Include SASE. Responds in 4 months. Accepts simultaneous submissions.

Artwork/Photography Publishes artwork and photography for children. Will review all varieties of ms/illustration packages. Wants comics, cartoons, b&w photos, paintings, drawings (preferably ink & pen or pencil), 8×10, color photos OK. Subjects include children, people, celebrations, nature, ecology, multicultural. Pays in contributor's copies.

Terms "*Skipping Stones* is a labor of love. You'll receive complimentary contributor's (up to 4) copies depending on the extent/length of your contribution. 25% discount on additional copies. We may allow others to reprint (including by electronic means) articles and art or photographs." Responds to artists in 4 months. Sample copy for $5 and 4 first-class stamps.

Tips "Let the 'inner child' within you speak out—naturally, uninhibited." Wants "material that gives insight on cultural celebrations, lifestyle, custom and tradition, glimpse of daily life in other countries and cultures. Please, no mystery for the sake of mystery! Photos, songs, artwork are most welcome if they illustrate/highlight the points. Upcoming features: Living abroad, turning points, inspirations and magical moments in life, cultural celebrations around the world, folktales, caring for the earth, endangered species, your dreams and visions, heroes, kid-friendly analysis of current events, resolving conficts, summer experiences, poetry, and minority experiences."

SPRING TIDES

824 Stillwood Dr., Savannah GA 31419. (912)925-8800. Annual magazine. Audience consists of children 5-12 years old. Purpose in publishing works by young people: to promote and encourage writing. Requirements to be met before work is published: must be 5-12 years old. Writers guidelines available on request.

Magazines 100% of magazine written by young people. Uses 5-6 fiction stories (1,200 words maximum); autobiographical experiences (1,200 words maximum); 15-20 poems (20 lines maximum) per issue. Writers are not paid. Submit complete ms or teacher may submit. Will accept typewritten mss. SASE.

Artwork Publishes artwork by children. "We have so far used only local children's artwork because of the complications of keeping and returning pieces."

STONE SOUP, The Magazine by Young Writers and Artists

Children's Art Foundation, P.O. Box 83, Santa Cruz CA 95063-0083. (831)426-5557. Fax: (831)426-1161. E-mail: editor@stonesoup.com. Web site: www.stonesoup.com. **Articles/Fiction Editor, Art Director:** Ms. Gerry Mandel. Magazine published 6 times/year. Circ. 20,000. "We publish fiction, poetry and artwork by children through age 13. Our preference is for work based on personal experiences and close observation of the world. Our audience is young people through age 13, as well as parents, teachers, librarians." Purpose in publishing works by young people: to encourage children to read and to express themselves through writing and art. Writer's guidelines available upon request with a SASE.

Magazines Uses animal, contemporary, fantasy, history, problem-solving, science fiction, sports, spy/mystery/ adventure fiction stories. Uses 5-10 fiction stories (150-2,500 words); 5-10 nonfiction stories (150-2,500 words); 2-4 poems per issue. Does not want to see classroom assignments and formula writing. Buys 65 mss/year.

Byline given. Pays on publication. Buys all rights. Pays $40 each for stories and poems, $40 for book reviews. Contributors also receive 2 copies. Sample copy $4. Free writer's guidelines. "We don't publish straight nonfiction, but we do publish stories based on real events and experiences." Send complete ms to editor. Will accept typewritten and legibly handwritten mss. Do not include SASE. Send copies, not originals. "If we are interested in publishing your work, you will hear from us in 6 weeks. If you don't hear from us, it means we could not use your work. Don't be discouraged. Try again."

Artwork/Photography Does not publish artwork other than illustrations. Pays $25 for color illustrations. Contributors receive 2 copies. Sample copy $ 5. Free illustrator's guidelines. Send color copies, not originals. If you would like to illustrate for *Stone Soup*, send us 2 or 3 samples (color copies) of your work, along with a letter telling us what kinds of stories you would like to illustrate. We are looking for artists who can draw complete scenes, including the background. Send submissions to editor. Include SASE. Responds in 6 weeks. All artwork must be by children through age 13.

Tips "Only work by young people through age 13 is considered. Whether your work is about imaginary situations or real ones, use your own experiences and observations to give your work depth and a sense of reality. Read a few issues of our magazine to get an idea of what we like."

⚡ WHAT IF?, Canada's Fiction Magazine for Teens

19 Lynwood Place, Guelph ON N1G 2V9 Canada. (519)823-2941. Fax: (519)823-8081. E-mail: editor@whatifmag azine.com. Magazine. Published 5 times/year. Writer's guidelines available on request.

● See full listing for *What If?* in Magazines section.

Magazines 100% of magazine written by Canadians 19 and under. Pays in copies. Submit mss to Mike Leslie, managing editor. Submit complete ms. Responds in 3 months.

Artwork Publishes artwork by Canadians 19 and under. Submit artwork to Jean Leslie, production manager. Include SASE for return of samples. Responds in 1 month.

Tips "Your chances for publication are better if you submit work other than contemporary fiction. We would like to see more science-fiction, fantasy, and other genres."

WHOLE NOTES

P.O. Box 1374, Las Cruces NM 88004-1374. (505)541-5744. E-mail: rnhastings@zianet.com. **Editor:** Nancy Peters Hastings. Magazine published twice yearly. "We encourage interest in contemporary poetry by showcasing outstanding creative writing. We look for original, fresh perceptions in poems that demonstrate skill in using language effectively, with carefully chosen images and clear ideas. Our audience (general) loves poetry. We try to recognize excellence in creative writing by children as a way to encourage and promote imaginative thinking." Writer's guidelines available for SASE.

Magazines Every fourth issue is 100% by children. Writers should be 21 years old or younger. Uses 30 poems/issue (length open). Pays complimentary copy. Submit mss to editor. Submit complete ms. "No multiple submissions, please." Will accept typewritten and legibly handwritten mss. SASE. Responds in 2 months.

Artwork/Photography Publishes artwork and photographs by children. Looks for b&w line drawings which can easily be reproduced; b&w photos. Pays complimentary copy. Send clear photocopies. Submit artwork to Nancy Peters Hastings, editor. SASE. Responds in 2 months.

Tips Sample issue is $3. "We welcome translations. Send your best work. Don't send your only copy of your poem. Keep a photocopy."

THE WRITERS' SLATE

The Writing Conference, Inc., P.O. Box 669, Ottawa KS 66067. Phone/fax: (785)242-1995. E-mail: jbushman@w ritingconference.com. Web site: www.writingconference.com. Magazine. Publishes 3 issues/year. *The Writers' Slate* accepts original poetry and prose from students enrolled in kindergarten-12th grade. The audience is students, teachers and librarians. Purpose in publishing works by young people: to give students the opportunity to publish and to give students the opportunity *to read* quality literature written by other students. Writer's guidelines available on request.

Magazines 90% of magazine written by young people. Uses 10-15 fiction, 1-2 nonfiction, 10-15 other mss per issue. Submit mss to Shelley McNerney, editor, 7619 Hemlock St., Overland Park KS 66204. Submit complete ms. Will accept typewritten mss. Responds in 1 month. Include SASE with ms if reply is desired.

Artwork Publishes artwork by young people. Bold, b&w, student artwork may accompany a piece of writing. Submit to Shelley McNerney, editor. Responds in 1 month.

Tips "Always accompany submission with a letter indicating name, home address, school, grade level and teacher's name. If you want a reply, submit a SASE."

Agents & Art Reps

T his section features listings of literary agents and art reps who either specialize in, or represent a good percentage of, children's writers and/or illustrators. While there are a number of children's publishers who are open to non-agented material, using the services of an agent or rep can be beneficial to a writer or artist. Agents and reps can get your work seen by editors and art directors more quickly. They are familiar with the market and have insights into which editors and art directors would be most interested in your work. Also, they negotiate contracts and will likely be able to get you a better deal than you could get on your own.

Agents and reps make their income by taking a percentage of what writers and illustrators receive from publishers. The standard percentage for agents is 10 to 15 percent; art reps generally take 25 to 30 percent. We have not included any agencies in this section that charge reading fees.

WHAT TO SEND

When putting together a package for an agent or rep, follow the guidelines given in their listings. Most agents open to submissions prefer initially to receive a query letter describing your work. For novels and longer works, some agents ask for an outline and a number of sample chapters, but you should send these only if you're asked to do so. Never fax or e-mail query letters or sample chapters to agents without their permission. Just as with publishers, agents receive a large volume of submissions. It may take them a long time to reply, so you may want to query several agents at one time. It's best, however, to have a complete manuscript considered by only one agent at a time. Always include a self-addressed, stamped envelope (SASE).

For initial contact with art reps, send a brief query letter and self-promo pieces, following the guidelines given in the listings. If you don't have a flier or brochure, send photocopies. Always include a SASE.

For those who both write and illustrate, some agents listed will consider the work of author/illustrators. Read through the listings for details.

As you consider approaching agents and reps with your work, keep in mind that they are very choosy about who they take on to represent. Your work must be high quality and presented professionally to make an impression on them. For additional listings of art reps see *Artist's & Graphic Designer's Market* (Writer's Digest Books).

For an agent's perspective on children's publishing, see the Insider Report with **Anna Olswanger** of Liza Dawson Associates on page 276.

Information on agents and art reps listed in the previous edition but not included in this edition of *Children's Writer's & Illustrator's Market* may be found in the General Index.

AGENTS

ADAMS LITERARY

7845 Colony Rd., #215, Charlotte NC 28226. (212)786-9140. Fax: (212)786-9170. E-mail: info@adamsliterary.c om. Web site: www.adamsliterary.com. **Contact:** Tracey Adams. Estab. 2004. Member of AAR and SCBWI. 20% of clients are new/previously unpublished writers. 100% of material handled is books for young readers.

- Prior to becoming an agent, Tracey Adams worked in the editorial and marketing departments at several children's publishing houses.

Represents Considers fiction, picture books, middle grade, young adult. "We place authors' work based on insight and experience. Adams Literary offers editorial guidance and marketing knowledge."

How to Contact Adams Literary is closed to unsolicited e-mails, queries and submissions. See Web site for updates on submission policy.

Terms Agent receives 15% commission on domestic sales; 20% on foreign sales. Offers written contract.

Writers' Conferences Attends Bologna Book Fair in Bologna, Italy. Other conferences listed on Web site.

Tips "We represent authors, not books, so we enjoy forming long-term relationships with our clients. We work hard to be sure we are submitting work which is ready to be considered, but we respect the role of editors and don't over-edit manuscripts ourselves. Our style is assertive yet collaborative."

BOOKSTOP LITERARY AGENCY

67 Meadow View Rd., Orinda CA 94563. Web site: www.bookstopliterary.com. Seeking both new and established writers. Estab. 1983. 100% of material handled is books of young readers.

Represents Considers fiction, nonfiction, picture books, middle grade, young adult. "Special interest in Hispanic writers and illustrators for children."

How to Contact Send entire ms with SASE. Considers simultaneous submissions. Responds in 6 weeks. Responds and returns material only with SASE.

Terms Agent receives 15% commission on domestic sales. Offers written contract, binding for 1 year.

ANDREA BROWN LITERARY AGENCY, INC.

1076 Eagle Dr., Salinas CA 93905. (831)422-5925. Web site: www.andreabrownlit.com. **President:** Andrea Brown. Estab. 1981. Member of SCBWI and WNBA. 10% of clients are new/previously unpublished writers. Specializes in "all kinds of children's books—illustrators and authors."

- Prior to opening her agency, Andrea Brown served as an editorial assistant at Random House and Dell Publishing and as an editor with Alfred A. Knopf.

Member Agents Andrea Brown, president; Laura Rennert, senior agent; Caryn Wiseman, Jennifer Jaeger, Rob Welsh, associate agents.

Represents 98% juvenile books. Considers: nonfiction (animals, anthropology/archaeology, art/architecture/

An Organization for Agents

In some listings of agents you'll see references to AAR (The Association of Authors' Representatives). This organization requires its members to meet an established list of professional standards and code of ethics.

The objectives of AAR include keeping agents informed about conditions in publishing and related fields; encouraging cooperation among literary organizations; and assisting agents in representing their author-clients' interests. Officially, members are prohibited from directly or indirectly charging reading fees. They offer writers a list of member agents on their Web site. They also offer a list of recommended questions an author should ask an agent and other FAQs, all found on their Web site. They can be contacted at AAR, P.O. Box 237201, Ansonia Station NY 10003. E-mail: info@aar-online.org. Web site: www.aar-online.org.

design, biography/autobiography, current affairs, ethnic/cultural interests, history, how-to, nature/environment, photography, popular culture, science/technology, sociology, sports); fiction (historical, science fiction); picture books, young adult.

How to Contact Query. Responds in 3 months to queries and mss. E-mail queries only.

Needs Mostly obtains new clients through recommendations, editors, clients and agents.

Recent Sales *Fire on Ice*, autobiography of Sasha Cohen (HarperCollins); Five Ancestors series, by Jeff Stone (Random House); *Downside Up*, by Neal Shusterman (Simon & Schuster).

Terms Agent receives 15% commission on domestic sales; 20% on foreign sales. Written contract.

Writers' Conferences Agents at Andrea Brown Literary Agency attend Austin Writers League; SCBWI; Columbus Writers Conference; Willamette Writers Conference; Orange County Conferences; Mills College Childrens Literature Conference (Oakland CA); Asilomar (Pacific Grove CA); Maui Writers Conference; Southwest Writers Conference; San Diego State University Writer's Conference; Big Sur Children's Writing Workshop (Director); BookExpo America/Writer's Digest Books Writing Conference.

Tips Query first. "Taking on very few picture books. Must be unique—no rhyme, no anthropomorphism. Do not call or fax queries or manuscripts. E-mail queries accepted. Check Web site for details."

CURTIS BROWN, LTD.

Ten Astor Place., New York NY 10003. (212)473-5400. Fax: (212)598-0917. Seeking both new and established writers. Estab. 1914. Member of AAR. Signatory of WGA. SCBWI. **Staff:** Elizabeth Harding and Ginger Knowlton.

Represents Considers fiction, nonfiction, picture books, middle grade, young adult.

How to Contact Query with SASE. If a picture book, send only one picture book ms. Considers simultaneous queries. Returns material only with SASE. Obtains clients through recommendations from others, queries/ solicitations, conferences.

Terms Agent receives 15% commission on domestic sales; 20% on foreign sales. Offers written contract. 75 days notice must be given to terminate contract.

BROWNE & MILLER LITERARY ASSOCIATES, LLC

410 S. Michigan Ave., Suite 460, Chicago IL 60605. (312)922-3063. Fax: (312)922-1905. E-mail: mail@brownean dmiller.com. Web site: www.browneandmiller.com. **Contact:** Danielle Egan-Miller, president. Prefers to work with established writers. Handles only certain types of work. Estab. 1971. Member of AAR, RWA, MWA. Represents 85+ clients. 5% of clients are new/previously unpublished writers. 15% of material handled is books for young readers.

• Prior to opening the agency, Danielle Egan-Miller worked as an editor.

Represents Considers primarily YA fiction, fiction, young adult. "We love great writing and have a wonderful list of authors writing YA in particular." Not looking for picture books, middle grade.

How to Contact Query with SASE. Accepts queries by e-mail. Considers simultaneous queries. Responds in 2-4 weeks to queries; 4-6 months to mss. Returns material only with SASE. Obtains clients through recommendations from others.

Recent Sales Sold 10 books for young readers in the last year.

Terms Agent receives 15% commission on domestic sales; 20% on foreign sales. Offers written contract. Offers written contract, binding for 2 years. 30 days notice must be given to terminate contract.

Tips "We are very hands-on and do much editorial work with our clients. We are passionate about the books we represent and work hard to help clients reach their publishing goals."

⚆ LIZA DAWSON ASSOCIATES

240 W. 35th St., Suite 500, New York NY 10001. (201)791-4699. E-mail: anna@olswanger.com. Web site: www.annaolswanger.com. **Contact:** Anna Olswanger. Member of SCBWI, WNBA, Authors Guild. Represents 10 clients. 30% of clients are new/unpublished writers. 50% of material handled is books for young readers.

• Anna Olswanger coordinates the Jewish Children's Book Writers' Conference each fall at the 92nd Street Y in New York City and is a children's book author.

Represents Fiction, nonfiction; no picture books.

How to Contact Query with SASE and first 5 pages. Considers simultaneous queries. Responds in 3 weeks to queries; 6 weeks to mss. Obtains most new clients through recommendations and queries.

Terms Agent receives 15% commission on domestic sales; 20% commission on foreign sales. Offers written contract. Charges client for photocopying and overseas postage.

DUNHAM LITERARY, INC.

156 Fifth Ave., Suite 625, New York NY 10010-7002. Web site: www.dunhamlit.com. **Contact:** Jennie Dunham. Seeking both new and established writers but prefers to work with established writers. Estab. 2000. Member

Resources

of AAR, signatory of SCBWI. Represents 50 clients. 15% of clients are new/previously unpublished writers. 50% of material handled is books of young readers.

Represents Considers fiction, picture books, middle grade, young adult. Most agents represent children's books or adult books, and this agency represents both. Actively seeking mss with great story and voice. Not looking for activity books, workbooks, educational books, poetry.

How to Contact Query with SASE. Consider simultaneous queries and submissions. Responds in 2 week s to queries; 2 months to mss. Returns material only with SASE. Obtains clients through recommendations from others.

Recent Sales Sold 30 books for young readers in the last year. *Winter's Tale*, by Robert Sabuda (Little Simon); *Willa and the Wind*, illustrated by Heather Solomon (Marshall Cavendish); *Cinderella*, by Barbara McClintock (Scholastic); *Sweetgrass Basket*, by Marlene Carvell (Dutton); *While You Were Out*, by Judith Irvin Kuns (Dutton); *How I Found the Strong*, by Margaret McMullan (Houghton Mifflin).

Terms Agent receives 15% commission on domestic sales; 20-25% on foreign sales. Offers written contract. 60 days notice must be given to terminate contract.

Fees The agency takes expenses from the clients' earnings for specific expenses documented during the marketing of a client's work in accordance with the AAR (Association of Authors' Representatives) Canon of Ethics. For example, photocopying, messenger, express mail, UPS, etc. The client is not asked to pay for these fees up front.

DWYER & O'GRADY, INC.

P.O. Box 790, Cedar Key FL 32625. (352)543-9307. Fax: (603)375-5373. E-mail: eogrady@dwyerogrady.com. Web site: www.dwyerogrady.com. **Contact:** Elizabeth O'Grady. Estab. 1990. Member of SCBWI. Represents 25 clients. Represents both writers and illustrators.

• Dwyer & O'Grady is currently not accepting new clients.

Member Agents Elizabeth O'Grady (children's books); Jeff Dwyer (children's books).

Represents 95% juvenile books. Considers: nonfiction, fiction, picture books, young adult.

How to Contact Does not accept unsolicited mss.

Needs Obtains new clients through referrals or direct approach from agent to writer whose work they've read.

Recent Sales Clients include: Kim Ablon Whitney, Tom Bodett, Odds Bodkin, James Rumford, Nat Tripp, Geoffrey Norman, Clemence McLaren, Lita Judge, Steve Schuch, Virginia Stroud, Natasha Tarpley, Zong-Zhou Wang, Peter Sylvada, Mary Azarian, E.B. Lewis, Rich Michelson, Barry Moser, Stan Fellows, Lynda Jones, Irving Toddy and Tom Sanders.

Terms Agent receives 15% commission on domestic sales; 20% on foreign sales. Offers written contract. Thirty days notice must be given to terminate contract. Charges for "photocopying of longer manuscripts or mutually agreed upon marketing expenses."

Writers' Conferences Agents from Dwyer & O'Grady attend Book Expo; American Library Association; Society of Children's Book Writers & Illustrators conferences.

⊡ EDUCATIONAL DESIGN SERVICES INC.

7238 Treviso Lane, Boynton Beach FL 33437. E-mail: linder.eds@adelphianet. **Contact:** B. Linder. Handles only certain types of work. Estab. 1981. 80% of clients are new/previously unpublished writers.

Represents Considers text materials for K-12 market. "We specialize in educational materials to be used in classrooms (in class sets) or in teacher education classes." Actively seeking educational, text materials. Not looking for picture books, story books, fiction; no illustrators.

How to Contact Query with SASE or send outline and 1 sample chapter. Considers simultaneous queries and submissions if so indicated. Responds in 608 weeks to queries/mss. Returns material only with SASE. Obtains clients through recommendations from others, queries/solicitations, or through conferences.

Recent Sales *How to Solve Word Problems in Mathematics*, by Wayne (McGraw-Hill); *Reviewing U.S. & New York State History*, by Farran-Paci (Amsco); *Minority Report*, by Gunn-Singh (Scarecrow Education); *No Parent Left Behind*, by Petrosino & Spiegel (Rowman & Littlefield); The Human Factor in Change, by Zimbalist (Scarecrow Education).

Terms Agent receives 15% commission on domestic sales; 25% on foreign sales. Offers written contract, binding until any party opts out. Terminate contract through certified letter.

ETHAN ELLENBERG LITERARY AGENCY

548 Broadway, #5-E, New York NY 10012. (212)431-4554. Fax: (212)941-4652. E-mail: agent@ethanellenberg.com. Web site: EthanEllenberg.com. **Contact:** Ethan Ellenberg. Estab. 1983. Represents 80 clients. 10% of clients are new/previously unpublished writers. "Children's books are an important area for us."

• Prior to opening his agency, Ethan Ellenberg was contracts manager of Berkley/Jove and associate contracts manager for Bantam.

Represents "We do a lot of children's books." Considers: picture books, middle grade, YA and selected.

How to Contact Picture books—send full ms with SASE. Young adults—send outline plus 3 sample chapters with SASE. Accepts queries by e-mail; does not accept attachments to e-mail queries or fax queries. Considers simultaneous queries and submissions. Responds in 10 days to queries; 1 month to mss. Returns materials only with SASE. "See Web site for detailed instructions, please follow them carefully."

Terms Agent receives 15% on domestic sales; 20% on foreign sales. Offers written contract, "flexible." Charges for "direct expenses only: photocopying for manuscript submissions, postage for submission and foreign rights sales."

Tips "We do consider new material from unsolicited authors. Write a clear letter with a succinct description of your book. We prefer the first three chapters when we consider fiction, but for children's book submissions, we prefer the full manuscript. For all submissions you must include SASE for return or the material is discarded. It's always hard to break in, but talent will find a home. We continue to seek natural storytellers and nonfiction writers with important books." This agency sold over 100 titles per year in the last 4 years (combining adult and children's books).

FLANNERY LITERARY

1155 South Washington St., Suite 202, Naperville IL 60540-3300. (630)428-2682. Fax: (630)428-2683. **Contact:** Jennifer Flannery. Estab. 1992. Represents 40 clients. 95% of clients are new/previously unpublished writers. Specializes in children's and young adult, juvenile fiction and nonfiction.

● Prior to opening her agency, Jennifer Flannery was an editorial assistant.

Represents 100% juvenile books. Considers: nonfiction, fiction, picture books, middle grade, young adult.

How to Contact Query. "No e-mail or fax queries, please." Responds in 2 weeks to queries; 5 weeks to mss.

Needs Obtains new clients through referrals and queries.

Terms Agent receives 15% commission on domestic sales; 20% on foreign sales. Offers written contract, binding for life of book in print, with 30-day cancellation clause. 100% of business is derived from commissions on sales.

Tips "Write an engrossing succinct query describing your work." Flannery Literary sold 20 titles in the last year.

BARRY GOLDBLATT LITERARY AGENCY INC.

320 Seventh Ave., #266, Brooklyn NY 11215. (718)832-8787. Fax: (718)832-5558. E-mail: bgliterary@earthlink.n et. Web site: www.bgliterary.com. **Contact:** Barry Goldblatt. Estab. 2000. Member of AAR, SCBWI. Represents 35 clients. 40% of clients are new/previously unpublished writers. 100% of material handled is books for young readers. Staff includes Barry Goldblatt (picture books, middle grade, and young adult novels).

Represents Considers picture books, fiction, middle grade, young adult.

How to Contact Send queries only; no longer accepting unsolicited manuscript submissions. Prefers to read material exclusively. Responds in 3 weeks to queries; 2 months to mss. Returns material only with SASE. Obtains clients through recommendations from others.

Recent Sales *City of Bones*, by Cassandra Clare; *The Getaway*, by Ed Vere; *Victim Soul*, by Laura Wiess.

Terms Agent receives 15% commission on domestic sales; 20% on foreign and dramatic sales.

Tips "I structure my relationship with each client differently, according to their wants and needs. I'm mostly hands-on, but some want more editorial input, others less. I'm pretty aggressive in selling work, but I'm fairly laid back in how I deal with clients. I'd say I'm quite friendly with most of my clients, and I like it that way. To me this is more than just a simple business relationship."

ASHLEY GRAYSON LITERARY AGENCY

1342 18th St., San Pedro CA 90732. (310)514-0267. Fax: (310)514-1148. Seeking both new and established writers. Estab. 1976. Agency is member of AAR, SCBWI, SFWA, RWA. Represents 75 clients. 5-10% new writers. 25% books for young readers. **Staff includes:** Ashley Grayson, young adult and middle grade; Carolyn Grayson, young adult, middle grade, some picture books; Denise Dumars, young adult.

Represents Handles fiction, middle grade, young adult. "We represent top authors in the field and we market their books to publishers worldwide." Actively seeking fiction of high commercial potential.

How to Contact Query with SASE. Include first 3 pages of manuscript; if querying about a picture books, include entire text. Accepts queries by mail and e-mail. Considers simultaneous queries. Responds 1 month after query, 2-3 months after ms. Returns mss only with SASE. Obtains new clients through recommendations from others, queries/solicitations, conferences.

Recent Sales Sold 25+ books last year. *Juliet Dove, Queen of Love*, by Bruce Coville (Harcourt); *Alosha*, by Christopher Pike (TOR); *Sleeping Freshmen Never Lie*, by David Lubar (Dutton); *Ball Don't Lie*, by Matt de la Peña (Delacorte); Wiley & Grampa's Creature Features, by Kirk Scroggs (6-book series, Little Brown); *Street Pharm*, by Allison van Diepen (Simon Pulse). Also represents: J.B. Cheaney (Knopf), Bruce Wetter (Atheneum).

Terms Agent receives 15% on domestic sales, 20% on foreign sales. Offers written contract. Contract binding for 1 year. 30 days notice must be given for termination of contract.

Anna Olswanger

Be optimistic, think big & have vision

Have you ever attended a writers' conference featuring an agent who's just hung out her shingle? She's easy to find. She's the one with the group of writers waiting in line to talk to her after a session or huddled around her in the hallway. A new agent—an agent who is actually looking for clients—is the most popular person in any room full of budding writers.

Anna Olwanger is ready to be popular. After years of interviewing industry professionals, teaching writing classes, running a Web site that promotes Jewish books, coordinating the annual Jewish Children's Book Writers' Conference, and penning a few picture books, in 2005 she joined Liza Dawson Associates in Manhattan as a literary agent.

Here Olswanger talks about what she looks for in a potential author, her agenting style, her own experience as a writer, and what she's learned from industry luminaries, and she offers some great advice. Visit her Web site www.olswanger.com and see the listing for Liza Dawson Associates for more.

You've been involved in the writing/publishing for many years. What made you decide to join Liza Dawson Associates as a literary agent?

When I moved to the metro NYC area in January 2001, I enrolled in the Certificate in Book Publishing program at NYU. I thought I might want to work in publishing, but after I took a course on how to be a literary agent, I knew I wanted to be an agent. I interned with the agent who taught that course, and at the end of that internship, started an internship with Liza Dawson Associates. Liza later offered to bring me into the agency as an agent.

What are you doing to build your roster of authors?

I have placed announcements in SCBWI newsletters (regional and national), as well as in national newsletters for children's book writers, I read my slush carefully, and I look at referrals from current clients and friends.

What are you looking for when authors approach you?

Like every agent (and editor), I'm looking for "something different." Right now, I'm looking for historical fiction or historical mysteries, with a touch of fantasy. Maybe "mystical" describes what I'm looking for. I like writing that takes risks in some way, either in subject matter or form. I'm both Jewish and from the South, so books with those elements will pique my interest.

For you, what makes a good author/agent relationship?

I like to work with mature authors, but I don't mean mature in career. I mean mature in personality. I can't do much for a writer who expects publishing to give her the happiness

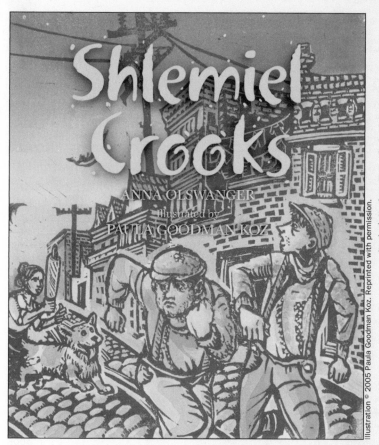

Illustration © 2005 Paula Goodman Koz. Reprinted with permission.

"This tale is a pleasure and a hoot," says *School Library Journal* of Anna Olswanger's picture book *Shlemiel Crooks*. "It rings so true with the voice of a Yiddishe grandmother that it's practically historical fiction." Olswanger has a second picture book, *Chicken Bone Man*, in the works with NewSouth, but as an agent she gravitates toward books for mid-grade and YA audiences.

she hasn't already given herself. I can't validate anyone's life with a book contract. On a practical level, I like to work with authors who are members of writers groups because they have wrestled with their manuscripts before they send them to me and aren't daunted if I ask for revisions.

Will you be specializing in books for young readers? What type of material interests you most?

I don't know yet what I'll be specializing in, but I like sophisticated writing, so when it comes to children's books, I gravitate towards middle grade or YA, not picture book texts.

How would you describe your agenting style?

If I think a manuscript has potential but isn't ready to send out, I will ask the author to make revisions. Any author who isn't willing to revise shouldn't approach me as an agent. I try to work fast and efficiently, so I tend to communicate with authors and editors by e-mail, although I prefer to receive submissions by regular mail.

When and why did you create your Web site, www.olswanger.com?

I created it in 1999 to promote Jewish books to librarians and booksellers. At the time, I was writing and editing "Jewish Book & Author News," a column that appeared in the newsletter of the Association of Jewish Libraries, and that I archived on my Web site. Because of my agenting job, I've had to give up the column, and my Web site now focuses on other ways to promote Jewish books, such as linking to book conferences, interviews with book industry professionals, lecture bureaus, discussion groups, book publishers, literary magazines, and book clubs, all with a Jewish connection.

You've interviewed many editors, authors and agents over the years (a number of them for this book). What have you learned from all these industry insiders that will help you as you begin your agenting career?

From Steve Mooser and Barry Moser, I learned that the author or illustrator who succeeds is the one who works hard. From Erin Murphy, I learned that writers have to pay their dues. They have to go to conferences, join writers' groups, network. From Ann Tobias, I learned that an agent should take on only books that she loves, because if she doesn't love them, she will end up hating them. But from Liza Dawson, the head of the agency where I work, I learned the most important things—to be optimistic, to think big, and to have a vision as an agent.

Tell me about your experience with the publication of your picture book *Shlemiel Crooks*, which was named a Sydney Taylor Honor Book by the Association of Jewish Libraries. Do you have more books on the horizon?

NewSouth, a small publisher in Alabama, turned out to be the best publisher for *Shlemiel Crooks*. Although the book is set in 1918 St. Louis and told in a Yiddish-American voice, the editor at NewSouth, a non-Jewish Southerner, immediately grasped the rhythm of the language. So, I trusted his editing suggestions. And the publisher has been tireless is sending the book out to reviewers and to bookstores. I had large book signings in Memphis and Baltimore, which was probably unusual for a first children's book. Although as an agent, I know that my clients will want to work with the publisher who brings the most money to the table, I can say that my experience with a small publisher has been a happy one. NewSouth will also publish my next picture book *Chicken Bone Man*, which takes place in the Jewish community of Memphis in 1927.

You do a lot to promote Jewish-themed books. Why is this important to you?

I'm a religious Jew who believes that Judaism, and that includes Jewish books, can change the world and make it a more just and humane place.

What advice can you offer to unpublished writers?

Think of all the book reviews you read in your Sunday paper. Each of those books is probably well written, but how many do you actually go out and buy? It's the same for agents and editors. Many of the books that cross our desk are well written, but how many do we actually accept? It's just a matter of taste. It has nothing to do with the quality of your work. Your job is to keep sending your work out until you find the agent or editor who likes it.

Each fall when I coordinate the Jewish Children's Book Writers' Conference at the 92nd Street Y, I share this advice with the audience: Think about the Torah reading for the first day of Rosh Hashanah. In the Torah reading, Abraham prays that the women of Avimelech's court will be able to conceive. As soon as he prayed for them, Abraham's wife Sarah conceived. The commentator Rashi says that when we pray on behalf of another, our prayer is answered first. It follows that if writers and illustrators help someone else get published, they'll get published first. I tell the audience, "Just try it."

—Alice Pope

Resources

KIRCHOFF/WOHLBERG, AUTHORS' REPRESENTATION DIVISION

866 United Nations Plaza, #525, New York NY 10017. (212)644-2020. Fax: (212)223-4387. Web site: www.kirch offwohlberg.com. **Director of Operations:** John R. Whitman. Estab. 1930s. Member of AAR. Represents 50 authors. 10% of clients are new/previously unpublished writers. Specializes in juvenile through young adult trade books and textbooks.

Member Agents Liza Pulitzer-Voges (juvenile and young adult authors).

Represents 80% juvenile books, 20% young adult. "We are interested in any original projects of quality that are appropriate to the juvenile and young adult trade book markets. But we take on very few new clients as our roster is full."

How to Contact "Send a query that includes an outline and a sample; SASE required." Responds in 1 month to queries; 2 months to mss. Please send queries to the attention of Liza Pulitzer-Voges.

Needs "Usually obtains new clients through recommendations from authors, illustrators and editors."

Terms Agent receives standard commission "depending upon whether it is an author only, illustrator only, or an author/illustrator book." Offers written contract, binding for not less than 1 year.

Tips "Kirchoff/Wohlberg has been in business since 1930 and sold over 50 titles in the last year."

BARBARA S. KOUTS, LITERARY AGENT

P.O. Box 560, Bellport NY 11713. (631)286-1278. **Contact:** Barbara Kouts. Currently accepting new clients. Estab. 1980. Member of AAR. Represent 50 clients. 10% of clients are new/previously unpublished writers. Specializes in children's books.

Represents 100% juvenile books. Considers: nonfiction, fiction, picture books, ms/illustration packages, middle grade, young adult.

How to Contact Accepts queries by mail only. Responds in 1 week to queries; 6 weeks to mss.

Needs Obtains new clients through recommendations from others, solicitation, at conferences, etc.

Recent Sales *Code Talker*, by Joseph Bruchac (Dial); *The Penderwicks*, by Jeanne Birdsall (Knopf); *Frogg's Baby Sister*, by Jonathan London (Viking).

Terms Agent receives 10% commission on domestic sales; 20% on foreign sales. Charges for photocopying.

Tips "Write, do not call. Be professional in your writing."

GINA MACCOBY LITERARY AGENCY

P.O. Box 60, Chappaqua NY 10514. (914)238-5630. **Contact:** Gina Maccoby. Estab. 1986. Represents writers and illustrators of children's books.

Represents 33% juvenile books. Considers: nonfiction, fiction, young adult.

How to Contact Query with SASE. "Please, no unsolicited manuscripts." Considers simultaneous queries and submisssions. Responds to queries in 3 months. Returns materials only with SASE.

Needs Usually obtains new clients through recommendations from own clients and/or editors.

Terms Agent receives 15% commission on domestic sales; 25% on foreign sales. Charges for photocopying. May recover certain costs such as airmail postage to Europe or Japan or legal fees.

Tips This agency sold 21 titles last year.

McINTOSH & OTIS, INC.

353 Lexington Ave., New York NY 10016. (212)687-7400. Fax: (212)687-6894. **Contact:** Edward Necarsulmer IV. Seeking both new and established writers. Estab. 1927. Member of AAR and SCBWI. 20% of clients are new/previously unpublished writers. 100% of material handled is books for young readers.

Represents Considers fiction, middle grade, young adult. "McIntosh & Otis has a long history of representing authors of adult and children's books. The children's department is a separate division." Actively seeking "books with memorable characters, distinctive voice, and a great plot." Not looking for educational, activity books, coloring books.

How to Contact Query with SASE. Exclusive submission only. Responds in 6 weeks. Returns material only with SASE. Obtains clients through recommendations from others or through conferences.

Terms Agent receives 15% commission on domestic sales; 20% on foreign sales.

Writers' Conferences Attends Bologna Book Fair, in Bologna Italy in April, SCBWI Conference in New York in February, and regularly attends other conferences and industry conventions.

Tips "No e-mail or phone calls!"

MEWS BOOKS

20 Bluewater Hill, Westport CT 06880. (203)227-1836. Fax: (203)227-1144. E-mail: mewsbooks@aol.com. **Contact:** Sidney B. Kramer. Seeking both new and established writers. Estab. 1974. 50% of material handled is books for young readers. Staff includes Sidney B. Kramer and Fran Pollak.

Resources

● Previously Sidney Kramer was Senior Vice President and founder of Bantam Books, President of New American Library, Director and Manager of Corgi Books in London, and attorney.

Represents Considers adult nonfiction, fiction; picture books, middle grade, young adult with outstanding characters and stories. Actively seeking books that have continuity of character and story. Not looking for unedited, poorly written mss by authors seeking learning experience.

How to Contact Query with SASE, send outline and 2 sample chapters. Accepts shrot queries by e-mail—no attachments. Prefers to read material exclusively. Responds in a few weeks to queries. Returns material only with SASE. Obtains clients through recommendations from others, clients through conferences.

Recent Sales Sold 10 books for young readers in the last year.

Terms Agent receives 15% commission on domestic sales; 20% on foreign sales. Offers written contract, binding for 1-2 years. "We never retain an unhappy author, but we cannot terminate in the middle of activity. If submission is accepted, we ask for $100 against all expenses. We occasionally make referrals to editing services."

ERIN MURPHY LITERARY AGENCY

2700 Woodlands Village, #300-458, Flagstaff AZ 86001-7127. (928)525-2056. Closed to unsolicited queries and submissions. Considers both new and established writers, by referral or personal contact (such as conferences) only. Estab. 1999. Member of SCBWI and AAR. Represents 50 clients. 50% of clients are new/previously unpublished writers. 100% of material handled is books of young readers.

● Prior to opening her agency, Erin Murphy was editor-in-chief at Northland Publishing/Rising Moon. Agency is not currently accepting unsolicited queries or submissions.

Represents Picture books, middle grade, young adult.

Terms Agent receives 15% commission on domestic sales; 20% on foreign sales. Offers written contract. 30 days notice must be given to terminate contract.

Recent sales Sold 30 books for young readers in the last year. Recent sales: *The Three Bears' Christmas*, by Kathy Duval (Holiday House), *Fame, Glory, and Other Things on My To-Do List*, by Janette Rallison (Walker); *Trigger*, by Susan Vaught (Bloomsbury); *Beyond the Dragon Portal* and *The Pluto Project*, by Melissa Glenn Haber (Dutton); *Werewolf Rising*, by R.L. LaFevers (Dutton).

ALISON PICARD, LITERARY AGENT

P.O. Box 2000, Cotuit MA 02635. Phone/fax: (508)477-7192. E-mail: ajpicard@aol.com. **Contact:** Alison Picard. Seeking both new and established writers. Estab. 1985. Represents 50 clients. 40% of clients are new/previously unpublished writers. 20% of material handled is books for young readers.

● Prior to opening her agency, Alison Picard was an assistant at a large New York agency before co-founding Kidde, Hoyt & Picard in 1982. She became an independent agent in 1985.

Represents Considers nonfiction, fiction, a very few picture books, middle grade, young adult. "I represent juvenile and YA books. I do not handle short stories, articles, poetry or plays. I am especially interested in commercial nonfiction, romances and mysteries/suspense/thrillers. I work with agencies in Europe and Los Angeles to sell foreign and TV/film rights. "Actively seeking middle grade fiction. Not looking for poetry or plays.

How to Contact Query with SASE. Accepts queries by e-mail with no attachments. Considers simultaneous queries and submissions. Responds in 2 weeks to queries; 4 months to mss. Returns material only with SASE. Obtains clients through queries/solicitations.

Recent Sales *Funerals and Fly Fishing*, by Mary Bartek (Henry Holt & Co.), *Stage Fright*, by Dina Friedman (Farrar Straus & Giroux), *Escaping into the Night*, by Dina Friedman (Simon & Schuster), *Celebritrees* and *The Peace Bell*, by Margi Preus (Henry Holt & Co.)

Terms Receives 15% commission on domestic sales; 20-25% on foreign sales. Offers written contract, binding for 1 year. 1-week notice must be given to terminate contract.

Tips "We currently have a backlog of submissions."

WENDY SCHMALZ AGENCY

P.O. Box 831, Hudson NY 12534. (518)672-7697. Fax: (518)672-7662. E-mail: wendy@schmalzagency.com. **Contact:** Wendy Schmalz. Seeking both new and established writers. Estab. 2001. Member of AAR. Represents 30 clients. 10% of clients are new/previously unpublished writers. 50% of material handled is books for young readers.

● Prior to opening her agency, Wendy Schmalz was an agent for 23 years at Harold Ober Associates.

Represents Considers nonfiction, fiction, middle grade, young adult. Actively seeking young adult novels, middle grade novels. Not looking for picture books, science fiction or fantasy.

How to Contact Query with SASE. Accepts queries by e-mail. Considers simultaneous queries. Responds in 2 weeks to queries; 4-6 weeks to mss. Returns material only with SASE. Obtains clients through recommendations from others.

Recent Sales Sold 15 books for young readers in the last year.

Terms Agent receives 15% commission on domestic sales; 20% on foreign sales. Fees for photocopying and FedEx.

[N] SUSAN SCHULMAN LITERARY AGENCY

454 W. 44th, New York NY 10036. (212)713-1633. Fax: (212)581-8830. E-mail: schulman@aol.com. Web site: www.schulmanagency.com. **Contact:** Susan Schulman. Seeking both new and established writers. Estab. 1980. Member of AAR, WGA, SCBWI, Dramatists Guild. 15% of material handled is books for young readers. Staff includes Emily Uhry, YA; Linda Megalti, picture books.

Represents Handles nonfiction, fiction, picture books, middle grade, young adult. Actively seeking well-written, original stories for any age group.

How to Contact Query with SASE. Accepts queries by e-mail, mail. Considers sumultaneous queries and submissions. Returns mss only with SASE. Obtains new clients through recommendations from others, queries/solicitations, conferences.

Recent Sales Of total agency sales, approximately 20% is children's literature. Recent sales include: 10-book deal to Scholastic for Jim Arnosky; *Remarkable Girl*, by Pamela Lowell (Marshall Cavendish); *I Get All Better*, by Vickie Cobb (4-book series with Lerner); film rights to *Geography Club*, by Brent Hartinger (East of Doheny); television rights to Louis Sachar's *Sideways Stories from Wayside School* (Nickelodeon).

Terms Agent receives 15% on domestic sales, 20% on foreign sales.

Writers' Conferences Attending IWWG in Geneva, Switzerland and New York and Columbus Writer's Conference.

Tips Schulman decribes her agency as ''professional boutique, long-standing, eclectic.''

STIMOLA LITERARY STUDIO

308 Chase Court, Edgewater NJ 07020. Phone/fax: (201)945-9353. E-mail: LtryStudio@aol.com. **Contact:** Rosemary B. Stimola. Seeking both new and established writers. Estab. 1997. Member of AAR, SCBWI, ALA. Represents 45+ clients. 25% of clients are new/previously unpublished writers. 85% of material handled is books for young readers.

● Prior to opening her agency Rosemary Stimola was an independent children's bookseller.

Represents Preschool through young adult, fiction and nonfiction. ''Agency is owned and operated by a former educator and children's bookseller with a Ph.D. in Linguistics.'' Actively seeking ''remarkable young adult fiction.'' Not looking for novelty books.

How to Contact Query with SASE or e-mail. ''No attachments, please!'' Considers simultaneous queries. Responds in 3 weeks to queries; 4-6 weeks to mss. Returns material only with SASE. While unsolicited queries are welcome, most clients come through editor, agent, client referrals.

Recent Sales Sold 25 books for young readers in the last year. *Beauty Shop for Rent*, by Laura Bowers (Harcourt); *Rucker Park*, by Paul Volponi (Viking/Penguin); *An Orange in January*, by Dianna Aston (Dial/Penguin); *Lobsterland*, by Susan Carlton (Henry Holt); *Ernestina and Enriquito*, by Enrique Flores Galbis (Roaring Brook Press); *Max and Pinky*, by Maxwell Eaton III (Knopf/Random House); *Pilot Pups*, by Michelle Meadows (Simon & Schuster); *Woolbur*, by Leslie Helakoski (Harper Collins); *Swords*, by Ben Boos (Candlewick Press); *Gregor and the Code of Claw*, by Suzanne Collins (Scholastic).

Terms Agent receives 15% commission on domestic sales; 20% on foreign sales (if subagents used). Offers written contract, binding for all children's projects. 60 days notice must be given to terminate contract. ''Charges $85 one-time fee per project to cover expenses. Client provides all copies of submission. Fee is taken from first advance payment and is payable *only* if manuscript is sold.''

Writers' Conferences Will attend: ALA Midwinter, BEA, Bologna Book Fair, SCBWI-Michigan regional conference; SCBWI Annual Winter Conference in New York.

Tips ''Agent is hands-on, no-nonsense. May request revisions. Does not edit but may offer suggestions for improvement. Well-respected by clients and editors. A firm but reasonable deal negotiator.''

ANN TOBIAS—A LITERARY AGENCY FOR CHILDREN'S BOOKS

520 E. 84th St., Apt. 4L, New York NY 10028. **Contact:** Ann Tobias. Seeking both new and established writers. Handles only certain types of work. Estab. 1988. Represents 25 clients. 50% of clients are new/previously unpublished writers. 100% of material handled is books for children.

● Prior to opening her agency, Ann Tobias worked as a children's book editor at Harper, William Morrow, Scholastic.

Represents Fiction, nonfiction, middle grade, picture books, poetry, young adult, young readers.

How to Contact Send entire ms for picture books; 30 pages and synopsis for longer works. No e-mail, fax or phone queries. Cannot sign for receipt of ms. Accepts simultaneous submissions for queries only. Must have 1 month exclusive basis for considering an entire ms after inviting author to submit. Responds to all queries

Resources

accompanied by SASE; 2 months to mss. Returns material only with SASE. Obtains clients through recommendations from editors.

Recent Sales Sold 12 titles in the last year.

Terms Agent receives 15% commission on domestic sales; 20% on foreign sales.

Tips "Read at least 200 children's books in the age group and genre in which you hope to be published. Follow this by reading another 100 children's books in other age groups and genres so you will have a feel for the field as a whole."

S©OTT TREIMEL NY

434 Lafayette St., New York NY 10003. (212)505-8353. Fax: (212)505-0664. E-mail: st@verizon.net. **Contact:** Scott Treimel. Estab. 1995. Represents 40 clients. 5% of clients are new/unpublished writers. Specializes in children's books, all genres: tightly focused segments of the trade. Member AAR, Author's Guild, SCBWI.

• Prior to opening his agency, Scott Treimel was an assistant to Marilyn E. Marlow of Curtis Brown; a rights agent for Scholastic, Inc.; a book packager and rights agent for United Feature Syndicate; the founding director of Warner Bros. Worldwide Publishing; a freelance editor; and a rights consultant for HarperCollins Children's Books.

Represents 100% juvenile books.

How to Contact Does not accept unsolicited mss; requires referral via clients or editors.

Recent Sales Sold 30 titles in the last year including *Megiddo's Shadow*, by Arthur Slade (HarperCanada and Random-House/Wendy Lamb); *Friends/Unfriends*, by Barbara Joosse (Greenwillow); *Fragments*, by Jeffry Johnston (Simon & Schuster); *What Happened to Cass McBride?*, by Gail Giles (Little, Brown); *Me & Death*, by Richard Scrimger (Tundra Books); *But That's Another Story*, by Mary Hanson (Random House/Schwartz & Wade); *Kimchi & Calamari*, by Rose Kent (HarperCollins); *When Louis Armstrong Taught Me Scat*, by Muriel Weinstein (Chronicle Books); *Beyond the Mask*, by David Ward (Scholastic Canada); *The Knoodles Celebrate Hanukkah*, by Barbara Goldin (Marshal Cavendish).

Terms Agent receives 15-20% commission on domestic sales; 20-25% on foreign sales. Offers verbal or written contract, binding on a "contract-by-contract basis." Charges for photocopying, overnight/express postage, messengers and books ordered for subsidiary rights sales. Offers editorial guidance, if extensive charges higher commission.

Writer's Conferences Speaks at Society of Children's Book Writers and Illustrators conferences in Hawaii and New Jersey. SouthWest Writers Workshop, Pike's Peak Writers Conference, Kindling Words Retreat; participates in local and national panel discussions.

WRITERS HOUSE

21 W. 26th St., New York NY 10010. (212)685-2400. Fax: (212)685-1781. Web site: www.writershouse.com. Estab. 1974. Member of AAR. Represents 280 clients. 50% of clients were new/unpublished writers. Specializes in all types of popular fiction and nonfiction. No scholarly, professional, poetry or screenplays.

Member Agents Amy Berkower (major juvenile authors); Merrilee Heifetz (quality children's fiction); Susan Cohen (juvenile and YA authors and illustrators), Jodi Reamer (juvenile and young adult fiction and nonfiction); Steven Malk (YA fiction and picture books); Robin Rue (YA fiction); Rebecca Sherman (picture books, picture book illustrators, middle grade fiction and YA fiction); Daniel Lazar (middle grade and YA fiction).

Represents 35% juvenile books. Considers: nonfiction, fiction, picture books, young adult.

How to Contact Query. Responds in 4-6 weeks on queries. Check Web site for submission guidelines.

Needs Obtains new clients through recommendations from others.

Terms Agent receives 15% commission on domestic sales; 20% on foreign sales. Offers written contract, binding for 1 year.

Tips "Do not send manuscripts. Write a compelling letter. If you do, we'll ask to see your work."

WRITERS HOUSE

(West Coast Office), 3368 Governor Dr., Suite 224F, San Diego CA 92122. (858)678-8767. Fax: (858)678-8530. **Contact:** Steven Malk.

• See Writers House listing above for more information.

Represents Nonfiction, fiction, picture books, middel-grade novels, young adult, illustrators.

WYLIE-MERRICK LITERARY AGENCY

1138 S. Webster St., Kokomo IN 46902. (765)459-8258. E-mail: smartin@wylie-merrick.com or rbrown@wylie-merrick.com. Web site: www.wylie-merrick.com. **Contact:** Sharene Martin or Robert Brown. Works with both new and established writers. Estab. 1999. Member of SCBWI and Romance Writers of America (RWA). Represents 22 clients. 20% of clients are new/previously unpublished writers. 30% of material handled is books for young readers. Staff includes Sharene Martin (children's and adult fiction and selected commercial nonfiction), Robert Brown (adult and young adult novels).

Resources

- Always visit Web site before querying.

Represents Considers mainstream and genre fiction, nonfiction, picture books, middle grade, young adult.

How to Contact "We prefer e-mail queries; no phone queries please."

Recent Sales *Whiskey and Tonic* and *Whiskey Straight Up*, by Nina Wright (Llewellyn); *Mineral Spirits*, by Heather Sharfeddin (Bridge Works); *Derailed*, by Jon Ripslinger (Flux).

Terms Agent receives 15% commission on domestic sales; 20% on foreign sales. Offers written contract. Charges no fees prior to sale.

Writers' Conferences 2006 conference appearances: Frontiers in Writing (June 9-10); Midwest Writers Conference (July 27-29); Florida Writer's Conference (November 10-12).

Tips "Write what is in your heart, but do it in a professional manner."

ART REPS

ART FACTORY

925 Elm Grove Rd., Elm Grove WI 53122. (262)785-1940. Fax: (262)785-1611. E-mail: tstocki@artfactoryltd.com. Web site: www.artfactoryltd.com. **Contact:** Tom Stocki. Commercial illustration representative. Estab. 1978. Represents 9 illustrators including: Tom Buchs, Tom Nachreiner, Todd Dakins, Linda Godfrey, Larry Mikec, Bill Scott, Gary Shea, Terry Herman, Troy Allen. 10% of artwork handled is children's book illustration. Currently open to illustrators seeking representation. Open to both new and established illustrators.

Handles Illustration.

Terms Receives 25-30% commission. Offers written contract. Advertising costs are split: 75% paid by illustrators; 25% paid by rep. "We try to mail samples of all our illustrators at one time and we try to update our Web site; so we ask the illustrators to keep up with new samples." Advertises in *Picturebook*, *Workbook*.

How to Contact For first contact, send query letter, tearsheets. Responds only if interested. Call to schedule an appointment. Portfolio should include tearsheets. Finds illustrators through queries/solicitations.

Tips "Have a unique style."

ASCIUTTO ART REPS., INC.

1712 E. Butler Circle, Chandler AZ 85225. (480)899-0600. Fax: (480)899-3636. E-mail: Aartreps@cox.net. **Contact:** Mary Anne Asciutto, art agent. Children's illustration representative since 1980. Specializing in childrens illustrations for childrens educational text books, grades K thru 8, childrens trade books, childrens magazines, posters, packaging, etc.

Recent Sales *Bats, Sharks, Whales, Snakes, Penguins, Alligators and Crocodiles*, illustrated by Meryl Henderson for Boyds Mills Press.

Terms Agency receives 25% commission. No geographic restrictions. Advertising and promotion costs are split: 75% paid by talent; 25% paid by representative.

How to Contact Send samples via email with a cover letter résumé. Submit sample portfolio for review with an SASE for it's return. Responds in 2 to 4 weeks. Portfolio should include at least 12 samples of original art, printed tearsheets, photocopies or color prints of most recent work.

Tips In obtaining representation, "Be sure to connect with an agent who handles the kind of work, you (the artist/writer) *want*."

CAROL BANCROFT & FRIENDS

4 Old Mill Plain Road., Danbury CT 06811. (203)730-8270 or (800)720-7020. Fax: (203)730-8275. E-mail: artists @carolbancroft.com. Web site: www.carolbancroft.com. **Owner:** Carol Bancroft. Illustration representative for children's publishing. Estab. 1972. Member of SPAR, Society of Illustrators, Graphic Artists Guild, SCBWI. Represents 40 illustrators. Specializes in illustration for children's publishing-text and trade; any children's-related material. Clients include, but not limited to, Scholastic, Houghton Mifflin, HarperCollins, Dutton, Harcourt.

Handles Illustration for children of all ages.

Terms Rep receives 25-30% commission. Advertising costs are split: 75% paid by talent; 25% paid by representative. For promotional purposes, talent must provide "laser copies (not slides), tearsheets, promo pieces, good color photocopies, etc.; 6 pieces or more is best; narrative scenes and children interacting." Advertises in RSVP, Picture Book, Directory of Illustration.

How to Contact "Send either 2-3 samples with your Web site address to the e-mail address above or mail 6-10 samples, along with a self Addressed, stamped envelope (SASE) to the street address provided."

SHERYL BERANBAUM

(401)737-8591. Fax: (401)739-5189. E-mail: sheryl@beranbaum.com. Web site: www.beranbaum.com. Commercial illustration representative. Estab. 1985. Member of Graphic Artists Guild. Represents 17 illustrators. 75% of artwork handled is children's book illustration. Currently open to illustrators seeking representation. Open to new and established illustrators only. Submission guidelines available by phone.

● Sheryl Beranbaum is currently not taking on new artists.

Handles Illustration. "My illustrators are diversified and their work comes from a variety of the industry's audiences."

Terms Receives 30% commission. Charges marketing-plan fee or Web-only fee. Offers written contract. Advertising costs are split: 75% paid by illustrators; 25% paid by rep. Requires Itoya portfolio; postcards only for promotion.

How to Contact For first contact, send direct mail flier/brochure, tearsheets, photocopies. Responds only if interested. Portfolio should include photocopies.

PEMA BROWNE LTD.

11 Tena Place, Valley Cottage NY 10989. (845)268-0029. **Contact:** Pema Browne. Estab. 1966. Represents 2 illustrators. 10% of artwork handled is children's book illustration. Specializes in general commercial. Markets include: all publishing areas; children's picture books. Clients include HarperCollins, Holiday House, Bantam Doubleday Dell, Nelson/Word, Hyperion, Putnam. Client list available upon request.

Handles Fiction, nonfiction, picture books, middle grade, young adult, manuscript/illustration packages. Looking for "professional and unique" talent.

Recent Sales *The Daring Ms. Quimby*, by Suzanne Whitaker (Holiday House).

Terms Rep receives 30% illustration commission; 15% author commission. Exclusive area representation is required. For promotional purposes, talent must provide color mailers to distribute. Representative pays mailing costs on promotion mailings.

How to Contact For first contact, send query letter, direct mail flier/brochure and SASE. If interested will ask to mail appropriate materials for review. Portfolios should include tearsheets and transparencies or good color photocopies, plus SASE. Accepts queries by mail only. Obtains new talent through recommendations and interviews (portfolio review).

Tips "We are doing more publishing—all types—less advertising." Looks for "continuity of illustration and dedication to work."

CATUGEAU: ARTIST AGENT, LLC

3009 Margaret Jones Lane, Williamsburg VA 23185. (757)221-0666. Fax: (757)221-6669. E-mail: chris@catugea u.com. Web site: www.CATugeau.com. **Owner/Agent:** Chris Tugeau. Children's publishing trade book, mass market, educational. Estab. 1994. Member of SPAR, SCBWI, Graphic Artists Guild. Represents 35 illustrators. 95% of artwork handled is children's book illustration.

● Not actively accepting new artists.

Handles Illustration ONL Y.

Terms Receives 25% commission. "Artists responsible for providing samples for portfolios, promotional books and mailings." Exclusive representation required in educational. Trade "house accounts" acceptable. Offers written contract. Advertises in *Picturebook*, *RSVP*, *Directory of Illustration*.

How to Contact For first contact, e-mail samples with note. No CDs. Responds ASAP. Finds illustrators through recommendations from others, conferences, personal search.

Tips "Do research, look at artists' Web sites, talk to other artists and buyers. Do make sure you're comfortable with personality of rep. Be professional. . . know what you do best, and be prepared to give rep what they need to present you! Do have e-mail and scanning capabilities, too."

CORNELL & MCCARTHY, LLC

2-D Cross Hwy., Westport CT 06880. (203)454-4210. Fax: (203)454-4258. E-mail: cmartreps@aol.com. Web site: www.cornellandmccarthy.com. **Contact:** Merial Cornell. Children's book illustration representatives. Estab. 1989. Member of SCBWI and Graphic Artists Guild. Represents 30 illustrators. Specializes in children's books: trade, mass market, educational.

Handles Illustration.

Terms Agent receives 25% commission. Advertising costs are split: 75% paid by talent; 25% paid by representative. For promotional purposes, talent must provide 10-12 strong portfolio pieces relating to children's publishing.

How to Contact For first contact, send query letter, direct mail flier/brochure, tearsheets, photocopies and SASE. Responds in 1 month. Obtains new talent through recommendations, solicitation, conferences.

Tips "Work hard on your portfolio."

CREATIVE FREELANCERS, INC.

4 Greenwich Hills Drive, Greenwich CT 06831 (800)398-9541. Fax: (203)532-2927. Web site: www.freelancers.c

om. **Contact:** Marilyn Howard. Commercial illustration representative. Estab. 1988. Represents over 30 illustrators. "Our staff members have art direction, art buying or illustration backgrounds." Specializes in children's books, advertising, architectural, conceptual. Markets include: advertising agencies; corporations/client direct; design firms; editorial/magazines; paper products/greeting cards; publishing/books; sales/promotion firms.
Handles Illustration. Artists must have published work.
Terms Rep receives 30% commission. Exclusive area representation is preferred. Advertising costs are split: 75% paid by talent; 25% paid by representative. For promotional purposes, talent must provide "printed pages to leave with clients. Must provide scans of artwork." Advertises in *American Showcase*, *Workbook*.
How to Contact For first contact, send tearsheets or "whatever best shows work." Responds back only if interested.
Tips Looks for experience, professionalism and consistency of style. Obtains new talent through "word of mouth and Web site."

DIMENSION
13420 Morgan Ave. S., Burnsville MN 55337. (952)201-3981. Fax: (952)895-9315. E-mail: jkoltes@dimensioncreative.com. Web site: www.dimensioncreative.com. **Contact:** Joanne Koltes. Commercial illustration representative. Estab. 1982. Member of MN Book Builder. Represents 12 illustrators. 45% of artwork handled is children's book illustration. Staff includes Joanne Koltes.
Terms Advertises in *Picturebook* and *Minnesota Creative*.
How to Contact Contact via phone or e-mail. Responds only if interested.

DWYER & O'GRADY, INC.
P.O. Box 790, Cedar Key FL 32625-0790. (352)543-9307. Fax: (603)375-5373. E-mail: eogrady@dwyerogrady.com. Web site: www.dwyerogrady.com. **Contact:** Elizabeth O'Grady. Agents for children's artists and writers, "small career development agents." Estab. 1990. Member of Society of Illustrators, Graphic Artist's Guild, SCBWI, ABA. Represents 18 illustrators and 7 writers. Staff includes Elizabeth O'Grady, Jeffrey Dwyer. Specializes in children's books (picture books, middle grade and young adult). Markets include: publishing/books, audio/film.
● Dwyer & O'Grady is currently not accepting new clients.
Handles Illustrators and writers of children's books.
Recent Sales *Don't Touch My Hat*, by James Rumford (Knopf); *Funny Cide*, illustrated by Barry Moser (Putnam); *Animals Anonymous*, by R. Michelson (Simon & Schuster); *China Alphabet*, by Zong-Zhou Wang (Sleeping Bear); *Native American Alphabet*, by Irving Toddy (Sleeping Bear); *How to Catch a Fish*, by Peter Sylvada (Roaring Brook).
Terms Receives 15% commission domestic, 20% foreign. Additional fees are negotiable. Exclusive representation is required (world rights). Advertising costs are paid by representative.
How to Contact For first contact, send query letter by postal mail only.

PAT HACKETT/ARTIST REP
7014 N. Mercer Way, Mercer Island WA 98040-2130. (206)447-1600. Fax: (206)447-0739. Web site: www.pathackett.com. **Contact:** Pat Hackett. Commercial illustration representative. Estab. 1979. Member of Graphic Artists Guild. Represents 12 illustrators. 10% of artwork handled is children's book illustration. Currently open to illustrators seeking representation. Open to both new and established illustrators.
Handles Illustration. Looking for illustrators with unique, strong, salable style.
Represents Bryan Ballinger, Kooch Campbell, Jonathan Combs, Eldon Doty.
Terms Receives 25-33% commission. Advertising costs are split: 75% paid by illustrators; 25% paid by rep. Illustrator must provide portfolios (2-3) and promotional pieces. Advertises in *Picturebook*, *Workbook*.
How to Contact For first contact, send query letter, tearsheets, SASE, direct mail flier/brochure. Responds only if interested. Wait for response. Portfolio should include tearsheets. Lasers OK. Finds illustrators through recommendations from others, queries/solicitations.
Tips "Send query plus 1-2 samples, either by regular mail or e-mail."

HANNAH REPRESENTS
14431 Ventura Blvd., #108, Sherman Oaks CA 91423. (818)378-1644. E-mail: hannahrepresents@yahoo.com. **Contact:** Hannah Robinson. Literary representative for illustrators. Estab. 1997. 100% of artwork handled is children's book illustration. Looking for established illustrators only.
Handles Manuscript/illustration packages. Looking for illustrators with picture book story and illustration proposal.
Terms Receives 15% commission. Offers written contract.
How to Contact For first contact, send SASE and tearsheets. Responds only if interested. Call to schedule an

Resources

appointment. Portfolio should include photocopies. Finds illustrators through recommendations from others, conferences, queries/solicitations, international.

Tips "Present a carefully developed range of characterization illustrations that are world-class enough to equal those in the best children's books."

HERMAN AGENCY

350 Central Park West, New York NY 10025. (212)749-4907. Fax: (212)662-5151. E-mail: ronnie@hermanagenc yinc.com. Web site: www.hermanagencyinc.com. **Contact:** Ronnie Ann Herman. Literary and artistic agency. Estab. 1999. Member of SCBWI and Graphic Artists Guild. Illustrators include: Joy Allen, Dawn Apperley, Tom Arma, Durga Bernhard, Ann Catherine Blake, Mary Bono, Seymour Chwast, Pascale Constantin, Doreen Gay-Kassel, Jan Spivey Gilchrist, Barry Gott, Steve Haskamp, Aleksey Ivanov, Gideon Kendall, Ana Martin Larranaga, Mike Lester, Scott McDougall, Bob McMahon, Alexi Natchev, Jill Newton, John Nez, Anna Nilsen, Betina Ogden, Tamara Petrosino, Michael Rex, Pete Whitehead, Wendy Rouillard, David Sheldon, Mark Weber, Nick Zarin-Ackerman, Deborah Zemke. Authors include: Anne Foster, Deloris Jordan. 90% of artwork handled is children's book illustration and related markets. Currently open to illustrators and authors seeking representation who are widely published by trade publishing houses.

• Looking for established illustrators and authors only.

Handles Illustration, manuscript/illustration packages and mss.

Terms Receives 25% commission for illustration assignments; 15% for ms assignments. Artists pay 75% of costs for promotional materialabout $300 a year. Exclusive representation usually required. Offers written contract. Advertising costs are split: 75% paid by illustrator; 25% paid by rep. Advertises in *Picturebook*, *Directory of Illustration*, *Promo Pages*.

How to Contact For first contact, send samples, SASE, direct mail flier/brochure, tearsheets, photocopies. Authors should e-mail with a query. Responds in 1 month or less. I will contact you if I like your samples. Portfolio should include tearsheets, photocopies, books, dummies. Finds illustrators and authors through recommendations from others, conferences, queries/solicitations.

HK PORTFOLIO

10 E. 29th St., 40G, New York NY 10016. (212)689-7830. E-mail: mela@hkportfolio.com. Web site: www.hkportf olio.com. **Contact:** Mela Bolinao. Illustration representative. Estab. 1986. Member of SPAR, Society of Illustrators and Graphic Artists Guild. Represents 44 illustrators. Specializes in illustration for juvenile markets. Markets include: advertising agencies; editorial/magazines; publishing/books.

Handles Illustration.

Recent Sales *Sweet Tooth*, illustrated by Jack E. Davis (Simon & Schuster); *Henry and the Buccaneer Bunnies*, illustrated by John Manders (Candlewick Press); *Bubble Gum, Bubble Gum*, illustrated by Laura Huliska Beith (Little Brown/Megan Tingley); *Pajamas Anytime*, illustrated by Hiroe Nakata (Putnam); *Way Up High in a Tall Green Tree*, illustrated by Valeria Petrone (Simon & Schuster).

Terms Rep receives 25% commission. No geographic restrictions. Advertising costs are split: 75% paid by talent; 25% paid by representative. Advertises in *Picturebook*, *Directory of Illustration* and *Workbook*.

How to Contact No geographic restrictions. For first contact, send query letter, direct mail flier/brochure, Web site address, tearsheets, slides, photographs or color copies and SASE. Responds in 1 week. After initial contact, send in appropriate materials for review. Portfolio should include tearsheets, slides, photographs or photocopies.

KIRCHOFF/WOHLBERG, ARTISTS' REPRESENTATION DIVISION

866 United Nations Plaza, #525, New York NY 10017. (212)644-2020. Fax: (212)223-4387. Web site: www.kirch offwohlberg.com. **Director of Operations:** John R. Whitman. **Artist's Representative:** Elizabeth Ford. Estab. 1930. Member of SPAR, Society of Illustrators, AIGA, Association of American Publishers, Bookbuilders of Boston, New York Bookbinders' Guild. Represents over 50 illustrators. Specializes in juvenile and young adult trade books and textbooks. Markets include: publishing/books.

Handles Illustration (juvenile and young adult).

Terms Rep receives 25% commission. Exclusive representation to book publishers is usually required. Advertising costs paid by representative ("for all Kirchoff/Wohlberg advertisements only"). Keeps some original work on file. Advertises in *Art Directors' Index*, *Society of Illustrators Annual*, children's book issues of *Publishers Weekly*.

How to Contact Please send all correspondence to the attention of Elizabeth Ford. For first contact, send query letter, "any materials artists feel are appropriate." Responds in 6 weeks. "We will contact you for additional materials." Portfolios should include "whatever artists feel best represents their work. We like to see children's illustration in any style. To see illustrators currently represented, visit Web site."

LEVY CREATIVE MANAGEMENT

300 E. 46th St., Suite 8E, New York NY 10017. (212)687-6465. Fax: (212)661-4839. E-mail: info@levycreative.c

Resources

om. Web site: www.levycreative.com. **Contact:** Sari Levy. Estab. 1998. Member of Society of Illustrators, Graphic Artists Guild, Art Directors Club. Represents 13 illustrators including: Alan Dingman, Marcos Chin, Thomas Fluharty, Max Gafe, Liz Lomax, Oren Sherman, Jason Tharp. 30% of artwork handled is children's book illustration. Currently open to illustrators seeking representation. Open to both new and established illustrators. Submission guidelines available on Web site.

Handles Illustration, manuscript/illustration packages.

Terms Exclusive representation required. Offers written contract. Advertising costs are split: 75% paid by illustrators; 25% paid by rep. Advertises in *Picturebook*, *American Showcase*, *Workbook*, *Alternative Pick*, *Contact*.

How to Contact For first contact, send tearsheets, photocopies, SASE. "See Web site for submission guidelines." Responds only if interested. Portfolio should include professionally presented materials. Finds illustrators through recommendations from others, word of mouth, competitions.

LINDGREN & SMITH

630 Ninth Ave., New York NY 10036. (212)397-7330. E-mail: inquiry@lindgrensmith.com. Web site: www.lindgrensmith.com. **Contact:** Pat Lindgren, Piper Smith. Illustration representative. Estab. 1984. Member of SCBWI. Markets include children's books, advertising agencies; corporations; design firms; editorial; publishing.

Handles Illustration.

Terms Exclusive representation is required. Advertises in *The Workbook*.

How to Contact For first contact, send postcard or e-mail a link to a Web site or send one JPEG file. Responds only if interested via e-mail or phone.

Tips "Check to see if your work seems appropriate for the group."

MARLENA AGENCY, INC.

322 Ewing St., Princeton NJ 08540. (609)252-9405. Fax: (609)252-1949. E-mail: marlena@marlenaagency.com. Web site: www.marlenaagency.com. Commercial illustration representative. Estab. 1990. Member of Society of Illustrators. Represents 30 international illustrators including: Marc Mongeau, Gerard Dubois, Linda Helton, Paul Zwolak, Martin Jarrie, Serge Bloch, Hadley Hooper and Carmen Segovia. Staff includes Marlena Torzecka, Simone Stark, Ella Lupo. Currently open to illustrators seeking representation. Open to both new and established illustrators. Submission guidelines available for #10 SASE.

Handles Illustration.

Recent Sales *Pebble Soup*, by Marc Mongeau (Rigby); *Sees Behind Trees*, by Linda Helton (Harcourt Brace & Company); *New Orleans Band*, by Marc Mongeau (Scott Foresman); and *My Cat*, by Linda Helton (Scholastic).

Terms Exclusive representation required. Offers written contract. Requires printed portfolios, transparencies, direct mail piece (such as postcards) printed samples. Advertises in *Creative Blackbook*, *Workbook*.

How to Contact For first contact, send tearsheets, photocopies. Responds only if interested. Drop off or mail portfolio, photocopies. Portfolio should include tearsheets, photocopies. Finds illustrators through queries/solicitations, magazines and graphic design.

Tips "Be creative and persistent."

THE NEIS GROUP

P.O. Box 174, 11440 Oak Dr., Shelbyville MI 49344. (269)672-5756. Fax: (269)672-5757. E-mail: neisgroup@wmis.net. Web site: www.neisgroup.com. **Contact:** Judy Neis. Commercial illustration representative. Estab. 1982. Represents 45 illustrators including: Lyn Boyer, Pam Thomson, Dan Sharp, Terry Workman, Liz Conrad, Garry Colby, Clint Hansen, Don McLean, Julie Borden, Johnna Bandle, Jack Pennington, Gary Ferster, Erika LeBarre, Joel Spector, John White, Neverne Covington, Ruth Pettis, Matt LeBarre. 60% of artwork handled is children's book illustration. Currently open to illustrators seeking representation. Looking for established illustrators only.

Handles Illustration, photography and calligraphy/manuscript packages.

Terms Receives 25% commission. Advertising costs are split: 75% paid by illustrator; 25% paid by rep. "I prefer porfolios on CD, color printouts and e-mail capabilities whenever possible." Advertises in *Picturebook*, *American Showcase*, *Creative Black Book*.

How to Contact For first contact, send bio, tearsheets, direct mail flier/brochure. Responds only if interested. After initial contact, drop off portfolio of nonreturnables. Portfolio should include tearsheets, photocopies. Obtains new talent through recommendations from others and queries/solicitations.

WANDA NOWAK/CREATIVE ILLUSTRATORS AGENCY

231 E. 76th St., 5D, New York NY 10021. (212)535-0438, ext. 1624. Fax: (212)535-1629. E-mail: wanda@wandanow.com. Web site: www.wandanow.com. **Contact:** Wanda Nowak. Commercial illustration representative. Estab. 1996. Represents 20 illustrators including: Emilie Chollat, Thea Kliros, Pierre Pratt, Frederique Bertrand, Ilja Bereznickas, Boris Kulikov, Yayo, Laurence Cleyet-Merle, E. Kerner, Ellen Usdin, Marie Lafrance, Stephane

Jorisch. 50% of artwork handled is children's book illustration. Staff includes Wanda Nowak. Open to both new and established illustrators.

Handles Illustration. Looking for "unique, individual style."

Terms Receives 30% commission. Exclusive representation required. Offers written contract. Advertising costs are split: 70% paid by illustrators; 30% paid by rep. Advertises in *Picturebook*, *Workbook*, *The Alternative Pick*, *Black Book*.

How to Contact For first contact, send SASE. Responds only if interested. Drop off portfolio. Portfolio should include tearsheets. Finds illustrators through recommendations from others, sourcebooks like *CA*, *Picture Book*, *Creative Black Book*, exhibitions.

Tips "Develop your own style. Send a little illustrated story, which will prove you can carry a character in different situations with facial expressions, etc."

REMEN-WILLIS DESIGN GROUP—ANN REMEN-WILLIS

2964 Colton Rd., Pebble Beach CA 93953. (831)655-1407. Fax: (831)655-1408. E-mail: remenwillis@comcast.net. Web sites: www.annremenwillis.com or www.picture-book.com. **Contact:** Ann Remen-Willis. Specializes in childrens' book illustration trade/education. Estab. 1984. Member of SCBWI. Represents 18 illustrators including: Christine Benjamin, Domini Catalano, Siri Weber Feeney, Doug Roy, Susan Jaekel, Dennis Hockerman, Rosiland Solomon, Meredith Johnson, Renate Lohmann, Loretta Lustig, Robin Kerr, Len Ebert, Gary Undercuffler. 100% of artwork handled is children's book illustration.

Terms Offers written contract. Advertising costs are split: 50% paid by illustrators; 50% paid by rep. Illustrator must provide small precise portfolio for promotion. Advertises in *Picturebook*, *Workbook*.

How to Contact For first contact, send tearsheets, photocopies. Responds in 1 week. Mail portfolio to set up an interview or portfolio review. Portfolio should include tearsheets, photocopies.

Tips "Send samples of only the type of work you are interested in receiving. Check out rep's forte first."

RENAISSANCE HOUSE

9400 Lloydcrest Dr., Beverly Hills CA 90210. (800)547-5113. Fax: (310)860-9902. E-mail: info@renaissancehouse.net. Web site: www.renaissancehouse.net or www.illustratorsonline.net. **Contact:** Raquel Benatar. Children's, educational, multicultural, and textbooks, advertising rep. Estab. 1991. Represents 80 illustrators. 95% of artwork handled is children's book illustration and photography. Currently open to illustrators and photographers seeking representation. Open to both new and established illustrators.

Handles Illustration and photography.

Recent Sales Maribel Suarez (Little Brown, Hyperion); Ana Lopez (Scholastic); Ruth Araceli (Houghton Mifflin); Vivi Escriva (Albert Whitman); Marie Jara (Sparknotes); Sheli Petersen (McGraw-Hill).

Terms Exclusive and non-exclusive representation. Illustrators must provide scans of illustrations. Advertises in *Picturebook*, *Directory of Illustration*, own Web site and *Catalog of Illustrators*.

How to Contact For first contact send tearsheets. Responds in 2 weeks. Finds illustrators through recommendations from others, conferences, direct contact.

S.I. INTERNATIONAL

43 E. 19th St., New York NY 10003. (212)254-4996. Fax: (212)995-0911. E-mail: info@si-i.com. Web site: www.si-i.com. Commercial illustration representative. Estab. 1983. Member of SPAR, Graphic Artists Guild. Represents 50 illustrators. Specializes in license characters, educational publishing and children's illustration, digital art and design, mass market paperbacks. Markets include design firms; publishing/books; sales/promotion firms; licensing firms; digital art and design firms.

Handles Illustration. Looking for artists "who have the ability to do children's illustration and to do license characters either digitally or reflectively."

Terms Rep receives 25-30% commission. Advertising costs are split: 70% paid by talent; 30% paid by representative. "Contact agency for details. Must have mailer." Advertises in *Picturebook*.

How to Contact For first contact, send query letter, tearsheets. Responds in 3 weeks. After initial contact, write for appointment to show portfolio of tearsheets, slides.

N SALZMAN INTERNATIONAL

824 Edwards St., Box 41, Trinidad CA 95570. (707)677-0241. Fax: (707)677-0242. E-mail: rs@slazint.com. Web site: www.salzint.com. Commercial illustration representative. Estab. 1982. Represents 20 illustrators. 20% of artwork is children's book illustration. **Staff includes:** Richard Salzman and Brian McMahon. Open to illustrators seeking representation. Accepting both new and established illustrators.

Handles Accepts illustration.

Terms Receives 25% commission. Offers written contract. 100% of advertising costs paid by illustrator. Advertises in *Workbook*, ispot.com, altpick.com.

How to Contact For first contact, send link to Web site or printed samples. Portfolio should include tearsheets, photocopies; "best to post samples on Web site and send link." Finds illustrators through queries/solicitations.

LIZ SANDERS AGENCY

2415 E. Hangman Creek Lane, Spokane WA 99224-8514. E-mail: liz@lizsanders.com. Web site: www.lizsanders .com. **Contact:** Liz Sanders. Commercial illustration representative. Estab. 1985. Represents Craig Orback, Amy Ning, Tom Pansini, Chris Lensch, Kate Endle, Susan Synarski, Sudi McCollum, Sue Rama, Suzanne Beaky and more. Currently open to illustrators seeking representation. Open to both new and established illustrators.
Handles Illustration. Markets include publishing, entertainment, giftware and advertising.
Terms Receives 30% commission against pro bono mailing program. Offers written contract. Advertises in *Picturebook* and picture-book.com, *Workbook* and workbook.com, theispot.com, folioplanet.com. No geographic restrictions.
How to Contact For first contact, send tearsheets, direct mail flier/brochure, color copies, non-returnables or e-mail. Responds only if interested. After initial contact, submit portfolio. Portfolio should include tearsheets, photocopies. Obtains new talent through recommendations from others, conferences and queries/solicitations, Literary Market Place.

THOROGOOD KIDS

5 Dryden Street, Covent Garden, London WC2E 9NW United Kingdom. (44)(207)829-8468. Fax: (44)(208)8597507. E-mail: kids@thorogood.net. Web site: www.thorogood.net/kids. Commercial illustration representative. Estab. 1978. Represents 30 illustrators including: Nicola Slater, Anne Yvonne Gilbert, Olivier Latyk, Sophie Allsopp, Carol Morley, Philip Nicholson, Dan Hambe, Bill Dare, Christiane Engel, Robin Heighway-Bury, Leo Timmers, Kanako & Yuzuru, Shaunna Peterson, Daniel Egneus, Al Sacui, John Woodcock. Staff includes Doreen Thorogood, Steve Thorogood, Tom Thorogood. Open to illustrators seeking representation. Accepting both new and established illustrators. Guidelines not available.
Handles Accepts illustration, illustration/manuscript packages.
Recent Sales *Have You Seen Elvis?*, Princess Diaries Series, (UK Editions) illustrated by Nicola Slater (Macmillan); Wizardology (Templar); *Night Before Christmas*, illustrated by Anne Yvonne Gilbert (Dorling Kindersley); *Goldilocks and The Three Bears*, illustrated by Anne Yvonne Gilbert (Ladybird); *Have You Seen Elvis?*, illustrated by Nicola Slater (Pan Macmillan); *Marsha Mellow & Me*, illustrated by Kanako Yuzuru (Random House); *Louis & Bobo Are Moving*, illustrated by Christiane Engel (Topaz Books); The Five Ancestors Series, illustrated by Kanako and Yuzuru (Hodder).
How to Contact For first contact, send tearsheets, photocopies, SASE, direct mail flyer/brochure. After initial contact, we will contact the illustrator if we want to see the portfolio. Portfolio should include tearsheets, photocopies. Finds illustrators through queries/solicitations, conferences.
Tips "Be unique and research your market. Talent will win out!"

TUGEAU 2, INC.

2225 Bellfield Ave., Cleveland Heights OH 44106. (216)707-0854. Fax: (216)795-8404. E-mail: nicole@tugeau2.c om. Web site: www.tugeau2.com. Children's publishing art/illustration representative. Estab. 2003. Member of SCBWI, Graphic Artists Guild. Represents 27 illustrators. **Staff includes:** Nicole Tugeau and Jeremy Tugeau. Open to illustrators seeking representation. Accepting both new and established illustrators.
Handles Accepts illustration.
Terms Receives 25% commission. Exclusive representation in the children's industry required. Offers written contract. Illustrator must provide digital portfolio (for Web and e-mail proposals) as well as 50-100 tearsheets (postcards or otherwise) with agency name and logo—to be kept inhouse for promotion. Advertises in *Picturebook*, *Directory of Illustration Play* (Sherbin Communications).
How to Contact For first contact, e-mail with 4 or 5 digital files of artwork. Responds immediately. Agency will request full portfolio with SASE if interested. Finds illustrators through recommendations from others, queries/ solicitations.
Tips "Do not look for representation until you have a portfolio (12-15 pieces) geared toward the children's market. Hone in on your personal style, consistency, and diversity of scenes and characters. Be ready to articulate your ambitions in the industry and the time you will be able to commit to those ambitions."

GWEN WALTERS ARTIST REPRESENTATIVE

1801 S. Flagler Dr., #1202, W. Palm Beach FL 33401. (561)805-7739. E-mail: artincgw@aol.com. Web site: www.gwenWaltersartrep.com. **Contact:** Gwen Walters. Commercial illustration representative. Estab. 1976. Represents 18 illustrators. 90% of artwork handled is children's book illustration. Currently open to illustrators seeking representation. Looking for established illustrators only.
Handles Illustration.

Recent Sales Sells to "All major book publishers."

Terms Receives 30% commission. Artist needs to supply all promo material. Offers written contract. Advertising costs are split: 70% paid by illustrator; 30% paid by rep. Advertises in *Picturebook*, *RSVP*, *Directory of Illustration*.

How to Contact For first contact, send tearsheets. Responds only if interested. Finds illustrators through recommendations from others.

Tips "Go out and get some first-hand experience. Learn to tell yourself to understand the way the market works."

WENDYLYNN & CO.

504 Wilson Rd., Annapolis MD 21401. (401)224-2729. Fax: (410)224-2183. E-mail: wendy@wendylynn.com. Web site: wendylynn.com. **Contact:** Wendy Mays. Children's illustration representative. Estab. 2002. Member of SCBWI. Represents 16 illustrators. 100% of artwork handled is children's illustration. Staff includes Wendy Mays, Janice Onken. Currently open to illustrators seeking representation. Open to both new and established illustrators. Submission guidelines available on Web site.

Handles Illustration.

Terms Receives 25% commission. Exclusive representation required. Offers written contract. Requires 15-20 images submitted on disk. Advertises in *Picturebook* or *CreativeBlack Book*.

How to Contact For first contact, e-mail or send color photocopies or tearsheets with bio; e-mail is preferred. Responds ASAP. After initial contact mail artwork on CD and send tearsheets. Portfolio should include a minimum of 15 images. Finds illustrators through recommendations from others and from portfolio reviews.

Tips "Show a character developed consistently in different settings in a series of illustrations interacting with other children, animals or adults."

DEBORAH WOLFE LTD.

731 N. 24th St., Philadelphia PA 19130. (215)232-6666. Fax: (215)232-6585. E-mail: inquiry@illustrationonline.com. Web site: www.illustrationOnline.com. **Contact:** Deborah Wolfe. Commercial illustration representative. Estab. 1978. Member of Graphic Artist Guild. Represents 30 illustrators. Currently open to illustrators seeking representation.

Handles Illustration.

Terms Receives 25% commission. Exclusive representation required. Offers written contract. Advertising costs are split: 75% paid by illustrators; 25% paid by rep. Advertises in *Picturebook*, *Directory of Illustration*, *The Workbook*, *The Black Book*.

How to Contact Responds in 2 weeks. Portfolio should include "anything except originals." Finds illustrators through queries/solicitations.

Clubs & Organizations

Contacts made through organizations such as the ones listed in this section can be quite beneficial for children's writers and illustrators. Professional organizations provide numerous educational, business, and legal services in the form of newsletters, workshops, or seminars. Organizations can provide tips about how to be a more successful writer or artist, as well as what types of business records to keep, health and life insurance coverage to carry, and competitions to consider.

An added benefit of belonging to an organization is the opportunity to network with those who have similar interests, creating a support system. As in any business, knowing the right people can often help your career, and important contacts can be made through your peers. Membership in a writer's or artist's organization also shows publishers you're serious about your craft. This provides no guarantee your work will be published, but it gives you an added dimension of credibility and professionalism.

Some of the organizations listed here welcome anyone with an interest, while others are only open to published writers and professional artists. Organizations such as the Society of Children's Book Writers and Illustrators (SCBWI, www.scbwi.org) have varying levels of membership. SCBWI offers associate membership to those with no publishing credits, and full membership to those who have had work for children published. International organizations such as SCBWI also have regional chapters throughout the U.S. and the world. Write or call for more information regarding any group that interests you, or check the Web sites of the many organizations that list them. Be sure to get information about local chapters, membership qualifications, and services offered.

Information on organizations listed in the previous edition but not included in this edition of *Children's Writer's & Illustrator's Market* may be found in the General Index.

Resources

AMERICAN ALLIANCE FOR THEATRE & EDUCATION

7475 Wisconsin Avenue, Suite 300A Bethesda, MD 20814. (301)951-7977. E-mail: info@aate.com. Web site: www.aate.com. Purpose of organization: to promote standards of excellence in theatre and drama education. "We achieve this by assimilating quality practices in theatre and theatre education, connecting artists, educators, researchers and scholars with each other, and by providing opportunities for our members to learn, exchange and diversify their work, their audiences and their perspectives." Membership cost: $110 annually for individual in U.S. and Canada, $220 annually for organization, $60 annually for students, $70 annually for retired people; add $30 outside Canada and U.S. Holds annual conference (July). Newsletter published quarterly (on Web site only). Contests held for unpublished play reading project and annual awards in various categories. Awards plaque and stickers for published playbooks. Publishes list of unpublished plays deemed worthy of performance and stages readings at conference. Contact national office at number above or see Web site for contact information for Playwriting Network Chairpersons.

AMERICAN SOCIETY OF JOURNALISTS AND AUTHORS

1501 Broadway, Suite 302, New York NY 10036. Web site: www.asja.org. **Executive Director:** Brett Harvey. Qualifications for membership: "Need to be a professional nonfiction writer. Refer to Web site for further qualifications." Membership cost: Application fee—$25; annual dues—$195. Group sponsors national conferences; monthly workshops in New York City. Workshops/conferences open to nonmembers. Publishes a newsletter for members that provides confidential information for nonfiction writers.

ARIZONA AUTHORS ASSOCIATION

P.O. Box 87857, Phoenix AZ 85080-7857. E-mail: info@azauthors.com. Web site: www.azauthors.com. **President:** Toby Heathcotte. Purpose of organization: to offer professional, educational and social opportunities to writers and authors, and serve as a network. Members must be authors, writers working toward publication, agents, publishers, publicists, printers, illustrators, etc. Membership cost: $45/year writers; $30/year students; $60/year other professionals in publishing industry. Holds regular workshops and meetings. Publishes bimonthly newsletter and Arizona Literary Magazine. Sponsors Annual Literary Contest in poetry, essays, short stories, novels, and published books with cash prizes and awards bestowed at a public banquet in Phoenix. Winning entries are also published or advertised in the *Arizona Literary Magazine.* Send SASE or view Web site for guidelines.

ASSITEJ/USA

724 Second Ave South, Nashville TN 37210. (615)254-5719. Fax: (615)254-3255. E-mail: usassitej@aol.com. Web site: www.assitej-usa.org. Purpose of organization: to promote theater for children and young people by linking professional theaters and artists together; sponsoring national, international and regional conferences and providing publications and information. Also serves as U.S. Center for International Association of Theatre for Children and Young People. Different levels of membership include: organizations, individuals, students, retirees, libraries. *TYA Today* includes original articles, reviews and works of criticism and theory, all of interest to theater practitioners (included with membership). Publishes journal that focuses on information on field in U.S. and abroad.

THE AUTHORS GUILD

31 E. 28th St., 10th Floor, New York NY 10011. (212)563-5904. Fax: (212)564-5363. E-mail: staff@authorsguild.org. Web site: www.authorsguild.org. **Executive Director:** Paul Aiken. Purpose of organization: to offer services and materials intended to help authors with the business and legal aspects of their work, including contract problems, copyright matters, freedom of expression and taxation. Guild has 8,000 members. Qualifications for membership: Must be book author published by an established American publisher within 7 years or any author who has had 3 works (fiction or nonfiction) published by a magazine or magazines of general circulation in the last 18 months. Associate membership also available. Annual dues: $90. Different levels of membership include: associate membership with all rights except voting available to an author who has a firm contract offer or is currently negotiating a royalty contract from an established American publisher. "The Guild offers free contract reviews to its members. The Guild conducts several symposia each year at which experts provide information, offer advice and answer questions on subjects of interest and concern to authors. Typical subjects have been the rights of privacy and publicity, libel, wills and estates, taxation, copyright, editors and editing, the art of interviewing, standards of criticism and book reviewing. Transcripts of these symposia are published and circulated to members. The *Authors Guild Bulletin,* a quarterly journal, contains articles on matters of interest to writers, reports of Guild activities, contract surveys, advice on problem clauses in contracts, transcripts of Guild and League symposia and information on a variety of professional topics. Subscription included in the cost of the annual dues."

Resources

CANADIAN SOCIETY OF CHILDREN'S AUTHORS, ILLUSTRATORS AND PERFORMERS, (CANSCAIP)

104-40 Orchard View Blvd., Toronto ON M4R 1B9 Canada. (416)515-1559. E-mail: office@canscaip.org. Web site: www.cansaip.org. **Office Manager:** Lena Coakley. Purpose of organization: development of Canadian children's culture and support for authors, illustrators and performers working in this field. Qualifications for membership: Members—professionals who have been published (not self-published) or have paid public performances/records/tapes to their credit. Friends—share interest in field of children's culture. Membership cost: $75 (Members dues), $35 (Friends dues), $45 (Institution dues). Sponsors workshops/conferences. Publishes newsletter: includes profiles of members; news round-up of members' activities countrywide; market news; news on awards, grants, etc; columns related to professional concerns.

LEWIS CARROLL SOCIETY OF NORTH AMERICA

P.O. Box 204, Napa CA 94559. E-mail: hedgehog@napanet.net. Web site: www.lewiscarroll.org/lcsna.html. **Secretary:** Cindy Watter. "We are an organization of Carroll admirers of all ages and interests and a center for Carroll studies." Qualifications for membership: "An interest in Lewis Carroll and a simple love for Alice (or the Snark for that matter)." Membership cost: $20 (regular membership), $50 (contributing membership). The Society meets twice a year—in spring and in fall; locations vary. Publishes a quarterly newsletter, *Knight Letter*, and maintains an active publishing program.

THE CHILDREN'S BOOK COUNCIL, INC.

12 W. 37th St., 2nd Floor, New York NY 10018. (212)966-1990. Fax: (212)966-2073. E-mail: info@cbcbooks.org. Web site: www.cbcbooks.org. **President:** Paula Quint. Purpose of organization: A nonprofit trade association of children's and young adult publishers and packagers, CBC promotes the enjoyment of books for children and young adults and works with national and international organizations to that end. The CBC has sponsored Children's Book Week since 1945 and Young People's Poetry Week since 1999. Qualifications for membership: trade publishers and packagers of children's and young adult books and related literary materials are eligible for membership. Publishers wishing to join should contact the CBC for dues information. Sponsors workshops and seminars for publishing company personnel. Individuals wishing to receive the CBC semi-annual journal, *CBC Features* with articles of interest to people working with children and books and materials brochures, may be placed on CBC's mailing list for a one-time-only fee of $60. Sells reading encouragement posters and graphics and informational materials suitable for libraries, teachers, booksellers, parents, and others working with children.

FLORIDA FREELANCE WRITERS ASSOCIATION

Cassell Network of Writers, P.O. Box A, North Stratford NH 03590. (603)922-8338. E-mail: FFWA@Writers-Editors.com. **Executive Director:** Dana K. Cassell. Purpose of organization: To provide a link between Florida writers and buyers of the written word; to help writers run more effective editorial businesses. Qualifications for membership: "None. We provide a variety of services and information, some for beginners and some for established pros." Membership cost: $90/year. Publishes a newsletter focusing on market news, business news, how-to tips for the serious writer. Annual *Directory of Florida Markets* included in FFWA newsletter section and electronic download. Publishes annual *Guide to CNW/Florida Writers*, which is distributed to editors around the country. Sponsors contest: annual deadline March 15. Guidelines on Web site. Categories: juvenile, adult nonfiction, adult fiction and poetry. Awards include cash for top prizes, certificate for others. Contest open to nonmembers.

GRAPHIC ARTISTS GUILD

90 John St., Suite 403, New York NY 10038. (212)791-3400. E-mail: membership@gag.org. Web site: www.gag.org. **President:** John P. Schmelzer. Purpose of organization: "To promote and protect the economic interests of member artists. It is committed to improving conditions for all creators of graphic arts and raising standards for the entire industry." Qualification for full membership: 50% of income derived from the creation of artwork. Associate members include those in allied fields, students and retirees. Initiation fee: $30. Full memberships: $200; student membership: $75/year. Associate membership: $170/year. Publishes *Graphic Artists Guild Handbook, Pricing and Ethical Guidelines* (free to members, $34.95 retail). "The Graphic Artists Guild is a national union that embraces all creators of graphic arts intended for presentation as originals or reproductions at all levels of skill and expertise. The long-range goals of the Guild are: to educate graphic artists and their clients about ethical and fair business practices; to educate graphic artists about emerging trends and technologies impacting the industry; to offer programs and services that anticipate and respond to the needs of our members, helping them prosper and enhancing their health and security; to advocate for the interests of our members in the legislative, judicial and regulatory arenas; to assure that our members are recognized financially and

professionally for the value they provide; to be responsible stewards for our members by building an organization that works efficiently on their behalf.''

HORROR WRITERS ASSOCIATION

P.O. Box 50577, Palo Alto CA 94303. E-mail: hwa@horror.org. Web site: www.horror.org. **Office Manager:** Nancy Etchemendy. Purpose of organization: To encourage public interest in horror and dark fantasy and to provide networking and career tools for members. Qualifications for membership: Complete membership rules online at www.horror.org/memrule.htm. At least one low-level sale is required to join as an affiliate. Non-writing professionals who can show income from a horror-related field may join as an associate (booksellers, editors, agents, librarians, etc.) To qualify for full active membership, you must be a published, professional writer of horror. Membership cost: $65 annually in North America; $75 annually elsewhere. Holds annual Stoker Awards Weekend and HWA Business Meeting. Publishes monthly newsletter focusing on market news, industry news, HWA business for members. Sponsors awards. We give the Bram Stoker Awards for superior achievement in horror annually. Awards include a handmade Stoker trophy designed by sculptor Stephen Kirk. Awards open to nonmembers.

INTERNATIONAL READING ASSOCIATION

800 Barksdale Rd., P.O. Box 8139, Newark DE 19714-8139. (302)731-1600, ext. 293. Fax: (302)731-1057. E-mail: pubinfo@reading.org. Web site: www.reading.org. **Public Information Associate:** Beth Cady. Purpose of organization: ''Formed in 1956, the International Reading Association seeks to promote high levels of literacy for all by improving the quality of reading instruction through studying the reading process and teaching techniques; serving as a clearinghouse for the dissemination of reading research through conferences, journals, and other publications; and actively encouraging the lifetime reading habit. Its goals include professional development, advocacy, partnerships, research, and global literacy development.'' **Open to students.** Basic membership: $36. Sponsors annual convention. Publishes a newsletter called ''Reading Today.'' Sponsors a number of awards and fellowships. Visit the IRA Web site for more information on membership, conventions and awards.

THE INTERNATIONAL WOMEN'S WRITING GUILD

P.O. Box 810, Gracie Station, New York NY 10028. (212)737-7536. Fax: (212) 737-9469. E-mail: dirhahn@aol.com. Web site: www.iwwg.org. **Executive Director and Founder:** Hannelore Hahn. IWWG is ''a network for the personal and professional empowerment of women through writing.'' Qualifications: open to any woman connected to the written word regardless of professional portfolio. Membership cost: $45 annually. ''IWWG sponsors several annual conferences a year in all areas of the U.S. The major conference is held in June of each year at Skidmore College in Saratoga Springs, NY. It is a week-long conference attracting over 500 women internationally.'' Also publishes a 32-page newsletter, *Network*, 6 times/year; offers dental and vision insurance at group rates, referrals to literary agents.

⚡ LEAGUE OF CANADIAN POETS

920 Yonge St., Suite 608, Toronto ON M4W 3C7 Canada. (416)504-1657. Fax: (416)504-0096. Web site: www.poets.ca. **Acting Executive Director:** Joanna Poblocka. President: Mary Ellen Csamer. Inquiries to Program Manager: Joanna Poblocka. The L.C.P. is a national organization of published Canadian poets. Our constitutional objectives are to advance poetry in Canada and to promote the professional interests of the members. Qualifications for membership: full—publication of at least 1 book of poetry by a professional publisher; associate membership—an active interest in poetry, demonstrated by several magazine/periodical publication credits; student—an active interest in poetry, 12 sample poems required; supporting—any friend of poetry. Membership fees: full—$175/year, associate—$60, student—$20, supporting—$100. Holds an Annual General Meeting every spring; some events open to nonmembers. ''We also organize reading programs in schools and public venues. We publish a newsletter which includes information on poetry/poetics in Canada and beyond. Also publish the books *Poetry Markets for Canadians*; *Who's Who in the League of Canadian Poets*; *Poets in the Classroom* (teaching guide), and online publications. The Gerald Lampert Memorial Award for the best first book of poetry published in Canada in the preceding year and The Pat Lowther Memorial Award for the best book of poetry by a Canadian woman published in the preceding year. Deadline for awards: November 1. Visit www.poets.ca for more details. Sponsors youth poetry competition. Visit www.youngpoets.ca for details.

LITERARY MANAGERS AND DRAMATURGS OF THE AMERICAS

P.O. Box 728, New York NY 10014. E-mail: lmda@lmda.org or lmdanyc@hotmail.com. Web site: www.lmda.org. LMDA is a not-for-profit service organization for the professions of literary management and dramaturgy. Student Membership: $25/year. Open to students in dramaturgy, performing arts and literature programs, or related disciplines. Proof of student status required. Includes national conference, New Dramaturg activities, local symposia, job phone and select membership meetings. Active Membership: $60/year. Open to full-time and part-time professionals working in the fields of literary management and dramaturgy. All privileges and services including voting rights and eligibility for office. Associate Membership: $45/year. Open to all performing arts professionals and academics, as well as others interested in the field. Includes national conference, local symposia and select membership meetings. Institutional Membership: $135/year. Open to theaters, universities, and other organizations. Includes all privileges and services except voting rights and eligibility for office. Publishes a newsletter featuring articles on literary management, dramaturgy, LMDA program updates and other articles of interest.

THE NATIONAL LEAGUE OF AMERICAN PEN WOMEN

1300 17th St. N.W., Washington DC 20036-1973. (202)785-1997. E-mail: nlapw1@verizon.net. Web site: www.americanpenwomen.org. **President:** Dr. Bernice Strand Reid. Purpose of organization: to promote professional work in art, letters, and music since 1897. Qualifications for membership: An applicant must show "proof of sale" in each chosen category—art, letters, and music. Membership cost: $40 ($10 processing fee and $30 National dues); Annual fees—$30 plus Branch/State dues. Different levels of membership include: Active, Associate, International Affiliate, Members-at-Large, Honorary Members (in one or more of the following classifications: Art, Letters, and Music). Holds workshops/conferences. Publishes magazine 6 times/year titled *The Pen Woman.* Sponsors various contests in areas of Art, Letters, and Music. Awards made at Biennial Convention. Biannual scholarships awarded to non-Pen Women for mature women. Awards include cash prizes—up to $1,000. Specialized contests open to nonmembers.

NATIONAL WRITERS ASSOCIATION

10940 S. Parker Rd., #508, Parker CO 80138. (303)841-0246. Fax: (303)841-2607. E-mail: info@nationalwriters.com. Web site: www.nationalwriters.com. **Executive Director:** Sandy Whelchel. Purpose of organization: association for freelance writers. Qualifications for membership: associate membership—must be serious about writing; professional membership—must be published and paid writer (cite credentials). Membership cost: $65 associate; $85 professional; $35 student. Sponsors workshops/conferences: TV/screenwriting workshops, NWAF Annual Conferences, Literary Clearinghouse, editing and critiquing services, local chapters, National Writer's School. Open to non-members. Publishes industry news of interest to freelance writers; how-to articles; market information; member news and networking opportunities. Nonmember subscription: $20. Sponsors poetry contest; short story contest; article contest; novel contest. Awards cash for top 3 winners; books and/or certificates for other winners; honorable mention certificate places 5-10. Contests open to nonmembers.

NATIONAL WRITERS UNION

113 University Place, 6th Floor, New York NY 10003. (212)254-0279. E-mail: nwu@nwu.org. Web site: www.nwu.org. **Open to students.** Purpose of organization: Advocacy for freelance writers. Qualifications for membership: "Membership in the NWU is open to all qualified writers, and no one shall be barred or in any manner prejudiced within the Union on account of race, age, sex, sexual orientation, disability, national origin, religion or ideology. You are eligible for membership if you have published a book, a play, three articles, five poems, one short story or an equivalent amount of newsletter, publicity, technical, commercial, government or institutional copy. You are also eligible for membership if you have written an equal amount of unpublished material and you are actively writing and attempting to publish your work." Membership cost: annual writing income under $5,000—$95/year or $55/½ year; annual writing income $5,000-25,000—$155/year or $85/½ year; annual writing income $25,000-50,000—$210/year or $110/½ year; over $50,000—$260/year or $135/½ year. Holds workshops throughout the country. Offers national union newsletter quarterly, *American Writer,* issues related to freelance writing and to union organization for members. Offers contract and grievance advice.

PEN AMERICAN CENTER

588 Broadway, Suite 303, New York NY 10012. (212)334-1660. Fax: (212)334-2181. E-mail: pen@pen.org. Web site: www.pen.org. Purpose of organization: "An associate of writers working to advance literature, to defend free expression, and to foster international literary fellowship." Qualifications for membership: "The standard qualification for a writer to become a member of PEN is publication of two or more books of a literary character, or one book generally acclaimed to be of exceptional distinction. Also eligible for membership: editors who have demonstrated commitment to excellence in their profession (usually construed as five years' service in book editing); translators who have published at least two book-length literary translations; playwrights whose works have been produced professionally; and literary essayists whose publications are extensive even if they have not yet been issued as a book. Candidates for membership may be nominated by a PEN member or they may nominate themselves with the support of two references from the literary community or from a current PEN member. Membership dues are $75 per year and many PEN members contribute their time by serving on committees, conducting campaigns and writing letters in connection with freedom-of-expression cases, contributing to the PEN journal, participating in PEN public events, helping to bring literature into underserved

communities, and judging PEN literary awards. PEN members receive a subscription to the PEN journal, the PEN Annual Report, and have access to medical insurance at group rates. Members living in the New York metropolitan and tri-state area, or near the Branches, are invited to PEN events throughout the year. Membership in PEN American Center includes reciprocal privileges in PEN American Center branches and in foreign PEN Centers for those traveling abroad. Application forms are available on the Web at www.pen.org. Associate Membership is open to everyone who supports PEN's mission, and your annual dues ($40; $20 for students) provides crucial support to PEN's programs. When you join as an Associate Member, not only will you receive a subscription to the PEN Journal http://pen.org/page.php/prmID/150 and notices of all PEN events but you are also invited to participate in the work of PEN. PEN American Center is the largest of the 141 centers of International PEN, the world's oldest human rights organization and the oldest international literary organiza- tion. International PEN was founded in 1921 to dispel national, ethnic, and racial hatreds and to promote understanding among all countries. PEN American Center, founded a year later, works to advance literature, to defend free expression, and to foster international literary fellowship. The Center has a membership of 2,900 distinguished writers, editors, and translators. In addition to defending writers in prison or in danger of imprisonment for their work, PEN American Center sponsors public literary programs and forums on current issues, sends prominent authors to inner-city schools to encourage reading and writing, administers literary prizes, promotes international literature that might otherwise go unread in the United States, and offers grants and loans to writers facing financial or medical emergencies. In carrying out this work, PEN American Center builds upon the achievements of such dedicated past members as W.H. Auden, James Baldwin, Willa Cather, Robert Frost, Langston Hughes, Thomas Mann, Arthur Miller, Marianne Moore, Susan Sontag, and John Stein- beck. The Children's Book Authors' Committee sponsors annual public events focusing on the art of writing for children and young adults and on the diversity of literature for juvenile readers. The PEN/Phyllis Naylor Working Writer Fellowship was established in 2001 to assist a North American author of fiction for children or young adults (E-mail: awards@pen.org). Visit www.pen.org for complete information. Sponsors several competitions per year. Monetary awards range from $2,000-35,000.

🌐 PLAYMARKET

P.O. Box 9767, Te Aro Wellington New Zealand. (64)4 3828462. Fax: (64)4 3828461. E-mail: info@playmarket.o rg.nz. Web site: www.playmarket.org.nz. **Director:** Mark Amery. Script Development: Kathy McRae, Jean Betts. Administrato r: Katrina Chandra. Purpose of organization: funded by Creative New Zealand, Playmarket serves as New Zealand's script advisory service and playwrights' agency. Playmarket offers script assessment, develop- ment and agency services to help New Zealand playwrights secure professional production for their plays. Playmarket runs the NZ Young Playwrights Competition, The Aotearoa Playwrights Conference and the Adam Playreading Series and administers the annual Bruce Mason Playwrighting Award. The organization's magazine, *Playmarket News*, is published biannually. Inquiries e-mail info@playmarket.org.nz.

PUPPETEERS OF AMERICA, INC.

P.O. Box 330, West Liberty IA 52776. (888)568-6235. Fax: (440)843-7867. E-mail: pofajoin@puppeteers.org. Web site: www.puppeteers.org. **Membership Officer:** Jean K. Newkirk. Purpose of organization: to promote the art of puppetry as a means of communications and as a performing art. Qualifications for membership: interest in the art form. Membership cost: single adult, $50; youth member, $30 (6-17 years of age); full- time college student, $30; family, $70; couple, $60. Membership includes a bimonthly newsletter (*Playboard*). Discounts for workshops/conferences, access to the Audio Visual Library & Consultants in many areas of Puppetry. *The Puppetry Journal*, a quarterly periodical, provides news about puppeteers, puppet theaters, exhibitions, touring companies, technical tips, new products, new books, films, television, and events sponsored by the Chartered Guilds in each of the 8 P of A regions. *The Puppetry Journal* is the only publication in the United States dedicated to puppetry in the United States. Subscription: $40 (libraries only). The Puppeteers of America sponsors an annual National Day of Puppetry the last Saturday in April.

SCIENCE-FICTION AND FANTASY WRITERS OF AMERICA, INC.

P.O. Box 877, Chestertown MD 21620. E-mail: execdir@sfwa.org. Web site: www.sfwa.org. **Executive Director:** Jane Jewell. Purpose of organization: to encourage public interest in science fiction literature and provide organization format for writers/editors/artists within the genre. Qualifications for membership: at least 1 profes- sional sale or other professional involvement within the field. Membership cost: annual active dues—$50; affiliate—$35; one-time installation fee of $10; dues year begins July 1. Different levels of membership include: active—requires 3 professional short stories or 1 novel published; associate—requires 1 professional sale; or affiliate—which requires some other professional involvement such as artist, editor, librarian, bookseller, teacher, etc. Workshops/conferences: annual awards banquet, usually in April or May. Open to nonmembers. Publishes quarterly journal, the SFWA *Bulletin*. Nonmember subscription: $18/year in U.S. Sponsors Nebula Awards for best published science fiction or fantasy in the categories of novel, novella, novelette and short story.

Awards trophy. Also presents the Damon Knight Memorial Grand Master Award for Lifetime Achievement, and, beginning in 2006, the Andre Norton Award for Outstanding Young Adult Science Fiction or Fantasy Book of the Year.

SOCIETY OF CHILDREN'S BOOK WRITERS AND ILLUSTRATORS

8271 Beverly Blvd., Los Angeles CA 90048. (323)782-1010. E-mail: info@scbwi.org (autoresponse). Web site: www.scbwi.org. **President:** Stephen Mooser. Executive Director: Lin Oliver. Chairperson, Board of Advisors: Sue Alexander. Purpose of organization: to assist writers and illustrators working or interested in the field. Qualifications for membership: an interest in children's literature and illustration. Membership cost: $60/year. Plus one time $15 initiation fee. Different levels of membership include: full membership—published authors/illustrators; associate membership—unpublished writers/illustrators. Holds 100 events (workshops/conferences) worldwide each year. National Conference open to nonmembers. Publishes a newsletter focusing on writing and illustrating children's books. Sponsors grants for writers and illustrators who are members.

SOCIETY OF ILLUSTRATORS

128 E. 63rd St., New York NY 10021-7303. (212)838-2560. Fax: (212)838-2561. E-mail: info@societyillustrators. org. Web site: www.societyillustrators.org. **Contact:** Terrence Brown, director. "Purpose is to promote interest in the art of illustration for working professional illustrators and those in associated fields." Cost of membership: Initiation fee is $250. Annual dues for nonresident members (those living more than 125 air miles from SI's headquarters): $287. Dues for Resident Artist Members: $475 per year; Resident Associate Members: $552." Artist Members shall include those who make illustration their profession and earn at least 60% of their income from their illustration. Associate Members are those who earn their living in the arts or who have made a substantial contribution to the art of illustration. This includes art directors, art buyers, creative supervisors, instructors, publishers and like categories. The candidate must complete and sign the application form which requires a brief biography, a listing of schools attended, other training and a résumé of his or her professional career. Candidates for Artist membership, in addition to the above requirements, must submit examples of their work." Sponsors contest. Sponsors "The Annual of American Illustration," which awards gold and silver medals. Open to nonmembers. Deadline: October 1. Also sponsors "The Original Art: The Best of Children's Book Illustration." Deadline: mid-August. Call for details.

SOCIETY OF MIDLAND AUTHORS

P.O. 10419, Chicago IL 60610-0419. Web site: www.midlandauthors.com. **Membership Secretary:** Thomas Frisbie. Purpose of organization: create closer association among writers of the Middle West; stimulate creative literary effort; maintain collection of members' works; encourage interest in reading and literature by cooperating with other educational and cultural agencies. Qualifications for membership: membership by invitation only. Must be author or co-author of a book demonstrating literary style and published by a recognized publisher and be identified through residence with Illinois, Indiana, Iowa, Kansas, Michigan, Minnesota, Missouri, Nebraska, North Dakota, Ohio, South Dakota or Wisconsin. **Open to students** (if authors). Membership cost: $35/year dues. Different levels of membership include: regular—published book authors; associate, nonvoting—not published as above but having some connection with literature, such as librarians, teachers, publishers and editors. Program meetings held 5 times a year, featuring authors, publishers, editors or the like individually or on panels. Usually second Tuesday of October, November, February, March and April. Also holds annual awards dinner in May. Publishes a newsletter focusing on news of members and general items of interest to writers. Sponsors contests. "Annual awards in six categories, given at annual dinner in May. Monetary awards for books published which premiered professionally in previous calendar year. Send SASE to contact person for details." Categories include adult fiction, adult nonfiction, juvenile fiction, juvenile nonfiction, poetry, biography. No picture books. Contest open to nonmembers. Deadline for contest: January 30.

SOCIETY OF SOUTHWESTERN AUTHORS

P.O. Box 30355, Tucson AZ 85751-0355. Fax: (520)296-5562. E-mail: wporter202@aol.com. Web site: www.azst arnet.com/nonprofit/ssa. **President:** Chris Stern. Purpose of organization: to promote fellowship among professional and associate members of the writing profession, to recognize members' achievements, to stimulate further achievement, and to assist persons seeking to become professional writers. Qualifications for membership: Professional Membership: proof of publication of a book, articles, TV screenplay, etc. Associate Membership: proof of desire to write, and/or become a professional. Self-published Author Membership: book must be published. Membership cost: $25 initiation plus $25/year dues. The Society of Southwestern Authors has annual 2-day Writers' Conference held the last weekend in January (check Web site for updated information). Publishes a bimonthly newsletter, *The Write Word*, about members' activities, achievements, and up-to-the-minute trends in publishing and marketing. Yearly writing contest open to all writers. Applications are available in January. Send SASE to the P.O. Box, Attn: Contest.

SOUTHWEST WRITERS

3721 Morris NE, Suite A, Albuquerque NM 87111. (505)265-9485. Fax: (505)265-9483. E-mail: swwriters@juno. com. Web site: www.southwestwriters.org. Non-profit organization dedicated to helping members of all levels in their writing. Members enjoy perks such as networking with professional and aspiring writers; substantial discounts on mini-conferences, workshops, and annual and monthly SWW writing contest; monthly newsletter; two writing programs per month; critique groups, critique service (also for nonmembers); discounts at book-stores and other businesses; Web site linking; and health and dental group insurance for New Mexico residents. Cost of membership: Individual, $60/year, $100/2 years; Two People, $50 each/year; Student, $40/year; Outside U.S., $65/year; Lifetime, $750. See Web site for information.

TEXT AND ACADEMIC AUTHORS ASSOCIATION

P.O. Box 76477, St. Petersburg FL 33734-6477. (727)563-0020. Fax: (727)563-2409. E-mail: TEXT@tampabay.rr. com. Web site: www.taaonline.net. **President:** John Wakefield. Purpose of organization: to address the profes-sional concerns of text and academic authors, to protect the interests of creators of intellectual property at all levels, and support efforts to enforce copyright protection. Qualifications for membership: all authors and prospective authors are welcome. Membership cost: $30 first year; $75 per year following years. Workshops/ conferences: June each year. Newsletter focuses on all areas of interest to text authors.

VOLUNTEER LAWYERS FOR THE ARTS

1 E. 53rd St., 6th Floor, New York NY 10022-4201. (212)319-ARTS, ext. 1 (the Art Law Line). Fax: (212)752-6575. E-mail: askvla@vlany.org. Web site: www.vlany.org. **Executive Director:** Elena M. Paul. Purpose of organization: Volunteer Lawyers for the Arts is dedicated to providing free arts-related legal assistance to low-income artists and not-for-profit arts organizations in all creative fields. Over 800 attorneys in the New York area donate their time through VLA to artists and arts organizations unable to afford legal counsel. There is no membership required for our services. Everyone is welcome to use VLA's Art Law Line, a legal hotline for any artist or arts organization needing quick answers to arts-related questions. VLA also provides clinics, seminars and publications designed to educate artists on legal issues which affect their careers. Membership is through donations and is not required to use our services. Members receive discounts on publications and seminars as well as other benefits. Some of the many publications we carry are *All You Need to Know About the Music Business*; *Business and Legal Forms for Fine Artists, Photographers & Authors & Self-Publishers*; *Contracts for the Film & TV Industry*, plus many more.

WESTERN WRITERS OF AMERICA, INC.

1012 Fair St., Franklin TN 37064-2718. (615)791-1444. Fax: (615)791-1444. E-mail: candywwa@aol.com, tncrut ch@aol.com. Web site: www.westernwriters.org. Secretary/Treasurer: James A. Crutchfield. Open to students. Purpose of organization: to further all types of literature that pertains to the American West. Membership requirements: must be a published author of Western material. Membership cost: $75/year ($90 foreign). Different levels of membership include: Active and Associate-the two vary upon number of books published. Holds annual conference. The 2006 conference held in Cody WY, 2007 in Springfield MO and 2007 in Flagstaff AZ. Publishes bimonthly magazine focusing on western literature, market trends, bookreviews, news of mem-bers, etc. Nonmembers may subscribe for $30 ($50 foreign). Sponsors youth writing contests. Spur awards given annually for a variety of types of writing. Awards include plaque, certificate, publicity. Contest and Spur Awards open to nonmembers.

WOMEN WRITING THE WEST

8547 E. Arapahoe Rd., #J-541, Greenwood Village CO 80112. (303)773-8349. E-mail: WWWAdmin@lohseworks .com. Web site: www.womenwritingthewest.org. **Contact:** Joyce Lohse, administrator. Purpose of organization: "To gather and unite writers and other literature professionals writing and promoting the Women's West. The heart of this organization's interest is in the written record of women fo the American West." Qualifications for membership: Open to all interested persons worldwide. **Open to students.** Cost of membership: annual membership dues $50. Along with the annual dues there is an option to become a sustaining member for $100. Publisher dues are $50. "Sustaining members receive a WWW enamal logo pin, prominent listing in WWW publications, and the knowledge that they are assiting the organization.Members actively exchange ideas on a listserv e-bulletin board. Note: WWW membership also allows the choice of participation in our marketing marvel, the annual *WWW Catalog of Author's Books*." Holds an annual conference the third weekend in October. Publishes newsletter. "The focus of the WWW newsletter is current WWW activities; feature market, research, and experience articles of interest pertaining to American West literature; and member news." Spon-sors annual WILLA Literary Award. "The WILLA Award is given in several catagories for outstanding literature featuring women's stories set in the West." The winner of a WILLA Literary Award receives $100 and a plaque at the annual conference luncheon. Contest open to non-members.

Resources

▓ WRITERS GUILD OF ALBERTA

11759 Groat Rd., Edmonton AB T5M 3K6 Canada. (780)422-8174. Fax: (780)422-2663. E-mail: mail@writersguil d.ab.ca. Web site: www.writersguild.ab.ca. Purpose of organization: to provide meeting ground and collective voice for the writers in Alberta. Membership cost: $60/year; $30 for seniors/students. Holds workshops/conferences. Publishes a newsletter focusing on markets, competitions, contemporary issues related to the literary arts (writing, publishing, censorship, royalties etc.). Nonmembers may subscribe to newsletter. Subscription cost: $60/year. Sponsors annual literary awards program in 7 categories (novel, nonfiction, short fiction, children's literature, poetry, drama, best first book). Awards include $1,000, leather-bound book, promotion and publicity. Open to nonmembers.

WRITERS OF KERN

P.O. Box 6694, Bakersfield CA 93386-6694. (661)399-0423. E-mail: sm@sandymoffett.com. Web site: http:// home.bak.rr.com/writersofkern/. **Membership:** Sandy Moffett. Open to published writers and any person interested in writing. Dues: $45/year, $20 for students. Types of memberships: professional, writers with published work; associate—writers working toward publication, affiliate—beginners and students. Monthly meetings held on the third Saturday of every month. Bi- or tri-annual writers' workshops, with speakers who are authors, agents, etc., on topics pertaining to writing; critique groups for several fiction genres, poetry, children's, nonfiction, journalism and screenwriting which meet bimonthly. Members receive a monthly newsletter with marketing tips, conferences and contests; access to club library; discount to annual CWC conference.

▓ WRITERS' FEDERATION OF NEW BRUNSWICK

Box 37, Station A, 404 Queen St., Fredericton NB E3B 4Y2 Canada. (506)459-7228. E-mail: wfnb@nb.aibn.com. Web site: www.umce.ca/wfnb. **Executive Director:** Mary Hutchman. Purpose of organization: "to promote New Brunswick writing and to help writers at all stages of their development." Qualifications for membership: interest in writing. Membership cost: $40, basic annual membership; $45, family membership; $50, institutional membership; $100, sustaining member; $250, patron; and $1,000, lifetime member. Holds workshops/conferences. Publishes a newsletter with articles concerning the craft of writing, member news, contests, markets, workshops and conference listings. Sponsors annual literary competition. Categories: fiction, nonfiction, poetry, children's literature—3 prizes per category of $150, $75, $50; Alfred Bailey Prize of $400 for poetry ms; The Richards Prize of $400 for short novel, collection of short stories or section of long novel; The Sheree Fitch Prize for writing by young people (14-18 years of age). Contest open to nonmembers (residents of Canada only).

Conferences & Workshops

Writers and illustrators eager to expand their knowledge of the children's publishing industry should consider attending one of the many conferences and workshops held each year. Whether you're a novice or seasoned professional, conferences and workshops are great places to pick up information on a variety of topics and network with experts in the publishing industry, as well as with your peers.

Listings in this section provide details about what conference and workshop courses are offered, where and when they are held, and the costs. Some of the national writing and art organizations also offer regional workshops throughout the year. Write, call or visit Web sites for information.

Writers can find listings of approximately 1,000 conferences (searchable by type, location, and date) at The Writer's Digest/Shaw Guides Directory to Writers' Conferences, Seminars, and Workshops—www.writersdigest.com/conferences.

Members of the Society of Children's Book Writers and Illustrators can find information on conferences in national and local SCBWI newsletters. Nonmembers may attend SCBWI events as well. SCBWI conferences are listed in the beginning of this section under a separate subheading. For information on SCBWI's annual national conferences, contact them at (323)782-1010 or check their Web site for a complete calendar of national and regional events (www.scbwi.org).

CONFERENCES & WORKSHOPS CALENDAR

To help you plan your conference travel, here is a month-by-month calendar of all the conferences, workshops and retreats included in this section. The calendar lists conferences alphabetically by the month in which they occur.

January
Butler University Children's Literature Conference (Indianapolis IN)
Central Ohio Writers of Literature for Children Conference (Columbus OH)
Kindling Words (Essex VT)
San Diego State University Writers' Conference (San Diego CA)
SCBWI—Florida Regional Conference (Miami FL)
Society of Southwestern Authors' Wrangling with Writing (Tucson AZ)
Winter Poetry & Prose Getaway in Cape May (Cape May NJ)

February
Fishtrap, Inc. (Enterprise OR)
San Francisco Writers Conference (San Francisco CA)

SCBWI; Annual Conference on Writing and Illustrating for Children (New York NY)
SCBWI—Norca (San Francisco/South); Retreat at Asilomar (Pacific Grove CA)
South Coast Writers Conference (Gold Beach OR)

March
AEC Conference on Southern Literature (Chattanooga TN)
Florida Christian Writers Conference (Bradenton FL)
Gig Harbor Writer's Conference (Gig Harbor WA)
Kentucky Writer's Workshop (Pineville KY)
SCBWI—Pocono Mountains Retreat (Sterling PA)
SCBWI—Southern Breeze; Springmingle (location varies; GA in 2007)
Virginia Festival of the Book (Charlottesville VA)
Whidbey Island Writers' Conference (Langley WA)

April
Children's Literature Conference (Hempstead NY)
Festival of Children's Literature (Minneapolis MN)
Festival of Faith and Writing (Grand Rapids MI)
Mount Hermon Christian Writers Conference (Mount Hermon CA)
Perspectives in Children's Literature Conference (Amherst MA)
SCBWI; Before-Bologna Conference (Bologna Italy)
SCBWI—Iowa Conferences (Des Moines IA)
SCBWI New Mexico Handsprings: A Conference for Children's Writers and Illustrators (Albu-
    querque NM)
SCBWI—Northern Ohio; Annual Writers' Retreat (Delroy OH)

May
Annual Spring Poetry Festival (New York NY)
Celebration of Children's Literature (Germantown MD)
Moondance International Film Festival (Boulder CO)
Oklahoma Writers' Federation, Inc. Annual Conference (Oklahoma City OK)

June
Conference for Writers & Illustrators of Children's Books (Corte Madera CA)
East Texas Christian Writers Conference (Marshall TX)
Great Lakes Writers Conference (Milwaukee WI)
Highland Summer Conference (Radford VA)
International Creative Writing Camp (Minot ND)
International Women's Writing Guild "Remember the Magic" Annual Summer Conference
    (Saratoga Spring NY)
Iowa Summer Writing Festival (Iowa City IA)
NEW-CUE Writers' Conference and Workshop in Honor of Rachel Carson (Boothbay Harbor
    ME)
Outdoor Writers Association of America Annual Conference (Lake Charles LA)
SCBWI—Florida Mid-Year Writing Workshop (Orlando FL)
SCBWI—New Jersey; Annual Spring Conference (Caldwell NJ)
UMKC/Writers Place Writers Workshops (Kansas City MO)
Wesleyan Writers Conference (Middleton CT)
Write! Canada (Markham ON Canada)
Write-by-the-Lake Writer's Workshop & Retreat (Madison WI)

Resources

Write-to-Publish Conference (Wheaton IL)
Writing and Illustrating for Young Readers Workshop (Provo UT)

July
Highlights Foundation Writers Workshop at Chautauqua (Chautaqua NY)
Hofstra University Summer Workshop (Hempstead NY)
Institute for Readers Theatre Annual Workshop (Toronto Canada or London England)
Ligonier Valley Writers Conference (Ligonier PA)
Maritime Writers' Workshop (Fredericton NB Canada)
Midwest Writers Workshop (Muncie IN)
Montrose Christian Writer's Conference (Montrose PA)
Pacific Northwest Children's Book Conference (Portland OR)
Pacific Northwest Writer Assn. Summer Writer's Conference (Seattle WA)
Robert Quackenbush's Children's Book Writing and Illustrating Workshop (New York NY)
Sage Hill Writing Experience (Saskatoon SK Canada)
Saskatchewan Festival of Words and Workshops (Moose Jaw SK Canada)
The Victoria School of Writing (Victoria BC Canada)

August
Cape Cod Writer's Conference (Osterville MA)
The Columbus Writers Conference (Columbus OH)
Green Lake Writers Conference (Green Lake WI)
SCBWI; Annual Conference on Writing and Illustrating for Children (Los Angeles CA)
Sunshine Coast Festival of the Written Arts (Sechelt BC Canada)
Willamette Writers Annual Writers Conference (Portland OR)

September
East of Eden Writers Conference (Santa Clara CA)
League of Utah Writers' Roundup (Provo UT)
Maui Writers Conference (Kihei HI)
SCBWI—Northern Ohio; Annual Conference (Cleveland OH)
SCBWI—Eastern Pennsylvania; Fall Philly Conference (Exton PA)

October
Flathead River Writers Conference (Whitefish MT)
La Jolla Writers Conference (San Diego CA)
SCBWI—Iowa Conference (Iowa City IA)
SCBWI—Midatlantic; Annual Fall Conference (Arlington VA)
SCBWI—Oregon Conferences (Portland OR)
SCBWI—Southern Breeze; Writing and Illustrating for Kids (Birmingham AL)
SCBWI—Ventura/Santa Barbara; Fall Conference (Thousand Oaks CA)
Surrey International Writer's Conference (Surrey BC Canada)
Vancouver Internatinoal Writers Festival (Vancouver BC Canada)
Write on the Sound Writers Conference (Edmonds WA)

November
North Carolina Writers' Network Fall Conference (Durham NC)
Ohio Kentucky Indiana Children's Literature Conference (Cincinnati OH)
SCBWI—Missouri; Children's Writer's Conference (St. Peters MO)
SCBWI—Wisconsin; Fall Retreat for Working Writers (Racine WI)

December
Big Sur Writing Workshop (Big Sur CA)

Multiple Events
The conference listings below include information on multiple or year-round events. Please read the listings for more information on the dates and locations of these events and check the conferences' Web sites.

Cat Writers Association Annual Writers Conference
Children's Authors' Bootcamp
Peter Davidson's How to Write a Children's Picture Book Seminar
The DIY Book Festival
Duke University Youth Programs: Creative Writer's Workshop
Duke University Youth Programs: Young Writer's Camp
Fishtrap, Inc. (Enterprise OR)
Gotham Writers' Workshop
Publishinggame.com Workshop
SCBWI—Alaska; Events
SCBWI—Arizona; Events
SCBWI—Los Angeles; Events
SCBWI—Metro New York; Professional Series (New York NY)
SCBWI—Michigan; Conferences (location varies)
SCBWI—Rocky Mountains; Events (location varies)
SCBWI—Oregon Conferences
Southwest Writers Conferences
Split Rock Arts Program (St. Paul MN)
University of the Nations School of Writing and Writers Workshops
Writers' League of Texas Workshop Series (Austin TX)

Information on conferences listed in the previous edition but not this edition of *Children's Writer's & Illustrator's Market* may be found in the General Index.

SCBWI CONFERENCES

SCBWI—ALASKA; EVENTS
P.O. Box 84988, Fairbanks AK 99708-4988. (907)474-2138. E-mail: stihlerunits@mosquitonet.com. Web site: www.scbwialaska.org. **Conference Organizer:** Cherie Stihler. SCBWI Alaska holds a conference every other year, Raven Under the Northern Lights, held in even numbered years (2006, 2008, 2010). Editors Days held September 2006, March 2007, September 2007. Coffee Chats: Held first Saturday of each month, year round from 4-5 p.m. Artists Field Trips: Held Second Saturdays during summer months. Visit Web site for details.

SCBWI; ANNUAL CONFERENCES ON WRITING AND ILLUSTRATING FOR CHILDREN
8271 Beverly Blvd., Los Angeles CA 90048. (323)782-1010. Fax: (323)782-1892. E-mail: scbwi@scbwi.org. Web site: www.scbwi.org. **Conference Director:** Lin Oliver. Writer and illustrator workshops geared toward all levels. **Open to students.** Covers all aspects of children's book and magazine publishing—the novel, illustration techniques, marketing, etc. Annual conferences held in August in Los Angeles and in New York in February. Cost of conference (LA): approximately $390; includes all 4 days and one banquet meal. Write for more information or visit web site.

SCBWI—ARIZONA; EVENTS
P.O. Box 26384, Scottsdale AZ 85255-0123. E-mail: rascbwiaz@aol.com. Web site: www.scbwi-az.org. **Regional Advisor:** Michelle Parker-Rock. SCBWI Arizona will offer a variety of workshops, retreats, conferences, meetings and other industry-related events throughout 2006-2007. Open to members and nonmembers, published and nonpublished. Registration to major events is usually limited. Pre-registration always required. Visit Web site, write or e-mail for more information.

🌐 SCBWI; BEFORE-BOLOGNA CONFERENCE
0 (1-323)782-1010 (PST). E-mail: SCBWIBologna@yahoo.com. Web site: www.scbwi.org. **Contact:** Lawrence Schimel, SCBWI/Bologna Day-Before Conference Organizer. Annual writer and illustrator conference for children's book professionals held in association with the largest international children's book rights fair in the world, the Bologna Children's Book Fair (www.bookfair.bolognafiere.it). **Open to students**. Conference held annually in the spring, the day(s) before the Bologna International Children's Book Fair. A craft-based conference, with talks, panels, and hands-on workshops, plus an introduction to the Bologna International Book Fair. A chance to meet editors, art directors and agents before the rights fair gets going. Registration limited to 100. Cost of conference: "We try to keep it under 100€." Attendance fee covers presentations and workshops; lunch, closing cocktail party (to which many industry professionals are invited). Manuscript and illustration critiques available by reservation for additional fee (deadline for manuscripts to be received is January 31, 2006). Registration at www.scbwi.org Events page; PayPal payment accepted. Register early and reserve affordable rooms at local bed & breakfast establishments. 2006 topics and speakers include: Synopsis writing workshop, with special emphasis on both stand-alone and multi-volume series, with Justine Larbalestier (*Magic or Madness*); "Voice in young adult fiction" with award-winning author Scott Westerfeld (Midnighters series; *So Yesterday*); "Co-editions and their impact on the creative process"; a two-day hands-on illustration workshop with special emphasis on creating animal characters and tips from the world of animation for visualizing your characters in other positions, with best-selling artist Doug Cushman (*What Dads Can't Do*, Aunt Eater series) and Sara Rojo Pérez (artist and former Artistic Director of animation studio Sopa de Sobre); Q&A with acquiring editors, and more.

🌐 SCBWI—BRITISH ISLES; ILLUSTRATOR'S DAY (SPRING)/WRITER'S DAY (FALL)
(44)(208)249-9716. E-mail: ra@britishscbwi.org. Web site: www.britishscbwi.org. **Regional Advisor:** Natascha Biebow. SCBWI Illustrator Coordinator: Anne-Marie Perks. Writer and illustrator conference geared toward beginner, intermediate and advanced levels. Open to students. Writer's Day: Sessions include for What to Write Down, What to Throw Out—Selection & Revision, Visual Thinking for Picture Book Writers; Creative Ways Into Non-Fiction: Non-fiction for Storytellers, Approaching Publishers and Handling Rejections; Novelties and Picture Books-Publishing Opportunities with a Packager; Capturing & Creating Memorable Characters; Getting Your First Novel Published: That First Crucial Page & Getting It Past the Reader; Editor's Panel. Illustrator's Day: Making Cracking Picture Books Using QuarkXPress, Photoshop and Freehand Drawing; Creating Winning Characters; Meet the Art Director; Writing With Pictures; Brilliant School Visits; Panel on Marketing Yourself: An editor, an art director and an artist's agent talk about How to Create Portfolios That Stand Out. Annual conference. Cost of conference: $105 for SCBWI members/$125 for nonmembers; includes tuition and lunch. "Both conferences offer the opportunity for manuscripts or portfolio critiques with editors and art directors." SCBWI—British Isles also offers a Professional Series of bi-monthly talks in London.

SCBWI—DAKOTAS; WRITERS CONFERENCE IN CHILDREN'S LITERATURE

Grand Forks ND 58202-7209. (701)777-3321. E-mail: jean@jeanpatrick.com. Web site: www.und.edu/dept/
english/ChildrensLit.html. **Regional Advisor:** Jean Patrick. Writer workshops geared toward all levels. "Although the conference attendees are mostly writers, we encourage & welcome illustrators of every level." Open
to students. "Our conference offers 3-4 children's authors, editors, publishers, illustrators, or agents. Past
conferences have included Kent Brown (publisher, Boyds Mills Press); Stephanie Lane (editor, Random House);
Jane Kurtz (author); Anastasia Suen (author); and Karen Ritz (illustrator). Conference held each fall. "Please
call or e-mail to confirm dates. Writers and illustrators come from throughout the northern plains, including
North Dakota, South Dakota, Montana, Minnesota, Iowa, and Canada." Writing facilities available: campus of
University of North Dakota. Local art exhibits and/or concerts may coincide with conference. Cost of conference
includes Friday evening reception and sessions, Saturday's sessions, and lunch. A manuscript may be submitted
1 month in advance for critique (extra charge). E-mail for more information.

SCBWI—EASTERN CANADA; ANNUAL EVENTS

E-mail: webinfo@SCBWIcanada.org; noreen@SCBWIcanada.org. Web site: www.scbwicanada.org. **Regional
Advisor:** Noreen Violetta. Writer and illustrator event geared toward all levels. Offers speakers forums, book
sale, portfolio displays, one-on-one critiques and a silent auction. Annual spring event held in May. SCBWI
Eastern Canada also holds Fall Retreats usually in September.

SCBWI—EASTERN PENNSYLVANIA; FALL PHILLY CONFERENCE

Whitford Country Club, Exton PA. E-mail: juliewinkler1@comcast.net. Web site: www.scbwiepa.org. **Conference Director:** Julie Winkler. Conference focuses on writing skills, the publishing market, and finding inspiration. Manuscript and Portfolio critiques with editors available for an additional fee. Registration is limited to
150. Information will be posted on the web site in July. Conference held in September. Cost: $90-100. Registration includes buffet lunch.

SCBWI—FLORIDA; MID-YEAR WRITING WORKSHOP

(305)382-2677. E-mail: lindabernfeld@hotmail.com. Web site: www.scbwiflorida.com. **Regional Advisor:**
Linda Rodriguez Bernfeld. Annual workshop held in June in Orlando. Workshop is geared toward helping
everyone hone their writing skills. Attendees choose one track and spend the day with industry leaders who
share valuable information about that area of children's book writing. There are a minimum of 3 tracks, picture
book, middle grade and young adult. The 4th track is variable, covering subjects such as nonfiction, humor or
writing for magazines. Speakers in 2006 included Sue Corbett, Nancy Mercado (editor, Dial), Lisa Yee, Gloria
Rothstein, Bill Farnsworth, Alexandra Penfold (assistant editor at Paula Wiseman Books), Tara Weikum (executive editor, HarperCollins), Dorian Cirrone, Ed Bloor and Paula Morrow. E-mail for more information.

SCBWI—FLORIDA; REGIONAL CONFERENCE

(305)382-2677. E-mail: lindabernfeld@hotmail.com. Web site: www.scbwiflorida.com. **Regional Advisor:**
Linda Rodriguez Bernfeld. Assistant Regional Advisor: Vivian Fernandez. Annual conference held in January
in Miami in 2007. Confirmed speakers include Bruce Hale (Chet Gecko series) and Barbara Seuling (*How to
Write a Children's Book and Get it Published*). Cost of conference: approximately $175. The 3-day conference
will have workshops Friday afternoon, open mic and informal critique groups Friday evening. There will be a
general session all day Saturday covering all aspects of writing for children. There will be hands on workshops
Sunday morning led by industry leaders. There is a Saturday only option. Past speakers have included Judy
Blume, Paula Danziger, Bruce Coville, Arthur Levine, Libba Bray and Kate DiCamillo. For more information,
contact by e-mail Linda Rodriguez Bernfeld.

SCBWI—HOFSTRA UNIVERSITY CHILDREN'S LITERATURE CONFERENCE

250 Hofstra University, U.C.C.E., Hempstead NY 11549. (516)463-5993. Fax: (516)463-4833. E-mail: judith.reed@ho
fstra.edu. Web site: www.hofstra.edu/ucce/childlitconf. **Contact:** Judith Reed, Program Director, Personal Enrichment. Writer and illustrator workshops geared toward all levels. Emphasizes: fiction, nonfiction, poetry, submission
procedures, picture books. Workshops will be held in April. Length of each session: 1 hour. Cost of workshop
(2006 rates): $77 members; $82 nonmembers; includes continental breakfast and full luncheon. Each year the
workshop is organized around a theme, and includes 2 general sessions and 6 breakout groups, and a panel of
children's book editors who critique randomly selected first-manuscript pages submitted by registrants. The conference takes place at the Student Center Building of Hofstra University, located in Hempstead, Long Island. Write for
more information or visit Web site. Co-sponsored by Society of Children's Book Writers & Illustrators.

SCBWI—ILLINOIS; A PRAIRIE WRITER'S DAY

Chicago IL 60614. E-mail: esthersh@aol.com. Web site: www.scbwi-illinois.org. **Regional Advisor:** Esther
Hershenhorn. Workshop held in early November at Dominican University in River Forest. Highlights 3 newly-

published members and their editors, along with agents, booksellers and reviewers. Ms critiques and First Page readings are on the program. Visit Web site for more information on this and other SCBWI—Illinois events.

SCBWI—IOWA CONFERENCES

E-mail: hecklit@aol.com. Web site: www.schwi-iowa.org. **Regional Advisor:** Connie Heckert. Writer and illustrator workshops geared toward all levels. The Iowa Region will offer 2 conferences in 2006: April 21-23 at Airport Holiday Inn, Des Moines featuring Cecile Goyette, Executive Editor, Alfred A. Knopf Books for Young Readers; Mark McVeigh, Senior Editor, Dutton Children's Books; Patrick Collins, Art Director, Henry Holt Books for Young Readers and Kathleen O'Dell, MG author, Dial Books for Young Readers. October 20-22 at Sheraton Iowa City featuring Bruce Coville, SCBWI Board Member and Author; Michael Stearns, Editorial Director and Foreign Acquisitions Manager, HarperCollins Children's Books; Lin Oliver, Executive Director, SCBWI and Co-Author of the Hank Zipzer series. Individual critiques and portfolio review offerings various with the program and presenters. For more information e-mail or visit Web site.

SCBWI—LOS ANGELES; EVENTS

P.O. Box 1728, Pacific Palisades CA 90272. (310)573-7318. Web site: www.scbwisocal.org. **Co-regional Advisors:** Claudia Harrington (claudiascbwi@earthlink.net) and Edie Pagliasotti (edie_pagliasotti@paramount.com). SCBWI—Los Angeles hosts 7 major events each year: **Writer's Workshop** (winter)—half-day workshop featuring speaker demonstrating nuts and bolts techniques on the craft of writing for childrens (*new*); **Writer's Day** (spring)—a one-day conference featuring speakers, a professional forum, writing contests and awards; **Critiquenic** (summer)—a free informal critiquing session for writers and illustrators facilitated by published authors/illustrators, held after a picnic lunch; **Writers & Illustrator's Sunday Field Trip** (summer)—hands-on creative field trip for writers and illustrators (*new*); **Working Illustrators Retreat** (summer)—a 3-day, 2-night retreat featuring an editor, art director, illustrators, and workshops on layout, design, portfolio presentation, and book dummies; **Illustrator's Day** (fall)—a 1-day conference featuring speakers, juried art competition, contests, and portfolio review/display; **Working Writer's Retreat** (winter)—a 3-day, 2-night retreat featuring an editor, speakers, and intensive critiquing. See calendar of events on Web site for more details and dates.

SCBWI—METRO NEW YORK; PROFESSIONAL SERIES

P.O. Box 1475, Cooper Station, New York NY 10276-1475. (212)545-3719. E-mail: scbwi_metrony@yahoo.com. Web site: www.home.nyc.rr.com/scbwimetrony. **Regional Advisor:** Nancy Lewis. Writer and illustrator workshops geared toward all levels. **Open to students.** The Metro New York Professional Series generally meets the second Tuesday of each month, from October to June, 7-9 p.m. Check Web site to confirm location, dates, times and speakers. Cost of workshop: $12 for SCBWI members; $15 for nonmembers. ''We feature an informal, almost intimate evening with coffee, cookies, and top editors, art directors, agents, publicity and marketing people, librarians, reviewers and more.''

SCBWI—MICHIGAN; CONFERENCES

4299 E. Highland Rd., Howell MI 48855. Web site: www.Kidsbooklink.org. **Co-Regional Advisors:** Mindy Crasner and Lisa Davis. One-day conference held in June and 3-day fall conference held in October. One day, $80 includes registration and lunch. Weekend, $270 includes registration, 6 meals and room. Speakers TBA. See Web site for details on all upcoming events.

SCBWI—MIDATLANTIC; ANNUAL FALL CONFERENCE

Mid-Atlantic SCBWI, P.O. Box 3215, Reston, VA 20195-1215. E-mail: sydney.dunlap@adelphia.net or midatlanticscbwi@tidalwave.net. Web site: www.scbwi-midatlantic.org. **Conference Chair:** Sydney Dunlap. Regional Advisor: Ellen Braaf. Conference takes place Saturday, October 27, 2007 in Arlington, VA from 8 to 5. Keynote speaker: Bruce Coville. For updates and details visit Web site. Registration limited to 200. Conference fills quickly. Cost: $85 for SCBWI members; $110 for nonmembers. Includes continental breakfast.

SCBWI—MISSOURI; CHILDREN'S WRITER'S CONFERENCE

St. Charles County Community College, P.O. Box 76975, 103 CEAC, St. Peters MO 63376-0975. (314)213-8000, ext. 4108. E-mail: suebradfordedwards@yahoo.com. Web site: www.geocities.com/scbwimo. **Regional Advisor:** Sue Bradford Edwards. Writer and illustrator conference geared toward all levels. **Open to students.** Speakers include editors, writers, and other professionals. Topics vary from year to year, but each conference offers sessions for both writers and illustrators as well as for newcomers and published writers. Previous topics included: ''What Happens When Your Manuscript is Accepted'' by Dawn Weinstock, editor; ''Writing—Hobby or Vocation?'' by Chris Kelleher; ''Mother Time Gives Advice: Perspectives from a 25 Year Veteran'' by Judith Mathews, editor; ''Don't Be a Starving Writer'' by Vicki Berger Erwin, author; and ''Words & Pictures: History in the Making,'' by author-illustrator Cheryl Harness. Annual conference held in early November. For exact date, see SCBWI Web site www.scbwi.org or the events page of the Missouri SCBWI Web site. Registration limited to 75-90. Cost of conference includes one-day workshop (8 a.m. to 5 p.m.) plus lunch. Write for more information.

SCBWI—NEW JERSEY; ANNUAL SPRING CONFERENCE

E-mail: njscbwi@newjerseyscbwi.com. Web site: www.newjerseyscbwi.com. **Regional Advisor:** Kathy Temean. This day-long conference brings in editors from top houses, an agent, art director and art rep to speak to small groups about timely topics. With various writer workshops running throughout the day, all writers will find workshops to fit their level of expertise. Illustrators can attend special sessions with an art director and art rep. Published authors attending the conference are invited to sign and sell their books in the afternoon. Illustrators have the opportunity to display their artwork during the day. Editors will do one-on-one manuscript critiques and portfolio critiques will be available for the illustrators who attend for an additional cost. Continental breakfast and lunch is included with the cost of admission. Conference is traditionally held during the beginning of June at Caldwell College, Caldwell, New Jersey. E-mail njscbwi@newjerseyscbwi.com for more information or see www.scbwi.org/events.htm.

SCBWI—NEW MEXICO; HANDSPRINGS: A CONFERENCE FOR CHILDREN'S WRITERS AND ILLUSTRATORS

P.O. Box 1084, Socorro NM. E-mail: scbwi_nm@blarg.net. Web site: www.scbwi-nm.org. **Writers contact:** Chris Eboch, SCBWI-NM Regional Advisor. Conference level for writers: beginner, intermediate. Conference level for illustrators: beginner, intermediate. **Open to students.** "Each conference features three keynote speakers—editors, agents, and/or art directors. This year's speakers include Paula Morrow, Executive Editor of Carus Publishing (Cricket Magazine Group) and artist rep Melissa Turk, as well as a book editor TBA. Writers and illustrators lead breakout sessions. Past workshop topics included: Get Published Now!, Children's Books in Rhyming Verse, Writing Easy Readers, The Art & Magic of Storytelling, Spectacular Sentences, New Markets for Illustrators, and Twelve Ways to Make Your Novel Stand Out." Annual event. Workshop held in April in Albuquerque. "Offers classroom-style workshops and large-group presentations." Cost: $80-110. Registration includes full day of speakers and breakout workshops, plus morning coffee and lunch; a Friday night cocktail party, panel discussion, and Illustrator's Display is an additional $10-20. For an additional fee, conference attendees can sign up for manuscript critiques with one of the editors or agents. Illustrators can schedule portfolio reviews with the art director or artist rep. Contact at address above for more information.

SCBWI—NORCA (SAN FRANCISCO/SOUTH); RETREAT AT ASILOMAR

Web site: www.scbwinorca.org. **Regional Advisor:** Jim Averbeck. While we welcome "not-yet-published" writers and illustrators, lectures and workshops are geared toward professionals and those striving to become professional. Program topics cover aspects of writing or illustrating picture books to young adult novels. Past speakers include editors, art directors, Newbery Award-winning authors, and Caldecott Award-winning illustrators. Annual conference, generally held last weekend in February; Friday evening through Sunday lunch. Registration limited to 100. Most rooms shared with one other person. Additional charge for single when available. Desks available in most rooms. All rooms have private baths. Conference center is set in wooded campus on Asilomar Beach in Pacific Grove, California. Approximate cost: $365 for SCBWI members, $500 for nonmembers; includes shared room, 6 meals, ice breaker party and all conference activities. Vegetarian meals available. One full scholarship is available to SCBWI members. Registration opens at the end of September and the conference sells out very quickly. A waiting list is formed. "Coming together for shared meals and activities builds a strong feeling of community among the speakers and conferees. For more information, including exact costs and dates, visit our Web site in September."

SCBWI—NORTHERN OHIO; ANNUAL CONFERENCE

225 N. Willow Street, Kent OH 44240-2561. (330)678-2900. E-mail: jdaigneau@sbcglobal.net. Web site: www.scbwiohio.org. **Regional Advisor:** Jean Daigneau. Writer and illustrator conference for all levels. **Open to students.** "This conference is the premier marketing/networking event of the year for Northern Ohio SCBWI. The emphasis is on current market trends; what the market is publishing; getting manuscripts/portfolios market-ready; and staying alive in the market post-publication, and the nuts and bolts of writing and illustrating for children. Additional emphasis is on meeting/networking with peers." Annual event. Workshop held in September—2006 event held September 8-9 at the Cleveland Airport Sheraton Hotel. Registration limited to 200. Conference costs will be posted on Web site with registration information. SCBWI members receive a discount. Additional fess for late registration and critiques or portfolio reviews may apply. Cost includes an optional Friday evening Opening Banquet with keynote speaker from 6-10 p.m. and Saturday event from 8:30 a.m. to 5 p.m., including continental breakfast, full-day conference with breakout sessions, headliner presentations, lunch, and panel discussions. Conference schedule includes four headliners and a total of 16 breakout session. Also offered is an Illustrator Showcase open to all illustrators at no additional cost.

SCBWI—NORTHERN OHIO; ANNUAL WRITERS' RETREAT

225 N. Willow Street, Kent OH 44240-2561. (303)678-2900. E-mail: jdaigneau@sbcglobal.net. Web site: www.sc bwiohio.org. **Regional Advisor:** Jean Daigneau. Writer retreat for advanced, professional levels. This Workshop focuses on specific aspects of writing. Bi-annual event. Last workshop held April 2005 at Atwood Lake Resort, Delroy, Ohio. Registration is limited; varies from year to year. See Web site for details. (For 2005, limit was 45.) Retreat costs posted on Web site with registration information.

SCBWI—OREGON CONFERENCES

E-mail: robink@scbwior.com. Web site: www.scbwior.com. **Regional Advisor:** Robin Koontz. Writer and illustrator workshops and presentations geared toward all levels. "We invite editors, teachers, agents, attorneys, authors, illustrators and others in the business of writing and illustrating for children. They present lectures, workshops, and on-site critiques on a first-registered basis." Critique group network for local group meetings and regional retreats; see Web site for details. Two main events per year: Writers and Illustrators Retreat: Retreat held near Portland Thursday-Sunday the 2nd weekend in October. Cost of retreat: $325 plus critique fee includes double occupancy and all meals; Spring Conference: Held in the Portland area (1-day event in May); cost for presentations and workshops: about $95 includes continental breakfast and lunch. Registration limited to 300 for the conference and 55 for the retreat. SCBWI Oregon is a regional chapter of the SCBWI. SCBWI Members receive a discount for all events.

SCBWI—POCONO MOUNTAINS RETREAT

(610)255-0514. Fax: (610)255-5715. E-mail: Lkiernan@tacsolutions.com. Web site: www.scbwiepa.org. **Regional Advisor:** Laurie Krauss Kiernan. Held in the spring at Sterling Inn, Sterling PA. Faculty addresses writing, illustration and publishing. Registration limited to 100. Cost of retreat: tuition $140, room and board averages $200. For information and registration form, visit Web site.

SCBWI—ROCKY MOUNTAIN; EVENTS

E-mail: denise@rmcscbwi.org or colin@rmcscbwi.org. Web site: www.rmcscbwi.org. Co-Regional Advisors: Denise Vega and Colin Murcray. SCBWI Rocky Mountain chapter will offer these upcoming events in 2006/ 2007: Spring Workshop 2006, April 8, Golden, CO; Summer Retreat 2006, June 23-25, Colorado Springs, CO; Fall 2006 Conference, Golden CO (date TBA), Spring Workshop 2007 (TBA), variety of mini-workshops. For more information check Web site.

SCBWI—SOUTHERN BREEZE; SPRINGMINGLE

P.O. Box 26282, Birmingham AL 35260. E-mail: JSKittinger@bellsouth.net. Web site: www.southern-breeze.o rg. **Regional Advisors:** Jo Kittinger and Donna Bowman. Writer and illustrator workshops geared toward intermediate, advanced and professional levels. Speakers typically include agents, editors, authors, art directors, illustrators. **Open to SCBWI members, non-members and college students.** Annual conference held in one of the three states comprising the Southern Breeze region; Georgia in 2007. Usually held in March. Registration limited. Cost of conference: approximately $225; includes Friday dinner, Saturday lunch and Saturday banquet. Pre-registration is necessary. Send a SASE to Southern Breeze, P.O. Box 26282, Birmingham AL 35260 for more information or visit Web site www.southern-breeze.org.

SCBWI—SOUTHERN BREEZE; WRITING AND ILLUSTRATING FOR KIDS

P.O. Box 26282, Birmingham AL 35260. E-mail: jskittinger@bellsouth.net. Web site: www.southern-breeze.org. **Regional Advisors:** Jo Kittinger and Donna Bowman. Writer and illustrator workshops geared toward all levels. Open to SCBWI members, non-members and college students. All sessions pertain specifically to the production and support of quality children's literature. This one-day conference offers 30 workshops on craft and the business of writing. Picture books, chapter books, novels covered. Entry and professional level topics addressed by published writers and illustrators, editors and agents. Annual conference. Fall conference is held the third weekend in October in the Birmingham, AL metropolitan area. (Museums, shopping, zoo, gardens, universities and colleges are within a short driving distance.) All workshops are limited to 25 or fewer people. Pre-registration is necessary. Some workshops fill quickly. Cost of conference: approximately $90 for members, $105 for non-members, $95 for students; program includes keynote speaker, 4 workshops (selected from 30), lunch, and Friday night dessert party. Mss critiques and portfolio reviews are available for an additional fee; mss must be sent early. Registration is by mail ahead of time. Manuscript and portfolio reviews must be pre-paid and scheduled. Send a SASE to: Southern Breeze, P.O. Box 26282, Birmingham AL 35260 or visit Web site. Fall conference is always held in Birmingham, Alabama. Room block at a hotel near conference site (usually a school) is by individual reservation and offers a conference rate. Keynote speakers to be announced.

SCBWI—TAIWAN; EVENTS

Fax: (886)2363-5358. E-mail: scbwi_taiwan@yahoo.com. Web site: http://groups.yahoo.com/group/scbwi_tai

wan. **Regional Advisor:** Kathleen Ahrens. Writer and illustrator workshops geared toward intermediate level. Open to students. Topics emphasized: "We regularly hold critiques for writers and for illustrators, and invite authors and illustrators visiting Taipei to give talks. See our Web site for more information."

SCBWI—VENTURA/SANTA BARBARA; FALL CONFERENCE

Simi Valley CA 93094-1389. (805)581-1906. E-mail: alexisinca@aol.com. Web site: www.scbwisocal-org/calendar.h tm. Writers' conference geared toward all levels. Speakers include editors, authors, illustrators and agents. Fiction and nonfiction picture books, middle grade and YA novels, and magazine submissions addressed. Annual writing contest in all genres. Conference held October 28, 2006 at California Lutheran University in Thousand Oaks, California in cooperation with the School of Education. For fees and other information e-mail or go to Web site.

SCBWI—VENTURA/SANTA BARBARA; PROFESSIONAL RETREAT FOR CHILDREN'S AUTHORS AND ILLUSTRATORS

E-mail: alexisinca@aol.com. Web site: www.scbwisocal.org. The Winter Retreat is for published or experienced pre-published children's book professionals. Go to Web site or e-mail for current theme and fee.

SCBWI—WESTERN WASHINGTON STATE; CONFERENCE

P.O. Box 799, Woodinville WA 98072-0799. (425)744-2359. E-mail: scbwiwa@oz.net. Web site: www.scbwi-washington.org. **Co-Regional Advisors:** Cathy Benson and Jolie Stekley. Writer workshops geared toward all levels. **Open to students.** All aspects of writing and illustrating children's books are covered from picture books to YA novels, from contracts to promotion. Editors, an art director, an agent and authors and published illustrators serve as conference faculty. Registration limited to about 350. Cost of conference: $110-135; includes registration, morning snack and lunch. A One-on-one portfolio reviews and an art sample show are available for illustrators. The conference is a one-day event held in the spring at Meyedenbauer Center in Bellevue, WA. "We've added Professional Writer's and Illustrator's Retreats which will be held the day before our conference with editor, award-winning author or illustrator and art director. These one-day events are held at a club in Bellevue, WA. Cost included critiques or portfolio reviews, continental breakfast, lunch, and afternoon snacks. Please check out Web site for updates."

SCBWI—WISCONSIN; FALL RETREAT FOR WORKING WRITERS

3446 Hazelnut Lane, Milton WI 53563. E-mail: fpberes@ticon.net. Web site: www.scbwi-wi.com. **Regional Advisor:** Pam Beres. Writer and illustrator conference geared toward all levels. All our sessions pertain to children's writing/illustration. Faculty addresses writing/illustrating/publishing. Annual conference held late October/early November (November 3-5, 2006) in Racine WI. Registration limited to 70. Bedrooms have desks/ conference center has small rooms—can be used to draw/write. Program has free time scheduled in. Cost of conference: $375 for SBCWI member; $450 for non-members; includes program, meals, lodging, ms critique. Write or go to our Web site for more information: www.geocities.com/scbwiwi.

OTHER CONFERENCES

Many conferences and workshops included here focus on children's writing or illustrating and related business issues. Others appeal to a broader base of writers or artists, but still provide information that can be useful in creating material for children. Illustrators may be interested in painting and drawing workshops, for example, while writers can learn about techniques and meet editors and agents at general writing conferences. For more information visit the websites listed or contact conference coordinator.

AEC CONFERENCE ON SOUTHERN LITERATURE

3069 South Broad Street, Suite 2, Chattanooga TN 37408-3056. (423)267-1218. Fax: (423)267-1018. E-mail: info@artsedcouncil.org. Web site: www.artsedcouncil.org. **Executive Director:** Susan Robinson. **Open to students.** Conference is geared toward readers. Biennial conference held March 28-31, 2007. Cost of conference: $75; $15 for students. Visit Web site for more information. Features panel discussions, readings and commentaries for adults and students by today's foremost Southern writers.

AMERICAN CHRISTIAN WRITERS CONFERENCE

P.O. Box 110390, Nashville TN 37222-0390. 1(800)21-WRITE or (615)834-0450. Fax: (615)834-7736. E-mail: detroitwriters@aol.com. Web site: www.ACWriters.com. **Director:** Reg Forder. Writer and illustrator workshops geared toward beginner, intermediate and advanced levels. Classes offered include: fiction, nonfiction, poetry, photography, music, etc. Workshops held in 3 dozen U.S. cities. Call or write for a complete schedule of conferences. 75 minutes. Maximum class size: 30 (approximate). Cost of conference: $99, 1-day session; $169, 2-day session (discount given if paid 30 days in advance) includes tuition only.

ANNUAL SPRING POETRY FESTIVAL

City College, New York NY 10031. (212)650-6343. E-mail: barrywal23@aol.com. **Director, Poetry Outreach Center:** Barry Wallenstein. Writer workshops geared to all levels. **Open to students.** Annual poetry festival. Festival held May 16, 2006. Registration limited to 325. Cost of workshops and festival: free. Write for more information.

ARKANSAS WRITERS' CONFERENCE

6817 Gingerbread Lane, Little Rock AR 72204. (501)565-8889. Fax: (501)907-1055. E-mail: pvining@aristotle.net. **Director:** Barbara Malkey. Writer workshops geared toward beginner, intermediate and advanced levels. **Open to students.** ''We have children's writers for hourly lectures on occasions.'' 60th annual conference. Conference always held the first full weekend in June. Cost of conference: $7.50/day; includes registration and workshops. Contest fees, lodging and food are not included. Send SASE for brochure after February 1. Offers 34 different awards for various types of writing, poetry and essay. ''This conference is sponsored by the AR Pioneer Branch of the National League of American Penwomen. It is the 60th annual conference (150 to 200 in attendance yearly). Registration fee is supplemented by money from trust fund. Conferences of this quality usually are $75 to $100 registration fee.''

Ⓝ BIG SUR WRITING WORKSHOP

Henry Miller Library, Highway One, Big Sur CA 93920. Phone/fax: (831)667-2574. E-mail: magnus@henrymiller.org. Web site: www.henrymiller.org/CWW.html. **Contact:** Magnus Toren, executive director. Annual workshop held in December focusing on children's and young adult writing. Workshop help in Big Sur Lodge in Pfeiffer State Park. Cost of workshop: $595; included meals, lodging, workshop, Saturday evening reception; $385 if lodging not needed.

Ⓒ BOOMING GROUND WRITER'S COMMUNITY

Buch E-462, 1866 Main Mall, UBC, Vancouver BC VGT 1Z1 Canada. (604)822-2469. Fax: (604)648-8848. E-mail: bg@arts.ubc.ca. Web site: www2.arts.ubc.ca/bg. **Director:** Andrew Gray. Writer workshops geared toward beginner and advanced levels. **Open to students.** ''We emphasize writing for children, both novel correspondence and writing illustrated books.'' Annual workshop. Workshop held July. Registration limited to 7 for novel writing and 10 for other genres. Cost of workshop: $650; includes workshops, seminars, and correspondence for 16 weeks following the workshop for novel class. Send manuscript sample with application. No art classes offered. Write for more information.

BUTLER UNIVERSITY CHILDREN'S LITERATURE CONFERENCE

2060 E. 54th Street, Indianapolis IN 46220. (317)254-0830. E-mail: kidsink@indy.net. Web site: www.butler.edu/childlit/about.htm. **Contact:** Shirley Mullin. Writer and illustrator conference geared toward all levels. **Open to college students.** Annual conference held the last Saturday of the month of January each year featuring top writers in the field of children's literature. Includes sessions such as Nuts and Bolts for Beginning Writers. Registration limited to 350. Cost of conference: $85; includes SCBWI Networking Luncheon, registration, 3 plenary addresses, 2 workshops, book signing, reception and conference bookstore. Write for more information. ''The conference is geared toward three groups: teachers, librarians and writers/illustrators.''

CAPE COD WRITER'S CONFERENCE

Cape Cod Writer's Center, P.O. Box 408, Osterville MA 02655. (508)420-0200. Fax: (508)420-0212. E-mail: writers@capecodwriterscenter.org. Web site: www.capecodwriterscenter.org. Courses and workshops geared toward beginner, intermediate and professional levels. Courses include: fiction, nonfiction, poetry, journalism, screenwriting, and writing for the young reader. Evening programs include speakers, a master class, panels, poetry, and prose reading. Manuscript evaluations and personal conferences with faculty, the agent and editor, are available. The Young Writers' Workshop for student interested in prose and poetry is held concurrent with the conference for 12- to 16-year-olds. Annual conference held third week in August on Cape Cod; 44th annual conference held August 20-25, 2006. Cost of conference: $70 to register; $100 for courses.

CAT WRITERS ASSOCIATION ANNUAL WRITERS CONFERENCE

% President Fran Pennock Shaw, 1761 Wickersham Lane, Lancaster PA 17603. (717)397-9531. E-mail: franshaw1@juno.com. Web site: www.catwriters.org. The Cat Writers' Association holds an annual conference at varying locations around the US. The agenda for the conference is filled with seminars, editor appointments, an autograph party, networking breakfast, reception and annual awards banquet, as well as the annual meeting of the association. See Web site for details.

Resources

CELEBRATION OF CHILDREN'S LITERATURE

Montgomery College, Germantown Campus, Germantown MD 20850. (240)683-2589. Fax: (240)683-1890. E-mail: theguild@childrensbookguild.org. Web site: www.childrensbookguild.org. Writer and illustrator conference co-sponsored by The Children's Book Guild of Washington, D.C., Montgomery County Public Libraries, Montgomery College and Montgomery County Public Schools. **Open to students.** Annual workshop held in May. Manuscript & portfolio reviews for a small fee. Keynote lectures by nationally recognized authors, artists, editors. Registration limited to 200. Art display facilities, continuing education classrooms and large auditorium. Cost of workshop: approximately $90; includes workshops, box lunch and coffee. Contact The Children's Book Guild of Washington D.C. for more information.

CENTRAL OHIO WRITERS OF LITERATURE FOR CHILDREN, A Conference for Teachers, Parents, Librarians, Writers & Illustrators

933 Hamlet St., Columbus OH 43201-3595. (614)291-8644. E-mail: cowriters@mail.com. Web site: www.sjms. net/conf. **Director:** Hari Ruiz. Writer and illustrator conference geared toward beginner, intermediate and advanced levels. **Also open to full-time high school and college students.** Annual conference. Held Saturday, January 27, 2007. Registration limited to 180. Cost of conference: students and seniors $70; all others early-bird before November $110; regular before January $120 (approximately); late after December $135. $40 additional charge for ms or portfolio evaluations by editors and workshops for writers and illustrators led by published authors and illustrators. $30 additional charge for "pitch sessions" with literary agent. "Event will be an all-day affair with one keynote speaker."

CHILDREN'S AUTHORS' BOOTCAMP

P.O. Box 231, Allenspark CO 80510. (303)747-1014. E-mail: CABootcamp@aol.com. Web site: www.WeMakeWriter s.com. **Contact:** Linda Arms White. Writer workshops geared toward beginner and intermediate levels. "Children Authors' Bootcamp provides two full, information-packed days on the fundamentals of writing fiction for children. The workshop covers developing strong, unique characters; well-constructed plots; believable dialogue; seamless description and pacing; point of view; editing your own work; marketing your manuscripts to publishers, and more. Each day also includes in-class writing exercises and small group activities." Workshop held 4 times/year at various locations throughout the United States. Bootcamps are generally held in March, April, June, September, October and November. Please check our Web site for upcoming dates and locations. Maximum size is 55; average workshop has 40-50 participants. Cost of workshop varies; see Web site for details. Cost includes tuition for both Saturday and Sunday (9:00 a.m. to 4:30 p.m.); morning and afternoon snacks; lunch; handout packet.

CHILDREN'S LITERATURE CONFERENCE

250 Hofstra University, U.C.C.E., Hempstead NY 11549. (516)463-5172. Fax: (516)463-4833. E-mail: uccelibarts @hofstra.edu. Web site: www.hofstra.edu. **Contact:** Judith Reed, director, arts, culture and leisure. Writer and illustrator workshops geared toward all levels. Emphasizes: fiction, nonfiction, poetry, submission procedures, picture books. Workshops will be held in April. Length of each session: 1 hour. Cost of workshop: approximately $85; includes 2 workshops, reception, lunch, 2 general sessions, and panel discussion with guest speakers and critiquing of randomly selected first-manuscript pages submitted by registrants. Write for more information. Co-sponsored by Society of Children's Book Writers & Illustrators.

THE COLUMBUS WRITERS CONFERENCE

P.O. Box 20548, Columbus OH 43220-0176. (614)451-3075. Fax: (614)451-0174. E-mail: angelaPL28@aol.com. Web site: www.creativevista.com. **Director:** Angela Palazzolo. Sessions geared toward all levels. "In addition to consultations with agents and editor, this two-day conference offers a wide variety of topics and has included writing in the following markets: children's, young adult, screenwriting, historical fiction, humor, suspense, science fiction/fantasy, travel, educational and greeting card. Other topics have included writing the novel, the short story, the nonfiction book; playwriting; finding and working with an agent; independent publishing; book reviewing; technical writing; and time management for writers. Specific sessions that have pertained to children: fiction, nonfiction, children's writing, children's markets, young adult and publishing children's poetry and stories. Annual conference. Conference held in August. Cost of conference is TBA. E-mail, call or write for more information; or visit Web site.

CONFERENCE FOR WRITERS & ILLUSTRATORS OF CHILDREN'S BOOKS

51 Tamal Vista Blvd., Corte Madera CA 94925. (415)927-0960, ext. 238. Fax: (415)924-3838. E-mail: conferences@b ookpassage.com. Web site: www.bookpassage.com. **Conference Coordinator:** Karen West. Writer and illustrator conference geared toward beginner and intermediate levels. Sessions cover such topics as the nuts and bolts of writing and illustrating, publisher's spotlight, market trends, developing characters/finding voice in your writing. Two-day conference held each June. Registration limited to 80. Includes 3 lunches and a closing reception.

PETER DAVIDSON'S HOW TO WRITE A CHILDREN'S PICTURE BOOK SEMINAR

982 S. Emerald Hills Dr., Arnolds Park IA 51331-0497. E-mail: Peterdavidson@mchsi.com. **Seminar Presenter:** Peter Davidson. "This seminar is for anyone interested in writing and/or illustrating children's picture books. Beginners and experienced writers alike are welcome." **Open to students.** How to Write a Children's Picture Book is a one-day seminar devoted to principles and techniques of writing and illustrating children's picture books. Topics include Definition of a Picture Book, Picture Book Sizes, Developing an Idea, Plotting the Book, Writing the Book, Illustrating the Book, Formatting Your Manuscript, Copyrighting Your Work, Marketing Your Manuscript and Contract Terms. Seminars are presented year-round at community colleges. Even-numbered years, presents seminars in Minnesota, Iowa, Nebraska, Kansas, Colorado and Wyoming. Odd-numbered years, presents seminars in Illinois, Minnesota, Iowa, South Dakota, Missouri, Arkansas and Tennessee (write for a schedule). One day, 9 a.m.-4 p.m. Cost of workshop: varies from $40-59, depending on location; includes approximately 35 pages of handouts. Write for more information.

THE DIY BOOK FESTIVAL

7095 Hollywood Blvd., Suite 864, Los Angeles CA 90028-0893. (323)665-8080. Fax: (323)660-1776. E-mail: diyconvention@aol.com. Web site: www.diyconvention.com. **Managing Director:** Bruce Haring. Writer and illustrator workshops geared toward beginner and intermediate levels. **Open to students.** Festival focus on getting your book into print, book marketing and promotion. Annual workshop. Workshop held February-October, various cities. Cost of workshop: $50; includes admission to event, entry to prize competition, lunch for some events. Check out our Web site for current dates and locations: www.diyconvention.com.

DUKE UNIVERSITY YOUTH PROGRAMS: CREATIVE WRITER'S WORKSHOP

P.O. Box 90702, Durham NC 27708. (919)684-6259. Fax: (919)681-8235. E-mail: youth@duke.edu. Web site: www.learnmore.duke.edu/youth. **Contact:** Duke Youth Programs. Writer workshops geared toward intermediate to advanced levels. **Open to students.** The Creative Writer's Workshop provides an intensive creative writing experience for advanced high school age writers who want to improve their skills in a community of writers. "The interactive format gives participants the opportunity to share their work in small groups, one-on-one with instructors, and receive feedback in a supportive environment. The review and critique process helps writers sharpen critical thinking skills and learn how to revise their work." Annual workshop. Every summer there is one 2-week residential session. Costs for 2005—$1,565 for this 2-week residential session. Visit Web site or call for more information.

DUKE UNIVERSITY YOUTH PROGRAMS: YOUNG WRITER'S CAMP

P.O. Box 90702, Durham NC 27708. (919)684-2827. Fax: (919)681-8235. E-mail: youth@duke.edu. Web site: www.learnmore.duke.edu/youth. **Contact:** Duke Youth Programs (919)684-6259. Beginner and intermediate levels writing workshops for middle and high school students. **Open to students** (grades 6-11). Summer Camp. The Young Writer's Camp offers courses to enhance participants skills in creative and expository writing. "Through a core curriculum of short fiction, poetry, journalism and playwriting students choose two courses for study to develop creative and analytical processes of writing. Students work on assignments and projects in and out of class, such as newspaper features, short stories, character studies, and journals." Annual workshop. Every summer there are three 2-week sessions with residential and day options. Costs for 2006—$1,565 for residential campers and $1,025 for extended/$775 for day campers. Visit Web site or call for more information.

EAST OF EDEN WRITERS CONFERENCE

California Writers Club, P.O. Box 3254, Santa Clara, CA 95055. (408)247-1286. Fax: (408)927-5224. E-mail: eastofeden@southbaywriters.com. Web site: www.southbaywriters.com. **Conference Director:** Beth Proudfoot. Writer workshops geared toward beginner, intermediate and advanced levels. Open to students. Bi-annual conference. Next held September 8-10, 2006, in Salinas, CA (at the National Steinbeck Center and the Salinas Community Center.) Registration limited to 400. Cost of conference: around $300, depending on options chosen; includes Friday night dinner and program; Saturday breakfast, lunch, and full day of workshops and panels; "Night Owl" sessions; Saturday dinner program and Sunday brunch at John Steinbeck's family home are available for a small additional fee. "This conference, run by the nonprofit California Writers Club, will include many top-notch seminars on the art and business of writing. We'll have panels where writers can meet literary agents and editors and an Ask-A-Pro program, where writers can sign up to speak individually with faculty members of their choice."

EAST TEXAS CHRISTIAN WRITERS CONFERENCE

East Texas Baptist University, 1209 North Grove Street, Marshall TX 75670. (903)923-2269. Fax: (903)938-7798. E-mail: jhopkins@etbu.edu. Web site: www.etbu.edu/cwc2006. **Humanities Secretary:** Donna Gribble. Writer workshops geared toward beginner, intermediate and advanced levels. **Open to students.** Children's literature, books, stories, plays, art, and general literature. Annual conference. Workshop held first Saturday in June each year. Cost of workshop: $50/individual; $40/student; includes 5 writing workshops, materials, luncheon. Write for more information.

FESTIVAL OF CHILDREN'S LITERATURE

The Loft Literary Center, Suite 200, Open Book, 1011 Washington Avenue South, Minneapolis MN 55415. (612)379-8999. E-mail: loft@loft.org. Web site: www.loft.org. Writer workshops geared toward all levels. Workshops have included: "Nuts and Bolts of Publishing Nonfiction for Children" (by 4 writers with multi-titles published); Annual conference held in April; speakers for 2006 included Caitlyn Dlouhy, executive editor, Atheneum Books for Young Readers along with many more writers, editors, publishers, and illustrators of children's literature. Registration limited to 185 people; smaller groups for breakout sessions. Writing facilities available with a performance hall, classrooms and writers studios. Cost of conference: approximately $153 for Friday and Saturday; $142 for Loft members; includes admission to full and break-out sessions, Saturday lunch, discount on hotel room (hotel 3 blocks from Loft Literary Center). Write for more information.

FESTIVAL OF FAITH AND WRITING

Department of English, Grand Rapids MI 49546. (616)526-6770. Fax: (616)526-8508. E-mail: ffw@calvin.edu. Web site: www.calvin.edu/festival. E-mail all inquiries about attendance (for registration brochures, program information, etc.). Geared toward all levels of readers and writers. **Open to students.** "The Festival of Faith and Writing has talks, panel discussions, and workshops by artists who compose, write, illustrate, and publish children's books and books for young adults. Each break-out session will have a session on children's books/young adult books. Please see Web site for list of authors and illustrators joining us for 2006." Conference held every other year in April. Registration limited to approximately 1,800 people. Cost of conference in 2006: $160 ($80 for students); includes all sessions, workshops, evening speakers. Cost subject to change in 2008. E-mail for more information. "This conference is geared towards a variety of writers. The Festival brings together writers and readers who wonder about the intersections of faith with words on a page, lyrics in a melody, or images on a screen. Novelists, publishers, musicians, academics, poets, playwrights, editors, screenwriters, agents, journalists, preachers, students, and readers of every sort sit down together for three days of conversation and celebration."

FISHTRAP, INC.

400 Grant Street, P.O. Box 38, Enterprise OR 97828-0038. (541)426-3623. Fax: (541)426-3324. E-mail: rich@fishtrap. Web site: www.fishtrap.org. **Director:** Rich Wandschneider. Writer workshops geared toward beginner, intermediate, advanced and professional levels. **Open to students.** Not specifically writing for children, although we have offered occasional workshops in the field. A series of eight writing workshops (enrollment 12/workshop) and a writers' gathering is held each July; a winter gathering concerning writing and issues of public concern held in February. Dates for the winter gathering are February 24-26, 2006; and for the summer gathering July 9-15, 2006. A Children's Writing Workshop is held each fall. Check Web site for details. During the school year Fishtrap brings writers into local schools and offers occasional workshops for teachers and writers of children's and young adult books. Also brings in "Writers in Residence" (10 weeks). Cost of Fishtrap workshops varies with length and format—$30 for short workshop to several hundred for weeklong intensive workshop. College credit is available. See Web site for full program descriptions and to get on the e-mail and mail lists.

FLATHEAD RIVER WRITERS CONFERENCE

P.O. Box 7711, Kalispell MT 59937. E-mail: conference@authorsoftheflathead.com. **Director:** Jake How. Writer workshops geared toward beginner, intermediate, advanced and professional levels. **Open to students.** Along with our presenters, we periodically feature a children's writer workshop. Annual conference held mid-October. Registration limited to 100. Cost of workshop: $150; includes all lectures and a choice of workshops plus breakfast and lunch. Write for more information.

FLORIDA CHRISTIAN WRITERS CONFERENCE

2344 Armour Ct., Titusville FL 32780. (321)269-5831. Fax: (321)264-0037. E-mail: billiewilson@cfl.rr.com. Web site: www.flwriters.org. **Conference Director:** Billie Wilson. Writer workshops geared toward all levels. **Open to students.** "We offer 56 one-hour workshops and 8 six-hour classes. Approximately 15 of these are for the children's genre." Annual workshop held in March. "We have 30 publishers and publications represented by editors teaching workshops and reading manuscripts from the conferees. The conference is limited to 200 people. Advanced or professional workshops are by invitation only via submitted application. Cost of workshop: $350; includes tuition and ms critiques and editor review of your ms plus personal appointments with editors. Write or e-mail for more information.

GIG HARBOR WRITER'S CONFERENCE

PMB #153, 3110 Judson St., Gig Harbor WA 98335-0826. (253)851-2444. Fax: (253)265-8532. E-mail: Director@peni nsulawritersassociation.org. Web site: www.peninsulawritersassociation.org. **Director:** Jan Walker. Writer workshops geared toward beginner, intermediate, advanced and professional levels. **Open to students.** Annual workshop. Workshop held Spring. Registration limited to 150. Cost of workshop: $100, nonmember; $75 members; includes workshops, welcome reception, keynote speaker, and several presenters. Write for more information.

GOTHAM WRITERS' WORKSHOP
New York NY 10023. (877)974-8377. (212)307-6325. E-mail: dana@write.org. Web site: www.WritingClasses.com. **Director, Student Affairs:** Dana Miller. Creative writing workshops taught by professional writers are geared toward beginner, intermediate and advanced levels. **Open to students.** "Workshops cover the fundamentals of plot, structure, voice, description, characterization, and dialogue appropriate to all forms of fiction and nonfiction for pre-schoolers through young adults. Students can work on picture books or begin middle-readers or young adult novels." Annual workshops held 4 times/year (10-week and 1-day workshops). Workshops held January, April, July, September/October. Registration limited to 14 students/in-person (NYC) class; 18 students/online class; 40 students for in-person (NYC) one-day workshops. Cost of workshop: $420 for 10-week workshops; $150 for 1-day workshops; 10-week NYC classes meet once a week for 3 hours; 10-week online classes include 10 week-long, asynchronous "meetings"; 1-day workshops are 7 hours and are held 8 times/year. E-mail for more information.

GREAT LAKES WRITER'S WORKSHOP
Milwaukee WI 53234-3922. (414)382-6176. Fax: (414)382-6332. E-mail: nancy.krase@alverno.edu. Web site: www.alverno.edu. **Program Assistant:** Nancy Krase. Writing workshops geared toward beginner and intermediate levels; subjects include publishing, short story writing, novel writing, poetry, writing techniques/focus in character development, techniques for overcoming writers block. Annual workshop. Workshop held 3rd or 4th weekend in June, Friday evening and all day Saturday. Average length of each session: 2 hours. Cost of workshop: $115/entire workshop; $99 if you register before June 1. See online brochure. Lunch is included in Saturday program with a featured author as keynote speaker. Write for more information or call.

GREEN LAKE WRITERS CONFERENCE
Green Lake Conference Center, W2511 State Hwy 23, Green Lake WI 54941. (800)558-8898. Fax: (920)294-3848. E-mail: program@glcc.org. Web site: www.glcc.org. **Program Coordinator:** Russann Devine. Writing workshops for beginning through advanced professional levels. **Open to students.** Participants under the age of 21 must be accompanied by an adult. Writing for Children, manuscript critique, publishing. Annual weeklong event. Workshop held early August. Writing facilities available: classrooms, library. Cost of workshop: $697/person; includes program fee and meals. Housing is double occupancy. Single rooms available at additional cost. Write for more information. Evening critique groups, editors on-hand for lecture and information. Per-page fee for additional manuscript critique.

HIGHLAND SUMMER CONFERENCE
P.O. Box 7014, Radford University, Radford VA 24142-7014. (540)831-5366. Fax: (540)831-5951. E-mail: jasbury@radford.edu. Web site: www.radford.edu/ ~ arsc. **Director:** Grace Toney Edwards. **Assistant to the Director:** Jo Ann Asbury. **Open to students.** Writer workshops geared toward beginner, intermediate and advanced levels. Emphasizes Appalachian literature, culture and heritage. Annual workshop. Workshop held first 2 weeks in June annually. Registration limited to 20. Writing facilities available: computer center. Cost of workshop: Regular tuition (housing/meals extra). Must be registered student or special status student. E-mail, fax or call for more information. Past visiting authors include: Wilma Dykeman, Sue Ellen Bridgers, George Ella Lyon, Lou Kassem.

HIGHLIGHTS FOUNDATION FOUNDERS WORKSHOPS
Dept. CWF, 814 Court St., Honesdale PA 18431. (570)253-1192. Fax: (570)253-0179. E-mail: contact@highlightsfoundation.org. Web site: www.highlightsfoundation.org. **Contact:** Kent Brown, director. Workshops geared toward those interested in writing and illustrating for children, intermediate and advanced levels. Classes offered include: Writing Novels for Young Adults, Biography, Nonfiction Magazine Writing, Writing Historical Fiction, Wordplay: Writing Poetry for Children, Heart of the Novel, Nature Writing for Kids, Visual Art of the Picture Book, Writing Books for Today's Kids, and more (see Web site for updated list). Workshops held in March, April, May, June, July, September, October and November near Honesdale, PA. Workshops limited to between 8 and 14 people. Cost of workshops range from $495 and up. Cost of workshop includes tuition, meals, conference supplies and housing. Call for application and more information.

HIGHLIGHTS FOUNDATION WRITERS WORKSHOP AT CHAUTAUQUA
Dept. CWL, 814 Court St., Honesdale PA 18431. (570)253-1192. Fax: (570)253-0179. E-mail: contact@highlightsfoundation.org. Web site: www.highlightsfoundation.org. **Contact:** Kent Brown, Director. Writer Workshops

geared toward those interested in writing for children; beginner, intermediate and advanced levels. Classes include: Writing Poetry, Book Promotion, Characterization, Developing a Plot, How to Promote Your Book, and many many more. Annual workshop held: July 15-22, 2006, at Chautauqua Institution, Chautauqua, NY. Registration limited to 100. Cost of workshop: $2,200; $1,785 if registered by February 26, 2006. Includes tuition, meals, conference supplies. Cost does not include housing. Call for availability and pricing. Scholarships are available for first-time attendees. Call for more information or visit the Web site.

HOFSTRA UNIVERSITY SUMMER WRITERS' WORKSHOP

250 Hofstra University, UCCE, Hempstead NY 11549. (516)463-5016. Fax: (516)463-4833. E-mail: uccelibarts@hofstra.edu. Web site: www.hofstra.edu/ucce/summerwriting. **Contact:**Richard Pioreck, director or summer writing workshops; or Judith Reed, administrator. Writer workshops geared toward all levels. Classes offered include fiction, nonfiction, poetry, children's literature, stage/screenwriting and other genres. Annual workshop. Workshops held for 2 weeks in mid-July. Each workshop meets for 2½ hours daily for a total of 25 hours. Students can register for 2 workshops, schedule an individual conference with the writer/instructor and submit a short ms (less than 10 pages) for critique. Enrollees may register as noncredit students or credit students. Cost of workshop: noncredit students' enrollment fee is approximately $425; 2-credit student enrollment fee is approximately $1,100/workshop undergraduate and graduate (2 credits); $2,100 undergraduate and graduate (4 credits). On-campus accommodations for the sessions are available for approximately $350/person for the 2-week conference. Students may attend any of the ancillary activities, a private conference, special programs and social events. All workshops include critiquing. Each participant is given one-on-one time for a half hour with workshop leader. Accepts inquiries by fax or e-mail. Web site includes details on dates, faculty, general description and tuition.

INSTITUTE FOR READERS THEATRE ANNUAL WORKSHOP

P.O. Box 421262, San Diego CA 92142. (858)277-4274. Fax: (858)576-7369. E-mail: wadams1@san.rr.com. Web site: www.readerstheatre.net. **General Manager:** Arlene McCoy. Writer workshops geared toward beginner, intermediate and advanced levels. **Open to students.** Topics include oral interpretation; script writing (converting literary material into performable scripts); journal writing (for credit participants). Annual workshop held in July. Registration limited to 50. Cost of workshop: $1,795; includes 2 weeks room in either Toronto, Canada or London, England. Airfare and university credit (optional) are extra. Write for more information.

INTERNATIONAL CREATIVE WRITING CAMP

1930 23rd Ave., SE, Minot ND 58701-6081. (701)838-8472. Fax: (701)838-8472. E-mail: info@internationalmusiccamp.com. Web site: www.internationalmusiccamp.com. **Camp Director:** Joseph T. Alme. Writer and illustrator workshops geared toward beginner, intermediate and advanced levels. **Open to students.** Sessions offered include those covering poems, plays, mystery stories, essays. Workshop held June 25-July 1, 2006. Registration limited to 20. The summer camp location at the International Peace Garden on the Border between Manitoba and North Dakota is an ideal site for generating creative thinking. Excellent food, housing and recreation facilities are available. Cost of workshop: $275. Write for more information.

INTERNATIONAL WOMEN'S WRITING GUILD "REMEMBER THE MAGIC" ANNUAL SUMMER CONFERENCE

P.O. Box 810, Gracie Station, New York NY 10028-0082. (212)737-7536. Fax: (212)737-9469. E-mail: iwwg@iwwg.org. Web site: www.iwwg.org. **Executive Director:** Hannelore Hahn. Writer and illustrator workshops geared toward all levels. Offers 65 different workshops—some are for children's book writers and illustrators. Also sponsors 13 other events throughout the U.S. Annual workshops. "Remember the Magic" workshops held 2nd or 3rd week in June. Length of each session: 1 hour-15 minutes; sessions take place for an entire week. Registration limited to 500. Cost of workshop: $995/single, $860/double (includes complete program, room and board). Write for more information. "This workshop always takes place at Skidmore College in Saratoga Springs NY."

IOWA SUMMER WRITING FESTIVAL

C215 Seashore Hall, Iowa City IA 52242. (319)335-4160. Fax: (319)335-4743. E-mail: iswfestival@uiowa.edu. Web site: www.uiowa.edu/~iswfest. **Director:** Amy Margolis. Writer workshops geared toward beginner, intermediate and advanced levels. Open to writers age 21 and over. "We offer writing workshops across the genres, including workshops for children's writers in picture books, structuring writing for children, the young adult novel, and nonfiction." Annual workshop. Workshop held June and July. Registration limited to 12/workshop. Workshops meet in university classrooms. Cost of workshop: $475-500/week-long session; $225/weekend; includes tuition. Housing is separate and varies by facility. Write or call for more information.

JEWISH CHILDREN'S BOOK WRITERS' CONFERENCE

New York NY. E-mail: anna@olswanger.com. **Contact:** Anna Olswanger, conference coordinator. The 2005 conference faculty included editor-in-chief Regina Griffin of Holiday House, editor Jodi Kreitzman Keller of Delacorte Press, marketing and sales director Michael J. Miller of Pitspopany Press, publicist Susan Salzman Raab of Raab Associates, literary agent Rebecca Sherman of Writers House, and production editor Aviva Werner of BabagaNewz magazine. Author Michelle Edwards, winner of a national Jewish Book Award, gave opening remarks. And the day included First Pages and Query Letter Clinic with the editors; talks on the Association of Jewish Libraries' Sydney Taylor Manuscript Competition, Sippurim: Israel Books for Kids, and Israel Beyond the Headlines; and door prizes. Held in November, the Sunday before Thanksgiving. Cost of workshop: includes Kosher breakfast and lunch. E-mail for more information.

KENTUCKY WRITER'S WORKSHOP

1050 State Park Road, Pineville KY 40977. (606)337-3066. Fax: (606)337-7250. E-mail: Dean.Henson@ky.gov. Web site: http://parks.ky.gov/resortparks/pm. **Event Coordinator:** Dean Henson. Writer and illustrator workshops geared toward beginner and intermediate levels. **Open to students.** Annual workshop held in March. Writing facilities available: classroom setup. Cost of workshop: $179/single package; $249/double; cost includes two nights accommodations, two evening buffet meals, and admission to all sessions. Write or call for more information.

ℕ KINDLING WORDS

Web site (for registration and information): www.kindlingwords.org. Annual retreat held in late-January near Burlington, Vermont. A retreat with three strands: writer, illustrator and editor; professional level. Intensive workshops for each strand, and an open schedule for conversations and networking. Registration limited to approximately 60. Tuition: $195. Hosted by the 4-star Inn at Essex (room and board extra). Participants must be published by a CCBC listed publisher, or if in publishing, occupy a professional position. Registration opens July 1, and fills quickly. Check Web site to see if spaces are available, to sign up to be notified when registration opens each year, or for more information.

LAJOLLA WRITERS CONFERENCE

P.O. Box 178122, San Diego CA 92177. (858)467-1978. E-mail: jkuritz@san.rr.com. Web site: www.lajollawriter sconference.com. **Founder:** Antoinette Kuritz. Writer workshop geared toward beginner and intermediate levels. Illustrator workshops geared toward beginner and intermediate. **Open to students.** ''We offer sessions with children's book agents and editors; read-and-critique sessions with young adult authors, editors, agents and publishers, including Laura Rennert of the Andrea Brown Agency; IRA Award winner, John H. Ritter; Harcourt Children's Book Editor, Deborah Halverson. Annual workshop. Workshop held in October. Registration limited to 200. Cost of workshop: $325; early bird, $265; includes classes Friday-Sunday, lunch and dinner Saturday. Write for more information.

LEAGUE OF UTAH WRITERS' ROUNDUP

P.O. Box 18430, Kearns UT 84118. (435)313-4459. E-mail: president_andy@luwrite.com. Web site: www.luwrite.c om. **President Elect:** Meredith ''Andy'' Anderson. **Membership Chairman:** Dorothy Crofts. Writer workshops geared toward beginner, intermediate or advanced. Annual workshop. Roundup usually held 3rd weekend of September. 2006 conference held at Christ Evangelical Church, Orem UT September 15-16. Registration limited to 300. Cost is $77 for members/$109 for nonmembers registering before August 19. Late registration will be $100 for members; $150 non-members after August 19. Cost includes 3 meals, all workshops, general sessions, a syllabus, hand outs and conference packet. Contact Andy with questions at (801)427-1385 or e-mail president _andy@luwrite. com. Send registration to Dorothy Crofts, Membership Chairman, P.O. Box 18430, Kearns, UT 84118.

LIGONIER VALLEY WRITERS CONFERENCE

P.O. Box B, Ligonier PA 15658-1602. (724)537-3341. Fax: (724)537-0482. E-mail: sarshi@wpa.net. Web site: www.ligoniervalleywriters.org. **Contact:** Sally Shirey. Writer programs geared toward all levels. **Open to students.** Annual conference features fiction, nonfiction, poetry and other genres. Annual conference. Held in July. Cost of workshop: $200; includes full weekend, some meals, all social events. Write or call for more information and conference dates.

MANHATTANVILLE SUMMER WRITERS' WEEK

2900 Purchase Street, Purchase NY 10577-2103. (914)694-3425. Fax: (914)694-3488. E-mail: dowdr@mville.e du. Web site: www.manhattanville.edu. **Dean, School of Graduate & Professional Studies:** Ruth Dowd. Writer workshops geared toward writers and aspiring writers. **Open to students.** Writers' week offers a special workshop for writers interested in children's/young adult writing. We have featured such workshop leaders as: Patricia Gauch, Richard Peck, Elizabeth Winthrop and Janet Lisle. Roni Schotter led the 2006 workshop. Annual workshop held last week in June. Length of each session: one week. Cost of workshop: $695 (non-credit);

includes a full week of writing activities, 5-day workshop on children's literature, lectures, readings, sessions with editors and agents, etc. Workshop may be taken for 2 graduate credits. Write for more information.

■ MARITIME WRITERS' WORKSHOP

UNB College of Extended Learning, P.O. Box 4400, Fredericton NB E3B 5A3 Canada. E-mail: k4jc@unb.ca. Web site: unb.ca/extend/writers/. **Coordinator:** Andrew Titus. Week-long workshop on writing for children, general approach, dealing with submitted material, geared to all levels and held in July. Annual workshop. 3 hours/day. Group workshop plus individual conferences, public readings, etc. Registration limited to 10/class. Cost of workshop: $395 tuition; meals and accommodations extra. Room and board on campus is approximately $320 for meals and a single room for the week. 10-20 ms pages due before conference (deadline announced). Limited scholarships available.

MAUI WRITERS CONFERENCE

P.O. Box 1118, Kihei HI 96753. (888)974-8373 or (808)879-0061. Fax: (808)879-6233. E-mail: writers@maui.net. Web site: www.mauiwriters.com. **Director:** Shannon Tullius. Writer workshops geared toward beginner, intermediate, advanced. **Open to students.** "We offer a small children's writing section covering picture books, middle grade and young adult. We invite one *New York Times* Bestselling Author and agents and editors, who give consultations." Annual workshop. Workshop held Labor Day weekend (usually early September). Cost includes admittance to all conference sessions and classes only—no airfare, food or consultations.

MIDLAND WRITERS CONFERENCE

Grace A. Dow Memorial Library, Midland MI 48640-2698. (517)837-3435. Fax: (517)837-3468. E-mail: ajarvis@midland-mi.org. Web site: www.midland-mi.org/gracedowlibrary. **Conference Chair:** Ann Jarvis. **Open to students.** Writer and illustrator workshops geared toward all levels. "Each year, we offer a topic of interest to writers of children's literature." Last year's workshops: (Cynthia Laferle—Marketing Essays; Margo Lagattua—Dreaming of Getting Your Poetry Published?; Boyd Miller—Self-publishing; John Smolens-Perils of Publishing. Annual workshop. Workshops held usually second Saturday in June. Length of each session: concurrently, 4 1-hour sessions repeated in the afternoon. Maximum class size: 50. "We are a public library." Cost of workshop: $60; includes choice of workshops and the keynote speech given by a prominent author (last year Michael Beschloss). Write for more information.

MIDWEST WRITERS WORKSHOP

Department of Journalism, Ball State University, Muncie IN 47306. (765)282-1055. Fax: (765)285-7997. Web site: www.midwestwriters.org. **Director:** Earl L. Conn. Writer workshops geared toward intermediate level. Topics include most genres. Past workshop presenters include Joyce Carol Oates, James Alexander Thom, Bill Brashler and Richard Lederer. Workshop also includes ms evaluation and a writing contest. Annual workshop. Workshop will be held July 28-30, 2005. Registration tentatively limited to 125. Most meals included. Offers scholarships. Write for more information.

MISSOURI WRITERS' GUILD ANNUAL STATE CONFERENCE

(816)361-1281. E-mail: mwgconfernece@earthlink.net. Web site: www.missouriwritersguild.org. **Contact:** Margo Dill, vice president and conference chairman. Writer and illustrator workshops geared to all levels. **Open to students.** Annual conference held late April or early May each year. Cost of conference: $125-175.

MONTROSE CHRISTIAN WRITER'S CONFERENCE

Montrose PA 18801-1112. (570)278-1001. Fax: (570)278-3061. E-mail: mbc@montrosebible.org. Web site: www.montrosebible.org. **Executive Director:** Jim Fahringer. **Secretary-Registrar:** Donna Kosik. **Open to adults and students.** Writer workshops geared toward beginner, intermediate and advanced levels. Annual workshop held in July. Cost of workshop: $140 tuition. Write for more information.

MOONDANCE INTERNATIONAL FILM FESTIVAL

970 Ninth St., Boulder CO 80302. (303)545-0202. E-mail: info@moondancefilmfestival.com (with MIFF or MOONDANCE in the subject line). Web site: www.moondancefilmfestival.com. **Executive Director:** Elizabeth English. Moondance Film Festival Workshop Sessions include screenwriting, playwriting, short stories, filmmaking (feature, documentary, short, animation), TV and video filmmaking, writing for TV (MOW, sitcoms, drama), writing for animation, adaptation to screenplays (novels and short stories), how to get an agent, what agents want to see, and pitch panels. 2006 workshops and film festival held June, 2006 (exact date and location TBA). Cost of workshops, seminars, panels, pitch session: $50 each. Check Web site for more information and registration forms. The 2006 competition deadline for entries is April 1, 2006. "The Moondance competition

includes special categories for writers and filmmakers who create work for the children's market!'' Entry forms and guidelines are on the Web site.

MOUNT HERMON CHRISTIAN WRITERS CONFERENCE

Mount Hermon Christian Conference Center, Mount Hermon CA 95041-0413. (831)335-4466. Fax: (831)335-9413. E-mail: rachelw@mhcamps.org. Web site: www.mounthermon.org/writers. **Director of Adult Ministries:** David R. Talbott. Writer workshops geared toward all levels. **Open to students over 16 years.** Emphasizes religious writing for children via books, articles; Sunday school curriculum; marketing. 70 workshops offered include: Suitable Style for Children; Everything You Need to Know to Write and Market Your Children's Book; Take-Home Papers for Children. Workshops held annually over Palm Sunday weekend: April 7-11, 2006 and March 30-April 3, 2007. Length of each session: 5-day residential conferences held annually. Registration limited 45/class, but most are 20-30. Conference center with hotel-style accommodations. Cost of workshop: $660-990 variable; includes tuition, resource notebook, refreshment breaks, full room and board for 13 meals and 4 nights. Conference information posted annually on Web site by December 1. Write or e-mail for more information or call toll-free to 1-888-MH-CAMPS.

THE NEW-CUE WRITERS' CONFERENCE AND WORKSHOP IN HONOR OF RACHEL CARSON

The Spruce Point Inn, Boothbay Harbor ME. (845)398-4247. Fax: (845)398-4224. E-mail: info@new-cue.org. Web site: www.new-cue.org. **President:** Barbara Ward Klein. Writer and illustrator workshops geared toward beginner, intermediate, advanced and professional levels. "Our conference emphasizes environmental and nature writing for juvenile fiction and non-fiction. Workshop held in June every 2 years on the even numbered year. Registration limited to 100 participants. Writing/art facilities available: Large meeting rooms for featured speakers, including Jean Craighead George. Smaller break-out rooms for concurrent sessions. Cost of workshop: $388/returning participants; $430/new-before 5/1/06. Includes all featured and keynote addresses, performance of one-woman play, *A Sense of Wonder*, concurrent sessions, workshops, guided outdoor activities and almost all meals. Submit writing sample, no longer than 3 pages. Write for more information. Additional information about featured speakers, The Spruce Point Inn, and the Boothbay Harbor Area is available on-line at www.new-cue.org.

NORTH CAROLINA WRITERS' NETWORK FALL CONFERENCE

P.O. Box 954, Carrboro NC 27510-0954. (919)967.9540. Fax: (919)929.0535. E-mail: mail@ncwriters.org. Web site: www.ncwriters.org. Writing workshops geared toward beginning, intermediate and advanced or published levels. **Open to students.** We offer workshops, keynote, presentations and critique sessions in a variety of genres: fiction, poetry, creative nonfiction, children's/youth, etc. Past youth and children's writing faculty include Louise Hawes, Jackie Ogburn, Clay Carmichael, Carole Boston Weatherford, Susie Wilde. Annual Conference to be held next in Research Triangle Park (Sheraton Imperial) November 10-12, 2006. (Most recent was in Asheville, November 4-6, 2005.) Cost of conference usually $250/members, $350/nonmembers, including all workshops, panels, roundtables, social activities and four meals. Extra costs for accommodations, master classes and critique sessions.

OHIO KENTUCKY INDIANA CHILDREN'S LITERATURE CONFERENCE

% Greater Cincinnati Library Consortium (GCLC), Cincinnati OH 45206-2855. (513)751-4422. Fax: (513)751-0463. E-mail: gclc@gclc-lib.org. Web site: www.gclc-lib.org. **Staff Development Coordinator:** Judy Malone. Writer and illustrator conference geared toward all levels. **Open to students.** Annual conference. Emphasizes multicultural literature for children and young adults. Conference held annually in November. Contact GCLC for more information. Registration limited to 250. Cost of conference: $50; includes registration/attendance at all workshop sessions, Tri-state Authors and Illustrators of Childrens Books Directory, continental breakfast, lunch, author/illustrator signings. E-mail or write for more information.

OKLAHOMA WRITERS' FEDERATION, INC. ANNUAL CONFERENCE

P.O. Box 2654, Stillwater OK 74076-2654. (405)762-6238. Fax: (405)377-0992. E-mail: wileykat@cox.net. Web site: www.owfi.org. **President:** Moira Wiley. Writer workshops geared toward all levels. Illustrator workshops geared toward beginner level. **Open to students.** "During 2003 event, Emily Mitchell, assistant editor with Charlesbridge Publishing, presented a session titled The Basics of Children's Book Contracts (Law Degree Not Required). Other noteworthy topics cover the basics of writing, publishing and marketing in any genre." Annual conference. Held first Friday and Saturday in May each year. Registration limited to 420. Writing facilities available: book room, autograph party, free information room. Cost of workshop: $125 (early bird); $150 after (early bird date); $60 for single days; full tuition includes 2-day conference—all events including 2 banquets and one 10-minute appointment with an attending editor or agent of your choice (must be reserved in advance). "If writers would like to participate in the annual writing contest, they must become members of OWFI. You don't have to be a member to attend the conference." Write or e-mail for more information.

Resources

OUTDOOR WRITERS ASSOCIATION OF AMERICA ANNUAL CONFERENCE
158 Lower Georges Valley Rd., Spring Mills PA 16875. (814)364-9557. Fax: (814)364-9558. E-mail: eking4owaa @cs.com. **Meeting Planner:** Eileen King. Writer workshops geared toward all levels. Annual 5-day conference. Craft Improvement seminars; newsmaker sessions. Workshop held in June. 2007 conference to be held in Roanoke, Virginia. Cost of workshop: $325; includes attendance at all workshops and most meals. Attendees must have prior approval from Executive Director before attendance is permitted. Write for more information.

THE PACIFIC COAST CHILDREN'S WRITERS WORKSHOP, From Master Class to Masterpiece: Crafting Characters Through Scenes,
P.O. Box 244, Aptos CA 95001. (831)684-2042. E-mail: nancy.sondel@chidrenswritersworkshop.com. Web site: www.childrenswritersworkshop.com. **Founding Director:** Nancy Sondel. Conference geared toward intermediate and professional levels; beginners may attend with some limits in participation. **Open to students.** "As with all enrollees, students must demonstrate competence in story crafting and/or come prepared to learn from highly skilled writers. Our keynotes, master class clinics, and hands-on focus sessions explore topics such as 'How to Craft Scenes Integrating Character, Plot and Theme in MG and YA Novels.'" Annual conference held late July or early/mid-August. Registration limited to 40. Sleeping rooms have DSL Internet access. Cost of Conference: $149-378 (disount for students ages 16-24). Fee is based on number and type of critiques (multiple options), number of days enrolled (2 or 3), and early bird/student discounts. Cost includes most meals (gourmet, with faculty). Saturday includes 1-2 editor/agent critiques in an intensive 9½-hour program— largely team-taught manuscript clinics among savvy, congenial writers. Application includes thought-provoking questions about writer's manuscripts; sample chapters must be submitted. E-mail for more information. "We focus on literary, character-driven, realistic novels with protagonists age 11 or older. Our seminar-style, master class format is highly interactive, with continuous dialogues between top-notch faculty and writers. Pre-workshop prep (personalized manuscript assignments and peer-manuscript critiques) maximizes learning and networking with pros."

PACIFIC NORTHWEST CHILDREN'S BOOK CONFERENCE
Portland State University Haystack Program, P.O. Box 1491, Portland OR 97207. (503)725-4186 or (800)547-8887, ext. 4186. Fax: (503)725-4840. E-mail: snydere@pdx.edu. Web site: www.haystack.pdx.edu/children. **Contact:** Elizabeth Snyder, Haystack program coordinator. Focus on the craft of writing and illustrating for children while working with an outstanding faculty of acclaimed editors, authors, and illustrators. Daily afternoon faculty-led writing and illustration workshops. Acquire specific information on how to become a professional in the field of children's literature. Annual workshop for all levels. Conference held in July on the campus of Reed College, Portland, Oregon. Cost of conference: $595 noncredit; $865 for 3 graduate credits; individual ms/portfolio reviews for an additional fee. Call for more information. Linda Zuckerman, editor, coordinates conference and collects knowledgeable and engaging presenters every year.

PACIFIC NORTHWEST WRITER ASSN. SUMMER WRITER'S CONFERENCE
P.O. Box 2016, Edmonds WA 98020. (425)673-2665. E-mail: staff@pnwa.org. Web site: www.pnwa.org. **Association Executive:** Dana Murphy-Love. Writer conference geared toward beginner, intermediate, advanced and professional levels. **Open to students.** New in 2006—conference sessions will be run in genre tracks. Annual conference held in July. Cost of conference: discounted conference rate for members (limited scholarships available to members); includes all conference materials, continental breakfasts, refreshments, awards ceremony dessert reception, keynote dinners, appointments with editors/agents. "There are approximately 30 agents/editors that attend this conference. The Literary Contest Winners are announced as well. Conference is at the Hilton Seattle Airport, Seattle, WA."

PERSPECTIVES IN CHILDREN'S LITERATURE CONFERENCE
School of Education, 226 Furcolo Hall, Amherst MA 01003-3035. (413)545-4190 or (413)545-1116. Fax: (413)545-2879. E-mail: childlit@educ.umass.edu. Web site: www.umass.edu/childlit. **Conference Coordinators:** Katelyn McLaughlin and Laura Ptaszynski. Writer and illustrator workshops geared to all levels. Presenters talk about what inspires them, how they bring their stories to life and what their visions are for the future. Conference held in April. For more information contact coordinators by phone, fax or e-mail."

PIMA WRITERS' WORKSHOP
Pima College, 2202 W. Anklam Rd., Tucson AZ 85709-0170. (520)206-6084. Fax: (520)206-6020. E-mail: mfiles @pima.edu. **Director:** Meg Files. Writer conference geared toward beginner, intermediate and advanced levels. **Open to students.** The conference features presentations and writing exercises on writing and publishing stories for children and young adults, among other genres. Annual conference. Workshop held in May. Cost of workshop: $75; includes tuition, manuscript consultation. Write for more information.

PUBLISHINGGAME.COM WORKSHOP

Newton MA 02459. (617)630-0945. E-mail: Alyza@publishinggame.com. Web site: publishinggame.com. **Coordinator:** Alyza Harris. Fern Reiss, author of the popular "Publishing Game" book series and CEO of Expertizing.-com, will teach this one-day workshop. Writer workshops geared toward beginner, intermediate and advanced levels. **Open to students.** Sessions will include: Find A Literary Agent, Self-Publish Your Children's Book, Book Promotion For Children's Books. September—New York, NY; October—Boston, MA; November—TBD; December—Philadelphia, PA; January—Washington, DC; February—Boca Raton, FL; March—New York, NY; April—TBD; May—Washington, DC; June—Los Angeles, CA; July—San Francisco, CA; August—Seattle, WA. Registration limited to 18. Fills quickly! Cost of workshop: $195. Write for more information. Workshop now available as a 5-CD audio workshop.

ROBERT QUACKENBUSH'S CHILDREN'S BOOK WRITING AND ILLUSTRATING WORKSHOP

Studio address: 223 East 79th St., New York, NY 10021. Mailing address: 460 East 79th St., New York, NY 10021. (212)744-3822. Fax: (212)861-2761. E-mail: Rqstudios@aol.com. Web site: www.rquackenbush.com. **Contact:** Robert Quackenbush. A four-day extensive workshop on writing and illustrating books for young readers held annually the second week in July at author/artist Robert Quackenbush's Manhattan studio. The focus of this workshop is on creating manuscripts and/or illustrated book dummies from start to finish for picture books and beginning reader chapter books ready to submit to publishers. Also covered is writing fiction and nonfiction for middle grades and young adults, if that is the attendee's interest. In addition, attention is given to review of illustrator's portfolios and new trends in illustration, including animation for films, are explored. During the four days, the workshop meets from 9 a.m-4 p.m. including one hour for lunch. Registration is limited to 10. Some writing and/or art supplies are available at the studio and there is an art store nearby, if needed. There are also electrical outlets for attendee's laptop computers. Cost of workshop is $650. Attendees are responsible for arranging for their own hotel and meals. On request, suggestions are given for economical places to stay and eat. Recommended by Foder's *Great American Learning Vacations*, which says, "This unique workshop, held annually since 1982, provides the opportunity to work with Robert Quackenbush, a prolific author and illustrator of children's books with more than 185 fiction and nonfiction books for young readers to his credit, including mysteries, biographies and songbooks. The workshop attracts both professional and beginning writers and artists of different ages from all over the world." Brochure available. Also inquire about fall, winter and spring workshops that meet once a week for ten weeks each that are offered to artists and writers in the New York area.

ROCKY MOUNTAIN RETREATS FOR WRITERS & ARTISTS

81 Cree Court, Lyons CO 80540. (303)823-0530. E-mail: ddebord@indra.com. Web site: www.expressionretreats .com. **Director:** Deborah DeBord. Writers and illustrator workshops geared to all levels. **Open to students.** Includes information on releasing creative energy, identifying strengths and interests, balancing busy lives, marketing creative works. Monthly conference. Registration limited to 4/session. Writing studio, weaving studio, private facilities available. Cost of workshop: $1,234/week; includes room, meals, materials, instruction." Treat yourself to a week of mountain air, sun, and personal expression. Flourish with the opportunity for sustained work punctuated by structured experiences designed to release the artist's creative energies. Relax over candlelit gourmet meals followed by fireside discussions of the day's efforts. Discover the rhythm of filling the artistic well and drawing on its abundant resources."

⚑ SAGE HILL WRITING EXPERIENCE, Writing Children's & Young Adult Fiction Workshop

Box 1731, Saskatoon SK S7K 3S1 Canada. Phone/fax: (306)652-7395. E-mail: sage.hill@sasktel.net. Web site: www.sagehillwriting.ca. **Executive Director:** Steven Ross Smith. Writer conference geared toward intermediate level. This program occurs every 2 or 3 years, but the Sage Hill Conference is annual. Conference held in July. Registration limited to 6 participants for this program, and to 37 for full program. Cost of conference approximately $895; includes instruction, meals, accommodation. Require ms samples prior to registration. Write or visit the Web site for more information and workshop dates.

SAN DIEGO STATE UNIVERSITY WRITERS' CONFERENCE

The College of Extended Studies, San Diego CA 92182-1920. (619)594-2517. Fax: (619)594-8566. E-mail: extended.std@sdsu.edu. Web site: www.neverstoplearning.net. **Conference Facilitator:** Becky Ryan. Writer workshops geared toward beginner, intermediate and advanced levels. Emphasizes nonfiction, fiction, screenwriting, advanced novel writing; includes sessions specific to writing and illustrating for children. Workshops offered by children's editors, agents and writers. Annual workshops. Workshops held January 27-29, 2006. Registration limited. Cost of workshops: approximately $300. Call for more information or visit Web site.

SAN FRANCISCO WRITERS CONFERENCE

1029 Jones St., San Francisco CA 94109. (415)673-0939. E-mail: sfwc@aol.com. Web site: www.sanfranciscowri

tersconference.com. **Co-Founder:** Elizabeth Pomada. Writer workshops geared toward beginner, intermediate, advanced and professional levels. **Open to students.** Annual conference. Conference held President's Day weekend in mid-February. Registration limited to 700. Cost of workshop: $425-495 depending on time of registration; includes continental breakfast and sit-down brunch. Write or visit Web site for more information. The preliminary program for the following year's conference will be on the Web site by October.

⬛ SASKATCHEWAN FESTIVAL OF WORDS AND WORKSHOPS

217 Main Street, Moose Jaw SK S6H 0W1 Canada. (306)691-0557. Fax: (306)693-2994. E-mail: word.festival@sasktel.net. Web site: www.festivalofwords.com. **Artistic Coordinator:** Gary Hyland. Writer workshops geared toward beginner and intermediate levels. **Open to students.** Readings that include a wide spectrum of genres—fiction, creative non-fiction, poetry, songwriting, screenwriting, playwriting, children's writing, panels, interviews and performances. Annual festival. Workshop held third weekend in July. Cost of workshop: $8/session—$125 for full festival pass. Write, e-mail, or visit Web site for more information.

SOCIETY OF SOUTHWESTERN AUTHORS' WRANGLING WITH WRITING

P.O. Box 30355, Tucson AZ 85751-0355. (520)546-9382. Fax: (520)296-0409. E-mail: wporter202@aol.com; barbara@clariticom.com. Web site: www.azstarnet.com/nonprofit/ssa. **Conference Director:** Penny Porter. Writer workshops geared toward all genres. "Limited scholarships available." Sessions include Writing and Publishing the Young Adult Novel, What Agents Want to See in a Children's Book, Writing Books for Young Children. "We always have several children's book editors and agents interested in meeting with children's writers." Annual workshop held January 30-31, 2004. Registration limited to 500—usually 300-400 people attend. Hotel rooms have dataports for internet access. Tucson has many art galleries. Tentative cost: $250 nonmembers, $225 for SSA members; includes 3 meals and 2 continental breakfasts, all workshop sessions—individual appointments with agents and editors are extra. Hotel accommodations are not included. "Some editors and agents like to see mss prior to the conference; information about requirements is in the brochure. If you want a portfolio of artwork critiqued, please contact us directly, and we'll try to accommodate you." Write for more information. SSA has put on this conference for over 25 years now. "It's hands-on, it's friendly, and every year writers sell their manuscripts."

SOUTH COAST WRITERS CONFERENCE

P.O. Box 590, 29392 Ellensburg Ave., Gold Beach OR 97444. (541)247-2741. E-mail: scwc@socc.edu. **Coordinator:** Janet Pretti. Writer workshops geared toward beginner, intermediate levels. **Open to students.** Include s fiction, nonfiction, nuts and bolts, poetry, feature writing, children's writing, publishing. Annual workshop. Workshop held Friday and Saturday of President's day weekend in February. Registration limited to 25-30 students/workshop. Cost of workshop: $50 before January 31, $60 after; includes Friday night author's reading and book signing, Saturday conference, choice of 4 workshop sessions, Saturday evening writers' circle (networking and critique). Write for more information. "We also have two six-hour workshops Friday for more intensive writing exercises. The cost is an additional $35."

SOUTH FLORIDA WRITERS' CONFERENCE

P.O. Box 570415, Miami FL 33257-0415. (786)877-0136. Fax: (305)233-8680. E-mail: greenfie@hotmail.com. **Conference Director:** Henry Greenfield. Writer conference geared toward beginner and intermediate levels. **Open to students.** Sample of sessions include Finding a Niche in the Children's Market, Riding the Boon in Young Adult Fiction, Finding Your Audience, How to Make Plots Work, Preparing a Manuscript for Submission. Annual conference. Conference held the week after Mother's Day at Barry University in Miami, FL. Writing facilities available: classrooms, dorms. Cost of conference: $200 (20% early registration by April 15th); includes all events beginning Friday afternoon through Sunday noon; banquet and continental breakfast; provides overnight accommodations: double $65/night with meals, single $75 with meals. Individual ms evaluations $35 for 15 minutes with agent, editor or author. Sponsors contest. Judges are professional writers. Prizes of $3,200 total for plays, novels, short fiction, poetry, nonfiction, juveniles. Deadline is in April. Send for Guidelines with SASE. Write for more information. "Conference focuses on short fiction, novels, poetry, juveniles, nonfiction, freelancing, playwriting, screenwriting, self-promotion, publication, e-books. Site: Barry University main campus. Tropical setting, university-type classrooms, theaters, meal service, housing. Last year's events included stage and play readings and individual manuscript evaluations by agents, editors, authors. Panelists included authors Edna Buchanan, John Dufresne, Joyce Sweeney, Marcia Preston and others. Agents included Jeff Herman, Elizabeth Pomada, Michael Larsen, James Schiavone, Janell Agyeman, Mandy Greenfield, Lois Blume, Michael Sasser, Carey Martin, Susan Cumins, Judi Welsh, and others among conference editors, packagers, publishers, poets, playwrights, etc."

SOUTHEASTERN WRITERS ASSOCIATION—ANNUAL WRITERS WORKSHOP

P.O. Box 82115, Athens GA 30608. E-mail: purple@southeasternwriters.com. Web site: www.southeasternwrite

rs.com. **CFO:** Tim Hudson. **Open to all writers and students.** Students must be in high school or college. Scholarships available for college and high school students. See Web site. Classes offered in fiction, nonfiction, juvenile, inspirational writing, and poetry. Intensive workshop in screenwriting offered in 2006. Annual workshop held in June. Cost of workshop (2005): $265 before April 15; $305 after April 15; $85 daily tuition. Accommodations: Offers overnight accommodations on workshop site. Visit Web site for more information and cost of overnight accommodations. E-mail or send SASE for brochure.

SOUTHWEST WRITERS CONFERENCES
3721 Morris NE, Suite A, Albuquerque NM 87111. (505)265-9485. Fax: (505)265-9483. E-mail: swwriters@juno. com. Web site: www.southwestwriters.org. **Open to adults and students.** Writer workshops geared toward all genres at all levels of writing. Various aspects of writing covered, including children's. Quarterly mini-conference and occasional workshops. Examples from mini-conferences: Beyond the Unknown conference: Steve Saffel of Del Rey and Liz Scheier of Penguin Groups lectured on science fiction/fantasy/horror and had one-on-one meetings with attendees for acquiring manuscripts. Included other speakers, lunch, midnight reading event and Old Town Ghost Tour. Cracking the Code: Secrets of Writing and Selling Compelling Nonfiction conference featured literary agents Michael Larsen, Elizabeth Pomoda and Jeff Herman; Lee Gutkind, publisher; David Fryxell, editor; Lucinda Schroeder, criminologist/writer; and a panel of New Mexico publishers. Making a Good Script Great: All-day seminar with Dr. Linda Seger and other speakers. Dimension in Fiction and Nonfiction: All-day workshop with Sean Murphy. Prices vary, but usually $99-$159. Also offers annual and monthly contests, two monthly programs, monthly newsletter, occasional workshops, critique service, Web site: linking and various discount perks. See Web site for information.

SPLIT ROCK ARTS PROGRAM
University of Minnesota, Twin Cities Campus, 360 Coffey Hall, 1420 Eckles Ave., St. Paul MN 55108-6084. (612)625-8100. Fax: (612)624-6210. E-mail: srap@cce.umn.edu. Web site: www.cce.umn.edu/splitrockarts . Workshop topics, including poetry, short fiction, memoir, novel, personal essay, young-adult literature, and children's picture books, among others, are taught by renowned writers, and geared toward students of intermediate, advanced, and professional levels. Weeklong and three-day workshops run June through August. Registration limited to 16/workshop. Graduate/Undergraduate credit and scholarships available. Cost of workshop: $365-545 and up. On-campus apartment-style housing available. Printed and online catalogs available in February.

⚅ SUNSHINE COAST FESTIVAL OF THE WRITTEN ARTS
P.O. Box 2299, Sechelt BC V0N-3A0 Canada. (604)885-9631, 1-800-565-9631. Fax: (604)885-3967. E-mail: info@ writersfestival.ca. Web site: www.writersfestival.ca. **Festival Producer:** Gail Bull. Writer and illustrator workshops geared toward professional level. **Open to Students.** Annual literary festival held every August. Pavilion seating 500/event. Festival pass $175; individual events $12. Fee schedule available upon request.

⚅ SURREY INTERNATIONAL WRITER'S CONFERENCE
Guildford Continuing Education, 10707 146th St., Surrey BC U3R IT5 Canada. (604)589-2221. Fax: (604)588-9286. E-mail: l.mason@siwc.ca. Web site: www.siwc.ca. **Coordinator:** Lisa Mason. Writer and illustrator workshops geared toward beginners, intermediate and advanced levels. Topics include marketing, children's agents and editors. Annual Conference. Conference held in October. Cost of conference includes all events for 3 days and most meals. Check our Web site for more information.

⊕ SYDNEY CHILDREN'S AND ILLUSTRATORS NETWORK
The Hughenden Boutique Hotel, Woollahra NSW 2025 Australia. (61)(29)363-4863. Fax: (61)(293)719-645. E-mail: gervays@bigpond.com. Web site: www.hughendenhotel.com.au. **Contact:** Susanne Gervay. Writer and illustrator workshops geared toward professionals. Topics emphasized include networking, information and expertise about Australian children's publishing industry. Workshop held the first Wednesday of every month, except for January, commencing at 10:30 a.m. Registration limited to 30. Writing facilities available: internet and conference facilities. Cost of workshop: $150 AUS; includes accommodation for one night at The Hughenden Boutique Hotel, breakfast. As a prerequisite must be published in a magazine of have a book contract. E-mail for more information. "This is a professional meeting which aims at an interchange of ideas and information between professional children's authors and illustrators. Editors and other invited guests speak from time to time."

TEXAS MOUNTAIN TRAIL WRITERS' WINTER RETREAT
HC 65 Box 20P, Alpine TX 79830. (432)364-2399. E-mail: bakedalaska@wfisp.com. **President:** Jackie Siglin. Writer and illustrator workshops geared toward beginner, intermediate and advanced levels. **Open to students.**

Topics emphasized include: inside information from editors of children's magazines; children's illustrator hints on collaboration; children's writer tips toward publication. Other genres are also covered. Conference held in April. Registration limited to 30-35. Writing facilities available: large comfortable conference room, nearby dining, mountain tourist attractions. Cost of workshop: $120; includes casual, friendly entertainment, weekend conference and 4 meals, one-on-one visits with authors, illustrators, etc. Write for more information. "Nearby attractions include McDonald Observatory, Ft. Davis and Big Bend National Park."

UMKC/WRITERS PLACE WRITERS WORKSHOPS

5300 Rockhill Rd., Kansas City MO 64110-2450. (816)235-2736. Fax: (816)235-5279. E-mail: seatons@umkc.e du. **Contact:** Kathi Wittfield. New Letters Writer's Conference and Mark Twain Writer's Workshop geared toward intermediate, advanced and professional levels. Workshops open to students and community. Annual workshops. Workshops held in Summer. Cost of workshop varies. Write for more information.

UNIVERSITY OF THE NATIONS SCHOOL OF WRITING AND WRITERS WORKSHOPS

YWAM Woodcrest, P.O. Box 1380, Lindale TX 75771-1380. (903)882-WOOD [9663]. Fax: (903)882-1161. E-mail: writingschooltx@yahoo.com. Web site: www.ywamwoodcrest.com. **School Leader:** Carol Scott. Writer workshops geared toward beginner, intermediate, advanced levels. **Open to students.** Children's writing workshops include: Writing Children's Picture Books with Mona Gansberg Hodgson. Workshops held during various weeks between September and December. Cost for workshop: $20 registration fee (nonrefundable) plus $175 tuition per week (the 1st week) plus $175/week if staying on our campus. ($125 tuition each additional week.) $175 tuition/week covers lectures, critique groups, hands-on-training. Students may make own arrangements for lodging and meals. If you want college credit for the workshop or are taking the entire 12-week school of writing, you must have completed the YWAM's Discipleship Training School first. Write for more information. "Although we are associated with the Youth with A Mission missionary group, we welcome inquiries from all interested parties—not only missionaries."

⚡ VANCOUVER INTERNATIONAL WRITERS FESTIVAL

1398 Cartwright St., Vancouver BC V6H 3R8 Canada. (604)681-6330. Fax: (604)681-8400. E-mail: viwf@writersf est.bc.ca. Web site: www.writersfest.bc.ca. **Artistic Director:** Alma Lee. Annual literary festival. The Vancouver International Writers Festival strives to encourage an appreciation of literature and to promote literacy by providing a forum where writers and readers can interact. This is accomplished by the production of special events and an annual Festival which feature writers from a variety of countries whose work is compelling and diverse. The Festival attracts over 11,000 people and presents approximately 50 events in six venues during six days on Granville Island, located in the heart of Vancouver. The first 4 days of the festival are programmed for elementary and secondary school students and teachers. Held in late October (6-day festival). All writers who participate are invited by the A.D. The events are open to anyone who wishes to purchase tickets. Cost of events ranges from $10-25.

⚡ THE VICTORIA SCHOOL OF WRITING

306-620 View St., Victoria BC V8W 1J6 Canada. (250)595-3000. E-mail: info@victoriaschoolofwriting.org. Web site: www.victoriaschoolofwriting.org. **Director:** Jill Margo. Annual 5-day intensive session geared toward intermediate level. In the 2006 conference there will include 1 workshop that includes writing for children and young adults. Workshop held July 16-21. Registration limited to 12/workshop. Session includes close mentoring from established writers. Cost of session: $585 (Canadian); includes tuition and some meals. Please see Web site, e-mail or call for details.

VIRGINIA FESTIVAL OF THE BOOK

145 Ednam Dr., Charlottesville VA 22903. (434)924-6890. Fax: (434)296-4714. E-mail: vabook@virginia.edu. Web site: www.vabook.org. **Program Director:** Nancy Damon. **Open to Students.** Readings, panel discussions, presentations and workshops by author, and book-related professionals for children and adults. Most programs are free and open to the public. Held in March. See Web site for more information.

WESLEYAN WRITERS CONFERENCE

Wesleyan University, Middletown CT 06459. (860)685-3604. Fax: (860)685-2441. E-mail: agreene@wesleyan.e du. Web site: www.wesleyan.edu/writers. **Director:** Anne Greene. Seminars, workshops, readings, ms advice; geared toward all levels. "This conference is useful for writers interested in how to structure a story, poem or nonfiction piece. Although we don't always offer classes in writing for children, the advice about structuring a piece is useful for writers of any sort, no matter who their audience is." One of the nation's best-selling children's authors was a student here. Classes in the novel, short story, fiction techniques, poetry, journalism and literary nonfiction. Guest speakers and panels offer discussion of fiction, poetry, reviewing, editing and publishing. Individual ms consultations available. Conference held annually the third week in June. Length of each session: 5 days. Usually, there are 100 participants at the Conference. Classrooms, meals, lodging and word processing facilities available on campus. Cost of workshop: tuition—$570, room—$170, meals (required of all participants)—$210. "Anyone may register; people who want financial aid must submit their work and be selected by scholarship judges." Call for a brochure or check Web site.

WHIDBEY ISLAND WRITERS' CONFERENCE

P.O. Box 1289, Langley WA 98260. (360)331-6714. E-mail: writers@whidbey.com. Web site: www.writeonwhid bey.org. **Writers Contact:** Elizabeth Guss, conference director. Three days focused on the tools you need to become a great writer. Learn from a variety of award-winning children's book authors and very experienced literary agents. Topics include: "Putting the character back in character"; "Contemporary and Historical Fiction for Children." Conference held March 2-4, 2007. Registration limited to 275. Cost: $360. Registration includes workshops, fireside chats, high tea book-signing reception, various activities, and daily luncheons. The conference offers consultation appointments with editors and agents as well as opportunities for critiques from authors in many genres. A preconference workshop highlights children's writing. Registrants may reduce the cost of their conference by volunteering. See the Web site for more information. "The uniquely personal and friendly weekend is designed to be highly interactive."

WILLAMETTE WRITERS ANNUAL WRITERS CONFERENCE

9045 SW Barbur Blvd., Suite 5A, Portland OR 97219. (503)452-1592. Fax: (503)452-0372. E-mail: wilwrite@willa mettewriters.com. Web site: www.willamettewriters.com. **Office Manager:** Bill Johnson. Writer workshops geared toward all levels. Emphasizes all areas of writing, including children's and young adult. Opportunities to meet one-on-one with leading literary agents and editors. Workshops held in August. Cost of conference: $285-350; includes membership.

TENNESSEE WILLIAMS/NEW ORLEANS LITERARY FESTIVAL

938 Lafayette St., Suite 328, New Orleans LA 70113. (504)581-1144. Fax: (504)523-3680. E-mail: info@tennessee williams.net. Web site: www.tennesseewilliams.net. **Executive Director:** Paul J. Willis. Writer workshops geared toward beginner, intermediate, advanced, and professional levels. **Open to students.** Annual workshop. Workshop held around the third week in March. Master classes are limited in size to 100—all other panels offered have no cap. Cost of workshop: prices range from $15-35. Visit Web site for more information. "We are a literary festival and may occasionally offer panels/classes on children's writing and/or illustration, but this is not done every year."

WINTER POETRY & PROSE GETAWAY IN CAPE MAY

18 N. Richards Ave., Ventnor NJ 08406. (609)823-5076. E-mail: info@wintergetaway.com. Web site: www.wint ergetaway.com. **Director:** Peter E. Murphy. Writer workshops geared toward all levels. **Open to students** (18 years and over). "Writing for Children: You will learn to develop character, plot, setting, points of view. There will also be a discussion of genres in juvenile literature, voice, detail and revision. Choose 1 of 2 sections— picture books and younger readers or middle graders and teens." Annual workshop. Workshop held January 12-15, 2007. Registration limited to 8 writers in each workshop. Writing/art facilities available in hotel meeting and ballrooms. Cost of workshop: $345, includes lunches and evening receptions. Single and shared rooms, which include breakfast, are available for an additional cost. Prices will be posted on the Web site in September, 2006. "The Winter Poetry & Prose Getaway is well known for its challenging and supportive atmosphere which encourages imaginative risk taking and promotes freedom and transformation in each participant's creative work."

WRITE ON THE SOUND WRITERS CONFERENCE

700 Main St., Edmonds WA 98020-3032. (425)771-0228. Fax: (425)771-0253. E-mail: wots@ci.edmonds.wa.us. Web site: www.ci.edmonds.wa.us/ArtsCommission/index.stm. **Conference Coordinator:** Kris Gillespie. Writer workshops geared toward beginner, intermediate, advanced and professional levels with some sessions on writing for children. Annual conference held in Edmonds, on Puget Sound, on the first weekend in October with 2 full days of workshops. Registration limited to 200. Cost of conference: approximately $104 for early registration, $125 for late registration; includes two days of workshops plus one ticket to keynote lecture. Brochures are mailed in August. Attendees must pre-register. Write, e-mail or call for brochure. Writing contest and critiques for conference participants.

⚑ WRITE! CANADA

P.O. Box 487, Markham ON L3P 3R1 Canada. (905)471-1447. Fax: (905)471-6912. E-mail: info@thewordguild.c om. Web site: www.thewordguild.com. Estab. 1984. Annual conference for writers who are Christian. Hosted

Resources

by The Word Guild, an association of Canadian writers and editors who are Christian. The Word Guild seeks to connect, develop, and promote its members. Keynote speaker, continuing classes, workshops, panels, editor appointments, reading times, critiques, and more. For all levels of writers from beginner to professional. Held at a retreat center in Guelph ON in mid-June.

WRITE-BY-THE-LAKE WRITER'S WORKSHOP & RETREAT

610 Langdon St., Room 621, Madison WI 53703. (608)262-3447. E-mail: cdesmet@dcs.wisc.edu. Web site: www.dcs.wisc.edu/lsa/writing. **Coordinator:** Christine DeSmet. Writer workshops geared toward beginner and intermediate levels. **Open to students** (1-3 graduate credits available in English). "One week-long session is devoted to juvenile fiction." Annual workshop. Workshop held the third week of June. Registration limited to 15. Writing facilities available: computer labs. Cost of workshop: $325 before May 23; $355 after May 23. Cost includes instruction, reception, and continental breakfast each day. Write for more information. "Brochure goes online every January for the following June."

WRITE-TO-PUBLISH CONFERENCE

9118 W. Elmwood Dr., #1G, Niles IL 60714-5820. (847)296-3964. Fax: (847)296-0754. E-mail: lin@writetopublish.com. Web site: www.writetopublish.com. **Director:** Lin Johnson. Writer workshops geared toward all levels. **Open to students.** Conference is focused for the Christian market and includes classes on writing for children. Annual conference held in June. Cost of conference approximately: $400; includes conference and banquet. For information, call or e-mail brochure@writetopublish.com. Conference takes place at Wheaton College in the Chicago area.

WRITERS RETREAT WORKSHOP

(formerly Gary Provost's Writers Retreat Workshop), (800)642-2494 (for brochure). E-mail: jssitzes@aol.com. Web site: www.writersretreatworkshop.com. **Director:** Jason Sitzes. Writer workshops geared toward beginner, intermediate and advanced levels. Workshops are appropriate for writers of full length novels for children/YA. Also, for writers of all novels or narrative nonfiction. Annual workshop. Workshops held last 10 days of May. Registration limited to small groups: beginners and advanced. Writing facilities available: private rooms with desks. Cost of workshop: $1,695; includes tuition, food and lodging for nine nights, daily classes, writing space, time and assignments, consultation and instruction. Requirements: short synopsis required to determine appropriateness of novel for our nuts and bolts approach to getting the work in shape for publication. Write for more information. For complete details, call 800 number or e-mail.

WRITERS' LEAGUE OF TEXAS WORKSHOP SERIES

1501 W. Fifth St., Suite E-2, Austin TX 78703. (512)499-8914. Fax: (512)499-0441. E-mail: wlt@writersleague.org. Web site: www.writersleague.org. **Contact:** Kristy Bordine. Writer workshops and conferences geared toward adults. Annual agents and editors conferences. Classes are held during weekend, and retreats/workshops are held throughout the year. Annual Teddy Children's Book Award of $1,000 presented each fall to book published from June 1 to May 1. Write for more information.

WRITING AND ILLUSTRATING FOR YOUNG READERS WORKSHOP

Brigham Young University, 348 Harman Continuing Education Bldg., Provo UT 84602-1532. (801)442-2568. Fax: (801)422-0745. E-mail: cw348@byu.edu. Web site: http://wifyr.byu.edu. Annual workshop held in June. Five-day workshop designed for people who want to write for children or teenagers. Participants focus on a single market during daily four-hour morning writing workshops: picture books, book-length fiction (novels), fantasy/science fiction, nonfiction, mystery, beginning writing or illustration. Afternoon workshop sessions feature a variety of topics of interest to writers for all youth ages. Workshop cost: $439—includes all workshop and breakout sessions plus a banquet on Thursday evening. Afternoon-only registration available; participants may attend these sessions all five days for a fee of $109. Attendance at the Thursday evening banquet is included in addition to the afternoon mingle, plenary, and breakout sessions.

WRITING CHILDREN'S FICTION

Rice University, Houston TX 77005. (713)348-4803. Fax: (713)348-5213. E-mail: scs@rice.edu. Web site: www.scs.rice.edu. **Contact:** School of Continuing Studies. Weekly evening children's writing courses and workshops geared toward all levels held in most fall and spring semesters. Topics include issues in children's publishing, censorship, multiculturalism, dealing with sensitive subjects, submissions/formatting, the journal as resource, the markets—finding your niche, working with an editor, the agent/author connection, the role of research, and contract negotiation. Contact Rice Continuing Studies for current information on course offerings.

Contests, Awards & Grants

Publication is not the only way to get your work recognized. Contests and awards can also be great ways to gain recognition in the industry. Grants, offered by organizations like SCBWI, offer monetary recognition to writers, giving them more financial freedom as they work on projects.

When considering contests or applying for grants, be sure to study guidelines and requirements. Regard entry deadlines as gospel and follow the rules to the letter.

Note that some contests require nominations. For published authors and illustrators, competitions provide an excellent way to promote your work. Your publisher may not be aware of local competitions such as state-sponsored awards—if your book is eligible, have the appropriate person at your publishing company nominate or enter your work for consideration.

To select potential contests and grants, read through the listings that interest you, then send for more information about the types of written or illustrated material considered and other important details. A number of contests offer information through websites given in their listings.

If you are interested in knowing who has received certain awards in the past, check your local library or bookstores or consult *Children's Books: Awards & Honors*, compiled and edited by the Children's Book Council (www.cbcbooks.org). Many bookstores have special sections for books that are Caldecott and Newbery Medal winners. Visit the American Library Association website, www.ala.org, for information on the Caldecott, Newbery, Coretta Scott King and Printz Awards. Visit www.hbook.com for information on The Boston Globe-Horn Book Award. Visit www.scbwi.org/awards.htm for information on The Golden Kite Award.

For a contest success story see the Insider Report with **Paula Yoo**, a winner of the Lee & Low New Voices Award, on page 338.

Information on contests listed in the previous edition but not included in this edition of *Children's Writer's & Illustrator's Market* may be found in the General Index.

Ⓝ Ⓦ ACADEMY OF CHILDREN'S WRITERS' WRITING FOR CHILDREN COMPETITION

Academy of Children's Writers, P.O. Box 95, Huntington Cambridgeshire PE28 5RL England. 01487 832752. Fax: 01487 832752. E-mail: per_ardua@lycos.co.uk. **Contact:** Roger Dewar, contest director. Annual contest for the best unpublished short story writer for children. **Deadline:** March 31. Guidelines for SASE. **Charges $5 (US); £ (UK).** Prize: 1st Prize: £1,000; 2nd Prize: £300; 3rd Prize: £100. Judged by a panel appointed by the Academy of Children's Writers. Open to any writer.

ACORN CONTESTS, SHEPHERD CONTEST

Acorn, 1530 Seventh St., Rock Island IL 61201. (309)788-3980. **Submit entries to:** Betty Mowery, editor. Open to students. Annually. "Purpose of contest: to help young authors compete with others and to obtain discipline in preparing and submitting entries." Submissions must be unpublished. Submissions made by author. Rules/entry forms are available for SASE. Entry fee: six 37¢ stamps. Awards subscription to Acorn. Judging by Acorn staff member. "Open to all young authors ages K-12th grade. Entries without SASE will not be returned and will not receive a reply. Entries without entry fee will not be judged."

JANE ADDAMS CHILDREN'S BOOK AWARDS

Jane Addams Peace Association, Inc./Women's International League for Peace and Freedom, 777 United Nations Plaza, New York NY 10017. (212)682-8830. Fax: (212)286-8211. E-mail: japa@igc.org. Web site: www.janeadda mspeace.org. **Contact:** Linda Belle. "Two copies of published books the previous year only." Annual award. Estab. 1953. Previously published submissions only. Submissions made by author, author's agent, person, group or publisher, submitted by the publisher. Must be published January 1-December 31 of preceding year. Deadline for entries: December 31. Check Web site for all submission information. Cash awards and certificate, $1,000 to winners (winning book) and $500 each to Honor Book winners (split between author and illustrator, if necessary). Judging by national committee from various N.S. regions (all are members of W.I.L.P.F.). The award ceremony is held in New York the third Friday October annually.

AIM MAGAZINE SHORT STORY CONTEST

P.O. Box 1174, Maywood IL 60153-8174. (773)874-6184. **Contest Director:** Ruth Apilado, associate editor. Annual contest. **Open to students.** Estab. 1983. Purpose of contest: "We solicit stories with lasting social significance proving that people from different racial/ethnic backgrounds are more alike than they are different." Unpublished submissions only. Deadline for entries: August 15. SASE for contest rules and entry forms. SASE for return of work. No entry fee. Awards $100. Judging by editors. Contest open to everyone. Winning entry published in fall issue of *AIM*. Subscription rate: $20/year. Single copy: $5.

Ⓦ ALCUIN CITATION AWARD

The Alcuin Society, P.O. Box 3216, Vancouver BC V6B 3X8 Canada. (604)732-5403. E-mail: leahgordon@shaw. ca. Web site: www.alcuinsociety.com. Annual award. Estab. 1981. Purpose of contest: Alcuin Citations are awarded annually for excellence in Canadian book design. Previously published submissions from the year prior to the Award's Call for Entries (i.e., 2005 awards went to books published in 2004). Submissions made by the publisher, author or designer. Deadline for entries: mid-March. Entry fee is $20/book; include cheque and entry form with book. Awards certificate. Winning books are exhibited nationally, and internationally at the Frankfurt and Leipzig Book Fairs. Winning books are Canada's entries in the international competition in Leipzig, "Best Book Design from all over the World" in the following Spring. Judging by professionals and those experienced in the field of book design. Requirements for entrants: Winners are selected from books designed and published in Canada. Awards are presented annually at an appropriate ceremony held in early June each year.

AMERICA & ME ESSAY CONTEST

Farm Bureau Insurance, P.O. Box 30400, 7373 W. Saginaw, Lansing MI 48909-7900. (517)323-7000. Fax: (517)323-6615. E-mail: lfedewa@fbinsmi.com. Web site: www.farmbureauinsurance-mi.co. **Contest Coordinator:** Lisa Fedewa. Annual contest. **Open to students only.** Estab. 1968. Purpose of the contest: to give Michigan 8th graders the opportunity to express their thoughts/feelings on America and their roles in America. Unpublished submissions only. Deadline for entries: mid-November. SASE for contest rules and entry forms. "We have a school mailing list. Any school located in Michigan is eligible to participate." Entries not returned. No entry fee. Awards savings bonds and plaques for state top ten ($500-1,000), certificates and plaques for top 3 winners from each school. Each school may submit up to 10 essays for judging. Judging by home office employee volunteers. Requirements for entrants: "Participants must work through their schools or our agents' sponsoring schools. No individual submissions will be accepted. Top ten essays and excerpts from other essays are published in booklet form following the contest. State capitol/schools receive copies."

AMERICAN ASSOCIATION OF UNIVERSITY WOMEN, NORTH CAROLINA DIVISION, AWARD IN JUVENILE LITERATURE

North Carolina Literary and Historical Association, 4610 Mail Service Center, Raleigh NC 27699-4610. (919)807-7290. Fax: (919)733-8807. E-mail: michael.hill@ncmail.net. **Award Coordinator:** Mr. Michael Hill. Annual award. Purpose of award: to recognize the year's best work of juvenile literature by a North Carolina resident. Book must be published during the year ending June 30. Submissions made by author, author's agent or publisher. Deadline for entries: July 15. SASE for contest rules. Awards a cup to the winner and winner's name inscribed on a plaque displayed within the North Carolina Office of Archives and History. Judging by Board of Award selected by sponsoring organization. Requirements for entrants: Author must have maintained either legal residence or actual physical residence, or a combination of both, in the state of North Carolina for three years immediately preceding the close of the contest period. Only published work (books) eligible.

AMERICAS AWARD

CLASP Committee on Teaching and Outreach, % Center for Latin American and Caribbean Studies, P.O. Box 413, Milwaukee WI 53201. (414)229-5986. Fax: (414)229-2879. E-mail: jkline@uwm.edu. Web site: www.uwm.edu/Dept/CLACS/outreach/americas.html. **Coordinator:** Julie Kline. Annual award. Estab. 1993. Purpose of contest: Up to two awards are given each spring in recognition of U.S. published works (from the previous year) of fiction, poetry, folklore or selected nonfiction (from picture books to works for young adults) in English or Spanish which authentically and engagingly relate to Latin America, the Caribbean, or to Latinos in the United States. By combining both and linking the "Americas," the intent is to reach beyond geographic borders, as well as multicultural-international boundaries, focusing instead upon cultural heritages within the hemisphere. Previously published submissions only. Submissions open to anyone with an interest in the theme of the award. Deadline for entries: January 15. Visit Web site or send SASE for contest rules and any committee changes. Awards $500 cash prize, plaque and a formal presentation at the Library of Congress, Washington DC. Judging by a review committee consisting of individuals in teaching, library work, outreach and children's literature specialists.

⊞ HANS CHRISTIAN ANDERSEN AWARD

IBBY International Board on Books for Young People, Nonnenweg 12, Postfach CH-4003 Basel Switzerland. (004161)272 29 17. Fax: (004161)272 27 57. E-mail: ibby@ibby.org. Web site: www.ibby.org. **Adminstrative Director:** Liz Page. Award offered every two years. Purpose of award: A Hans Christian Andersen Medal shall be awarded every two years by the International Board on Books for Young People (IBBY) to an author and to an illustrator, living at the time of the nomination, who by the outstanding value of their work are judged to have made a lasting contribution to literature for children and young people. The complete works of the author and of the illustrator will be taken into consideration in awarding the medal, which will be accompanied by a diploma. Published work only. Submissions are nominated by National Sections of IBBY in good standing. The National Sections select the candidates. The Hans Christian Andersen Award, named after Denmark's famous storyteller, is the highest international recognition given to an author and an illustrator of children's books. The Author's Award has been given since 1956, the Illustrator's Award since 1966. Her Majesty Queen Margrethe of Denmark is the Patron of the Hans Christian Andersen Awards. The Hans Christian Andersen Jury judges the books submitted for medals according to literary and artistic criteria. The awards are presented at the biennial congresses of IBBY.

ARTS RECOGNITION AND TALENT SEARCH (ARTS)

National Foundation for Advancement in the Arts, 444 Brickell Ave., P-14, Miami FL 33131. (305)377-1140. Fax: (305)377-1149. E-mail: info@nfaa.org. Web site: www.ARTSaward.org. **Contact:** Christopher D. Schram. Open to students/high school seniors or 17- and 18-year-olds. Annual award. Estab. 1981. "Created to recognize and reward outstanding accomplishment in dance, music, jazz, voice, theater, photography, film and video, visual arts and/or writing. Arts Recognition and Talent Search (ARTS) is an innovative national program of the National Foundation for Advancement in the Arts (NFAA). Established in 1981, ARTS touches the lives of gifted young people across the country, providing financial support, scholarships and goal-oriented artistic, educational and career opportunities. Each year, from a pool of more than 8,000 applicants, an average of 800 ARTS winners are chosen for NFAA support by panels of distinguished artists and educators. Deadline for entries: June 1 and October 1. Entry fee is $30/40. Fee waivers available based on need. Awards $100-10,000—unrestricted cash grants. Judging by a panel of authors and educators recognized in the field. Rights to submitted/winning material: NFAA/ARTS retains the right to duplicate work in an anthology or in Foundation literature unless otherwise specified by the artist. Requirements for entrants: Artists must be high school seniors or, if not enrolled in high school, must be 17 or 18 years old. Applicants must be U.S. citizens or residents, unless applying in jazz. Works will be published in an anthology distributed during ARTS Week, the final adjudication phase which takes place in Miami. NFAA will invite 2% of artists to participate in "ARTS Week 2005," in January in Miami-Dade County, Florida. ARTS Week is a once-in-a-lifetime experience consisting of performances, master classes, workshops, readings, exhibits, and enrichment activities with renowned artists and arts educators. All expenses are paid by NFAA, including airfare, hotel, meals and ground transportation.

THE ASPCA HENRY BERGH CHILDREN'S BOOK AWARD

The American Society For the Prevention of Cruelty to Animals, 424 E. 92nd St., New York NY 10128-6804. (212)876-7700, ext. 4409. Fax: (212)860-3435. E-mail: education@aspca.org. Web site: www.aspca.org/booka ward. **Award Manager:** Miriam Ramos, assistant director, National Education Programs. Competition open to authors, illustrators, and publishers. Annual award. Estab. 2000. Purpose of contest: To honor outstanding children's literature that fosters empathy and compassion for all living things. Awards presented to authors. Previously published submissions only. Submissions made by author or author's agent. Must be published between January 2006-December 2006. Deadline for entries: October 31, 2006. Awards foil seals, plaque, certificate. Judging by professionals in animal welfare and children's literature. Requirements for entrants: Open to children's literature about animals and/or the environment published in 2006. Includes fiction, nonfiction and poetry in 5 categories: Companion Animals, Ecology and Environment, Humane Heroes, Illustration, and Young Adult.

ⓝ ⬚ ASTED/GRAND PRIX DE LITTERATURE JEUNESSE DU QUEBEC-ALVINE-BELISLE

Association pour l'avancement des sciences et des techniques de la documentation, 3414 Avenue du Parc, Bureau 202, Montreal QC H2X 2H5 Canada. (514)281-5012. Fax: (514)281-8219. E-mail: info@asted.org. Web site: www.asted.org. **Contact:** Magdalena Michalowska, president. "Prize granted for the best work in youth literature edited in French in the Quebec Province. Authors and editors can participate in the contest." Offered annually for books published during the preceding year. **Deadline: June 1.** Prize: $1,000.

⬚ ATLANTIC WRITING COMPETITION

Writer's Federation of Nova Scotia, 1113 Marginal Rd., Halifax NS B3H 4P7 Canada. (902)423-8116. Fax: (902)422-0881. E-mail: talk@writers.ns.ca. Web site: www.writers.ns.ca/competitions.html. Annual contest. Purpose is to encourage emerging writers in Atlantic Canada to explore their talents by sending unpublished work to any of five categories: novel, short story, poetry, writing for younger children, writing for juvenile/ young adult or essay/magazine article. Unpublished submissions only. Only open to residents of Atlantic Canada who are unpublished in category they enter. Visit Web site for more information.

BAKER'S PLAYS HIGH SCHOOL PLAYWRITING CONTEST

Baker's Plays, P.O. Box 6992222, Quincy MA 02269-9222. Fax: (617)745-9891. Web site: www.bakersplays.com. **Contest Director:** Deirdre Shaw. **Open to any high school student.** Annual contest. Estab. 1990. Purpose of the contest: to encourage playwrights at the high school level and to ensure the future of American theater. Unpublished submissions only. Postmark deadline: January 31. Notification: May. SASE for contest rules and entry forms. No entry fee. Awards $500 to the first place playwright with publication by Baker's Plays; $250 to the second place playwright with an honorable mention; and $100 to the third place playwright with an honorable mention in the series. Judged anonymously. Plays must be accompanied by the signature of a sponsoring high school drama or English teacher, and it is recommended that the play receive a production or a public reading prior to the submission. "To ensure return of manuscripts, please include SASE, otherwise the script paper will be recycled." Teachers must not submit student's work. The winning work will be listed in the Baker's Plays Catalogue, which is distributed to 50,000 prospective producing organizations.

JOHN AND PATRICIA BEATTY AWARD

California Library Association, 717 20th Street, Suite 200, Sacramento CA 95814. (916)447-8541. Fax: (916)447-8394. E-mail: info@cla-net.org. Web site: www.cla-net.org. **Executive Director:** Susan Negreen. Annual award. Estab. 1987. Purpose of award: "The purpose of the John and Patricia Beatty Award is to encourage the writing of quality children's books highlighting California, its culture, heritage and/or future." Previously published submissions only. Submissions made by the author, author's agent or review copies sent by publisher. The award is given to the author of a children's book published the preceding year. Deadline for entries: Submissions may be made January-December. Contact CLA Executive Director who will liaison with Beatty Award Committee. Awards cash prize of $500 and an engraved plaque. Judging by a 5-member selection committee appointed by the president of the California Library Association. Requirements for entrants: "Any children's or young adult book set in California and published in the U.S. during the calendar year preceding the presentation of the award is eligible for consideration. This includes works of fiction as well as nonfiction for children and young people of all ages. Reprints and compilations are not eligible. The California setting must be depicted authentically and must serve as an integral focus for the book." Winning selection is announced through press release during National Library Week in April. Author is presented with award at annual California Library Association Conference in November.

[N] [symbol] THE GEOFFREY BILSON AWARD FOR HISTORICAL FICTION FOR YOUNG PEOPLE

The Canadian Children's Book Centre, 40 Orchard View Blvd., Suite 101, Toronto ON M4R 1B9 Canada. (416)975-0010. Fax: (416)975-8970. E-mail: brenda@bookcentre.ca. Web site: www.bookcentre.ca. **Contact:** Brenda Halliday, librarian. Created in Geoffrey Bilson's memory in 1988. Offered annually for a previously published "outstanding work of historical fiction for young people by a Canadian author." Open to Canadian citizens and residents of Canada for at least 2 years. Deadline: January 15. Prize: $1,000. Judged by a jury selected by the Canadian Children's Book Centre.

THE IRMA S. AND JAMES H. BLACK BOOK AWARD

Bank Street College of Education, New York NY 10025-1898. (212)875-4450. Fax: (212)875-4558. E-mail: lindag @bnkst.edu. Web site: http://streetcat.bnkst.edu/html/isb.html. **Contact:** Linda Greengrass. Annual award. Estab. 1972. Purpose of award: "The award is given each spring for a book for young children, published in the previous year, for excellence of both text and illustrations." Entries must have been published during the previous calendar year (between January '06 and December '06 for 2007 award). Deadline for entries: mid-December. "Publishers submit books to us by sending them here to me at the Bank Street Library. Authors may ask their publishers to submit their books. Out of these, three to five books are chosen by a committee of older children and children's literature professionals. These books are then presented to children in selected second, third and fourth grade classes here and at a number of other cooperating schools. These children are the final judges who pick the actual award winner. A scroll (one each for the author and illustrator, if they're different) with the recipient's name and a gold seal designed by Maurice Sendak are awarded in May."

WALDO M. AND GRACE C. BONDERMAN/IUPUI NATIONAL YOUTH THEATRE PLAYWRITING COMPETITION AND DEVELOPMENT WORKSHOP AND SYMPOSIUM

Bonderman Youth Theatre Playwriting Workshop, 1114 Red Oak Drive, Avon, IN 46123. E-mail: bonderma@iupui.edu. Web site: www.liberalarts.iupui.edu/bonderman. **Director:** Dorothy Webb. **Open to students.** Chairperson, Canadian Association of Children's Librarians. Annual award. Estab. 1947. "The main purpose of the award is to encourage writing and publishing in Canada of good books for children up to and including age 14. If, in any year, no book is deemed to be of award calibe r, the award shall not be given that year. To merit consideration, the book must have been published in Canada and its author must be a Canadian citizen or a permanent resident of Canada." Previously published submissions only; must be published between January 1 and December 1 of the previous year. Deadline for entries: January 1. SASE for award rules. Entries not returned. No entry fee. Judging by committee of members of the Canadian Association of Children's Librarians. Requirements for entrants: Contest open only to Canadian authors or residents of Canada.

[N] [symbol] BOOKTRUST EARLY YEARS AWARDS

Booktrust, Book House, 45 E. Hill, Wandsworth, London SW18 2QZ United Kingdom. Fax: (00 44)20 8516 2978. E-mail: tarryn@booktrust.org.uk. Web site: www.booktrusted.com. **Contact:** Tarryn McKay. The Booktrust Early Years Awards were initially established in 1999 and are awarded annually. The awards are given to the best books, published between September 1 and the following August 31, in the opinion of the judges in each category. The categories are: Baby Book Award, Pre-School Award, and Best New Illustrator Award. Authors and illustrators must be of British nationality, or other nationals who have been residents in the British Isles for at least 10 years. Books can be any format. Deadline: June. Prize: £2,000 and a crystal award to each winner. In addition, the publisher receives a crystal award naming them as "The Booktrust Early Years Awards Publisher of the Year."

THE BOSTON GLOBE-HORN BOOK AWARDS

The Boston Globe & The Horn Book, Inc., The Horn Book, 56 Roland St., Suite 200, Boston MA 02129. (617)628-0225. Fax: (617)628-0882. E-mail: info@hbook.com. Web site: www.hbook.com/awards/bghb/submissions_bghb.asp. Annual award. Estab. 1967. Purpose of award: To reward literary excellence in children's and young adult books. Awards are for picture books, nonfiction, fiction and poetry. Up to two honor books may be chosen for each category. Books must be published between June 1, 2005 and May 31, 2006. Deadline for entries: May 2005. Textbks, e-books, and audiobooks will not be considered, nor will manuscripts. Books should be submitted by publishers, although the judges reserve the right to honor any eligible book. Award winners receive $500 and silver engraved bowl, honor book winners receive a silver engraved plate. Judging by 3 judges involved in children's book field. *The Horn Book Magazine* publishes speeches given at awards ceremonies. The book must have been published in the U.S.

ANN ARLYS BOWLER POETRY CONTEST

Bowler Poetry Contest, Weekly Reader Corporation, 200 First Stamford Place, P.O. Box 120023 Stamford, CT 06912-0023. Web site: http://www.weeklyreader.com/teens/read/bowlers_poetry_contest.asp. **Open to stu-**

Resources

dents. Annual contest. Estab. 1988. Purpose of the contest: to reward young-adult poets (grades 6-12). Unpublished submissions only. Submissions made by the author or nominated by a person or group of people. Entry form must include signature of teacher, parent or guardian, and student verifying originality. Maximum number of submissions per student: 3 poems. Deadline for entries: mid-January. SASE for contest rules and entry forms. No entry fee. Awards 6 winners $100 each, medal of honor and publication in *Read.* Semifinalists receive $50 each. Judging by *Read* and *Weekly Reader* editors and teachers. Requirements for entrants: the material must be original. Winning entries will be published in an issue of *Read.*

ANN CONNOR BRIMER AWARD

Nova Scotia Library Association, P.O. Box 36036, Halifax NS B3J 3S9 Canada. (902)490-5875. Fax: (902)490-5893. Web site: http://nsla.ns.ca/aboutnsla/brimeraward.html. **Award Director:** Heather MacKenzie. Annual award. Estab. 1991. Purpose of the contest: to recognize excellence in writing. Given to an author of a children's book who resides in Atlantic Canada. Previously published submissions only. Submissions made by the author's agent or nominated by a person or group of people. Must be published in previous year. Deadline for entries: October 15. SASE for contest rules and entry forms. No entry fee. Awards $1,000 and framed certificate. Judging by a selection committee. Requirements for entrants: Book must be intended for use up to age 15; in print and readily available; fiction or nonfiction except textbooks.

BUCKEYE CHILDREN'S BOOK AWARD

Ada Kent % Ohio School for the Deaf, 500 Morse Rd., Columbus OH 43214. (614)728-1414. E-mail: agkent@columbus.rr.com. Web site: www.bcbookaward.info. **President:** Ada G. Kent. Correspondence should be sent to Ada Kent at the above address. **Open to students.** Award offered every 2 years. Estab. 1981. Purpose of the award: "The Buckeye Children's Book Award Program was designed to encourage children to read literature critically, to promote teacher and librarian involvement in children's literature programs, and to commend authors of such literature, as well as to promote the use of libraries. Awards are presented in the following three categories: grades K-2, grades 3-5, grades 6-8 and grades 9-12 (Teen Buckeye)." Previously published submissions only. Deadline for entries: February 1. "The nominees are submitted by the students by this date during the even year and the votes are submitted by this date during the odd year. This award is nominated and voted upon by children in Ohio. It is based upon criteria established in our bylaws. The winning authors are awarded a special plaque honoring them at a banquet given by one of the sponsoring organizations. The BCBA Board oversees the tallying of the votes and announces the winners in March of the voting year at www.bcbookaward.info and in a number of national journals. The book must have been written by an author, a citizen of the United States and originally copyrighted in the U.S. within the last three years preceding the nomination year. The award-winning books are displayed in a historical display housed at the Reinberger Children's Library at Kent State Library School."

BYLINE MAGAZINE CONTESTS

P.O. Box 5240, Edmond OK 73083-5240. E-mail: mpreston@bylinemag.com. Web site: www.bylinemag.com. **Contest Director:** Marcia Preston. Purpose of contest: *ByLine* runs 4 contests a month on many topics to encourage and motivate writers. Past topics include first chapter of a novel, children's fiction, children's poem, nonfiction for children, personal essay, general short stories, valentine or love poem, etc. Send SASE for contest flier with topic list and rules, or see Web site. Unpublished submissions only. Submissions made by the author. "We do not publish the contests' winning entries, just the names of the winners." Entry fee is $3-5. Awards cash prizes for first, second and third place. Amounts vary. Judging by qualified writers or editors. List of winners will appear in magazine.

BYLINE MAGAZINE STUDENT PAGE

P.O. Box 5240, Edmond OK 73083-5240. (405)348-5591. E-mail: mpreston@bylinemag.com. Web site: www.bylinemag.com. **Contest Director:** Marcia Preston, publisher. **Open to students.** Estab. 1981. "We offer writing contests for students in grades 1-12 on a monthly basis, September through May, with cash prizes and publication of top entries." Previously unpublished submissions only. "This is not a market for illustration." Deadline for entries varies. "Entry fee usually $1." Awards cash and publication. Judging by qualified editors and writers. "We publish top entries in student contests. Winners' list published in magazine dated 2 months past deadline." Send SASE for details.

RANDOLPH CALDECOTT MEDAL

Association for Library Service to Children, Division of the American Library Association, 50 E. Huron, Chicago IL 60611. (312)280-2163. E-mail: alsc@ala.org. Web site: www.ala.org. **Executive Director:** Malore I. Brown. Annual award. Estab. 1938. Purpose of the award: to honor the artist of the most outstanding picture book for children published in the U.S. (Illustrator must be U.S. citizen or resident.) Must be published year preceding award. Deadline for entries: December 31. SASE for award rules. Entries not returned. No entry fee. "Medal given at ALA Annual Conference during the Newbery/Caldecott Banquet."

CALIFORNIA YOUNG PLAYWRIGHTS CONTEST

Playwrights Project, 450 B St., Suite 1020, San Diego CA 92101. (619)239-8222. Fax: (619)239-8225. E-mail: write@playwrightsproject.com. Web site: www.playwrightsproject.com. **Director:** Deborah Salzer. **Open to Californians under age 19.** Annual contest. Estab. 1985. "Our organization and the contest is designed to nurture promising young writers. We hope to develop playwrights and audiences for live theater. We also teach playwriting." Submissions required to be unpublished and not produced professionally. Submissions made by the author. Deadline for entries: April 1. SASE for contest rules and entry form. No entry fee. Award is professional productions of 3-5 short plays each year, participation of the writers in the entire production process, with a royalty awarded. Judging by professionals in the theater community, a committee of 5-7; changes somewhat each year. Works performed in San Diego at the Cassius Carter Centre Stage of the Old Globe. Writers submitting scripts of 10 or more pages receive a detailed script evaluation letter upon request.

CALLIOPE FICTION CONTEST

Writers' Specialized Interest Group (SIG) of American Mensa, Ltd., P.O. Box 466, Moraga CA 94556-0466. E-mail: cynthia@theriver.com. Web site: www.us.mensa.org. **Fiction Editor:** Sandy Raschke. **Open to students.** Annual contest. Estab. 1991. Purpose of contest: "To promote good writing and opportunities for getting published. To give our member/subscribers and others an entertaining and fun exercise in writing." Unpublished submissions only (all genres, no violence, profanity or extreme horror). Submissions made by author. Deadline for entries: changes annually but usually around September 15. Entry fee is $2 for nonsubscribers; subscribers get first entry fee. Awards small amount of cash (up to $75 for 1st place, to $10 for 3rd), certificates, full or mini-subscriptions to *Calliope* and various premiums and books, depending on donations. All winners are published in subsequent issues of *Calliope*. Judging by fiction editor, with concurrence of other editors, if needed. Requirements for entrants: winners must retain sufficient rights to have their stories published in the January/February issue, or their entries will be disqualified; one-time rights. Open to all writers. No special considerations—other than following the guidelines. Contest theme, due dates and sometimes entry fees change annually. Always send SASE for complete rules; available after April 15 each year. Sample copies with prior winners are available for $3.

◆ CANADA COUNCIL GOVERNOR GENERAL'S LITERARY AWARDS

350 Albert St., Ottawa ON K1P 5V8 Canada. (613)566-4410, ext. 4582. Fax: (613)566-4410. E-mail: joanne.laroc que-poirier@canadacouncil.ca. **Program Officer, Writing and Publishing Section:** TBA. Annual award. Estab. 1937. Purpose of award: given to the best English-language and the best French-language work in each of the seven categories of Fiction, Literary Nonfiction, Poetry, Drama, Children's Literature (text), Children's Literature (illustration) and Translation. Books must be first-edition trade books that have been written, translated or illustrated by Canadian citizens or permanent residents of Canada. In the case of Translation, the original work written in English or French, must also be a Canadian-authored title. English titles must be published between September 1, 2005 and September 30, 2006. Books must be submitted by publishers. Books must reach the Canada Council for the Arts no later than August 7, 2006. The deadlines are final; no bound proofs or books that miss the applicable deadlines will be given to the peer assessment committees. The awards ceremony is scheduled mid-November. Amount of award: $15,000 to winning authors; $1,000 to nonwinning finalists.

◆ SANDRA CARON YOUNG ADULT POETRY PRIZE

National League of American Pen Women, Nob Hill, San Francisco Branch, 1544 Sweetwood Dr., Colma CA 94015-2029. E-mail: pennobhill@aol.com. Web site: www.soulmakingcontest.us. **Contact:** Eileen Malone. **Open to students.** Three poems/entry; one poem/page; one-page poems only from poets in grades 9-12. Annually. Deadline:November 30. Guidelines for SASE. Charges $5/entry (make checks payable to NLAPW, Nob Hill Branch). Prize: 1st Place: $100; 2nd Place: $50; 3rd Place: $25. Open to any writer in grade 9-12.

◆ CHILDREN'S AFRICANA BOOK AWARD

African Studies Association, % Rutgers University, 132 George St., New Brunswick NJ 08901. (732)932-8173. Fax: (732)932-3394. Web site: www.africanstudies.org. Administered by Africa Access, 2204 Quinten Rd., Silver Springs MD 20910. (301)562-5239. Fax: (301)562-5244. E-mail: africaaccess@aol.com. Web site: www.africaacc essreview.org. **Director:** Brenda Randolph. Annually. Estab. 1991. Purpose of contest: "The Children's Africana Book Awards are presented annually to the authors and illustrators of the best children's books on Africa published or republished in the U.S. The awards were created by the African Studies Association (ASA) to encourage the publication and use of accurate, balanced children's materials about Africa. The awards are presented in 2 categories: Young Children and Older Readers. Since 1991, 44 books have been recognized."

Submissions must be previously published. Entries must have been published in the calendar year previous to the award. No entry fee. Awards plaque, announcement at Library of Congress, reviews published at H-AFRTEACH and Africa Access Review, and in *Sankofa: Journal of African Children's & Young Adult Literature*. Judging by Committee of African Studies and children's literature scholars. "Work submitted for awards must be suitable for children ages 4-18; a significant portion of books' content must be about Africa; must by copyrighted in the calendar year prior to award year; must be published or republished in the US."

CHILDREN'S WRITER WRITING CONTESTS

93 Long Ridge Rd., West Redding CT 06896-1124. (203)792-8600. Fax: (203)792-8406. Web site: www.childrens writer.com. Contest offered twice per year by *Children's Writer*, the monthly newsletter of writing and publishing trends. Purpose of the award: To promote higher quality children's literature. "Each contest has its own theme. Any original unpublished piece, not accepted by any publisher at the time of submission, is eligible." Submissions made by the author. Deadline for entries: Last weekday in February and October. "We charge a $10 entry fee for nonsubscribers only, which is applicable against a subscription to *Children's Writer* Awards: 1st place—$250 or $500, a certificate and publication in *Children's Writer*; 2nd place—$100 or $250, and certificate; 3rd-5th places—$50 or $100 and certificates. To obtain the rules and theme for the current contest go to the Web site: and click on "Writing Contests," or send a SASE to *Children's Writer* at the above address. Put "Contest Request" in the lower left of your envelope. Judging by a panel of 4 selected from the staff of the Institute of Children's Literature. "We acquire First North American Serial Rights (to print the winner in *Childre n's Writer*), after which all rights revert to author." Open to any writer. Entries are judged on age targeting, originality, quality of writing and, for nonfiction, how well the information is conveyed and accuracy. "Submit clear photocopies only, not originals; submission will *not* be returned. Manuscripts should be typed double-spaced. No pieces containing violence or derogatory, racist or sexist language or situations will be accepted, at the sole discretion of the judges."

CHILDREN'S WRITERS FICTION CONTEST

Stepping Stones, P.O. Box 601721, Miami Beach FL 33160. (305)944-6491. E-mail: verwil@alumni.pace.edu. **Director:** V.R. Williams. Annual contest. Estab. 1993. Purpose of contest: to promote writing for children by giving children's writers an opportunity to submit work in competition. Unpublished submissions only. Submissions made by the author. Deadline for entries: August 31. SASE for contest rules and entry forms. Entry fee is $10. Awards cash prize, certificate; certificates for Honorable Mention. Judging by Williams, Walters & Associates. First rights to winning material acquired or purchased. Requirements for entrants: Work must be suitable for children and no longer than 1,500 words. Send SASE for list of winners. "Stories should have believable characters. Work submitted on colored paper, in book format, illustrated, or with photograph attached is not acceptable."

COLORADO BOOK AWARDS

1490 Lafayette St., Suite 101, Denver CO 80218. (303)894-7951, ext 19. Fax: (303)864-9361. E-Mail: ccftb@ceh.-org. Web site: www.coloradocenterforthebook.org. Annual award. Estab. 1993. Previously published submissions only. Submissions are made by the author, author's agent, nominated by a person or group of people. Requires Colorado residency by authors. Deadline for entries: January 15. SASE for contest rules and entry forms. Entry fee is $45. Awards $250 and plaque. Judging by a panel of literary agents, booksellers and librarians. "Please note, we *also* have periodic competitions for illustrators to design a poster and associated graphics for our other book programs. The date varies. Inquiries are welcomed." See Web site for complete contest guidelines and entry form.

THE COMMONWEALTH CLUB'S BOOK AWARDS CONTEST

The Commonwealth Club of California, 595 Market St., San Francisco CA 94105. (415)597-4846. Fax: (415)597-6729. E-mail: blane@commonwealthclub.org. Web site: www.commonwealthclub.org/bookawards. **Contact:** Barbara Lane. Chief Executive Officer: Gloria Duffy. Annual contest. Estab. 1932. Purpose of contest: the encouragement and production of literature in California. Juvenile categories included. Previously published submissions; must be published from January 1 to December 31, previous to contest year. Deadline for entries: January 31. SASE for contest rules and entry forms. No entry fee. Awards gold and silver medals. Judging by the Book Awards Jury. The contest is only open to California writers/illustrators (must have been resident of California when ms was accepted for publication). "The award winners will be honored at the Annual Book Awards Program." Winning entries are displayed at awards program and advertised in newsletter.

CRICKET LEAGUE

Cricket magazine, P.O. Box 300, 315 Fifth St., Peru IL 61354. (815)224-5803. Web site: www.cricketmag.com/cricketleague.htm. Address entries to: Cricket League. **Open to students.** Monthly contest. Estab. 1973. "The purpose of Cricket League contests is to encourage creativity and give young people an opportunity to express themselves in writing, drawing, painting or photography. There is a contest each month. Possible categories include story, poetry, or art. Each contest relates to a *specific theme* described on each *Cricket* issue's Cricket League page. Signature verifying originality, age and address of entrant and permission to publish required. Entries which do not relate to the current month's theme cannot be considered." Unpublished submissions only. Deadline for entries: the 25th of each month. Cricket League rules, contest theme, and submission deadline information can be found in the current issue of *Cricket* and via Web site. "We prefer that children who enter the contests subscribe to the magazine or that they read *Cricket* in their school or library." No entry fee. Awards certificate suitable for framing and children's books or art/writing supplies. Judging by *Cricket* editors. Obtains right to print prizewinning entries in magazine. Refer to contest rules in current *Cricket* issue. Winning entries are published on the Cricket League pages in the *Cricket* magazine 3 months subsequent to the issue in which the contest was announced. Current theme, rules, and prizewinning entries also posted on the Web site.

DELACORTE DELL YEARLING CONTEST FOR A FIRST MIDDLE-GRADE NOVEL

Delacorte Press, Random House, Inc., 1745 Broadway, 9th Floor, New York NY 10019. Estab. 1992. Web site: www.randomhouse.com/kids/writingcontests/#middlegrade. Annual award. Purpose of the award: to encourage the writing of fiction for children ages 9-12, either contemporary or historical; to encourage unpublished writers in the field of middle grade fiction. Unpublished submissions only. No simultaneous submissions. Length: between 96-160 pages. Submissions made by author or author's agent. Entries should be postmarked between April 1 and June 30. SASE for award rules. No entry fee. Awards a $1,500 cash prize plus a hardcover and paperback book contract with a $7,500 advance against a royalties to be negotiated. Judging by Delacorte Press Books for Young Readers editorial staff. Open to U.S. and Canadian writers who have not previously published a novel for middle-grade readers (ages 9-12).

DELACORTE PRESS CONTEST FOR A FIRST YOUNG ADULT NOVEL

Delacorte Press, Books for Young Readers Department, 1745 Broadway, 9th Floor, New York NY 10019. Web site: www.randomhouse.com/kids/writingcontests/#middlegrade. Annual award. Estab. 1982. Purpose of award: to encourage the writing of contemporary young adult fiction (for readers ages 12-18). Previously unpublished submissions only. Manuscripts sent to Delacorte Press may not be submitted to other publishers while under consideration for the prize. "Entries must be submitted between October 1 and New Year's Day. The real deadline is a December 31 postmark. Early entries are appreciated." Length: between 100-224 pages. SASE for award rules. No entry fee. Awards a $1,500 cash prize and a $7,500 advance against royalties for world rights on a hardcover and paperback book contract. Works published in an upcoming Delacorte Press, an imprint of Random House, Inc., Books for Young Readers list. Judged by the editors of the Books for Young Readers Department of Delacorte Press. Requirements for entrants: The writer must be American or Canadian and must *not* have previously published a young adult novel but may have published anything else. Foreign-language mss and translations and mss submitted to a previous Delacorte Press are not eligible. Send SASE for new guidelines. Guidelines are also available on our Web site.

MARGARET A. EDWARDS AWARD

50 East Huron St., Chicago IL 60611-2795. (312)280-4390 or (800)545-2433. Fax: (312)664-7459. E-mail: yalsa@ ala.org. Web site: http://www.ala.org/ala/yalsa/booklistsawards/margaretedwards/margaretedwards.htm. Annual award administered by the Young Adult Library Services Association (YALSA) of the American Library Association (ALA) and sponsored by *School Library Journal* magazine. Purpose of award: "ALA's Young Adult Library Services Association (YALSA), on behalf of librarians who work with young adults in all types of libraries, will give recognition to those authors whose book or books have provided young adults with a window through which they can view their world and which will help them to grow and to understand themselves and their role in relationships, society and the world." Previously published submissions only. Submissions are nominated by young adult librarians and teenagers. Must be published five years before date of award. SASE for award rules and entry forms. No entry fee. Judging by members of the Young Adult Library Services Association. Deadline for entry: December 1. "The award will be given annually to an author whose book or books, over a period of time, have been accepted by young adults as an authentic voice that continues to illuminate their experiences and emotions, giving insight into their lives. The book or books should enable them to understand themselves, the world in which they live, and their relationship with others and with society. The book or books must be in print at the time of the nomination."

DOROTHY CANFIELD FISHER CHILDREN'S BOOK AWARD

Vermont Department of Libraries, Northeast Regional Library, 23 Tilton Rd., St. Johnsbury VT 05819. (802)828-6954. Fax: (802)828-2199. E-mail: grace.greene@dol.state.vt.us. Web site: www.dcfaward.org. **Chair:** Steve Madden. Annual award. Estab. 1957. Purpose of the award: to encourage Vermont children to become enthusias-

Resources

tic and discriminating readers by providing them with books of good quality by living American authors published in the current year. Deadline for entries: December of year book was published. SASE for award rules and entry forms or e-mail. No entry fee. Awards a scroll presented to the winning author at an award ceremony. Judging is by the children grades 4-8. They vote for their favorite book. Requirements for entrants: "Titles must be original work, published in the United States, and be appropriate to children in grades 4 through 8. The book must be copyrighted in the current year. It must be written by an American author living in the U.S."

⟦N⟧ ⟦⟧ THE NORMA FLECK AWARD FOR CANADIAN CHILDREN'S NONFICTION

The Canadian Children's Book Centre, 40 Orchard View Blvd., Suite 101, Toronto ON M4R 1B9 Canada. (416)975-0010. Fax: (416)975-8970. E-mail: info@bookcentre.ca. Web site: www.bookcentre.ca. **Contact:** Shannon Howe, program coordinator. The Norma Fleck Award was established by the Fleck Family Foundation in May 1999 to honor the life of Norma Marie Fleck, and to recognize exceptional Canadian nonfiction books for young people. Publishers are welcome to nominate books using the online form. Offered annually for books published between May 1, 2005, and April 30, 2006. Open to Canadian citizens or landed immigrants. The jury will always include at least 3 of the following: a teacher, a librarian, a bookseller, and a reviewer. A juror will have a deep understanding of, and some involvement with, Canadian children's books. The Canadian Children's Book Centre will select the jury members. **Deadline: March 31 (annually).** Prize: $10,000 goes to the author (unless 40% or more of the text area is composed of original illustrations, in which case the award will be divided equally between the author and the artist).

FLICKER TALE CHILDREN'S BOOK AWARD

Flicker Tale Award Committee, North Dakota Library Association, Mandan Public Library, 609 West Main St., Mandan ND 58554. Web site: www.ndla.info/ftaward.htm. **Contact:** Kelly Loftis. Estab. 1979. Purpose of award: to give children across the state of North Dakota a chance to vote for their book of choice from a nominated list of 20: 4 in the picture book category; 4 in the intermediate category; 4 in the juvenile category (for more advanced readers); 4 in the upper grage level non-fiction category. Also, to promote awareness of quality literature for children. Previously published submissions only. Submissions nominated by librarians and teachers across the state of North Dakota. Awards a plaque from North Dakota Library Association and banquet dinner. Judging by children in North Dakota. Entry deadline in June.

FLORIDA STATE WRITING COMPETITION

Florida Freelance Writers Association, P.O. Box A, North Stratford NH 03590. (603)922-8338. Fax: (603)922-8339. E-mail: contest@writers-editors.com. Web site: www.writers-editors.com. **Executive Director:** Dana K. Cassell. Annual contest. Estab. 1984. Categories include children's literature (length appropriate to age category). Entry fee is $5 (members), $10 (nonmembers) or $10-20 for entries longer than 3,000 words. Awards $100 first prize, $75 second prize, $50 third prize, certificates for honorable mentions. Judging by teachers, editors and published authors. Judging criteria: interest and readability within age group, writing style and mechanics, originality, salability. Deadline: March 15. For copy of official entry form, send #10 SASE or visit Web site. List of winners on Web site.

DON FREEMAN MEMORIAL GRANT-IN-AID

Society of Children's Book Writers and Illustrators, 8271 Beverly Blvd., Los Angeles CA 90048. E-mail: scbwi@scbwi.org. Web site: www.scbwi.org. Estab. 1974. Purpose of award: to "enable picture book artists to further their understanding, training and work in the picture book genre." Applications and prepared materials are available in October and must be postmarked between February 1 and March 1. Grant awarded and announced in August. SASE for award rules and entry forms. SASE for return of entries. No entry fee. Annually awards one grant of $1,500 and one runner-up grant of $500. "The grant-in-aid is available to both full and associate members of the SCBWI who, as artists, seriously intend to make picture books their chief contribution to the field of children's literature."

⟦N⟧ FRIENDS OF THE AUSTIN PUBLIC LIBRARY AWARD FOR BEST CHILDREN'S AND BEST YOUNG ADULT'S BOOK

Web site: www.wtamu.edu/til/awards.htm. Offered annually for work published January 1-December 31 of previous year to recognize the best book for children and young people. Writer must have been born in Texas or have lived in the state for at least 2 consecutive years at one time, or the subject matter must be associated with the state. See Web site for information on eligibility, deadlines, and the judges names and addresses to whom the books should be sent. Prize: $500 for each award winner.

⟦N⟧ THEODOR SEUSS GEISEL AWARD

Association for Library Service to Children, Division of the American Library Association, 50 E. Huron, Chicago

IL 60611. (312)280-2163. E-mail: alsc@ala.org. Web site: www.ala.org. The Theodor Seuss Geisel Award, established in 2004, is given annually beginning in 2006 to the author(s) and illustrator(s) of the most distinguished contribution to the body of American children's literature known as beginning reader books published in the United States during the preceding year. The award is to recognize the author(s) and illustrator(s) of a beginning reader book who demonstrate great creativity and imagination in his/her/their literary and artistic achievements to engage children in reading. The award is named for the world-renowned children's author, Theodor Geisel. "A person's a person no matter how small," Theodor Geisel, a.k.a. Dr. Seuss, would say. "Children want the same things we want: to laugh, to be challenged, to be entertained and delighted." Brilliant, playful and always respectful of children, Dr. Seuss charmed his way into the consciousness of four generations of youngsters and parents. In the process, he helped them to read.

AMELIA FRANCES HOWARD GIBBON AWARD FOR ILLUSTRATION

Canadian Library Association, 328 Frank St., Ottawa ON K2P 0X8 Canada. (613)232-9625. Web site: www.cla. ca. **Contact:** Chairperson, Canadian Association of Children's Librarians. Annual award. Estab. 1971. Purpose of the award: "to honor excellence in the illustration of children's book(s) in Canada. To merit consideration the book must have been published in Canada and its illustrator must be a Canadian citizen or a permanent resident of Canada." Previously published submissions only; must be published between January 1 and December 31 of the previous year. Deadline for entries: December 31. SASE for award rules. Entries not returned. No entry fee. Judging by selection committee of members of Canadian Association of Children's Librarians. Requirements for entrants: illustrator must be Canadian or Canadian resident.

GOLD MEDALLION BOOK AWARDS

Evangelical Christian Publishers Association, 4816 South Ash, Suite 101, Tempe AZ 85282. (480)966-3998. Fax: (480)966-1944. E-mail: mkuyper@ecpa.org. Web site: www.ecpa.org. **President:** Mark W. Kuyper. Annual award. Estab. 1978. Categories include Childrens and Youth. "All entries must be evangelical in nature and cannot be contrary to ECPA's Statement of Faith (stated in official rules)." Deadlines for entries: January (see Web site for specific date). Guidelines available on Web site in November. SASE for award rules and entry form. "The work must be submitted by an ECPA member." Entry fee is $300/title for nonmembers. Awards a Gold Medallion plaque.

GOLDEN KITE AWARDS

Society of Children's Book Writers and Illustrators, 8271 Beverly Blvd., Los Angeles CA 90048. (323)782-1010. E-mail: scbwi@scbwi.org. Web site: www.scbwi.org. **Contact:** SCBWI Golden Kite Coordinator. Annual award. Estab. 1973. "The works chosen will be those that the judges feel exhibit excellence in writing, and in the case of the picture-illustrated books—in illustration, and genuinely appeal to the interests and concerns of children. For the fiction and nonfiction awards, original works and single-author collections of stories or poems of which at least half are new and never before published in book form are eligible—anthologies and translations are not. For the picture-illustration awards, the art or photographs must be original works (the texts—which may be fiction or nonfiction—may be original, public domain or previously published). Deadline for entries: December 15. SASE for award rules. No entry fee. Awards statuettes and plaques. The panel of judges will consist of professional authors, illustrators, editors or agents." Requirements for entrants: "must be a member of SCBWI and books must be published in that year." Winning books will be displayed at national conference in August. Books to be entered, as well as further inquiries, should be submitted to: The Society of Children's Book Writers and Illustrators, above address.

GOVERNOR GERERAL'S LITERARY AWARD FOR CHILDREN'S LITERATURE

Canada Council for the Arts, 350 Albert St., P.O. Box 1047, Ottawa ON K1P 5V8 Canada. (613)566-4414, ext. 5576. Fax: (613)566-4582. E-mail: caroline.lecours@canadacouncil.ca. Web site: www.canadacouncil.ca/prizes/ggla. Offered for work published September 1-September 30. Submissions in English must be published between September 1, 2005 and September 30, 2006; submissions in French between July 1, 2005 and June 30, 2006. Publishers submit titles for consideration. Deadline: March 15, June 1 and August 7, depending on the book's publication date. Prize: Each laureate receives $15,000; nonwinning finalists receive $1,000.

GUIDEPOSTS YOUNG WRITERS CONTEST

Guideposts, 16 E. 34th St., New York NY 10016. (212)251-8100. E-mail: ywcontest@guideposts.org. Web site: gp4teens.com. Offered annually for unpublished high school juniors and seniors. Stories "needn't be about a highly dramatic situation, but it should record an experience that affected you and deeply changed you. Remember, *Guideposts* stories are true, not fiction, and they show how faith in God has made a specific difference in a person's life. We accept submissions after announcement is placed in the October issue each year. If the manuscript is place, we require all rights to the story in that version." Open only to high school juniors or

Resources

seniors. Deadline: November 24. Prize: 1st Place: $10,000; 2nd Place: $8,000; 3rd Place: $6,000; 4th Place: $4,000; 5th Place: $3,000; 6th-10th Place: $1,000; 11th-20th Place: $250 gift certificate for college supplies.

THE MARILYN HALL AWARDS FOR YOUTH THEATRE

Beverly Hills Theatre Guild, P.O. Box 39729, Los Angeles CA 90039-0729. Web site: www.beverlyhillstheatreguild.org. **Contact:** Dick Dotterer. **Open to students.** Annual contest. Estab. 1998/99. Purpose of contest: "To encourage the creation and development of new plays for youth theatre." Unpublished submissions only. Authors must be U.S. citizens or legal residents and must sign entry form personally. Deadline for entries: between January 15 and last day of February each year (postmark accepted). Playwrights may submit up to two scripts. One nonprofessional production acceptable for eligibility. SASE for contest rules and entry forms. No entry fee. Awards: $500, 1st prize; $300, 2nd prize; $200, 3rd prize. Judging by theatre professionals cognizant of youth theatre and writing/producing.

HIGHLIGHTS FOR CHILDREN FICTION CONTEST

803 Church St., Honesdale PA 18431-1895. (570)253-1080. Fax: (570)251-7847. Web site: www.highlights.com. **Fiction Contest Editor:** Christine French Clark. Annual contest. Estab. 1980. Purpose of the contest: to stimulate interest in writing for children and reward and recognize excellence. Unpublished submissions only. Deadline for entries: February 28; entries accepted after January 1 only. SASE for contest rules and return of entries. No entry fee. Awards 3 prizes of $1,000 each in cash and a pewter bowl (or, at the winner's election, attendance at the Highlights Foundation Writers Workshop at Chautauqua) and a pewter bowl. Judging by a panel of *Highlights* editors and outside judges. Winning pieces are purchased for the cash prize of $1,000 and published in *Highlights*; other entries are considered for purchase at regular rates. Requirements for entrants: open to any writer 16 years of age of older. Winners announced in June. Length up to 800 words. Stories for beginning readers should not exceed 500 words. Stories should be consistent with *Highlights* editorial requirements. No violence, crime or derogatory humor. Send SASE or visit Web site for guidelines and current theme.

HRC SHOWCASE THEATRE

Hudson River Classics, Inc., P.O. Box 940, Hudson NY 12534. (518)828-0175. Fax: (518)828-1480. E-mail: jangrice2002@yahoo.com. **President:** Jan M. Grice. Annual contest. Estab. 1992. HRCs Showcase Theatre is a not-for-profit professional theater company dedicated to the advancement of performing in the Hudson River Valley area through reading of plays and providing opportunities for new playwrights. Unpublished submissions only. Submissions made by author and by the author's agent. Deadlines for entries: May 1st. SASE for contest rules and entry forms. Entry fee is $5. Awards $500 cash plus concert reading by professional actors. Judging by panel selected by Board of Directors. Requirements for entrants: Entrants must live in the northeastern U.S.

IMPRINT OF MIDLAND COMMUNITY THEATRE

Midland Community Theatre, 2000 W. Wadley, Midland TX 79705. (432)682-2544. Fax: (432)682-6136. E-mail: mclaren@mctmidland.org. Web site: www.mctmidland.org. **Co-Chairmen:** Harry Harrison and Alathea Blischke. Estab. 1989. Open to students. Annual contest. Purpose of conference: "The McLaren Memorial Comedy Play Writing Competition was established in 1989 to honor long-time MCT volunteer Mike McLaren who loved a good comedy, whether he was on stage or in the front row." Unpublished submissions only. Submissions made by author. Deadline for entries: January 31st (scripts are accepted from December 1st through January 31st each year). SASE for contest rules and entry forms. Entry fee is $10 per script. Awards $400 for full-length winner and $200 for one-act winner as well as staged readings for 3 finalists in each category. Judging by the audience present at the McLaren festival when the staged readings are performed. Rights to winning material acquired or purchased. 1st right of production or refusal is acquired by MCT. Requirements for entrants: "Yes, the contest is open to *any* playwright, but the play submitted must be unpublished and never produced in a for-profit setting. One previous production in a *nonprofit* theatre is acceptable. 'Readings' do not count as productions."

INSIGHT WRITING CONTEST

Insight Magazine, 55 W. Oak Ridge Dr., Hagerstown MD 21740-7390. Web site: www.insightmagazine.org. **Open to students.** Annual contest. Unpublished submissions only. Submissions made by author. Deadline for entries: June. SASE for contest rules and entry forms. Awards first prizes, $100-250; second prizes, $75-200; third prizes, $50-150. Winning entries will be published in *Insight*. Contest includes three catagories: Student Short Story, General Short Story and Student Poetry. You must be age 22 or under to enter the student catagories. Entries must include cover sheet form available with SASE or on Web site.

IRA CHILDREN'S BOOK AWARDS

International Reading Association, 800 Barksdale Rd., P.O. Box 8139, Newark DE 19714-8139. (302)731-1600.

Paula Yoo

'Winning was just the encouragement I needed to keep writing'

P aula Yoo is not an athlete, nor can she dive. "I'm not even a good swimmer!" she says. Yet, once she stumbled upon the story of Korean American Olympic champion diver Dr. Sammy Lee, she was drawn to it.

For several weeks after learning of Lee as she researched for a thesis, Yoo continued to delve into his life as his story brewed in her mind. "I learned about how Sammy Lee's Korean immigrant father wanted him to become a doctor. I was inspired by how Sammy fulfilled his father's dream as well as his own dream of becoming an Olympic champion," she says. She also found that there was little to nothing in the way of books about the Olympic hero—so Yoo decided to write one herself. Her picture book about Sammy Lee, *Sixteen Years in Sixteen Seconds*, went on to win the Lee & Low New Voices Awards and was published by Lee & Low in 2005 with illustrations by Dom Lee.

"As a Korean American, I was so proud that he was the first Korean American to win a Gold Medal despite the obstacles he faced. I realized Sammy Lee's story was inspirational to people of all different ethnic backgrounds," Yoo says. "That's why I decided to write a children's book of Dr. Lee's life. I wanted readers of all ages and nationalities to learn about his achievements and how persistence and hard work are key to making your dreams come true."

Why did you choose to write about Sammy Lee in picture book form? Had you written picture books before? Tell me about your process.

[As I researched] I found many historical photographs of Sammy Lee's dives—he looked like he was flying! That made me realize a picture book would be the perfect form to tell his story because of the beautiful visual images of his dives. I also thought a picture book would be a great way to help parents and teachers discuss the difficult topic of racial discrimination with their children and students.

I began writing a draft of the book after two weeks of research. I struggled with the opening paragraph, trying to find the perfect opening image that would encapsulate Sammy Lee's desire to dive and his struggle to overcome prejudice. And then it hit me—when Sammy was 12 years old, he was forbidden from entering his town's public swimming pool except on Wednesdays because he was not white. I suddenly imagined Sammy as a young boy, standing outside the fence, looking in longingly at the other children splashing about the pool on a hot summer day.

As soon as I settled on that image as my opening paragraph, the rest of the picture book manuscript flowed out of me quite easily. It took about a week to come up with a draft, and then about a month of revisions and polishing and tightening the language until I was satisfied that it was ready to submit.

Had you ever aspired to write nonfiction books before you wrote *Sixteen Years in Sixteen Seconds*?

I was a journalist for ten years before I wrote my first picture book. During my years as a reporter for *The Seattle Times*, *The Detroit News*, and *PEOPLE Magazine*, I had always aspired to write books—both fiction and nonfiction. Writing a nonfiction picture book was the perfect transition from my full-time job as journalist to my new career in books. Journalism had taught me how to finish a story on a tight deadline, how to communicate the main point of a story right away, and how to write with active, specific language where not one word was wasted.

What made you decide to submit your book for the Lee & Low's New Voices Award? How did you feel when you found out you'd won for *Sixteen Years*?

I decided to enter because I thought Sammy Lee's story would be the perfect match for this publisher, whose books I admired and also owned. In addition, I was a *huge* fan of illustrator Dom Lee, who has illustrated many of their wonderful books, including the classic *Baseball Saved Us*. I received the

Author Paula Yoo read about Olympic Gold Medalist diver Dr. Sammy Lee as she researched Korean American History for a thesis, and she was fascinated by his story. "I was drawn to his story because I admired how he overcame prejudice to achieve his dreams," says Yoo. After a few weeks of research, she began writing a children's picture book about the physician-athlete. Her manuscript *Sixteen Years in Sixteen Seconds* went on to win the Lee & Low New Voices Award and was published in 2005 with illustrations by Dom Lee.

good news two days before Christmas! Talk about the perfect present! My husband and I were on our vacation, driving from the Grand Canyon to Las Vegas, when editor Philip Lee called. I was so excited that I squealed! I was grateful I wasn't driving at the time! And then to find out Dom Lee would be my illustrator was the icing on the cake.

How did winning the award help your writing career?

Winning gave me the confidence boost I needed to continue writing. Being a writer is very difficult—you're always faced with rejection. You have to believe in yourself and constantly strive to become a better writer by taking writing workshop classes and studying and reading great books and learning from your mistakes. We hear "Sorry, this just isn't right for us" and "I'm sorry to inform you that your book has been rejected by..." so often that it can sometimes hurt us creatively because we lose confidence in ourselves. Winning the Lee & Low contest was just the encouragement I needed to keep writing.

***Sixteen Years* is your first published book. Had you shopped your children's book to publishers before you entered Lee & Low's contest?**

I had already written three novels and had signed with an agent. My first novel, an adult novel, failed to find a publisher. My agent specializes in children's literature and encouraged me to try writing children's picture books and young adult novels because he felt I could capture a young voice in my writing. I took his advice and wrote two middle grade novels. Although these were very solid, good drafts, we both agreed they were not quite ready to submit and needed some revisions. While I was taking a break from revising those novels, I learned about Sammy Lee and decided to submit my picture book manuscript about him to Lee & Low's contest. Ironically, I had submitted a fictional picture book manuscript to the same contest a few years earlier, only to receive a rejection letter. I guess the lesson is never give up and try, try again!

You're a graduate of Yale and Columbia, you've been a staff correspondent for *PEOPLE Magazine*, written scripts for shows like *The West Wing* and *Angel*, written an award-winning picture book, have a novel on the horizon, you're a professional violinist, and you're in a band. Any advice for writers on how to successfully juggle projects?

I've always juggled many different projects at the same time. A lot of people shake their heads and say, "How can you handle so many things at once?" It's funny because I don't think it's difficult at all to balance these different worlds—children's book writing, TV writing, journalism, and music. All these different jobs require creative thinking, so they have more in common than people realize.

For example, being a musician has helped my writing skills. Practicing the violin on a daily basis, going out on auditions and performing music in public taught me discipline— practicing a difficult concerto or sitting in orchestra rehearsal for three hours taught me how to sit still and concentrate and focus on getting the job done. That classical music discipline spilled over into my writing—I would not leave my desk until I finished a story or a chapter. I also improvise in rehearsals with my rock band, so the brainstorming techniques used during these jam sessions are easily transferable to my writing side, where often I have to brainstorm new ideas or solutions to problems I'm having with a particular character or storyline. In fact, when I'm "stuck" on a writing project, I'll pick up my violin and practice. I find that my subconscious starts to work while I'm playing my violin. Plus, I love playing my violin, so it puts me in a good mood! After I'm done practicing, I'll go back to the computer and voila! Suddenly I have a solution to a writing problem!

Finally, TV writing is very similar to novels and picture books—in all genres, you have a character who has a desire to do something but faces an obstacle preventing him or her from achieving that goal. The collaborative brainstorming you do in a TV writers' room where there are usually about a half-dozen or so screenwriters brainstorming a new episode taught me how to collaborate and work with my book editors when brainstorming how to revise a manuscript.

As for juggling multiple projects successfully, my advice is—don't panic. And don't procrastinate. (My writer friends are now laughing at me because I do both all the time!) But seriously—I tend to write very detailed schedules every day of what I plan to do, project-wise. But I never expect to meet all those goals by the end of the day. Instead, as long as I've accomplished at least *one* goal for the day, I'm happy. It could be anything from writing two to 20 new pages of a draft to learning a new piece on my violin to revising a chapter to reading a book (reading books helps you become a better writer, so I'm constantly reading a new novel). Step by step, I meet all my goals. In addition, I love deadlines. As long as I have a deadline, I'll get it done. Journalism taught me that skill. So deadlines help when you're working on more than one project at the same time.

You've said, "Anyone can relate to the universal theme of Dr. Lee's struggle to balance his dreams with his parents' dreams." Is this something you've experienced?

I think we all have struggled to balance our own personal dreams with our parents' dreams. For me, I had always wanted to be a book author *and* a professional musician, but my parents wanted me to have a "normal" job—i.e. become a lawyer. Of course they supported my writing dreams but they also wanted me to have a good education and financial security. They were worried because being a writer (and a musician) involves so much sacrifice and rejection. So I became a fulltime journalist because it satisfied my writing dreams at the time, plus it also satisfied my parents, knowing that I had a steady paycheck. (As for music, I pursued it on a freelance basis, performing in chamber music recitals, playing with community orchestras, and jamming with various rock bands.) When I decided to leave journalism and pursue fiction writing fulltime, it was scary but my parents supported my decision.

Tell me about your upcoming novel with HarperCollins? What's it about? How did it end up with Harper?

Believe it or not, I wrote this novel in about six weeks straight. A TV show I was writing for had just been cancelled and I was in a panic about finding a new TV job and afraid of being unemployed. Well, I was unemployed and stressed, and then I realized this is actually a blessing in disguise! Look at all this free time I have to write! So I started writing a funny story about some stuff that happened to me in high school, and before I knew it, the words kept pouring out of me. I wrote in this feverish daze, literally eight hours a day and then into the late night, for six straight weeks and produced a 300-page novel. My book agent loved it, submitted it to publishers, and after a few weeks of anxious nail-biting, we heard from the good news from HarperCollins.

My novel is called *Good Enough* and it will be published sometime in 2007. It's a funny-but-poignant YA novel poking fun at the stereotypes of the Asian American overachiever/model minority myth. My main character is a 17-year-old Korean American girl who is an accomplished violinist and valedictorian who struggles with the pressure to please her parents' expectations of getting accepted into an Ivy League along with her own secret dream of pursuing music instead. (Plus, there's a cute new guy at her school whom she has a crush on!) Note—I swear this is *not* an autobiography! Let's just say it was "inspired" by my own experiences growing up.

—Alice Pope

Fax: (302)731-1057. E-mail: exec@reading.org. Web site: www.reading.org. Annual award. Awards are given for an author's first or second published book for fiction and nonfiction in three categories: primary (ages preschool-8), intermediate (ages 9-13), and young adult (ages 14-17). This award is intended for newly published authors who show unusual promise in the children's book field. Deadline for entries: November 1. Awards $500. For guidelines write or e-mail exec@reading.org.

JOSEPH HENRY JACKSON AND JAMES D. PHELAN LITERARY AWARDS

Sponsored by The San Francisco Foundation. Administered by Intersection for the Arts, 446 Valencia St., San Francisco CA 94103. (415)626-2787. Fax: (415)626-1636. Web site: www.theintersection.org/resource_awards. php. Submit entries to Awards Coordinator. **Open to Students.** Annual award. Estab. 1937. Purpose of award: to encourage young writers for an unpublished manuscript-in-progress. Submissions must be unpublished. Submissions made by author. Deadline for entry: January 31. SASE for contest rules and entry forms. Judging by established peers. All applicants must be 20-35 years of age. Applicants for the Henry Jackson Award must be residents of northern California or Nevada for 3 consecutive years immediately prior to the January 31 deadline. Applicants for the James D. Phelan awards must have been born in California but need not be current residents.

THE EZRA JACK KEATS NEW WRITER AND NEW ILLUSTRATOR AWARDS

Ezra Jack Keats Foundation/Administered by The Office of Children's Services, The New York Public Library, 455 Fifth Ave., New York NY 10016. (212)340-0906. Fax: (612)626-0377. E-mail: mtice@nypl.org. Web site: www.ezra-jack-keats.org. **Program Coordinator:** Margaret Tice. Annual awards. Purpose of the awards: "The awards will be given to a promising new writer of picture books for children and a promising new illustrator of picture books for children. Selection criteria include books for children (ages 9 and under) that reflect the tradition of Ezra Jack Keats. These books portray: the universal qualities of childhood, strong and supportive family and adult relationships, the multicultural nature of our world.'' Submissions made by the publisher. Must be published in the preceding year. Deadline for entries: mid-December. SASE for contest rules and entry forms. No entry fee. Awards $1,000 coupled with Ezra Jack Keats Bronze Medal. Judging by a panel of experts. ''The author or illustrator should have published no more than 3 children's books. Entries are judged on the outstanding features of the text, complemented by illustrations. Candidates need not be both author and illustrator. Entries should carry a 2005 copyright (for the 2006 award).'' Winning books and authors to be presented at reception at The New York Public Library.

EZRA JACK KEATS/KERLAN COLLECTION MEMORIAL FELLOWSHIP

University of Minnesota, 113 Elmer L. Andersen Library, Minneapolis MN 55455. (612)624-4576. Fax: (612)625-5525. E-mail: clrc@tc.umn.edu. Web site: special.lib.umn.edu/clrc/. Offered annually. Deadline for entries: May 1. Send request with SASE (6×9 or 9×12 envelope), including 60¢ postage. The Ezra Jack Keats/Kerlan Collection Memorial Fellowship from the Ezra Jack Keats Foundation will provide $1,500 to a ''talented writer and/or illustrator of children's books who wishes to use the Kerlan Collection for the furtherance of his or her artistic development. Special consideration will be given to someone who would find it difficult to finance the visit to the Kerlan Collection.'' The fellowship winner will receive transportation and per diem. Judging by the Kerlan Award Committee—3 representatives from the University of Minnesota faculty, one from the Kerlan Friends, and one from the Minnesota Library Association.

KENTUCKY BLUEGRASS AWARD

Kentucky Reading Association, % Carrie L. Cooper, Eastern Kentucky University Libraries, Richmond KY 40475. (859)622-1778. Fax: (859)622-1174. E-mail: carrie.cooper@eku.edu. Web site: www.kyreading.org. **Award Director:** Carrie L. Cooper. Submit entries to: Carrie L. Cooper. Annual award. Estab. 1983. Purpose of award: to promote readership among young children and young adolescents. Also to recognize exceptional creative efforts of authors and illustrators. Previously published submissions only. Submissions made by author, made by author's agent, nominated by teachers or librarians. Must be published no more than 3 years prior to the award year. Deadline for entries: March 15. Contest rules and entry forms are available from the Web site. No entry fee. Awards a framed certificate and invitation to be recognized at the annual luncheon of the Kentucky Bluegrass Award. Judging by children who participate through their schools or libraries. ''Books are reviewed by a panel of teachers and librarians before they are placed on a Master List for the year. These books must have been published within a three year period prior to the review. Winners are chosen from this list of preselected books. Books are divided into four divisions, K-2, 3-5, 6-8, 9-12 grades. Winners are chosen by children who either read the books or have the books read to them. Children from the entire state of Kentucky are involved in the selection of the annual winners for each of the divisions.''

CORETTA SCOTT KING AWARD

Coretta Scott King Committee, Ethnic and Multicultural Information Exchange Round Table, American Library Association, 50 E. Huron St., Chicago IL 60611. (312)280-4297. Fax: (312)280-3256. E-mail: olos@ala.org. Web site: www.ala.org/csk. ''The Coretta Scott King Award is an annual award for books (1 for text and 1 for illustration) that convey the spirit of brotherhood espoused by Martin Luther King, Jr.—and also speak to the Black experience—for young people. There is an award jury of children's librarians that judges the books—reviewing over the year—and making a decision in January. A copy of an entry must be sent to each juror by December 1 of the juried year. A copy of the jury list can be found on Web site. Call or e-mail ALA Office for Literary Services for jury list. Awards breakfast held on Tuesday morning during A.L.A. Annual Conference. See schedule at Web site.

LOUISE LOUIS/EMILY F. BOURNE STUDENT POETRY AWARD

Poetry Society of America, 15 Gramercy Park South, New York NY 10003-1705. (212)254-9628. Fax: (212)673-2352. E-mail: eve@poetrysociety.org. Web site: www.poetrysociety.org. **Contact:** Program Director. **Open to students.** Annual award. Purpose of the award: award is for the best unpublished poem by a high or preparatory school student (grades 9-12) from the U.S. and its territories. Unpublished submissions only. Deadline for entries: Oct. 1 to Dec. 22. SASE for award rules and entry forms. Entries not returned. ''High schools can send an unlimited number of submissions with one entry per individual student for a flat fee of $20. (High school students may send a single entry for $5.)'' Award: $250. Judging by a professional poet. Requirements for entrants: Award open to all high school and preparatory students from the U.S. and its territories. School attended, as well as name and address, should be noted. PSA submission guidelines must be followed. These are printed in our fall calendar on our Web site and are readily available if those interested send us a SASE. Line limit: none. ''The award-winning poem will be included in a sheaf of poems that will be part of the program at the award ceremony and sent to all PSA members.''

MCLAREN MEMORIAL COMEDY PLAY WRITING COMPETITION

Midland Community Theatre, Inc., 2000 W. Wadley, Midland TX 79705.(432)682-2554. Web site: www.mctmidland
.org. Contact: Alathea Blischke. Annual competition. Accepts submissions in 2 division: one-act and full-length.
Accepts submissions December 1, 2006-January 31, 2007 for 2007 competition. Entries must be comedies for adults,
teens or children; musical comedies not accepted. Work must never have been produced professionally or published.
See Web site for competitions guidelines and required brochure with entry form. Entry fee: $15/script. Awards
$400 for winning full-length play; $200 for winning one-act play; staged reading for finalists in each catagory.

[N] [C] THE VICKY METCALF AWARD FOR CHILDREN'S LITERATURE

The Writers' Trust of Canada, 90 Richmond St. E., Suite 200, Toronto ON M5C 1P1 Canada. (416)504-8222.
Fax: (416)504-9090. E-mail: info@writerstrust.com. Web site: www.writerstrust.com. **Contact:** James Davies.
The Vicky Metcalf Award is presented each spring to a Canadian writer for a body of work in children's literature
at The Writers' Trust Awards event in Toronto: Prize: $15,000. Open to Canadian residents only.

MILKWEED PRIZE FOR CHILDREN'S LITERATURE

Milkweed Editions, 1011 Washington Ave. S., Suite 300, Minneapolis MN 55415-1246. (612)332-3192. Fax:
(612)215-2550. E-mail: editor@milkweed.org. Web site: www.milkweed.org. **Award Director:** Daniel Slager,
editor-in-chief. Annual award. Estab. 1993. Purpose of the award: to recognize an outstanding literary novel
for readers ages 8-13 and encourage writers to turn their attention to readers in this age group. Unpublished
submissions only "in book form." Please send SASE or visit Web site for award guidelines. The prize is awarded
to the best work for children ages 8-13 that Milkweed agrees to publish in a calendar year by a writer not
previously published by Milkweed. The Prize consists of a $5,000 advance against royalties agreed to at the
time of acceptance. Submissions must follow our usual children's guidelines.

MINNESOTA BOOK AWARDS

Minnesota Humanities Commission, 987 E. Ivy Ave., St. Paul MN 55106-2046. (651)724-4245 or (866)268-
7293 (toll free). E-mail: martha@minnesotahumanities.org. Web site: www.minnesotahumanities.org. **Contact:**
Martha Davis Beck. Annual award. Estab. 1988. Purpose of contest: To recognize and honor achievement by
members of Minnesota's book community. Previously published submissions only. Submissions made by author, publisher or author's agent. Fee for some categories. Work must hold copyright from the year previous
to that in which award is given (2005 copyright for 2006 award). Deadline for entries: late-December. Awards to
winners and finalists, some cash. Judging by members of Minnesota's book community: booksellers, librarians,
teachers and scholars, writers, reviewers and publishers. Requirements for entrants: Author must be a Minnesota author, editor or primary artistic creator. The Minnesota Book Awards includes 13 awards categories for
children and young adult fiction and nonfiction titles and designs. For complete guidelines, visit Web site.

NATIONAL CHILDREN'S THEATRE FESTIVAL

Actors' Playhouse at the Miracle Theatre, 280 Miracle Mile, Coral Gables FL 33134. (305)444-9293, ext. 615.
Fax: (305)444-4181. E-mail: maulding@actorsplayhouse.org. Web site: www.actorsplayhouse.org. **Director:**
Earl Maulding. **Open to students.** Annual contest. Estab. 1994. Purpose of contest: to bring together the excitement of the theater arts and the magic of young audiences through the creation of new musical works and to
create a venue for playwrights/composers to showcase their artistic products. Submissions must be unpublished. Submissions are made by author or author's agent. Deadline for entries: May 1. Visit Web site or send
SASE for contest rules and entry forms. Entry fee is $10. Awards: first prize of $500, full production, and
transportation to Festival weekend based on availability. Final judges are of national reputation. Past judges
include Joseph Robinette, Moses Goldberg and Luis Santeiro.

NATIONAL PEACE ESSAY CONTEST

United States Institute of Peace, 1200 17th St. NW, Washington DC 20036. (202)429-3854. Fax: (202)429-6063.
E-mail: education@usip.org. Web site: www.usip.org. **Open to high school students.** Annual contest. Estab.
1987. "The contest gives students the opportunity to do valuable research, writing and thinking on a topic of
importance to international peace and conflict resolution. Teaching guides are available for teachers who allow
the contest to be used as a classroom assignment." Deadline for entries is February 1, 2007. "Interested students,
teachers and others may write or call to receive free contest kits. Please do not include SASE." Guidelines and
rules on Web site. No entry fee. State Level Awards are $1,000 college scholarships. National winners are
selected from among the 1st place state winners. National winners receive scholarships in the following
amounts: first place $10,000; second $5,000; third $2,500. National amount includes State Award. First place
state winners invited to an expenses-paid awards program in Washington, DC in June. Judging is conducted
by education professionals from across the country and by the Board of Directors of the United States Institute
of Peace. "All submissions become property of the U.S. Institute of Peace to use at its discretion and without

royalty or any limitation. Students grades 9-12 in the U.S., its territories and overseas schools may submit essays for review by completing the application process. U.S. citizenship required for students attending overseas schools. National winning essays will be published by the U.S. Institute of Peace.''

NATIONAL WRITERS ASSOCIATION NONFICTION CONTEST

10940 S. Parker Rd., #508, Parker CO 80134. (303)841-0246. **Executive Director:** Sandy Whelchel. Annual contest. Estab. 1971. Purpose of contest: ''to encourage and recognize those who excel in nonfiction writing.'' Submissions made by author. Deadline for entries: December 31. SASE for contest rules and entry forms. Entry fee is $18. Awards 3 cash prizes; choice of books; Honorable Mention Certificate. ''Two people read each entry; third party picks three top winners from top five.'' Judging sheets sent if entry accompanied by SASE. Condensed version of 1st place published in *Authorship*.

NATIONAL WRITERS ASSOCIATION SHORT STORY CONTEST

10940 S. Parker Rd., #508, Parker CO 80134. (303)841-0246. **Executive Director:** Sandy Whelchel. Annual contest. Estab. 1971. Purpose of contest: ''To encourage writers in this creative form and to recognize those who excel in fiction writing.'' Submissions made by the author. Deadline for entries: July 1. SASE for contest rules and entry forms. Entry fee is $15. Awards 3 cash prizes, choice of books and certificates for Honorable Mentions. Judging by ''two people read each entry; third person picks top three winners.'' Judging sheet copies available for SASE.

THE NENE AWARD

Hawaii State Library, Honolulu HI 96813. (808)586-3510. Fax: (808)586-3584. E-mail: hslear@netra.lib.state.hi. us. Estab. 1964. ''The Nene Award was designed to help the children of Hawaii become acquainted with the best contemporary writers of fiction, become aware of the qualities that make a good book and choose the best rather than the mediocre.'' Previously published submissions only. Books must have been copyrighted not more than 6 years prior to presentation of award. Work is nominated. Ballots are usually due around the beginning of March. Awards plaque. Judging by the children of Hawaii in grades 4-6. Requirements for entrants: books must be fiction, written by a living author, copyrighted not more than 6 years ago and suitable for children in grades 4, 5 and 6. Current and past winners are displayed in all participating school and public libraries. The award winner is announced in April or May.

〈N〉 ⊕ NESTLÉ CHILDREN'S BOOK PRIZE

Booktrust, Book House, 45 East Hill, Wandsworth London SW18 2QZ United Kingdom. Fax: (00 44)20 8516 2978. E-mail: hannah@booktrust.org.uk. Web site: www.booktrusted.com. **Contact:** Hannah Rutland. ''The Nestlé Children's Book Prize was established in 1985 to encourage high standards and stimulate interest in children's books. The prize is split into 3 age categories: 5 and under, 6-8, 9-11. The books are judged by our adult panel, who shortlist 3 outstanding books in each category, and the final decision of who gets Gold, Silver and Bronze is left to the young judges. The young judges are chosen from classes of school children who complete a task for their age category; the best 50 from each category go on to judge the 3 books in their age category. From the 150 classes who judge the books, 1 class from each category is invited to present the award at the ceremony in London. The children are chosen from projects they submit with their votes.'' Open to works of fiction or poetry for children written in English by a citizen of the UK, or an author residing in the UK. All work must be submitted by a UK publisher. Deadline: July. Prize: Gold Award winners in each age category: £2,500; Silver Award winners in each age category: £1,500; Bronze Award winners in each age category: £500.

NEW ENGLAND BOOK AWARDS

New England Booksellers Association, 1700 Massachusetts Ave., Suite 332, Cambridge MA 02140. (617)576-3070. Fax: (617)576-3091. E-mail: rusty@neba.org. Web site: www.newenglandbooks.org/NE_awards.html. **Executive Director:** Rusty Drugan. Annual award. Estab. 1990. Purpose of award: ''to promote New England authors who have produced a body of work that stands as a significant contribution to New England's culture and is deserving of wider recognition.'' Previously published submissions only. Submissions made by New England booksellers; publishers. ''Award given to authors 'body of work' not a specific book.'' Entries must be still in print and available. SASE for contest rules and entry forms. No entry fee. Judging by NEBA membership. Requirements for entrants: Author/illustrator must live in New England. Submit written nominations only; actual books should not be sent. Member bookstores receive materials to display winners' books.

NEW VOICES AWARD

Lee & Low Books, 95 Madison Ave., New York NY 10016. (212)779-4400. Fax: (212)532-6035. E-mail: general@l eeandlow.com. Web site: www.leeandlow.com/editorial/voices.html. **Editor-in-chief:** Louise May. **Open to**

students. Annual award. Estab. 2000. Purpose of contest: Lee & Low Books is one of the few publishing companies owned by people of color. We have published over 50 first-time writers and illustrators. Titles include *In Daddy's Arms I Am Tall: African Americans Celebrating Fathers*, winner of the Coretta Scott King Illustrator Award; *Passage to Freedom: The Sugihara Story*, an American Library Association Notable Book; and *Crazy Horse's Vision*, a Bank Street College Children's Book of the Year. Submissions made by author. Deadline for entries: October 31. SASE for contest rules. No entry fee. Awards New Voices Award—$1,000 prize and standard publication contract (regardless of whether or not writer has an agent) along with an advance on royalties; New Voices Honor Award—$500 prize. Judging by Lee & Low editors. Restrictions of media for illustrators: The author must be a writer of color who is a resident of the U.S. and who has not previously published a children's picture book. For additional information, send SASE or visit Lee & Low's Web site, (www.leeandlow.com/editorial/voices3.html).

JOHN NEWBERY MEDAL

Association for Library Service to Children, Division of the American Library Association, 50 E. Huron, Chicago IL 60611. E-mail: alsc@ala.org. Web site: www.ala.org. **Executive Director, ALSC:** Malore Brown. Annual award. Estab. 1922. Purpose of award: to recognize the most distinguished contribution to American children's literature published in the U.S. Previously published submissions only; must be published prior to year award is given. Deadline for entries: December 31. SASE for award rules. Entries not returned. No entry fee. Medal awarded at Caldecott/Newbery banquet during ALA annual conference. Judging by Newbery Award Selection Committee.

NORTH AMERICAN INTERNATIONAL AUTO SHOW HIGH SCHOOL POSTER CONTEST

Detroit Auto Dealers Association, 1900 W. Big Beaver Rd., Troy MI 48084-3531. (248)643-0250. Fax: (248)283-5148. E-mail: sherp@dada.org. Web site: www.naias.com. **Contact:** Sandy Herp. **Open to students.** Annual contest. Submissions made by the author and illustrator. Contact D.A.D.A. for contest rules and entry forms or retrieve rules from Web site. No entry fee. Awards in the High School Poster Contest are as follows: Chairman's Award—$1,000; Designer's Best of Show (Digital and Traditional)—$500; Best Theme—$250; Best Use of Color—$250; Most Creative—$250. A winner will be chosen in each category from grades 10, 11 and 12. Prizes: 1st place in 10, 11, 12—$500; 2nd place—$250; 3rd place—$100. The winners of the Designer's Best of Show Digital and Traditional will each receive $500. The winner of the Chairman's Award will receive $1,000. Entries will be judged by an independent panel of recognized representatives of the art community. Entrants must be Michigan high school students enrolled in grades 10-12. Winning posters may be displayed at the NAIAS 2006 and reproduced in the official NAIAI program, which is available to the public, international media, corporate executives and automotive suppliers. Winning posters may also be displayed on the official NAIAS Web site at the sole discretion of the NAIAS.

OHIOANA AWARD FOR CHILDREN'S LITERATURE: ALICE LOUISE WOOD MEMORIAL

Ohioana Library Association, 274 E. First Ave., Suite 300, Columbus OH 43201. (614)466-3831. Fax: (614)728-6974. E-mail: ohioana@sloma.state.oh.us. Web site: www.ohioana.org. **Director:** Linda R. Hengst. Annual award. Estab. 1991. Purpose of award: ''to recognize an Ohio author whose body of work has made, and continues to make a significant contribution to literature for children or young adults.'' Deadline for entries: December 31. SASE for award rules and entry forms. Award: $1,000. Requirements for entrants: ''must have been born in Ohio, or lived in Ohio for a minimum of five years; established a distinguished publishing record of books for children and young people; body of work has made, and continues to make, a significant contribution to the literature for young people; through whose work as a writer, teacher, administrator, and community service, interest in children's literature has been encouraged and children have become involved with reading.''

OHIOANA BOOK AWARDS

Ohioana Library Association, 274 E. First Ave., Suite 300, Columbus OH 43201. (614)466-3831. Fax: (614)728-6974. E-mail: ohioana@sloma.state.oh.us. Web site: www.OHIOANA.org. **Director:** Linda R. Hengst. Annual award. ''The Ohioana Book Awards are given to books of outstanding literary quality. Purpose of contest: to provide recognition and encouragement to Ohio writers and to promote the work of Ohio writers. Up to six are given each year. Awards may be given in the following categories: fiction, nonfiction, children's/juvenile, poetry and books about Ohio or an Ohioan. Books must be received by the Ohioana Library during the calendar year prior to the year the award is given and must have a copyright date within the last two calendar years.'' Deadline for entries: December 31. SASE for award rules and entry forms. No entry fee. Winners receive citation and glass sculpture. ''Any book that has been written or edited by a person born in Ohio or who has lived in Ohio for at least five years is eligible.''

OKLAHOMA BOOK AWARDS

Oklahoma Center for the Book, 200 NE 18th, Oklahoma City OK 73105. (405)521-2502. Fax: (405)525-7804. E-mail: gcarlile@oltn.odl.state.ok.us. Web site: www.odl.state.ok.us/ocb. **Executive Director:** Glenda Carlile. Annual award. Estab. 1989. Purpose of award: "to honor Oklahoma writers and books about our state." Previously published submissions only. Submissions made by the author, author's agent, or entered by a person or group of people, including the publisher. Must be published during the calendar year preceding the award. Awards are presented to best books in fiction, nonfiction, children's, design and illustration, and poetry books about Oklahoma or books written by an author who was born, is living or has lived in Oklahoma. Deadline for entries: early January. SASE for award rules and entry forms. No entry fee. Awards a medal—no cash prize. Judging by a panel of 5 people for each category—a librarian, a working writer in the genre, booksellers, editors, etc. Requirements for entrants: author must be an Oklahoma native, resident, former resident or have written a book with Oklahoma theme. Winner will be announced at banquet in Oklahoma City. The Arrell Gibson Lifetime Achievement Award is also presented each year for a body of work.

ONCE UPON A WORLD CHILDREN'S BOOK AWARD

Simon Wiesenthal Center's Museum of Tolerance Library and Archives, 1399 S. Roxbury Dr., Los Angeles CA 90035-4709. (310)772-7605. Fax: (310)772-7628. E-mail: bookaward@wiesenthal.net. Web site: www.wiesenth al.com/library. **Award Director:** Adaire J. Klein. Submit 4 copies of each entry to: Adaire J. Klein, Director of Library and Archival Services. Annual award. Estab. 1996. Previously published submissions only. Submissions made by publishers, author or by author's agent. Must be published January-December of previous year. Deadline for entries: April 1. SASE for contest rules and entry forms. Awards $1,000. Judging by 3 independent judges familiar with children's literature. Award open to any writer with work in English language on subjects of tolerance, diversity, human understanding, and social justice for children 6-10 years old. The next award will be presented on October 29, 2006. Book Seals available from the library.

ORBIS PICTUS AWARD FOR OUTSTANDING NONFICTION FOR CHILDREN

The National Council of Teachers of English, 1111 W. Kenyon Rd., Urbana IL 61801-1096. (217)328-3870. Fax: (217)328-0977. E-mail: dzagorski@ncte.org. Web site: www.ncte.org/elem/awards/orbispictus. **Chair , NCTE Committee on the Orbis Pictus Award for Outstanding Nonfiction for Children:** Sandip Wilson, Husson College, Bangor ME. Annual award. Estab. 1989. Purpose of award: To promote and recognize excellence in the writing of nonfiction for children. Previously published submissions only. Submissions made by author, author's agent, by a person or group of people. Must be published January 1-December 31 of contest year. Deadline for entries: November 30. Call for award information. No entry fee. Awards a plaque given at the NCTE Elementary Section Luncheon at the NCTE Annual Convention in November. Judging by a committee. "The name Orbis Pictus commemorates the work of Johannes Amos Comenius, 'Orbis Pictus—The World in Pictures' (1657), considered to be the first book actually planned for children."

THE ORIGINAL ART

Society of Illustrators, 128 E. 63rd St., New York NY 10021-7303. (212)838-2560. Fax: (212)838-2561. E-mail: dir@societyillustrators.org. Web site: www.societyillustrators.org. Annual contest. Estab. 1981. Purpose of contest: to celebrate the fine art of children's book illustration. Previously published submissions only. Deadline for entries: August 20. Request "call for entries" to receive contest rules and entry forms. Entry fee is $20/book. Judging by seven professional artists and editors. Works will be displayed at the Society of Illustrators Museum of American Illustration in New York City October-November annually. Medals awarded; catalog published.

HELEN KEATING OTT AWARD FOR OUTSTANDING CONTRIBUTION TO CHILDREN'S LITERATURE

Church and Synagogue Library Association, P.O. Box 19357, Portland OR 97280-0357. (503)244-6919. Fax: (503)977-3734. E-mail: csla@worldaccessnet.com. Web site: www.worldaccessnet.com/ ~ csla. **Chair of Committee:** Barbara Graham. Annual award. Estab. 1980. "This award is given to a person or organization that has made a significant contribution to promoting high moral and ethical values through children's literature." Deadline for entries: April 1. "Recipient is honored in July during the conference." Awards certificate of recognition and a conference package consisting of all meals, day of awards banquet, two nights' housing and a complimentary 1 year membership. "A nomination for an award may be made by anyone. It should include the name, address and telephone number of the nominee, plus the church or synagogue relationship where appropriate. Nominations of an organization should include the name of a contact person. A detailed description of the reasons for the nomination should be given, accompanied by documentary evidence of accomplishment. The person(s) making the nomination should give his/her name, address and telephone number and a brief explanation of his/her knowledge of the nominee's accomplishments. Elements of creativity and innovation will be given high priority by the judges."

PATERSON PRIZE FOR BOOKS FOR YOUNG PEOPLE

Poetry Center at Passaic County Community College, One College Blvd., Paterson NJ 07505-1179. (973)684-

Resources

6555. Fax: (973)523-6085. E-mail: mgillan@pccc.edu. Web site: www.pccc.edu/poetry. **Director:** Maria Mazziotti Gillan. Estab. 1996. Part of the Poetry Center's mission is "to recognize excellence in books for young people." Published submissions only. Submissions made by author, author's agent or publisher. Must be published between January 1-December 31 of year previous to award year. Deadline for entries: March 15. SASE for contest rules and entry forms or visit Web site. Awards $500 for the author in either of 3 categories: PreK-Grade 3; Grades 4-6, Grades 7-12. Judging by a professional writer selected by the Poetry Center. Contest is open to any writer/illustrator.

PEN/PHYLLIS NAYLOR WORKING WRITER FELLOWSHIP

PEN, 588 Broadway, New York NY 10012. (212)334-1660, ext. 108. Fax: (212)334-2181. E-mail: awards@pen.org. Web site: www.pen.org. Submit entries to: awards coordinator. Must have published 2 books to be eligible. Annual contest. Estab. 2001. To support writers with a financial need and recognize work of high literary caliber. Unpublished submissions only. Submissions nominated. Deadline for entries: mid-January. Awards $5,000. Upon nomination by an editor or fellow writer, a panel of judges will select the winning book. Open to a writer of children's or young adult fiction in financial need, who has published at least two books, and no more than five during the past ten years. Please visit our Web site for full guidelines.

PENNSYLVANIA YOUNG READERS' CHOICE AWARDS PROGRAM

Pennsylvania School Librarians Association, 148 S. Bethelehem Pike, Ambler PA 19002-5822. (215)643-5048. Fax: (215)646-7250. E-mail: bellavance@verizon.net. Web site: www.psla.org. **Coordinator:** Jean B. Bellavance. Annual award. Estab. 1991. Submissions nominated by a person or group. Must be published within 5 years of the award for example, books published in 2002 to present are eligible for the 2006-2007 award. Deadline for entries: September 1. SASE for contest rules and entry forms. No entry fee. Framed certificate to winning authors. Judging by children of Pennsylvania (they vote). Requirements for entrants: currently living in North America. Reader's Choice Award is to promote reading of quality books by young people in the Commonwealth of Pennsylvania, to promote teacher and librarian involvement in children's literature, and to honor authors whose work has been recognized by the children of Pennsylvania. Four awards are given, one for each of the following grade level divisions: K-3, 3-6, 6-8, YA View information at the Pennsylvania School Librarians Web site.

JAMES D. PHELAN AWARD

Intersection for the Arts, 446 Valencia Street, San Francisco CA 94103. (415)626-2787. Fax: (415)626-1636. E-mail: info@theintersection.org. Web site: www.theintersection.org. **Contest Director:** Kevin B. Chen. Submit entries to: Awards Coordinator. Annual contest. Estab. 1935. Purpose of contest: "To support unpublished manuscripts in progress." Unpublished submissions only. Submissions made by author. Deadline for entries: January 31. SASE for contest rules and entry forms. No entry fee. Awards: $2,000. Judging by 3 independent judges to be determined. "Must be born in California and must be between ages 20-35."

PLEASE TOUCH MUSEUM® BOOK AWARD

Please Touch Museum, 210 N. 21st St., Philadelphia PA 19103-1001. (215)963-0667. Fax: (215)963-0424. E-mail: kmiller@pleasetouchmuseum.org. Web site: www.pleasetouchmuseum.org. **Contact:** Kathleen Miller. Annual award. Estab. 1985. Purpose of the award: "to recognize and encourage the publication of high-quality books for young children. The award is given to books that are imaginative, exceptionally illustrated and help foster a child's life-long love of reading. Each year we select one winner in two age categories—ages 3 and under and ages 4 to 7. These age categories reflect the age of the children Please Touch Museum serves. To be eligible for consideration, a book must: (1) Be distinguished in text, illustration, and ability to explore and clarify an idea for young children (ages 7 and under). (2) Be published within the last year by an American publisher. (3) Be by an American author and/or illustrator." SASE for award rules and entry forms. No entry fee. Publishing date deadlines apply. Judging by selected jury of children's literature experts, librarians and early childhood educators. Education store purchases books for selling at Book Award Ceremony and throughout the year. Autographing sessions may be held at Please Touch Museum, and at Philadelphia's Early Childhood Education Conference.

PNWA LITERARY CONTEST

Pacific Northwest Writers Association, P.O. Box 2016, Edmonds WA 98020-9516. (425)673-2665. E-mail: staff@pnwa.org. Web site: www.pnwa.org. **Contest/Award Director:** Dana Murphy-Love. **Open to students.** Annual contest. Purpose of contest: "Valuable tool for writers as contest submissions are critiqued (2 critiques)." Unpublished submissions only. Submissions made by author. Deadline for entries: late February. SASE for contest rules and entry forms. Entry fee is $35/entry for members, $45/entry for nonmembers. Awards $600-1st; $300-2nd; $150-3rd. Awards in all 11 categories.

POCKETS MAGAZINE FICTION CONTEST

Pockets Magazine, The Upper Room, P.O. Box 340004, Nashville TN 37203-0004. (615)340-7333. Fax: (615)340-7267. E-mail: pockets@upperroom.org. Web site: www.pockets.org. **Contact:** Lynn W. Gilliam, senior editor. The purpose of the contest is to "find new freelance writers for the magazine." Annual competition for short stories. Award: $1,000 and publication in *Pockets* Competition receives 250-325 submissions. Judged by *Pockets* editors and 3 other editors of other Upper Room publications. Guidelines available on Web site or upon request and SASE. No entry fee. No entry form. Note on envelope and first sheet: Fiction Contest. Submissions must be postmarked between March 1 and August 15 of the current year. Former winners are not eligible. **Unpublished submissions only.** Word length: 1,000-1,600 words. Winner notified November 1. Submissions returned if accompanied by SASE.

EDGAR ALLAN POE AWARD

Mystery Writers of America, Inc., 6th Floor, 17 E. 47th St., New York NY 10017. (212)888-8171. Fax: (212)888-8107. E-mail: mwa@mysterywriters.org. Web site: www.mysterywriters.org. **Office Manager:** Margery Flax. Annual award. Estab. 1945. Purpose of the award: to honor authors of distinguished works in the mystery field. Previously published submissions only. Submissions made by the author, author's agent; "normally by the publisher." Work must be published/produced the year of the contest. Deadline for entries: November 30 "except for works only available in the month of December." SASE for award rules and entry forms. No entry fee. Awards ceramic bust of "Edgar" for winner; scrolls for all nominees. Judging by professional members of Mystery Writers of America (writers). Nominee press release sent after first Wednesday in February. Winner announced at the Edgar Banquet, held in late April/early May.

MICHAEL L. PRINTZ AWARD

Young Adult Library Services Association, Division of the American Library Association, 50 E. Huron, Chicago IL 60611. Fax: (312)664-7459. E-mail: yalsa@ala.org. Web site: www.ala.org/yalsa. Annual award. The Michael L. Printz Award is an award for a book that exemplifies literary excellence in young adult literature. It is named for a Topeka, Kansas school librarian who was a long-time active member of the Young Adult Library Services Association. It will be selected annually by an award committee that can also name as many as 4 honor books. The award-winning book can be fiction, nonfiction, poetry or an anthology, and can be a work of joint author-ship or editorship. The books must be published between January 1 and December 31 of the preceding year and be designated by its publisher as being either a young adult book or one published for the age range that YALSA defines as young adult, e.g. ages 12 through 18. The deadline for both committee and field nominations will be December 1.

⚏ PRIX ALVINE-BELISLE

Association pour l'avancement des sciences et des techniques de la documentation (ASTED) Inc., 3414 Avenue Du Parc, Bureau 202, Montreal QC H2X 2H5 Canada. (514)281-5012. Fax: (514)281-8219. E-mail: info@asted.o rg. **Executive Director:**Louis Cabral. Award open to children's book editors. Annual award. Estab. 1974. Pur-pose of contest: To recognize the best children's book published in French in Canada. Previously published submissions only. Submissions made by publishing house. Must be published the year before award. Deadline for entries: June 1. Awards $1,000. Judging by librarians jury.

QUILL AND SCROLL INTERNATIONAL WRITING/PHOTO CONTEST

Quill and Scroll, School of Journalism and Mass Communication, University of Iowa, Iowa City IA 52242-1528. (319)335-3457. Fax: (319)335-3989. E-mail: quill-scroll@uiowa.edu. Web site: www.uiowa.edu/~quill-sc. **Contest Director:** Richard Johns. **Open to students.** Annual contest. Previously published submissions only. Submissions made by the author or school newspaper adviser. Must be published within the last year. Deadline for entries: February 5. SASE for contest rules and entry forms. Entry fee is $2/entry. Awards engraved plaque to junior high level sweepstakes winners. Judging by various judges. *Quill and Scroll* acquires the right to publish submitted material in the magazine if it is chosen as a winning entry. Requirements for entrants: must be students in grades 9-12 for high school division. Entry form available on Web site.

⊕ REDHOUSE CHILDREN'S BOOK AWARD

(formerly Children's Book Award), Federation of Children's Book Groups, 2 Bridge Wood View, Horsforth, Leeds LS18 5PE England. (44)(113)258-8910. Fax: (44)(113)258-8920. E-mail: marianneadey@aol.com. Web site: www.redhousechildrensbookawards.co.uk. **Coordinator:** Marianne Adey. Purpose of the award: "The R.H.B.A. is an annual prize for the best children's book of the year judged by the children themselves." Categories: (I) books for younger children, (II) books for younger readers, (III) books for older readers. Estab. 1980. Works must be published in the United Kingdom. Deadline for entries: December 31. SASE for rules and entry forms. Entries not returned. Awards "a magnificent silver and oak trophy worth over $6,000 and a portfolio of children's work." Silver dishes to each category winner. Judging by children. Requirements for entrants: Work must be fiction and published in the UK during the current year (poetry is ineligible). Work will be published in current "Pick of the Year" publication.

TOMAS RIVERA MEXICAN AMERICAN CHILDREN'S BOOK AWARD

Texas State University-San Marcos, EDU, 601 University Dr., San Marcos TX 78666-4613. (512)245-2357. Fax: (512)245-7911. E-mail: jb23@txstate.edu. **Award Director:** Dr. Jennifer Battle. Competition open to adults. Annual contest. Estab. 1995. Purpose of award: "To encourage authors, illustrators and publishers to produce books that authentically reflect the lives of Mexican American children and young adults in the United States." Unpublished mss not accepted. Submissions made by "any interested individual or publishing company." Must be published the year prior to the year of consideration. Deadline for entries: November 1 of publication year. Contact Dr. Jennifer Battle for nomination forms, or send copy of book. No entry fee. Awards $3,000 per book. Judging of nominations by a regional committee, national committee judges finalists. Annual ceremony honoring the book and author/illustrator is held during Hispanic Heritage Month at Texas State University-San Marcos.

ROCKY MOUNTAIN BOOK AWARD: ALBERTA CHILDREN'S CHOICE BOOK AWARD

Rocky Mountain Book Award Committee, Box 42, Lethbridge AB T1J 3Y3 Canada. (403)381-0855. E-mail: rockymountainbookaward@shaw.ca. Web site: http://rmba.lethsd.ab.ca. **Contest Director:** Michelle Dimnik. Submit entries to: Richard Chase, board member. Open to students. Annual contest. Estab. 2001. Purpose of contest: "Reading motivation for students, promotion of Canadian authors, illustrators and publishers." Previously unpublished submissions only. Submissions made by author's agent or nominated by a person or group. Must be published between 2003-2005. Deadline for entries: January 17, 2007. SASE for contest rules and entry forms. No entry fee. Awards: Gold medal and author tour of selected Alberta schools. Judging by students. Requirements for entrants: Canadian authors and illustrators only.

SASKATCHEWAN BOOK AWARDS: CHILDREN'S LITERATURE

Saskatchewan Book Awards, 205B-2312 11th Avenue, Regina SK S4P 0K1 Canada. (306)569-1585. Fax: (306)569-4187. E-mail: director@bookawards.sk.ca. Web site: www.bookawards.sk.ca. **Award Director:** Glenda James. Open to Saskatchewan authors only. Annual award. Estab. 1995. Purpose of contest: to celebrate Saskatchewan books and authors and to promote their work. Previously published submissions only. Submissions made by author, author's agent or publisher by September 15. SASE for contest rules and entry forms. Entry fee is $20 (Canadian). Awards $2,000 (Canadian). Judging by two children's literature authors outside of Saskatchewan. Requirements for entrants: Must be Saskatchewan resident; book must have ISBN number; book must have been published within the last year. Award-winning book will appear on TV talk shows and be pictured on bookmarks distributed to libraries, schools and bookstores in Saskatchewan.

SCBWI MAGAZINE MERIT AWARDS

Society of Children's Book Writers and Illustrators, 8271 Beverly Blvd., Los Angeles CA 90048. Fax: (323)782-1010. E-mail: scbwi@scbwi.org. Web site: www.scbwi.org. **Award Coordinator:** Dorothy Leon. Annual award. Estab. 1988. Purpose of the award: "to recognize outstanding original magazine work for young people published during that year and having been written or illustrated by members of SCBWI." Previously published submissions only. Entries must be submitted between January 1 and December 15 of the year of publication. For rules and procedures see Web site. No entry fee. Must be a SCBWI member. Awards plaques and honor certificates for each of 4 categories (fiction, nonfiction, illustration, poetry). Judging by a magazine editor and two "full" SCBWI members. "All magazine work for young people by an SCBWI member—writer, artist or photographer—is eligible during the year of original publication. In the case of co-authored work, both authors must be SCBWI members. Members must submit their own work." Requirements for entrants: 4 copies each of the published work and proof of publication (may be contents page) showing the name of the magazine and the date of issue. The SCBWI is a professional organization of writers and illustrators and others interested in children's literature. Membership is open to the general public at large.

SCBWI WORK-IN-PROGRESS GRANTS

Society of Children's Book Writers and Illustrators, 8271 Beverly Blvd., Los Angeles CA 90048. (323)782-1010. Fax: (323)782-1892. E-mail: scbwi@scbwi.org. Web site: www.scbwi.org. Annual award. "The SCBWI Work-in-Progress Grants have been established to assist children's book writers in the completion of a specific project." Four categories: (1) General Work-in-Progress Grant. (2) Grant for a Contemporary Novel for Young People. (3) Nonfiction Research Grant. (4) Grant for a Work Whose Author Has Never Had a Book Published. Requests for applications may be made beginning October 1. Completed applications accepted February 1-April 1 of each year. SASE for applications for grants. In any year, an applicant may apply for any of the grants except the one awarded for a work whose author has never had a book published. (The recipient of this grant will be chosen from entries in all categories.) Five grants of $1,500 will be awarded annually. Runner-up grants of $500 (one in each category) will also be awarded. "The grants are available to both full and associate members of the SCBWI. They are not available for projects on which there are already contracts." Previous recipients not eligible to apply.

SEVENTEEN FICTION CONTEST
1440 Broadway, 13th Floor, New York NY 10018. Fax: (212)204-3977. Web site: www.seventeen.com. **Open to students.** Annual contest. Estab. 1945. Purpose of contest: To recognize and encourage talented, young writers. Unpublished submissions only. Deadline for entries: April 30. SASE for contest rules and entry forms; contest rules also published in December issue of *Seventeen.* Entries not returned. Submissions accepted by mail only. No entry fee. Awards $1,000 cash prize and possible publication in *Seventeen.* Judging by "inhouse panel of editors, external readers." If 1st, 2nd or 3rd prize, acquires first North American rights for piece to be published. Requirements for entrants: "Our annual fiction contest is open to anyone between the ages of 13 and 21 who submit on or before April 30. Submit only original fiction that has not been published in any form other than in school publications. Stories should be between 1,500 and 3,000 words in length (6-12 pages). All manuscripts must be typed double-spaced on a single side of paper. Submit as many original stories as you like, but each story must include your full name, address, birth date, e-mail address, and signature in the top right-hand corner of the first page. Your signature on submission will constitute your acceptance of the contest rules."

SHUBERT FENDRICH MEMORIAL PLAYWRITING CONTEST
Pioneer Drama Service, Inc., P.O. Box 4267, Englewood CO 80155-4267. Fax: (303)779-4315. E-mail: submission a@pioneerdrama.com. Web site: www.pioneerdrama.com. **Director:** Lori Conary. Annual contest. **Open to students.** Estab. 1990. Purpose of the contest: "To encourage the development of quality theatrical material for educational and family theater." Previously unpublished submissions only. Deadline for entries: December 31. SASE for contest rules and guidelines. No entry fee. Cover letter, SASE for return of ms, and proof of production or staged reading must accompany all submissions. Awards $1,000 royalty advance and publication. Upon receipt of signed contracts, plays will be published and made available in our next catalog. Judging by editors. All rights acquired with acceptance of contract for publication. Restrictions for entrants: Any writers currently published by Pioneer Drama Service are not eligible.

SKIPPING STONES BOOK AWARDS
Skipping Stones, P.O. Box 3939, Eugene OR 97403-0939. (541)342-4956. E-mail: skipping@efn.org. Web site: www.skippingstones.org. Open to published books, magazines, educational videos, and DVDs. Annual awards. Purpose of contest: To recognize contributions to children's literature, teaching resources and educational audio/ video resources in the areas of multicultural awareness, nature and ecology, social issues, peace and nonviolence. Submissions made by the author or publishers and/or producers. Deadline for entries: February 1. Send request for contest rules and entry forms. Entry fee is $50; 50% discount for small/nonprofit publishers. Each year, about 15-20 books and A/V resources are selected by a multicultural team of editors, reviews, parents, teachers and librarians. Winners receive gold honor award seals, certificates and publicity via multiple outlets. Many educational publications announce the winners of our book awards. The reviews of winning books and educational videos/DVDs are published in the May-August issue of *Skipping Stones,* now in 18th year.

SKIPPING STONES YOUTH HONOR AWARDS
Skipping Stones, P.O. Box 3939, Eugene OR 97403-0939. (541)342-4956. E-mail: editor@SkippingStones.org. Web site: www.SkippingStones.org. **Open to students.** Annual awards. Purpose of contest: "to recognize youth, 7 to 17, for their contributions to multicultural awareness, nature and ecology, social issues, peace and nonviolence. Also to promote creativity, self-esteem and writing skills and to recognize important work being done by youth organizations." Submissions made by the author. Deadline for entries: June 25. SASE for contest rules. Entries must include certificate of originality by a parent and/or teacher and background information on the author written by the author. Entry fee is $3. Everyone who enters the contest receives the September-October issue featuring Youth Awards. Judging by *Skipping Stones'* staff. "Up to ten awards are given in three categories: (1) Compositions—(essays, poems, short stories, songs, travelogues, etc.) should be typed (double-spaced) or neatly handwritten. Fiction or nonfiction should be limited to 1,000 words; poems to 30 lines. Non-English writings are also welcome. (2) Artwork—(drawings, cartoons, paintings or photo essays with captions) should have the artist's name, age and address on the back of each page. Send the originals with SASE. Black & white photos are especially welcome. Limit: 8 pieces. (3) Youth Organizations—Tell us how your club or group works to: (a) preserve the nature and ecology in your area, (b) enhance the quality of life for low-income, minority or disabled or (c) improve racial or cultural harmony in your school or community. Use the same format as for compositions." The winners are published in the September-October issue of *Skipping Stones.*

Now in it's 18th year, *Skipping Stones*, is a winner of N.A.M.E., EDPRESS and Parent's Choice Awards.

KAY SNOW WRITERS' CONTEST
Williamette Writers, 9045 SW Barbur Blvd. #5A, Portland OR 97219-4027. (503)452-1592. Fax: (503)452-0372. E-mail: wilwrite@willamettewriters.com. Web site: www.willamettewriters.com. **Contest Director:** Patricia MacAodha. Annual contest. **Open to students.** Purpose of contest: "to encourage beginning and established writers to continue the craft." Unpublished, original submissions only. Submissions made by the author. Deadline for entries: May 15. SASE for contest rules and entry forms. Entry fee is $10, Williamette Writers' members; $15, nonmembers; free for student writers grades 1-12. Awards cash prize of $300 per category (fiction, nonfiction, juvenile, poetry, script writing), $50 for students in three divisions: 1-5, 6-8, 9-12. Judges are anonymous.

SOCIETY OF MIDLAND AUTHORS AWARDS
Society of Midland Authors, P.O. Box 10419, Chicago IL 60610-0419. E-mail: writercc@aol.com. Web site: www.midlandauthors.com. Annual award. Society estab. 1915. Purpose of award: "to stimulate creative literary effort," one of the goals of the Society. There are six categories, including children's fiction and nonfiction, adult fiction and nonfiction, biography and poetry. Previously published submissions only. Submissions made by the author or publisher. Must be published during calendar year previous to deadline. Deadline for entries: February 15th. SASE for award rules and entry forms or check Web site. No entry fee. Awards plaque given at annual dinner, cash ($300). Judging by panel (reviewers, university faculty, writers, librarians) of 3 per category. Author must be currently residing in, born in, or have strong connections to the Midlands, i.e., Illinois, Indiana, Iowa, Kansas, Michigan, Minnesota, Missouri, Nebraska, North Dakota, South Dakota, Ohio or Wisconsin.

SOUTHWEST WRITERS ANNUAL CONTEST
SouthWest Writers, 3721 Morris NE, Suite A, Albuquerque NM 87111. (505)265-9485. Fax: (505)265-9483. E-mail: swwriters@juno.com. Web site: www.southwestwriters.org. Submit entries to: Contest Chair. **Open to adults and students.** Annual contest. Estab. 1982. Purpose of contest: to encourage writers of all genres. Also offers quarterly mini-conferences, critique groups (for $60/year, offers 2 monthly programs, monthly newsletter, annual writing and monthly writing contests, other workshops, various discount perks, Web site linking and critique service (open to nonmembers). See Web site for more information or call or write.

GEORGE G. STONE CENTER FOR CHILDREN'S BOOKS RECOGNITION OF MERIT AWARD
George G. Stone Center for Children's Books, Claremont Graduate University, 740 N. College Ave., Claremont CA 91711-6188. (909)607-3670. **Award Director:** Carolyn Angus. Annual award. Estab. 1965. Purpose of the award: to recognize an author or illustrator of a children's book or a body of work exhibiting the "power to please and expand the awareness of children and teachers as they have shared the book in their classrooms." Previously published submissions only. SASE for award rules and entry forms. Entries not returned. No entry fee. Awards a scroll. Judging by a committee of teachers, professors of children's literature and librarians. Requirements for entrants: Nominations are made by students, teachers, professors and librarians. Award given in April.

THE JOAN G. SUGARMAN CHILDREN'S BOOK AWARD
Washington Independent Writers Legal and Educational Fund, Inc., P.O. Box 70437, Washington DC 20024-8437. (202)466-1344. E-mail: sugarman@Lefund.org. Web site: www.Lefund.org/sugarman.html. **Award Director:** Rob Anderson. Submit entries to: Rob Anderson. Award offered annually. Estab. 1987. Previously published submissions only during the two-year time frame specified for each award. Submissions made by author. No entry fee. Awards $1,000 cash prize for book judged best overall. Three honorable mentions in the categories of early readers, middle readers, and young adult readers are also recognized. Judging by a committee drawn from selected fields of children's literature, such as library science, editing, teaching, and psychology. Books eligible for the award must be written by an author residing in Virginia, Maryland or the District of Columbia and be published works with the copyright of 2002 or 2003. The books must be geared for children 15 years or younger, be original and have universal appeal. Since the books are judged on the basis of their written content, picture books without text are not eligible.

SUGARMAN FAMILY AWARD FOR JEWISH CHILDREN'S LITERATURE
Washington District of Columbia Jewish Community Center, 1529 16th St. N.W., Washington DC 20036. (202)518-9400. Fax: (202)518-9420. E-mail: jessikac@dcjcc.org. Web site: www.dcjcc.org. **Award Director:** Jessika Cirkus. **Open to students.** Biannual award. Estab. 1994. Purpose of contest: to enrich all children's appreciation of Jewish culture and to inspire writers and illustrators for children. Newly published submissions only. Submissions are made by the author, made by the author's agent. Must be published January-December of year previous to award year. Deadline: May 2005. SASE for entry deadlines, award rules and entry forms. Entry fee is $25. Award at least $750. Judging by a panel of three judges—a librarian, a children's bookstore

owner and a reviewer of books. Requirements for entrants: must live in the United States. Work displayed at the DC Jewish Community Center Library.

[N] SYDNEY TAYLOR BOOK AWARD

Association of Jewish Libraries, % NFJC, 330 7th Ave., 21st Floor, New York NY 10001. (212)725-5359. E-mail: heidi@cbiboca.org or ajllibs@osu.edu. Web site: www.jewishlibraries.org. **Contact:** Heidi Estrin, chair. Offered annually for work published in the year of the award. "Given to distinguished contributions to Jewish literature for children. One award for older readers, one for younger." Publishers submit books.Deadline: December 31.Guidelines for SASE. Awards certificate, cash award, and gold seal for cover of winning book.

SYDNEY TAYLOR MANUSCRIPT COMPETITION

Association of Jewish Libraries, 315 Maitland Ave., Teaneck NJ 07666. Fax: (201)862-0362. E-mail: rkglasser@a ol.com. Web site: www.jewishlibraries.org. **Coordinator:** Rachel Glasser. **Open to students** and any unpublished writer of fiction. Annual contest. Estab. 1985. Purpose of the contest: "This competition is for unpublished writers of fiction. Material should be for readers ages 8-11, with universal appeal that will serve to deepen the understanding of Judaism for all children, revealing positive aspects of Jewish life." Unpublished submissions only. Deadline for entries: December 30. Download rules and forms from Web site or send SASE for contest rules and entry forms must be enclosed. No entry fee. Awards $1,000. Award winner will be notified in April, and the award will be presented at the convention in June. Judging by qualified judges from within the Association of Jewish Libraries. Requirements for entrants: must be an unpublished fiction writer; also, books must range from 64-200 pages in length. "AJL assumes no responsibility for publication, but hopes this cash incentive will serve to encourage new writers of children's stories with Jewish themes for all children."

[N] TEDDY AWARD FOR BEST CHILDREN'S BOOK

Writers' League of Texas, 1501 W. Fifth St., Suite E-2, Austin TX 78703. (512)499-8914. Fax: (512)499-0441. E-mail: wlt@writersleague.org. Web site: www.writersleague.org. **Contact:** Kristy Bordine, membership administrator. Offered annually for work published June 1-May 31. Honors 2 outstanding books for children published by members of the Writers' League of Texas. Writer's League of Texas dues may accompany entry fee. Deadline: May 31. Charges $25 fee. Prize: Two prizes of $1,000, and teddy bears.

[] THE TORONTO BOOK AWARDS

City of Toronto, 100 Queen St. W, 2nd Floor, West Tower, Toronto ON M5H 2N2 Canada. (416)392-8191. Fax: (416)392-1247. E-mail: bkurmey@toronto.ca. **Submit entries to:** Bev Kurmey, Protocol Officer. Annual award. Estab. 1974. Recognizes books of literary or artistic merit that are evocative of Toronto. Submissions made by author, author's agent or nominated by a person or group. Must be published the calendar year prior to the award year. Deadline for entries: last week day of February annually. Awards $15,000 in prize money. Judging by committee.

[] TORONTO MUNICIPAL CHAPTER IODE BOOK AWARD

Toronto Municipal IODE, 40 St. Clair Ave. E., Suite 205, Toronto ON M4T 1M9 Canada. (416)925-5078. Fax: (416)925-5127. E-mail: iodetoronto@bellnet.ca. **Contest Director:** Mary K. Anderson. Submit entries to: Theo Heras, Lillian Smith Library, 239 College St., Toronto. Annual contest. Estab. 1974. Previously published submissions only. Submissions made by author. Deadline for entries: November 1. No entry fee. Awards: $1,000. If the illustrator is different from the author, the prize money is divided. Judging by Book Award Committee comprised of members of Toronto Municipal Chapter IODE. Requirements for entrants: Authors and illustrators must be Canadian and live within the GTA.

VEGETARIAN ESSAY CONTEST

The Vegetarian Resource Group, P.O. Box 1463, Baltimore MD 21203. (410)366-VEGE. Fax: (410)366-8804. E-mail: vrg@vrg.org. Web site: www.vrg.org. Annual contest. **Open to students.** Estab. 1985. Purpose of contest: to promote vegetarianism in young people. Unpublished submissions only. Deadline for entries: May 1 of each year. SASE for contest rules and entry forms. No entry fee. Awards $50 savings bond. Judging by awards committee. Acquires right for The Vegetarian Resource Group to reprint essays. Requirements for entrants: age 18 and under. Winning works may be published in *Vegetarian Journal*, instructional materials for students. "Submit 2-3 page essay on any aspect of vegetarianism, which is the abstinence of meat, fish and fowl. Entrants can base paper on interviewing, research or personal opinion. Need not be vegetarian to enter."

VFW VOICE OF DEMOCRACY

Veterans of Foreign Wars of the U.S., 406 W. 34th St., Kansas City MO 64111. (816)968-1117. Fax: (816)968-1149. Web site: www.vfw.org. **Open to high school students.** Annual contest. Estab. 1960. Purpose of contest:

to give high school students the opportunity to voice their opinions about their responsibility to our country and to convey those opinions via the broadcast media to all of America. Deadline for entries: November 1. No entry fee. Winners receive awards ranging from $1,000-25,000. Requirements for entrants: "Ninth-twelfth grade students in public, parochial, private and home schools are eligible to compete. Former first place state winners are not eligible to compete again. Contact your participating high school teacher, counselor, our Web site www.vfw.org or your local VFW Post to enter."

WASHINGTON CHILDREN'S CHOICE PICTURE BOOK AWARD

Washington Library Media Association, P.O. Box 50194, Mukilteo WA 98275. E-mail: galantek@edmonds.wedn et.edu. Web site: www.wlma.org/Association/wccpba.htm. **Award Director:** Kristin Galante. Submit nominations to: Kristin Galante, chairman; mail to Kristin Galante, WCCPBA, Lynndale Elementary School, 7200 191st SW, Lynnwood WA 98036. Annual award. Estab. 1982. Previously published submissions only. Submissions nominated by a person or group. Must be published within 2-3 years prior to year of award. Deadline for entries: March 1. SASE for contest rules and entry forms. Awards pewter plate, recognition. Judging by WCCPBA committee.

WASHINGTON POST/CHILDREN'S BOOK GUILD AWARD FOR NONFICTION

E-mail: theguild@childrensbookguild.org. Web site: www.childrensbookguild.org. **President:** changes yearly. Annual award. Estab. 1977. Purpose of award: "to honor an author or illustrator whose total work has contributed significantly to the quality of nonfiction for children." Award includes a cash prize and an engraved crystal paperweight. Judging by a jury of Children's Book Guild specialists, authors, illustrators and a *Washington Post* book critic. "One doesn't enter. One is selected. Our jury annually selects one author for the award."

WE ARE WRITERS, TOO!

Creative With Words Publications, Carmel CA 93922. Fax: (831)655-8627. E-mail: cwwpub@usa.net. Web site: members.tripod.com/CreativeWithWords. **Contest Director:** Brigitta Geltrich. **Open to students.** Twice a year (January, August). Estab. 1975. Purpose of award: to further creative writing in children. Unpublished submissions only. Can submit year round on any theme (theme list available upon request and SASE). Deadlines for entries: year round. SASE for contest rules and entry forms. SASE for return of entries "if not accepted." No entry fee. Awards publication in an anthology. Judging by selected guest editors and educators. Contest open to children only (up to and including 19 years old). Writer should request contest rules. SASE with all correspondence. Age of child and home address must be stated and ms must be verified of its authenticity. Each story or poem must have a title. Creative with Words Publications (CWW) publishes the top 100-120 mss submitted to the contest. CWW also publishes anthologies on various themes throughout the year to which young writers may submit.

WESTERN HERITAGE AWARDS

National Cowboy & Western Heritage Museum, 1700 NE 63rd St., Oklahoma City OK 73111-7997. (405)478-2250. Fax: (405)478-4714. E-mail: editor@nationalcowboymuseum.org. Web site: www.nationalcowboymuseu m.org. **Director of Publications:** M.J. Van deventer. Annual award. Estab. 1961. Purpose of award: The WHA are presented annually to encourage the accurate and artistic telling of great stories of the West through 13 categories of western literature, television, film and music; including fiction, nonfiction, children's books and poetry. Previously published submissions only; must be published the calendar year before the awards are presented. Deadline for literary entries: November 30. Deadline for film, music and television entries: December 31. Entries not returned. Entry fee is $45/entry. Awards a Wrangler bronze sculpture designed by famed western artist, John Free. Judging by a panel of judges selected each year with distinction in various fields of western art and heritage. Requirements for entrants: The material must pertain to the development or preservation of the West, either from a historical or contemporary viewpoint. Literary entries must have been published between December 1 and November 30 of calendar year. Film, music or television entries must have been released or aired between January 1 and December 31 of calendar year of entry. Works recognized during special awards ceremonies held annually at the museum. There is an autograph party preceding the awards. Awards ceremonies are sometimes broadcast.

JACKIE WHITE MEMORIAL NATIONAL CHILDREN'S PLAY WRITING CONTEST

Columbia Entertainment Company, 309 Parkade Blvd., Columbia MO 65202-1447. (573)874-5628. E-mail: bybet sy@yahoo.com. Web site: www.cectheatre.org. **Contest Director:** Betsy Phillips. **Open to students.** Annual contest. Estab. 1988. Purpose of contest: "To encourage writing of family-friendly scripts." Previously unpublished submissions only. Submissions made by author. Deadline for entries: June 1. SASE for contest rules and entry forms. Entry fee is $10. Awards $500 with production possible. Judging by current and past board members of CEC and at least one theater school parent. Play may be performed during the following season. 2006 winner may be presented during CEC's 2006-07 season. We reserve the right to award 1st place and prize monies without a production. All submissions will be read by at least three readers. Author will receive a written evaluation of the script.

LAURA INGALLS WILDER AWARD

Association for Library Service to Children, Division of the American Library Association, 50 E. Huron, Chicago IL 60611. (312)280-2163. E-mail: alsc@ala.org. Web site: www.ala.org/ala/alsc/awardsscholarships/literarya wds/wildermedal/wildermedal.htm. **Executive Director:** Malore Brown. Award offered every 2 years. Purpose of the award: to recognize an author or illustrator whose books, published in the U.S., have over a period of years made a substantial and lasting contribution to children's literature. The candidates must be nominated by ALSC members. Medal presented at Newbery/Caldecott banquet during annual conference. Judging by Wilder Award Selection Committee.

⃞N⃞ RITA WILLIAMS YOUNG ADULT PROSE PRIZE

National League of American Pen Women, Nob Hill, San Francisco Branch, 1544 Sweetwood Dr., Colma CA 94015-2029. E-mail: pennobhill@aol.com. Web site: www.soulmakingcontest.us. **Contact:** Eileen Malone. **Open to students.** Up to 3,000 words in story, essay, journal entry, creative nonfiction, or memoir by writers in grades 9-12. Annual prize. Deadline: November 30. Guidelines for SASE. Charges $5/entry (make checks payable to NLAPW, Nob Hill Branch). Prize: 1st Place: $100; 2nd Place: $50; 3rd Place: $25. Open to any writer in grade 9-12.

PAUL A. WITTY OUTSTANDING LITERATURE AWARD

International Reading Association, Special Interest Group, Reading for Gifted and Creative Learning, School of Education, P.O. Box 297900, Fort Worth TX 76129. (817)257-6938. Fax: (817)257-7480. E-mail: clock@tcu.edu. **Award Director:** Dr. Cathy Collins Block. **Open to students.** Annual award. Estab. 1979. Categories of entries: poetry/prose at elementary, junior high and senior high levels. Unpublished submissions only. Deadline for entries: February 1. SASE for award rules and entry forms. SASE for return of entries. No entry fee. Awards $25 and plaque, also certificates of merit. Judging by 2 committees for screening and awarding. Works will be published in International Reading Association publications. "The elementary students' entries must be legible and may not exceed 1,000 words. Secondary students' prose entries should be typed and may exceed 1,000 words if necessary. At both elementary and secondary levels, if poetry is entered, a set of five poems must be submitted. All entries and requests for applications must include a self-addressed, stamped envelope."

PAUL A. WITTY SHORT STORY AWARD

International Reading Association, P.O. Box 8139, 800 Barksdale Rd., Newark DE 19714-8139. (302)731-1600. E-mail: exec@reading.org. Web site: www.reading.org. "The entry must be an original short story appearing in a young children's periodical for the first time during 2005. The short story should serve as a literary standard that encourages young readers to read periodicals." Deadline for entries: The entry must have been published for the first time in the eligibility year; the short story must be submitted during the calendar year of publication. Anyone wishing to nominate a short story should send it to the designated Paul A. Witty Short Award Subcommittee Chair by December 1. Award is $1,000 and recognition at the annual IRA Convention.

WOMEN IN THE ARTS ANNUAL CONTESTS

Women In The Arts, P.O. Box 2907, Decatur IL 62524-2907. (217)872-0811. **Open to students.** Annual contest. Estab. 1995. Purpose of contest: to encourage beginning writers, as well as published professionals, by offering a contest for well-written material in plays, fiction, essay and poetry. Submissions made by author. Deadline for entries: November 1 annually. SASE for contest rules and entry forms. Entry fee is $2/ms. Prize consists of $50—1st place; $35—2nd place; $15—3rd place. Send SASE for complete rules.

JOHN WOOD COMMUNITY COLLEGE CREATIVE WRITING CONTEST

John Wood Community College, Quincy IL 62305. (217)641-4903 or (217)641-4905. Fax: (217)228-9483. Web site: www.jwcc.edu. **Contact:** Sherry Sparks. The college sponsors a writing contest for poetry, fiction and nonfiction. Entries for the contest are accpeted March-April of each year. Please see the JWCC Web site for more details or e-mail Janet McGovern at jmcgovern@jwcc.edu for more information. In addition, the college sponsors writing workshops, readings, speakers, a humanities series, a photography show in spring, and an art competition in the fall.

⃞N⃞ ALICE WOOD MEMORIAL OHIOANA AWARD FOR CHILDREN'S LITERATURE

Ohioana Library Association, 274 E. First Ave., Suite 300, Columbus OH 43201. (614)466-3831. Fax: (614)728-6974. E-mail: ohioana@sloma.state.oh.us. Web site: www.ohioana.org. **Contact:** Linda R. Hengst. Offered to an author whose body of work has made, and continues to make, a significant contribution to literature for children or young adults and through their work as a writer, teacher, administrator, and community member, interest in children's literature has been encouraged and children have become involved with reading. Nomination forms for SASE. Recipient must have been born in Ohio or lived in Ohio at least 5 years. Deadline: December 31. Awards $1,000 cash prize.

WRITE IT NOW!

SmartWriters.com, 10823 Worthing Ave., San Diego CA 92126-2665. (858)689-2665. E-mail: editor@smartwrite rs.com. Web site: www.SmartWriters.com. **Editorial Director:** Roxyanne Young. Estab. 1994. Annual contest. "Our purpose is to encourage new writers and help get their manuscripts into the hands of people who can help further their careers." Unpublished submissions only. Submissions made by author. Deadline for entries: February 1. SASE for contest rules and entry forms; also see Web site. Entry fee is $10. Awards a cash prize, books about writing, and an editorial review of the winning manuscripts. 2005's cash prize was $500. Judging by published writers and editors. Requirement for entrants: "This contest is open to all writers age 18 and older. There are 6 categories: Young Adult, Mid-grade, Picture Book, Poetry, Non-Fiction, and Illustration." See Web site for more details.

WRITER'S INT'L FORUM CONTESTS

Bristol Services Int'l., P.O. Box 1000, Carlsborg WA 98324-1000. Web site: www.bristolservicesintl.com. Estab. 1997. Purpose of contest: to inspire excellence in the traditional short story format. "In fiction we like identifiable characters, strong storylines, and crisp, fresh endings. Open to all ages." SASE or see Web site to determine if a contest is currently open. Only send a ms if an open contest is listed at Web site. Read past winning mss online. Judging by Bristol Services Int'l staff.

WRITING CONFERENCE WRITING CONTESTS

The Writing Conference, Inc., P.O. Box 664, Ottawa KS 66067. Phone/fax: (785)242-1995. E-mail: jbushman@w ritingconference.com. Web site: www.writingconference.com. **Contest Director:** John H. Bushman. **Open to students.** Annual contest. Estab. 1988. Purpose of contest: to further writing by students with awards for narration, exposition and poetry at the elementary, middle school and high school levels. Unpublished submissions only. Submissions made by the author or teacher. Deadline for entries: January 8. SASE for contest rules and entry form or consult Web site. No entry fee. Awards plaque and publication of winning entry in *The Writers' Slate*, March issue. Judging by a panel of teachers. Requirements for entrants: must be enrolled in school—K-12th grade.

▟ WRITING FOR CHILDREN COMPETITION

90 Richmond St. E, Suite 200, Toronto ON M5C 1P1 Canada. (416)703-8982, ext. 223. Fax: (416)504-9090. E-mail: projects@writersunion.ca. Web site: www.writersunion.ca. **Open to students** and Canadian citizens or landed immigrants who have not had a book published. Annual contest. Estab. 1997. Purpose of contest: to discover, encourage and promote new writers of children's literature. Unpublished submissions only. Submissions made by author. Deadline for entries: April 24. Entry fee is $15. Awards $1,500 and submission of winner and finalists to 3 publishers of children's books. Judging by members of the Writers Union of Canada (all published writers with at least one book). Requirements for entrants: Open only to unpublished writers. Please do not send illustrations.

YEARBOOK EXCELLENCE CONTEST

Quill and Scroll Society, School of Journalism and Mass Communication, 100 Adler Building, Room E346, Iowa City IA 52242- 2004. (319)335-3457. Fax: (319)335-3989. E-mail: quill-scroll@uiowa.edu. Web site: www.uiowa .edu/ ~ quill-sc. **Executive Director:** Richard Johns. **Open to students whose schools have Quill and Scroll charters.** Annual contest. Estab. 1987. Purpose of contest: to recognize and reward student journalists for their work in yearbooks and to provide student winners an opportunity to apply for a scholarship to be used freshman year in college for students planning to major in journalism. Previously published submissions only. Submissions made by the author or school yearbook adviser. Must be published between in the 12-month span prior to contest deadline. Deadline for entries: November 1. SASE for contest rules and entry form. Entry fee is $2 per entry. Awards National Gold Key; sweepstakes winners receive plaque; seniors eligible for scholarships. Judging by various judges. Winning entries may be published in *Quill and Scroll* magazine.

▟ YOUNG ADULT CANADIAN BOOK AWARD

The Canadian Library Association, 328 Frank St., Ottawa ON K2P 0X8 Canada. (613)232-9625. Fax: (613)563-9895. Web site: www.cla.ca. **Contact:** Committee Chair. Annual award. Estab. 1981. Purpose of award: "to recognize the author of an outstanding English-language Canadian book which appeals to young adults between the ages of 13 and 18 that was published the preceding calendar year. Information is available upon request.

We approach publishers. Entries are not returned. No entry fee. Awards a leather-bound book. Requirement for entrants: must be a work of fiction (novel or short stories), the title must be a Canadian publication in either hardcover or paperback, and the author must be a Canadian citizen or landed immigrant. Award given at the Canadian Library Association Conference.

YOUNG READER'S CHOICE AWARD

3738 W. Central, Missoula MT 59804. (406)542-4055. Fax: (406)543-5358. E-mail: monlux@montana.com. Web site: www.PNLA.org. **Award Director:** Carole Monlux, chair YRCA. "This award is not for unsolicited books—the short list for this award is nominated by students, teachers and librarians and it is only for students in the Pacific Northwest to vote on the winner." YRCA is intended to be a Book Award chosen by students—not adults. It is the oldest children's choice award in U.S. and Canada. Previously published submissions only (the titles are 3 years old when voted upon). Submissions nominated by a person or group in the Pacific Northwest. Deadline for entries: February 1—Pacific Northwest nominations only. SASE for contest rules and entry forms. Awards medal made of Idaho silver, depicting eagle and salmon in northwest. Native American symbols. Judging by students in Pacific Northwest. "The Pacific Northwest Library Association's Young Reader's Choice Award is the oldest children's choice award in the U.S. and Canada. Only 4th- through 12th-graders in the Pacific Northwest are eligible to vote. PNLA strongly encourages people to nominate titles to be included in the ballot."

THE YOUTH HONOR AWARD PROGRAM

Skipping Stones, P.O. Box 3939, Eugene OR 97403. (514)342-4956. E-mail: editor@skippingstones.org. Web site: www.skippingstones.org. **Director of Public Relations:** Arun N. Toke. **Open to students.** Annual contest. Estab. 1994. Purpose of contest: "To recognize creative and artistic works by young people that promote multicultural awareness and nature appreciation." Unpublished submissions only. Submissions made by author. Deadline for entries: June 25. SASE for contest rules and entry forms. Entry fee is $3; low-income entrants, free. "Ten winners will be published in our fall issue. Winners will also receive an Honor Award Certificate, a subscription to *Skipping Stones* and five nature and/or multicultural books." Requirements for entrants: Original writing (essays, interviews, poems, plays, short stories, etc.) and art (photos, paintings, cartoons, etc.) are accepted from youth ages 7 to 17. Non-English and bilingual writings are welcome. Also, you must include a certificate of originality signed by a parent or teacher. "Include a cover letter telling about yourself and your submissions, your age, and contact information. Every student who enters will receive a copy of *Skipping Stones* featuring the ten winning entries."

THE ANNA ZORNIO MEMORIAL CHILDREN'S THEATRE PLAYWRITING AWARD

University of New Hampshire, Department of Theatre and Dance, Paul Creative Arts Center, 30 College Rd., Durham NH 03824-3538. (603)862-3038. Fax: (603)862-0298. E-mail: mike.wood@unh.edu. Web site: www.unh.edu/theatre-dance. **Contact:** Michael Wood. Contest every 4 years; next contest is November 2008 for 2009-2010 season. Estab. 1979. Purpose of the award: "to honor the late Anna Zornio, an alumna of The University of New Hampshire, for dedication to and inspiration of playwriting for young people, K-12th grade. Open to playwrights who are residents of the U.S. and Canada. Plays or musicals should run about 45 minutes." Unpublished submissions only. Submissions made by the author. Deadline for entries: March 3, 2008. SASE for award rules and entry forms. No entry fee. Awards $1,000 plus guaranteed production. Judging by faculty committee. Acquires rights to campus production. Write for details.

Helpful Books & Publications

The editors of *Children's Writer's & Illustrator's Market* suggest the following books and periodicals to keep you informed on writing and illustrating techniques, trends in the field, business issues, industry news and changes, and additional markets.

BOOKS

An Author's Guide to Children's Book Promotion, Ninth edition, by Susan Salzman Raab, 345 Millwood Rd., Chappaqua NY 10514. (914)241-2117. E-mail: info@raabassociates.com. Web site: www.raabassociates.com/authors.htm.

The Business of Writing for Children, by Aaron Shepard, Shepard Publications. Web site: www.aaronshep.com/kidwriter/Business.html. Available on www.amazon.com.

Children's Writer Guide, (annual), The Institute of Children's Literature, 93 Long Ridge Rd., West Redding CT 06896-0811. (800)443-6078. Web site: www.writersbookstore.com.

The Children's Writer's Reference, by Berthe Amoss and Eric Suben, Writer's Digest Books, 4700 E. Galbraith Rd., Cincinnati OH 45236. (800)448-0915. Web site: www.writersdigest.com.

Children's Writer's Word Book, Second edition, by Alijandra Mogilner & Tayopa Mogilner, Writer's Digest Books, 4700 E. Galbraith Rd., Cincinnati OH 45236. (800)448-0915. Web site: www.writersdigest.com.

The Complete Idiot's Guide® to Publishing Children's Books, Second Edition, by Harold D. Underdown, Alpha Books, 201 W. 103rd St., Indianapolis IN 46290. Web site: www.underdown.org/cig.htm.

Creating Characters Kids Will Love, by Elaine Marie Alphin, Writer's Digest Books, 4700 E. Galbraith Rd., Cincinnati OH 45236. (800)448-0915. Web site: www.writersdigest.com.

Formatting & Submitting Your Manuscript, Second Edition, by Cynthia Laufenberg and the editors of *Writer's Market*, Writer's Digest Books, 4700 E. Galbraith Rd., Cincinnati OH 45236. (800)448-0915. Web site: www.writersdigest.com.

Guide to Literary Agents, edited by Joanna Masterson, Writer's Digest Books, 4700 E. Glabraith Rd., Cincinnati OH 45236. (800)448-0915. Web site: www.writersdigest.com.

Resources

How to Write a Children's Book and Get It Published, Third Edition, by Barbara Seuling, John Wiley & Sons, 111 River St., Hoboken NJ 07030. (201)748-6000. Web site: www.wiley.com.

How to Write and Illustrate Children's Books and Get Them Published, edited by Treld Pelkey Bicknell and Felicity Trottman, Writer's Digest Books, 4700 E. Galbraith Rd., Cincinnati OH 45236. (800)448-0915. Web site: www.writersdigest.com.

How to Write Attention-Grabbing Query & Cover Letters, by John Wood, Writer's Digest Books, 4700 E. Galbraith Rd., Cincinnati OH 45236. (800)448-0915. Web site: www.writersdigest.com.

Illustrating Children's Books: Creating Pictures for Publication, by Martin Salisbury, Barron's Educational Series, 250 Wireless Blvd., Hauppauge NY 11788. (800)645-3476. Web site: www.barronseduc.com.

It's a Bunny-Eat-Bunny World: A Writer's Guide to Surviving and Thriving in Today's Competitive Children's Book Market, by Olga Litowinsky, Walker & Company, 104 Fifth Ave., New York NY 10011. (212)727-8300. Web site: www.walkerbooks.com.

Page After Page: discover the confidence & passion you need to start writing & keep writing (no matter what), by Heather Sellers, Writer's Digest Books, 4700 E. Galbraith Rd., Cincinnati OH 45236. (800)448-0915. Web site: www.writersdigest.com.

Picture Writing: A New Approach to Writing for Kids and Teens, by Anastasia Suen, Writer's Digest Books, 4700 E. Galbraith Rd., Cincinnati OH 45236. (800)448-0915. Web site: www.writersdigest.com.

Story Sparkers: A Creativity Guide for Children's Writers, by Marcia Thornton Jones and Debbie Dadey, Writer's Digest Books, 4700 E. Galbraith Rd., Cincinnati OH 45236. (800)448-0915. Web site: www.writersdigest.com.

N **Take Joy: A Writer's Guide to Loving the Craft**, by Jane Yolen, Writer's Digest Books, 4700 E. Galbraith Rd., Cincinnati OH 45236. (800)448-0915. Web site: www.writersdigest.com.

A Teen's Guide to Getting Published; Publishing for Profit, Recognition and Academic Success, Second edition, by Jessica Dunn & Danielle Dunn, Prufrock Press, P.O. Box 8813, Waco TX 76714-8813. (800)998-2208.

The Writer's Guide to Crafting Stories for Children, by Nancy Lamb, Writer's Digest Books, 4700 E. Galbraith Rd., Cincinnati OH 45236. (800)448-0915. Web site: www.writersdigest.com.

Writing and Illustrating Children's Books for Publication: Two Perspectives, Revised Edition, by Berthe Amoss and Eric Suben, Writer's Digest Books, 4700 E. Galbraith Rd., Cincinnati OH 45236. (800)448-0915. Web site: www.writersdigest.com.

Writing for Children & Teenagers, Third Edition, by Lee Wyndham, revised by Arnold Madison, Writer's Digest Books, 4700 E. Galbraith Rd., Cincinnati OH 45236. (800)448-0915. Web site: www.writersdigest.com.

Writing for Young Adults, by Sherry Garland, Writer's Digest Books, 4700 E. Galbraith Rd., Cincinnati OH 45236. (800)448-0915. Web site: www.writersdigest.com.

Writing With Pictures: How to Write and Illustrate Children's Books, by Uri Shulevitz, Watson-Guptill Publications, 770 Broadway, New York NY 10003. (800)278-8477.

You Can Write Children's Books, by Tracey E. Dils, Writer's Digest Books, 4700 E. Galbraith Rd., Cincinnati OH 45236. (800)448-0915. Web site: www.writersdigest.com.

You Can Write Children's Books Workbook, by Tracey E. Dils, Writer's Digest Books, 4700 E. Galbraith Rd., Cincinnati OH 45236. (800)448-0915. Web site: www.writersdigest.com.

The Young Writer's Guide to Getting Published, by Kathy Henderson, Writer's Digest Books, 4700 E. Galbraith Rd., Cincinnati OH 45236. (800)448-0915. Web site: www.writersdigest.com.

PUBLICATIONS

Book Links: Connecting Books, Libraries and Classrooms, editor Laura Tillotson, American Library Association, 50 E. Huron St., Chicago IL 60611. (800)545-2433. Web site: www.ala.org/BookLinks. *Magazine published 6 times a year (September-July) for the purpose of connecting books, libraries and classrooms. Features articles on specific topics followed by bibliographies recommending books for further information. Subscription: $28.95/year.*

Children's Book Insider, editor Laura Backes, 901 Columbia Rd., Ft. Collins CO 80525-1838. (970)495-0056 or (800)807-1916. E-mail: mail@write4kids.com. Web site: www.write4kids.com. *Monthly newsletter covering markets, techniques and trends in children's publishing. Subscription: $29.95/year; electronic version $29.95/year.*

Children's Writer, editor Susan Tierney, The Institute of Children's Literature, 93 Long Ridge Rd., West Redding CT 06896-0811. (800)443-6078. Web site: www.childrenswriter.com. *Monthly newsletter of writing and publishing trends in the children's field. Subscription: $24/year; special introductory rate: $15.*

The Five Owls, editor Dr. Mark West, 2000 Aldrich Ave. S., Minneapolis MN 55405. (612)890-0404. Web site: www.fiveowls.com. *Bimonthly newsletter for readers personally and professionally involved in children's literature. Subscription: $35/year.*

The Horn Book Magazine, editor-in-chief Roger Sutton, The Horn Book Inc., 56 Roland St., Suite 200, Boston MA 02129. (800)325-1170. E-mail: info@hbook.com or cgross@hbook.com. Web site: www.hbook.com. *Bimonthly guide to the children's book world including views on the industry and reviews of the latest books. Subscription: $34.95/year for new subscriptions; $49/year for renewals.*

The Lion and the Unicorn: A Critical Journal of Children's Literature, editors Jack Zipes and Louisa Smith, The Johns Hopkins University Press, P.O. Box 19966, Baltimore MD 21211-0966. (800)548-1784 or (410)516-6987 (outside the U.S. and Canada). E-mail: jlorder@jhu.edu. Web site: www.press.jhu.edu/journals/lion_and_the_unicorn/. *Magazine published 3 times a year serving as a forum for discussion of children's literature featuring interviews with authors, editors and experts in the field. Subscription: $31/year.*

Once Upon a Time, editor Audrey Baird, 553 Winston Court, St. Paul MN 55118. (651)457-6223. E-mail: audreyouat@comcast.net. Web site: www.onceuponatimemag.com. *Quarterly support magazine for children's writers and illustrators and those interested in children's literature. Subscription: $26/year.*

Resources

Publishers Weekly, editor-in-chief Sara Nelson, Reed Business Information, a division of Reed Elsevier Inc., 360 Park Ave. S., New York NY 10010. (800)278-2991. Web site: www.publishersweekly.com. *Weekly trade publication covering all aspects of the publishing industry; includes coverage of the children's field and spring and fall issues devoted solely to children's books. Subscription: $199/year. Available on newsstands for $8/issue. (Special issues are higher in price.)*

Society of Children's Book Writers and Illustrators Bulletin, editors Stephen Mooser and Lin Oliver, SCBWI, 8271 Beverly Blvd., Los Angeles CA 90048. (323)782-1010. Web site: www.scbwi.org/pubs.htm. *Bimonthly newsletter of SCBWI covering news of interest to members. Subscription with $60/year membership.*

Useful Online Resources

The editors of *Children's Writer's & Illustrator's Market* suggest the following Web sites to keep you informed on writing and illustrating techniques, trends in the field, business issues, industry news and changes, and additional markets.

Amazon.com: www.amazon.com
Calling itself "A bookstore too big for the physical world," Amazon.com has more than 3 million books available on their Web site at discounted prices, plus a personal notification service of new releases, reader reviews, bestseller and suggested book information.

America Writes for Kids: http://usawrites4kids.drury.edu
Lists book authors by state along with interviews, profiles and writing tips.

Artlex Art Dictionary: www.artlex.com
Art dictionary with more than 3,200 terms

Association for Library Service to Children: www.ala.org
This site provides links to information about Newbery, Caldecott, Coretta Scott King, Michael L. Printz and Theodor Seuss Geisel Awards as well as a host of other awards for notable children's books.

Association of Illustrators: www.theaoi.com
This U.K.-based organization has been working since 1973 to promote illustration, illustrators' rights and standards. The Web site has discussion boards, artists' directories, events, links to agents and much more.

Authors and Illustrators for Children Webring: http://t.webring.com/hub?ring=aicwebring
Here you'll find a list of link of sites of interest to children's writers and illustrators or created by them.

The Authors Guild Online: www.authorsguild.org
The Web site of The Authors Guild offers articles and columns dealing with contract issues, copyright, electronic rights and other legal issues of concern to writers.

Barnes & Noble Online: www.barnesandnoble.com
The world's largest bookstore chain's Web site contains 600,000 in-stock titles at discount prices as well as personalized recommendations, online events with authors and book forum access for members.

The Book Report Network: includes www.bookreporter.com; www.readinggroupguides.com; www.authorsontheweb.com; www.teenreads.com and www.kidsreads.com.

All the sites feature giveaways, book reviews, author and editor interviews, and recommended reads. A great way to stay connected.

Bookwire: www.bookwire.com
A gateway to finding information about publishers, booksellers, libraries, authors, reviews and awards. Also offers frequently asked publishing questions and answers, a calendar of events, a mailing list and other helpful resources.

Canadian Children's Book Centre: www.bookcentre.ca
The site for the CCBC includes profiles of illustrators and authors, information on recent books, a calendar of upcoming events, information on CCBC publications, and tips from Canadian children's authors.

Canadian Society of Children's Authors, Illustrators and Performers: www.canscaip.org
This organization promotes all aspects of children's writing, illustration and performance.

The Children's Book Council: www.cbcbooks.org
This site includes a complete list of CBC members with addresses, names and descriptions of what each publishes, and links to publishers' Web sites. Also offers previews of upcoming titles from members; articles from *CBC Features*, the Council's newsletter; and their catalog.

Children's Literature: www.childrenslit.com
Offers book reviews, lists of conferences, searchable database, links to over 1,000 author/illustrator Web sites and much more.

Children's Literature Web Guide: www.ucalgary.ca/~dkbrown
This site includes stories, poetry, resource lists, lists of conferences, links to book reviews, lists of awards (international), and information on books from classic to contemporary.

Children's Writer's & Illustrator's Market Web Page: www.cwim.com
Visit the new web page for market updates and sign up for a free e-newsletter.

Children's Writing Supersite: www.write4kids.com
This site (formerly Children's Writers Resource Center) includes highlights from the newsletter *Children's Book Insider*; definitions of publishing terms; answers to frequently asked questions; information on trends; information on small presses; a research center for Web information; and a catalog of material available from *CBI*.

The Colossal Directory of Children's Publishers Online: www.signaleader.com/childrens-writers
This site features links to Web sites of children's publishers and magazines and includes information on which publishers offer submission guidelines online.

Cynthia Leitich Smith's Web site: www.cynthialeitichsmith.com
In addition to information about her books and appearances and a blog, Cynthia Leitich Smith has assembled a site chock full of great useful and inspiring information including interviews with writers and illustrators, favorite reads, awards, bibliographies, and tons of helpful links, many to help writers explore diversity.

Database of Award-Winning Children's Literature: www.dawcl.com
A compilation of over 4,000 records of award-winning books throughout the U.S., Canada, Australia, New Zealand and the U.K. You can search by age level, format, genre, setting, historical period, ethnicity or nationality of the protagonist, gender of protagonist, publication year, award name, or even by keyword. Begin here to compile your reading list of award-winners.

Resources

The Drawing Board: http://members.aol.com/thedrawing
This site for illustrators features articles, interviews, links and resources for illustrators from all fields.

Editor & Publisher: www.editorandpublisher.com
The Internet source for *Editor & Publisher*, this site provides up-to-date industry news, with other opportunities such as a research area and bookstore, a calendar of events and classifieds.

Imaginary Lands: www.imaginarylands.org
A fun site with links to Web sites about picture books, learning tools and children's literature.

International Board on Books for Young People: www.ibby.org
Founded in Switzerland in 1953, IBBY is a nonprofit that seeks to encourage the creation and distribution of quality children's literature. They cooperate with children's organizations and children's book institutions around the world.

International Reading Association: www.reading.org
This Web site includes articles; book lists; event, conference and convention information; and an online bookstore.

Kid Magazine Writers: www.kidmagwriters.com
Writer Jan Fields created this site to offer support and information to the often-neglected children's magazine writer. The Web site features editor interviews, articles on technique, special reports, an A to Z magazine market guide, and archives of monthly features.

National Association for the Education of Young Children: www.naeyc.org.
This organization is comprised of over 100,000 early childhood educators and others interested in the development and education of young children. Their Web site makes a great introduction and research resource for authors and illustrators of picture books.

National Writers Union: www.nwu.org
The union for freelance writers in U.S. Markets. The NWU offers contract advice, greviance assistance, health and liability insurance and much more.

Once Upon a Time: www.onceuponatimemag.com
This companion site to *Once Upon A Time* magazine offers excerpts from recent articles, notes for prospective contributors, and information about *OUAT*'s 11 regular columnists.

Picturebook: www.picture-book.com
This site brought to you by *Picturebook* sourcebook offers tons of links for illustrators, portfolio searching, and news, and offers a listserv, bulletin board and chatroom.

Planet Esmé: A Wonderful World of Children's Literature: www.planetesme.com
This site run by author Esmé Raji Codell, offers extensive lists of children's book recommendations, including the latest titles of note for various age groups, a great list of links, and more. Be sure to click on "join the club" to receive Codell's delightful e-mail newsletter.

Publishers' Catalogues Home Page: www.lights.com/publisher/index.html
A mammoth link collection of more than 6,000 publishers around the world arranged geographically. This site is one of the most comprehensive directories of publishers on the Internet.

Resources

The Purple Crayon: www.underdown.org

Editor Harold Underdown's site includes articles on trends, business, and cover letters and queries as well as interviews with editors and answers to frequently asked questions. He also includes links to a number of other sites helpful to writers and excerpts from his book *The Complete Idiot's Guide to Publishing Children's Books*.

Slantville: www.slantville.com

An online artists community, this site includes a yellow pages for artists, frequently asked questions and a library offering information on a number of issues of interest to illustrators. This is a great site to visit to view artists' portfolios.

Smartwriters.com: www.smartwriters.com

Writer, novelist, photographer, graphic designer, and co-founder of 2-Tier Software, Inc., Roxyanne Young, runs this online magazine, which is absolutely stuffed with resources for children's writers, teachers and young writers. It's also got contests, interviews, free books, advice and well—you just have to go there.

Society of Children's Book Writers and Illustrators: www.scbwi.org

This site includes information on awards and grants available to SCBWI members, a calendar of events listed by date and region, a list of publications available to members, and a site map for easy navigation. Follow the Regional Chapters link to find the SCBWI chapter in your area.

The Society of Illustrators: www.societyillustrators.org

Since 1901, this organization has been working to promote the interest of professional illustrators. Information on exhibitions, career advice, and many other links provided.

U.K. Children's Books: www.ukchildrensbooks.co.uk

Filled with links to author sites, illustrator sites, publishers, booksellers, and organizations—not to mention help with Web site design and other technicalities—visit this site no matter which side of the Atlantic you rest your head.

United States Board on Books for Young People: www.usbby.org

Serves as the U.S. national section of the International Board on Books for Young People.

United States Postal Service: www.usps.com

Offers domestic and International postage rate calculator, stamp ordering, zip code look up, express mail tracking and more.

Verla Kay's Web site: www.verlakay.com

Author Verla Kay's Web site features writer's tips, articles, a schedules of online workshops (with transcripts of past workshops), a good news board and helpful links.

Writersdigest.com: www.writersdigest.com

Brought to you by *Writer's Digest* magazine, this site features articles, resources, links, writing prompts, a bookstore, and more.

Writersmarket.com: www.writersmarket.com

This gateway to the *Writer's Market* online edition offers market news, FAQs, tips, featured markets and web resources, a free newsletter, and more.

Writing-world.com: www.writing-world.com/children/index.shtml

Site features reams of advice, links and offers a free bi-weekly newsletter.

Glossary

AAR. Association of Authors' Representatives.

ABA. American Booksellers Association.

ABC. Association of Booksellers for Children.

Advance. A sum of money a publisher pays a writer or illustrator prior to the publication of a book. It is usually paid in installments, such as one half on signing the contract, one half on delivery of a complete and satisfactory manuscript. The advance is paid against the royalty money that will be earned by the book.

ALA. American Library Association.

All rights. The rights contracted to a publisher permitting the use of material anywhere and in any form, including movie and book club sales, without additional payment to the creator.

Anthology. A collection of selected writings by various authors or gatherings of works by one author.

Anthropomorphization. The act of attributing human form and personality to things not human (such as animals).

ASAP. As soon as possible.

Assignment. An editor or art director asks a writer, illustrator or photographer to produce a specific piece for an agreed-upon fee.

B&W. Black and white.

Backlist. A publisher's list of books not published during the current season but still in print.

Biennially. Occurring once every 2 years.

Bimonthly. Occurring once every 2 months.

Biweekly. Occurring once every 2 weeks.

Book packager. A company that draws all elements of a book together, from the initial concept to writing and marketing strategies, then sells the book package to a book publisher and/or movie producer. Also known as book producer or book developer.

Book proposal. Package submitted to a publisher for consideration usually consisting of a synopsis, outline and sample chapters. (See Before Your First Sale, page 7.)

Business-size envelope. Also known as a #10 envelope. The standard size used in sending business correspondence.

Camera-ready. Refers to art that is completely prepared for copy camera platemaking.

Caption. A description of the subject matter of an illustration or photograph; photo captions include persons' names where appropriate. Also called cutline.

Clean-copy. A manuscript free of errors and needing no editing; it is ready for typesetting.

Clips. Samples, usually from newspapers or magazines, of a writer's published work.

Concept books. Books that deal with ideas, concepts and large-scale problems, promoting an understanding of what's happening in a child's world. Most prevalent are alphabet and counting books, but also includes books dealing with specific concerns facing young people (such as divorce, birth of a sibling, friendship or moving).

Contract. A written agreement stating the rights to be purchased by an editor, art director or producer and the amount of payment the writer, illustrator or photographer will receive for that sale. (See Running Your Business, page 13.)

Contributor's copies. The magazine issues sent to an author, illustrator or photographer in which her work appears.

Co-op publisher. A publisher that shares production costs with an author, but, unlike subsidy publishers, handles all marketing and distribution. An author receives a high percentage of royalties until her initial investment is recouped, then standard royalties. (*Children's Writer's & Illustrator's Market* does not include co-op publishers.)

Copy. The actual written material of a manuscript.

Copyediting. Editing a manuscript for grammar usage, spelling, punctuation and general style.

Copyright. A means to legally protect an author's/illustrator's/photographer's work. This can be shown by writing ©, the creator's name, and year of work's creation. (See Running Your Business, page 13.)

Cover letter. A brief letter, accompanying a complete manuscript, especially useful if responding to an editor's request for a manuscript. May also accompany a book proposal. (See Before Your First Sale, page 8.)

Cutline. See caption.

Division. An unincorporated branch of a company.

Dummy. A loose mock-up of a book showing placement of text and artwork.

Electronic submission. A submission of material by modem or on computer disk.

Final draft. The last version of a polished manuscript ready for submission to an editor.

First North American serial rights. The right to publish material in a periodical for the first time, in the United States or Canada. (See Running Your Business, page 13.)

F&Gs. Folded and gathered sheets. An early, not-yet-bound copy of a picture book.

Flat fee. A one-time payment.

Galleys. The first typeset version of a manuscript that has not yet been divided into pages.

Genre. A formulaic type of fiction, such as horror, mystery, romance, science fiction or western.

Glossy. A photograph with a shiny surface as opposed to one with a non-shiny matte finish.

Gouache. Opaque watercolor with an appreciable film thickness and an actual paint layer.

Halftone. Reproduction of a continuous tone illustration with the image formed by dots produced by a camera lens screen.

Hard copy. The printed copy of a computer's output.

Hardware. All the mechanically-integrated components of a computer that are not software—circuit boards, transistors and the machines that are the actual computer.

Hi-Lo. High interest, low reading level.

Home page. The first page of a Web site.

IBBY. International Board on Books for Young People.

Imprint. Name applied to a publisher's specific line of books.

Internet. A worldwide network of computers that offers access to a wide variety of electronic resources.

IRA. International Reading Association.

IRC. International Reply Coupon. Sold at the post office to enclose with text or artwork sent to a recipient outside your own country to cover postage costs when replying or returning work.

Keyline. Identification of the positions of illustrations and copy for the printer.

Layout. Arrangement of illustrations, photographs, text and headlines for printed material.

Line drawing. Illustration done with pencil or ink using no wash or other shading.

Mass market books. Paperback books directed toward an extremely large audience sold in supermarkets, drugstores, airports, newsstands, online retailers, and bookstores.

Mechanicals. Paste-up or preparation of work for printing.

Middle grade or mid-grade. See middle reader.

Middle reader. The general classification of books written for readers approximately ages 9-11. Also called middle grade.

Ms (mss). Manuscript(s).

Multiple submissions. See simultaneous submissions.

NCTE. National Council of Teachers of English.

One-time rights. Permission to publish a story in periodical or book form one time only. (See Running Your Business, page 13.)

Outline. A summary of a book's contents; often in the form of chapter headings with a descriptive sentence or two under each heading to show the scope of the book.

Package sale. The sale of a manuscript and illustrations/photos as a "package" paid for with one check.

Payment on acceptance. The writer, artist or photographer is paid for her work at the time the editor or art director decides to buy it.

Payment on publication. The writer, artist or photographer is paid for her work when it is published.

Picture book. A type of book aimed at preschoolers to 8-year-olds that tells a story using a combination of text and artwork, or artwork only.

Print. An impression pulled from an original plate, stone, block, screen or negative; also a positive made from a photographic negative.

Proofreading. Reading text to correct typographical errors.

Query. A letter to an editor or agent designed to capture interest in an article or book you have written or propose to write. (See Before Your First Sale, page 7.)

Reading fee. Money charged by some agents and publishers to read a submitted manuscript. (*Children's Writer's & Illustrator's Market* does not include agencies that charge reading fees.)

Reprint rights. Permission to print an already published work whose first rights have been sold to another magazine or book publisher. (See Running Your Business, page 13.)

Response time. The average length of time it takes an editor or art director to accept or reject a query or submission and inform the creator of the decision.

Rights. The bundle of permissions offered to an editor or art director in exchange for printing a manuscript, artwork or photographs. (See Running Your Business, page 13.)

Rough draft. A manuscript that has not been checked for errors in grammar, punctuation, spelling or content.

Roughs. Preliminary sketches or drawings.

Royalty. An agreed percentage paid by a publisher to a writer, illustrator or photographer for each copy of her work sold.

SAE. Self-addressed envelope.

SASE. Self-addressed, stamped envelope.

SCBWI. The Society of Children's Book Writers and Illustrators. (See listing in Clubs & Organizations section.)

Second serial rights. Permission for the reprinting of a work in another periodical after its first publication in book or magazine form. (See Running Your Business, page 13.)

Semiannual. Occurring every 6 months or twice a year.

Semimonthly. Occurring twice a month.

Semiweekly. Occurring twice a week.

Resources

Serial rights. The rights given by an author to a publisher to print a piece in one or more periodicals. (See Running Your Business, page 13.)

Simultaneous submissions. Queries or proposals sent to several publishers at the same time. Also called multiple submissions. (See Before Your First Sale, page 7.)

Slant. The approach to a story or piece of artwork that will appeal to readers of a particular publication.

Slush pile. Editors' term for their collections of unsolicited manuscripts.

Software. Programs and related documentation for use with a computer.

Solicited manuscript. Material that an editor has asked for or agreed to consider before being sent by a writer.

SPAR. Society of Photographers and Artists Representatives.

Speculation (spec). Creating a piece with no assurance from an editor or art director that it will be purchased or any reimbursements for material or labor paid.

Subsidiary rights. All rights other than book publishing rights included in a book contract, such as paperback, book club and movie rights. (See Running Your Business, page 13.)

Subsidy publisher. A book publisher that charges the author for the cost of typesetting, printing and promoting a book. Also called a vanity publisher. (*Children's Writer's & Illustrator's Market* does not include subsidy publishers.)

Synopsis. A brief summary of a story or novel. Usually a page to a page and a half, single-spaced, if part of a book proposal.

Tabloid. Publication printed on an ordinary newspaper page turned sideways and folded in half.

Tearsheet. Page from a magazine or newspaper containing your printed art, story, article, poem or photo.

Thumbnail. A rough layout in miniature.

Trade books. Books sold in bookstores and through online retailers, aimed at a smaller audience than mass market books, and printed in smaller quantities by publishers.

Transparencies. Positive color slides; not color prints.

Unsolicited manuscript. Material sent without an editor's or art director's request.

Vanity publisher. See subsidy publisher.

Work-for-hire. An arrangement between a writer, illustrator or photographer and a company under which the company retains complete control of the work's copyright. (See Running Your Business, page 13.)

YA. See young adult.

Young adult. The general classification of books written for readers approximately ages 12-18. Often referred to as YA.

Young reader. The general classification of books written for readers approximately ages 5-8.

Names Index

This new index lists the editors, art directors, agents and art reps listed in *Children's Writer's & Illustrator's Market*, along with the publishers, publications or companies for which they work. Names were culled from Book Publishers, Canadian & International Book Publishers, Magazines, Young Writer's & Illustrator's Markets, and Agents & Art Reps.

Age-Level Index

This index lists book and magazine publishers by the age-groups for which they publish. Use it to locate appropriate markets for your work, then carefully read the listings and follow the guidelines of each publisher. Use this index in conjunction with the Subject Index to further narrow your list of markets. **Picture Books** and **Picture-Oriented Material** are for preschoolers to 8-year-olds; **Young Readers** are for 5- to 8-year-olds; **Middle Readers** are for 9- to 11-year-olds; and **Young Adults** are for ages 12 and up.

BOOK PUBLISHERS

Picture Books

Tingley Books, Megan 189
Tormont Publications 210
Tricycle Press 190
Turtle Books 190
Two Lives Publishing 191
Two-Can Publishing 191
Tyndale House Publishers, Inc. 192
Unity House 192
URJ Press 192
Viking Children's Books 192
VSP Books 193
Walker & Company 193
WestWinds Press/Alaska Northwest Books 194
Whitman & Company, Albert 194
Wiseman Books, Paula 196
Wright Group/McGraw Hill, The 197

Young Readers

Abingdon Press 106
Abrams Books for Young Readers, Harry N. 106
Advocacy Press 107
Alaska Northwest Books 107
All About Kids Publishing 108
Allen & Unwin 199
Amirah Publishing 109
Annick Press Ltd. 199
Atheneum Books for Young Readers 110
Ballyhoo BookWorks Inc. 110
Bantam Books for Young Readers 111
Barefoot Books 111
Barrons Educational Series 112
Benchmark Books 113
Benefactory, The 113
Bess Press 114
Bethany House Publishers 114
Beyond Words Publishing, Inc. 114
Birdsong Books 115
Blooming Tree Press 115
Bloomsbury Childrens Books 120
Blue Sky Press 120
Boyds Mills Press 121
Bright Ring Publishing, Inc. 121
Broadman & Holman Publishers 121
Calkins Creek Books 121
Candlewick Press 122
Carolrhoda Books, Inc. 122

Cartwheel Books 123
Cavendish Children's Books, Marshall 123
Charlesbridge 123
Chicago Review Press 124
Children's Book Press 124
Child's Play (International) Ltd. 199
Christian Ed. Publishers 125
Chronicle Books 125
Concordia Publishing House 126
Coteau Books Ltd. 200
Creative Education 127
Cricket Books 127
Darby Creek Publishing 128
Delacorte and Doubleday Books for Young Readers 129
Dial Books for Young Readers 129
DNA Press, LLC 133
Dutton Children's Books 134
EDCON Publishing 134
Eerdman's Books for Young Readers 135
Enslow Publishers Inc. 136
Faith Kidz 136
Farrar, Straus & Giroux Inc. 137
Fickling Books, David 201
Free Spirit Publishing 138
Freestone/Peachtree, Jr. 139
Geringer Books, Laura 139
Godine, Publisher, David R. 140
Golden Books 140
Greene Bark Press 141
Greenwillow Books 141
Grosset & Dunlap Publishers 141
Groundwood Books 201
Hachai Publishing 142
Harcourt, Inc. 142
HarperCollins Children's Books 143
Health Press 143
Hendrick-Long Publishing Company 147
Holiday House Inc. 147
Holt & Company, Henry 148
Houghton Mifflin Co. 148
Hyperion Books for Children 149
Impact Publishers, Inc. 150
Jewish Lights Publishing 150
Kamehameha Schools Press 151
Kar-Ben Publishing, Inc. 151
Key Porter Books 202

Young Adult/Teen

MAGAZINES
Picture-Oriented Material

Young Readers

Subject Index

This index lists book and magazine publishers by the fiction and nonfiction subject area in which they publish. Use it to locate appropriate markets for your work, then carefully read the listings and follow the guidelines of each publisher. Use this index in conjunction with Age-Level Index to further narrow your list of markets.

Animal

Fantasy

Humor

Multicultural

Problem Novels

Religious

Suspense/Mystery

BOOK PUBLISHERS: NONFICTION

Activity Books

Dog-Eared Publications 134
Emma Treehouse 200
Farrar, Straus & Giroux Inc. 137
Gibbs Smith, Publisher 139
Godine, Publisher, David R. 140
Gryphon House 142
Houghton Mifflin Co. 148
Jewish Lights Publishing 150
Kar-Ben Publishing, Inc. 151
Kids Can Press 202
Lark Books 153
Magination Press 156
Master Books 156
Meadowbrook Press 157
Meriwether Publishing Ltd. 160
Milet Publishing Ltd. 160
Nomad Press 163
NorthWord Books for Young Readers 163
Pitspopany Press 171
Players Press, Inc. 172
Playne Books Limited 205
Price Ltd., Mathew 206
QED Publishing 206
Rainbow Publishers 174
Running Press Kids 177
Speech Bin, Inc., The 186
Teora USA 188
TOKYOPOP Inc. 189
Tormont Publications 210
Wiley & Sons, Inc., John 195
Windward Publishing 195

Animal

Alaska Northwest Books 107
All About Kids Publishing 108
Bancroft Press 111
Benefactory, The 113
Birdsong Books 115
Boyds Mills Press 121
Cartwheel Books 123
Charlesbridge 123
Child's Play (International) Ltd. 199
Creative Education 127
Dawn Publications 128
Dog-Eared Publications 134
Emma Treehouse 200
Enslow Publishers Inc. 136

Facts on File 136
Farrar, Straus & Giroux Inc. 137
Freestone/Peachtree, Jr. 139
Godine, Publisher, David R. 140
Harcourt, Inc. 142
Holiday House Inc. 147
Holt & Company, Henry 148
Houghton Mifflin Co. 148
Key Porter Books 202
Kids Can Press 202
Lark Books 153
Lobster Press 203
Master Books 156
Milet Publishing Ltd. 160
NorthWord Books for Young Readers 163
Owen Publishers, Inc., Richard C. 166
Peachtree Publishers, Ltd. 168
Pineapple Press, Inc. 170
Pitspopany Press 171
Playne Books Limited 205
Price Ltd., Mathew 206
Putnam's Sons, G.P. 174
QED Publishing 206
RGU Group, The 176
Ronsdale Press 208
Running Press Kids 177
Scholastic Canada Ltd. 208
Scholastic Library Publishing 178
Seedling Publications 178
Smooch 186
Stemmer House Publishing 187
Teora USA 188
Tingley Books, Megan 189
Tricycle Press 190
Two-Can Publishing 191
Viking Children's Books 192
WestWinds Press/Alaska Northwest Books 194
Whitman & Company, Albert 194
Windward Publishing 195
Wiseman Books, Paula 196
World Book, Inc. 196
Wright Group/McGraw Hill, The 197

Arts/Crafts

American Girl Publications 109
Ballyhoo BookWorks Inc. 110

Hobbies

How-to

Writer's Digest
WRITE BETTER
GET PUBLISHED

DISCOVER A WORLD OF WRITING SUCCESS!

Are you ready to be praised, published, and paid for your writing? It's time to invest in your future with *Writer's Digest!* Beginners and experienced writers alike have been relying on *Writer's Digest*, the world's leading magazine for writers, for more than 80 years — and it keeps getting better! Each issue is brimming with:

Get a FREE ISSUE of *Writer's Digest!*

- Technique articles geared toward specific genres, including fiction, nonfiction, business writing and more

- Business information specifically for writers, such as organizational advice, tax tips, and setting fees

- Tips and tricks for rekindling your creative fire

- The latest and greatest markets for print, online and e-publishing

- And much more!

NO RISK!
Send No Money Now!

☐ **Yes!** Please rush me my FREE issue of *Writer's Digest* — the world's leading magazine for writers. If I like what I read, I'll get a full year's subscription (6 issues, including the free issue) for only $19.96. That's 44% off the newsstand rate! If I'm not completely satisfied, I'll write "cancel" on your invoice, return it and owe nothing. The FREE issue is mine to keep, no matter what!

Name (please print)

Address

City   State   ZIP

E-mail (to contact me regarding my subscription)

☐ YES! Also e-mail me *Writer's Digest*'s FREE e-newsletter and other information of interest. *(We will not sell your e-mail address to outside companies.)*

Subscribers in Canada will be charged an additional US$10 (includes GST/HST) and invoiced. Outside the U.S. and Canada, add US$10 and remit payment in U.S. funds with this order. Annual newsstand rate: $35.94. Please allow 4-6 weeks for first-issue delivery.

Writer's Digest   www.writersdigest.com

J6FCMK

Get a **FREE** TRIAL ISSUE of **Writer's Digest**

WRITE BETTER
GET PUBLISHED

Packed with creative inspiration, advice, and tips to guide you on the road to success, *Writer's Digest* offers everything you need to take your writing to the next level! You'll discover how to:

- Create dynamic characters and page-turning plots
- Submit query letters that publishers won't be able to refuse
- Find the right agent or editor
- Make it out of the slush-pile and into the hands of publishers
- Write award-winning contest entries
- And more!

See for yourself — order your FREE trial issue today!

RUSH! Free Issue!

BUSINESS REPLY MAIL
FIRST-CLASS MAIL   PERMIT NO. 340   FLAGLER BEACH FL

POSTAGE WILL BE PAID BY ADDRESSEE

Writer's Digest

PO BOX 421365
PALM COAST FL 32142-7104

NO POSTAGE
NECESSARY
IF MAILED
IN THE
UNITED STATES

Photography Index

This index lists markets that buy photos from freelancers and is divided into book publishers, magazines, and greeting cards. It's important to carefully read the listings and follow the guidelines of each publisher to which you submit.

BOOK PUBLISHERS

General Index

Market listings that appeared in the 2006 edition of *Children's Writer's & Illustrator's Market* but do not appear in this edition are identified with a two-letter code explaining why the listing was omitted: **(NR)**—no response to our requests for updated information; **(OB)**—out of business; **(RP)**—business restructured or purchased; **(RR)**—removed by request; **(UC)**—unable to contact.

General Index

Eike Batista — net present value

Eike's city — he wants to help his country — macro world — infrastructure — power plants

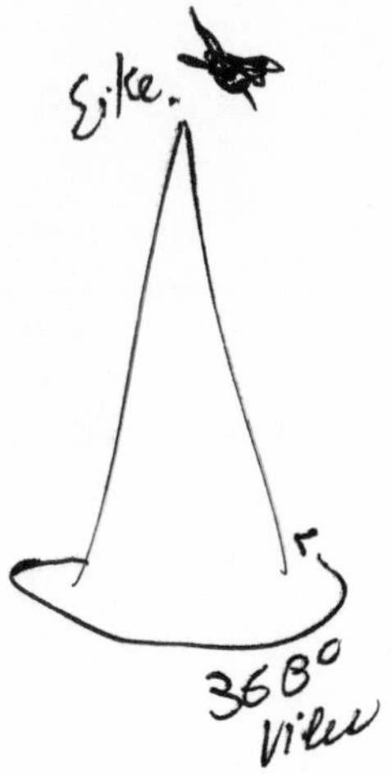

good politics / good Gov Systems

• Chile
• Colombia
• Brasil

a mature democracy

Eike.

360° view

(China for Chinese)

Brasil's credit rating better than Germany

populist Gov → "poor people of ! (Vzla) Argentina" — he says

{ Rolls Royce driven by an Egyptian chauffeur)

oil producer 3 : , 4 : position — Brasil

"open an office) you are one of us" — Brasilian for the world

oil Auction new rules

don't change the past but change the future of the grandfather

Eike's views
Peru leftist Gov

Mex Ø

Paraguay / Uruguay / 6

Lula
82%
acceptance
Rate

Model for Latin American leader
respect for business & the people

More great resources from Writer's Digest Books!

Children's Writer's Word Book, 2nd edition—Revised and updated to address the changing trends in children's literature, this new edition provides even more of the essential information for children's writers that made author Alijandra Mogilner's first edition a success. With lists of reading-level-specific words and a thesaurus of words annotated with reading levels, this invaluable guide saves writers time by collecting everything they need to know about age-appropriate language in one handy book.
ISBN-13: 978-1-58297-413-2
ISBN-10: 1-58297-413-6, paperback, 352 pages, $16.99, #11031

Take Joy: A Writer's Guide to Loving the Craft—Author Jane Yolen combats the perception that writing is a strenuous, solitary craft in this sweet, insightful book. She reveals the silver lining of the writing life through 15 easy-to-digest essays on plot, beginnings and endings, voice, point of view, writing poetry, and more. This optimistic guide urges writers to re-experience the joy of doing what matters most to them.
ISBN-13: 978-1-58297-385-2
ISBN-10: 1-5829-385-7, paperback, 208 pages, $14.99, #11008

The Write-Brain Workbook: 366 Exercises to Liberate Your Writing—Writers will never have to face a blank page again with this one-of-a-kind guide that provides a full year of writing exercises and games designed to get thoughts brewing and the pen moving across the page. The book includes 366 10-minute exercises to help build momentum and turn on the right side of the brain, painlessly leading writers to new writing every day—all in a stunning 4-color package.
ISBN-13: 978-1-58297-355-5
ISBN-10: 1-58297-355-5, paperback, 384 pages, $19.99, #10986

The Writer's Book of Matches: 1,001 Prompts to Ignite Your Fiction—Designed to help writers find inspiration anytime, anywhere, this book is both muse and exercise partner for beginning and advanced writers. It's jam-packed with 1,001 creative prompts, including situation, dialogue-oriented and point-of-view changing exercises, along with dozens of sidebars containing humorous and inspiring quotes from famous authors about the writing life, idea creation, and writer's block.
ISBN-13: 978-1-58297-411-8
ISBN-10: 1-5829-411-X, pob, 272 pages, $19.99, #11030

You Can Write Children's Books Workbook—In this companion to the best-selling *You Can Write Children's Books*, author Tracey E. Dils provides aspiring children's authors with hands-on instruction for finishing their manuscripts, preparing them for publication, and getting them published. The book includes 48 exercises that take readers step-by-step through identifying a project, writing and revising a manuscript, researching the marketplace, targeting publishers, and preparing a professional submission.
ISBN-13: 978-1-58297-248-0
ISBN-10: ISBN: 1-58297-248-6, paperback, 160 pages, $14.99, #10899

These and other fine Writer's Digest Books are available at your local bookstore or online supplier.

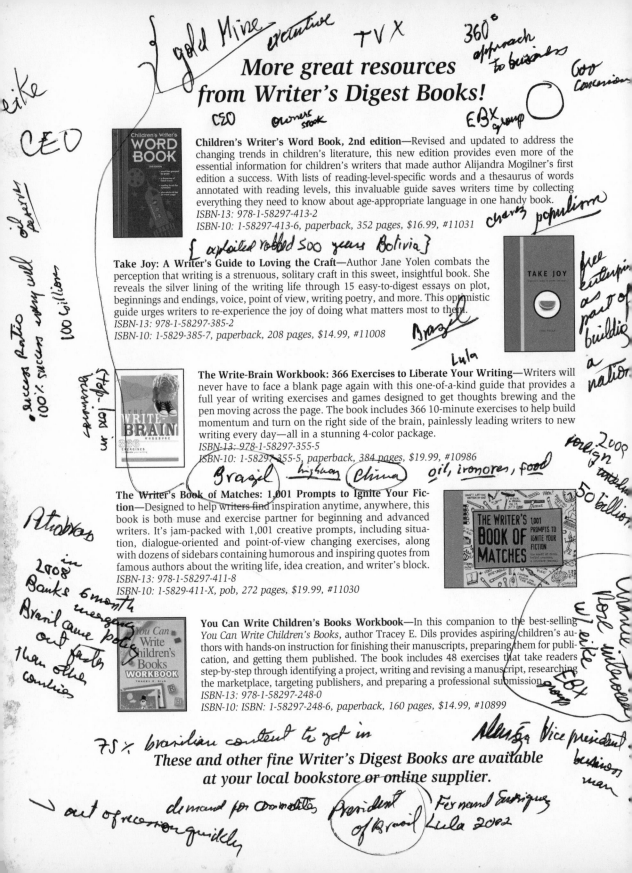